If you're wondering why you should buy this new edition of *European Politics Today*, here are 14 good reasons!

1. Chapter 1, "The European Context," describes the historical development of European nations and provides updated information **on the social, economic and ethnic-racial characteristics of these societies**.

2. Chapter 2, "Democratic Political Culture and Political Action," uses new findings from several recent cross-national surveys to describe the **political values of European republics and differences in their styles of political action**.

3. Chapter 3, "European Interest Groups and Parties," presents the more recent evidence on the **patterns of interest group representation in Europe** and the **patterns of party competition in the East and West**.

4. Chapter 4, "Government and Public Policy," adds new material on the **policy challenges facing European societies at present** and their **policy performance**.

5. Chapter 5, "Politics in Britain," covers the domestic and international issues confronting the Labour government and **the transition from Tony Blair to Gordon Brown**.

6. Chapter 6, "Politi... affects of **Nicolas Sarkozy's hotly contested election** in 2007.

7. Chapter 7, "Politics in Germany," details the **challenges facing Chancellor Angela Merkel** and the Grand Coalition as they struggle with policy reform.

8. Chapter 8, "Politics in Spain," shows how **the surprising victory of the PSOE** in 2004 has changed Spanish policy and covers the reelection of the Socialists in 2008.

9. Chapter 9, "Politics in Russia," covers **Vladimir Putin's transition from president to prime minister**, the country's economic resurgence, and attempts to reassert power at home and abroad.

10. Chapter 10, "Politics in Poland," tracks **Poland's rightward shift** in government and policy direction in the aftermath of the **2005 and 2007 elections**.

11. Chapter 11, "Politics in Bulgaria," is a new country study that brings you up to date on **Bulgaria's EU membership** and the country's transition to democracy.

12. Chapter 12, "Politics in the European Union," discusses the struggle for constitutional reform and the **issues surrounding EU expansion**.

13. Every country study includes the **latest political events, scholarship, and data**, including revised Country Bios and Current Policy Challenges.

14. New and updated **internet sources and suggested readings** help you make the most of your course and further independent study.

CONTRIBUTORS

GABRIEL A. ALMOND
Late, Stanford University

RUSSELL J. DALTON
University of California, Irvine

G. BINGHAM POWELL, Jr.
University of Rochester

KAARE STRØM
University of California, San Diego

TATIANA KOSTADINOVA
Florida International University

THOMAS F. REMINGTON
Emory University

RICHARD ROSE
University of Aberdeen

ALBERTA SBRAGIA
University of Pittsburgh

MARTIN A. SCHAIN
New York University

DONALD SHARE
University of Puget Sound

FRANCESCO STOLFI
University College Dublin

RAY TARAS
Tulane University

FOURTH EDITION

EUROPEAN POLITICS TODAY

Gabriel A. Almond
Late, Stanford University

Russell J. Dalton
University of California, Irvine

G. Bingham Powell, Jr.
University of Rochester

Kaare Strøm
University of California, San Diego

Longman

New York   San Francisco   Boston
London   Toronto   Sydney   Tokyo   Singapore   Madrid
Mexico City   Munich   Paris   Cape Town   Hong Kong   Montreal

Acquisition Editor: Vikram Mukhija
Editorial Assistant: Toni Magyar
Marketing Manager: Lindsey Prudhomme
Production Manager: Eric Jorgensen
Project Coordination, Text Design, and Electronic Page Makeup: GGS Higher Education Resources,
   A division of PreMedia Global, Inc.
Cover Designer/Manager: John Callahan
Cover Image: Corbis, Inc.
Senior Manufacturing Buyer: Alfred C. Dorsey
Text printer and binder and cover printer: Command Web

Library of Congress Cataloging-in-Publication Data

European politics today / Gabriel A. Almond . . . [et al]. — 4th ed.
        p. cm.
    Includes bibliographical references and index.
    ISBN-13: 978-0-205-72389-8
    ISBN-10: 0-205-72389-6
1. Europe, Western—Politics and government.   2. Europe—Politics and government—1989–
3. Democracy—Europe.   4. Europe, Eastern—Politics and government—1989–
5. Democratization—Europe.   I. Almond, Gabriel A. (Gabriel Abraham), 1911–2002.
  JN94.A58E89 2010
  320.94—dc22   2009019108

1 2 3 4 5 6 7 8 9 10—CW—12 11 10 09

Longman
is an imprint of

www.pearsonhighered.com

ISBN 13: 978-0-205-72389-8
ISBN 10:   0-205-72389-6

BRIEF CONTENTS

DETAILED CONTENTS

PART III
Political Transitions

CHAPTER 9

Politics in Russia *Thomas F. Remington*   280

CHAPTER 10

Politics in Poland *Ray Taras*   326

CHAPTER 11

Politics in Bulgaria *Tatiana P. Kostadinova*   374

This new edition of *European Politics Today* updates our introduction to the politics of the new Europe in the twenty-first century. Unlike most European politics textbooks, it bridges the East/West divide, celebrating the extraordinary changes since the fall of the Berlin Wall. A continent historically torn by division and conflict now encompasses forty-one nations that are almost all democratic in reality or aspiration and oriented toward market, rather than command, economies. Many nations in new Europe, including some countries of the former Soviet orbit, have joined the European Union and the NATO military alliance. Where once Europe was divided at the Berlin Wall, now ten East European nations have joined the EU. This book recognizes the many implications of this unity, as well as the great diversity that still remains within Europe. The success of the first three editions has led to this new fourth edition.

Given its historical and cultural commonalities, Europe is a natural unit for an area studies approach to political science. Its nations have borrowed from each other and imitated each other, as well as competing against each other, for a very long time. Today their economies and cultures are more closely interdependent than ever before. Europe's political cultures share many historical and political reference points. Its societies were all affected, in varying ways, by the Renaissance, by the Reformation and the subsequent religious wars, by the Enlightenment and the French Revolution, by the formation and later collapse of European-centered international empires, by the industrial revolution, by fascism and communism, by the terrible wars of the twentieth century and the Holocaust, and by the Cold War. Learning about the general European setting helps us to understand the politics of each European country. Conversely, of course, the dynamic forces of the region cannot be understood independently of the politics of individual countries.

European Politics Today responds to the dissolving barriers between Eastern and Western Europe by offering teacher and student the opportunity to engage in political analysis on a truly European scale. We can appreciate the commonalities between nations and also *take advantage of the differences* across them. We can apply the theories of modern political science in an analysis of countries sharing the common European experience, but recently differentiated by history into quite different introductions to democratic politics and its concomitants.

In our analysis of Western Europe, we examine politics in established democracies. Our chapters show the richness and variety of the democratic experience, comparing the politics of consensual and conflictual cultures, majoritarian and proportional institutional rules, two-party and multiparty electoral competition, and interventionist or market-dominated economic policies. We also track how democracy has taken root in several Western European nations, such as Germany and Spain.

In studying Eastern Europe, we use modern political science techniques to observe the interaction between political culture and the formation of new political institutions. The new party systems of Eastern Europe provide natural experiments where we can study processes of forming identities, organizations, and strategies. Furthermore, Eastern Europeans are experimenting with new forms of democratic institutions and new political economies. Of course, democracy itself faces severe challenges in some parts of Eastern Europe, with fundamental consequences for both European stability and world politics.

FEATURES

This book builds upon the highly successful model of Almond, Powell, Dalton, and Strøm's introductory text, *Comparative Politics Today*. We use the well-tested conceptual framework in describing political cultures and structures. Four of our country chapters (Britain, France, Germany, and Russia) are derived from that text, although completely revised for this volume. However, it is not necessary to understand the formal theoretical framework of *Comparative Politics Today* in order to study the European experience in this volume.

As a text studying a specific geographic region, this book can be used in various ways. The simplest, of course, is to follow the chapters in consecutive order. We begin with four chapters that consider the European experience as a whole. Chapter 1 describes the geography and history of the contemporary nations, as well as the two critical features differentiating them: the sharply varying levels of economic development and the patterns of ethnic and religious division. The chapter also introduces the student to the theme of Europe's special relationship with democracy and democratization. While providing a thorough overview, we define key terms and keep our use of more technical political science vocabulary to a minimum. We suggest that all courses begin with this introductory chapter.

Chapters 2 through 4 discuss the nature, bases, and variety of democracy across the European systems. Chapter 2 examines how Europeans think and act in politics, focusing especially on the mutual expectations of citizens and policymakers in democracies. Chapter 3 examines political organizations—interest groups and parties—and their roles within the democratic process. Chapter 4 offers an overview of the main constitutional arrangements and policymaking processes in European democracies. These chapters assume no specific background in political science or the individual countries. They provide concepts and generalizations that can help students understand the working of politics in specific countries. Thus, it may be helpful for students to read and discuss these chapters, considering their concepts and generalizations, before turning to the individual countries presented in the rest of the book. Alternatively, students may read and discuss the politics of one or more specific countries and then return to Chapters 2 through 4 to see how the detailed play of the political culture and political process in a given country fits into the broader concepts and patterns.

The country authors thus introduce their materials with sufficient clarity and autonomy to make it possible for the students to read them after, before, or concurrently with Chapters 2 through 4. Chapters 5 and 6 introduce the politics of two well-established democracies (Britain and France), while Chapters 7 and 8 describe the political systems in two more recently consolidated ones (Germany and Spain). Chapters 9 through 11 (on Russia, Poland, and Bulgaria) describe political systems that began transitions to democratic politics in the 1990s and for which the issues of democratic consolidation are paramount. Chapter 12 describes the political system of the European Union. In this way, we conclude with an account of this complex political confederation of twenty-seven European countries so far (and more applicants waiting in the wings).

In addition, the book contains an **analytic index** to help instructors coordinate the presentation of material in the introductory chapters and specific country chapters. The index outlines the framework of specific topics that are discussed in the introductory chapters and in each country study, indicating the pages where these topics are presented.

Each of the country chapters includes the following features:

- **A Country Bio** with a map at the beginning of the chapter gives students a quick factual overview of the nation: its size, social composition, leadership, and so on.
- **A Current Policy Challenges** section helps students focus on the important issues and contemporary problems facing that nation.
- **Example Boxes** provide students with current and topical examples that illustrate key concepts and theories in the text, increase student interest, and add visual appeal to the layout of the book.
- **Review Questions, Key Terms, Internet Resources, and Suggested Readings** reinforce the chapter material and give students an opportunity to further explore government agencies, news media, and other information sources.

NEW TO THIS EDITION

European Politics Today marks a new era in Europe's history: a continent made up of free, democratic, and market-oriented societies. We also hope that this new edition will continue the progress toward a new era in the study of European politics, where a comprehensive study of the European political experience replaces a curriculum dividing Europe in half. *European Politics Today* will help students and scholars understand the new Europe and the contribution this region continues to make to the development of political science.

In addition to a new chapter on Bulgaria, all of the country chapters have undergone major revision and updating. A brief summary of the major changes follows:

- **Britain**—The transition from Prime Minister Tony Blair to Gordon Brown and the building domestic and international problems facing the Labour government.
- **France**—The hotly contested presidential election of 2007 and the victory of Nicolas Sarkozy, who has begun to chart a new policy course for France.
- **Germany**—The struggle of the Grand Coalition, headed by Germany's first woman chancellor, Angela Merkel, to deal with Germany's need for policy reform.
- **Spain**—The surprising PSOE electoral victory in 2004, which led to a change in Spain's policy direction and a narrow reelection for the Socialists in 2008.
- **Russia**—Vladimir Putin's transition from president to prime minister and the government's attempts to reassert the domestic and international power of Russia based on its economic resurgence.
- **Poland**—The presidential and parliamentary elections of 2005, which expressed a sharp turn to the right in party and policy terms, followed by the parliamentary election of 2007, which resulted in another change of government.
- **Bulgaria**—Bulgaria's accession to the European Union in 2007, which hopefully marks a positive milestone in the nation's consolidation of democracy.
- **European Union**—The European Union's continued struggle with the need for constitutional reform—thwarted by the Irish veto of the Lisbon Treaty—and the new challenges of an expanded membership of twenty-seven nations. (The European Union is also more extensively discussed throughout the book as the integration process affects the policies of its member states.)

ACKNOWLEDGMENTS

This book began as a product of Gabriel A. Almond's comparative analysis of political science, first represented in *Comparative Politics Today* and then *European Politics Today*. Gabriel passed away in December 2002; we retain Gabriel Almond as a coeditor on this edition to acknowledge his formative influence on this project.

The development of a book requires the support and advice of many people, and we want to acknowledge their contributions. Because this book builds on the success of *Comparative Politics Today,* we benefited from the contributors to this global introduction to comparative politics. Four of the chapters from *Comparative Politics Today* appear here in revised and updated form. As editors, we owe a special debt to the contributors to *European Politics Today*. They produced excellent accounts of politics in their nations of specialization, linked to the larger issues of comparative political studies. We want to acknowledge our debt to their written contribution and our admiration for their tolerance of our frequent editorial requests. We also want to welcome Tatiana Kostadinova and Francesco Stolfi as new authors in this edition and to thank Kathleen Montgomery, who authored the chapter on Hungary in previous editions. It has been a pleasure working with all of our contributors.

The support of the publisher is also essential to a book's success. Vikram Mukhija and Eric Stano have managed this book and *Comparative Politics Today* with admirable success. Their advice and constant support are appreciated. We also thank Toni Magyar for preparing this manuscript for production with care and attention to detail, Suganya Karuppasamy for her efforts in editing and preparing the manuscript, Eric Jorgensen for seeing it through to print, and Lindsey Prudhomme for her marketing efforts.

We also profited from the advice of many colleagues. The following colleagues read all or portions of the manuscript and offered their advice: Emily Beaulieu, University of Kentucky; Amy Mazur, Washington State University; Nancy Nicas, University of Nebraska–Omaha; Shannon Peterson, Utah State University; Jefferey Sellers, University of Southern California; and Margit Tavits, Washington University, St. Louis.

Paulina Marek, Jennifer Burkem, Natalie Michael, and Devesh Tiwari provided valuable research assistance for the editors. We also want to thank Willy Jou for indexing the book and developing the analytic index. The book is much improved because of all of these contributions.

RUSSELL J. DALTON
G. BINGHAM POWELL, JR.
KAARE STRØM

A GUIDE TO COMPARING NATIONS

This analytic index provides a guide to the specific themes addressed in each chapter.

Topics	Chs. 1–4	Britain	France	Germany	Spain	Russia	Poland	Bulgaria	EU
History	3–7	87–90	131	181–186	232–234	284–288	330–335	377–379	420–426
Social Conditions	9–18	—	131–133	186–188	—	314–315	—	379–383	—
Executive	63–66	90–96	133–134	191–192	238–240	288–290	337–338 339–340	385–387	426–431
Parliament	66–67	97–99	134–136	190	240–242	290–292	338–339	383–385	431–432
Judiciary	67	100–101	136	192	242–244	292 317–318	340	387	432 449–450
Provincial Government	—	84–86	167–169	—	244–245	292–295	—	387–388	433–435*
Political Culture	24–33	99–100	136–140	193–197	245–247	295–298	341–345	388–391	440–443
Political Socialization	—	102–105	140–143	197–199	247–248	299–300	345–348	391–394	—
Recruitment/ Participation	33–37	105–108	143–145	199–202	—	300–302	348–350	394–397	—
Interest Groups	42–46	108–111	145–149	202–205	248–253	302–306	350–355	397–399	438–440
Parties and Elections	46–54 67–70	111–116	149–162	205–213	253–265	306–311	355–361	399–406	435–438
Policy Process	71–73	116–120	162–167	213–217	—	—	361–363	406–409	444–449
Outputs and Outcomes	73–74	121–124	169–173	217–224	265–273	311–314	363–369	409–412	453–456
International Relations	—	—	173	224–225	274–275	319–320	—	—	451–452

*relation with member states

EUROPEAN POLITICS TODAY

THE EUROPEAN CONTEXT

For centuries Europeans have dreamed of a prosperous continent leading the world in the pursuit of human well-being and peace. Mikhail Gorbachev, the last General Secretary of the Soviet Union, expressed this feeling in his 1987 book *Perestroika (Opening)*. Gorbachev foresaw an end to the **Cold War** that had split Europe for more than half a century: "Europe from the Atlantic to the Urals is a cultural-historical entity united by the common heritage of the Renaissance and Enlightenment. . . . Europe's historic chance and its future lie in peaceful cooperation between the states of that continent."[1] Just a few years later the Cold War ended, not as Gorbachev had expected, but still creating a unique opportunity for European peace and integration.

Gorbachev's image of a cooperative and peaceful Europe seemed unrealistic at the time because it contrasted sharply with Europe's history. During the twentieth century, Europe experienced not only the tensions of the Cold War, but also the horrors of two World Wars and the barbarisms, holocausts, and mass oppression of totalitarian governments in several nations. And previous centuries had seen repeated warfare and often brutal imperial conquests.

Yet, historic Europe has been an ambivalent force—destructive and creative at the same time. In the Middle Ages and early Renaissance, Europe was relatively backward and defensive, divided into a large number of kingdoms, principalities, dukedoms, and independent cities. War, economic struggle, and autocracy were often the norms of life. Much of Europe was guided by a hierarchical and sometimes corrupt Roman Catholic Church establishment.

On the creative side, however, the dominant forms of political and economic organization in the world today—the effective service-producing state, the industrial market economy, representative democracy, and the ideas of universal human rights and freedoms—originated in Europe. They were created in a tempestuous period during which Europe changed from a comparative backwater to the most powerful and prosperous region in the world. A series of costly wars stretching from the seventeenth century to the twentieth shaped the modern state. The industrial **market economy** emerged in Protestant Europe and America. It has transformed these and other societies with its class structures and patterns of social interaction. The Industrial Revolution began in Britain around 1770, vastly changing the working lives and improving the standard of living of the citizenry. These changes also sowed new democratic impulses. Representative democracy traces its modern origins to the British struggle to democratize Parliament and contain the arbitrary power of the king and to the American and French revolutions of 1776 and 1789, respectively. The first wave of democratization in the modern world occurred in Europe and some of its former colonies, and subsequent waves spread to more countries around the world.

In three fateful centuries, the **Renaissance**, the **Protestant Reformation**, the **Enlightenment**, and the **Industrial Revolution** transformed Europe in basic ways—in its aspirations and ideas, its technology, its social structure, and its political organization. Europe was reorganized into a small number of centralized states. These states drew on growing industrial and commercial sectors and developed professional and technologically advanced armed forces. Europe became the proactive continent, its nations imposing colonial empires on technologically less developed peoples. Yet, while Europe was outwardly expansive, it was inwardly divided into states that were repeatedly at war with one another. Only after the fall of Napoleon in 1814 and with the emergence of British dominance did Europe experience a long spell of relative peace (*Pax Britannica*). This was also a period of unprecedented economic and technological progress.

In the twentieth century, however, Europe's divisions and rivalries produced two World Wars. Since the end of World War II, Europe has tamed its national rivalries and relaxed its imperial ambitions. But Europe has left its values and institutions implanted throughout the world, where they have combined and interacted with indigenous forms and practices. Thus, Europe has had a disproportionate influence on the contemporary world.

The European project is still developing. The **European Union (EU)** creates new institutions and processes for European cooperation. Originally formed by 6 Western European nations in 1957, the EU had expanded to a dozen states by 1981 and now includes twenty-seven nations—spanning the continent from Portugal and Ireland in the West to Bulgaria and the Baltic States in the East. The European dream of a common society from the Atlantic to the Urals is making progress.

THE PURPOSE AND ORGANIZATION OF THIS BOOK

This book celebrates a new Europe. Primarily democratic in reality or in aspiration and broadly committed to market exchange and freedoms, the 41 nations of this new Europe are no longer divided into hostile ideological camps or challenging each other with threats of war. Large parts of this new Europe, including many countries formerly in the Soviet orbit, have a new cooperative history through the EU and other international agreements.

European Politics Today is about Europe, not just about Western Europe or Eastern Europe. Our first goal is to introduce Europe as a cultural and political region. Europe is an idea and a set of values, as well as a geographic region. The nations of Europe have different histories, but they share common social, economic, and political experiences. The Renaissance, the Protestant

Reformation, the Enlightenment, and the Industrial Revolution affected them all to different degrees. They actively or passively experienced the rising nationalism of the nineteenth century, as well as **communism**, **fascism**, and the terrible wars of the twentieth century. The European experience is also relevant to Americans, who live in a modern state that began as a European transplant. The United States inevitably was drawn into Europe's politics and wars and accepted successive generations of European refugees.

We use the European political experience to introduce important concepts and theories in political science. Much of modern political science attempts to understand and explain the workings of the political and economic structures that originated in Europe: the bureaucratic state, the industrial market economy, and representative democratic government. Thus, the unique European experience is relevant to anyone trying to utilize modern political science. We use the concepts and tools of political science to examine European political histories, values, institutions, and processes. We also believe in the dictum that "a person who knows only one country knows no country."[2] Political science should be comparative. The best way to understand what is distinctive about Britain (or any other nation) is to compare it to other nations. Similarly, to understand what is common across democracies or advanced industrial societies, we need to compare them.

European Politics Today contains four introductory chapters, seven chapters on specific nations, and one chapter on the European Union. The first four chapters introduce the European experience and the concepts used in this book. The first chapter describes Europe geographically, socially, and historically. International relations continue to be an important part of European politics; the recent changes in Eastern Europe and the increasing integration of the EU have given new forms to such relations. This chapter discusses critical features of each country, such as economic conditions, religious diversity, and ethnic divisions. It also introduces a continuing theme of our book: Europe's special relationship with democracy and democratization.

Interest in the nature and varieties of democracy in Europe also shapes the subsequent chapters. Chapter 2 describes how Europeans think and act politically. It focuses especially on what democracy expects of its citizens and what citizens in old and new democracies expect of their governments. Chapter 3 offers a similar overview of European interest groups and political parties. Finally, Chapter 4 presents the main features of European constitutions, government institutions, and policymaking processes.

Chapters 5 through 11 apply these themes to specific European political systems, including two democracies that are well established (England and France), two that secured democracy only after World War II (Germany and Spain), and three that have only in the last 15 years grappled with transitions to democratic politics (Russia, Poland, and Bulgaria). Finally, Chapter 12 describes the European Union, which since 2007 has included 27 countries, 10 of which are from Eastern Europe. Of the countries highlighted in this book, only Russia is not a member of the EU. The EU is an increasingly important, though sometimes complex and inscrutable, supranational organization. It influences the political decisions of all European states, including those that are not members.

The front matter for this book includes an analytic index that presents the specific topics discussed in the introductory chapters and in each country study and indicates the pages where these topics are discussed. This index links the general topics from the introductory chapters to the specific country chapters.

THE EMERGENCE OF TODAY'S EUROPE

Europe is not one thing, but many. There is a geographical Europe, a cultural Europe, and a political Europe. Moreover, the boundaries of Europe have changed and are changing over time. Geographically, Europe is a fairly small continent, a peninsula extending out of the Eurasian landmass. Its eastern border runs along the Ural Mountains, and its western border edges into the Atlantic Ocean. It extends from the Arctic Ocean south to the Mediterranean Sea, almost touching Africa at the Straits of Gibraltar. It is the second smallest of the seven continents, larger only than Australia, at roughly 4 million square miles, with some three-quarters of a billion inhabitants.

Culturally, Europe is far larger, since it has influenced much of the rest of the world through conquest, emigration, and example. Though they are scattered throughout the world, countries such as Canada, Argentina, Uruguay, Israel, and New Zealand share a lot of similarities with the nations of Europe.

Politically, Europe is yet another entity that has evolved out of centuries of internal and external struggles. A series of treaties following major European wars formalized the major changes in the political map of Europe over the past several centuries. These treaties are shown in Figure 1.1. The **Peace of Westphalia** ended the Thirty Years War (1618–1648), a religious struggle triggered by the Protestant Reformation. The treaty tried to resolve these conflicts by dividing Europe into Catholic countries (mainly in the south) and Protestant countries (mainly in the north and west). This peace settlement also established the principle of national sovereignty, according to which each country has the right to determine its internal affairs, including religion, as it sees fit.

Figure 1.2 presents Europe following the Peace of Westphalia (1648). Southeastern Europe lived within the Ottoman Empire under the Turkish sultanate. Central Europe—in the form of Austria, Prussia, Switzerland, and Poland—was just beginning to take political shape. Northern Europe was dominated by Sweden, which in the 1600s was at the peak of its power. But more than anything else, Europe's future lay with a set of countries—Spain, Portugal, England, the Netherlands, and France—that bordered on the Atlantic Ocean, giving them maritime access to the rest of the world. This part of Europe evolved into a set of powerful states much earlier than did the rest of the continent. In Italy and Germany, in contrast, political control was split among loose and ineffective empires, city-states, and small principalities. The Atlantic states' size, seafaring capacity, and resources enabled them to create colonial empires. For two centuries after the Peace of Westphalia, France and England were the leading European powers.

The French Revolution of 1789 happened in the wake of the American Revolution. But unlike the latter, the French Revolution did not lead to stable democracy. Eventually, Napoleon Bonaparte seized power as an autocrat (1799–1814) and engaged France in a series of wars. Napoleon's expansionist policies led to many military conquests in Europe, but eventually his enemies defeated him. The **Treaty of Vienna** (1815) ended the Napoleonic Wars (see Figure 1.1). Prussia emerged as a powerful state. Russia gobbled up Poland and Finland. Europe of the early nineteenth century was dominated by a "Holy Alliance" of conservative monarchs trying to preserve their power and to prevent further social revolutions.

Later in the nineteenth century, the Prussians created a unified Germany that became an increasingly powerful and expansive state. A united Italian state emerged at about the same time. In the East the Ottoman Empire gradually weakened; it lost a part of

Milestones in European History

FIGURE 1.1

1618–48	Thirty Years War
1648	*Peace of Westphalia*
1688	Glorious Revolution in Britain, beginning of parliamentary democracy
1770	Industrial Revolution begins in Britain
1789	French Revolution
1799	Napoleon becomes French emperor, Napoleonic wars
1815	*Treaty of Vienna* ends Napoleonic wars
1870–71	German unification; Italian unification
1914–18	World War I
1917	Russian Revolution, Communists come to power
1919	*Treaty of Versailles* ends World War I
1933	Hitler creates Third Reich
1939–45	World War II
1945	*United Nations* founded; Germany divided into East and West
1949	NATO formed
1957	*European Community* (later *European Union—EU*) founded
1973–77	Greece, Portugal, and Spain democratize
1989–90	Berlin Wall Falls, Germany is reunified
1991	Collapse of Soviet Union
2004	EU expands to 25 members and takes in 8 Eastern countries
2007	EU expands to 27 members, Bulgaria and Romania join

Greece in the early nineteenth century and Bulgaria in the early twentieth.

World War I (1914–1918) was the disastrous result of the great power rivalries of the period. It involved most nations in Europe, at least indirectly, and produced death and destruction on a previously unimaginable scale. The **Treaty of Versailles** (1919) following the war established the national right to self-determination. Each nation (a people having a common self-defined identity and sharing a common territory) should have the right to determine whether to form its own state. The military results of World War I were hard on empires, and the Treaty of Versailles was not friendly to them. The defeated Ottoman Empire was driven back to its Turkish base, and the Austro-Hungarian Empire was split into Austria, Hungary, Yugoslavia, and Czechoslovakia. The German Empire crumbled and was replaced by a fragile democratic republic. The Russian Empire collapsed in 1917; the ensuing revolution led to a radical, Bolshevik Russia, which became the Soviet Union. Devastated by war and internal conflict, Russia lost control of Finland, Estonia, Latvia, Lithuania, and Poland. The map of Europe "between the wars" was much like contemporary Europe, except that Ukraine, Belarus, and Moldova were parts of the Soviet Union.

The aggressions of the Axis powers (Nazi [National Socialist] Germany, fascist Italy, and authoritarian Japan) brought on World War II. These countries had largely been left behind in the age of imperial conquest. Within the first years of World War II, almost all of Western Europe, with the notable exception of the United Kingdom, was overpowered and "coordinated" by Nazi armies. Nazi-occupied Europe was subjected to a reign of terror and a campaign of extermination directed against Jews, various other minorities, and opponents of the regime in general. The Nazi hold on Europe was broken in 1945 by the bloodied troops of the Soviet Union from the east and the armed forces of the United States, Britain, and their allies from the west. World War II led to the formation of the United Nations in 1945 and to the proclamation

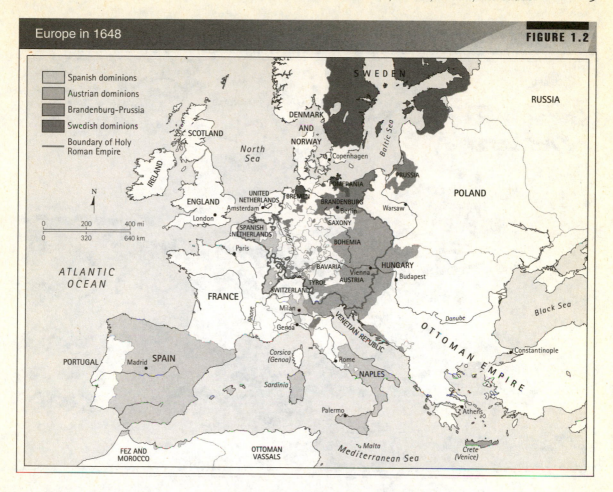

Europe in 1648

FIGURE 1.2

Legend:
- Spanish dominions
- Austrian dominions
- Brandenburg-Prussia
- Swedish dominions
- Boundary of Holy Roman Empire

of the Universal Declaration of Human Rights three years later. In 1948 a Communist coup in Czechoslovakia and a Soviet blockade of Berlin dashed hopes for a peaceful postwar Europe. The line separating the Soviet and the Western Allies' forces in mid-Germany became the **Iron Curtain** of the next generation.

Figure 1.3 depicts the Europe of the Cold War—a sharply divided continent. Its eastern part lay under Soviet political control and military occupation. Its western part was drawn together under American leadership. A few countries, such as Switzerland and Sweden, were neutral. Europe was frozen in what seemed a permanent confrontation.

This East-West division contributed to the development of European integration in the West (see Chapter 12). The **European Economic Community (EEC)**, formed in 1957, originally consisted of six countries: France, Germany, Italy, Belgium, the Netherlands, and Luxembourg.[3] The organization gradually expanded and in 1995 renamed itself the European Union. Until 2004 the EU included only Western European countries (at that time, 15 in all). International security policy also evolved. The **North Atlantic Treaty Organization (NATO)**, formed early in the Cold War (1949) under American leadership, mobilized Western European countries against the communist threat. NATO included the majority of West European nations, plus Turkey, Canada, and the United States. The Soviet bloc formed the **Warsaw Pact** (1955) to counter NATO. The **Council for Mutual Economic Assistance (COMECON)**, formed in 1959, coordinated the Eastern European economies.

The collapse of the communist regimes in the East in 1989 produced the most recent redrawing of the European map. The Berlin Wall, which had separated East and West Germany for almost thirty years,

Europe in the Cold War   **FIGURE 1.3**

was torn down by ordinary people on both sides, while armed border guards stood by and watched. Popular uprisings in Poland, Czechoslovakia, Hungary, and other Eastern European states brought down their communist governments. The Soviet Union accepted these events, withdrew from Eastern Europe, and in 1991 split into 15 independent political entities, 7 of which are considered to be European. Four of these states (Russia, Belarus, Ukraine, and Moldova) retain close, but sometimes tense, ties to one another. In contrast, the Baltic countries—Estonia, Latvia, and Lithuania—quickly reasserted their independence and successfully sought close ties with Western Europe. Five countries initially emerged from the dissolution of Yugoslavia in 1991–1992: Slovenia, Croatia, Macedonia, Bosnia-Herzegovina, and Serbia and Montenegro. Montenegro split off from Serbia in 2006 and Kosovo seceded in 2008. In

addition, two nations emerged from the peaceful breakup of the former Czechoslovakia in 1993: the Czech Republic and Slovakia.

Figure 1.4 presents a map of contemporary Europe. It is still common to think of Europe as divided into Western and Eastern parts, a view surviving from the Cold War and reflecting these nations' different experiences in the second half of the twentieth century. From this perspective 21 of the current 41 countries are the Eastern successors to the old Communist bloc: the 7 European successor states to the Soviet Union and the 7 components of the former Yugoslavia, plus Albania, Bulgaria, the Czech Republic, Hungary, Poland, Romania, and Slovakia. The remaining 20 Western countries include the 15 states that made up the EU until 2004.

In 2004 the EU admitted ten new states. These included eight Eastern European countries—Estonia,

Europe Today

FIGURE 1.4

Latvia, Lithuania, Poland, the Czech Republic, Slovakia, Hungary, and Slovenia—plus two smaller "Western" Mediterranean island states, Cyprus and Malta. In 2007 the EU added Bulgaria and Romania. Three Western states remain outside the EU: Iceland, Norway, and Switzerland. With patience, you should be able to count 41 "European" countries in Figure 1.4. Appendix 1.1 contains basic data on all of them. However, the political boundaries of Europe are far from settled. Many people in the states that bridge Europe and Asia—such as Georgia, Armenia, Azerbaijan, and especially Turkey—have aspirations to join the EU and be members of the European family.

NATO is still operating in Europe today and has expanded and redefined its role, for example, by supporting the new democratically elected government in Afghanistan. Like the EU, NATO has added ten Eastern European nations. Yet, NATO's role in the new Europe is uncertain. Russia opposes further NATO expansion to the east, viewing it as a threat to isolate Russia internationally. The close Cold War security relationship between the United States and Europe is no longer justified by a Soviet threat, even though some Eastern European countries still worry about their Russian neighbor. While substantial parts of Eastern Europe are now part of a greater Europe of democracy and relative prosperity, there are still areas of internal and international instability.

DESCRIBING EUROPE: LARGE AND SMALL COUNTRIES

One important way that European countries vary is by their size. Table 1.1 describes the differences in population for the Western and Eastern European

National Characteristics					TABLE 1.1
Comparing European Nations in Terms of Their Size and Economic Characteristics					

	Population (millions)	Geographic Area (thousands of sq mi)	Per Capita PPP, 2006 (U.S. Dollars)	Per Capita GDP Growth, 2002–2006 (percentages)	Average Inflation, 2002–2006 (percentages)	Labor Force in Agriculture (percentages)
Bulgaria	7.7	42.9	$10,274	5.7	5.3	9
France	61.3	212.9	31,992	1.7	1.9	4
Germany	82.4	137.9	32,322	0.9	1.6	2
Poland	38.1	120.7	14,836	4.1	1.9	17
Russia	142.5	6601.7	13,116	6.4	12.6	10
Spain	44.1	195.1	28,649	3.3	3.2	
United Kingdom	60.6	94.1	33,087	2.6	2.7	1

Source: World Bank. Retrieved June 18, 2008, from web.worldbank.org/wbsite/external/datastatistics

countries covered in this book. Russia is the giant, with over 140 million inhabitants. Some 30 million Russians live east of the Urals, in the Asian part of the country. Even if we subtract these eastern residents, European Russia has a population almost 50 percent larger than that of Germany, the second most populous European country. European Russia's population is almost 400 times that of Iceland, which has fewer than 300,000 inhabitants. France is third in population size, with over 60 million residents. The United Kingdom is very close behind; Spain and Poland are next among the countries covered in this book. Bulgaria is a relatively small nation, with just over 7 million inhabitants.

Out of all 41 European countries, 9 have populations of 20 million or more. Six of them are covered in this book; the remaining ones are Ukraine, Italy, and Romania. There are 15 medium-sized countries, with populations ranging from 5 million to about 15 million; 9 of these are in Western Europe, and the remaining 6 are in Eastern Europe. The populations in the 17 smallest European countries range from about 300,000 in Iceland to fewer than 5 million. Appendix 1.1 gives the population of each of these countries.[4]

In terms of geographic area (the second column in Table 1.1), Russia is again the leader; the ratio of its area to that of the second largest country is even greater than for its population. Although European Russia is only half again as populous as Germany, it has ten times the territory. The larger Western European countries (with areas exceeding 100,000 square miles or about the size of Oregon) are France, Spain, Sweden, Norway, Germany, Finland, and Italy. The United Kingdom is slightly smaller. In addition to Russia, the Eastern European giants include Ukraine and Poland.

Population and geographic area do not directly explain a nation's politics. The biggest states in terms of territory or population are not necessarily the richest or most powerful ones. For example, the small country of Switzerland has been an independent, free, and prosperous country for centuries, whereas Ukraine is a large, but comparatively poor country that has only recently gained its independence. Size, of course, does make a difference in warfare, as Napoleon and Hitler discovered on the wintry steppes of Russia. It also makes a difference in the availability of resources, in the problems of government centralization, and in other policy matters. Similarly, the relationship between area and population is important. Asian Russia (Siberia) has been a sparsely populated frontier open to settlement and economic exploitation. The Netherlands and other densely populated European countries have very different and powerful geographic constraints on their economic development.

One of the most important population issues is the rate of increase, which has crucial implications for economic growth and social policy. Europe now has the smallest population growth rate of all the

BOX 1.1

The Vanishing European

Steadily declining birthrates have created a population implosion within much of Europe. Because fewer children are being born, the overall population is decreasing and the average age is increasing. The United Nations estimates that the average age of Europeans has increased from 29.7 years in 1950 to 39.8 years in 2005 and will reach 48.9 years in 2050. In addition, the total population of Europe will decrease from 761 million in 2005 to 664 million in 2050. Europe's share of the global population will decrease from just over 20 percent in 1950 to about 7 percent in 2050. If it were not for immigration into Europe, the total population would drop even more dramatically.

Sources: United Nations, *World Population Prospects, 2006 Revision* (New York: United Nations, 2007); United Nations, *World Population Assessment and Projection,* 1996 ed. (New York: United Nations, 1997).

---

world regions (see Box 1.1). Around 2006 Europe had only a 0.1 percent average annual increase, in comparison with the Middle East and North Africa (1.8%), Sub-Saharan Africa (2.5%), South Asia (1.6%), Latin America (1.3%), and East Asia (.8%).[5] The low European birthrates are raising serious concerns about the sustainability of that continent's welfare states as their populations become steadily older.

DESCRIBING EUROPE: RICH AND POOR COUNTRIES

We can also think of large and small countries in terms of economic size. Germany is at the top among the European countries, with close to a $3,000 billion economy as of 2006, contrasted with a Montenegrin economy of around $2.5 billion. The economic output of Germany is thus over 1,000 times that of Montenegro. The other large Western European economies—France, the United Kingdom, and Italy—generate around $2,000 billion each year, while the larger Eastern European economies range from $1,000 billion for Russia to $340 billion for Poland and $100 billion for Hungary and Ukraine. By this measure the German economy in 2006 was about three times the size of that of Russia, with only a little more than half the population.

Table 1.1 also compares the economic performance of the seven countries in this book. An important measure of economic conditions is the average income level of people in a country. The third column in Table 1.1 shows a per capita measure of income. PPP stands for **purchasing power parity**, which is an attempt to measure the true values of different currencies, based on their respective capacities to purchase goods and services in domestic markets.[6] The economic contrasts between Western and Eastern Europe are striking. The average per capita income among the nations of Western Europe in 2006 was close to $36,000, while in Eastern Europe it was about $13,000, or only a little more than a third. These economic conditions shape the needs of each country's citizens, the resources available to address social and political needs, and thus the agenda of politics.

The structure of the labor force also differs between West and East. East European economies still have substantial agricultural sectors, in comparison with the heavily industrialized and urbanized societies of Western Europe. In all four Western European countries in this book, the agricultural workers account for 5 percent or less of the labor force. In contrast, 17 percent of Poland's labor force works in agriculture. A large agricultural labor force usually indicates lower economic development and productivity. Highly productive modern economies manage their agricultural needs with small, but very efficient farm populations. Also, a large agricultural sector usually means strong interest groups that protect the farm sector, and these interests often resist economic modernization policies and international integration.

These East-West differences, while large, can and will change over time, just as other differences have grown or disappeared. At the end of World War II, East and West Germany were equally devastated. When Germany was reunified 45 years later, the capitalist West had far outgrown the communist East. Similarly, 30 years ago Ireland was one of the poorest countries in Western Europe; today it is one of the richest. The gap between Western and most Eastern European economies grew larger in the 1990s. All the Western European countries had positive economic growth rates for the 1990s, averaging about 2 percent a year. In contrast, most Eastern European countries struggled with the very difficult transition from communist "command" economies to market economies. The average Eastern European country saw its economy decline nearly 2.5 percent a year. By the late 1990s, this trend changed, and since 1998 the Eastern European countries have generally grown more than those in the West, as seen in the fourth column in Table 1.1.

The average growth rate in Eastern Europe conceals great differences in how these countries are managing the economic transition. Poland is among the most successful Eastern European economies, and its average gains of 3 to 5 percent per year are larger than those of most Western European countries. Russia's economy was greatly affected by the collapse of its military sector and the obsolescence of much of its heavy industry; it experienced economic decline in the 1990s that was worse than the U.S. experience of the Great Depression of the 1930s. Fortunately, since around 1998 the Russian economy, fueled in part by its production of oil and other raw materials, has produced rapid economic growth, even though drastic poverty persists.

Inflation has been a major problem for many Western European countries in the past, especially in the 1920s and again from the 1960s through the 1980s. In recent years, however, Western Europe has worried much less about this problem, as Table 1.1 indicates. In Eastern Europe inflation was a serious, and largely unfamiliar, phenomenon in the 1990s. These price increases directly followed from the economic transitions. Inflation rates have greatly improved in much of Eastern Europe since 2000, but Table 1.1 shows that Russia still had nearly 13 percent yearly inflation in 2002–2006.

SOCIAL DEVELOPMENT AND WELFARE IN EUROPE

Economic conditions and public policies jointly shape the welfare of citizens and, in turn, their satisfactions or frustrations with their government's politics. Table 1.2 presents four measures of social development and welfare in European countries: education, computer ownership, income distribution, and infant mortality. These measures show different aspects of wealth and resources, as well as the past performance of national governments.

Most European countries, East and West, successfully educate their youth. All over Europe, and including most Eastern European countries, about half of all

National Social Development
Comparing European Nations in Terms of Their Social Development, Income Inequality, and Health

TABLE 1.2

	College (Tertiary School) Attendance as a Percentage of Age Group, 2006	Computers per 1,000 Population, 2006	Income Going to Top Fifth of Income Recipients* (percentages)	Infant Mortality per 1,000 births, 2006
Bulgaria	44	63	38.3	12
France	56	575	40.2	4
Germany	46	606	36.9	4
Poland	64	242	42.5	6
Russia	70	122	46.6	14
Spain	66	277	42.0	4
United Kingdom	59	600	40.2	5

*The income share numbers for France date back to 1995.
All other income share numbers range from 1999 to 2005.

Source: World Bank. Retrieved June 18, 2008, from web.worldbank.org/wbsite/external/datastatistics young adults attend some level of college or university. In some countries, including Russia, the percentage is much higher. Even in the poorer European countries, college education is far more widespread than in many low-income countries in other parts of the world. And in the East as well as the West, both boys and girls have ready access to secondary education, and large numbers complete their education at this level. High levels of literacy in these countries follow from these education levels. Public expenditures on education are also relatively similar across the seven nations in this book. In 2005 Germany spent 5.1 percent of its gross domestic product (GDP) on education and the United Kingdom 6.2 percent, compared with Russia's 3.8 percent and Poland's 5.9 percent.[7] However, the GDPs of the Western countries are several times larger than those of some Eastern countries, which translates into substantially larger Western European spending on such things as construction and maintenance of schools, teacher salaries, and educational equipment.

Table 1.2 also shows computer ownership as a measure of access to information and resources in the new electronic age. In this respect the richer Western European countries are significantly ahead of the Eastern European states. Yet, computer access is growing rapidly in all parts of Europe.

The distribution of income reported in Table 1.2 reflects an ironic situation. For 75 years Russia had a government ostensibly committed to social equality and the eradication of class differences. Today, only a few years after the introduction of a market economy, Russia has the most unequal distribution of income among all the countries listed. Nearly half of Russia's total income goes to the top fifth of income recipients, and less than 5 percent goes to the bottom fifth. Although some developing nations are even more unequal, Russia has one of the world's least egalitarian distributions of income, which contributes to its political tensions. This situation has arisen because many "entrepreneurs" (often well-connected former managers from the communist period or friends of the new power-holders) scooped up huge fortunes through shady deals when government assets were sold off after the collapse of the Soviet system (see Chapter 9). In contrast, Poland and Bulgaria are more egalitarian, with around 40 percent of income going to the top fifth. Distributions in most of Western Europe are fairly similar to these.

Table 1.2 includes infant mortality as an indicator of public health. Here again, the main difference runs not so much between East and West as between the poorer countries of the East and the rest. Russia's death rate is significantly higher than that of any other country in the table, and Bulgaria's is not far behind. Differences between the various Western European countries are small, and health conditions are generally excellent.

The European Dream?   BOX 1.2

American author and social critic Jeremy Rifkin has argued that an emerging "European Dream" is challenging and eclipsing the global appeal of the "American Dream." The American Dream, he argues, is about individual freedom, hard work, personal success, and financial independence. The European Dream, on the other hand, is more about quality of life, community, peaceful coexistence, and the enjoyment of leisure. Rifkin argues that European countries have achieved a standard of living that rivals that of the United States, but with less emphasis on work and more on quality of life. Whereas Americans live to work, he argues, Europeans work to live. According to Rifkin, the appeal of the European Dream is seen both in the inflow of immigrants into Europe and in the success of European ideas in the world community.

Not everyone agrees with Rifkin's ideas. For one thing, the European Dream is surely more evident in the richer countries of Western Europe than in the East. And some of the Western countries have experienced their own problems of stagnant economies and ethnic tension. Moreover, Europeans sometimes experience the "leisure" that Rifkin praises as unemployment that particularly hits the young and the immigrant population.

Source: Jeremy Rifkin, *The European Dream* (Cambridge, MA: Polity Press, 2004).

DEVELOPMENT, MODERNIZATION, AND DEMOCRACY

According to the various economic and social statistics we have presented, most Eastern European countries fall into the World Bank classification of "middle income countries," ranging from "lower middle income" (e.g., Albania, Bosnia, Moldova, and Ukraine) to "upper middle income" (e.g., Bulgaria, Poland, and Russia). At the same time, Eastern European economies have been growing rapidly in recent years, and most Eastern Europeans are educated and literate people, exposed to the world culture. Although long limited by communist control, they have the makings of civil societies, interest groups, and voluntary associations (see Chapter 3). Competitive communications media are growing.

The economic fortunes of the Eastern European countries bear on some of the major debates about the relationship between economic development and democratization. Indeed, the great ideological struggles of the past two centuries turned on these issues. Karl Marx claimed that the development of capitalism and the rise of the **bourgeoisie** would signal the decline of feudalism and the introduction of bourgeois democracy. This, in turn, would produce socialist democracy after the working class ousted the bourgeoisie and introduced a classless society.

There is little in the history of Eastern Europe to support this theory. The Eastern countries did not become communist because they were rich or because their workers rose up, but rather because the Soviet Union imposed this system of government. All the Eastern European countries were forcibly assimilated into the communist orbit at the end of World War II, and except for Yugoslavia it was mainly due to Soviet military and political control. Efforts to break free in Hungary in 1956 and in Czechoslovakia in 1968 were repressed by Soviet troops. And contrary to Marx, communist dominance did not lead to much social or economic progress or to a classless society.

Modern political science replaced the Marxist view with a different model of the economics-politics relationship, often referred to as a theory of **modernization** or development. Political scientists observe a strong association among economic development, social and political mobilization, and democracy.[8] Economic growth and **industrialization** are associated with urbanization, the spread of education and literacy, and exposure to the mass media of communication. Their studies argued that these conditions would result in greater political awareness and activity (mobilization), the formation of voluntary associations and competitive political parties, and the attainment of what is called **civil society**. These elements of a civil society would both demand and support more-democratic political systems.

But these theories did not always seem correct either. Spain and Portugal came through World War II as authoritarian regimes; Greece and Turkey also fell under military control in the 1960s. It became evident that the road to economic development could be long and hard—and that, at least in the short run, economic development did not ensure political development.[9]

However, the long-term implications of development became more apparent in the late 1970s and 1980s. Rapid and sustained economic growth in authoritarian Spain (see Chapter 8), Portugal, and Greece weakened the legitimacy of their authoritarian regimes. This democratic trend culminated in the dramatic collapse of the communist regimes in East Europe and the establishment of new democracies. The dominant political ideas of the 1990s were democracy and the market economy.

The experiences of the last decades, as well as the European historical experience, have produced a better understanding of the complex interaction of economic, social, and political processes. There is no doubt that stable or consolidated democracy is strongly associated with a high level of economic development. But the relationship occurs over the long run. It is shaped by the more dispersed power resources in a complex economy, the more participatory citizen values, the demands of an educated and organized citizenry, and the growth of socioeconomic resources to meet human needs.[10]

There remains in Europe a serious division of realities and prospects. Most Western European countries—economically developed, democratically consolidated, and largely organized in a confederation—have democracies that seem as stable as those anywhere in the world. Many Eastern European countries are approaching the Western European economic level, and many of these have joined the EU. But several Eastern European nations are far less economically productive, are often plagued by continuing economic difficulties, and are struggling with democratic ways of coping with change and conflict. Sadly, democratic freedoms are under pressure in nearly half of Eastern Europe, especially in the countries with lower levels of economic development, and are severely threatened in several nations, especially Belarus, Russia, and Moldova.

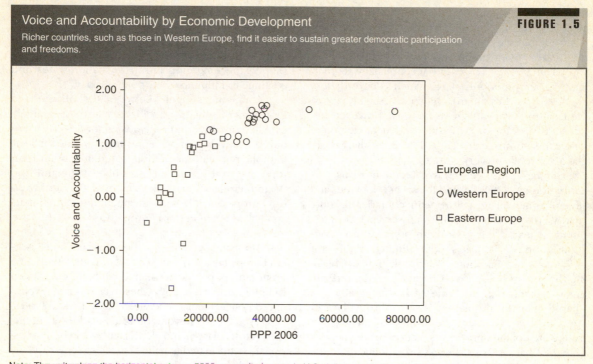

Voice and Accountability by Economic Development

FIGURE 1.5

Richer countries, such as those in Western Europe, find it easier to sustain greater democratic participation and freedoms.

Note: The units along the horizontal axis are 2006 per capita income in U.S. dollars, controlling for purchasing power parities.

Figure 1.5 depicts the relationship between economic development and the Voice and Accountability measure from the World Bank's Worldwide Governance Indicators for Europe. The Voice and Accountability scores in the figure draw on citizen and expert perceptions of "the extent to which a country's citizens are able to participate in selecting their government, as well as freedom of expression, freedom of association and a free media."[11] A score of zero means that the country is at the world average (mean) in voice and accountability. A positive score means the country is more democratic than the world's average; a negative score means the country is less democratic than the world's average. The economic development measure is **gross domestic product (GDP)** per capita in U.S. dollars, corrected for purchasing power parities, as of 2006 (see Table 1.1). Each circle in the figure represents a single country in Western Europe and each square an Eastern European country. Note that most countries in both East and West Europe score above zero: Compared to the rest of the world, Europe has much to be proud of in its record of voice and accountability. Note also that even within Europe affluence tends to

go hand in hand with democratic performance, although the relationship is far from perfect.

The small circles that represent the Western European countries appear at the top and from the center to the right of the figure. Nearly all are more affluent than most of the Eastern European countries, and all receive Voice and Accountability scores that rank them roughly in the top one-sixth of all the nations in the world. The poorest Western European countries, Portugal and Malta, have income levels only slightly below that of the richest Eastern European country (Slovenia). Their Voice and Accountability scores of about 1.2 put them at roughly the same level as Spain, Greece, and Italy, but significantly below the scores of Germany, France, and the United Kingdom, which are close to the Western European average of 1.4. There is clearly work still to do in both economic and democratic development in Western Europe.

In Eastern Europe, as shown by the small squares toward the left of the figure, the majority of the most successful economies are associated with strong democratic performance, with Slovenia, the Czech Republic, Hungary, Estonia, Poland, Slovakia, and Lithuania all showing PPP levels near or over

$15,000 and Voice and Accountability scores around 1.0. However, the less economically and socially developed countries, especially the successor states of the former Soviet Union and Yugoslavia, score less well. The average Voice and Accountability score in Eastern Europe is only 0.34 (which is nevertheless above the world's mean). Bulgaria is slightly above the Eastern European average at 0.56. However, Belarus, Russia, Moldova, Ukraine, and Montenegro are below the world average, and Albania, Bosnia, Serbia, and Macedonia are very close to it.

Similarly, the well-known Freedom House organization rates Belarus and Russia as "Not Free" and several other Eastern European countries as only "Partly Free." Freedom House's observers report frequent issues having to do with pressures and constraints on the mass media, limited rights for individuals and minorities, and problems in establishing the rule of law.[12] (See Chapter 4 on the difficulties of establishing the rule of law generally and Chapter 9 on this problem in Russia in particular.)

Of course, economic development and modernization are not the only factors that encourage democracy. In Chapter 2 we discuss how political culture may sustain or hinder democracy. International norms and institutions may also help support democracy. In contrast, religious and ethnic cleavages create potential tensions in many of the newly independent Eastern European countries. Democracy can arouse new expectations from suppressed minorities, and in poorer countries the absence of resources can make it difficult to accommodate such expectations. Yet, democracy may nonetheless provide a way to address ethnic and other social divisions that might otherwise be repressed and unresolved.

ETHNIC AND RELIGIOUS DIVISIONS IN EUROPE

Over the course of European history, economic growth, migration, warfare, famine, disease, and other factors have created a complex ethno-religious patchwork. Religion has been one central basis of differentiation among European states. The great religions of the world offer coherent value systems and standards of behavior. Before the Protestant Reformation, the Catholic Church provided much of the cultural unity for the fragmented politics of Christian Europe. Its magnificent cathedrals and splendid artworks inspire us even today. The birth

of modern Europe in the Renaissance and the Protestant Reformation shattered religious unity. The religious wars of the sixteenth and seventeenth centuries created Catholic-Protestant divisions that shaped the emerging European nation-states and continue to influence their politics today.[13]

When the struggle between Catholicism and Protestant dissent had stabilized, many states largely expelled or converted religious minorities. This produced relatively homogeneous religious nationalities. Catholic populations predominated in Southern Europe, as well as in nations such as Ireland and Poland. Protestant churches dominated in Northwestern Europe, usually without much internal religious conflict. Much of Eastern Europe was tied to the Eastern Orthodox Church.

Along the fault line between Northern and Southern Europe lay a series of states with both Catholic and Protestant populations—including both the United Kingdom and Germany. These states often experienced political tension between Catholics and Protestants. The French Revolution of 1789 added a conflict between secularism and clericalism, which became especially acute in traditionally Catholic societies. Followers of different faiths and worldviews tended to organize into separate communities with distinct social and political organizations. Such divisions often endure. Disagreements between these groups have focused on education, family law, abortion, and the rights and roles of women—areas in which religious and secular values often clash. A decline in church attendance and other religious practices since World War II has shifted the political balance in most of Western Europe in secular directions and decreased the intensity of divisions among Christian groups. Nonetheless, church attendance is still a potent predictor of vote choice in many countries, especially those with substantial Catholic populations (see Chapter 3).

Ethnicity is another source of social differentiation. Ethnic groups see themselves as having a common identity and believe that they share a common descent or history. Ethnicity is sometimes associated with religion, but it can also be related to language, custom, and historical memories. It provides an important basis for mobilizing communities based on common interests and deeply felt personal identities.

Ethnicity can be especially potent when allied with **nationalism**, the belief that an ethnic group should have the right, if it so chooses, to form a geographically defined independent state. The large nation-states that formed in the sixteenth through the nineteenth centuries often suppressed local identities in favor of a dominant national identity. With the spread of printing, mass education, and literacy, a state-supported national language replaced both Latin (the international language of the educated) and various local dialects. People came to identify with a larger nationality. They were French, Spanish, English, or German first—rather than a regional or ethnic minority within the nation. Nation-states became the foci of political activity and the key actors in international politics. World trade became dominated by nation-states and their respective colonies. And instead of being struggles between different monarchs and dynasties, wars became conflicts between nations and races. Nationalism helped bond people from different regions and social classes, and it became the banner under which many peoples freed themselves from the autocratic empires (such as the Austro-Hungarian Empire, Russia, and the Ottoman Empire) that dominated much of Europe until the early twentieth century. But nationalism also led to ethnic divisions and conflicts within and between states.

While ethnic divisions within European states were often deemphasized during the Cold War, the collapse of the communist bloc produced new expressions of these differences. Even though bureaucracies and party organizations in the Soviet Union and Yugoslavia were constructed to recognize and even encourage ethnic minorities, they had in practice mostly repressed these minorities' political aspirations. The overthrow of the authoritarian political systems and the introduction of free speech and independent mass media, especially in the absence of well-entrenched democratic parties, created political space for new ethnic and religious demands. Even within Western Europe ethnic groups seeking greater autonomy from the national government have become increasingly influential in such countries as Britain and Spain.

Table 1.3 highlights the diversity of ethno-religious divisions in six of the seven core nations examined in this book. Fewer than half of all European countries, mainly smaller ones, are free of significant ethnic or cultural divisions. The remaining European countries manifest more substantial ethno-religious divisions. In countries such as Switzerland, different language or denominational groups have long been able to coexist without much tension. In others, such as Belgium, ethnic divisions are deep and troubling, but have given rise to little or no organized violence in recent years. Yet, in some European countries, ethnic or religious divisions are sharp and explosive. After the breakup of Yugoslavia, Bosnia and later Kosovo erupted into civil war in the 1990s. For many decades terrorism in Northern Ireland and in Basque Spain has taken many lives and shattered the peace of these countries. In the Russian region of Chechnya, separatist terrorism and guerrilla warfare have been met by harsh Russian repression and have resulted in large-scale violence and devastation (see Chapter 9). The substantial Russian populations left in most of the countries bordering the Russian Federation are a source of tension vis-à-vis their national governments, as well as their relationships with the

| Ethno-religious Divisions | | TABLE 1.3 |
| Examples of Major Ethnic or Religious Divisions in Western and Eastern Europe | | |
Nation	**Groups**	**Bases of Conflict**
Bulgaria	Bulgarians v. Turks	Language, Religion
France	French v. Immigrants	Language, Religion
Germany	Germans v. Immigrants	Language, Religion
	Catholics v. Protestants	Religion
Russia	Russians v. Muslims	Language, Religion
	Russians v. Ethnic Minorities	Language, Religion
Spain	Spanish v. Basques and Catalans	Language
United Kingdom	British v. Irish in Northern Ireland	Religion
	British v. Scottish, Welsh	Language, Ethnicity
	British v. Immigrants	Language, Religion

Russian government. And the Russian incursions into Georgia in 2008 illustrate that such ethnic tension may even lead to cross-border warfare.

It is difficult to solve disputes over nation-state boundaries through democratic procedures. If the conflict comes to violence, it can quickly degenerate into *ethnic cleansing,* the forcible eviction or destruction of local minorities. Ethnic divisions and national grievances can lead to dehumanizing behavior and cruelties of enormous proportions, as has occurred in several parts of the former Yugoslavia.

While ethnic conflict can inflict terrible costs, it need not. Three strategies have often been employed to solve ethnic conflict: consociationalism, federalism, and secession. *Consociationalism* (or **consociational democracy**) involves (1) sharing political power by bringing all the different ethnic or religious groups into the national government, (2) decentralizing decisions by giving each group control over its own affairs (for example, separate school systems for different language or religious groups), (3) allowing each group to veto important collective policies that it believes will affect it adversely, and (4) proportionally sharing national offices and resources.[14] In Austria, for example, Socialists and Catholics in the 1950s and 1960s developed elaborate power-sharing arrangements to prevent a recurrence of the civil war of the early 1930s. But consociationalism is not always successful. Consociational efforts have thus far failed to solve the ethnic conflict in Cyprus and have long met with limited success in Northern Ireland.

The other two strategies are geographic. **Federalism** means geographic decentralization and the sharing of power between the central government and subnational regions. Generally speaking, it is most feasible when minorities are geographically concentrated, as in Switzerland and the Tatar Republic in Russia. Russia seems to have created a more or less successful federal relationship with the Tatars. **Secession** involves redefining state boundaries, allowing an ethnic group to form a new nation-state or to join with a neighboring one. Like federalism, it is realistic only when the different ethnic groups can be geographically separated, as in the breakup of Czechoslovakia into the Czech Republic and Slovakia.

Minorities that are territorially dispersed cannot easily be accommodated through either federalism or secession. Bulgaria, for example, has worked to accept Turkish residents into the political mainstream, in part through a Turkish political party. There are also ethnic parties in the Basque country and Catalonia in Spain. Britain has devolved some political authority to new regional assemblies in Scotland and Wales. While these strategies suggest that ethnic violence can be avoided or contained, this sometimes comes at substantial cost and requires tolerance from leaders and followers on all sides.

INTERNATIONAL MIGRATION

While European countries have thus struggled to overcome long-standing ethnic or religious divisions, recent surges of immigration have added new challenges. The rapidly growing presence of recent immigrants and foreign workers, primarily in Western Europe, is an important source of ethnic (and sometimes racial) division.[15] In 1960 Western Europe had a total of 14.2 million international migrants; by 2005 the number had risen to 64.2 million. As a share of the European population, immigrants went from 3.4 to 8.8 percent.[16] These minorities have produced new sources of cultural diversity, but also political tensions.

Table 1.4 gives some data on international migration for our core European countries. Note the substantial differences between East and West. Whereas most Eastern European countries (though not Russia) have a net outflow of migrants, most Western European states have become countries of substantial net immigration. This is true even of Spain and Ireland, which until the last decade or two used to have a net outflow. Many Western European countries now have a foreign-born population of 10–12 percent, which is not much smaller than that of the United States (12.9%). In contrast, a country such as Bulgaria has very few immigrants and a small net outward flow.

Immigration has come in many different forms. During the economic boom of the 1960s and early 1970s, several Western European countries invited foreign workers to fill vacancies in the labor force. Many came, and their families often followed. Germany has in this way attracted almost 2 million Turks and Kurds. Although many do not have formal citizenship, these workers and their families have become long-term residents.

The opening up of Eastern Europe produced new waves of migrants to Western European countries. Refugees sought to escape conflict in the Balkans, and people from many Eastern European

Immigrants Flow to the West	TABLE 1.4
Foreign-Born Population and Net Migration	

Country	Foreign-Born Population, 2005 (percentages)	Net Annual Migration per 1,000 Population, 2000–2005
Bulgaria	1.3	−1.0
France	10.7	1.0
Germany	12.3	2.7
Poland	1.8	−0.4
Russia	8.4	0.6
Spain	11.1	10.0
United Kingdom	9.1	2.3

Source: United Nations, *International Migration 2006* (New York: United Nations, 2006).

countries were looking for greater freedom and economic opportunities in the West. Conflicts in other regions of the globe, often in Europe's former colonies, have also stimulated migration to a stable and prosperous Europe. Europe has received a steady stream of refugees and asylum seekers from all parts of the world. While the United States is currently the world's single largest recipient of asylum seekers, the European nations jointly account for about two-thirds of all such migrants that come to the industrialized world. Immigrants have come from North Africa to France, from South Asia and the Caribbean to Britain, and from Surinam to the Netherlands. More than 3 million Algerian Muslims now reside in France. Often the cultural differences with the population of the host nation are heightened because the immigrants have a different language, religion, or race.

Immigration has brought new cultural richness and diversity to Europe. In most major European cities, it is now common to find ethnic restaurants run by immigrants, stores offering a global marketplace of products, a diversity of cultural events, and a wider range of political experiences among the citizenry. At the same time, increased ethnic diversity can create new sources of cultural contrast and conflict. One of the most troubling issues for European governments has been to integrate and find work for their often unskilled immigrants and to distinguish among legitimate refugees and asylum seekers, those falsely claiming such identities, and those involved in cross-border crime, smuggling,

and human trafficking. Most European governments today have tight restrictions on regular immigration, but maintain a generous policy toward refugees.

In many Western European nations—including Britain, France, Germany, and Spain—tensions with recent Muslim immigrants have increased in recent years. Some of these tensions arise from the immigrants' poor economic conditions and the struggle to provide for their families when jobs and welfare benefits are limited. In many European countries, strict labor market regulations make it difficult for immigrants to find jobs. A 2008 study found that in the state of Minnesota, almost 70 percent of Somali immigrants had found jobs; however, in Norway, the percentage was only 28.[17] Other tensions reflect cultural clashes over social, religious, and political values. Some members of ethnic majorities feel that their cultural and religious customs, as well as long-standing policies regulating church-state relations, are threatened (see Box 1.3). New political parties have arisen to express concerns that core values and identities are threatened by these new citizens (see Chapter 3 on the new "radical right" parties). Tensions have also occasionally boiled over into protest and violence, as in France in 2005 and 2006 (see Chapter 6).

These tensions have been magnified by the battle against Jihadist terrorism. The September 11 attacks in the United States were followed by several visible terrorist attacks in Europe, and other attempts were thwarted by authorities. On March 11, 2004, the deadly terrorist attack on the Madrid train

Headscarves: Contentious Cloths

BOX 1.3

A number of European countries have been struggling with the dilemmas posed by the Muslim headscarf, which throws up a variety of difficult issues relating to tolerance and equality. France is introducing a ban on the wearing of veils in schools, while in Germany, two states have proposed legislation which would also bar the scarf from educational institutions. In both countries it is argued that the covering of the head is a symbol of women's oppression which has no place in a democratic society—and certainly not in a school. Some female Muslims, feminists note, are forced into wearing the scarves by men—fathers, brothers, boyfriends, and husbands. But there are undeniably Muslim women and girls who of their own accord believe they should be covered up. They declare they are suffering discrimination at the hands of the state and being denied their right to freedom of religion. For both countries, efforts to prevent the headscarf appearing in civic spaces have raised serious questions about religious tolerance, and fueled the ongoing row about the relative benefits of assimilation as opposed to multiculturalism in an age of immigration.

Source: Clare Murphy, "Headscarves: Contentious Cloths," BBC Online, December 11, 2003.

station killed or wounded hundreds of people. In July 2005 there were several terrorist bomb attacks on the London Underground. In response, the EU has strengthened antiterrorism cooperation. Furthermore, these events have generally intensified European concerns about immigrants and prompted debates on the meaning of citizenship and the rights and obligations of minorities.

EUROPEAN POLITICS TODAY

Given its social and political history, Europe has been a primary laboratory of political innovation. The modern bureaucratic state, representative parliamentary institutions, various electoral systems, political parties and party systems, interest groups, and specialized communications media—the whole modern political apparatus—emerged first in Europe and its colonies. Most of the rest of the world has now incorporated these institutions and practices and has combined them (more and less successfully) with indigenous cultures and institutions. Europe is thus the location of both some of the greatest triumphs of democratic politics and some of the greatest horrors of totalitarian oppression.

Europe's global relevance continues. As the third wave of democracy seems to be reaching its peak, the 21 Eastern European countries—now free to shape their own futures after more than half a century of suppression—are a crucial battleground in the long human struggle for freedom and welfare. Nothing would affect the balance of this struggle more than rapid economic growth and consolidated democratization in such countries as the Russian Federation, Ukraine, Belarus, Bulgaria, and Romania. Moreover, the consolidated democracies of Western Europe can still go further to make public policies more responsive to a participating and confident citizenry. The newly enlarged EU, cutting across both Eastern and Western Europe, adds a dimension of the greatest relevance in an age of **globalization:** how to make citizen democratic control visible and viable, while reconciling different interests in an enormously complex institution that incorporates 27 economically and ethnically diverse national units.

At the same time, the challenges of aging populations, global economic competitors, and ethnically diverse immigrants that face the nations of Western Europe are increasingly felt also in the United States, Japan, and other economically developed countries. Europe's responses to these challenges, drawing on its historic experiences, can help us understand the range of possible answers and inject new creativity into the efforts to deal with them.

REVIEW QUESTIONS

- In what ways has historical Europe been both a creative and a destructive force?
- Discuss the historical and contemporary features that distinguish nations in "Western" and "Eastern" Europe.
- Why do higher levels of economic development help encourage and sustain democracy?
- Why are religious and ethnic divisions found within many European nations?
- Discuss the promises and problems associated with recent immigration trends in Europe.
- How has the European Union helped control Europe's national divisions?

KEY TERMS

bourgeoisie
civil society
Cold War
communism
Consociational democracy
Council for Mutual Economic Assistance (COMECON)
Enlightenment
ethnicity
European Economic Community (EEC)
European Union (EU)
fascism
federalism
globalization
gross domestic product (GDP)
industrialization
Industrial Revolution
Iron Curtain
market economy
modernization
nationalism
Nazism–National Socialism
North Atlantic Treaty Organization (NATO)
Peace of Westphalia
Protestant Reformation
purchasing power parity (PPP)
Renaissance
secession
Treaty of Versailles
Treaty of Vienna
Warsaw Pact

SUGGESTED READINGS

Dahl, Robert A. *Democracy and Its Critics*. New Haven, CT: Yale University Press, 1989.

———. *Polyarchy: Participation and Opposition*. New Haven, CT: Yale University Press, 1971.

Davies, Norman. *Europe: A History*. New York: Viking, 1997.

Diamond, Larry. *Developing Democracy: Toward Consolidation*. Baltimore, MD: Johns Hopkins University Press, 1999.

Fukuyama, Francis. *The End of History and the Last Man*. New York: Avon Books, 1992.

Hall, Peter, and David Soskice. *Varieties of Capitalism: The Institutional Foundations of Comparative Advantage*. Oxford, England: Oxford University Press, 2001.

Heywood, Paul, Erik Jones, Martin Rhodes, and Ulrich Sedelmeier, eds. *Developments in European Politics*. London: Palgrave Macmillan, 2002.

Horowitz, Donald. *Ethnic Groups and Conflict*. Berkeley: University of California Press, 1985.

Huntington, Samuel. *The Third Wave: Democratization in the Late Twentieth Century*. Norman: University of Oklahoma Press, 1991.

Koslowski, Rey. *Migrants and Citizens: Demographic Change in the European State System*. Ithaca, NY: Cornell University Press, 2000.

Roberts, J. M. *Europe 1880–1945*. 3rd ed. New York: Longman, 2000.

Sbragia, Alberta, ed. *Europolitics, Institutions, and Policy Making in the New European Community*. Washington, DC: Brookings Institution, 1992.

ENDNOTES

1. Mikhail Gorbachev, *Perestroika: New Thinking for Our Country and the World* (New York: Harper and Row, 1987), pp. 190, 197.

2. "Without comparisons to make, the mind does not know how to proceed," wrote Alexis de Tocqueville in a letter to Ernest de Chabrol in 1831 [*Alexis de Tocqueville: Selected Letters on Politics and Society*, ed. Roger Boesche (Berkeley: University of California Press, 1985), p. 59]. This theme has been repeated by many contemporary social scientists.

3. See Chapter 12; also see Leon Lindberg, *The Political Dynamics of European Economic Integration* (Stanford, CA: Stanford University Press, 1963).

4. We have consistently excluded from our analysis the "micro-states" of Andorra, Liechtenstein, Monaco, San Marino, and Vatican City, all of them with populations of less than 50,000 permanent residents and sustained by varying complex treaties and agreements with their surrounding nation-states.

5. World Bank, *World Development Indicators 2000*. Retrieved May 3, 2000, from www.worldbank.org/data/wdi2000/pdfs/tab1_4.pdf.

6. Most cross-national economic comparisons now calculate purchasing power parities (PPPs) to adjust for international differences in price levels, rather than simply relying on currency exchange rates. Goods generally cost less in poor, agricultural societies than in urbanized, industrial societies; thus, the PPP adjustments take into account the lower prices in Eastern Europe, compared with Western Europe.

7. Organisation for Economic Co-operation and Development (OECD), *Education at a Glance 2008: Education Indicators* (Paris: OECD, 2008).

8. See, for example, Daniel Lerner, *The Passing of Traditional Society* (New York: Free Press, 1958); Karl W. Deutsch, "Social Mobilization and Political Development," *American Political Science Review* Vol. 55 (September 1961): pp. 493–515; Seymour Martin Lipset, "Some Social Requisites of Democracy," *American Political Science Review* Vol. 53 (September 1959): pp. 69-105; Gabriel A. Almond and James S. Coleman, *The Politics of the Developing Areas* (Princeton, NJ: Princeton University Press, 1960); Robert Dahl, *Polyarchy: Participation and Opposition* (New Haven, CT: Yale University Press, 1971); Samuel Huntington, *Political Order in Changing Societies* (New Haven, CT: Yale University Press, 1968).

9. A "dependency" school of political economy argued that the idea of development was a sham that concealed the exploitation of poor peoples by capitalist powers. Dependency theorists saw global political reality as control of the third world periphery by American and European multinational capitalist corporations, backed up by military force and also by indigenous henchmen serving international capitalism. These theorists believed that the authoritarian governments in many developing countries in the 1960s and 1970s enforced this systematic exploitation. The dependency school gradually lost support among social scientists during the 1980s and has generated little scholarly research since then.

10. On the connections among modernization, citizen attitudes, and democracy, see especially Gabriel A. Almond and Sidney Verba, *The Civic Culture: Political Attitudes and Democracy in Five Nations* (Princeton, NJ: Princeton University Press, 1963), and Ronald Inglehart, *Modernization and Postmodernization: Cultural, Economic and Political Change in 43 Societies* (Princeton, NJ: Princeton University Press, 1997), chap. 6. On the dispersion of potential political resources in modernized societies, see especially Tatu Vanhanen, *Prospects of Democracy: A Study of 172 Countries* (New York: Routledge, 1997).

11. See Daniel Kaufmann, Aart Kraay, and Massimo Mastruzzi, "Governance Matters VII: Aggregate and Individual Governance Indicators 1996–2007" (unpublished World Bank paper, June 2008), pp. 7, 76–78. Retrieved June 24, 2008, from www.govindicators.org,

12. See www.freedomhouse.org.

13. Seymour Martin Lipset and Stein Rokkan, "Cleavage Structures, Party Systems and Voter Alignments: An Introduction," in *Party Systems and Voter Alignments*, ed. Seymour Martin Lipset and Stein Rokkan (New York: Free Press, 1967). The authors present a detailed analysis of the impact of religion on European nation-building and party formation.

14. Arend Lijphart, *The Politics of Accommodation: Pluralism and Democracy in the Netherlands* (Berkeley: University of California Press, 1968); Arend Lijphart, *Democracy in Plural Societies* (New Haven, CT: Yale University Press, 1977).

15. Rey Koslowski, *Migrants and Citizens: Demographic Change in the European State System* (Ithaca, NY: Cornell University Press, 2000); James Hollifield, *Immigrants, Markets and States: The Political Economy of Postwar Europe* (Cambridge: Harvard University Press, 1992).

16. United Nations, *World Migrant Stock: The 2005 Revision Population Database*. Retrieved July 24, 2008, from esa.un.org/migration/p2k0data.asp.

17. *Aftenposten*, October 4, 2008. Retrieved October 4, 2008, from aftenposten.no.

APPENDIX 1.1

The States of Contemporary Europe

Name	Population	Area (sq mi)	EU	NATO	Former USSR	Former Yugoslavia	Warsaw Pact
Albania	3,510,000	11,100					1955–1961
Austria	8,193,000	32,380	1995				
Belarus	10,293,000	80,130			X		
Belgium	10,379,000	11,780	1957	1949			
Bosnia and Herzegovina	4,499,000	19,740				X	
Bulgaria	7,385,000	42,810	2007	2004			X
Croatia	4,495,000	21,830				X	
Cyprus	784,000	3,570	2004				
Czech Republic	10,235,000	30,440	2004	1999			Czechoslovakia
Denmark	5,451,000	16,630	1973	1949			
Estonia	1,324,000	17,460	2004	2004	X		
Finland	5,231,000	130,520	1995				
France	62,752,000	246,360	1957	1949			
Germany	82,422,000	137,810	1957	1955			East Germany
Greece	10,688,000	50,930	1981	1952			
Hungary	9,981,000	35,910	2004	1999			X
Iceland	299,000	39,760		1949			
Ireland	4,062,000	27,130	1973				
Italy	58,134,000	116,270	1957	1949			
Kosovo	2,325,000	4,200				X	
Latvia	2,275,000	24,930	2004	2004	X		
Lithuania	3,586,000	25,170	2004	2004	X		
Luxembourg	474,000	1,000	1957	1949			
Macedonia	2,051,000	9,780				X	
Malta	400,000	120	2004				
Moldova	4,467,000	13,060			X		
Montenegro	631,000	5,410				X	
Netherlands	16,491,000	16,030	1957	1949			
Norway	4,611,000	124,990		1949			
Poland	38,537,000	120,700	2004	1999			X
Portugal	10,606,000	35,660	1986	1949			
Romania	22,304,000	91,680	2007	2004			X
Russia	142,894,000	6,591,030			X		
Serbia	7,071,000	29,910				X	
Slovakia	5,439,000	18,850	2004	2004			Czechoslovakia
Slovenia	2,010,000	7,830	2004	2004		X	
Spain	40,398,000	194,850	1986	1982			
Sweden	9,017,000	173,690	1995				
Switzerland	7,524,000	15,940					
Ukraine	46,711,000	233,030			X		
United Kingdom	60,609,000	86,780	1973	1949			

Source: Population as of 2005–2007 and area: Retrieved from www.theodora.com/wfb.

Kosovo area and estimated population as of 2001 (last official census was conducted in 1991): Retrieved from www.encyclopedia.com/doc/1B1-369404.html.

DEMOCRATIC POLITICAL CULTURE AND POLITICAL ACTION

If you travel across Europe on a long-distance Eurail Pass, maybe on the Orient Express from Paris to Istanbul, you see the diversity of the European continent. On such a trip, you see how Europeans differ in their languages, their styles of dress, their eating habits, their music preferences, their patterns of social relations, and even their definitions of humor. These elements make up the social culture of a nation. In addition, Europeans differ in their basic political values—that is, their political cultures. These are the so-called habits of the heart that shape political attitudes and actions. Like the social culture, the political culture is a shared set of norms about what is considered appropriate in the political system. It reflects the history of each nation, its social conditions, and the values transmitted by its parents and other political actors.

Nearly all the nations of Europe claim to follow the democratic model. There is wide variation, however, in the institutions and practice of democracy (see Chapters 3 and 4). These cross-national institutional differences partially reflect variations in how people think politics should function, as well as historical experiences and traditions. Citizens in Western Europe have a long experience with democratic elections and autonomous social groups that represent their interests. These experiences have nurtured attachments to democratic values and more activist norms of citizenship. Even within Western Europe, however, people emphasize different aspects of the democratic model. The French revolutionary tradition often encourages protest activity; the British tradition of moderation prompts more conventional political

action. The citizens of some nations believe in a more activist role for government, and in other nations people are more skeptical of government. Such variations in political norms shape how politics functions in a nation.

The question of political norms has special relevance to the study of Eastern Europe. Scholars claim that democracy requires a supportive public with democratic values if it is to endure. Indeed, the failure of European democracies in the 1930s and later is often linked to these nations' lack of democratic norms. To what extent have democratic values and norms developed in the new democracies of the East? Furthermore, East Europeans may have different expectations about the democratic process and their role within this new political system. What is the legacy of their communist histories? The nature of Eastern Europeans' political values is an important factor in the study of contemporary European politics.

By examining citizen attitudes and behavior, this chapter describes what democracy expects of its citizens, what citizens expect of their government, and the variations in how Europeans can participate in the political process.

THE CULTURAL FOUNDATIONS OF DEMOCRACY

Most Eastern European nations have made remarkable democratic progress since the democratic transitions of the 1990s. Despite initial economic problems, struggles with new democratic procedures, and a host of

Although Britain follows democratic procedures, it remains a constitutional monarchy, and its traditions underscore the importance attached to the Crown. For example, the Queen of England presides over the opening of the new Parliament following the general elections. The Lords and Ladies assemble in the House of Lords, along with the Bishops of the Church, foreign ambassadors, members of the royal family, and other dignitaries. When the Queen arrives from the palace, the members of the House of Commons are summoned by Blackrod, following a centuries-old tradition. When both houses of Parliament are assembled, the Queen delivers an address outlining the policies of "her" government during the next legislative session.

(The opening of Parliament, as well as weekly Question Hours in the House of Commons, is broadcast in the United States on C–SPAN.)

social problems, most of these nations have maintained their democratic course. But beyond the institutional changes, there is a deeper question of whether East Europeans accept democratic principles and their rights and responsibilities under a democratic system. The futures of these new democracies partially depend on the values and beliefs of their citizens. If the people share the values of the political system, then it is more likely that they and the system can function more effectively. If the people reject the values of the system, it can lead to revolts like those that swept across Eastern Europe in the early 1990s, when communist regimes fell in a series of largely bloodless revolutions.

At issue is the content of each nation's **political culture**.[1] The political culture includes what the people think and feel about politics, attitudes that have evolved from history and traditions. Scholars argue that a stable political system requires a political culture that is congruent with the style of government. Thus, a democratic political system must be based on a democratic political culture, while an autocratic state has different expectations of the public.

During times of regime change, agreement between the public's political norms and the institutions and procedures of the new political system is especially important. For example, most scholars believe that the Weimar Republic collapsed in the 1930s partially because many Germans did not believe in the new democratic system that had been created in 1919. Prior experiences had taught these Germans to accept authoritarian and ethnocentric values, attitudes that made them susceptible to Hitler's demagogic appeals. Thus, post–World War II West Germany again faced the question of whether the new institutions of democracy could succeed if Germans lacked democratic values. Fortunately, military defeat and postwar economic growth led to a transformation of the political culture in West Germany (see Chapter 7). The Spanish transition to democracy generated similar questions—and fortunately similarly positive answers (see Chapter 8).

East Europe faces the same kinds of questions. What are the enduring historical, political, and cultural legacies of communism for the region? Do Poles, Czechs, Russians, and the other nationalities of Eastern European hold political values that support the democratic process? Or has prior communist rule created undemocratic and authoritarian values that may produce a fragile new political order? We need to assess the contemporary political cultures of our set of European nations in order to answer these questions.

Furthermore, the West European political experiences and political cultures are changing. Analysts make conflicting claims about whether decreasing electoral engagement and increasing political cynicism signal an emerging crisis of democracy in the West. In addition, the increasing ethnic and racial diversity of European societies raises new questions about possible divisions in political norms. There are common worries that diversity may erode support for pluralist democratic norms. Thus, a study of political culture allows us to address these questions of change for both East and West Europe.

THE LEVELS OF A POLITICAL CULTURE

A nation's political culture includes citizen orientations at three levels: (1) the political system, (2) the political and policymaking process, and (3) policy outputs (Table 2.1). The **system level** involves citizens' orientations toward the political community and the values and organizations that constitute the political system. Do citizens identify with the nation and generally accept the political system?

The **process level** taps expectations of how politics should function and how individuals should relate to the process. For instance, attitudes toward government procedures and political institutions, such as the principles of pluralist democracy and support for parliamentary government, are important in defining how politics actually functions.

The **policy level** deals with what citizens expect from the government. What should the government's policy goals be, and how are they to be achieved?

The System Level

If you grew up in the United States, you remember the common school-time expressions of our national identity that develop feelings of patriotism: saying the pledge of allegiance and singing the national anthem. Such an orientation toward the nation and the political system is one of our basic political identities—and an important component of a political culture. These sentiments are often acquired early in life, taught by parents and the education system. Therefore, these are fairly stable orientations that are relatively independent of attitudes toward the political issues of the day.

The legitimacy of the political system is another aspect of system orientations. Legitimacy provides a foundation for a successful, or at least enduring, polity. When citizens believe that they ought to obey the laws, then legitimacy is high. If they question the authority of the state or if they comply only from fear, then legitimacy is low. A new political system often faces a challenge in convincing the people that the new government is legitimate and thus that its directives should be followed voluntarily.

A strong emotional identity with the nation can also reinforce acceptance of the polity and can maintain a political system through temporary periods of political stress. The deep sense of national pride and national destiny voiced by Winston Churchill during World War II struck a responsive chord with the British public, thus enabling Britain to endure in the midst of an intense military conflict. However, Scottish and Welsh regional identities have seemingly grown in recent years, accompanied by the devolution of political institutions. Divided ethnic or historical identities still exist in many West European democracies (see Table 1.3), but in most countries a single national identity unites the citizenry.

Among the nations of Eastern Europe, some, such as Poland, have a strong national identity, but many others are relatively new political constructs that lack public identifications. Virtually all East European nations have new constitutions written during the 1990s, and most have existed as independent nations for barely a decade. For instance, Yugoslavia fragmented after the collapse of communism because the public lacked a common national identity as Yugoslavs. Thus, we might ask whether European publics—in West and East—have a strong sense of national identity.

Feelings of pride in one's nation illustrate this aspect of the political culture, as shown in Figure 2.1. In the mid-2000s, the upheavals of the political transition are past in most of Eastern Europe, and enduring national traits are more apparent. Strong feelings of national pride exist in both Western and Eastern Europe—the Poles express as much pride as the Spaniards, for example. National pride is not a function of the longevity or past political form of the nation.

More questionable are the cases where the populace does not identify with the nation. This raises warning signals for a political system. For example, national pride was relatively low in Czechoslovakia in a 1990 survey—within three years, the nation had split in two.

Political Culture	TABLE 2.1
Defining the three key aspects of political culture	

Aspects of Political Culture

	Examples
System	Pride in nation
	National identity
	Legitimacy of government
Process	Role of citizens
	Perceptions of political rights
	Norms of political process
Policy	Role of government
	Government policy priorities

National Pride

FIGURE 2.1

Most Europeans feel proud about their nationality and supportive of the political community.

West Europe/United States	East Europe
	Poland (100)
Spain, Finland, USA	
Britain	
Sweden, France, Switzerland (90)	Slovenia (90)
	Russia/Romania
Netherlands (80)	Bulgaria
	Ukraine
Germany (70)	

Note: The figure presents the percentages that are "very proud" and "proud"; missing data are not included in the calculation of percentages.

Source: Selected nations from the 2005–08 World Values Survey.

German political leaders have consciously avoided the nationalism of the past, and it shows even in this recent survey. National pride is also relatively restrained in several Eastern European nations that have struggled throughout the 1990s: Russia, Bulgaria, and Ukraine.

While system orientations normally focus on the nation, this aspect of the political culture is becoming more complex in Europe. The process of European integration and the development of the European Union (EU) have created supranational identities, often in tandem with national attachments (see Chapter 12). For instance, a recent survey found that more than 90 percent of the public identified themselves as citizens of their nation in eight EU member states; at the same time, about two-thirds also identified themselves as citizens of the EU.[2] Furthermore, the supranational umbrella of the EU appears to strengthen regional identities in some divided nations.

As the EU's membership and policy responsibilities have expanded in recent years, opinions about the integration process are evolving. Most Europeans are still positive about the EU and its benefits, but opinions have become more changeable, and the factors influencing opinions have become more variable.[3] Concerns about the EU's expanded policy role and desires for more citizen input into the integration process have slowed recent efforts at constitutional reform (see Chapter 12). Increasingly, Europeans are balancing their European, national, and regional identities in defining their own sense of community.

The Process Level

The second level of the political culture involves public expectations for the political process. What do Bulgarians think is expected of them as citizens, and what do they expect of their government? Are their views different from those of British or Spanish citizens?

Political theorists generally stress three norms as the basis of the democratic process. The first is the Lockean emphasis on popular sovereignty as the basis of government authority and the final arbiter of politics. Democracy must, above all, be based on the rule of the people. The second is a commitment to the equality of citizens based on the arguments of Jefferson, Bentham, and Paine. The third is the principle of majoritarian decisionmaking, with adequate protection of minority rights. These principles lead to specific procedures by which democratic processes are ensured, such as Robert Dahl's conditions of polyarchy.[4] In short, the political culture approach argues that democracies require a citizenry (and elites) who endorse the core values of a democratic regime.

Research on West European countries generally finds broad public support for **democratic values**.[5] Citizens and elites accept the principle of organizing political institutions based on popular control through regular elections, as well as party competition and the selection of leadership through elections. Most Western Europeans recognize the legitimacy of conflict over political means and ends, while opposing violence as a political tool. Europeans also broadly endorse the right of individual participation and majority rule, paired with the protection of minority rights.

At the same time, we cannot become complacent about public support for democracy in Western

Europe. Often there is a gap between public support for these democratic principles and public support for their application in specific cases. Many people say they support free speech, but they are less willing to actually grant this right to groups that challenge their values. Still, most citizens in the established democracies of Western Europe accept the principles on which their democratic systems were founded and function today.

Earlier transitions from authoritarianism to democracy in West Europe show how a prior authoritarian state could leave a negative cultural heritage. After World War II, Italy had a cultural legacy of fascist attitudes that were not conducive to the workings of democracy. But the Italian culture was transformed and democratic values became the norm.[6] The postwar Germans and Austrians held broadly undemocratic views, and the remaking of their political cultures over the next generation was quite remarkable. The more recent democratic transitions in Spain and Portugal reflected this same pattern. The Francoist regime was antidemocratic and based on authoritarian norms, but after Franco's death the Spanish process of cultural transformation created a new political culture that is more conducive to democracy (see Chapter 8). In short, each of these new democratic regimes inherited a public that was critical of its institutions and unsupportive of its norms. These West European states had to remold citizen beliefs into a culture compatible with democratic processes—and they were successful in this task.

Communism raises a similar question about the cultural legacy of Eastern Europe. In the early 1990s, it was difficult to know whether these nations would face the same cultural problems as the countries that previously underwent authoritarian/democratic transitions in Western Europe. The communist system was full of internal contradictions. Although the Soviet Union and other Eastern European states suppressed dissent and prohibited meaningful forms of representative democracy, the official rhetoric of these regimes often endorsed democratic principles. Elections were regularly held, and turnout routinely topped 90 percent of the eligible electorate. Many of these governments also mobilized people into an array of political organizations, ranging from labor unions to women's federations and state-sanctioned environmental groups. While some communist regimes were openly authoritarian, others displayed examples of a nascent form of democracy. Gorbachev's reforms of *perestroika* and

glasnost built on these tendencies, and reform movements existed within Eastern Europe.[7]

Almost as soon as the Berlin Wall fell, survey researchers found surprisingly high levels of support for basic democratic principles in the former Soviet Union and other East European nations.[8] Figure 2.2 compares the opinions of Western and Eastern Europeans on two current examples of democratic values: willingness to allow a revolutionary to publish a book and opposition to the government detaining individuals without a trial when it suspects terrorists are about to act. These questions posed difficult choices to respondents in order to test their support for democratic values. Almost two-thirds of Western Europeans would allow even a revolutionary the opportunity to publish a book; a majority of East Europeans shared this opinion, although their rate of support was about 10 percent less. Even more challenging was the question on detaining individuals without trial. Most Western Europeans opposed such detention. The opposition was markedly lower in Britain, however, which had experienced terrorist attacks on London the year before the survey and has broad detention laws. The opinions in East Europe are as varied as in the West, with almost a majority opposed to detention even in these circumstances. There was a surprising opposition to government detention in Russia, perhaps because it evoked images of the communist past. Indeed, since the earliest surveys after the collapse of communism, East Europeans have displayed surprising support for democratic values.[9]

The support for democratic principles in Eastern Europe is somewhat surprising, given the attempts of the prior regimes to instill communist values among the citizenry. To many Eastern Europeans, however, these democratic rights represent a new reality for which they had fought the old regime. The Solidarity demonstrations in Poland, the protests in central Prague, the candlelight marches in Leipzig, and the public response to the August 1991 Russian coup demonstrate this commitment. Having newly won these freedoms, Eastern Europeans openly endorse them.

After half a century or more of communism, how did these publics come to express such support for democratic norms? There is no single answer, and researchers point to several factors. The limited empirical evidence suggests that support for the prior communist system eroded during the 1980s. Eastern Europeans saw their living standards decline during the decade, and their governments seemed unwilling or unable to

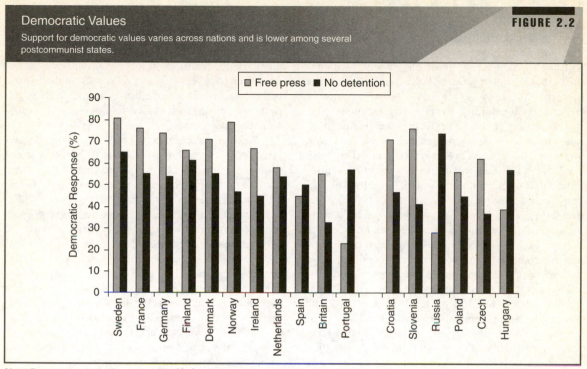

Democratic Values

FIGURE 2.2

Support for democratic values varies across nations and is lower among several postcommunist states.

Note: Percentages indicate agreement with the statement that "revolutionaries should be allowed to publish books expressing their views" and disagreement with the statement that "the government could detain people for as long as it wants without putting them on trial" if the government suspected a terrorist act was about to happen. Missing data are excluded from the calculations of percentages.

Source: International Social Survey Program 2006 (www.issp.org).

respond. This eroded popular support for the communist system and its values. And, ironically, the old regimes had voiced support for democratic principles, even if the reality of the communist system was much different. These democratic sentiments were further encouraged by *perestroika* and *glasnost* reforms—albeit with different consequences than Gorbachev had envisioned. The positive model of Western Europe also appealed to many Easterners, as seen in the mass exodus from East Germany in 1989. Furthermore, the euphoria of the democratization wave in 1989–1991 undoubtedly boosted support for the new political creed. Even with these explanations, however, the broad support for democratic principles in Eastern Europe was still a surprising starting point for these democratic transitions—much different from the democratic transitions in West Europe in the 1940s and 1970s.

Although expressed support for democratic principles appears fairly similar in East and West, larger differences often appear in how people evaluate the actual functioning of democracy in their individual

nations. In some Eastern European nations, there is a substantial gap between the public's support for democratic principles and its views of the present political process. For instance, a recent poll found that only a third of the public in 11 Eastern European nations was satisfied with the way that democracy worked in their nation, compared to two-thirds in Western Europe.[10] People are frustrated by the inability of the new political institutions to deal with the economic and social problems existing in Eastern Europe.[11] Furthermore, realities such as the Bosnian and Kosovo conflicts, the rise of an authoritarian government in Belarus, and the increasingly autocratic government in Russia remind us that the prospects for democracy remain uncertain in many Eastern European states.

In the end, support for democracy and an understanding of the democratic process are still developing in Eastern Europe. It is difficult to evaluate the depth of Easterners' feelings about democracy or to judge whether these are enduring cultural norms. Still, even if public endorsement of democratic values cannot yet be described as an enduring political culture, the widespread expression of such values is a positive signal for democratic prospects in the East. The people in most postcommunist states espouse support for democratic principles, which facilitates the democratization process. Poland and several other Eastern European states have made impressive progress in developing competitive elections, ensuring the rule of law, and protecting democratic liberties. Democratic development in Bulgaria is slower, and previous progress in Russia has reversed in recent years. Most Russians value democracy and freedom—although a significant minority still longs for an autocratic leader. Rather than the apathy or hostility that greeted democracy after transitions from right-wing authoritarian governments in Western Europe, the cultural legacy of communism in Eastern Europe appears to be more supportive of democratization.

Western Europeans broadly endorse democratic values, but there are cultural challenges in the West as well.[12] One area involves the tensions associated with an increasingly diverse society, where tolerance for immigrants and minorities is under increasing challenge. Acceptance of these minorities and protection of their rights have become a growing source of tension and polarization within many nations.[13] In addition, publics are now more openly critical of politicians and the working of representative democracy. Many young, better-educated Europeans have raised their expectations for greater political influence and want to further strengthen the democratic process. These sentiments generate substantial pressure for political reform in the West and stimulate a more contentious style of politics. These critical citizens are pressing for more access to government decisionmakers, more transparency in government, and institutional reforms to expand the democratic process.[14] Similar concerns about a "democracy deficit" in EU institutions have grown in importance as the EU itself has expanded its policy role. Indeed, the goal of democratic politics is to give the public an institutionalized way to express its dissatisfaction by electing new public officials and changing the policies of government.

The Policy Expectations Level

What do you expect of your government? It should run the education and postal systems and manage foreign policy—but should it also provide jobs, guarantee health care, or decide whether stem cell research is allowed?

A third level of the political culture involves the public's expectations of the appropriate social and political role of government. These cultural norms involve the public's broad views about the scope of government, the needs and wants that government should address, and the areas that should remain in the private sphere. And because government adapts to these expectations, the political culture defines the broad framework of policymaking.

Western European democracies have experienced great conflict over these questions. The labor and social democratic movements of the nineteenth century focused on the government's rightful role in providing basic social services and managing the economy. Urbanization created new demands on municipal governments and raised new questions of urban development and redevelopment. More recently, the environmental movement has demanded that governments address the environmental costs of economic activity and ensure environmental quality. Other social interests press their government to be active in everything from training rock bands to preserving the nation's historic sites.

Indeed, government activity grew in nearly all Western European democracies during the latter half of the twentieth century (see Chapter 1). The various levels of government in the United States spend roughly a third of the gross national product (GNP), but many European governments account for half (or more) of the GNP (see Chapter 4). Governments are now responsible for a variety of social and personal conditions that were once outside the domain of government activity. Analysts attribute at least a portion of this growth to the public's expanding expectations.[15] People expect more of their government, and they are promised more by politicians; thus, government policymaking has grown to meet these expectations. As Anthony King has written: "Once upon a time, man looked to God to order the world. Then he looked to the market. Now he looks to government."[16]

These public expectations have several important implications for contemporary European politics. Although most Europeans expect an activist government, there are still sharp cross-national and domestic differences in exactly what is expected. Labor unions want government to expand the benefits given to workers; businesses want government to provide tax incentives and subsidies to spur economic growth. Environmentalists want government to spend more on protecting the environment; commuters want government to build more roads and expand public transportation. The essence of democratic politics is to find the balance between these competing interests.

Government and the Economy

As West European governments have grown over time, complaints about high taxation and the excess of government action became more commonplace. Some political analysts claim that contemporary interest groups are demanding more than what democratic government can provide in an effective and efficient way. Others maintain that government is usurping individual freedom and private initiative. Public opinion surveys show a renewed debate over government action as many citizens question government's appropriate role in addressing the economic downturn that began in 2008. Thus, the debate about the appropriate role of government is continuing.

The political changes in Eastern Europe and the Soviet Union added a new theme to this discussion on the role of government. State corporations and government agencies almost exclusively controlled the command economies in the East, and the government set both wages and prices. The government was also responsible for providing for individual needs, ranging from guaranteed employment to the provision of housing and health care. "Cradle to grave socialism" was more than just a slogan in Eastern Europe.

However, the socialist economies were unable to compete on the world market because they lacked the economic efficiencies of a market system. Posttransition governments therefore rushed to privatize their economies. Thus, the democratization of Eastern European political systems was paralleled by a privatization of their economies.

To what extent do Eastern Europeans carry forward their expectations for government activities from the experiences of the prior regimes? Do Poles and Bulgarians expect the new governments to guarantee employment despite the economic principles of their new market economies? Similarly, do Germans in the West and East have similar expectations about what services government should provide, or has unification created a public with sharply contrasting views of the government's appropriate role? The collapse of communism does not necessarily mean that Eastern Europeans reject the socialist principles of their former systems—principles that could often conflict with their new market economies.

We can describe Europeans' present policy norms by comparing opinions in several areas. At the heart of this debate is the government's role in managing the

economy and ensuring individual well-being. This separates both conservatives and liberals in the West, as well as forming a potential East-West divide. Comparative research shows that levels of national affluence affect these opinions; the citizens of less-affluent nations are generally more in favor of government action as a strategy for economic development.[17] In addition, we want to compare the nations in the West with established market economies with those in Eastern Europe with new market economies.

Figure 2.3 shows how several European nations differ in their support for government taking more

Government Responsibility

FIGURE 2.3

East Europeans are generally supportive of government action to ensure the public's well-being.

(%)	
80	Russia
	East Germany/Bulgaria
	Ukraine
70	Spain
	Slovenia/Moldova
	Romania
	West Germany/Italy
60	Poland
	Netherlands
50	
	France
	United States/Switzerland
	Britain/Finland
40	
	Sweden
30	

Note: The figure indicates approval of "government taking more responsibility for ensuring that everyone is provided for" versus "people should take responsibility to provide for themselves."

Source: 2005–2008 World Values Survey (www.worldvalues survey.org).

responsibility for ensuring that everyone is provided for (versus people taking individual responsibility for themselves). In the mid-2000s, the more affluent countries of Northern Europe (for example, France, Britain, Finland, and Sweden) were less likely to favor greater governmental responsibility—in part because the government's role is already quite large. Resistance to government action has grown over the past few decades, paralleling the privatization of government-owned businesses and the moderation in social service programs. The less affluent nations of Western Europe (Spain and Italy) were more supportive of government taking responsibility.

Equally interesting are the results for Eastern Europe. The dismantling of the socialist economies in the East was accompanied by popular endorsement of a greater role for a market economy. But East Europeans still favor a greater role for government in the economy. For example, almost four-fifths of the Russian public felt the government should take more responsibility—partially a reaction to economic problems that followed the transition to democracy and partially a persistence of socialist norms.[18] Similarly, support for government action remains high in most other East European states.

Comparing support for a government-managed economy in the various social strata in Eastern Europe illustrates the surprising legacy of the old communist system. The better educated are typically the "carriers of the creed" in most societies.[19] These individuals normally occupy positions of status and influence; they are the operators of the existing economic and political systems. In addition, accepting the regime norms was often required to gain access to higher education. One could not attend the university without being a member of the correct communist youth groups or without having a good family record of regime support. Thus, the better educated should espouse the values of the pre-1989 communist and socialist systems. In fact, the opposite occurs. When the old regimes were just ending in the early 1990s, most better-educated Eastern Europeans showed limited affection for socialism.[20] Instead of adhering to the values of the old regime, as is normally the case, the better educated were the strongest advocates for a privatized economy. Indeed, the intelligentsia of the communist society led the protests in East Berlin and Prague, and the faces of young university students were prominent in these crowds. Perhaps communism fell as rapidly as it did because it had lost the support of the managers and technicians of the old regimes.

The communist regimes more effectively socialized the less educated into believing in government management of the economy. This pattern holds in most of the nations in Eastern Europe. Think of the irony: These regimes claimed to represent workers and peasants, and the less educated actually adhered to these socialist principles. The true beneficiaries of these regimes—the better educated and those in the upper social strata—doubted their value. Possibly the better educated were more aware of the superior productivity of the market systems of the West.

The Government's Policy Responsibilities

Government management of the economy is one of the state's most basic policy activities. But many citizens believe the government should be involved in a great many other areas, from deterring crime to protecting the quality of the environment. Many citizens also feel the government is responsible for promoting individual well-being and guaranteeing the quality of life for its citizens—and both Westerners and Easterners share these expectations.

Table 2.2 displays the percentages of the public in several European nations in 2006 (and the United States) who think the government is "definitely responsible" for dealing with specific social problems. Residents of Russia, Poland, and Eastern Germany, who were conditioned by their former regimes to expect big government, have higher expectations of their democratic governments. Most citizens in Poland and Russia believe the government is definitely responsible for providing health care, providing a decent standard of living for the elderly, protecting the environment, aiding students, providing employment, and reducing income differences. There is also a clear contrast between the more modest expectations of West Germans and the more activist expectations of East Germans.

Many West Europeans share these high expectations of government. Spaniards, for instance, favor about as much government policy activity as do Poles or Russians. Support for government activity has decreased in Britain, but the French still see the government as definitely responsible in several policy areas. Thus, support for government action to resolve social needs is a common element of the European political culture. In comparison to most Europeans, Americans are more reserved in accepting government action, but support for government policy activity has increased significantly since the previous survey in 1996. Analysts often explain Americans' conservative

What Should Government Do?

Europeans, and especially East European publics, generally favor a large policy role for government

TABLE 2.2

	United States	Britain	France	West Germany	East Germany	Spain	Poland	Russia
Provide health care for the sick	55%	71%	58%	51%	62%	76%	71%	76%
Provide a decent living standard for the elderly	56	60	52	45	54	79	71	81
Enact strict environmental laws	61	48	72	45	51	62	54	64
Give aid to needy college students	55	34	56	38	46	70	58	62
Keep prices under control	45	32	48	31	46	55	36	71
Provide a job for everyone who wants one	16	17	33	30	46	43	58	63
Reduce income differences between rich and poor	27	27	53	26	50	50	54	53
Provide housing for those who need it	32	25	37	21	25	61	42	55
Provide a decent living standard for the unemployed	16	11	18	15	26	50	35	32
Provide industry with help	28	29	30	17	25	46	43	47
Average	39	35	46	32	43	59	62	60

Note: Table entries are the percentages who say that each area should definitely be the government's responsibility. Missing data are excluded in the calculation of percentages.

Source: 2006 International Social Survey Programs.

socioeconomic attitudes as the result of the individualist nature of the American political culture and the absence of a socialist working-class party.

The public sentiments expressed in Table 2.2 may partially explain why the scope of government has grown so large in Europe over the past generation. Others scholars claim that these opinions result from the growth of government activism, which conditions the public to expect even more from government.[21] In either case, these expectations are another example of how political culture and political outcomes tend to converge. Governments can grow more easily when the public accepts (and expects) that they will grow. Governments are more likely to shrink when public support for government activism wanes. Thus, it is more than a coincidence that the expansive welfare states in Scandinavia coincide with broad public support for social programs, while Margaret Thatcher's program of privatizing government-owned industries in Britain coincided with decreasing public support for nationalized industry.

Another new aspect of policy expectations involves the question of which level of government should be responsible in different policy domains. In many areas, such as science policy and environmental protection, a majority in most nations is willing to transfer policy responsibility to the EU in the belief that Europe-wide regulations are more appropriate. In other areas, such as education and social security, a large bias toward national responsibility remains.[22] Indeed, one of the central elements of the European integration process involves the public's (and the elites') willingness to transfer ever more policy responsibility to the EU (see Chapter 12).

Debates about the proper role of the national and EU governments will be a continuing feature of contemporary politics. However, it is clear that most Europeans expect their government to protect social welfare, help the economy, and guarantee the quality of life. The question is not whether government should act, but how it should manage the diverse demands the public makes on it.

THE CONGRUENCE PRINCIPLE

We study political culture to know what citizens think about politics and their governments. Moreover, the political culture approach argues that these sentiments are important in defining the nature of politics. Political culture theory says that the political institutions of a nation must be congruent with the political culture of the public. A stable democracy, for instance, requires a democratic social and political culture. Tocqueville, for instance, wrote that democracy should develop as a habit of the heart, reflecting basic values and patterns of social relations: "The manners of the people may be considered as one of the great general causes to which the maintenance of a democratic republic in the United States is attributable."[23] If democratic values are lacking, the system may succumb to the appeals of autocratic leaders or tolerate nondemocratic governments. Thus, both democratic and nondemocratic cultures tend to overlap with political systems congruent with these values. Similarly, expectations of government policy outputs tend to converge with what the government actually does. This convergence of citizen norms and politics is the essence of the political culture approach.

The congruence theory led to speculation about the popular base for democracy in Eastern Europe that we have discussed in this chapter. Although we have described broad support for democratic principles in many East European nations, these democratic aspirations often are accompanied by a thin understanding of the actual nature of democracy. Moreover, there is residual support for autocratic governments. Gradually, we would expect the political culture and political system to converge on a new equilibrium. This should be a mutual process. Sometimes the new institutions might reshape public values, and sometimes democratic orientations might facilitate changes in political institutions and practices.

A cross-national comparison of public opinion illustrates the link between the political culture and the political history of a nation. Researchers asked people in nearly three dozen European nations whether they approved of a government run by a strong leader who could act without parliamentary support—this measures a mix of people who favor dynamic leadership and outright support for an autocratic form of government. Figure 2.4 illustrates how opinions about government by a strong leader covary with the political

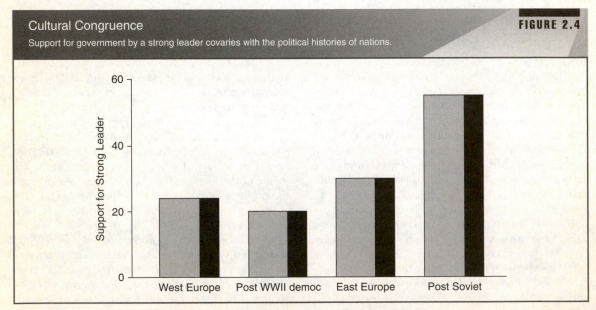

Cultural Congruence   **FIGURE 2.4**

Support for government by a strong leader covaries with the political histories of nations.

Note: For each group, the percentage who support "a strong leader who does not have to bother with parliament" is an average across the nations that were interviewed in the survey.

Source: 1999–2002 World Values Survey.

histories of nations.[24] Those West European countries with continuous democratic histories during the twentieth century display relatively low support for government by a strong leader. Nations that experienced authoritarian disruption in midcentury—such as Germany, Italy, Spain, and Portugal—are even less supportive of a strong leader, possibly as a socialized reaction to earlier negative experiences.

Support for a strong leader is generally higher in Eastern European states. This implies residual support for the strong autocratic governments of the past by a minority of the public. Yet, other questions from the same survey demonstrate that support for democracy is much greater in these nations. The greatest reservoir of support for government by a strong leader is found in the post-Soviet states, such as Russia, Belarus, and Ukraine. These sentiments provide a cultural basis for Putin's personalistic style in Russia and for the elitism in these nations (see Box 2.2). Even a decade after the end of communism, this cultural legacy remains.

One may ask whether a democratic political system creates a democratic political culture or whether a democratic political culture leads to a democratic political system. Obviously, it works both ways. For example, West Germans became more trustful as the nation democratized following World War II. This may have been a result of both Westerners living in a democratic system and democracy encouraging this aspect of the culture. Trend data from almost all East European nations suggest that these publics are becoming more supportive of democracy over time.[25]

The important conclusion is that in the long term there is a congruence between the political culture and the political process. It is difficult for democracy to endure when people are intolerant and lack democratic values and understanding. When these values exist, a democratic government must reinforce them; when they are lacking, an aspiring democracy must create them. The hope is that democratization will continue to change these norms among the publics of Eastern Europe.

Furthermore, we have stressed that the political culture also influences the style of politics within a political system. Czechoslovakia divided in 1993 into the Czech and Slovak republics because citizens in the two halves had different national identities despite their common political heritage. Their political identities were not congruent with their political institutions. Similarly, a government's level of activity and its style of policymaking should generally overlap with the public's expectations of how these processes should function. A nation's political culture thus identifies the broad parameters within which the people, elites, and political institutions are expected to function.

PARTICIPATION AND DEMOCRACY

If you wanted to change a government program or oppose new legislation under consideration, what would you do? One way to measure the growth of democracy is by the public's access to politics and the government's responsiveness to public demands. The history of modern democracies has been marked by a slow and sometimes conflictual expansion of the public's participation.

Modern democracy is **representative democracy**. It treats elections as the primary vehicle for public participation and democratic governance.

Vladimir Putin: Elected Leader or Czar

BOX 2.2

When Vladimir Putin finished his second term as president of Russia in 2008, he had overwhelming public approval in the polls and was quickly elected to Parliament and then appointed Russia's new premier. Many observers worry that Putin's strong-arm tactics—such as restricting the free press, taking over the oil industry, ending elections for regional governors, and pursuing a more nationalistic foreign policy—have reversed Russia's democratic development and that this will continue as long as he is premier. They see his tactics as reflecting a culture where support for a strong autocratic leader is nearly as widespread as support for democracy. Putin's supporters attribute his popularity in the polls to the government's policies of restoring order, strengthening the economy, and regaining some of Russia's lost international stature.

Through elections, the public controls the selection of political leaders, which determines the formation of government and the policies the government will likely implement.

Although **election turnout** is now a standard part of democratic participation, the expansion of the franchise in Europe occurred only during the past century. At the start of the twentieth century, most European democracies severely restricted the franchise. Britain, for instance, limited election rolls by implementing residency and financial restrictions and by allowing multiple votes for business owners and university graduates. In 1900 only 14 percent of the British adult population was eligible to vote. Almost without exception, governments denied women the right to vote.

During the twentieth century, governments gradually extended suffrage rights to the adult population. Women won the right in most nations in the century, but some countries delayed—most notably, France until 1944 and Switzerland until 1970. During the 1970s most nations also reduced the minimum voting age to 18. By the latter half of the twentieth century, voting rights were essentially universal among the adult populations in Western Europe.

Although the Communist parties of Eastern Europe did not permit open competition, these nations also held regular elections, sometimes with multiple parties or a unified slate of candidates. Voting turnout routinely exceeded 90 percent of the eligible electorate; the last Soviet-era election of 1984 had an official turnout rate of 99.9 percent. Elections were not a way to influence government; they were a means for the government to mobilize and indoctrinate the populace. Thus, voting levels were consistently high, even if some ballots had to be cast by election officials themselves. Nevertheless, elections were held, and the public learned the mechanics of campaigns and the voting process.

Today most eligible Europeans vote in national elections. Moreover, voting is a significant method of citizen influence because it selects political elites and determines the composition of the government. Elections also provide an opportunity for political activists to participate in the selection of party candidates and to try to influence the political views of others. Elections are national civics lessons in which voters learn about the past and future programs of the parties, participate in the democratic process, and decide about the issues facing their nation.

Figure 2.5 displays the election turnouts in West and East Europe in the most recent national

Voting   **FIGURE 2.5**

Most Europeans vote, but turnout is generally higher in Western European elections.

West Europe	East Europe
100	
Luxembourg	
Belgium/Cyprus 90	
Denmark	
	Turkey
Italy	
Sweden	
Netherlands 80	
Germany	
Norway	
Spain	
Austria/Greece	
70	
Ireland	
Finland	Moldova
Portugal	Czech Republic/Hungary
	Georgia/Russia
	Estonia/Ukraine
Britain	Latvia/Slovenia
France 60	Croatia
	Poland/Romania
	Bulgaria
	Slovakia
50	Albania
Switzerland	
	Lithuania
(%)	

Note: The figure shows the percentage of registered voters who cast a ballot in the most recent election. Voting in Belgium, Cyprus, and Luxembourg is compulsory.

Source: Institute for Democracy and Electoral Systems (www.idea.int).

parliamentary election for which data are available. What is most striking is the large range in voter turnout across these nations. The lowest level of involvement is in a well-established democracy, Switzerland, where less than half of the eligible electorate (48%) actually voted in 2007. Voting rates are consistently higher in most other European nations; in three nations where voting is still compulsory (Belgium, Cyprus, and Luxembourg), turnout tops 90 percent. Turnout rates in Eastern Europe were often quite high in the first elections after the democratic transition, but have decreased a bit in recent elections.

A range of factors affects levels of voter turnout.[26] Electoral laws and institutions, such as the type of electoral system and the registration regulations, influence participation rates. In addition, political competition and the structure of party choices strongly affect turnout levels. For example, turnout in U.S. elections is significantly below the norm for European democracies, and this can largely be explained by such uniquely American characteristics as complicated registration requirements and the frequency of elections.

Because voting is the most common form of political action and the basis of representative democracy, the declining turnout in Western Europe over the last few decades is a source of concern.[27] Furthermore, other forms of campaign activity are also declining in many nations. Fewer citizens, even in established democracies, attend a campaign rally or display their partisan support during a campaign. Similarly, high turnout levels in the first democratic elections in Eastern Europe often were followed by a drop-off in later elections. If elections are the celebration of democratic politics, fewer individuals seem to be joining in these celebrations.

The decrease in electoral participation is even more surprising when compared with the socioeconomic development of Europe described in the previous chapter. Contemporary electorates are better educated, better informed, and more interested in politics than were their predecessors. Europeans are also more democratic in their values than was the public a generation ago. Nevertheless, electoral participation has decreased. This creates a puzzle as to why electoral participation is limited and decreasing if the public's political skills and resources are increasing.

At the core of this puzzle is a concern with the vitality of the democratic process. Analysts view higher levels of voter turnout as a positive feature for

democracy. In general, this is correct; democratic nations with high levels of turnout for elections are involving their citizens in the political process. Consequently, decreasing turnout is often attributed to growing alienation from politics or a more general decline in civic life.[28]

Another explanation for reduced levels of electoral participation is the development of a new style of **participatory democracy** among West European publics. Instead of indirect influence through elected officials, many citizens now try to influence politics directly. Interest in contacting politicians or in participating in direct-action methods has grown as election turnout has decreased. Citizen-action groups and public interest groups are pressing for greater citizen input in policy formation and administration.[29]

The situation, of course, is different in Eastern Europe. These prior communist regimes involved the public in mass membership groups and state-sponsored political organizations.[30] In East Germany, for example, there were millions of members in the labor unions, the women's federation, and the German-Soviet Friendship Society. However, these groups were not autonomous, but rather were controlled by the Communist Party and state agencies. Gradually, civil society groups are developing in East Europe, but they are still less extensive than in the West. Slowly, but steadily, Easterners are learning to become good democratic citizens.

Figure 2.6 compares the average public involvement in various forms of political participation between West European and East European nations. Voting in elections is the most common activity, but there are a variety of political activities that citizens can use to influence the government. Many Europeans within the previous year signed a petition, donated money to a political cause, or boycotted a product for a political reason. Even more-demanding forms of activity—such as contacting a politician, attending a meeting, and participating in a demonstration—involved a significant minority on a yearly basis. Protest has become the extension of conventional politics used by the full range of societal interests. There are also specific cross-national differences in these patterns. For instance, the French score relatively high on contentious forms of action, reflecting their revolutionary tradition, while Russia and Bulgaria tend to score the lowest on protest activities.[31]

The second obvious pattern is the difference in activity between West and East. For each one of these activities, West Europeans were more active

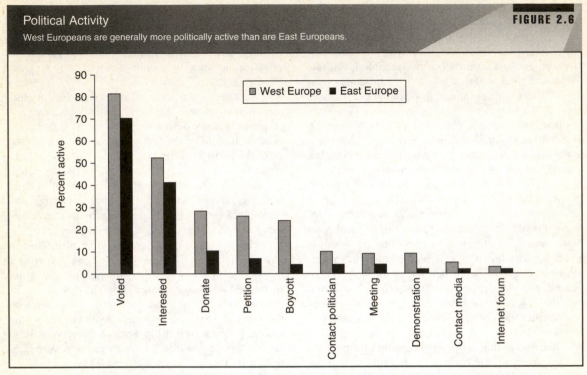

Political Activity

West Europeans are generally more politically active than are East Europeans.

FIGURE 2.6

Note: The figure presents reported turnout in the previous national election and participation in each of the other activities during the previous 12 months based on the ISSP survey. These results are the average of 15 West European nations and 9 East European nations.

Source: International Social Survey Program 2004.

than East Europeans. The gap is modest for voter turnout, but it widens for other forms of action. For instance, donating, signing petitions, and boycotting were more than twice as common in the West as in the East. The level of protest activity was also markedly lower across Eastern Europe, and protest there has declined as the tumultuous events of 1990–1991 have passed into history.

We also know that different kinds of people engage in these various forms of participation.[32] Because voting places the least demands on its participants, it is the most common form of political action and involves a diverse mix of people. By comparison, direct-action methods require greater personal initiative and more-sophisticated political skills. It is much more demanding to organize a letter-writing campaign or participate in a public interest group than to cast a ballot at the next election. Consequently, participation in direct forms of action often varies considerably by social status. While

voting is spread across the electorate, direct action is now disproportionately used by the affluent and better educated. Similarly, only those with strong political beliefs are likely to become active in single-issue groups. This situation increases the participation gap between lower-status and higher-status individuals. As the better educated expand their political influence through direct-action methods, less-educated citizens might be unable to compete on the same terms. Ironically, overall increases in political involvement may mask growing inequalities in citizen participation and influence, which run counter to democratic ideals.

In summary, European political participation has changed in three significant ways in recent decades. First, the obvious change has involved the democratic transition in the East. Even though East Europeans are generally less active than their cousins in the West, most Eastern European nations are now functioning democracies where citizens play a significant role in the political process. With the passage of time, these citizens are likely to expand their role and democratic influence.

Second, the Western public's involvement and interest in political matters are now widespread. Many Europeans turn out at the polls, contact their representative directly, and belong to local community organizations; others work on political campaigns; and large numbers are members of public interest groups.[33] Therefore, some analysts describe the last two decades as a **participatory revolution,** during which public involvement in the democratic process has grown.

Third, the patterns of political participation in the established democracies have changed in qualitative terms. The methods of representative democracy—voting and campaign work—are important activities because they determine the control of government. However, these are relatively blunt democratic tools, since the typical election involves many issues and candidates. Some theorists even criticize representative democracy as a mechanism designed to limit the public's influence over government by channeling participation through infrequent elections.

Participatory democracy produces a qualitatively different form of citizen input. Involvement in a citizen action group or direct contact with policymakers allows people to focus attention on a specific policy concern. The voice of the public is also louder when the citizens express their views themselves. Direct action gives citizens greater control over the timing and methods of participation, compared with the institutionalized framework of elections. Therefore, the growing use of citizen-initiated participation increases popular control of political elites. Citizen participation is becoming more closely linked to citizen influence.

These developments are changing the style of politics in advanced industrial democracies. New social movements have created an infrastructure for continued citizen policy involvement. For instance, in Germany administrative law now gives the public more say in policy administration; in Italy new legislation gives the public legal standing in defending the environment in court, and the use of initiatives and referendums is generally increasing. Citizen groups such as these have legitimated direct-action methods of participation for other citizens (see Chapter 4). Today Gray Panthers protest for senior citizen rights, consumers are active monitors

of industry, and citizen groups of all kinds are proliferating.

The strength of the democratic process is its ability to adapt, evolve, and become more democratic. In recent years the political systems in most West European states have adopted forms of participatory democracy and given their citizenry new methods by which to participate in the decisions affecting their lives. The nations of Western Europe vary in their emphasis on representative and participatory democracy, but nearly all are now characterized by a mix of these styles.

The challenge for established and emerging democracies is to expand the opportunities for citizens to participate in the political process. Meeting this challenge also means ensuring an equality of political rights and opportunities that will be even more difficult to guarantee with these new forms of participation.

THE PUBLIC AND DEMOCRACY

In many ways the citizenry defines the essence of democratic politics. In practice democracy is a German at the polls casting a vote for her preferred party, a French farmer driving his tractor to Paris to protest the government's agricultural policy, a Bulgarian writing a letter to a newspaper in the capital to criticize government policy, and a Polish health care worker protesting a cut in government health care spending.

Public wants and needs set the priorities that democratic governments strive to address. Citizen expectations of the political process influence the ways in which that process works and the kinds of policies it produces. Citizen political participation presses a democracy to match its lofty ideals.

This chapter's emphasis on the citizenry does not presume that political culture and citizen action determine policy outcomes. Other parts of the process—interest groups, political parties, and political leaders—also affect policy outcomes, and their direct impact is often greater in the short term. Similarly, if we want to predict the success of democracy in Eastern Europe, it is much more important in the short term to study the actions and values of elites and the role of institutions.

Thus, citizen politics does not primarily explain the daily outcomes of politics, but it determines the

BOX 2.3

France's National Sport: Protest

The French routinely display high levels of protest activity in comparative studies of political participation in Europe. A sample of the protests from 2007 illustrates this. During that year French labor unions protested the use of English language terms in the workplace, a campaign to help the homeless erected tent cities across France in protest, others demonstrated against a law using DNA tests in immigration hearings, farmers dumped dead sheep in front of a town hall to protest the reintroduction of bears who had killed the sheep, young people protested a proposal for a tax on Internet file sharing, transportation workers opposed government plans for pension reforms, students protested against policies giving universities more financial autonomy, and lawyers demonstrated against a proposed change in the divorce law. Indeed, the year began with a small protest in Nantes advocating that France say "no to 2007" and declare a moratorium on the future. Protest in France spreads across all of society.

---

broad boundaries of the political system. One political scientist described public opinion as a set of dikes, broadly channeling the course of democratic politics and defining its boundaries. The public's policy preferences influence policy outcomes in a democratic system—but through a complex and sometimes circuitous route.[34] In the same way, the public's expectations of politics and support for the political system determine the long-term functioning of the system. The immediate success of the new Eastern European democracies may depend on elite actions, but their long-term success depends on creating a democratic political culture among both the public and the elites. Democracy cannot endure in a nation without democrats.

This chapter illustrates the citizens' part of the democratic process in Europe. The citizens in these nations generally share a common democratic creed, and these political systems are built on common principles. Most Europeans express support for their political system and a sense of national identity; expectations about an activist government are also common.

These publics differ in their conceptions about *how* the democratic process should function. People in some nations display a more participatory style of democracy, with high levels of conventional and unconventional political action. The Danes (and the Americans), for example, are an activist public with institutional structures that encourage the representation of diverse political interests. Other Europeans, such as the British, accept a more representative style of democracy, placing greater reliance on elites and on elections as instruments of popular control. The

French seem to follow a more conflictual style of politics, where protest is almost routine. Democracy follows a single set of principles, but it takes life in many forms.

The nations of Eastern Europe are now making choices about how to practice democracy as the new system becomes institutionalized. Chapter 1 showed that several Eastern European nations still merit poor scores for political rights and civil liberties. Some political experts argue that another form of authoritarian state lies in the future for some of these nations, and political progress in Russia is uncertain.

We do not overlook these difficulties, but we also note that these democratic transitions generally began with a majority of the people and the elites supporting democratic principles. Moreover, the international community is actively working to encourage freedom and political liberties in Eastern Europe. The expansion of EU membership to ten East European states is a prime example. If democracy successfully takes root, Eastern Europeans will search for democratic forms that meet their particular histories and their expectations. Political debates over representative and participatory democracy and over various institutional choices for democratic politics are especially real in Eastern Europe as these systems are now taking shape. Thus, the evolution of democracy continues, with new trends emerging among the consolidated democracies in the West and still unclear trends developing among the nations in Eastern Europe. How these two democratization processes develop will define the political fate of Europe in this century.

REVIEW QUESTIONS

- What are the three key elements of a political culture?
- What are the cultural legacies of communism for the nations of East Europe?
- How does the political culture affect contemporary politics?

- What are the implications of congruence theory?
- What are the main ways in which citizens can participate in politics?
- Describe the differences in participation styles between West and East Europe

KEY TERMS

democratic values

election turnout

participatory democracy

participatory revolution

policy level of political culture

process level of political culture

political culture

representative democracy

system level of political culture

SUGGESTED READINGS

Almond, Gabriel, and Sidney Verba. *The Civic Culture*. Princeton, NJ: Princeton University Press, 1963.

_____, eds. *The Civic Culture Revisited*. Boston: Little Brown, 1980.

Blais, Andre. *To Vote or Not? The Merits and Limits of Rational Choice Theory*. Pittsburgh, PA: University of Pittsburgh Press, 2000.

Borre, Ole, and Elinor Scarbrough, eds. *The Scope of Government*. Oxford, England: Oxford University Press, 1995.

Dalton, Russell. *Citizen Politics: Public Opinion and Political Parties in Advanced Industrial Democracies,* 5th ed. Washington, DC: CQ Press, 2008.

_____ *Democratic Challenges, Democratic Choices: The Erosion of Political Support in Western Democracies*. Oxford, England: Oxford University Press, 2004.

Franklin, Mark. *Voter Turnout and the Dynamics of Electoral Competition in Established Democracies Since 1945*. New York: Cambridge University Press, 2004.

Inglehart, Ronald. *Culture Shift in Advanced Industrial Society*. Princeton, NJ: Princeton University Press, 1990.

Inglehart, Ronald, and Christian Welzel. *The Human Development Model and Value Change*. New York: Cambridge University Press, 2005.

Kaase, Max, and Ken Newton, eds. *Beliefs in Government*. Oxford, England: Oxford University Press, 1995.

Klingemann, Hans-Dieter, Dieter Fuchs, and Jan Zielonka, eds. *Democracy and Political Culture in Eastern Europe*. New York: Routledge, 2006.

Niemi, Richard, Lawrence LeDuc, and Pippa Norris, eds. *Comparing Democracies 3: New Challenges in the Study of Elections and Voting*. Newbury Park, CA: Sage, 2009.

Norris, Pippa. *Democratic Phoenix: Reinventing Political Activism*. New York: Cambridge University Press, 2002.

Pharr, Susan, and Robert Putnam, eds. *Discontented Democracies: What's Troubling the Trilateral Countries?* Princeton, NJ: Princeton University Press, 2000.

Putnam, Robert. *Bowling Alone: The Collapse and Revival of American Community*. New York: Simon and Schuster, 2000.

Putnam, Robert, ed. *Democracies in Flux: The Evolution of Social Capital in Contemporary Society*. Oxford, England: Oxford University Press, 2002.

Rose, Richard, William Mishler, and Christian Haerpfer. *Democracy and Its Alternatives: Understanding Postcommunist Societies*. Baltimore, MD: Johns Hopkins University Press, 1998.

Verba, Sidney, Kay Schlozman, and Henry Brady. *Voice and Equality: Civic Volunteerism in American Politics*. Cambridge: Harvard University Press, 1995.

White, Stephen, Richard Rose, and Ian McAllister. *How Russia Votes*. Chatham, NJ: Chatham House, 1996.

ENDNOTES

1. Gabriel Almond and Sidney Verba, *The Civic Culture* (Princeton, NJ: Princeton University Press, 1963); Gabriel Almond and Sidney Verba, eds., *The Civic Culture Revisited* (Boston: Little Brown, 1980).

2. 2005–08 World Values Survey (www.worldvaluessurvey.org). These comparisons are based on Cyprus, Finland, Germany, Italy, Poland, Slovenia, Spain, and Sweden. In the two East European states that were not yet EU members (Bulgaria and Romania), less than half saw themselves as EU citizens.

3. Liesbet Hooghe and Gary Marks, eds., "Understanding Euroscepticism," special issue of *Acta Politica* 42 (July 2007): 119–354.

4. Robert Dahl, *Polyarchy* (New Haven, CT: Yale University Press, 1971).

5. Russell J. Dalton, *Democratic Challenges, Democratic Choices* (Oxford, England: Oxford University Press, 2004); Jacques Thomassen, "Democratic Values," in *Oxford Handbook of Political Behavior*, ed. Russell J. Dalton and Hans-Dieter Klingemann (Oxford, England: Oxford University Press, 2007).

6. Giacomo Sani, "The Political Culture of Italy," in Almond and Verba, *The Civic Culture Revisited*.

7. Nicholai Petro provocatively argues that there are strong currents of democracy and civil society that predate the communist era in *The Rebirth of Russian Democracy: An Interpretation of Political Culture* (Cambridge: Harvard University Press, 1995); for a counter view, see Harry Eckstein et al., *Can Democracy Take Root in Post-Soviet Russia?* (Lanham, MD: Rowman & Littlefield, 1998).

8. Richard Rose, William Mishler, and Christian Haerpfer, *Democracy and Its Alternatives: Understanding Postcommunist Societies* (Baltimore, MD: Johns Hopkins University Press, 1998); William Reisinger, Arthur Miller, and Vicki Hesli, "Political Values in Russia, Ukraine, and Lithuania," *British Journal of Political Science* 24 (1994): 183–223; Russell Dalton, "Communists and Democrats: Attitudes Toward Democracy in the Two Germanies," *British Journal of Political Science* 24 (1994): 469–493. Compare with Robert Rohrschneider, *Learning Democracy: Democratic and Economic Values in Unified Germany* (New York: Oxford University Press, 1999).

9. Samuel H. Barnes and Janos Simon, eds., *The Postcommunist Citizen* (Budapest: Erasmus Foundation, 1998); Rose, Mishler, and Haerpfer, *Democracy and Its Alternatives*.

10. *Eurobarometer 65: Public Opinion and the European Union* (Brussels: Commission of the European Union, 2007), pp. 44–46.

11. Richard Rose, "Learning to Support New Regimes in Europe," *Journal of Democracy* 18 (2007): 111–125; Dieter Fuchs, Edeltraud Rolle, and K. Zagórski, eds., "The State of Democracy in Central and Eastern Europe," special issues of *International Journal of Sociology* 36, nos. 2 & 3 (2006).

12. Dalton, *Democratic Challenges, Democratic Choices*; Robert Putnam, ed., *Democracies in Flux* (Oxford, England: Oxford University Press, 2002); Fareed Zakaria, *The Future of Freedom: Illiberal Democracy at Home and Abroad* (New York: Norton, 2004); Susan Pharr and Robert Putnam, eds., *Discontented Democracies* (Princeton, NJ: Princeton University Press, 2000).

13. Paul Sniderman et al., *The Outsiders: Prejudice and Politics in Italy* (Princeton, NJ: Princeton University Press, 2002); Paul Sniderman and Louk Hagendoorn, *When Ways of Life Collide: Multiculturalism and Its Discontents in the Netherlands* (Princeton, NJ: Princeton University Press, 2007).

14. Bruce Cain, Russell Dalton, and Susan Scarrow, eds., *Democracy Transformed? Expanding Political Opportunities in Advanced Industrial Democracies* (Oxford, England: Oxford University Press, 2003).

15. Ole Borre and Elinor Scarbrough, eds., *The Scope of Government* (Oxford, England: Oxford University Press, 1995).

16. Anthony King, "Overload: Problems of Governing in the 1970s," *Political Studies* 23 (1975): 166.

17. Ronald Inglehart, *Culture Shift in Advanced Industrial Society* (Princeton, NJ: Princeton University Press, 1990), chap. 8; Ole Borre and Jose Manuel Viega, "Government Intervention in the Economy," in Borre and Scarborough, *The Scope of Government*.

18. See Raymond Duch, "Tolerating Economic Reform," *American Political Science Review* 87 (1993): 590–608; Richard Rose, *New Democracies Barometer V: A Twelve Nation Survey* (Glasgow, Scotland: University of Strathclyde, 1998).

19. For instance, the better educated are more likely to espouse democratic values if they live in a democratic system, and German public opinion surveys immediately after the collapse of the Third Reich found that the better educated were more likely to support the tenets of fascism. This point is, however, debated for postcommunist societies. See Ada Finifter, "Attitudes Toward Individual Responsibility and Political Reform in the Former Soviet Union," *American Political Science Review* 90 (1996): 138–152; Arthur Miller, William Reisinger, and Vicki Hesli, "Understanding Political Change in Post-Soviet Societies," *American Political Science Review* 90 (1996): 153–166.

20. See, for example, Figure 2.6 in the first edition of *European Politics Today*, p. 45.

21. Ole Borre, "Beliefs and the Scope of Government," in Borre and Scarbrough, *The Scope of Government*.

22. Lauren McLaren, "Explaining Mass-Level Euroscepticism: Identity, Interests, and Institutional Distrust," *Acta Politica* 42 (2007): 233–251; *Eurobarometer 65*.

23. Alexis de Tocqueville, *Democracy in America* (New York: Knopf, 1945), p. 299.

24. For an interesting comparison, earlier editions of *European Politics Today* include the same figure based on 1990–1991 and then 1995–1998 survey data, and the same pattern is apparent. The survey asks: "Can most people be trusted, or can't you be too careful when dealing with people?" Also see Inglehart, *Culture Shift*, chap. 1; Ronald Inglehart, *Modernism and Postmodernism* (Princeton, NJ: Princeton University Press, 1997).

25. Rose, "Learning to Support New Regimes in Europe*," Journal of Democracy* 18 (July 2007): 111–125.

26. Mark Franklin, *Voter Turnout and the Dynamics of Electoral Competition in Established Democracies Since 1945* (New York: Cambridge University Press, 2004); Andre Blais, *To Vote or Not to Vote? The Merits and Limits of Rational Choice Theory* (Pittsburgh, PA: University of Pittsburgh Press, 2000).

27. Mark Gray and Miki Caul, "The Decline of Election Turnout in Advanced Industrial Democracies," *Comparative Political Studies* 33 (2000): 1091–1122; Blais, *To Vote or Not to Vote?*

28. Putnam, *Democracies in Flux*.

29. Pippa Norris, *The Democratic Phoenix* (New York: Cambridge University Press, 2000); Dalton and Scarrow, eds. *Democracy Transformed? Expanding Citizen Access in Advanced Industrial Democracies* (Oxford, England: Oxford University Press, 2003).

30. Donald Schulz and Jan Adams, eds., *Political Participation in Communist Systems* (New York: Pergamon Press, 1981).

31. Russell Dalton, *The Good Citizen* (Washington, DC: CQ Press, 2007), chap. 9; Norris, *The Democratic Phoenix*.

32. Sidney Verba, Norman Nie, and Jae-on Kim, *Participation and Political Equality* (Cambridge: Cambridge University Press, 1978); Russell Dalton, *Citizen Politics* (Washington, DC: CQ Press, 2008), chaps. 3, 4.

33. Dalton, *Citizen Politics*, chaps. 3, 4; Norris, *The Democratic Phoenix*.

34. Benjamin Page and Robert Shapiro, *The Rational Public* (Chicago: University of Chicago Press, 1992); Christopher Wlezien, "Patterns of Representation: Dynamics of Public Preferences and Policy," *Journal of Politics* 66 (2004): 1–24.

EUROPEAN INTEREST GROUPS AND PARTIES

Citizens play a vital role in democratic politics. However, their impact on politics and policymaking is shaped and often overshadowed by the activities of political organizations. Politics in Western Europe has long been characterized by dense organizations of interest groups and political parties. The interest groups express the great variety of needs and demands in the society. The political parties run candidates for office. Both have developed complex, intimate connections with the policymaking process, even serving on policymaking bodies.

As we discussed in Chapter 2, new citizen movements, parties, and tactics are challenging the traditional organizations and approaches. But the traditional groups and parties retain great influence; we cannot understand Western European politics without taking account of them. In contrast, politics in Eastern Europe before 1989 was dominated by **Communist parties** that not only monopolized elections, but also controlled labor unions, professional associations, veterans' organizations, and all other organized groups. In these new democracies, organized interest groups and stable political parties have been struggling to emerge.

THE TYPES OF INTEREST GROUPS

Interest groups may take many forms. **Anomic interest groups** are generally spontaneous groups that form suddenly when many individuals respond to frustration, disappointment, or other strongly emotional events. They are flash affairs, rising and subsiding suddenly. Spontaneous student protesters about tuition and urban rioters sparked by rumors of police violence during arrests are examples of anomic groups. They normally act and then disperse. Like anomic groups, **nonassociational groups** rarely are well organized, and their activity is episodic. They differ from anomic groups because they are based on common interests of ethnicity, region, religion, occupation, or perhaps kinship. Because of these continuing economic or cultural ties, nonassociational groups have more continuity than anomic groups. **Institutional groups,** such as business corporations, legislatures, armies, bureaucracies, and churches, have a formal structure and have other political or social functions besides interest articulation. Either as corporate bodies or as smaller groups within these bodies (legislative blocs, officer cliques, groups in the clergy, or ideological factions in bureaucracies), such groups express their own interests or represent the interest of other groups in the society. The influence of institutional interest groups is usually derived from the strength of their primary organizational base—for instance, the resources of their affiliated businesses or the access to policymaking of their bureaucrats.

Political scientists often focus on **associational groups**. These groups are organized explicitly to represent a particular social interest or political issue. This type of group includes trade unions, chambers of commerce and manufacturers' associations, ethnic associations, professional organizations, and environmental associations. These organizations have orderly procedures for formulating interests and demands and often employ a full-time professional staff. Associational groups are frequently very active in representing the interests of their members in the policy process.

Thus, social interests can manifest themselves in many different ways. To highlight the different types of interest groups, we can describe those that involve members of the working class:

Anomic group: a spontaneous group of protesting working-class individuals

Nonassociational group: the working class as a collective

Institutional group: the labor department within the government

Associational group: a labor union

One of the distinctive features of Western European democracies is the richness of the organizational life—all of these different types of groups exist. A recent study of 15 Western European countries showed that about a fifth of the citizens were members of sports or recreational groups; nearly as many belonged to religious groups or trade unions; and about one-seventh belonged to cultural or educational groups.[1] In some countries these membership levels were much higher. Moreover, in recent decades there has been a flowering of new groups to protect the environment, ensure equal rights for women, and advocate other public interests. Overall, about 60 percent of Western European citizens belong to some kind of organized group; nearly a quarter belong to three or more.[2]

Analysts often describe this organizational activity as making up the **civil society** and maintain that a vibrant civil society is an essential base for a vibrant democracy.[3] Participation in associational and institutional groups socializes individuals into the types of political skills and cooperative relations that are part of a well-functioning society. Group activity also can help citizens to develop their own policy preferences, obtain important information about politics, and articulate their interests to policymakers. In large groups citizens with common interests may be inhibited from acting on those interests by the high costs of and low rewards for individual activity. But organizations can overcome these difficulties of collective action, drawing citizens into membership through individual benefits, often called *selective incentives,* and coordinating their political activities.[4] (See Box 3.1.) Thus, an active public involved in a diversity of interest groups provides a fertile ground for democracy.

The chapters in this book on Eastern European countries discuss the problems faced by the newly democratized nations in building a rich associational group life in societies where organized groups were

---

BOX 3.1

What Sustains Membership in Large Organizations: Selective Incentives in Swedish Unions

One of the puzzles of organizational membership is what sustains citizen involvement in large organizations. In large organizations citizens may have little expectation that their individual involvement will make a difference. Why, then, should they take the trouble to join? One answer is that some organizations can provide "selective" incentives—benefits that come to all members and only to members. Such selective incentives can encourage citizens to join and keep them involved.

In Sweden the many selective benefits that union members receive have probably helped keep membership high at a time when interest and memberships in unions are declining in many countries. The Swedish unions control the unemployment insurance system, which gives the union a very powerful selective incentive to help them recruit members. This also means that the unions handle the very difficult question of deciding who is really to be considered unemployed—that is, what type of work one has to accept or risk losing the benefits. In addition, many industrial laws and regulations give the local unions a say over working conditions, the implementation of work safety regulations, and who is laid off when there is a shortage of jobs. Thus, for many employees, membership in the union is not really a voluntary decision.

Source: Bo Rothstein, "Sweden: Social Capital in the Social Democratic State," in *Democracies in Flux,* ed., Robert D. Putnam (New York: Oxford University Press, 2002), pp. 310–311.

long suppressed or controlled.[5] The Communist Party and the government bureaucracy dominated these nations for over forty years, and the governments controlled associational life in order to pursue their own goals. The process of building new, independent associational groups to articulate different citizen interests is proving difficult. In the recent European Values Survey, average membership levels in sports, religious, education, and environmental associations in 14 Eastern European countries were less than half of those in the Western European countries.[6] Only membership levels in labor unions, a fundamental part of the communist regimes and still a conduit for many governmental benefits (see the discussion of Russia in Chapter 9), are more comparable between Western and Eastern Europe.

While Eastern Europe faces questions about how to develop a rich associational life, there are also new questions about whether existing civil society is declining in the West. Memberships in labor unions and religious associations are down in most Western European nations, as are memberships in some professional associations. Robert Putnam has found that Americans participate less than they used to in traditional group activities and has suggested that citizens in many countries may be disengaging themselves from groups all the way from bowling leagues to political parties.[7] Instead of getting together with others to solve community problems, as Tocqueville described the democratic ethos, Putnam claims that too many of us sit in front of our television screens and computer monitors experiencing a virtual reality. The evidence from Western Europe suggests that overall organizational involvement is increasing in some countries and declining in others. However, new styles of engagement are often replacing membership in some traditional associational groups.[8] These changes may also affect the types of citizens who are drawn into the political process through organizations. This debate is still unresolved, but it underscores the importance attached to organizational life as a foundation of democracy.

INTEREST GROUP SYSTEMS

In all modern societies, associational groups play major roles in shaping public policy. However, research in comparative politics shows that democratic nations differ significantly in how interest groups are organized and how they are connected to government.

The differences in organization and connections define different interest group systems in modern societies. Across the Western European democracies, interest group systems vary between two contrasting models: pluralist and corporatist.[9]

Pluralist interest group systems are characterized by several features that involve both how interests are organized and how they participate in the political process:

- Multiple groups may represent a single societal interest.
- Membership in associational groups is noncompulsory and limited.
- Groups often have a loose or decentralized organizational structure.
- Interest groups are clearly separated from the government.

For instance, not only are there different groups for each social sector—such as labor unions, business associations, and professional groups—but also there may be multiple labor unions or business associations within each sector. These groups compete among themselves for membership and influence, and all simultaneously press their demands on policymakers and the bureaucracies. The United States is the best-known example of a strongly pluralist interest group system. Britain (Chapter 5) is also usually characterized as pluralist, as is France (Chapter 6), because of the fragmentation of its interest organizations.

Corporatist interest group systems are more common in the Western European democracies. The most thoroughly corporatist interest group and policy systems were developed in the Scandinavian nations, such as Norway and Sweden, and in Austria. Substantial corporatist tendencies are also found in the Netherlands and Germany.

Corporatist systems are characterized by much more organized representation of interests:

- A single association normally represents each societal interest. (These are often called *peak associations*.)
- Membership in the peak association is often compulsory and nearly universal.
- Peak associations (also called umbrella groups) are centrally organized and direct the actions of their members.
- Corporatist groups are often systematically involved in making and implementing policy.

For instance, in a corporatist system there may be a single peak association that represents all the major business or industrial interests. The Federation of German Industry (BDI) is an example of a corporatist business association, which is matched by a corporatist labor organization: the German Federation of Trade Unions (DGB). This contrasts with the wide diversity of business groups and labor unions that act separately in a pluralist system.

In corporatist systems national wage and benefit policies and related employment issues have often been set through *tri-partism,* bargaining among the peak associations of labor and business and the government. The direct involvement of large interest groups and the government in negotiating national policy and also in seeing that it is implemented (a process of joint responsibility sometimes called *concerted action* or *concertation*) characterizes European corporatism in various policy areas.

Because different sectors of a society may vary in terms of their organized interest groups and their government relations, we must be cautious about generalizing too much about interest group systems. However, Figure 3.1 shows the striking differences in the organization of labor and wage bargaining in members of the European Union (EU). The countries are arrayed along the horizontal axis in terms of the percentage of the total labor force that belongs to a labor union. The vertical axis displays the organizational level at which wages are negotiated. At the bottom level, wages are negotiated at the level of individual industrial plants; at the middle levels, wages tend to cover specific industrial sectors, such as chemicals or food. At the top level in the figure are binding national contracts covering the entire economy.

The patterns in Figure 3.1 illustrate the institutional diversity of the labor movement and the likely potential for influencing and participating in policymaking. The labor movement is larger and more

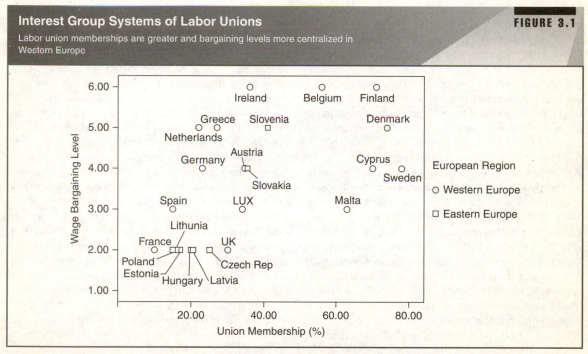

Interest Group Systems of Labor Unions

FIGURE 3.1

Labor union memberships are greater and bargaining levels more centralized in Western Europe

Source: Union membership as a percentage of the labor force and wage bargaining levels are from Sabina Avdagit and Colin Crouch, "Organized Economic Interests: Diversity and Change in an Enlarged Europe," in *Developments in European Politics,* ed. Paul M. Heywood, Erik Jones, Martin Rhodes, and Ulrich Sedelmeier (New York: Palgrave Macmillan, 2006,) pp. 207, 209; originally from European Commission, *Industrial Relations in Europe 2004* (Brussels: European Commission, 2004).

Note: Bargaining levels: 1 = company level only; 2 = predominately company level and some sector level; 6 = predominately national level; 5 = mixtures of national and sector levels; 3 and 4 are predominately or importantly sector level with some company level.

influential in the countries at the upper right of the figure because of the unions' size and bargaining co-ordination and generally less effective in the nations at the lower left. In Sweden, for example, nearly 80 percent of the nonagricultural workforce is organized into unions, and wages tend to be set through cen-tralized, sector-level bargaining. The United States would be at the lower left of the figure, the polar op-posite of the Scandinavian pattern; only about a sev-enth of the U.S. labor force is unionized, and negotiation is usually at the level of individual plants.

The best-studied consequences of democratic corporatist arrangements are found in the economic areas. Some studies indicate that countries with cor-poratist economic systems had better records than more pluralist countries in sustaining employment and restraining inflation in the 1970s and 1980s.[10] This might have occurred because the large groups were able to negotiate with each other and the gov-ernment and find common ground. Corporatist sys-tems were also associated with increased social spending and greater income equality.

In the 1990s the environment, groups, and conse-quences of corporatism changed. Independent central banks and, increasingly, the EU (Chapter 12) con-strained national economic and social policymaking in many ways. Membership in labor unions declined quite sharply in some countries; some bargaining patterns became less centralized; and problems of deadlock in corporatist negotiation became more prominent. Inter-estingly, the same countries that had relied earlier on corporatism policymaking tended to retain it, but in newly adapted forms with complex results.[11]

In Eastern Europe, Communist parties (govern-ments) penetrated and controlled virtually all organ-ized groups until the collapse of Soviet control in 1989. Since then there has been an explosion of new groups and splintering and division of the ones pre-viously dominated by the authoritarian governments. (See the discussions of interest groups in Russia, Poland, and Bulgaria in Chapters 9 through 11.) Yet, citizen memberships in these groups still lag far be-hind levels in Western Europe. These societies have been trying to bring some order into this chaotic sit-uation, while at the same time encouraging freedom in group formation and the representation of many varieties of interests. In Figure 3.1 the Eastern European members of the EU are shown with squares. As we can see, most of these countries are found in the lower left part of the graph, with rela-tively low membership levels and decentralized

bargaining. Poland provides an example.[12] Poland has attempted to use corporatist involvement of la-bor, business, and government in negotiating labor policy, but fragmentation of the groups has made this difficult (see Chapter 10).

Another problem in Eastern Europe has been to prevent the remaining institutional groups of the old communist systems—such as the government bu-reaucracy and the government-run industries and businesses—from dominating policymaking (see es-pecially Russia, discussed in Chapter 9). Often these groups have been restructured or "privatized," but in many instances, they have been run by the same people as during the communist era.

PARTIES AND PARTY COMPETITION

In liberal democracies political parties provide a criti-cal link between citizens and policymakers. Political parties run candidates for election. Before and during elections, they mobilize voters and structure their choices; after elections they organize governments and policymaking.

The party systems of Western Europe are highly developed. Party leaders and organizers have had many elections to build organizations, form alliances, and refine their strategies. Although each new elec-tion brings new challenges, new voters, and some-times new parties, many lessons of the past are encoded in the surviving organizations, as well as in the memories of voters, activists, and party leaders. The party system in a country—the number of parties, the partisan balance, the range and content of issues presented—tends to provide a fairly stable context from one election to the next.

In Eastern Europe, in contrast, until 20 years ago the Soviet-backed Communist parties permitted no competition. Only selected allies, at most, were permit-ted to offer candidates. Moreover, the Communist par-ties attempted to penetrate the entire society and pull all those interested in public life into their networks.

It has been very difficult to build new party organizations in the tumult-filled years since the democratic transitions in 1989–1991. The sudden ex-pansion of democratic opportunity initially over-whelmed the potential organizers of opposition parties, who had no experience with competitive politics. The absence of independent social and eco-nomic organizations, especially the trade unions and churches that were historically the focus of much initial party organization in Western Europe, has made building new party organizations far more difficult.[13] Democratic elections in Eastern Europe since 1989 have been typically characterized by many new parties, small parties, and independent candidates. Voter support for parties has been very volatile, shifting greatly between one election and the next.[14] After the elections the assemblies have frequently experienced lack of coherence within parties and the formation of new party groups, as well as difficulties in forming governments based on stable coalitions between parties. Building strong new parties is an important challenge facing many of the new democracies of Eastern Europe.

The Social Bases of Parties

Political sociologists Lipset and Rokkan observed that voter preferences based on such social divisions as class and religion (called *cleavages*) characterized most Western European party systems from the 1920s to the 1960s.[15] In the Catholic societies of Mediterranean Western Europe, for example, voters' frequency of church attendance was a strong predictor of their party attachments. In central Western Europe, religious affiliation as Protestant or Catholic often predicted party support. In Northern Europe, a voter's occupation most powerfully shaped his or her partisanship. These voter attachments were anchored by the alignments of social organizations (labor unions, churches, and voluntary associations) and party organizations. In some countries ethnicity and region were also important cleavages.

These historic cleavages continue to organize many Western European party systems today. But they have been diminished by the declines in church attendance and trade union strength, as well as by increased geographic mobility and the provision of welfare safety nets. New issues, such as immigration, and new values are also beginning to obscure the traditional cleavages,[16] as are more candidate-centered campaigns.

Religious, ethnic, and economic cleavages may yet crystallize in Eastern Europe, too. Analyses of voting in Poland, for example, show some of the effects of church attendance that we might expect in a Catholic nation. But at present the basis of voter support in Eastern Europe remains fluid, with less connection to social groups than in the West. Voter volatility, although perhaps diminishing in some countries, continues to be high, encouraged by fluctuating economic performance.[17]

The Number of Parties

Political scientists have emphasized two major distinctions in analyzing the performance of Western European party systems: (1) **number of parties** and (2) **extremist parties**. The first distinguishes **multiparty systems** from two-party systems, or at least **majority-electing party systems**. Multiparty systems seem to offer a wider range of choices to voters, explicit representation of social and political groups, and more inclusiveness in policymaking. Majority-electing systems seem to offer clearer political responsibility, more-stable governments, and the direct implementation of campaign promises.

Most Western European party systems fall clearly into the multiparty category. In the average Western European election, 6 or 7 parties win 1 percent of the vote or more, with as many as 12 such parties in the Netherlands in the 1970s and Belgium in the 1980s. These numbers pale, however, when compared with the numbers of parties competing in some of the new electoral landscapes in Eastern Europe. In Russia in 1995, for example, 18 parties won over 1 percent of the vote.

Such figures can be somewhat misleading if there are a few large parties together with many very small ones. It is more revealing to compare the relative numbers of parties through a weighting approach that calculates the "'effective' number" of parties in the election and in the legislature.[18] The average effective number of parties winning *votes* in Western Europe in the elections of the mid-2000s was about four and a half. Britain, Greece, Malta, Portugal, and Spain were at the low end with effectively no more than about three parties, while Belgium was at the high end with about nine. The average in Eastern Europe was somewhat higher: about five parties. Bosnia, Latvia, and Slovakia had effectively over six parties winning votes.

These numbers decline if we look at the legislature because the election laws prevent many smaller parties from winning seats in parliament. The average number of effective parties is less than four in the legislatures in both East and West. Figure 3.2 displays the distribution of the effective number of parties in **legislatures** in Western and Eastern European nations. The average reductions between election results and the legislature are greater in Eastern Europe because even low barriers shut out very small parties.

Figure 3.2 also displays quite wide variation across nations. In Western Europe, there are effectively two-party systems in the legislatures in Britain,

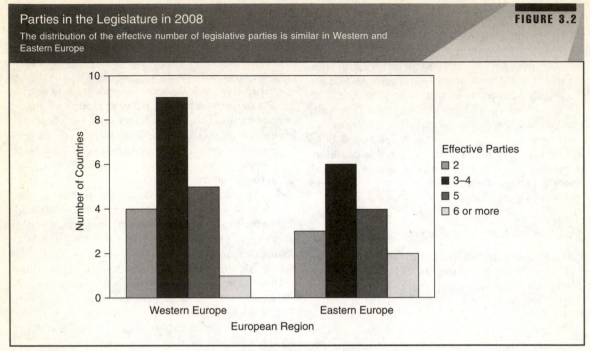

Parties in the Legislature in 2008   **FIGURE 3.2**

The distribution of the effective number of legislative parties is similar in Western and Eastern Europe

Source: See the discussion of the effective number of parties in this chapter and in Arend Lijphart, *Patterns of Democracy: Government Forms and Performance in Thirty-Six Countries* (New Haven, CT: Yale University Press, 1999), ch. 5.

France, Malta, and Spain.[19] We see that most countries have three or four effective parties in the legislature. At the more fragmented end, quite a few have five parties, although only Belgium has over six. In Eastern Europe there are several effective two-party systems, including those in Hungary, Moldova, and Russia. The modal country has three or four effective parties, as in Western Europe, but several have five or six parties.

The variety of party systems in Europe means that the context of party competition can be quite different in different countries. In the systems dominated by two large parties, each party must appeal to a sufficient range of voters to have a chance to win at least a large plurality. Each party faces pressures to reach out from its social or ideological "base" and seek centrist voters (as the British Labour Party did in 1997 and afterward).[20] In this context factions within the parties also know that if they split their party for the sake of offering another policy choice, they may bring an opposition to power and doom themselves for years to the role of a weak voice of protest. Citizens who do not want to "waste" their votes must

choose between the major alternatives, even if these seem less than ideal.

In multiparty contexts a party's leaders can seek a smaller and more focused constituency. Party policies may reflect the preferences of specific groups, such as labor unions, business associations, or religious and ethnic groups. Historical issue commitments and ideological traditions also play a role.[21] As no party will win a majority, small parties can still hope to shape policy through negotiation and coalition with other parties. (See the discussion of government formation in Chapter 4.) Issue factions can also split to form new parties and still expect to play a role in policymaking. Citizens will find a wide range of party choices to represent their interests. However, the parties will have to adjust their promises to the realities of building coalitions with other parties; citizens must anticipate this process.

Despite the general similarity in the distribution, Figure 3.2 overstates somewhat the comparability of Western and Eastern Europe. Some of the larger Eastern European "parties" are really electoral coalitions of several parties and are less cohesive in their behavior in the legislature. Moreover, the greater volatility between elections in Eastern Europe makes it harder for voters to learn what parties stand for and to anticipate the implications of their voting choices for government policy. Figure 3.2, like the voting averages, should also remind Americans how unusual their truly two-party system is.

Extremist Parties

A second distinction in the literature on political parties focuses on *extremism* (or *polarization*) in the party system. Many theorists suggest that the performance of democracy is threatened by **extremist parties**— parties espousing dramatically different policy packages (ideologies) or challenging the basic ground rules of the society.[22] Communist and neo-Fascist parties, for example, were extreme in both their attacks on democracy and the alienation of their supporters. Italian political scientist Giovanni Sartori argues that polarized systems enhance the ideological intensity of the policy debate, encouraging a pattern of irresponsible "outbidding" by extremist parties. Extremism also discourages turnovers of power that could keep incumbent parties responsible to citizens.[23]

Substantial research, based largely on Western Europe, suggests that support for extremist parties is associated with less durable governments, and probably with mass turmoil as well, although not necessarily with instability of democracy itself.[24]

Data from the late 1970s and early 1980s showed parties that could be classified as extremist—in terms of either their extreme policy positions or the alienation of their supporters—had the support of over 20 percent of the electorate in Belgium, Denmark, Finland, France, and Italy,[25] but substantially less in the rest of Western Europe. These percentages somewhat reduced by the early 1990s as the collapse of international communism moderated the position of some left parties. Moreover, before the 1990s Green parties were generally considered extremist parties, challenging environmental policies of other parties and attacking the political and economic establishment. But today they are a more accepted part of the political landscape, although this varies from country to country.

New populist (usually rightist) parties, attacking the political establishment and often appealing to concerns about immigrants and/or relations with the EU, have been a new source of extremism in the last decade (see Box 3.2). Voters in Western Europe, as in the United States, are concerned about the impact of economic globalization on the outsourcing of jobs and the consequent rise in unemployment. Increases in levels of crime and drug trafficking are also disturbing. Populist extremist parties have attacked the established parties as indifferent to all of these challenging issues. The extreme right parties particularly blame these problems on the high levels of immigration encouraged by the opening of borders and conflict in Eastern Europe, as well as by the loosening of internal controls within the EU. Immigration also threatens well-understood cultural communities. New differences of religion and custom raise a variety of issues, such as the conflict over wearing Muslim headscarves in schools in France.

In some countries, such as Sweden and the Netherlands, support for extreme right parties surged suddenly behind a popular leader and then declined. In others, they have become a more permanent part of the political landscape. Before it declined in the legislative election of 2007, the National Front in France, for example, had won 10 to 15 percent in elections since 1986. (See Chapter 6.) The National Front's controversial leader, Jean-Marie Le Pen, has called for expulsion of illegal immigrants and all immigrants after a maximum stay of a year or two, a ban on even tourist visas for Africans and Arabs from North Africa, preferential treatment of French citizens in jobs and public housing, and very tight citizenship requirements.[26]

In recent elections right-wing populist parties or presidential candidates won over 10 percent of the vote in Austria, Belgium, Denmark, France, Italy, Luxembourg, Norway, and Switzerland.[27] Such extremist parties pose and reflect the familiar potential for unstable government and citizen turmoil. In the European Parliament elections in 2004, new parties opposing membership in or extension of the EU won substantial support in a number of countries, including Britain.

In Western Europe most of the new radical right-wing parties at least formally support political democracy, although they have less tolerance for minorities. In Eastern Europe voters in a number of countries have given substantial support to extremist parties that could well be considered antidemocratic. Zhirinovsky's (ill-named) Liberal Democratic Party in Russia, which promises personal dictatorship at home and wildly aggressive foreign policy abroad, is one example. The Greater Romanian Party, the Slovakian SNS, and the Serbian SRS are other extremist parties whose commitment to basic democratic boundaries seems unclear.[28]

BOX 3.2

List Pim Fortuyn and the 2002 Dutch Election:
An Extreme Right Party

In a television interview on August 20, 2001, a political columnist and former professor named Pim Fortuyn announced his intention to run for the Dutch Parliament. He was not an ordinary member of the political establishment. He was "an outspoken homosexual with a flamboyant lifestyle—Ferrari, Bentley with chauffeur, butler, two lap dogs, portraits of John F. Kennedy in his lavishly decorated Rotterdam home which he referred to as Palazzo di Pietro." In short order he was chosen head of a small party, Livable Netherlands. His charismatic speeches and interviews attacked traditionally tolerant Dutch attitudes toward minority groups and brought his issues of foreigners, immigration policies, asylum seekers, and crime to the top of the political agenda. He put the traditional parties on the defensive. Then, on February 9, 2002, he published an interview that rocked Dutch politics, stating "that Islam was a backward culture, that no new asylum-seekers would be allowed, and that if necessary to protect Freedom of Speech, the first article of the Constitution [which forbids discrimination] should be repealed." His party immediately expelled him. But he formed his own party, List Pim Fortuyn, which immediately surged to second place in the public opinion polls. Pim Fortuyn himself became the center of the national election campaign. The country was shocked when he was assassinated 10 days before the election. However, his new party won 17 percent of the vote, becoming the second largest party in the fragmented Dutch Parliament, and soon joined two other parties in forming the next (short-lived) parliamentary government. Public opinion polls showed that the party's success was built on Fortuyn's personal popularity, general cynicism about Dutch politics and the incumbent government, and issues of sending back asylum seekers and requiring that "foreigners" adapt to Dutch culture and customs. By the 2006 election, the support for List Pim Fortuyn had faded to less than half of one percent of the vote, as often happens with populist parties.

Source: Joop J. M. Van Holsteyn and Galen Irwin, "Never a Dull Moment: Pim Fortuyn and the Dutch Parliamentary Election of 2002," *West European Politics* 26 (April 2003): 41–66. Also see "Pim Fortuyn and the 'New' Far Right in the Netherlands," *Representation* 40 (2004): 131–145.

More typical of Eastern European politics than these extreme right-wing parties has been a variety of populist parties, campaigning against all the main parties and their government failures. Support for such parties often changes greatly from one election to the next; a fifth or more of the electorate has voted for such parties in several Eastern European nations.[29] The rejection of moderate centrist parties apparent in such voting reflects the hardships of the political and economic transitions, but also contributes to the difficulties of government.

A critical question in most of Eastern Europe concerns the parties that are direct descendants of the authoritarian Communist parties that so long dominated the region. These parties generally call themselves "socialist" or "social democrat" (except in Russia) and claim to be democratic. (Many are required by the law or even the constitution to make this claim in order to compete in elections.) Some of them have undergone great changes in organization, people, and policies and have even proved their moderate credentials in office. A few are still largely unreconstructed in organization and personnel from their Communist predecessors. Some of them continue to adapt as circumstances change. The **formerly Communist parties** and their potential extremism must be evaluated individually in each country.

The Content of Party Competition

People often discuss party competition in the multiparty systems of Western Europe by relating the parties to different positions on a **left-right continuum**.[30] The left-right language, which originated in the physical placement of the new members of the Assembly during the French Revolution over two hundred years ago, has gradually become a shorthand summary of a number of the issues that are important to contemporary voters.

Economic or class differences are a long-term focus of party competition in Western Europe. Almost every party system has had one or more parties claiming to be on the "left" in the sense of representing the interests of the working class. In most Western European countries, socialist or **social democratic parties** are the predominant parties of the "left," with smaller Communist or New Left challengers. Economic issues continue to define the main differences between many established "left" and "right" parties in Western Europe. However, the substance of difference has changed substantially in recent years, anticipating, but also encouraged by, the collapse of international communism.

Most "left" parties in Western Europe have now abandoned the idea of full government ownership of the economy, which was a major element of classic socialism. The combination of support for a large welfare system, redistribution of income from the better off to the less fortunate through taxes and transfer payments, and a mixed (but predominately market) economy is often called a "social democratic" approach.

In contrast, a **"rightist" party** has traditionally stressed economic competition, less personal reliance on the government, and less government involvement of all kinds. In many nations the "right" is also a representative of religious or social conservative positions, often by a Christian democratic party.

Thus, the meaning of "left" and "right" can vary across individuals and party systems. To a German blue-collar worker, "left" may mean social welfare policies; to a young German college student, it may mean environmental protection and issues of gender equality. Indeed, the value of the left-right scale is its inclusive nature. allowing it to summarize the salient issues in each nation.

Figure 3.3 shows the parties on the left-right scale in most of the political systems with detailed case studies in this book.[31] The United States is shown for purposes of comparison. At the very bottom of the figure, we see the alignment of the party groups in the European Parliament. The position of the parties is based on their placement by all citizens or on the self-placement of citizens who voted for the party.[32] The height of the bars on the graph shows the voting support that each party received in the election year shown at the left of each line. Only parties getting about 4 percent of the vote or more are shown in the figure. The figure is best used as a guide to compare the distributions of party support within the countries, not to compare the centers of the party systems or the positions of specific parties across countries. The average European voter places herself somewhat to the left of the average American voter, but we do not know that the voters have similar issues in mind.

The United States has only two parties, of course. Its uniqueness as the only purely two-party system is striking in Figure 3.3. Among the other countries, only in Spain do the two largest parties get over 75 percent of the vote. The American parties have become somewhat more distinctive than they used to be, with the Democrats to the left and the Republicans similarly to the right of the average voter. The two main parties in Britain and Germany, in lines 2 and 3 of the figure, are about as far apart as the American parties. The main party groupings in the European Parliament, whose positions can also be described in general left-right language, are only slightly farther apart.

The figure also shows clearly the Communist or formerly Communist parties well on the left in France, Germany, and Spain, with more moderate social democratic or labor parties closer to the center. Each country also has one or more large parties of the moderate right. France stands out with 11 percent of the vote going to the right-extremist National Front Party, but parties equally far to the right on the left-right scale appear in several countries. The alignment of party groups in the European Parliament also looks like this configuration.

As shown toward the bottom of the figure, the left-right language also comfortably describes wide party ranges in the newer democracies of Poland and Bulgaria, with the former Communists (SLD in Poland and BSP in Bulgaria) rather far to the left, several parties in the center, and a cluster of parties to the right and even the far right. Both religious and economic issues shape the left-right dialogue in Poland (see Chapter 10). The party configurations that we see in Figure 3.3 are only snapshots of party competition in a single election. In all democracies voters may change their patterns of support. But especially in the new democracies of Eastern Europe, party support and even the identities of the competing parties have often changed drastically from one election to the next.

Figure 3.3 also shows why in some multiparty systems, such as that in France, the number of parties and their dispersion across the left-right spectrum make this language helpful for voters. Without something like a single dimension to organize political discussion, it is difficult for voters in any democracy to compare their wishes with the promises and actions of policymakers.[33] With many smaller parties offering

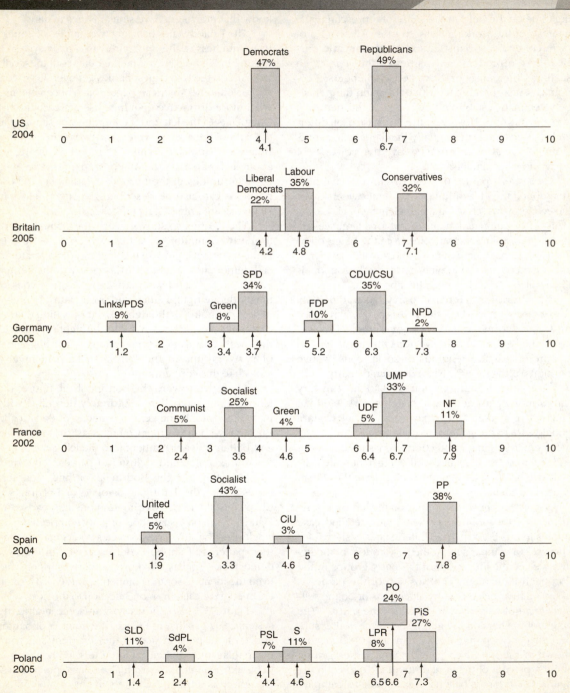

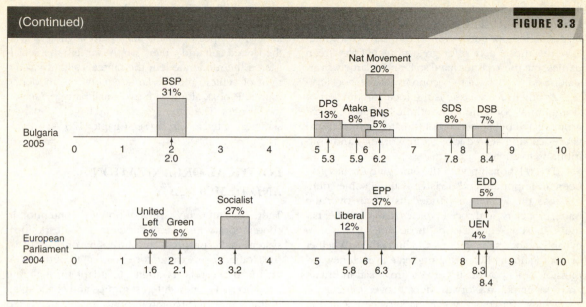

(Continued)

FIGURE 3.3

Sources: The party placements in the United States, Britain, Germany, France, Spain, and Poland are from the *Comparative Study of Electoral Systems Surveys* www.umich.edu/~cses in the years shown, using the party position estimated by all citizens in the surveys. In Bulgaria party positions are estimated from the self-placements of party voters in the election shown, using the European Social Surveys downloaded from www.europeansocialsurvey.org; European Parliament (EP) party group positions are from an expert survey reported in Gail McElroy and Kenneth Benoit, "Party Groups and Policy Positions in the European Parliament," *Party Politics* 13 (2007): 5–28.

Note: The height of the bar is the percentage of the vote won by the party in the parliamentary election shown on the left; for EP party groups, the height of the bar is the percentage of seats won in the EP.

a variety of alternatives, voters find it especially helpful to characterize debate in terms of something like "left" and "right." In addition to economic issues, the left-right language has begun to incorporate elements of the values distinction between welfare and security, on one hand, and quality of life issues, such as the environment, on the other.[34]

Economic issues have also been important in Eastern Europe, but they have often focused on the difficult transition from the old communist "command control" systems—in which the government owned the economy and directly decided wages, prices, investment, and so forth—to a system in which the market determines prices and government plays a lesser role.[35] While most contemporary parties favor the transition in general terms, they often disagree sharply on the pace and extent of this economic transition. For a variety of reasons, economic conditions have been difficult and quite painful for many groups in these societies. Not only did absolute living standards decline throughout Eastern Europe in the early 1990s, but also groups accustomed to guaranteed jobs have had to face

unemployment (real and potential); inflation, which has made saving difficult; and increased income disparities. Naturally, some political parties have appeared to express the grievances and fears of the disadvantaged and to call for moderation in the process or for protection of the vulnerable. In the early days of the transition, the issue of economic transformation was also entangled with the transition to political democracy.

Of course, other issues are involved in party competition, in both West and East. Clashes between parties representing "new" and "traditional" values, including religious values, continue to be prominent in several countries, especially those with Catholic populations. In the last two decades, **Green parties** have challenged the industrialization and pollution associated with economic growth policies. They have often forced older and larger parties to adopt at least some pro-environment programs, even at some cost to jobs and profits. They have a substantial party group in the European Parliament. In 1998 and 2002, the German Green Party joined with the SPD to form the governing coalition (see Chapter 7). Green parties have also participated in governing coalitions in France, Italy, Belgium, Ireland, and Finland. Because of the serious pollution inherited from Soviet rule, Eastern Europe may offer great potential for Green parties, but these issues have so far been largely overshadowed by those of the economy and democracy.

Another recent issue is the focus on the fear of "foreigners" or minority ethnic groups. These groups have been accused of threatening traditional values, taking scarce jobs from workers, and contributing to crime.

The relationship with the emerging EU has also been an important and divisive issue in some countries. As the EU has expanded its power over the trade, monetary, and social policies of the member nations, the consequences of those policies have inevitably helped some groups and hurt others. Whether or not to join the EU or to participate in each new expansion of its powers is very controversial in Britain and Denmark. In Norway debate over joining the EU, which Norwegian voters have twice rejected in referendums, reshaped party competition. In Eastern Europe many of the newly independent democracies wanted rapid incorporation into the EU to protect their political independence and encourage their economies. This has been achieved in many cases. But parties suspicious of EU policies gained surprising support in many of the new EU member countries (as well as some older members) in the European parliamentary elections in 2004 (see Chapter 12). At the bottom of Figure 3.3, we see the party groups in the European Parliament, which do not run directly in elections, but are formed from the various national parties elected in the European Parliament elections,

as described in Chapter 12. These party groups vote increasingly cohesively in the EU. They reflect a rather familiar European parliamentary party alignment, with the United Left and Greens on the far left; the Socialists on the moderate left; the Liberals slightly to the right of center; and the largest party, the moderate right EPP, next, along with two small party groups on the far right. The latter are made up largely of parties skeptical of the EU itself. (See Chapter 12.)

POLITICAL ORGANIZATIONS AND DEMOCRACY

There are still many issues of political contention in contemporary Europe. As society and the political system make progress in addressing one set of issues, others come to the fore. A strength of the democratic process is its ability to adapt to changing conditions. The new interest groups and challenging political parties force attention to new or neglected political issues.

This chapter described the importance of interest groups and political parties to this process. Although the method of interest group representation varies across Western European democracies, all contain a rich array of groups that articulate the public's policy interests. Similarly, the party systems in these nations represent these issues, offer a method for deciding between contrasting goals, and provide citizens a way to shape the policies of government. In Eastern Europe organized groups and political parties are developing as part of the new democratic order in most countries, but the process has been slow and uneven.

REVIEW QUESTIONS

- How did interest group systems and party systems change in Eastern Europe after 1989?

- Describe the similarities and differences between interest group systems in Western and Eastern Europe today.

- Why is a strong civil society important for a vigorous democracy?

- Describe the main differences between pluralist interest group systems, such as those in the United States and Britain, and the corporatist interest

group systems found in many Western European countries.

- How have the social cleavages of religion and class helped shape the European party systems?

- Discuss the advantages and disadvantages of multiparty systems compared to majority-electing party systems.

- What impact has the recent high level of immigration into Western Europe had on support for extremist political parties?

KEY TERMS

anomic interest group

associational interest group

civil society

Communist parties/ formerly Communist parties

corporatist interest group systems

extremist parties

Green parties

institutional groups

left-right continuum

legislatures

multiparty system/majority-electing party system

nonassociational group

number of political parties

pluralist interest group systems

rightist political parties

social democratic parties

SUGGESTED READINGS

Bartolini, Stefano, and Peter Mair. *Identity, Competition and Electoral Availability: The Stabilization of European Electorates*. New York: Cambridge University Press, 1990.

Cox, Gary. *Making Votes Count: Strategic Coordination in the World's Electoral Systems*. New York: Cambridge University Press, 1997.

Dalton, Russell J., and Martin Wattenberg, eds. *Parties Without Partisans: Political Change in Advanced Industrial Democracies*. Oxford, England: Oxford University Press. 2000.

Franklin, Mark, Thomas Mackie, and Henry Valen, eds. *Electoral Change: Responses to Evolving Social and Attitudinal Structures in Western Countries*. New York: Cambridge University Press, 1992.

Gallagher, Michael, Michael Laver, and Peter Mair. *Representative Government in Modern Europe*. New York: McGraw Hill, 2005.

Heywood, Paul M., Erik Jones, Martin Rhodes, and Ulrich Sedelmeier, eds. *Developments in European Politics*. New York: Palgrave Macmillan, 2006.

Howard, Marc Morje. *The Weakness of Civil Society in Post-communist Europe*. Cambridge, England: Cambridge University Press, 2000.

Kitschelt, Herbert, Zdenka Mansfedlova, Radoslaw Markowski, and Gabor Toka. *Post-communist Party Systems: Competition, Representation and Inter-Party Cooperation*. New York: Cambridge University Press, 1999.

LeDuc, Lawrence, Richard G. Niemi, and Pippa Norris, eds. *Comparing Democracies 3: Elections and Voting in the 21st Century*. London: Sage, forthcoming.

Lijphart, Arend. *Patterns of Democracy: Government Forms and Performance in Thirty-Six Countries*. New Haven, CT: Yale University Press, 1999.

Mudde, Cas. *Populist Radical Right Parties in Europe*. New York: Cambridge University Press, 2007.

Powell, G. Bingham. *Elections as Instruments of Democracy: Majoritarian and Proportional Visions*. New Haven, CT: Yale University Press, 2000.

Putnam, Robert, ed. *Democracies in Flux: The Evolution of Social Capital in Contemporary Society*. Oxford, England: Oxford University Press, 2002.

Rose, Richard, and Neil Munro. *Elections and Parties in the New European Democracies*. Washington, DC: CQ Press, 2003.

Webb, Paul, David M. Farrell, and Ian Holiday, eds. *Political Parties in Advanced Industrial Democracies*. Oxford, England: Oxford University Press, 2002.

ENDNOTES

1. These figures are based on the 1999 European Values Study, www.europeanvaluesstudy.eu. Fairly similar levels were reported in the 2000–2001 European Social Survey, www.europeansocialsurvey.org. Even higher membership levels were reported in the International Social Survey Program (ISSP) 2004 survey of 13 Western European countries, www.issp.org. As will be seen in Figure 3.1, union membership is, of course, much higher as a percentage of the labor force than of the adult population.

2. Calculated from the European Social Survey, www. europeansocialsurvey.org.

3. Robert Putnam, *Bowling Alone: The Collapse and Revival of American Community* (New York: Simon and Schuster, 2000); Grzegorz Ekiert and Jan Kubik,

Rebellious Civil Society: Popular Protest and Democratic Consolidation in Poland, 1989–1993 (Ann Arbor: University of Michigan Press, 1999); Jean Cohen and A. Arato, *Civil Society and Political Theory* (Cambridge, MA: MIT Press, 1992).

4. Studies of the problems of organizing large groups were stimulated by the now classic work of Mancur Olson, *The Logic of Collective Action* (Cambridge: Harvard University Press, 1965).

5. See Chapters 9–11. Also see Anna Seleny, "Old Political Rationalities and New Democracies: Compromise and Confrontation in Hungary and Poland," *World Politics* 51 (1999): 484–519.

6. Also see Marc Morje Howard, *The Weakness of Civil Society in Post-communist Europe* (Cambridge, England: Cambridge University Press, 2000), who reports even sharper differences, based on a slightly earlier set of World Value Surveys and a much smaller set of Western European countries. The ISSP 2004 surveys show average group memberships in their 13 Western European countries to be two to three times greater than memberships in their 8 Eastern European countries. However, there are substantial differences across countries and types of groups within both West and East. Poland, for example, showed high membership in churches and religious organizations, although low memberships in other types of organizations. Retrieved from www.za.uni_koeln.de/data/en/issp/codebooks/AZ3950.

7. Putnam, *Bowling Alone;* Robert Putnam, "Bowling Alone," *Journal of Democracy* 6 (1995): 65–78.

8. Robert Putnam, ed., *Democracies in Flux: The Evolution of Social Capital in Contemporary Society* (Oxford, England: Oxford University Press, 2002).

9. The classic statements in this very large literature are Philippe Schmitter, "Still the Century of Corporatism," *Review of Politics* 36 (1974): 85–131, and Gerhard Lehmbruch, "Liberal Corporatism and Party Government," *Comparative Political Studies* 10 (1977): 91–126. For a recent review of the evolution of the literature and its response to events of the 1990s, see Oscar Molina and Martin Rhodes, "Corporatism: The Past, Present and Future of a Concept," *Annual Review of Political Science* 5 (2002): 305–331. Also see Peter Katzenstein, *Small States in World Markets* (Ithaca, NY: Cornell University Press, 1985); Arend Lijphart, *Patterns of Democracy: Government Forms and Performance in 36 Countries* (New Haven, CT: Yale University Press, 1999), ch. 9; and Alan Siaroff, "Corporatism in 24 Industrial Countries: Meaning and Measurement," *European Journal of Political Research* 36 (1999): 175–205.

10. On the earlier relative success of the corporatist systems in economic performance, see, for example, Miriam Golden, "The Dynamics of Trade Unionism and National Economic Performance," *American Political Science Review* 87, no. 2 (June 1993): 439–454.

11. See Molina and Rhodes, "Corporatism," and Michael Wallerstein and Bruce Western, "Unions in Decline? What Has Changed and Why?" *Annual Review of Political Science* 3 (2000): 355–377.

12. Stephen Crowley and David Ost, eds., *Workers After Workers' States: Labor and Politics in Postcommunist Eastern Europe* (London: Rowman and Littlefield, 2001).

13. Barbara Geddes, "A Comparative Perspective on the Leninist Legacy in Eastern Europe," *Comparative Political Studies* 28 (July 1995): 239–274.

14. Paul G. Lewis, *Political Parties in Post-communist Elections in Eastern Europe* (London: Routledge, 2000); Richard Rose and Neil Munro, *Elections and Parties in New European Democracies* (Washington, DC: CQ Press, 2003), pp. 78–84; Sarah Birch, *Electoral Systems and Political Transformation in Post-communist Europe* (New York: Palgrave Macmillan, 2003); Scott Mainwaring and Edurne Zoco, "Political Sequences and the Stabilization of Interparty Competition," *Party Politics* 13 (2007): 155–178; Margit Tavits, "The Development of Stable Party Support: Electoral Dynamics in Post-communist Europe," *American Journal of Political Science* 49, no. 2 (April 2005): 283–298.

15. Seymour M. Lipset and Stein Rokkan, *Party Systems and Voter Alignments* (New York: The Free Press, 1967).

16. See Russell J. Dalton, "Political Cleavages, Issues, and Electoral Change," in *Comparing Democracies 2,* ed. Lawrence LeDuc, Richard G. Niemi, and Pippa Norris (Thousand Oaks, CA: Sage, 2002); Mark Franklin, Tom Mackie, and Henry Valen, eds., *Electoral Change: Responses to Evolving Social and Attitudinal Structures in Western Countries* (Cambridge, England: Cambridge University Press, 1992); and Paul Webb, "Political Parties and Democratic Control," in *Political Parties in Advanced Industrial Democracies*, ed. Paul Webb, David Farrell, and Ian Holiday (Oxford, England: Oxford University Press, 2002), pp. 438–460.

17. Tavits, "Stable Party Support," suggests that there are signs of stabilization after about 11 years of electoral competition.

18. This number tells us roughly how many parties of the same size would be the equivalent of the current distributions. From Markku Laakso and Rein Taagepera, "'Effective' Number of Parties: A Measure with Application to West Europe," *Comparative Political Studies* 12 (April 1979): 3–27. See also Lijphart, *Patterns of Democracy*, ch. 5. Mathematically, the number is

$$\frac{1}{\sum_i^n p_i^2}$$

where P_i is the proportion of votes or seats of the ith party.

19. Because of the working of the single-member districts on the French alignment in 2002, an effective number of more than five voted parties was reduced nearly to two in the French Assembly (see Chapter 6). Malta is Western Europe's most purely two-party system.

20. The classic analysis of the incentive for both parties in a two-party system to "converge to the median voter" is Anthony Downs, *An Economic Theory of Democracy* (New York: Harper and Row, 1957).

21. See, for example, Herbert Kitschelt, *The Transformation of European Social Democracy* (New York: Cambridge University Press, 1994); and Wolfgang C. Mueller and Kaare Strom, *Policy, Office or Votes? How Political Parties in Western Europe Make Hard Decisions* (New York: Cambridge University Press, 1999).

22. For example, Maurice Duverger, *Political Parties: Their Organization and Activity in the Modern State* [1954] (New York: John Wiley, 1963), pp. 419–420; see also the discussion in G. Bingham Powell, Jr., *Contemporary Democracies: Participation, Stability and Violence* (Cambridge: Harvard University Press, 1982), ch. 5.

23. Giovanni Sartori, *Parties and Party Systems* (New York: Cambridge University Press, 1976), ch. 6.

24. Paul Warwick, *Government Survival in Parliamentary Democracies* (New York: Cambridge University Press, 1994). A very large body of research exists on this topic, beginning especially with Michael Taylor and Valentine Herman, "Party Systems and Government Stability," *American Political Science Review* 65 (March 1971): 28–37; see the reviews in Powell, *Contemporary Democracies*, ch. 7; Warwick, *Government Survival*; and Michael Laver, "Government Termination," *Annual Review of Political Science* 6 (2003): 23–40.

25. See G. Bingham Powell, Jr., "Extremist Parties, Electoral Polarization, and Citizen Turmoil," *American Journal of Political Science* 30 (1986): 357–378.

26. See discussion in *The Economist,* November 23, 1991, pp. 56–57, "A Programme, or a Pogrom?" Vol. 321, and in Chapter 6.

27. For a detailed analysis describing and listing "populist radical right" and "populist neoliberal" parties, see Cas Mudde, *Populist Radical Right Parties in Europe* (New York: Cambridge University Press, 2007). On explanations of support for different kinds of extreme right parties, see Herbert Kitschelt, *The Radical Right in Western Europe* (Ann Arbor: University of Michigan Press, 1995); Matt Golder, "Explaining Variation in the Success of Extreme Right Parties in Western Europe," *Comparative Political Studies* 36 (2003): 432–466; Wouter van der Brug and Meindert Fennema, "Protest or Mainstream," *European Journal of Political Research* 42 (2003): 55–76; Elisabeth Carter, *The Extreme Right in Western Europe: Success or Failure* (New York: Manchester University Press, 2005); Mudde, *Populist Radical Right Parties*; and Bonnie M. Meguid, *Party Competition Between Unequals: Strategies and Electoral Fortunes in Western Europe* (New York: Cambridge University Press, 2008).

28. Grigore Pop-Eleches, "Romania's Politics of Dejection," *Journal of Democracy* 12 (2001): 156–169. The party, which had strongly attacked Hungarian, Jewish, and Gypsy minorities and published a list of "top intellectuals" who should be shot for the greater good of the country (p. 163), won a fifth of the vote in the 2000 election and 13 percent in 2004. In the elections of 2004–2008, parties identified by Mudde, *Populist Radical Right Parties*, won 8 percent or more of the vote in Bosnia, Bulgaria, Macedonia, Romania, Russia, Slovakia, and Serbia.

29. These countries include Bulgaria, Croatia, Estonia, Latvia, Lithuania, and Slovakia, with only slightly less backing in Moldova and Poland. See Grigore Pop-Eleches, "Throwing the Bums Out: Protest Voting and Anti-Establishment Parties after Communism," Chicago: Annual Meeting of American Political Science Association, 2007.

30. Americans use the terms *liberal* and *conservative* in roughly this sense; *liberal* means something quite different in Europe, so it is safer, as well as regionally correct, to stay with "left."

31. Because of the undemocratic nature of Russian party competition in recent elections, as discussed in Chapter 9, Russia is not shown.

32. The party placements in the United States, Britain, Germany, France, Spain, and Poland are from the *Comparative Study of Electoral Systems* Surveys, www.umich.edu/~cses, in the years shown, using the party position estimated by all citizens in the surveys. (We are grateful to Joshua Tucker and Radoslaw Markowski for providing the CSES data for Poland 2005.) In Bulgaria party positions are estimated from the self-placements of party voters in the election shown, using the European Social Surveys downloaded from www.europeansocialsurvey.org; European Parliament party group positions are from an expert survey reported in Gail McElroy and Kenneth Benoit, "Party Groups and Policy Positions in the European Parliament," *Party Politics* 13 (2007): 5–28. All scales are converted to 0–10.

33. See G. Bingham Powell, Jr., *Elections as Instruments of Democracy: Majoritarian and Proportional Visions* (New Haven, CT: Yale University Press, 2000), especially ch. 7 and references.

34. Ronald Inglehart, "The Changing Structure of Political Cleavages in Western Society," in *Electoral Change in Advanced Industrial Societies,* ed. Russell J. Dalton, Scott C. Flanagan, and Paul Allen Beck (Princeton, NJ: Princeton University Press, 1984), pp. 25–69. On the "post-materialist" values, especially those associated with generational differences, see Ronald Inglehart, *Culture Shift in Advanced Industrial Society* (Princeton, NJ: Princeton University Press, 1990).

35. See Joshua A. Tucker, *Regional Economic Voting: Russia, Poland, Hungary, Slovakia and the Czech Republic from 1990–99* (New York: Cambridge University Press, 2005); Timothy J. Colton, *Transitional Citizens: Voters and What Influences Them in the New Russia* (Cambridge: Harvard University Press, 2000); and Stephen White, Richard Rose, and Ian McAllister, *How Russia Votes* (Chatham, NJ: Chatham House, 1997).

GOVERNMENT AND PUBLIC POLICY

The great British wartime leader Winston Churchill famously observed, "Indeed, it has been said that democracy is the worst form of government, except all those other forms that have been tried from time to time." As Chapter 2 demonstrated, most Europeans share his view. And as this chapter will show, most European governments are indeed **liberal democracies** in practice, claim, or aspiration. In a liberal democracy, citizens must be free to organize and express their desires, and public policy must be shaped by these preferences—not by what leaders or experts claim is the people's true interest. Democratic leaders are supposed to do what their citizens want and be accountable to them through competitive elections. Moreover, liberal democracies protect the civil and political rights and liberties of individual citizens and the rights of minorities. Liberal democracy also implies the *rule of law,* which means that government can take no action that has not been authorized by law and that citizens can be punished only if they violate an existing law. The opposite of democratic government is *authoritarianism* or autocracy.

In Western Europe liberal democracy is well established. By the early 1980s, the last authoritarian governments (in Greece, Portugal, and Spain) had made successful transitions to democracy. Yet, democracies may backslide, and even democratic constitutions may fall far short of their citizens' expectations. In the early 1990s, for example, Italians expressed extreme dissatisfaction with their country's political performance, replaced most of its politicians, and voted to restructure its political processes. But despite occasional problems of violence, terrorism, and intolerance, all Western European countries now have competitive elections, representative assemblies, and civil rights.

The nations of Central and Eastern Europe present a more varied picture. Until 1989 the Soviet Union dominated most of Eastern Europe, which meant authoritarian rule and in large part foreign domination. While most citizens now support democratic freedoms and market economies (see Chapter 2), it has not always been easy to sustain these reforms. Consolidation is hampered not only by the lack of democratic experience, but also by unfavorable social and economic conditions in some countries. Some new democracies, such as Poland and Hungary, have consolidated. Others, such as Bulgaria, seem on their way to stable democracy. Democracy remains limited or fragile in some, including Moldova and Serbia, while authoritarianism prevails in Belarus and Russia. Most of the successor countries of Yugoslavia have experienced civil war or sharp ethnic tension. But despite their shortcomings, the nations of Eastern Europe offer intriguing experiences in democratic governance and new lessons on why some emerging democracies survive, while others fail.

CONSTITUTIONAL ORGANIZATION: RULES FOR MAKING RULES

Any new democracy requires a **constitution,** a general agreement on how laws are made and decision-makers are chosen. A constitution may be a single written document, a set of statutes and practices, or some combination of these. The most important question in constitutional design is who has authority to make political decisions. Democracies typically mix elements of *direct* governance, in which citizens make political decisions themselves through referendums, initiatives, town hall meetings, and the like, and *representative* rule, in which citizens elect politicians to make political decisions on their behalf. European democracies are primarily representative ones. Except for Switzerland, there is much less direct democracy than in many American states. Yet, many European constitutions require or permit referendums on major constitutional changes, such as whether or not to join the European Union (EU) or adopt a new constitution. The choice of constitutional arrangements may shape political decisions for generations. Because constitutional rules are so fundamental, radical changes in them are rare except after massive upheavals.

Separation of Government Powers

Since most political decisions in Europe are made by the people's representatives, rather than by the people themselves, it is important to understand what powers different branches of government possess. Whereas authoritarian political systems often lack any effective limitation on the power of the ruler(s), democracies need to constrain politicians. This is done in part by limiting the power of all politicians and in part by dividing power among them.

The theory of **separation of powers** has a long and venerable history, going back to Locke in Britain and Montesquieu in France.[1] Separation of powers, they argued, can prevent injustices that might result from an unchecked executive or legislature. James Madison, Alexander Hamilton, and John Jay elaborated this theory in *The Federalist,* which described and defended the institutional arrangements proposed by the U.S. Constitutional Convention of 1787. In modern democracies there are two basic ways to separate power: (1) a *geographic* distribution of authority between the central (national) government and lower levels, such as states, provinces, or local governments; and (2) a *structural* separation of powers among different branches of government, such as the legislature, the executive, and the judiciary.

Geographic Distribution of Government Power

The United States has a long history of geographic separation of power. The Articles of Confederation set up a *confederal* system: Ultimate power rested with the states. Under the Constitution of 1787, the U.S. government became *federal:* Both central and state governments have separate spheres of authority. Most European states are more geographically centralized. Britain, France, Poland, and many other European countries are *unitary,* with power concentrated in the central government. Regional and local units have only those powers specifically delegated to them by the central government, which may change or withdraw these powers at will. Thus, confederal systems represent the greatest degree of power dispersion, unitary systems represent the least dispersion, and federal systems are in the middle (see the vertical dimension of Figure 4.1).

There are several federal states in Europe, and especially in Central Europe. In Germany and Switzerland, for example, the national government shares power in many policy areas with regional governments (called *Länder* in Germany). Austria and Russia are also federal states, and Belgium became federal in 1993. Moreover, even such unitary countries as France and Spain have shifted some power from their national governments "downward" to regional ones. The EU is also becoming increasingly federal as power is shifted "upward" from the member states to this supranational body (see Chapter 12).

Federalism can have a number of advantages. In culturally divided societies, it may help protect ethnic, linguistic, or religious minorities, particularly if they are geographically concentrated. In Belgium, federalism was introduced to satisfy the country's two main language communities: the French-speaking Walloons and the Dutch-speaking Flemings. Federalism may also constrain overly ambitious rulers and thus protect the rights and freedoms of the citizens. Moreover, federalism may allow subunits (such as states) to experiment with different policy programs. One government may thus learn from the experiences of others. Besides, citizens can "vote with their feet" and choose the policy environment they like best.

While federalism promotes choice and diversity, it does so at the expense of equality. Since federalism allows different subnational governments to pursue distinct policies, citizens in different regions may get

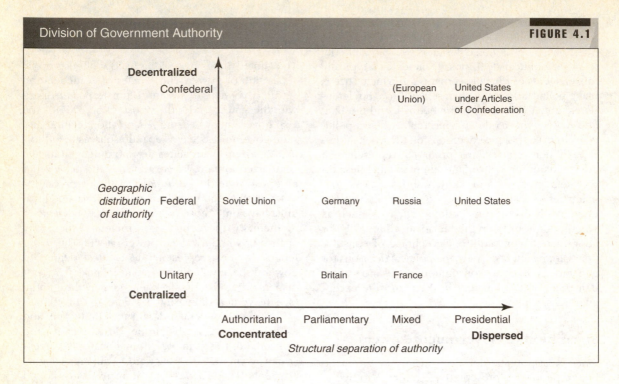

Division of Government Authority

FIGURE 4.1

different rules and benefits. In the United States, for example, some states permit marriage between two individuals of the same sex, but most states do not. Some people value this diversity; others would rather have the same rules apply everywhere. Federalism also typically limits the claims that residents of one region can make on those of another. Unitary governments may therefore be better able to redistribute resources from richer to poorer regions. Finally, national governments often fear that decentralization of power will put the country on a slippery slope toward a total breakup, as happened in the former Yugoslavia. But most federal states are stable. Even when federalism leads to a breakup, this is not always undesirable. Czechoslovakia is a positive example of a federal system that peacefully transformed itself into the separate states of the Czech Republic and Slovakia.

Parliamentary or Presidential Democracies

The second form of separation of power is *functional:* It runs between the different branches of government. The major distinction is between presidential and parliamentary systems. These alternatives specify the relationship between the **assembly** (or legislature or parliament),[2] which has primary authority to make laws, and the **executive**, which carries out these laws. In both parliamentary and presidential democracies, the assembly is directly elected by the citizens and has significant authority to make laws, tax, and spend.

In a **presidential democracy**, such as the United States, the people also elect the president separately. The president is both head of state and chief executive (head of government). He or she appoints a cabinet, which helps the president administer the executive agencies. Both president and assembly have fixed terms; neither can dismiss the other before the next election. (It may be possible to impeach the president or members of the cabinet, but only for serious criminal offenses and after an extraordinary vote that often requires a large majority.) While the primary authority to make laws and to raise and spend money usually rests with the assembly, the president often has veto power. In the United States, for example, Congress can pass legislation over the president's veto only if each house adopts it by a two-thirds majority. A presidential democracy typically implies such checks and balances between the different branches of government. Similar rules apply in Russia, which shares many of the features of presidential government, but has an even stronger president than does the United States (see Chapter 9).

The typical Western European government, in contrast, is a **parliamentary democracy**, in which the people do *not* directly elect the chief executive, the **prime minister**. Instead, the people elect the assembly (parliament), which then chooses and can dismiss the prime minister. This chief executive goes by different names in different countries (prime minister in Britain, premier in France, and chancellor in Germany, for example), but all function in a similar fashion. The prime minister heads the **cabinet**, which consists of the top executive policymakers, primarily the heads of the various executive agencies (known as departments or ministries). The prime minister, his or her cabinet members, and their party-affiliated staff and political advisors are collectively referred to as the *government*. The prime minister is the head of government, but not the ceremonial head of state. All authority to make and execute laws derives from the elected assembly, but in reality the cabinet dominates policymaking more than it does in presidential systems. Some of the typical features of presidential and parliamentary systems are shown in Table 4.1.

Most parliamentary systems have two critical constitutional provisions that distinguish them from presidential systems. One is the *vote of no confidence* or *vote of censure*. If a parliamentary majority expresses its lack of confidence in the government (the prime minister and his or her cabinet), then the government must resign.[3] (See Box 4.1.) The second distinctive feature is the power of *parliamentary dissolution*. Dissolution allows the government to end the assembly session and hold new elections before they would otherwise be due. In some parliamentary countries, such as Britain, the prime minister can effectively call new elections whenever he or she wants to. In other countries there may be constitutional restrictions on the prime minister's dissolution power, but virtually all parliamentary democracies allow for early parliamentary elections. Votes of no confidence are often followed by parliamentary dissolution. If the government resigns, it may call a new election at the same time. Alternatively, some of the parties in the assembly may try to form a new government without having an election. This depends on the constitutional rules, customs, and the political situation.

The confidence vote and the dissolution power ensure that the executive branch and the legislature share a common political view so that they do not work at cross-purposes or get bogged down in gridlock. Rather than a rivalry between government

Parliamentary Versus Presidential Democracies		TABLE 4.1
Distinguishing Features*	**Parliamentary Democracies**	**Presidential Democracies**
Title of chief executive	Prime minister (head of government)	President (head of state and government)
How is the assembly selected?	By citizens in competitive election	By citizens in competitive election
How is the chief executive selected?	By assembly after election or removal	By citizens in competitive election
Can the chief executive be removed before the end of his/her term?	Yes, by assembly through no-confidence vote	No
Can the assembly be dismissed before the end of its term?	Yes, the prime minister may call for early election[†]	No
Authority to legislate	Assembly only	Assembly plus president (e.g., veto)
Party control of assembly and executive	Same parties control both	Different party control possible
Party cohesion in assembly voting	Strong	Less strong

*These define the pure parliamentary and presidential types; as discussed in the text, many constitutional systems, especially in Eastern Europe, "mix" the features of the two types.

[†]Some constitutional systems that are parliamentary in all other ways do not allow for early legislative elections. All parliamentary democracies provide for legislative elections after some maximum time (from three to five years) since the last election.

BOX 4.1

The Confidence Vote in Parliamentary Democracies

In parliamentary democracies, **confidence votes** can be critical and dramatic events; if the governing party loses the vote, the prime minister and all members of the cabinet have to resign. A confidence vote can be called either by the opposition (a no-confidence motion) or by the prime minister (a confidence motion). In either case the government must win the vote or resign from office. But why would the prime minister ever voluntarily call for a confidence vote and risk being thrown out of office? The answer is that the prime minister typically attaches the confidence motion to a bill (a policy proposal) that he or she favors but that the parliamentary majority would not otherwise pass. Through the confidence motion, the prime minister forces parliament either to adopt the bill or to find another prime minister. This can be a particularly painful choice for dissident members of the prime minister's own party. If they don't vote for the bill, they may bring down their own government. Perhaps they will also immediately have to answer to the voters. Prime ministers can therefore use the confidence motion to bring rebellious members of their own party into line. Usually, the threat alone is enough to ensure party discipline and pass important legislation. The fact that the confidence vote does not exist in presidential democracies helps explain why party discipline tends to be stronger in parliamentary systems.

branches, as we often see in presidential systems, there is strong coordination. This promotes decisive government, but it also means fewer checks on officeholders and much less separation of power between the legislative and executive branches of government.

In almost all parliamentary systems, the executive branch is the major policymaker, while the parliament provides an arena for debate, questions, and final authorization. The assembly thus plays a more limited policymaking role than in presidential systems. Since most European countries are parliamentary democracies, the most powerful politician is usually the prime minister.

In European parliamentary systems, most governments depend on disciplined party support to survive. In particular, the elected representatives of the governing party tend to vote very cohesively. Partisan voting is further encouraged by the fact that members of parliament who want to be appointed to cabinet positions or other prestigious offices depend on the goodwill of their respective party leaders, since there is no direct election to these offices. The tendency of Europeans to vote for parties, not individual representatives, both reflects and encourages *party cohesion* (often called *discipline*). This party cohesion in European parliaments is an important feature of these governments and is frequently contrasted with the situation in the U.S. Congress, where party affiliation is only one of several features shaping voting decisions, along with constituency interests, interest group pressure, and personal opinions. On the average substantive "party" vote in the U.S. Congress in the 1990s, a little more than 80 percent of the members of each party voted together.[4] In the typical Western European parliamentary system, on the other hand, over 95 percent of the party members vote together on issues that the parties contest, and the major parties often exhibit nearly perfect internal cohesion.[5] These differences have been quite stable over time.

A second lesson of European parliamentary systems is that the party composition of the parliament greatly affects the cabinet's stability and strength. When a single party controls a parliamentary majority, it can also control the executive and carry out its election promises in predictable ways. By the same token, it may ignore the interests of minority parties. When elections instead produce an assembly divided among many parties, some of them must negotiate to form a coalition government. For better or worse, a coalition government is likely to pursue compromise policies that may not fully reflect anybody's election platform. If legislative negotiations are difficult, coalition governments may also be unstable (as in Italy, where the average cabinet since World War II has lasted only about a year). For these reasons, election rules that determine how many parties gain representation are especially important in parliamentary systems.

Heads of State

Presidential democracy is defined by its head of state, the president, who is at the same time the effective leader of the government and the symbolic representative of his or her country. Contrary to presidential systems, parliamentary democracies have a dual (or split) executive. One person (the prime minister) is the head of government and the effective leader of the executive branch. Another person, a president or a monarch, is the ceremonial representative of the country (the head of state). A hundred years ago the overwhelming majority of European heads of state were monarchs, but now there are only eight left (if we disregard such micro-states as Monaco and Liechtenstein). The last new European democracy that chose a monarchy was Spain in the 1970s. All the other European monarchies (those in Britain, Scandinavia, and the Low Countries) are at least a century old. There are no monarchs in Eastern Europe.

Figure 4.2 displays the constitutional structures of Western and Eastern Europe. There are no pure presidential systems. All Western European countries except Switzerland are parliamentary. Typically, the head of state is a president, rather than a monarch. But presidents may be selected in many different ways. The most important distinction is between those who are elected by the citizens and those who are selected by parliament.[6] In European countries with directly elected presidents, the most common election procedure begins with an open contest between as many different parties as wish to present a candidate. If no candidate wins a majority of votes in this first round (as has happened frequently in France, as well as in Poland in 1995 and in Russia in 1996), there is a runoff, normally between the two leading candidates from the first round.

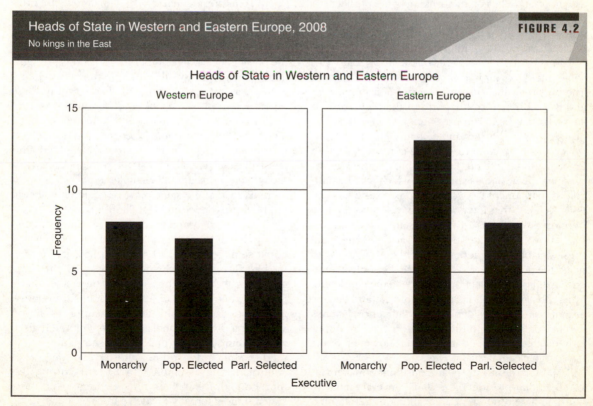

Heads of State in Western and Eastern Europe, 2008   **FIGURE 4.2**
No kings in the East

Heads of State in Western and Eastern Europe

Note: "Popularly Elected" executives include those that are *directly* elected by the citizens and those that are *indirectly* elected by them.

"Parliament Selected" executives may be elected solely by the parliament or by some combination of the parliament and other government officials.

Source: Central Intelligence Agency, *CIA World Factbook 2007 (Washington, DC: Central Intelligence Agency, 2008) retrieved February 2008.*

The power of European heads of state varies a great deal across countries.[7] Nowadays monarchs have only symbolic or ceremonial functions, though King Juan Carlos actually played a positive role in consolidating Spain's new democracy in the 1970s and early 1980s. Parliament-selected presidents, such as those in Germany, Hungary, and Italy, never have much policymaking authority and consistently rank well behind their respective prime ministers in real power. To find powerful heads of state we therefore have to look to countries with popularly elected presidents.

A handful of European countries, including France and Poland, have **semi-presidential systems**, which combine parliamentary and presidential features. In such systems the directly elected president appoints the prime minister. Moreover, the president can usually dissolve parliament and call new elections; he or she may also have some direct policymaking powers. Prime ministers in these countries are "jointly accountable": They depend on majority support in the assembly as well as on the backing of the president. If they fail to retain parliamentary support, they can be removed through a vote of no confidence. If they fail to please the president, they can often be fired.

Presidents in semi-presidential systems can sometimes play an important role in policymaking. The president may use his powers of appointment and the influence of his party in the legislature to shape the cabinet. The president may also have executive powers—for example, in foreign and defense policy—directly conferred by the constitution (as in France). Some, like the Russian (but not the French) president, have a legislative veto, which may be difficult for parliament to override. Some presidents can issue decrees that have the force of law for limited periods or even (as in the Russian case) until replaced by appropriate legislative action. Where the president's powers depend largely on her ability to name the government, as in France, her policy influence will largely reflect the balance in the legislature. Where the president has powers of veto and decree, as in Russia, the president's policy influence depends less on his support in the legislature. Not all popularly elected presidents are strong, however. Some have largely ceremonial powers.

Many Eastern European constitution makers favored a semi-presidential regime. Several countries partly imitated the French constitution. Yet about a third of the Eastern European constitutions are purely parliamentary and have weak, parliament-selected presidents. A similar number, including Bulgaria, have directly elected, but fairly weak and ceremonial, presidents. However, the popularly elected presidents in Lithuania, Poland, and Romania have powers at least equal to those of the French president. They appoint prime ministers and cabinets that are accountable to the assembly. The presidents of Croatia, Russia, and Ukraine have even greater policymaking powers. These are the only European countries in which the president is more powerful than the prime minister. Table 4.2 compares various powers of the five presidents covered in our text. The Russian president is the strongest of these five executives. He is the only one who names cabinet members directly. Thus, the Russian president, rather than the prime minister, controls the membership of the cabinet. It is also very difficult for the Russian assembly to override presidential vetoes. The German president, on the other hand, is the weakest of the five. He has no veto or decree powers and can only dismiss the assembly (the *Bundestag*) in narrowly defined emergency situations.

A semi-presidential system with a powerful president as well as a prime minister may experience *divided government* (known in France as *cohabitation*). This is where one party (or coalition of parties) holds the presidency, while another party controls the legislature and typically also the prime ministership. France has experienced such cohabitation in three different periods since 1986 and Poland twice in the 1990s. Divided government is most common when legislative and presidential elections are not held at the same time, since voters then often use "midterm" legislative elections to punish the president's party. If the two elections are held simultaneously, it is much more likely that the same party or coalition will control both presidency and legislature.[8]

Divided government can lead to conflict or complex political bargaining. While we are still learning about semi-presidential systems in Eastern Europe, the basic lessons from France are that (1) if the president's party controls the assembly, he or she can be the lead policymaker; (2) even without such control, a clever president with substantial support can prevail over a divided opposition; but (3) if the legislature is controlled by a united opposition, power will tend to shift to the prime minister and the parties controlling the assembly.[9] In Eastern Europe this third condition has been rare, as fragmented party systems and internally divided parties have facilitated presidential dominance.

Scholars disagree about the advantages of parliamentary versus presidential constitutions.[10] Based on

TABLE 4.2 Presidential Powers in Five European Countries
Popularly Elected Presidents Are More Powerful

Countries	Can the President Veto Laws? If So, How Does the Assembly Override?	Can the President Issue Decrees (Regulations Not Passed by the Assembly)?	Can the President Propose a Referendum?	What Is the Role of the President When a Cabinet Is Formed?	Can the President Dissolve the Assembly and Call New Elections?
Bulgaria (popularly elected)	Yes; override by simple majority	No	No; the president can only schedule referendums authorized by the assembly	The president names a prime minister, who must be approved by the assembly and who then names other ministers	Yes, but only after the assembly has three times failed to elect a prime minister
France (popularly elected)	Yes; override by simple majority	The president has limited authority to issue decrees	Yes, but only upon the request of the prime minister or both houses of the assembly	The president names a prime minister, who must be approved by the assembly and who then names other ministers	Yes, but not during the first year of the assembly's term
Germany (parliament selected)	Veto power not clearly established by constitution	No	No	The president names a prime minister, who must be approved by the assembly and who then names other ministers	Yes, but only after there has been a vote of no confidence in the prime minister
Poland (popularly elected)	Yes; override by absolute majority of all representatives	No	Yes, but only with the consent of the senate	The president names a prime minister, who must be approved by the assembly and who then names other ministers	Yes, but only after there has been a vote of no confidence in the prime minister
Russia (popularly elected)	Yes; override only by extraordinary majority in both chambers	The president has extensive power to issue decrees as long as they do not conflict with existing laws	Yes; there are no restrictions on this power	The president names cabinet ministers directly; they must then be approved by the Assembly.	Yes, but only after there has been a vote of no confidence in the prime minister

Sources: Albert P. Blaunstein and Gisbert H. Flanz, eds., *Constitutions of the Countries of the World* (Dobbs Ferry, NY: Oceana, 1971); *The Europa World Year Book*, various editions (New York: Europa Publications, various years); Lee Kendall Metcalf, "Measuring Presidential Power," *Comparative Political Studies* 33 (June 2000): 660–685; Matthew S. Shugart and John M. Carey, *Presidents and Assemblies: Constitutional Design and Electoral Dynamics* (New York: Cambridge University Press, 1992).

the favorable Western European experience with parliamentary systems (and the often unfavorable Latin American experience with presidential systems), many have tended to favor the parliamentary option. Parliamentary systems, their proponents argue, can represent a wide range of public opinion in the assembly and make sure that these views bear directly on the executive. And if the elected representatives of the people dislike the cabinet's policies, they can replace it. Another argument for the parliamentary option is that a strong president may use executive powers to repress democratic competition.

Moreover, a presidential system always holds the potential for a confrontation between a strong president who initiates a lot of legislation and also implements it and the assembly that must approve all laws and fund all government programs. Such confrontation is particularly likely when different political parties control these branches of government. Divided government is sometimes associated with policy deadlock. When the conflict is very severe, as in Chile in the early 1970s, the strife between these two branches of government can tear the political system apart.

On the other hand, advocates of presidential systems as well as many constitution makers in new democracies believe that direct presidential election and fixed terms improve efficiency and accountability. Election dates are predictable, and citizens and politicians do not constantly have to concern themselves with election campaigns and threats that new elections may be called. Another positive feature of presidential systems is that the head of government is chosen directly by the people, not through the political "wheeling and dealing" of parliamentary systems. Elected by and accountable to the whole nation, rather than the parliamentary majority, the president should be able to take a larger view of the national interest than can individual legislators or the prime ministers they choose. Defenders of presidential systems also argue that the instability of many presidential regimes in Latin America may have been due more to unfavorable social conditions and especially to military intervention than to presidential constitutions. Between the two world wars, parliamentary constitutions in Europe were no more stable than were presidential ones in Latin America.

In Eastern Europe government stability has been a problem both in a number of parliamentary systems and in some semi-presidential systems with moderately strong presidents. Ominously, all three countries with particularly strong presidents (Croatia, Russia, and Ukraine) have experienced at least temporary limitations on democracy and the freedom of speech. Only about a third of the countries with other types of constitutions have experienced such severe transition problems. The 2007 Freedom House report on **freedom of the press** tells a very similar tale (see Box 4.3).

The European countries most consistently ranked democratic and free include every constitutional type except the semi-presidential type with a strong president. Yet, this may be because the countries that have adopted strong presidencies are relatively poor and ethnically troubled. Countries with more advanced economies and fewer ethno-nationalist divisions have had easier transitions. Despite the many challenges, so far the transition to democracy has clearly failed only in Belarus and Russia—where strong presidents have ignored constitutional limits on their power and, in the Russian case, gradually undermined democratic freedoms (see Chapter 9)—and in Bosnia-Herzegovina—where the country was plunged into a civil war before democracy had had a chance to work. But even in Ukraine and Serbia, democracy seems fragile. Democracy faces many different risks, and there may not be any one constitution that fits all circumstances.

LIMITING AND DISPERSING POLICYMAKING POWER

European democracies are embedded in complex constitutional arrangements, many of which require the policymakers to secure the consent of more than a simple parliamentary majority. The British political system is one of the simplest because a government that controls the House of Commons need not share power with other institutions or political opponents. Most other European countries, however, constrain the parliamentary majority in different ways.

Besides direct democracy and federalism, many European democracies limit executive power through three kinds of institutional arrangements: strong legislative committees, bicameralism, and judicial review. The first approach, **strong legislative committees**, requires **power-sharing** with opposition parties within the parliament itself. Germany and Hungary delegate a large part of the process of drafting laws to parliamentary committees in which the chairmanships are shared proportionally between government and opposition parties. In such committees government majorities must usually take greater account of the parliamentary opposition parties.

Another approach is **bicameralism**—a separation of power between two parliamentary chambers. Germany and Switzerland, for example, have (as does the United States) a second (upper) legislative chamber with significant powers and a different method of election. In some countries, such as Germany, the upper house directly represents regional governments. If different parties control the two chambers, then policymaking may require more extensive bargaining and compromise.

Judicial review by special constitutional courts or councils is another way to constrain the government. Although most European courts are not as active as the U.S. Supreme Court, many have become more assertive in recent years.[11] The constitutions of the Eastern European nations generally provide for constitutional courts, many of which have been influential in constraining government policies and even defining new constitutional powers. However, in some countries, such as Russia, Belarus, and Albania, the constitutional courts have not been willing or able to crack down on abuses of power by the government.

All governments are constrained by international agreements and alliances and by the economies and societies in which they operate. For its 27 member countries, the EU is an especially important international commitment (see Chapter 12). The European Court of Justice (ECJ) has become an important check on national legislation in the sense that within its jurisdiction ECJ decisions supersede those of national courts. Moreover, the EU requires all its member states to respect basic democratic freedoms and civil rights. By virtue of its economic and political power, the EU also influences politics even in states that are not members, such as Switzerland and Turkey.

CONSTITUTIONAL ORGANIZATION: ELECTORAL RULES

Since European polities operate mainly as representative democracies, the rules for electing the people's representatives play a critical part in shaping the policy process. Most European democracies elect their assemblies through **proportional representation (PR)** in multimember districts, with parties represented in rough proportion to their vote. There are many forms of PR, and none is perfectly proportional. But the larger the number of representatives

elected in each district (known as **district magnitude**), the easier it is to reach proportionality. For example, it may take up to 33 percent of the vote to gain a seat in a three-member district, and parties that get less may get no representation. Electoral systems that have many such districts are not likely to be very proportional. In the Netherlands, in contrast, the entire 150-seat legislature is elected from the nation at large, permitting even very small parties to gain representation.

Proportional representation rules with large districts very accurately convert votes into legislative seats, but they can fragment the assembly into a multitude of little parties. Consequently, it may become difficult to build legislative majorities and pass coherent legislation. In order to limit the number of legislative parties, many countries have some minimum threshold of votes (for example, 2 or 5 percent) that parties must win in order to enter parliament. Such thresholds are often used in combination with so-called *supplementary seats,* which are elected from the country as a whole and given to parties that would otherwise be underrepresented.

The Swedish Parliament, for example, has 349 seats, 310 of which are given out in separate districts that have anywhere from 2 to 34 representatives each, depending on population. The remaining 39 seats are supplementary ones, given to parties that surpass the national threshold of 4 percent but that are underrepresented when all the district seats are added up. In this way, all Swedish parties that get at least 4 percent of the vote get highly proportional representation, whereas parties that fall below this threshold typically get nothing.

Figure 4.3 shows some features of European election laws. The first two bars in each region show countries with PR, but with different thresholds for representation. Eastern European PR systems are more likely to feature thresholds that require parties to win from 4 to as much as 9 percent of the vote to enter the national parliament. Even 4- or 5-percent thresholds can eliminate the representation of many voters (but also help constrain legislative fragmentation) if the party system is extremely splintered. A few PR countries such as Greece and Spain have small districts or other special rules that make it harder for small parties to enter the legislature and easier for large parties to win majorities. Nonetheless, under PR it is rare for individual parties to win legislative majorities.

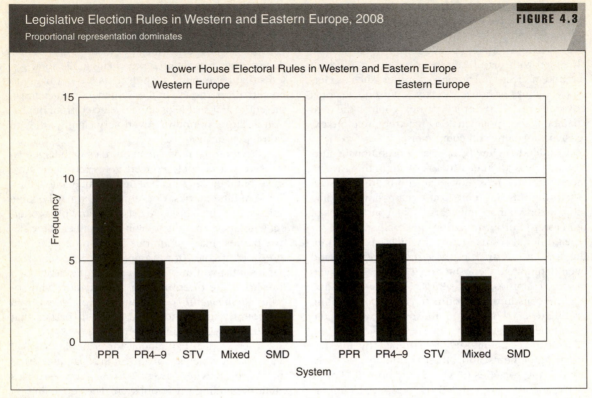

Legislative Election Rules in Western and Eastern Europe, 2008   FIGURE 4.3
Proportional representation dominates

Lower House Electoral Rules in Western and Eastern Europe

Notes:
PPR = pure proportional representation
PR4–9 = proportional representation with a 4–9 percent electoral threshold
STV = single transferable vote
Mixed = mixed proportional and plurality electoral system
SMD = single-member district system

Sources: Electionworld, *Elections Around the World,* retrieved February 2008, from www.electionworld.org; Harvard University, John F. Kennedy School of Government, *Kokkalis Program on Southeastern and East-Central Europe,* as updated July 12, 2004, from www.ksg. harvard.edu/kokkalis/region; Library of Congress, *Country Studies U.S.,* as updated in 2003, from countrystudies.us.

Single-Member District Plurality Systems

The best-known alternative to proportional representation is the first-past-the-post system, in which the country is divided into **single-member districts (SMDs),** each won by the candidate with the most votes (the plurality). This system is used in most elections in the United States and Canada. In Europe, only Britain and Belarus use simple first-past-the-post voting in national parliamentary elections, though some other countries (such as Germany) use SMDs for some of their legislative seats. France uses an SMD system, but with a majority requirement. If no candidate garners an outright majority, the leading candidates enter a runoff.

Plurality systems have some attractive features. Districts can be small, and voters can get to know their representative. Voting is simple and easy to understand, and the number of viable candidates is usually low. But plurality elections tend to yield disproportional results. The largest party often gains a majority in parliament even if it does not have a majority of the popular vote. Small parties are shut out unless their votes are concentrated in a few districts. Even medium-sized parties (25 percent or so) whose votes are spread evenly across many districts can come in second nearly everywhere and win few seats. In Britain in 2005, for example, the Liberal Democratic Party won 22 percent of the national vote, but carried only 9 percent of the parliamentary seats. In the same election, the Labour Party gained 55 percent of the parliamentary seats with only 35 percent of the vote (see Chapter 5). The problems of smaller parties are made worse because voters do not want to "waste" their votes on hopeless candidates. And knowing that, such candidates will not run. The tendency for SMD elections to foster two-party systems is known as Duverger's Law, after the distinguished French political scientist who described it.[12]

Mixed Electoral Systems

After World War II, the new German constitution pioneered a novel **mixed electoral system** that combines proportional representation and SMDs (see Figure 4.3). For elections to the German *Bundestag* (the lower house), the country is divided into SMDs. Half the members are elected from these districts; the other half are elected by proportional representation (with a 5-percent threshold). Each voter casts two votes: one for an individual district candidate and one for a party list of candidates from a larger area. In this way each voter has a representative from his or her geographic district to turn to on local issues, whereas the party-list seats are allocated so as to achieve partisan proportionality. Parties that are underrepresented in the SMDs receive a compensatory overrepresentation from the party-list seats. The result is very high proportionality.

Eastern Europe features a variety of electoral systems (see Figure 4.3). **Mixed electoral rules**, often inspired by the German system, initially found wide favor. However, many of these systems lacked the compensatory features found in Germany. If there is no such compensation and a large proportion of the seats is given to SMDs, as in Hungary, the results may be much less proportional. Some countries that experimented with mixed systems, such as Italy and Russia, have in recent years moved away from the German model.

Another type of electoral system is the **single transferable vote** (STV), which Ireland and Malta use. Under an STV system, the voters get to rank candidates from different parties in any order. Each party presents a slate of candidates, but voters get to pick and choose from different lists as they please. The votes are first counted according to the voters' first preferences. Whenever any candidate has reached enough first-preference votes to get elected, his or her surplus votes are distributed to other candidates according to the voters' second choices. The same thing happens to candidates who get too few votes to be elected: Their votes are instead given to the second choices of the respective voters. The STV system allows voters to "split their tickets" and therefore reduces the power of political parties over their candidates. Because it tends to lead to fairly proportional results, it is commonly counted as a special type of PR.

All electoral designs face the question of whether representation should be based strictly on the principle of "one person, one vote." Should each assembly member represent an equal number of citizens? Deviations from this principle are known as *malapportionment*. It may seem obvious that malapportionment should be avoided, and, indeed, it is generally viewed as undesirable. Serious malapportionment also makes it difficult to achieve proportionality in party representation. Yet, some assemblies feature malapportionment by design. This is most common in federal systems, where all states (or more generally, subnational units) may be represented equally, regardless of population. Thus, in the U.S. Senate, each state, whatever its population, has two seats. The same is true of the upper house of the Russian assembly. In the German upper house, the bigger states have more seats than the smaller ones, but not nearly as many as their populations would indicate. Deliberate malapportionment is less common in unitary states and in the lower houses of bicameral assemblies. Yet, the Chamber of Deputies in unitary Spain substantially underrepresents some regions and overrepresents others. And Scotland has more seats in the British House of Commons than its population would justify. Nevertheless, malapportionment in most European assemblies is modest, though in some countries it systematically benefits particular parties.

The Effects of Electoral Systems

Election laws and party competition both affect the number of parliamentary parties. Since most Western European countries use proportional representation, even rather small parties can gain seats in the legislature, and it is rare for any party to win a majority. In most of Western Europe, the electoral rules, constitutional provisions, and policymaking procedures work together to represent many different groups of citizens through multiple political parties. Only Britain, France, Greece, and Spain have rules that typically produce directly elected majority governments. In these systems single parties often win legislative majorities with far fewer than half of the votes. Some relatively recent electoral systems in Western Europe, such as those of Greece and Spain, have some basic features of proportional representation, but contain special provisions that reward large parties and often help them secure parliamentary majorities even when they have not won a popular majority.

Eastern Europe is different in two notable ways. First, electoral thresholds have been more consequential. Often many parties run unsuccessfully and fall below the electoral threshold. This is because many political party leaders (and followers) are only gradually learning enough about the electorate and the electoral rules to coalesce into viable parties. Eventually, the party leaders and organizers in these countries may come to build stable parties large enough to surmount these barriers. But there are still quite a few countries in which 10 to 20 percent of the voters support parties that are too small to get any representation. In countries with mixed electoral systems, such as Hungary and Lithuania, the SMD elections also reduce the number of legislative parties.

The second difference is the weakness of national parties in SMD elections in the East. To a degree unknown in contemporary Western Europe (except Ireland), many candidates in these elections campaign as independents, representing local rather than national interests. This was, for example, true of Russia in the 1990s. Weak national parties in these countries have also weakened their assemblies and contributed to presidential dominance.

The makers of the Eastern European constitutions were torn between their fear of strong government and their need for it. They were also torn between the desire to involve as many citizens as possible and the concern that a fragmented party system would create deadlock. As a result their constitutions frequently feature complex institutions, such as semi-presidential systems and mixed election rules, that strike a balance between their desires for inclusiveness, on one hand, and for effective government, on the other. Experience suggests that it is often difficult to predict what a particular package of institutional compromises will produce. This is in part because new and complex rules sometimes generate unexpected results and in part because politicians will always try to manipulate institutions to their advantage. It can take a number of elections before these effects are fully understood.

Stealing Elections   BOX 4.2

Elections are critical for democracy, but it is not enough that citizens have a chance to vote. Elections that are not free or fair mean a sham democracy, rather than a real one. Unfortunately, there is sometimes electoral fraud even in well-established democracies. Russia and some of the other Eastern European countries, however, have experienced voting fraud that has sometimes been quite blatant.

"Natalia" (who withheld her real name for fear of reprisals) was a teacher and a local election observer in the 2000 Russian presidential elections. When the voting was done and the ballot boxes were turned upside down for counting, Natalia noticed two big packets of ballots on top. They had clearly been inserted into the ballot box and not cast by individual voters. One packet even had a sheet around it. Natalia picked up the two packets, noticed that all the ballots in them had President Putin's name on them, and alerted the other observers to the fraud. Some observers from Putin's campaign just grabbed the packets of fake ballots out of her hands, unbundled them, and mixed them in with the other ballots so that they could no longer be recognized. In Bashkortostan, another election observer, Klavdiia Grigorieva, recorded the final voting results from her local precinct as 862 for Putin, 356 for Ziuganov (his main opponent), 24 for Zhirinovskii, 21 for Titov, and 12 for Lavlinskii. But the official election protocol listed 1,092 votes for Putin, 177 votes for Ziuganov, and no votes for anybody else. Grigorieva lodged a formal complaint, but never received a response. In 2002 Governor Aleksandr Prokhorov ran for reelection in Smolensk. Prokhorov had criticized President Putin and was challenged by the head of the regional FSB (the Russian secret police). During the campaign two cottages belonging to Prokhorov's supporters were burned, and his election headquarters were bombed. The son of his lawyer was beaten up, and his deputy was attacked by gunmen who killed his driver in the process. Not surprisingly, Prokhorov lost his bid for reelection.

Source: M. Steven Fish, *Democracy Derailed in Russia* (Cambridge, England: Cambridge University Press, 2005).

GOVERNMENT FORMATION AND POLICYMAKING

Forming Governments

Since in parliamentary and semi-presidential systems the head of government is not directly elected, parliamentary elections are followed by a period of bargaining over **government formation**. This process is sometimes straightforward, rapid, and simple. When a single political party wins a majority of the parliamentary seats, it almost always forms a government with its party leader as prime minister. It rarely shares cabinet posts with other parties. Such governments are very common in countries with SMD elections, but in Europe these are a minority. As Figure 4.4 shows, after the most recent elections five countries in Western Europe (Britain, France, Greece, Malta, and Portugal) and three in Eastern Europe (Belarus, Moldova, and Russia) had single-party majority governments.[13]

In most European elections, no single party comes away with a majority. In these cases there may be a **coalition government** of parties that jointly control a parliamentary majority. In fact, the tall middle bar in Figure 4.4 shows that such a multiparty majority coalition is the most common type of government in Eastern as well as Western Europe. The task of forming a coalition government can be easy or difficult. It is relatively simple when several parties agree before the election that they would like to govern together and then in fact go on to win a legislative majority.[14] Parties that are already involved in a **coalition government** may simply announce that they will continue to govern together if they keep their majority. Or a group of opposition parties may agree to join forces so that they present an alternative to the incumbent government. Such preelection agreements have been common in Germany, France, and the Scandinavian countries. They may be encouraged by election rules that favor electoral cooperation between parties. All told, about 20 percent of recent Western European governments have been such majority coalitions that were announced before the elections.

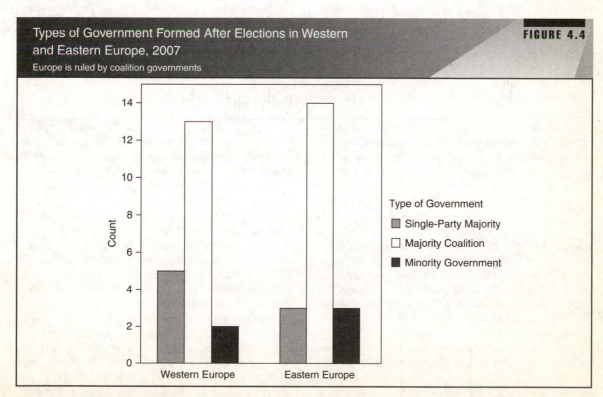

Types of Government Formed After Elections in Western and Eastern Europe, 2007

FIGURE 4.4

Europe is ruled by coalition governments

Type of Government
- Single-Party Majority
- Majority Coalition
- Minority Government

Note: "Single-party majority" refers to governments containing one party whose representatives constitute a majority in the legislature, even if additional parties also share cabinet seats.

Source: *Keesing's Contemporary Archives, Electoral Studies,* various issues.

When there is no parliamentary majority for parties that have agreed to govern together, the process of forming a government is less straightforward. What happens depends on constitutional rules as well as circumstances. Typically, the head of state will ask the leader of the largest political party to attempt to negotiate a government. If he or she fails, another party leader will be asked. If it is difficult to anticipate which coalitions may be feasible, the head of state may ask an *informateur* to sound out possible options. This kind of coalition bargaining, immediately after either an election or the breakup of a previous coalition government, is frequent throughout Europe. Virtually all governments in Belgium, Finland, and the Netherlands (as well as in pre-1994 Italy) have been formed in this way.

Sometimes the outcome of coalition bargaining is not what people expect. About a fifth of all European governments are **minority governments**, which consist of parties that between them do not control a parliamentary majority. Such governments therefore depend on support from one or several parties that have no representatives in the cabinet. By the rules of parliamentary democracy, minority governments live dangerously, and, in fact, they do tend to be shorter lived than majority governments. But in some countries minority governments can become a common occurrence. Norway, for example, had nothing but minority governments between 1985 and 2005. A minority government can be a stopgap until the next election provides a parliamentary majority (as in Britain in 1974). Or it can be an alternative to majority government where the rules permit even the opposition parties to have policy influence (as in Norway) so that they are less keen to defeat the incumbent government. Or a minority government may be a sign of parliamentary deadlock in which it is simply not possible to build any majority coalition (as has frequently happened in Italy). In semi-presidential systems a strong president may be able to use the threat of dissolving the assembly or other policymaking powers to sustain a minority government, as in France (1988–1993) and in Russia under President Yeltsin (1991–1999). As of 2007, five European countries, two in the West and three in the East, had minority governments.

After a coalition government has formed, the cabinet positions are shared among the participating parties, which usually receive such "portfolios" in proportion to their relative strength in parliament. They also tend to receive ministries reflecting their particular interests. Thus, the ministry of agriculture tends to go to parties with strong rural support and the ministry of labor to parties supported by labor unions. In semi-presidential systems the president may be able to influence the composition of the cabinet even if his or her party does not control the legislature.

Single-party majority governments usually endure until they lose an election, at least in mature party systems such as that in Britain. Coalition governments that are "minimal winning"—those that have a parliamentary majority, but cannot afford to shed any party without losing this majority—are also usually quite durable. Minority governments, on the other hand, last only about a year and a half on average and less in some countries. Very broad coalitions consisting of as many as five to seven different parties also tend to be fragile and short lived.

When governments fall between elections—either because they lose a confidence vote or because they resign in anticipation of this—the bargaining process must begin anew. This can be a serious liability if parties are so busy negotiating and renegotiating their coalitions that they have no time to govern. In France in the 1950s and Italy in the 1970s and 1980s, governments became so weak and unstable that little got done politically, and both countries experienced serious political crises.

Policymaking in Parliamentary Governments

Between elections the policymaking process in parliamentary systems is primarily, but not exclusively, shaped by the composition of the government. In systems with concentrated political power, such as those in Britain and France, the winning party or coalition expects and is expected to carry out its campaign promises. If competing parties or coalitions offer contrasting choices, a change of government usually makes a notable policy difference. When in 1981 a coalition government of socialists and communists came to power in France after more than 20 years of center-right rule, it made many dramatic policy changes, such as nationalizing private banks and the five largest industrial corporations and raising the minimum wage and social security benefits. In countries where parties outside of government have more influence or where governments are broad coalitions of very different parties, a change of government usually makes less of a dramatic policy difference. Frequent changes in government can also limit the impact of elections and parties on policy, as it takes time for new executives to affect policy.[15]

DEMOCRATIC POLICIES AND WELFARE IN EUROPE

Economic conditions and public policies jointly affect the welfare of citizens and, in turn, their satisfactions or frustrations with democratic politics. In general, the public policies that have emerged in Western Europe have responded to public demand for extensive social safety nets, substantial public services (that include, for example, government-run public transit systems), and relative economic equality. Governments have also contended with the economic problems of unemployment, inflation, and growth. Finally, in recent years governments have been responding to pressures from citizens and some parties to pay more attention to the environment.

Many social welfare benefits—such as unemployment benefits, social security, and public-sector health care—tend to be more extensive in Western Europe than in the United States or Japan. They also tend to be more thoroughly financed by the government. These and other social policy programs make up the **welfare state,** which is more extensive in many European countries than anywhere else. Historically, the Western European societies also developed these policies earlier. In many countries the benefits were markedly expanded during reconstruction after the two World Wars. Massive public involvement in housing was also stimulated by postwar reconstruction and remains a prominent, though generally declining, feature of the policies of many European nations. Public education, and especially university education, in contrast, was a policy priority in the United States before it became one in Europe. Only in recent decades have many Western European countries begun to offer public higher education to a large share of their cohorts of young people.

Extensive social services in large part account for the comparatively large size of government relative to the private sector in Western Europe. Whereas in the United States about 15 percent of all workers are employed by the government, this percentage ranges in Western Europe from about the same in Britain to more than 30 percent in some Scandinavian countries. The median government

expenditure in Western Europe is around 45 percent of the gross domestic product, as compared with around 35 percent in the United States and Japan. However, there is substantial variation across Europe, with Switzerland similar to the United States, but Denmark and Sweden approaching 60 percent of gross domestic product. The welfare state tends to be larger where social democratic parties have frequently been in government, where labor unions are strong, and where there is a tradition of a strong bureaucracy. In the 1990s budgetary pressures resulted in cutbacks in the public sector in some high-spending countries such as Sweden.

Some countries also have a large public sector because the government is directly involved in many large economic enterprises (for example, banks, oil companies, airlines, railroads, or defense industries). Such government ownership is often a hotly contested political issue. For example, in the early 1980s, conservative governments in Britain and Germany sold off many government enterprises (privatization), while the socialist government in France was acquiring them (nationalization). In both countries, the opposition parties strongly opposed these policies. Since about that time, the strong economic performance of market-oriented and free-enterprise economies have made privatization policies the dominant trend.

The Eastern European countries began their democratic experience in the early 1990s with controlled economies that guaranteed employment for able-bodied citizens of working age, fixed prices for goods and services, ensured relative income equality, and promised some modest welfare security for the young, the old, and those unable to work. Most of these countries also had great shortages of consumer goods, poor economic productivity, and a standard of living far below that of Western Europe. Most citizens were disillusioned with the communist governments.

The newly democratic Eastern European governments began by freeing prices, privatizing industry, and encouraging free competition and investment. Unfortunately, it proved difficult to move swiftly from a controlled economy to a competitive one. In some countries, as in Russia, it has been hard even to dismantle the old system, let alone to build a new one. Even where this was achieved most rapidly and successfully, as in Poland, it came at the cost of short-term drops in living standards and a great deal of confusion as citizens learned to live with economic uncertainties. The region also faces a huge task of cleaning up vast environmental damage created by the communist governments' ruthless industrialization, but this is for most citizens a lower priority. The costs of transition have brought many formerly communist parties back into power, though in most Eastern European countries these parties have now clearly committed themselves to a democratic polity. From about the late 1990s, the most difficult transition period was over in most Eastern European countries (though not in all parts of the former Yugoslavia), and many of them, such as Poland, have since grown strongly.

THE RULE OF LAW, CORRUPTION, AND DEMOCRACY

Democracy depends on competitive elections to link government policies to citizen preferences. To ensure that those policies are implemented fairly, democracy also requires the rule of law. The rule of law can fail in many ways. The president may decide to continue past the end of his term of office or ignore the rulings of a constitutional court (as in Belarus). Ruling parties may demand kickbacks from firms seeking public works contracts or bribes from interest groups asking for legislative favors (which unfortunately happens far too often in many countries). Tax officials or border authorities may take cash payments to overlook violations and illegal conduct. Or corruption may open the door to penetration of the government by organized crime.

No democracy is immune to such threats to the rule of law. But some countries suffer much more grievously than others from political corruption. When citizens are forced to participate in corrupt practices to gain even basic benefits, it surely weakens their confidence in government. A blatant example of public corruption emerged in Italy in the early 1990s, when a judicial investigation called "Operation Clean Hands" revealed that the governing political parties had demanded and received huge bribes from business organizations and used them to finance both political activities and lavish lifestyles for their leaders. Through bribery as well as violence, organized crime had deeply penetrated Italian politics, particularly in the south of the country. These revelations destroyed most of the political parties and leaders that had dominated Italian politics since World War II, sparking constitutional change and a new party system.

In Eastern Europe establishing the rule of law has been one of the most difficult parts of the transition to democracy.[16] Communist dictatorships had in many countries coexisted with widespread corruption. Sometimes the governments even encouraged corruption to overcome the inefficiencies of the vast bureaucracies. Abuse of power to gain personal benefits was common at all levels, especially where communism had been imposed on economically poor societies. Such habits were not easily overcome after democratization, especially in local government. They were sustained by poverty and exacerbated in the short run by the slumping economies and lagging salary payments that made life desperate for many government employees. Privatization of large enterprises also created unusual opportunities for insiders, such as the Russian "oligarchs," to abuse their positions and acquire much of this new wealth.

While it is difficult to study corruption and criminal activity systematically, interesting comparisons are offered by Transparency International, which surveys businesses to estimate corruption levels in different countries. Their Corruption Perceptions Index annually rates most countries of the world on a scale from 0 (most corrupt) to 10 (most clean). In 2007 no fewer than ten Western European countries, or half of all the states in this region, rated 8 or higher. Apart from Britain, though, these were all smaller countries. Denmark, Finland, and New Zealand shared the best score of all countries (9.4). The Western European average was similar to that of the United States (7.2). Spain (6.7) and especially Italy (5.2) were rated less "clean" than the United States.[17] All the Eastern European nations fell well below the Western European average. Slovenia and Estonia were rated highest for the region and well above Italy. Russia scored a discouraging 2.3, whereas at 2.1, Belarus had the worst perceived corruption problem in Europe, on a par with such notorious cases as Nigeria and Zimbabwe.

In Europe and across the world, economic development is a very powerful predictor of cleaner politics. Yet, presumably because of the problems of overcoming its communist heritage and managing an economic transition, Eastern Europe appears to be somewhat more corrupt than its economic development would lead us to expect. Corruption is recognized as a serious issue in most of these countries, but it is easier to raise it as an election issue than to solve the problem.

INTRODUCING AND SUSTAINING DEMOCRACY

A hundred years ago most of the world's democracies were European. Europe has thus been the source of much of our knowledge of democratic governance. It has also been the site of some of the most famous failures of democracy, most notably the collapse of Germany's Weimar Republic into Nazi dictatorship. While there are now more democracies outside of Europe, there is little doubt that the experiences of Eastern Europe will add greatly to our understanding of democratization.

In managing democratic conflict, Western European societies have tended to engage in power-sharing through a variety of constitutional and electoral devices, which has encouraged multiple political parties and multiple paths to policy influence. In some European countries such as the Netherlands, Austria, Belgium, and Switzerland, the efforts to overcome deep conflicts gave rise to a distinctive form of guaranteed power-sharing called *consociational democracy* (see Chapter 1).[18] Elite-negotiated agreements guaranteed both influence and benefits to all social segments (whether defined by religious, linguistic, or occupational criteria) and were buttressed by formal organizational arrangements. Consociational democracy has proven to be a valuable approach to conflict management in seriously divided societies, although it may work better in the short term than over the longer haul. This is because consociationalism isolates different social groups from one another. Such isolation can be beneficial when there is severe conflict, but as social groups become less distinctive and conflicts less intense, consociational arrangements may become confining and a barrier to fuller integration.

Studies of conflict in Europe and elsewhere suggest that power-sharing processes can help diminish riots and protests.[19] Such turmoil is likely to be more intense where there are fewer roads to influence, as in majoritarian democracies. In contrast, proportional representation and power-sharing strategies may bring turmoil "inside" the institutions, as extremist parties may gain access to the legislature and make

stable government more difficult. And once violent conflict is unleashed, elite agreements may be insufficient. Northern Ireland has demonstrated repeatedly that democratic power-sharing agreements cannot be sustained without the assent of the majority of citizens, who will simply replace leaders they believe are betraying their group interests.

Historically, Western Europe has experienced many threats to democracy by violence and military intervention. When such crises have happened, it has been critical for democratic political parties to rally behind the democratic constitution. In the 1930s the bitterly suspicious socialist and middle-class parties failed to unite against the Nazis in Germany, whereas in Austria similar parties careened into civil war. In Greece conservative fears of a new socialist government encouraged the military to overthrow democracy in 1967. In contrast, in France in 1961 and Spain in 1981, a united front of all major parties helped democratic heads of state defeat attempted coups by rallying citizens and loyal members of the military.

Western European countries continue to battle against terrorism and violence (especially violence against immigrant groups). In so doing, these democratic governments must maintain the critical balance between upholding the security of their residents and protecting their freedoms. This is, of course, easier to do when economic conditions are positive and when citizens share common democratic values. In Eastern Europe these conditions were often missing right after the collapse of communism, but in most countries the situation has improved a great deal since then. In most of Eastern Europe, the revolution that has occurred since 1989 has brought remarkable change with little violence. Democracy is shaky in some nations because of strong ethnic tension, gross corruption in government, and violations of the freedom of speech and other civil liberties (see Box 4.3). The devastating wars in Chechnya, Bosnia, and Kosovo show the potential cost of failure. This is a critical time for the region formerly dominated by the Soviet Union. As Russia has become more authoritarian and more assertive internationally, the risks to its neighbors have increased. These risks are particularly great in those states that used to be part of the Soviet Union and that have not become members of the EU, such as Ukraine, Moldova, and Georgia.

Democracy seems to be building a firm foundation elsewhere in the East. Parties are learning to develop internal cohesion and accommodate differences with

BOX 4.3

Democratic Failure: An Unfree Press

One of the surest threats to democracy is the failure to sustain free broadcast, electronic, and print media. Freedom House's annual Press Freedom Survey evaluates constraints on these freedoms in many countries. Europe scores comparatively high on press freedom, but the region is diverse and far from trouble free. In the report covering 2007, all Western and eight Eastern countries, including Poland, were classified as having a "Free" press.

Even though Western Europe boasts some of the world's highest levels of media freedom, things are not perfect. The ratings for some Scandinavian countries declined due to harassment from Islamist and far-right groups. Italy had been the only Western European country that was only "Partly Free," but it rejoined the ranks of the "Free" countries when Silvio Berlusconi resigned as prime minister. Berlusconi had been a threat to media freedom because at the same time that he served as prime minister, he owned or controlled so many of the Italian media. However, Berlusconi returned to office in 2008, and it remains to be seen whether Italy's press freedom ratings will fall once again.

Eastern Europe scores less favorably on press freedoms. Only a minority of these countries enjoy a free press, and a majority of its population lives in countries where the press is "Not Free." While the region shares a common history of communist oppression, the Soviet successor states, except for the Baltic States, are faring much worse than the neighboring countries in Central Europe, such as Poland and Hungary. Russia and Belarus are the only European countries rated "Not Free" in terms of press freedom. Central Europe and the Baltic States, by contrast, are all "Free." The remaining Eastern European states, including Bulgaria, Romania, Ukraine, and all the post-Yugoslavian states except Slovenia, are "Partly Free." The greater press freedom in the Baltic States, as compared to other parts of the former Soviet Union, shows that prior regime type is not the only thing that matters.

Perhaps the most troubling trend in Eastern Europe is the lack of improvement in press freedoms. The legal environment in Russia has worsened as the government has tightened its grip on all mass media and as harassment and crimes against journalists have occurred with little legal recourse. Given Russia's influence in several post-Soviet states, its disregard for media freedoms is a distressing sign for the future of the media in that region.

Source: Freedom House, Press Freedom Survey 2007. Retrieved February 2008 from freedomhouse.org.

---

political opponents. Governments are learning to deal with dissent without suppressing dissenters or the press, to manage capitalist economies, and to provide safety nets for citizens without destroying their incentives. Citizens are demanding a rule of law, and so are many international agencies and nongovernmental organizations. The prospects for democracy are particularly favorable in the ten Eastern European countries (including Poland and Bulgaria) that joined the EU in 2005 and 2007. This is both because they were selected for membership on the basis of their democratic credentials and because the EU itself will insist on and monitor democracy within its member states.

No one has yet found the perfect political institutions. Europe is no exception. It is easy to find flaws in constitutional arrangements, party systems, and policymaking processes. It is even easier to criticize a particular government, since democracy does not guarantee good leadership or wise policies. Yet, bitter experience in Europe and elsewhere shows that democracy is more likely than any other form of government to sustain personal freedoms, encourage equal treatment under the law, and protect the rights of minorities. Moreover, democracies seldom go to war against each other. Democratic government is the best security for the hard-won personal freedoms of the citizens of Eastern Europe and for the peace that has largely replaced Europe's destructive wars. Building democracy thus has profound consequences for all Europeans. And the European experiences will continue to hold valuable lessons for the world about the potentials and challenges of democratic government.

REVIEW QUESTIONS

- Why do democracies separate powers, and what is the difference between a geographic and a functional separation of powers?

- What is a parliamentary democracy, and how common are such governments across Europe?

- What are the advantages and disadvantages of federalism?

- How are European heads of state selected, and what powers do they have?

- What is a system of proportional representation, and what consequences does it have?

- Why does press freedom matter?

- What is a welfare state, and how do welfare states differ across Europe?

KEY TERMS

assembly

bicameralism

cabinet

coalition government

confidence vote

constitution

district magnitude

executive

federalism

freedom of the press

government
formation

judicial review

liberal democracy

minority government

mixed electoral system

parliamentary
democracy

power-sharing

presidential democracy

prime minister

proportional
representation
(PR)

semi-presidential
systems

separation of powers

single-member districts
(SMDs)

single transferable vote
(STV)

strong legislative
committees

welfare state

SUGGESTED READINGS

Bowler, Shaun, David M. Farrell, and Richard W. Katz. *Party Cohesion, Party Discipline and the Organization of Parliaments.* Columbus: Ohio State University Press, 1999.

Cheibub, Jose Antonio. *Presidentialism, Parliamentarism, and Democracy.* Cambridge, England: Cambridge University Press, 2007.

Cox, Gary. *Making Votes Count: Strategic Coordination in the World's Electoral Systems.* New York: Cambridge University Press, 1997.

Doering, Herbert, ed. *Parliaments and Majority Rule in Western Europe.* New York: St. Martin's, 1995.

Laver, Michael, and Kenneth A. Shepsle, eds. *Cabinet Ministers and Parliamentary Government.* New York: Cambridge University Press, 1994.

Lijphart, Arend. *Democracy in Plural Societies.* New Haven, CT: Yale University Press, 1977.

_____. *Electoral Systems and Party Systems: A Study of Twenty-Seven Democracies, 1945–1990.* New York: Oxford University, 1994.

_____. *Patterns of Democracy: Government Forms and Performance in Thirty-Six Countries.* New Haven, CT: Yale University Press, 1999.

Powell, G. Bingham, Jr. *Contemporary Democracies: Participation, Stability and Violence.* Cambridge: Harvard University Press, 1982.

_____. *Elections as Instruments of Democracy: Majoritarian and Proportional Visions.* New Haven, CT: Yale University Press, 2000.

Rose, Richard. *Do Parties Make a Difference?* 2nd ed. Chatham, NJ: Chatham House, 1984.

Sartori, Giovanni. *Comparative Constitutional Engineering.* New York: New York University Press, 1997.

Shugart, Matthew Soberg, and John Carey. *Presidents and Assemblies: Constitutional Design and Electoral Dynamics.* New York: Cambridge University Press, 1992.

Strøm, Kaare. *Minority Government and Majority Rule.* New York: Cambridge University Press, 1990.

Strøm, Kaare, Wolfgang C. Müller, and Torbjörn Bergman, eds. *Cabinets and Coalition Bargaining: The Democratic Life Cycle in Western Europe.* Oxford, England: Oxford University Press, 2008.

————. *Delegation and Accountability in Parliamentary Democracies.* Oxford, England: Oxford University Press, 2003.

Tsebelis, George. *Veto Players: An Introduction to Institutional Analysis.* Princeton, NJ: Princeton University Press and Russell Sage Foundation, 2002.

Volcansek, Mary L., ed. "Judicial Politics and Policymaking in Western Europe." *West European Politics* (Special Issue) 15, no. 3 (July 1992).

ENDNOTES

1. John Locke, *Two Treatises of Government,* ed. Peter Laslett (Cambridge, England: Cambridge University Press, 1960); Charles de Secondat, Baron de Montesquieu, *The Spirit of the Laws* (London: Hafner, 1960).

2. We occasionally use the term assembly, rather than legislature, to emphasize that legislation—making laws—may not be its most important function. The assembly may not have sole authority to make laws, and it is seldom the most important source of legislation.

3. The German, Hungarian, and Spanish constitutions feature a "constructive" vote of no confidence, under which the government is forced to resign only if a parliamentary majority explicitly designates and supports an alternative government.

4. Congressional Quarterly, Inc.: *Congressional Quarterly,* December 21, 1996, p. 3461. This analysis considers only votes in which the two major parties oppose each other and does not include voting for official leadership positions in the House of Representatives (for which voting tends to be strictly along party lines).

5. In the 1987–1992 British House of Commons, both parties were perfectly cohesive on 80 percent of the votes on which these parties took official stands (Philip Norton, "Parliamentary Behavior Since 1945," *Talking Politics* 8 (1995–1996): 112). For similar numbers for Germany in the 1970s and 1980s, see Thomas Saalfeld, "The West German Bundestag After Forty Years," *West European Politics* 13, no. 3 (July 1990): 74. On France, see Philip E. Converse and Roy Pierce, *Political Representation in France* (Cambridge: Harvard University Press, 1986), pp. 552–561. On party cohesion generally, see Shaun Bowler, David M. Farrell, and Richard W. Katz, *Party Cohesion, Party Discipline and the Organization of Parliaments* (Columbus: Ohio State University Press, 1999).

6. In some countries the president is elected by a special "electoral college" that includes both members of parliament and other public officials, such as representatives of local governments.

7. For simplicity we refer to heads of state as presidents or monarchs and to heads of government in parliamentary systems as prime ministers. The formal titles are sometimes different. Thus, the head of government is the president of the Council of Ministers in Spain and the federal chancellor in Germany. See the country chapters for details.

8. See Matthew Soberg Shugart, "The Electoral Cycle and Institutional Sources of Divided Presidential Government," *American Political Science Review* 89 (June 1995): 327–343.

9. See Chapter 6; Roy Pierce, "The Executive Divided Against Itself: Cohabitation in France 1986–1988," *Governance* 4, no. 3 (July 1991): 270–294; and John D. Huber, *Rationalizing Parliament: Legislative Institutions and Party Politics in France* (New York: Cambridge University Press, 1996).

10. See Arend Lijphart, ed., *Parliamentary Versus Presidential Government* (Oxford, England: Oxford University Press, 1992); Juan Linz and Arturo Valenzuela, eds., *The Failure of Presidential Government* (Baltimore. MD: Johns Hopkins University Press, 1994); G. Bingham Powell, Jr., *Contemporary Democracies: Participation, Stability and Violence* (Cambridge: Harvard University Press, 1982), chs. 6 and 10; Jose Antonio Cheibub, *Presidentialism, Parliamentarism, and Democracy* (Cambridge, England: Cambridge University Press, 2007).

11. See Mary L. Volcansek, ed., "Judicial Politics and Policymaking in Western Europe," *West European Politics* (Special Issue) 15, no. 3 (July 1992); and Martin Shapiro and Alec Stone, "The New Constitutional Politics of Europe," *Comparative Political Studies* (Special Issue) 26, no. 4 (January 1994).

12. Maurice Duverger, *Political Parties: Their Organization and Activity in the Modern State* [1954], trans. Barbara and Robert North (New York: Wiley, 1963).

13. Kosovo has been excluded from Figure 4.4 because it gained independence only in 2008.

14. Sona Nadenichek Golder, *The Logic of Pre-electoral Coalition Formation* (Columbus: Ohio State University Press, 2006).

15. See the classic analysis of France in the Fourth Republic by Philip Williams, *Crisis and Compromise:*

Politics in the Fourth Republic (Hamden, CT: Archon Press, 1964), esp. p. 405. But the issue is controversial; see John D. Huber, "How Does Cabinet Instability Affect Political Performance? Portfolio Volatility and Health Care Cost Containment in Parliamentary Democracies," *American Political Science Review* 92 (1996): 577–591.

16. See, for example, the essays by Stephen Holmes and others, "Crime and Corruption After Communism," *East European Constitutional Review* 6 (Fall 1997): 69–98.

17. All scores retrieved February 2008 from www.transparency .org.

18. The classical studies of consociationalism have been done by Arend Lijphart; see especially *Democracy in Plural Societies* (New Haven, CT: Yale University Press, 1977).

19. Powell, *Contemporary Democracies,* chs. 4, 5, and 10.

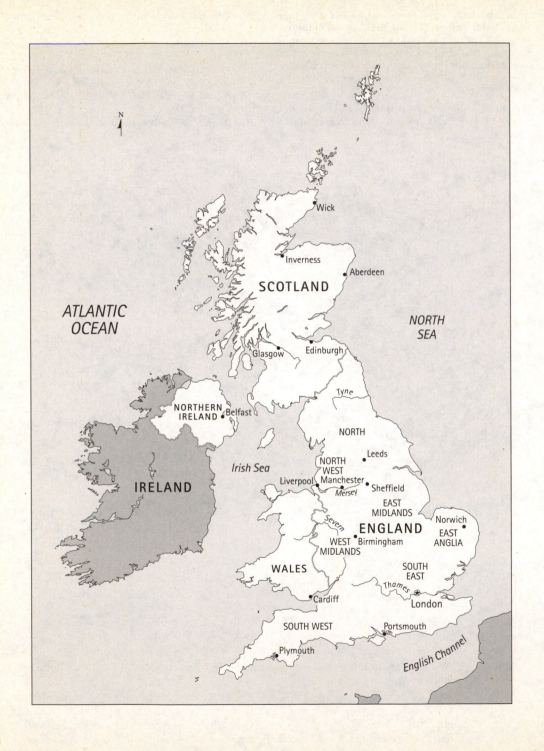

POLITICS IN BRITAIN

Richard Rose

Country Bio

UNITED KINGDOM

Population
60.6 Million

Territory
94,525 square miles

Year of Independence
From the twelfth century

Year of Current Constitution
Unwritten; partly statutes, partly common law and practice

Head of State
Queen Elizabeth II

Head of Government
Prime Minister Gordon Brown

Language
English plus about 600,000 who regularly speak Welsh and about 60,000 who speak Gaelic, plus immigrants speaking languages of the Indian subcontinent and elsewhere

Religion
Nominal identification in census: Church of England 26.1 million, Roman Catholic 5.7 million, Presbyterian 2.6 million, Methodist 1.3 million, other Christian 4.0 million, Muslim 1.5 million, Hindu 500,000, Sikh 330,000, Jewish 260,000, other 300,000, no religion 8.6 million, no reply 4.4 million

In a world of new democracies, Britain is different because it is an old democracy; its political system has been evolving for more than 850 years. In medieval times the King of England claimed to rule France and Ireland, as well as England. From the end of the fifteenth century onward, the claim to rule France was abandoned, and sovereignty was gained over Wales and Scotland. The government of the **United Kingdom** was created in 1801 by merging England, Scotland, Wales, and Ireland under the authority of Parliament in London.

Unlike new democracies in Eastern Europe, Latin America, and Asia, Britain did not become a democracy overnight. It became a democracy by evolution, rather than revolution. Democratization was a slow process. The rule of law was established in the seventeenth century, the accountability of the executive to Parliament was established by the eighteenth century, and national political parties organized in the nineteenth century. Even though competitive elections had been held for more than a century, the right of every adult man and woman to vote was not recognized until the twentieth century.

The evolution of democracy in Britain is in contrast with a European history of countries switching between democratic and undemocratic forms of government. Whereas older British people have lived in the same political system all their lives, the oldest Germans have lived under four or five constitutions, two democratic and two or three undemocratic.[1]

At no point in history did representatives of the British people meet to decide what kind of government they would like to have, as happened in America and France at the end of the eighteenth century and in many democracies since. British politicians have been socialized to accept institutions and rules of the game as a legacy from distant predecessors. Ordinary citizens have been socialized to accept established institutions, too.

The influence of British government can be found in places as far-flung as Australia, Canada, India, and the United States. Just as Alexis de Tocqueville travelled to the United States in 1831 to seek the secrets of democracy, so we can examine Britain for secrets of stable representative government. Yet, the limitations of Britain as a model are shown by the failure of many attempts to transplant its institutions to countries gaining independence from the British Empire—and even more by the failure of its institutions to bring political stability to Northern Ireland.

POLICY CHALLENGES FACING THE BRITISH GOVERNMENT

In Britain the term **government** is used in many senses. People may speak of the Queen's government to emphasize enduring and nonpartisan features, they may refer to a Labour or Conservative government or the government of the day to emphasize partisanship, or they may speak of Gordon Brown's government to stress its transitory personal feature. The departments headed by Cabinet ministers advised by senior civil servants are referred to collectively as **Whitehall,** after the London street on which many major government departments are located. **Downing Street,** where the prime minister works, is a short street off Whitehall. **Parliament**—that is, the popularly elected House of Commons and the nonelected House of Lords—is at one end of Whitehall. The term Parliament is often used as another way to refer to the House of Commons. Together, all of these institutions are often referred to as **Westminster,** after the district in London in which the principal offices of British government are located.

The constitutional doctrine that Parliament is sovereign was traditionally interpreted as holding that the government of the day can do whatever it wants, as long as it has the backing of a majority in the House of Commons. However, the claim to sovereignty of this island state stops at the water's edge.

In a world in which many policy issues transcend national boundaries, the first challenge facing governors is to answer this question: Where does Britain belong? Prime ministers from Winston Churchill to Gordon Brown have claimed that Britain is a major world power because of its close ties with Commonwealth countries, the United States, and Europe.

The British Empire was transformed after World War II into the Commonwealth, a free association of 54 sovereign states with members on every continent. The independent status of its chief members is shown by the absence of the word *British* from their names. Commonwealth countries from Antigua and Australia to Zambia and Zimbabwe differ from each other in wealth, language, culture, and religion. They also differ in their commitment to democracy.

Every British prime minister claims a special relationship with the United States. The traditional view, dating back to the time of Winston Churchill and Franklin D. Roosevelt, was that "America provides the brawn and we provide the brains." However, the number of countries with which America has a special relationship keeps expanding, whereas British prime ministers have not built equally strong relationships with other countries. After the end of the Cold War, the emergence of the United States as a unique global force has made the relationship more attractive to Britain. However, the unilateralist policy of Washington under President George W. Bush reduced the influence that Britain and other countries may have hoped to have on American foreign policy.

When President Bush formed a "coalition of the willing" to attack Iraq, Prime Minister Tony Blair was more than willing, believing it desirable to do so to make the world a safer place. In response to doubts raised in the House of Commons, Blair argued that allying with the United States in Iraq would give Britain greater influence. However, both British Members of Parliament (MPs) and the public have had their doubts. In a June 2006 Populus poll of public opinion, two-thirds said Britain's relationship with the United States had become less important than its other international ties.

As countries such as Germany and France have regained economic and political significance, the British government has looked to Europe. In the jet age, the English Channel is no longer a barrier to travel to the European continent, and a tunnel under the English Channel provides a rail and road link to Paris that is shorter than that to the North of England or Scotland. Manufacturers such as Ford Motor Company link their plants in Britain with factories across Western Europe, just as Ford links factories across the United States.

Although the European Economic Community (EEC) was established in 1957, Britain did not join it until 1973. Since then the EEC has grown in membership and powers and has become the European Union (EU). The EU has the power to impose regulations affecting British business and limiting the government's economic policies. Government ministers spend an increasing amount of their time negotiating with other countries of the EU on matters ranging from political fundamentals to whether British beer should be served in metric units or by the traditional measure of a British pint.

Britain's governors accept the inevitability of globalization: In 2005 the prime minister, the deputy prime minister, the foreign secretary, and the ministers of Defence, Trade and Industry, and Environment each averaged more than one day a week traveling abroad. However, commitment to the EU remains limited. In small countries, which have always recognized the influence of bigger neighbors, exchanging nominal sovereignty to participate in the EU presents no problems. However, it is a shock to Britain's governors, who pride themselves on having a major role in three different international settings—the Commonwealth, Europe, and Washington, D.C.

When a public opinion poll asks whether Britain should act like a leading world power or a small neutral country like Sweden or Switzerland, 49 percent favor being a small power, as compared to 34 percent wanting the country to be a world power.[2] However, Britain's island status cannot insulate it from the rest of the world. It is not possible for Britain to become a small, rich country like Switzerland or Sweden. The effective choice today is between Britain being a big, rich country and Britain being a big, relatively less prosperous country.

A second set of challenges in the economic field makes the link between international and domestic policy very visible. For centuries Britain has depended on world trade, importing much food and many raw materials. To pay for these imports, it exports manufactured goods and "invisible" services of banks and other financial institutions in the city of London, and it does a big trade in tourism. The British pound sterling (£) is an international currency, but speeches by the prime minister and head of the Treasury do not determine its international value. This is decided in international markets in which currency

speculators play a significant role. Since 1997 the value of the British pound in exchange for the dollar has ranged from $1.35 to $2.00.

Economic growth is important not only for British consumers, who borrow heavily, but also for the government, which usually runs a deficit to meet the bills for public spending. An aging population requires more health care and pensions, an educated population demands better education for their children, and a more prosperous society wants a better environment. However, the means of raising additional revenue without raising visible taxes are few. Moreover, any increase in deficit spending threatens inflation and a rise in interest rates by the independent Bank of England. The fiscal dividend of economic growth makes it much easier to meet these challenges.

Some challenges, such as fighting crime, cannot be resolved solely by spending money. Successive Conservative and Labour governments have spent more money on the police and built more prisons. However, their efforts have been accompanied by random crimes of street violence and stabbing, especially in London, and the use of guns in robberies and in shootings of police officers. Multiculturalism is another problem that cannot be met just by spending more money. The government seeks to promote a sense of "Britishness" among immigrants, giving lessons about the rights and obligations of citizens to immigrants wanting British passports. British-born offspring of immigrants automatically gain citizenship. Whether they choose to adopt British ways is greatly influenced by family and ethnic background and, in the case of a few Muslims, by jihadist activists.

Notwithstanding the power of the government of the day within Westminster, ministers are regularly confronted with challenges concerning the delivery of public services by local government, the National Health Service, and other institutions. Schools whose pupils have bad examination results embarrass the minister responsible for education, a social security official that loses computer disks with confidential details about millions of claims embarrasses the minister responsible for pensions, and the health minister is called to account when shortcomings of hospital cleaning staff lead to infections causing the death of patients These failings lead to calls for the government of the day to "do something," but it is not easy for a Cabinet minister in Whitehall to monitor the activities of more than a million health workers or millions of pupils. Whitehall has contracted with profit-making companies to deliver a variety of public services in a businesslike way. However, when these organizations make mistakes, the blame continues to fall on the government department that employed the faulty supplier.

With a general election due no later than Spring 2010, party leaders are concentrating on winning the next election. Gordon Brown, the leader of the **Labour Party,** faces a unique problem: As prime minister he must defend the record of a Labour government continuously in office since 1997. Labour's narrow margin of victory in 2005 makes its parliamentary majority vulnerable. After a "honeymoon" with the public after becoming prime minister in summer 2007, Brown has faced a legacy of taxing and spending problems and a worldwide economic and financial crisis. His hesitancy in making and explaining decisions, combined with a reserved personality, has led to an approval rating in the polls as low as that of his Labour predecessor, Tony Blair, at the end of Blair's prime ministership.

After losing three successive elections under three different leaders, the **Conservative Party,** the official Opposition, accepted the challenge to change by electing a youthful new leader, David Cameron. His strategy has much in common with that of Tony Blair in Opposition: to move the party from being promarket and antigovernment to occupying the political center by showing sympathy with measures to improve the environment, gay rights, and other liberal issues. Since Cameron has been an MP only since 2001, he cannot be identified with unpopular policies that led to his party's previous defeats. However, since neither he nor his principal associates have ever held office in government, inexperience raises questions about what a Cameron-led government would actually do if it were to win an election. As Opposition leader, Cameron has a problem in gaining public recognition. But since big majorities have come to disapprove of the Labour government's record under Blair and Brown, the Conservative Party has been ahead of Labour in the opinion polls because it offers a change from an unpopular government.

The **Liberal Democratic Party** is now the closest approximation to a "left" party that Britain has. It favors social and environmental policies and attacks government proposals that encroach on civil liberties. It is strongly in favor of the EU, where its leader, Nick Clegg, once worked as an official. It is also the only British party that opposed the Iraq War. Because of being third in seats in the House of Commons, the Liberal Democrats have no chance of forming a government on their own. But because the Conservative Party faces an uphill struggle to win an absolute majority in the House of Commons, it could hold the balance of power in the House of Commons after the next general election.

A change of government following the next general election would not change the problems facing government. A new government would then be challenged to realize its campaign promises. But this is easier said than done. As Tony Blair ruefully admitted five years after becoming prime minister, "In opposition, announcement is the reality. For the first period in government, there was a tendency to believe this is the case. It isn't. The announcement is only the intention."[3]

THE ENVIRONMENT OF POLITICS: ONE CROWN, BUT FIVE NATIONS

The Queen of England is the best known monarch in the world, yet there is no such entity as an English state. In international law the state is the United Kingdom of Great Britain and Northern Ireland. Great Britain is divided into England, Scotland, and Wales. The most distinctive feature of **Wales** is that one-quarter of the population speaks an old Celtic language, Welsh, as well as English. **Scotland,** once an independent kingdom, has been an integral part of Britain since 1707. However, the Scots have separate legal, religious, and education institutions. The fourth part of the United Kingdom, **Northern Ireland,** consists of six counties of Ulster. The remainder of Ireland rebelled against the Crown in 1916 and established a separate Irish state in Dublin in 1921. The current boundaries of the United Kingdom, colloquially known as Britain, were fixed in 1921.

The United Kingdom is a unitary state because there is a single source of authority, the British Parliament. However, the institutions of government are not uniform throughout the United Kingdom. In the minds of its citizens, it is a multinational state, for people differ in how they describe themselves (Table 5.1). In England people often describe themselves as English or British without considering the different meanings of these terms. This does not happen elsewhere in the United Kingdom. In Scotland three-quarters see themselves as Scots. In Wales three-fifths identify themselves as Welsh. In Northern Ireland people divide three ways: almost half see themselves as British, one-quarter see themselves as Irish, and

National Identities Identities vary within each nation	England	Scotland	Wales	Northern Ireland	TABLE 5.1

Self-identifying as:	England	Scotland	Wales	Northern Ireland
British	51%	19%	27%	47%
English, Scots, Welsh, Irish	38	75	60	27
Other, don't know	11	6	13	26*

Sources: England: British Social Attitudes Survey, 2004; Scotland: Scottish Social Attitudes Survey, 2004; Wales: Life and Times Survey, 2003; Northern Ireland: Life and Times Survey, 2004.
*Includes 21 percent identifying as Ulster.

another one-quarter identify with Ulster (i.e., Northern Ireland).

Historically, Scotland and Wales have been governed by British Cabinet ministers accountable to Parliament. After decades of campaigning by nationalist parties seeking independence, in 1997 the Labour government endorsed **devolution**; an Act of Parliament gave responsibilities for policy to elected assemblies in Scotland and in Wales, and they came into being in 1999. The revenue of both assemblies comes from Westminster. It is assigned by a formula relating it to public expenditures on comparable policies in England.

The Scottish Parliament in Edinburgh has powers to legislate and to initiate a wide variety of social and environmental policies, including those delivered by Scottish local government. Elections to the 129-seat Parliament mix the traditional British **first-past-the-post electoral system** and proportional representation (PR), which are discussed in more detail later in the chapter. After the 1999 and 2003 elections, the Labour Party in Scotland formed a coalition government with the Liberal Party. In the May 2007 Scottish election, the unpopularity of the British Labour Party resulted in a one-seat margin for the Scottish National Party (SNP) over the Labour Party, 47 to 46. The remaining seats were divided among the Conservatives, 17; Liberal Democrats, 16; and others, 3.

Under the leadership of Alex Salmond as First Minister, the SNP established a minority government. Its first aim has been to demonstrate that the SNP was not just a protest party, but a party that was capable of governing as well as or better than parties that appeal for votes across the whole of Britain. Its second aim is to promote a referendum on independence for Scotland. The three Opposition parties have reacted by establishing a commission to recommend increases in

powers devolved to Scotland, subject to approval by the British government in London. The chief dividing issue in Scotland today is what question or questions should be put to the Scottish people in a referendum that could take place in 2010 or 2011.

The 60-seat Welsh Assembly in Cardiff has power over a variety of local and regional services, and its activities are conducted in English and in Welsh. However, it does not have the power to enact legislation. It is elected by a mixed first-past-the-post and PR ballot. Labour has consistently been the biggest party at each election, but it has difficulty winning a majority of Assembly seats. After the May 2007 Assembly election, Labour held 26 seats, Plaid Cymru (the Welsh National Party) 14, Conservatives 12, Liberals 6, and others 2. Labour and Plaid Cymru together formed a coalition government. There is no effective political demand for independence.

Northern Ireland is the most un-English part of the United Kingdom. Formally, it is a secular polity, but differences between Protestants and Catholics about national identity dominate its politics. Protestants, who make up about three-fifths of the population, want to remain part of the United Kingdom. Until 1972 the Protestant majority governed through a home-rule Parliament at Stormont, a suburb of Belfast. Many of the Catholic minority did not support this regime, wanting to leave the United Kingdom and join the Republic of Ireland, which claims that Northern Ireland should be part of the Republic.

After Catholics launched protests against discrimination in 1968, demonstrations turned to violence in 1969. The illegal **Irish Republican Army (IRA)** was revived and in 1971 began a military campaign to remove Northern Ireland from the United Kingdom. Protestants organized illegal armed forces in response. More than 3,500 people have been killed in political violence since. After adjusting for population differences, this is equivalent to more than 140,000 political deaths in Britain or more than 700,000 such deaths in the United States.

In 1969 the British Army went into action in Northern Ireland to protect Catholics. In 1971 it helped intern hundreds of Catholics without trial in an unsuccessful attempt to break the IRA. In 1972 the British government abolished the Stormont Parliament, placing government in the hands of a Northern Ireland Office under a British Cabinet minister. In 1985 the British government took the unprecedented step of inviting the Dublin-based government of the Republic of Ireland to participate in institutions affecting the governance of Northern Ireland.

A stable settlement requires the support of paramilitary organizations, as well as political parties on both sides of the political divide. In 1994 the IRA announced a cessation of its military activity, and Sinn Fein, the political party of the Irish Republican movement, agreed to talks. Protestant paramilitary forces also announced a cessation of activities. On Good Friday of 1998, an agreement was reached that provided for an elected power-sharing executive and cross-border institutions involving both Dublin and Belfast. Contrary to the practice of government at Westminster, power-sharing means that whatever the outcome of a Northern Ireland election, government must be a coalition of parties representing both the pro–Britain Protestant majority and the pro–Irish Republic Catholic minority. The coalition government initially formed along these lines collapsed in a dispute about whether the IRA had decommissioned its arsenal of weapons.

An election for the 108-seat Northern Ireland Assembly in 2007 gave the Democratic Unionist Party led by Dr. Ian Paisley 36 seats, the Republican Sinn Fein 27, the Ulster Unionist Party 18, the pro-Irish Social Democratic and Labour Party 16, the cross-religious Alliance Party 7, and others 4. After intensive negotiations in which London and Dublin offered incentives to Irish Republicans and put pressure on Ulster Unionists, a coalition government was formed with Dr. Ian Paisley, an outspoken Unionist and Protestant, as First Minister and Martin McGuinness, a Sinn Fein politician who had been active in the IRA, as Deputy First Minister, plus representatives of the Ulster Unionist Party and the Social Democratic and Labour Party.

While there is no agreement about national identity within Britain, there is no doubt about which nationality is the most numerous. England dominates the United Kingdom. It accounts for 84 percent of the United Kingdom population, as compared to 8 percent in Scotland, 5 percent in Wales, and 3 percent in Northern Ireland. Previous editions of this chapter have been called "Politics in England" because, as Tony Blair once said, "Sovereignty rests with me, as an English MP, and that's the way it will stay."[4] However, changes in other parts of the United Kingdom have begun to affect politics in England. For example, in the 2005 British general election the Conservative Party won the most votes in England, but the Labour Party, thanks to its dominance in Scotland and Wales, won the most votes in the United Kingdom and a majority in the British Parliament. Demands by the Scottish National Party for independence have been met by English demands to reduce the share of British tax revenue that Westminster allocates to Scotland.

A Multiracial Britain

Throughout the centuries England has received a relatively small but noteworthy number of immigrants from other parts of Europe. The Queen herself is descended from a titled family that came from Hanover, Germany, to assume the English throne in 1714. Until the outbreak of anti-German sentiment in World War I, the surname of the royal family was Saxe-Coburg-Gotha. By royal proclamation King George V changed the family name to Windsor in 1917.

The worldwide British Empire was multiracial, and so is the Commonwealth. Since the late 1950s, job seekers have been arriving in Britain from the West Indies, Pakistan, India, Africa, and other parts of the Commonwealth. Hundreds of thousands of people from Australia, Canada, the United States, and the member countries of the EU flow in and out of Britain as students or as workers. A strong British economy attracts temporary workers from Central and Eastern European countries in the EU. Public opinion has opposed unlimited immigration, and both Labour and Conservative governments have passed laws trying to limit the number of immigrants. However, these laws contain many exceptions.

Political disturbances around the world in the past two decades have increased the number of immigrants claiming asylum as political refugees from troubled areas in the Balkans, the Middle East, and Africa. Some have valid credentials as refugees, whereas others have arrived with false papers or make claims to asylum that courts have not upheld.

In response to popular concern, the government has tried to make deportation of illegal immigrants easier. However, the government has admitted that hundreds of thousands of illegal immigrants now live in Britain.

The minority ethnic population of the United Kingdom has risen from 74,000 in 1951 to 4.6 million in the latest census, almost 8 percent of the total population. Official statistics define the minority population by the one characteristic that they have in common—they are not white. Because persons placed in this catchall category have neither culture nor religion in common, there is a further subdivision by race and ethnicity. West Indians speak English as their native language and have a Christian tradition, but this is often not the case for black Africans. Ethnic minorities from India, Pakistan, and Bangladesh are divided among Hindus, Muslims, and Sikhs, and most speak English as a second language. Chinese from Hong Kong have a distinctive culture. Altogether, almost half of the minority category comes from the Indian subcontinent, a quarter consists of black people from the Caribbean or Africa, one in seven is often of mixed British and minority origin, and the remainder come from many different countries.

With the passage of time, the ethnic minority population is becoming increasingly British-born and -educated. This raises an important issue: What is the position of British-born offspring of immigrants? Whatever their country of origin, they differ in how they see themselves: 64 percent of Caribbean origin identify themselves as British, as do more than three-fifths of Pakistanis, Indians, and Bangladeshis and two-fifths of Chinese. However, some offspring of immigrants have rejected integration. A coordinated terrorist attack in London on July 7, 2005, that killed more than fifty people was organized by British-born offspring of Pakistani immigrants who had been converted to jihadism at British mosques. British-born jihadists have been able to receive training in Pakistan and neighboring Afghanistan.

In response to terrorist attacks, the government has shifted from promoting multiculturalism to stressing the integration of immigrant families into the British way of life. It has greatly increased police powers, justifying shoot-to-kill policies even when people wrongly suspected of being terrorists are the victims. Its program of cooperating with people it identifies as leaders of the Muslim community has faced difficulties. Those cooperating with the British government have found themselves in dispute with their coreligionists. Moreover, they have criticized police methods used in surveillance of the Muslim community and British military actions in Afghanistan and Iraq.

Many immigrants and their offspring are being integrated into electoral politics, since residential concentration makes their votes important in some parliamentary constituencies. Some candidates from different immigrant groups compete with each other. There are now hundreds of elected minority ethnic councillors in local government. The 15 ethnic MPs in the Commons today come from diverse backgrounds—India, Pakistan, the West Indies, Ghana, and Aden—and sit for the Labour, Liberal Democratic, and Conservative parties. A disproportionate number of minority ethnic people have voted Labour.

THE LEGACY OF HISTORY

The legacy of the past limits current choices, and Britain has a very long past. Much of its legacy is positive, for many fundamental problems of governance were resolved centuries ago. The Crown was established as the central political authority in medieval times. The supremacy of the state over the church was settled in the sixteenth century when Henry VIII broke with the Roman Catholic Church to establish the Church of England. The power struggle between the English Crown and Parliament was resolved by a civil war in the seventeenth century in which Parliament triumphed and a weakened monarch was then restored. A Parliament chosen by an unrepresentative franchise was able to hold the Crown accountable in the eighteenth century.

The continuity of England's political institutions through the centuries is remarkable. Prince Charles, the heir to an ancient Crown, pilots jet airplanes, and a medieval-named chancellor of the Exchequer pilots the British economy through the deep waters of the international economy. Yet, symbols of continuity often mask great changes in English life. Parliament was once a supporter of royal authority. Today Parliament is primarily an electoral college deciding which party leader is in charge of government.

There is no agreement among political scientists about when England developed a modern system of government.[5] The most reasonable judgment is that modern government developed during the very long reign of Queen Victoria, from 1837 to 1901, when government institutions were created to cope with the problems of a society that was increasingly urban, literate, industrial, and critical of unreformed institutions. The creation of a modern system of government does not get rid of the problems of governing.

Developments since World War II can be divided into stages. The first stage, an all-party consensus on a mixed-economy Keynesian welfare state, built on the foundations of a wartime coalition government led by Winston Churchill. The Beveridge Report on social welfare, John Maynard Keynes's Full Employment White Paper, and the Butler Education Act of 1944 were initiatives named after Liberals and Conservatives. The 1945 British general election was won by a Labour government led by Clement Attlee. It combined social welfare policies, leading to the establishment of a comprehensive National Health Service, and socialist economic policies, under which many basic industries were taken into state ownership. Between 1951 and 1964, Conservative governments led by Winston Churchill, Sir Anthony Eden, and Harold Macmillan maintained a consensus about the mixed-economy welfare state. Keynesian techniques for promoting economic growth, full employment, and low inflation led to an era of consumer prosperity, and the availability of free university education was greatly expanded.

A flood of books on the theme "What's wrong with Britain?" proclaimed the need for faster economic growth and led to a second stage in which parties competed in innovation. The Labour Party under Harold Wilson won the 1964 election, campaigning with the vague activist slogan "Let's go with Labour." New names were given to government department offices, but behind their entrances many officials went through the same routines as before. The economy did not grow as predicted. In 1967 the government was forced to devalue the pound and seek a loan from the International Monetary Fund. Labour lost the 1970 election.

The major achievement of Edward Heath's 1970–1974 Conservative government was to make Britain a member of the EU. Doing so divided his own party and the Opposition. In trying to limit unprecedented inflation by controlling wages, Heath risked his authority in a confrontation with the left-wing-led National Union of Mineworkers, which struck for higher wages in what was then the state-owned coal industry. When Heath called the "Who Governs?" election in February 1974, no party won a majority of seats in the Commons. Labour formed a minority government, with Harold Wilson again as prime minister. A second election in October 1974 gave Labour a bare majority. Inflation, rising unemployment, and a contraction in the economy undermined Labour's program. James Callaghan succeeded Wilson as prime minister in 1976. Keynesian policies were abandoned in 1977 after Labour relied on a loan from the International Monetary Fund to stabilize the value of the pound in international markets.

When Margaret Thatcher won the 1979 election as leader of the Conservative Party, she became the first woman prime minister of a major European country (see Box 5.1). Thatcher's radical break with the economic policies of her predecessors introduced a third stage: She promoted free market policies and a reduction in the size of government. She regarded the economic failures of previous governments as arising from too much compromise. "The Old Testament prophets did not say 'Brothers, I want a consensus.' They said: 'This is my faith. This is what I passionately believe. If you believe it too, then come with me.'"[6]

Divisions among opponents enabled Thatcher to lead her party to three successive election victories, although never winning more than 43 percent of the total vote. Militant left-wing activists seized control of the Labour Party, and in 1981 four former Labour Cabinet ministers formed a centrist Social Democratic Party (SDP) in an alliance with the Liberal Party. The Labour Party's 1983 election manifesto was described as the longest suicide note in history. After Thatcher's third successive election victory in 1987, the SDP leadership merged with the Liberals to form the Liberal Democratic Party.

While proclaiming the virtues of the market and attacking big government, Thatcher did not court electoral defeat by imposing radical spending cuts on popular social programs. In consequence, public spending continued to grow in the Thatcher era. It was 40 percent of the gross domestic product in her last full year in office. While the Conservative majority in Parliament endorsed Thatcher's policies, it did not win the hearts and minds of the electorate. On the tenth anniversary of Thatcher's period as prime minister, an opinion poll asked whether people approved of "the Thatcher revolution." Less than one-third said they did.[7]

Within the Conservative Party, Thatcher's increasingly autocratic treatment of Cabinet colleagues created resentment, and during her third term of office, she became very unpopular in opinion polls. In autumn 1990 disgruntled Conservative MPs forced a ballot for the party leadership that caused her to resign. Conservative MPs elected a relatively unknown John

The Meaning of Thatcherism

BOX 5.1

Among modern British prime ministers, Margaret Thatcher has been unique in giving her name to a political ideology, **Thatcherism**.* Thatcher's central conviction was that the market offered a cure for the country's economic difficulties. She rejected the mixed-economy welfare state philosophy of her Conservative as well as her Labour predecessors. As Milton Friedman, the Nobel Prize–winning monetary economist, noted: "Mrs. Thatcher represents a different tradition. She represents a tradition of the nineteenth-century Liberal, of Manchester Liberalism, of free market free trade."†

In its economic policy, the Thatcher government experienced both successes and frustrations. The rate of economic growth increased and inflation dropped; however, unemployment rose. Industrial relations acts gave union members the right to elect their leaders and to vote on whether to hold a strike. State-owned industries and municipally owned council houses were sold to private owners. What were described as "businesslike" methods were introduced into managing everything from hospitals to museums.

As long as she was in control, Thatcher believed in strong government. In foreign policy she strongly promoted what she saw as Britain's national interest in dealings with the European Union and in alliance with President Ronald Reagan. The 1982 Argentine invasion of the Falkland Islands, a remote British colony in the South Atlantic, led to a brief and victorious war. Thatcher was also quick to assert her personal authority against colleagues in the Cabinet and against civil servants. The autonomy of local government was curbed, and a property tax on houses was replaced by a poll tax on each adult.

Following her departure from office, British Conservatives divided between those who sought to push market-oriented and anti–European Union measures further, the so-called Thatcherites, and those who believed the limits of cutbacks on the size of government had been reached.

*Cf. Margaret Thatcher, *The Downing Street Years* (New York: HarperCollins, 1993); Dennis Kavanagh, *The Reordering of British Politics* (Oxford, England: Oxford University Press, 1997).

†"Thatcher Praised by Her Guru," *The Guardian* (London), March 12, 1983.

Major as party leader. In 1992 Major won an unprecedented fourth consecutive term for the Conservative government. However, a few months afterward his economic policy, based on a strong British pound, crashed under pressure from foreign speculators. A division opened up within the Conservative Party between hard-line Thatcherite opponents of Europe and those who supported Major's acceptance of EU initiatives. The Major government held onto office and maintained such Thatcherite policies as the **privatization** of the coal mines and railways.

A fourth stage opened after Tony Blair became Labour leader in 1994. Blair was elected leader because he did *not* talk or look like an ordinary Labour Party member. Instead of being from a poor background, he was educated at boarding school and studied law at Oxford. Instead of having grown up in the Labour movement, his parents were Conservatives. He joined the Labour Party due to the encouragement of a girlfriend, Cherie Booth, now his wife and a successful lawyer.

Blair first won office by proclaiming that he represented New Labour, a vague Third Way philosophy modeled on that of President Bill Clinton. It was invoked to show that he rejected socialist values and principles. In setting out Labour's manifesto, Blair proclaimed, "We are proud now to be the party of modern, dynamic business, proud now to be the party of law and order, proud now to be the party of the family, and proud now to be the party pledged not to increase income tax."[8] He pledged a pragmatic government that would do "what works" and appealed to the voters to "trust me" (see Box 5.2).

The first term of the Blair government (1997–2001) was devoted to demonstrating that Labour was fit for government. Blair and his chancellor of the Exchequer, Gordon Brown, endorsed Thatcher's efforts to limit public spending and payments to private-sector businesses to manage the delivery of major health, education, and other services. Five months after re-election in 2001, Blair responded to the September 11 attack by closely aligning himself with U.S. policies.

Britain sent troops to Afghanistan and Iraq in 2003, but this policy lacked the full support of his party. It was endorsed in Parliament only with the support of Conservative MPs. In 2005 Labour again won a majority of seats in the House of Commons, making Blair Britain's second-longest-serving prime minister in more than a century.

Since a prime minister does not have a fixed term of office, when Blair fell in the opinion polls, he came under pressure to fulfill his promise to retire rather than fight a fourth election. He did so in June 2007. The Labour Party unanimously elected Gordon Brown as its leader on the basis of his record as the government's chief economic minister, the chancellor of the Exchequer. During Brown's period as chancellor, the economy grew steadily, inflation was low, and unemployment fell, and Brown claimed that he had put an end to the recurring cycle of economic boom and bust. However, the turmoil in the world economy in 2008 showed this was not the case. After blaming the country's financial problems on world rather than domestic economic mistakes, Brown has initiated measures involving tens of billions of pounds in efforts to prevent the recession in the economy turning into a major depression.

THE STRUCTURE OF GOVERNMENT

We must understand what government is as a precondition of evaluating what it does. Descriptions of a government often start with its constitution. However, Britain has never had a written constitution. In the words of constitutional lawyer J. A. G. Griffith, "The Constitution is what happens."[9]

The **unwritten constitution** is a jumble of acts of Parliament, court rulings, customs, and conventions that constitute the rules of the political game. The vagueness of the constitution makes it flexible, a point that political leaders such as Margaret Thatcher and Tony Blair have exploited to increase their own power. Comparing the written U.S. Constitution and the unwritten English constitution emphasizes how few are the constraints of an unwritten constitution (see Table 5.2). Whereas amendments to the U.S. Constitution must receive the endorsement of well over half the states and members of Congress, the unwritten constitution can be changed by a majority vote in Parliament or by the government of the day acting in an unprecedented manner.

The U.S. Constitution gives the Supreme Court the final power to decide what the government may or may not do. By contrast, in Britain the final authority is Parliament, where the government of the day commands a majority of votes. Courts do not have the power to declare an Act of Parliament unconstitutional; judges simply ask whether the executive acts within its authorized powers. Many statutes delegate broad discretion to a Cabinet minister or public authority. Even if the courts rule that the government has improperly exercised its authority, the effect of such a judgment can be annulled by a subsequent Act of Parliament retroactively authorizing the action.

The Bill of Rights in the U.S. Constitution allows anyone to turn to the courts for the protection of their personal rights. Instead of giving written guarantees to citizens, the rights of British people are meant to be secured by trustworthy governors. However, individuals who believed their personal rights infringed had no redress through the courts until the Blair government incorporated the European Convention of Human Rights into the country's laws.

In Britain the **Crown** is the abstraction that is used in place of the continental European idea of the state. It combines the dignified parts of the constitution, which sanctify authority by tradition and myth, with the efficient parts, which carry out the work of government. The Queen is only a ceremonial head of state. Some Britons argue that a monarchy is out of date, and the Labour government has sought to promote British values as an alternative focus of loyalty. The public reaction to the accidental death of Princess Diana was a media event, but not a political event like the assassination of President John Kennedy. Queen Elizabeth II does not influence the actions of what is described as Her Majesty's Government. While the Queen gives formal assent to laws passed by Parliament, she may not publicly state any opinion about legislation. The Queen is expected to respect the will of Parliament, as communicated to her by the leader of the majority party in Parliament, the prime minister.

What the Prime Minister Says and Does

Leading a government with a complex structure (see Figure 5.1) is a political rather than a managerial task. Within the Cabinet the **prime minister** occupies a unique position, sometimes referred to as *primus inter pares* (first among equals). But as Winston Churchill once wrote, "There can be no comparison

BOX 5.2

The Accomplishments and Frustrations of Tony Blair

Tony Blair became the leader of the Labour Party with the goal of winning elections. To make the party electable, he abandoned traditional commitments to trade unions and to socialist policies. Blair's personality and actions appealed to middle-class voters, whose support Labour needed to win elections. Blair's efforts to create what he called a **New Labour Party** were rewarded with three straight Labour election victories in 1997, 2001, and 2005.

After becoming prime minister, Blair gave priority to running a perpetual election campaign through the media and used his rare appearances in the House of Commons to play to the television cameras there. The number of political appointees at 10 Downing Street increased substantially. Although they usually had no prior experience working in government, they were given unprecedented power to give orders to civil servants.

Blair promoted reforms in state-financed health and education services through competition intended to give citizens a measure of "consumer" choice in health and education. However, the methods chosen to do so angered many doctors, teachers, and public employees, who saw it as making their professional judgments subject to targets laid down by management consultants, continuing Thatcher's emphasis on making government businesslike, rather than a public service. Given that it takes years to deliver changes in social policies, many effects of Blair's measures may become evident only years after he has left office.

Major constitutional reforms included the devolution of executive responsibilities to elected assemblies in Scotland and Wales and to a power-sharing government in Northern Ireland. London was given a popularly elected mayor. Human

rights laws were adopted. However, in the wake of terrorist attacks, the government drew protests from civil liberties groups because of the way it pursued terrorist suspects. Blair welcomed such criticism as proof of his toughness.

In international affairs Blair gave priority to close working relationships with Presidents Bill Clinton and George W. Bush. Following the September 11 attack on the United States, he committed British troops to Afghanistan and Iraq. Although Blair was successful in getting close to the White House, he failed in his declared goal of placing Britain at the heart of Europe—for example, by adopting the euro as Britain's currency. In his last full year in office, Blair was out of the country for 58 days on trips to more than two dozen different national capitals on six different continents.

Shortly after winning his first election victory, 75 percent approved of Blair as prime minister. Within a year of his second election victory, Blair's rating fell below 50 percent and never recovered. Blair's third election victory in 2005 was won with only 35.2 percent of the popular vote, a fall of 8.0 percent from his first victory. By June 2006, he reached a low: Only 23 percent approved of his performance as prime minister. A year later he resigned. Since then Blair has extended his public role as an envoy for peace between Israel and Palestine and has privately enriched himself through a part-time job advising Wall Street banker J.P. Morgan.

Tony Blair, *New Britain: My Vision of a Young Country* (London: Fourth Estate, 1996); Anthony Seldon, *Blair* (New York: Free Press, 2004); Anthony Seldon, Peter Snowdon, and Daniel Collings, *Blair Unbound* (New York: Simon and Schuster, 2007); Simon Jenkins, *Thatcher and Sons* (London: Allen Lane, 2006).

---

between the positions of number one, and numbers two, three or four."[10] The preeminence of the prime minister is ambiguous. A politician at the apex of government is remote from what is happening on the ground. The more responsibilities attributed to the prime minister, the less time there is to devote to any one task. Like a president a prime minister is the prisoner of the law of first things first. Regardless of personality, a prime minister wears multiple hats as party leader, head of government, and spokesperson

for the nation. Simultaneously, he or she is concerned with the following:

1. ***Winning elections.*** A prime minister may be self-interested, but he or she is not self-employed. To become prime minister, a politician must first be elected leader of his or her party. The only election that a prime minister must win is that of party leader. Seven prime ministers since 1945—Winston Churchill, Anthony Eden, Harold

Constitutional Comparison Comparing an Unwritten and a Written Constitution		TABLE 5.2
	Britain (unwritten)	**United States (written)**
Origin	Medieval customs	1787 Constitutional Convention
Form	Unwritten, indefinite	Written, precise
Final constitutional authority	Majority in Parliament	Supreme Court
Bill of individual rights	No	Yes
Amendment	Ordinary vote in Parliament; unprecedented action by government	More than majority vote in Congress, states
Policy relevance	Low	High

Structure of the British Government	FIGURE 5.1

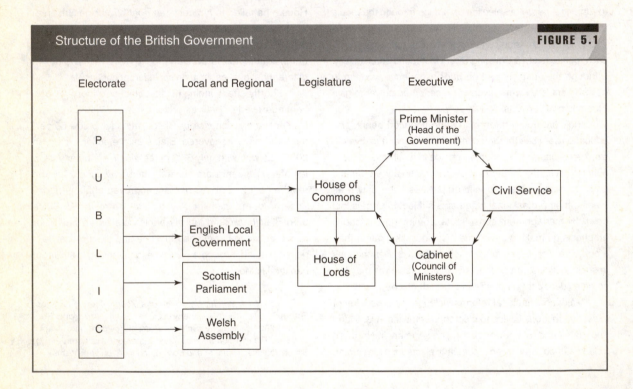

Macmillan, Alec Douglas-Home, James Callaghan, John Major, and Gordon Brown—initially entered Downing Street during the middle of a Parliament, rather than after a national election. In the 17 elections since 1945, the prime minister of the day has ten times led the governing party to victory and seven times to defeat.

2. ***Campaigning through the media.*** A prime minister does not need to attract publicity; it is thrust on him or her by the curiosity of television and newspaper reporters. During an election campaign, the prime minister gets four times as much coverage as any other member of his Cabinet team. Media eminence is a double-edged sword, for bad news puts the prime minister in an unfavorable light. The personality of a prime minister remains relatively constant, but during a term of office, his or her popularity can fluctuate by more than 45 percentage points in public opinion polls.[11]

3. ***Dispensing patronage.*** To remain prime minister, a politician must keep the confidence of a party. Potential critics can be silenced by appointing a quarter of MPs to posts as government ministers, who sit on front bench seats in the House of Commons. MPs not appointed to a post are backbenchers; many ingratiate themselves with the party leader in hopes of becoming a government minister. In dispensing patronage a prime minister can use any of four different criteria: (a) personal loyalty (rewarding friends), (b) cooption (silencing critics by giving them an office so that they are committed to support the government), (c) representativeness (for example, appointing a woman or someone from Scotland or Wales), and (d) competence in managing a large department.

4. ***Performing well in Parliament.*** The prime minister appears in the House of Commons weekly for half an hour of questions from MPs, engaging in rapid-fire repartee with a highly partisan audience. Unprotected by a speechwriter's script, the prime minister must show that he or she is a good advocate of government policy or suffer a reduction in confidence. By being in the Commons and participating in votes there, the prime minister is able to judge the mood of the governing party. Whereas his predecessors would participate in at least a third of the votes in the Commons, Tony Blair turned his back on Parliament, in some years participating in as little as 6 percent of votes there.

5. ***Making and balancing policies.*** The overriding concern of a prime minister is foreign affairs because as head of the British government he or she deals with heads of other governments around the world. When there are conflicts between international and domestic policy priorities, the prime minister is the one person who can strike a balance between pressures from the world "out there" and pressures from the domestic electorate. The number of "intermestic" policies (that is, problems combining both an international and a domestic element) is increasing. The prime minister also makes policy by striking a balance between ministers who want to spend more money to increase their popularity and a Treasury minister who wants to cut taxes in order to boost his or her popularity.

While the formal powers of the office remain constant, individual prime ministers (see Figure 5.2)

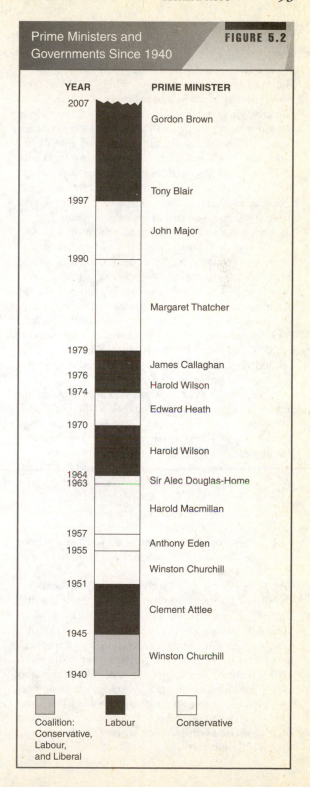

Prime Ministers and Governments Since 1940

FIGURE 5.2

YEAR	PRIME MINISTER
2007	Gordon Brown
1997	Tony Blair
	John Major
1990	
	Margaret Thatcher
1979	James Callaghan
1976	Harold Wilson
1974	Edward Heath
1970	
	Harold Wilson
1964	Sir Alec Douglas-Home
1963	
	Harold Macmillan
1957	Anthony Eden
1955	
	Winston Churchill
1951	
	Clement Attlee
1945	
	Winston Churchill
1940	

Coalition: Conservative, Labour, and Liberal   Labour   Conservative have differed in their electoral success, in how they view their job, and in their impact on government. Clement Attlee, Labour prime minister from 1945 to 1951, was a nonassertive spokesperson for the lowest common denominator of views within a Cabinet consisting of very experienced Labour politicians. When an aging Winston Churchill succeeded Attlee in 1951, he concentrated on foreign affairs and took little interest in domestic policy; the same was true of his successor, Anthony Eden. Harold Macmillan intervened strategically on a limited number of domestic and international issues, while giving ministers great scope on everyday matters. Alec Douglas-Home was weak because he lacked knowledge of economic affairs, the chief problem during his administration.

Both Harold Wilson and Edward Heath were initially committed to an activist definition of the prime minister's job. However, Wilson's major initiatives in economic policy were unsuccessful, and in 1974 the electorate rejected Heath's direction of the economy. Wilson won office again by promising to replace confrontation between management and unions with political conciliation. James Callaghan, who succeeded Wilson in 1976, also emphasized consensus, but economic crises continued.

Margaret Thatcher had strong views about many major policies; associates gave her the nickname TINA because of her motto: There Is No Alternative. Thatcher was prepared to push her views against the wishes of Cabinet colleagues and civil service advisors by any means necessary. In the end her "bossiness" caused a revolt of Cabinet colleagues that helped bring about her downfall. Her former colleagues welcomed John Major as a consensus replacement of a domineering Thatcher. However, his conciliatory manner was often interpreted as a sign of weakness. Sniping from ministers led Major to refer to his Cabinet colleagues as "bastards."

Tony Blair carried into the prime ministership the priority he gave in Opposition to campaigning through the media. Managing the flow of news to secure favorable media coverage was a top priority. Blair's communications director, Alastair Campbell, was given unprecedented powers to give orders to civil servants, and Cabinet ministers were supposed to support his media strategy on pain of losing favor with Downing Street. In the words of the former head of the civil service, the Blair government put "too much emphasis on selling" and "too little on careful deliberation."[12]

Gordon Brown came to the prime ministership with a reputation for success in managing the economy, which had enjoyed an unprecedented period of growth while he was in charge of the Treasury. He also used its power of the purse to influence Cabinet colleagues. Labour MPs unhappy with Tony Blair's endorsement of many policies of Margaret Thatcher hoped that Brown's left-wing views in youth would be reflected in policies promoting more egalitarian and socialist goals. After a brief honeymoon with public opinion, Brown fell out of favor. By the end of the summer of 2008, his approval ratings in opinion polls were at a historic low, the Labour Party had lost two by-elections, and Labour MPs afraid of defeat at the next general election were publicly discussing the desirability of another change of leadership, but the rules of the Labour Party make it difficult for dissatisfied members to mount an effective challenge to an incumbent.

Brown's quick response to the autumn 2008 financial crisis helped him regain some support, but continuing economic difficulties have continued to threaten his position.

Blair's innovations have led to charges that Britain now has a presidential system of government in which power is concentrated in the hands of one person. However, by comparison with a U.S. president, a British prime minister has less formal authority and less security of office (see Table 5.3). The president is directly elected for a fixed four-year term. A prime minister is chosen by his or her party for an indefinite term and is thus vulnerable to losing office if its confidence wanes. The president is the undoubted leader of the federal executive and can dismiss Cabinet appointees with little fear of the consequences; by contrast, senior colleagues of a prime minister are potential rivals for leadership and may be kept in the Cabinet to prevent them from challenging him or her.

However, with the support of the Cabinet and the majority of the governing party's MPs, a prime minister can be far more confident than a president that major legislative proposals will be enacted into law. Although the president is the chief of the executive branch of the federal government, the White House is without authority over Congress, state and local government, and the judiciary. By contrast, the prime minister is at the apex of a unitary government, with powers that are not limited by the courts or by a written constitution.[13]

	Britain (prime minister)	USA (president)
Media visibility	High	High
Route to top	Parliament	Governor, senator
Chosen by	Party vote	State primaries and caucuses
Elected by	Parliament	National election
Term of office	Flexible, insecure	Four years, secure
Constitution	Unitary	Federal
Domestic influence	High	So-so
International role	Semi-independent	Superpower
Checks	Informal	Congress, Supreme Court

Prime Minister and President
Comparing the powers of and processes for choosing a prime minister and a president

TABLE 5.3

Source: Adapted from Richard Rose, *The Prime Minister in a Shrinking World* (Boston: Polity Press, 2001), p. 242.

THE CABINET AND CABINET MINISTERS

The **Cabinet** consists of ministers appointed by the prime minister to head Whitehall departments. They must be members of either the House of Commons or the House of Lords. As ministers are leading figures in the majority party in Parliament, they contribute to what Walter Bagehot described as "the close union, the nearly complete fusion of the executive and legislative powers."[14]

Historically, the Cabinet was the forum in which the prime minister brought together leading members of the governing party, many with competing departmental interests and personal ambitions, to ensure agreement about major government policies. This was possible because the convention of Cabinet responsibility required that all Cabinet ministers give public support to, or at least refrain from public criticism of, what the government was doing, even if they opposed a policy in private. A minister unwilling to share responsibility was expected to resign from office.

The Cabinet is no longer a place for collective deliberation about policies. A half century ago there were usually two Cabinet meetings a week, and many took several hours to arrive at a political consensus. By the time of John Major, meetings were shorter and occurred less than once a week. Tony Blair further reduced the frequency of meetings and cut their average length to under an hour; he used them as a forum in which to exhort ministers to support Downing Street's media priorities. Gordon Brown has preferred to take charge of a wide range of issues, rather than trusting Cabinet colleagues.

Cabinet ministers remain important because the department that each heads is responsible for a major area of public policy and most decisions about what government does are taken within departments (see Box 5.3). Whitehall departments differ greatly from each other. For example, the Department of Business, Enterprise, and Regulatory Reform (DBER) has a larger staff than the Department of the Treasury. However, because of the importance of its responsibility for taxation and public expenditure, the Treasury has more senior civil servants. The DBER staff have a dispersed variety of concerns, including the competitiveness of industry, trade, employment, energy, and regulation. The Treasury staff concentrate on one big task, the management of the economy. The varied tasks of the DBER secretary make him or her much more vulnerable to adverse publicity if, for example, there is a financial scandal or energy prices rise. The job of the chancellor of the Exchequer is more important politically, insofar as economic performance affects the governing party's electoral fate.

A Cabinet minister is both the head of a government department and a party politician. As a department head, he or she can initiate policies, select among alternatives brought forward from within the department, and try to avoid making an unpopular decision. A minister is responsible for actions taken by thousands of civil servants nominally acting on the minister's behalf and must answer for agencies to

Departmental Organization and Reorganization

British government departments are multipurpose organizations created as a result of the growth of government. Some departments focus on a clearly defined major function, while others combine multiple functions. The names and functions of departments are often reorganized to reflect changes in policy, political expediency, or fashion. For example, since 1964 responsibilities for trade, industry, and technology have been placed in departments labeled Trade and Technology, then Trade and Industry, then separate departments for Trade and for Industry, and again reunited as a single Trade and Industry department. Today the policies are divided between departments for Business, Enterprise, and Regulatory Reform and for Innovation, Universities, and Skills. Each time that the title on the front door of the department was changed, most officials and programs continued as before.

In March 2009 the government of Gordon Brown was organized as follows:

1. *External affairs:* foreign and commonwealth affairs; defense; international development.
2. *Economic affairs:* treasury; business, enterprise, and regulatory reform; transport; innovation, universities, and skills; energy and climate change.
3. *Legal and constitutional issues:* justice; home office; law officer's department; equalities office.
4. *Social services:* health; children, schools, and families; work and pensions; culture, media, and sport.
5. *Territorial:* environment, food, and rural affairs; communities and local government; Northern Ireland office; Scotland office; Wales office.
6. *Managing government business:* Cabinet office; leader of the House of Commons; chief whip in the House of Commons; leader of the House of Lords; chancellor of the Duchy of Lancaster; Privy Council office.

Source: www.parliament.uk

---

which Whitehall is increasingly contracting out responsibility for delivering public services. In addition, a minister is a department's ambassador to the world outside, including Downing Street, Parliament, the mass media, and interest or pressure groups. Not least, Cabinet ministers are individuals with ambitions to rise in politics. The typical minister is not an expert in a subject, but an expert in politics, and is willing to deal with any department that offers opportunities to further his or her political career.

The political reputation of Cabinet ministers depends on their success in promoting the interests of their department in Parliament, in the media, and in battles within Whitehall. Cabinet ministers are willing to go along silently with their colleagues' proposals in exchange for endorsement of their own measures. However, ministers often have to compete for scarce resources, making conflict inevitable between departments. Regardless of party, the ministers responsible for defense and education will press for increased spending, while the Treasury minister will oppose such moves. Cabinet ministers sometimes resolve their differences in Cabinet committees that include all ministers whose departments are most affected by an issue.

Tony Blair sought to exercise control over ministers through his personal staff. However, Blair did not have time during the week to go into the details of policy. Because he had never been a departmental minister, his public remarks sometimes showed naiveté about how the government actually worked—and the same was even more true of his staff. After years in office, Blair attacked the consequences of government by political advisors and spin doctors. In a leaked memo to Cabinet ministers, he criticized them for "too often" rushing out policies "in ignorance of the risks," thus making the government look bad.[15]

The Civil Service

Although government could continue for months without new legislation, it would collapse overnight if hundreds of thousands of civil servants stopped administering laws and delivering public services that the government of the day had inherited from its predecessors. The largest number of civil servants are clerical staff with little discretion; they carry out the routine activities of a large bureaucracy. Only if these duties are executed satisfactorily can ministers have the time and opportunity to make new policies.

The most important group of civil servants is the smallest: the few hundred higher civil servants who advise ministers and oversee work of their departments. Top British civil servants deny they are politicians because of the partisan connotations of the term. However, their work is political because they are involved in formulating and advising on controversial policies. Thus, a publication aimed at recruiting bright graduates for the higher civil service declares: "You will be involved from the outset in matters of major policy or resource allocation and, under the guidance of experienced administrators, encouraged to put forward your own constructive ideas and to take responsible decisions."[16]

Top civil servants are not apolitical; they are bipartisan, being ready to work for whichever party wins an election. Their style is not that of the professional American athlete for whom winning is all-important. English civil servants have grown up playing cricket; its motto is that winning is less important than how one plays the game. However, ministers want to win.

The relationship between ministers and higher civil servants is critical. A busy politician does not have time to go into details; he or she wants a brief that can catch a headline or squash criticism. Ministers expect higher civil servants to be responsive to their political views and to give advice consistent with their outlook and that of the governing party and Downing Street. Civil servants like working for a political heavyweight who can carry the department's cause to victory in interdepartmental battles. Civil servants prefer to work for a minister who has clear views on policy, but they dislike it when a minister grabs a headline by expressing views that will get the department into trouble later because they are impractical.

Both ministers and civil servants are concerned with political management in complementary ways. High-level civil servants are expected to be able to think like politicians, anticipating what their minister would want and objections that would be raised by Parliament, interest or pressure groups, and the media. Ministers are expected to be able to recognize the obstacles to achieving desirable goals that civil servants identify for them, However, this has caused activist prime ministers such as Margaret Thatcher

and Tony Blair to regard much civil service advice as unhelpful to them in achieving their ambitions.

Ministers now have at hand political advisors to advise them on measures they can announce that will reflect credit on them in the media and in the governing party. This has caused civil servants to complain that ministers too often ignore advice that calls attention to the difficulties in achieving their intentions. In the words of a senior civil servant, "Just because ministers say to do something does not mean that we can ignore reality."[17] When ministerial decisions attract criticism, ministers may blame civil servants, rather than taking responsibility themselves. The head of the trade union of higher civil servants has argued, "There is a danger of descending into a search for scapegoats when problems emerge."[18]

The Thatcher government introduced a new phenomenon in Whitehall: a prime minister who believed civil servants were inferior to business people because they did not have to "earn" their living—that is, to make a profit. *Management* was made the buzzword in Whitehall, and departments were supposed to be run in a businesslike fashion, achieving value for money so that the government could profit politically by cutting taxes. Parts of government departments were "hived off" to form separate public agencies, with their own accounts and performance targets. The Blair government continued Thatcher's attempts to make the civil service more businesslike, in hopes of providing public services more cheaply.

During 11 years as head of the Treasury, Gordon Brown gathered around him a small team of political appointees and civil servants to further his efforts to manage the economy. As prime minister he has faced a different challenge: to concentrate attention on a few big decisions and to delegate tasks that he lacks the time to deal with. Cabinet ministers criticize Brown for trying to take charge of too many policies and then delaying decisions when all alternatives appear politically unpopular.

The Role of Parliament

The principal division in Parliament is between the party with a majority of the seats in the House of Commons and the Opposition parties. The government expects to get its way because its members are the leading politicians in the majority party. MPs in the majority party almost invariably vote as the party leadership instructs because only by voting as a bloc can their party maintain control of government. If a bill or a motion is identified as a vote of confidence in the government, the government will fall if it is defeated.

The government's state of mind is summed up in the words of a Labour Cabinet minister who declared, "It's carrying democracy too far if you don't know the result of the vote before the meeting."[19] In the great majority of House of Commons votes, MPs vote along party lines. If a handful of MPs votes against the party whip or abstains, this is headlined as a rebellion. The Opposition cannot expect to alter major government decisions because it lacks a majority of votes in the Commons. It accepts the frustrations going with its minority status for the life of a Parliament because it hopes to win a majority at the next election.

Whitehall departments draft bills presented to Parliament, and few amendments to legislation are carried without government approval. Laws are described as acts of Parliament, but it would be more accurate if they were stamped "Made in Whitehall." In addition, the government, rather than Parliament, sets the budget for government programs. The weakness of Parliament is in marked contrast to the U.S. Congress, where each house controls its own proceedings independent of the White House. A U.S. president may ask Congress to enact a bill, but cannot compel a favorable vote.

The chief functions of Parliament are political, rather than legislative. First of all, it weighs political reputations. MPs continually assess their colleagues as ministers or potential ministers and as allies or potential allies in internal party disputes about policy and personalities and promotion. A minister may win a formal vote of confidence, but lose status if his or her arguments are demolished in debate. They continually assess their leader as a person who will lead them to victory or defeat at the next election.

Second, backbench MPs can demand that the government do something about an issue and force a minister to explain and defend what he or she is responsible for. The party whip is expected to listen to the views of dissatisfied backbench MPs and to convey their concerns to ministers. In the corridors, dining rooms, and committees of the Commons, backbenchers can tell ministers what they think is wrong with government policy. If the government is unpopular and MPs feel threatened with losing their seats at the next election, they will be aggressive in demanding that something be done.

Publicizing issues is a third function of Parliament. MPs can use their position to call the media's attention to issues and to call the public's attention to themselves. Television cameras are now in Parliament, and a quick-witted MP can provide the media with sound bites.

Fourth, MPs can examine how Whitehall departments administer public policies. An MP may write to a minister about a department responsibility affecting a constituent or pressure group. MPs can request the parliamentary commissioner for administration (also known as the ombudsman, after the Scandinavian original) to investigate complaints about maladministration. Parliamentary committees scrutinize administration and policy, interviewing civil servants and ministers. However, as a committee moves from discussing details to discussing issues of government policy, it raises a question of confidence in the government, and this can divide a committee along party lines, with MPs in the governing party in the majority.

MPs are expected to promote the interests of their constituency and be helpful to individual constituents having trouble in dealing with a government department. However, the obligation to follow the party line when it comes to a vote limits the influence they can exert. Most MPs hold their seat by a comfortable majority conferred by partisan electors who identify with their party. When their party is in trouble nationally, constituency work and personal popularity cannot save MPs in seats held by a narrow margin from defeat.

A newly elected MP contemplating his or her role as one among 646 members of the House of Commons is faced with many choices. An MP may decide to be a party loyalist, voting as the leadership decides without participating in deliberations about policy. The MP who wishes more attention can make a mark by exhibiting brilliance in debates, by acting as an acknowledged representative of a pressure group, or by acting in a nonpartisan way—for example, helping look after unglamorous parliamentary services. An MP is expected to speak for constituency interests, but constituents accept that their MP will not vote against party policy if it is in conflict with local interests. The only role that an MP rarely undertakes is that of lawmaker—this job is undertaken in Whitehall departments.

Backbench MPs perennially demand changes to make their jobs more interesting and to give them more influence. However, the power to make major changes rests with the government, rather than the House of Commons. Whatever criticisms MPs made of Parliament while in Opposition, once in government they have an interest in existing arrangements that greatly limit the power of Parliament to influence or stop what ministers do.

The second chamber of the British Parliament, the House of Lords, is unique because it was initially composed of hereditary peers, now supplemented by lords appointed for life. However, in 1999 the Labour government abolished the right of all but 92 hereditary peers to sit in the House of Lords. Today a large majority of its members are life peers who have been given a title later in life for achievement in one or another public sphere, government ministers who have been appointed without having a seat in the House of Commons, and prominent donors of money to a party. In Tony Blair's third term of office, the police investigated allegations that he had raised $50 million from rich backers hoping to be made into a lord and thereby being given a seat in the upper chamber of Parliament.

No party has a majority of seats in the House of Lords, and more than one-fifth of its members are cross-benchers who do not identify with any party. The government often introduces relatively noncontroversial legislation in the Lords. and it uses the Lords as a revising chamber to amend bills. Members of the Lords can raise party political issues or issues that cut across party lines, such as problems of the fishing industry or pornography. The Lords cannot veto legislation, but it can and does amend or delay the passage of some government bills.

Although all parties accept the need for some kind of second chamber to revise legislation, there is no agreement about what its composition or its powers should be. Current methods of appointment have raised concerns about the abuse of appointment powers. In 2007 a majority of MPs voted in favor of a completely elected House of Lords. However, the government has made no commitment to implement so large a reform. The last thing the government of the day wants is a reform that gives the upper chamber enough electoral legitimacy to challenge government legislation.

Government as a Network

Policy making involves a network of prime minister, ministers, leading civil servants, and political advisors, all of whom share in what has been described as the "village life" of Whitehall. An English village is far smaller and more intimate than the city full of politicians inside the Washington, D.C., beltway.[20]

The growth of government has increased specialization so that policy makers see less and less of each other. For a given issue, a relatively small number of people are involved in the **core executive** group that makes a decision. However, members of the network are a floating population of people in Westminster; it is not the same for decisions about transport and agriculture or about health and defense.

The prime minister is the single most important person in government. Since there is no written constitution, a determined prime minister can challenge the status quo and turn government to fresh ends. But to say that the prime minister makes the most important decisions and leaves the less important ones to department ministers begs this question: What is an important decision? Decisions in which the prime minister is not involved are more numerous, require more money, and affect more lives than do most decisions taken at Downing Street. Scarcity of time is a major limitation on the influence of the prime minister. In the words of one Downing Street official, "It's like skating over an enormous globe of thin ice. You have to keep moving fast all the time."[21]

Within each department the permanent secretary, its highest-ranking civil servant, usually has much more knowledge of a department's problems than does a transitory Cabinet minister. Political advisors brought into a department to put the best spin on what their minister does know less about the department's work than its career civil servants. However, they have the political advantage of knowing the minister better.

POLITICAL CULTURE AND LEGITIMACY

Political culture refers to values and beliefs about how the country ought to be governed. For example, there is a consensus that Britain ought to have a government accountable to a popularly elected Parliament. This view is held not only by the major parties, but also by parties that demand independence, such as the Scottish National Party.

The values of the political culture impose limitations on what government can do and what it must do. Regardless of party preference, the great majority of British people today believe that government ought to provide education, health services, and social security. Cultural norms about freedom of speech prevent censorship of criticism, and liberal laws on sexual relations and abortion allow for great freedom of choice in sexual matters.

Today many limits on the scope of public policy are practical, rather than normative. Public expenditure on popular policies, such as the health service, are limited by the extent to which the economy grows and the reluctance of Labour or Conservative governments to raise more money by increasing taxes. Trying to introduce new legislation or reverse a major policy is difficult because of the need to take into account well-entrenched programs and interests.

There are three competing normative theories of how British government ought to operate. The **trusteeship theory of government** assumes that leaders ought to take the initiative in deciding what is collectively in the public interest. It is summed up in the epigram "The government's job is to govern." The trusteeship doctrine is always popular with the party in office because it justifies doing whatever the government wishes. The Opposition party rejects it because it is not in office.

The **collectivist theory** sees government as balancing the competing demands of collective groups in society. From this perspective, parties and pressure groups advocating group or class interests are more authoritative than individual voters.[22] Traditional Conservatives emphasized harmony between different classes in society, each with its own responsibilities and rewards. For socialists, group politics has been about class conflict. With changes in British society, party leaders have distanced themselves from close identification with representing collective interests, as they realize that votes are cast by individuals, rather than by business firms or trade unions.

The **individualist theory** postulates that political parties should represent people, rather than organized group interests. In the 1980s Margaret Thatcher was an outspoken advocate of economic individualism, regarding each person as responsible for his or her welfare. In an interview in 1987 she went so far as to declare, "There is no such thing as society." Liberal Democrats put emphasis on individual freedom from government enforcement of social norms, too. However, individuals are rarely offered a referendum allowing them to vote directly on what government does.

The Legitimacy of Government

The legitimacy of government is shown by the British people simultaneously valuing their form of government with free elections to a representative Parliament, while making many specific criticisms about how it works.

Dissatisfaction with government encourages protest, but it is normally kept within lawful bounds.

The World Values Survey finds that nearly every Briton says he or she might sign a petition and half might participate in a lawful demonstration. However, only one-sixth might participate in an illegal occupation of a building or factory. The readiness of groups in Northern Ireland to resort to armed action for political ends makes it the most "un-British" part of the United Kingdom.

The legitimacy accorded to British government is not the result of economic calculations about whether parliamentary democracy "pays" best. During the depression of the 1930s, Communist and Fascist parties received only derisory votes in Britain, while their support was great in Germany and Italy. Likewise, inflation and unemployment in the 1970s and 1980s did not stimulate extremist politics.

The symbols of a common past, such as the monarchy, are sometimes cited as major determinants of legitimacy. But surveys of public opinion show that the Queen has little political significance; her popularity derives from the fact that she is nonpolitical. The popularity of a monarch is a consequence, not a cause, of political legitimacy. In Northern Ireland, where the minority denies the legitimacy of British government, the Queen is a symbol of divisions between British Unionists and Irish Republicans, who reject the Crown. Habit and tradition appear to be the chief explanations for the persisting legitimacy of British government. A survey asking people why they support the government found that the most popular reason was "It's the best form of government we know."

Authority is not perfect or trouble free. Winston Churchill made this point when he told the House of Commons: "No one pretends that democracy is perfect or all wise. Indeed, it has been said that democracy is the worst form of government, except all those other forms that have been tried from time to time."[23] In the words of English writer E. M. Forster, people give "two cheers for democracy."

Courts and Abuses of Power

The Constitutional Reform Act of 2005 authorized the creation of a Supreme Court as the highest judicial authority in the United Kingdom, with effect from autumn 2009. It ends the centuries-old practice of having a committee of the House of Lords operate as the highest court. The new Supreme Court consists of a president and 11 other justices appointed by the prime minister. Its chief function is to serve as the final court of appeal on points of law in cases initially heard by courts in

England, Wales, and Northern Ireland and in some cases by courts in Scotland, which maintains a separate system of courts, albeit the content of laws is usually much the same. Although the name of the new British Supreme Court is the same as that of the highest court in the United States, its powers are much more limited. It cannot declare an Act of Parliament unconstitutional, for Parliament remains the supreme authority in deciding what government can and cannot do.

In constitutional theory Parliament can hold ministers accountable for abuses of power by the government. In practice Parliament is an ineffective check on abuses of executive power because the executive consists of the leaders of the majority party in Parliament. When the government is under attack, the tendency of MPs in the governing party is to close ranks in its defense. The government can use this shield to protect itself from charges of abusing its power.

The decline of ministerial accountability to Parliament in recent decades has encouraged the courts to become more active in making rulings against the elected government of the day if ministers can be shown to have acted inconsistently with grants of power contained in acts of Parliament. Governments of both parties have responded by including clauses in acts that give ministers broad grants of discretionary power.

Britain's membership in the EU offers additional channels for judicial influence. The United Kingdom is now bound to act within laws and directives authorized by the EU. British judges can use EU standards when evaluating government actions, and plaintiffs can challenge British government actions at the European Court of Justice. The 1998 Human Rights Act of the Westminster Parliament allows citizens to ask British courts to enforce rights conferred by the European Convention on Human Rights.

Terrorist activities challenge conventional norms about individual rights and the collective interests of the state. At times British government forces dealt with the violence of the IRA and illegal armed Protestant groups by "bending" the law, implementing shoot-to-kill policies and fabricating evidence to produce convictions of terrorist suspects that the courts have subsequently overturned. As a response to jihadist terrorist bombings in London, the police are ready to use harsh measures against suspects, including shoot-to-kill responses when arresting suspects. The Labour government's proposals for reducing the rights of suspect terrorists have been condemned by Opposition parties as creating a risk of a "siege" or "authoritarian" society.[24]

Tension is emerging between the principle that the elected government of the day should do what it thinks best and the judges' view that government should act in accord with the rule of law, whether an Act of Parliament or an obligation contained in a European treaty that the British government has endorsed. When judges make decisions that Labour government ministers do not like, the ministers have publicly attacked the decisions of the court. Judges reply by stating that they should not be attacked for enforcing the law. If the government does not like it, it should pass a new Act of Parliament or secure amendments to European treaties.

Both ministers and senior civil servants sometimes mislead Parliament and the public. A Conservative minister nominally responsible for open government told a Commons select committee in 1994 that "in exceptional cases it is necessary to say something that is untrue in the House of Commons." When accused in court of telling a lie about the British government's efforts to suppress an embarrassing memoir by an ex-intelligence officer, Robert Armstrong, then the head of the civil service and secretary to the Cabinet, described the government's statements as "a misleading impression, not a lie. It was being economical with the truth."

Whitehall practices of "cutting corners" or abusing powers have been protected from parliamentary scrutiny by legislation on **official secrecy**. This legislation treats information as a scarce commodity that should not be given out freely. Information about policy deliberations in departments is often deemed not in the "public" interest to disclose, for it can make government appear uncertain or divided. The Whitehall view is "The need to know still dominates the right to know."[25] Secrecy remains strong because it serves the interests of the most important people in government, Cabinet ministers and civil servants. A Freedom of Information Act has reduced, but not ended, the executive's power to keep secret the exchange of views within the Whitehall network. For example, in response to a request for information about its operation, a civil servant at the Histories, Openness, and Records Unit of the Cabinet Office wrote: "Releasing information which would allow analysis of policy decisions affecting the operation of the Act would of itself be detrimental to the Act's operation."[26]

Occasional abuses of executive power have created tensions for civil servants who believe that their job is not only to serve the elected government of the day, but also to maintain the integrity of government.

Conflicting Loyalties Among Civil Servants

BOX 5.4

The inability of Parliament to hold the government of the day accountable for palpable misdeeds disturbs senior civil servants who know what is going on and risk becoming accessories before the fact if they assist ministers in producing statements that mislead Parliament.

In one well-publicized case, a Ministry of Defence official, Clive Ponting, leaked to the House of Commons evidence that questioned the accuracy of government statements about the conduct of the Falklands War. He was indicted and tried for violating the Official Secrets Act. The judge asked the jury to think about the issue this way: "Can it then be in the interests of the state to go against the policy of the government of the day?" The jury concluded that it could be; Ponting was acquitted.

Most senior civil servants are unwilling to become whistle-blowers, challenging actions of ministers, and thereby jeopardizing their own careers. However, inquiries after major mistakes can show that these mistakes have occurred because ministers have refused to listen to cautions from civil servants or misrepresented their views. This was notably so in Tony Blair's justification of going to war in Iraq.

Graham Wilson and Anthony Barker, "Whitehall's Disobedient Servants? Senior Officials' Potential Resistance to Ministers in British Government Departments," *British Journal of Political Science* 27, no. 2 (1997): 223–246.

This has led civil servants at times to leak official documents with the intention of preventing government from carrying out a policy that the leaker believes to be unethical or inadvisable (see Box 5.4).

British citizens have reacted to abuses of public office by becoming distrusting. Only a third of Britons report that they have a great deal or quite a lot of confidence in Parliament. The press and trade unions—institutions that theories of civil society describe as important in holding government accountable—are trusted by even fewer people. The most trusted public institutions today are those that maintain authority, led by the armed forces and the police (see Figure 5.3).

POLITICAL SOCIALIZATION

Socialization influences the political division of labor between those who participate in politics and those who do not. The family's influence comes first chronologically; political attitudes learned within the family become intertwined with primary family loyalties. However, social change means that the views that parents transmit to their children may not be relevant by the time that their offspring have become 40 to 50 years old. In contemporary Britain whether one is a Christian or a Muslim is more relevant

than whether one was brought up in the Church of England or the Methodist Church.

Family and Gender

A child may not know what the Labour, Conservative, or Liberal Democratic Party stands for, but if it is the party of Mom and Dad, this can be enough to create a youthful identification with a party. However, the influence of family on voting is limited because 36 percent do not know how one or both of their parents usually voted or else their parents voted for different parties. Among those who report knowing which party both parents supported, just over half vote as their parents have. In the electorate as a whole, only 35 percent say that they know how both parents voted and that they vote for the same party.[27]

Children learn different social roles according to gender; yet, as adult citizens, men and women have the same legal right to vote and participate in politics. Bipartisan interest in appealing to women is illustrated by the 1976 Sex Discrimination Act, prohibiting discrimination in employment. It was enacted by a Labour government following a report by a Conservative government. For each general election, the votes of women are divided in much the same way as those of men.

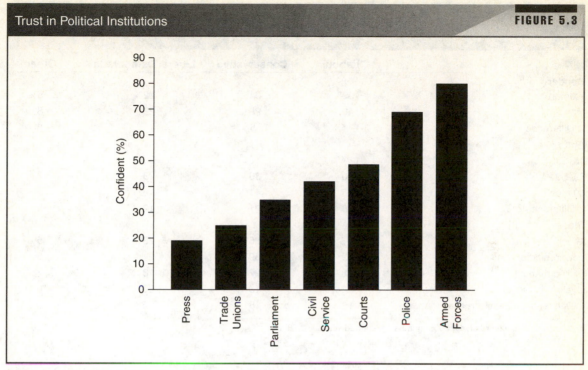

Trust in Political Institutions

FIGURE 5.3

Source: Ronald Inglehart et al., World Values Survey and European Values Survey, 1999–2001 (Ann Arbor, MI: Interuniversity Consortium for Political and Social Research). Interviews were conducted in Great Britain in October–November 1999 (N = 1,000).

Whether talking about economic, social, or international issues, politicians usually stress concerns common to both men and women. Men and women tend to have similar political attitudes. For example, more than half of women and half of men favor capital punishment, and a substantial minority in each group opposes it. Gender is less important than class, age, or education as an influence on party loyalties (see Table 5.4).

Gender differences do, however, lead to differences in political participation. Men are almost twice as likely as women to be local government councillors. Women are almost half the employees in the civil service, but are heavily concentrated in lower-level clerical jobs; women hold about 10 percent of the top appointments in the civil service. A record number of women candidates stood for the Commons in 2005, but male candidates still outnumbered women by a margin of four to one. A total of 128 women were elected to the House of Commons; it remains four-fifths male.

Education

The majority of the population was once considered fit for only a minimum of education, but that minimum has steadily risen. In today's electorate the oldest voters left school at the age of 14 and the median voter by the age of 17. Less than 6 percent of young persons attend "public" schools—that is, fee-paying schools, which are actually private schools. Whereas half a century ago Britain had few universities, today there are more than one hundred universities and almost one-half of young persons are in postsecondary institutions, many of which lack the facilities of established research universities.

The stratification of English education used to imply that the more education a person had, the more likely that person was to vote for Conservatives. This is no longer the case. People with a university degree or its equivalent now divide their votes among the Conservative, Labour, and Liberal Democratic parties.

Social Differences in Voting				TABLE 5.4
The Labour Party drew on a different electoral base than the Conservative Party in 2005				
	Labour	**Conservative**	**Liberal Democratic**	**Other**
Gender				
Women	39%	34%	22%	5%
Men	40	29	23	8
Difference	−1	5	−1	−3
Age				
18–29	44%	20%	30%	6%
30–59	40	30	23	7
60 plus	36	41	18	5
Difference	8	−21	12	2
Class				
Middle	36%	36%	23%	5%
Lower middle	32	39	24	5
Skilled manual	48	27	18	7
Unskilled manual	52	18	20	10
Difference, middle unskilled manual	−16	18	3	−5

Source: British Election Survey, 2005 (number of reported voters = 2,787).

Education is strongly related to active participation in politics. The more education a person has, the greater the possibility of climbing the political ladder. University graduates make up more than two-thirds of the members of the House of Commons. The expansion of universities has broken the dominance of Oxford and Cambridge; barely one-quarter of MPs went to these two institutions. The concentration of graduates from many different British universities in top jobs is a sign of a meritocracy, in which officials qualified by education have replaced an aristocracy based on birth and family.

Class

Historically, party competition has been interpreted in class terms; the Conservative Party has been described as a middle-class party and Labour as a working-class party. Class has appeared as relatively important in England because of the absence of major divisions of race, religion, or language, as are found in the United States, Canada, and Northern Ireland. The concept of **class** can refer to occupational status or serve as a shorthand term for the social status conferred by income and education. Occupation is the most commonly used indicator of class. Manual workers are usually described as the working class and nonmanual workers as the middle class.

Most Britons have a mixture of middle-class and working-class attributes. The mixed-class group has been increasing, as changes in the economy have led to a reduction in manual jobs and an increase in middle-class jobs. Many occupations such as computer technicians now have an indeterminate social status. When British citizens are asked whether they belong to a social class, 57 percent now reject placing themselves in either the middle or the working class.

The relationship between class and party has become limited. No party now wins as much as half the vote of middle-class electors. In the 2005 election, just over half of unskilled manual workers and just under half of skilled manual workers voted Labour (see Table 5.4). Due to the cross-class appeal of parties, less than half of the electorate conforms to the stereotypes of middle-class Conservative and working-class Labour voters.

Socioeconomic experiences other than occupation also influence voting. At each level of the class structure, people who belong to trade unions are more likely to vote Labour than Conservative. Housing creates neighborhoods with political relevance. People who live in municipally built council houses tend to vote Labour, while Conservatives do relatively well among homeowners, who are now a large majority of the electorate.

The focus of the mass media on what's happening today makes them an agency for resocializing people. The media's stress on what is new deemphasizes tradition. Today the upper class no longer commands deference, and celebrities owing their prominence to the media and achievements in sports, rock music, or the like are better known than most MPs and even some Cabinet ministers. Moreover, the Internet provides people with alternative sources of information and opinion, and most Britons old enough to vote are able to find information there.

The British press is sharply divided. A few quality newspapers such as *The Times, The Guardian, The Daily Telegraph, The Independent,* and *The Financial Times* carry news and comment at an intellectual level higher than most American newspapers. Mass-circulation tabloids such as *The Sun,* Britain's best-selling newspaper, concentrate on trivia and trash. Most papers tend to lean toward one party. However, if the party that a paper normally supports becomes very unpopular, then the paper will criticize it or even lean toward whichever party has risen in popularity.

In the aggressive pursuit of news and audiences, journalists are prepared to grab attention by making the government of the day look bad, and television interviewers can gain celebrity by insulting MPs and ministers on air. A majority of MPs think that the media are to blame for popular cynicism about politicians and parties. However, a Populus poll in 2007 found that a majority of the electorate thinks that the conduct of politicians is just as much to blame for cynicism about politics as is the conduct of the media.

Television is the primary source of political news. Historically, radio and television were a monopoly of the British Broadcasting Corporation (BBC). Seeking to educate and to elevate, the BBC was also very respectful of all forms of authority, including government. The introduction of commercial television in the 1950s and commercial radio in the following decades has made all broadcasting channels populist in competing for audiences. There are now many television channels and a great variety of radio stations. The law forbids selling advertising to politicians, parties, or political causes.

Current affairs programs often seek audiences by exposing alleged failings of government, and television personalities make their names by the tough cross-examination of politicians of all parties. However, the government of the day controls the renewal of the broadcasting companies' licenses, and it sets the annual fee that every viewer must pay for noncommercial BBC programs, currently about $250 a year. Broadcasters try to avoid favoring one party because over a period of time control of government is likely to shift between parties and, with it, the power to make decisions that affect the companies' revenue and licenses.

Since political socialization is a lifetime learning process, the loyalties of voters are shaped by an accumulation of influences over many decades. Today there are still some members of the electorate who are old enough to have voted for or against Winston Churchill when he led the Conservative Party. However, the youngest electors had not been born until after Margaret Thatcher retired as leader of the Conservative Party. The median elector in the next British general election cast his or her first vote in the 1992 election.

POLITICAL PARTICIPATION AND RECRUITMENT

Participation

An election is the one opportunity people have to influence government directly. Every citizen aged 18 or over is eligible to vote. Local government officials register voters, and the list is revised annually, ensuring that nearly everyone eligible to vote is actually registered. Turnout at general elections averaged 77 percent in the 50 years since 1950. However, in 2001 it fell to 59 percent. In an attempt to boost turnout, the Labour government has experimented with encouraging people to vote by post, rather than in person. When postal ballots were mailed out in several North of England constituencies during the 2004 European Parliament election, three-fifths of those receiving a ballot did not bother to return it. In the 2005 general election, postal voting on demand led to serious allegations of fraud in several inner-city constituencies. Even then, turnout was only 61 percent.

Between elections there are additional opportunities to express political opinions (Figure 5.4). More than one-third have signed a petition on a public issue, and more than one-fifth say that politics has affected their shopping by causing them to boycott a product. The most politically involved—those who say they are very interested in politics, take part in a demonstration, or are active in a political party—make

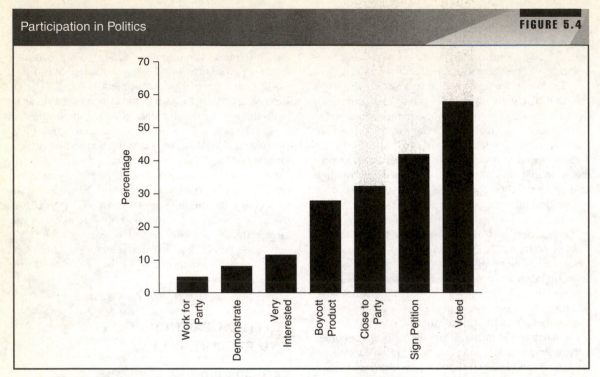

Participation in Politics

FIGURE 5.4

Source: Roger Jowell and the Central Coordinating Team, European Social Survey, 2002–2003 (London: Centre for Comparative Social Surveys, City University). Interviews were conducted in the United Kingdom from September 24, 2002, to February 4, 2003 (N = 1,908).

up no more than one-tenth of the electorate. However, a London-based protest by a few thousand people can get national media coverage, even though those participating make up only 0.01 percent of the electorate.

If political participation is defined as paying taxes and drawing benefits from public policies, then virtually every Briton is involved. Public programs provide benefits at each stage of the life cycle, from maternity allowances to mothers through education, employment and unemployment benefits, health care, and pensions in old age. The median British household receives two major benefits from public policies.

Political Recruitment

The most important political roles in Britain are those of Cabinet minister, higher civil servant, partisan political advisor, and intermittent public person, which is analogous to a Washington insider. Each group has its own recruitment pattern. To become a Cabinet

minister, an individual must first be elected to Parliament. Shortly after leaving university, ambitious politicians often become assistants to politicians and then "graduate" to becoming lobbyists, journalists, or MPs. Individuals enter the civil service shortly after leaving university by passing a highly competitive entrance examination; promotion is based on achievement and approval by seniors. Intermittent public persons gain access to ministers and civil servants because of the knowledge and position they have gained by making a career outside party politics.

In all political roles, starting early on a political career is usually a precondition of success because it takes time to build up the skills and contacts necessary to become a major political actor. Geography is a second major influence on recruitment. Ministers, higher civil servants, and other public persons spend their working lives in London. A change at Downing Street does not bring in policy makers from a different part of the country, as can happen in the White House when a president from Chicago succeeds a president from Texas. Since London is atypical of the cities and towns in which most British people live, there is a gap between the everyday lives of policy makers and those of the majority on whose behalf they act.

MPs and Cabinet Ministers

For a person with ambitions to be a Cabinet minister, becoming an MP is the necessary first step. An ambitious person is not expected to begin in local politics and work his or her way gradually to the top at Westminster. Instead, at an early age an individual becomes a "cadet" recruit to a junior position such as a parliamentary assistant to an MP or a "gofer" for a Cabinet minister.

Nomination for a winnable or safe seat in the House of Commons is in the hands of local party committees. A candidate does not have to be resident in the constituency in which he or she is nominated. Hence, it is possible for a young person to go straight from university to a job in the House of Commons or party headquarters and then look around the country for a winnable seat for which to be nominated, a process that usually takes years. Once selected for a constituency in which his or her party has a large majority, the MP can then expect to be reelected routinely for a decade or more.

After entering the House of Commons, an MP seeks to be noticed. Some ways of doing so—for example, grabbing headlines by questioning the wisdom of the party leadership—make it difficult to gain promotion to the ministerial ranks. Other approaches assist promotion, such as successfully attacking Opposition leaders in debate or being well informed about a politically important topic. So, too, does showing loyalty to the party leader.

Experience in the Commons does not prepare an individual for the work of a minister. An MP's chief concerns are dealing with people and talking about what government ought to do. A minister must also be able to handle paperwork, relate political generalities to specific technical problems facing his or her department, and make hard decisions when all the alternatives are unpopular.

The restriction of ministerial appointments to MPs prevents a nationwide canvass for appointees. A prime minister must distribute about 100 jobs among approximately 200 MPs in the governing party who are experienced in Parliament and have not ruled themselves out of consideration on grounds of parliamentary inexperience, old age, political extremism,

personal unreliability, or lack of interest in office. An MP has a better than even chance of a junior ministerial appointment if he or she serves three terms in Parliament. Exceptionally, Tony Blair gave a variety of ministerial posts to personal supporters whom he made life peers; they owed their posts to their patron, Blair, rather than to voters and to the Labour Party.

A minister learns on the job. Usually, an MP is first given a junior post as an under secretary and then promoted to minister of state before becoming a full member of the Cabinet. In the process an individual is likely to be shuffled from one department to another, having to learn new subject matter with each shift between departments. The average minister can expect to stay in a particular job for about two years and never knows when an accident of politics—a death or an unexpected resignation—will lead to a transfer to another department. The rate of ministerial turnover in Britain is one of the highest in Europe. The minister who gets a new job as the result of a reshuffle usually arrives at a department with no previous experience with its problems. Anthony Crosland, an able Labour minister, reckoned: "It takes you six months to get your head properly above water, a year to get the general drift of most of the field, and two years really to master the whole of a department."[28]

Higher Civil Servants

Whereas MPs come and go from ministerial office with great frequency, civil servants can be in Whitehall for the whole of their working lives. Higher civil servants are recruited without specific professional qualifications or training. They are meant to be "the best and the brightest"—a requirement that has traditionally meant getting a prestigious degree in history, literature, or languages. The Fulton Committee on the Civil Service recommended that recruits have "relevant" specialist knowledge, but the committee members could not decide what kind of knowledge was relevant to the work of government.[29] The Civil Service Commission tests candidates for their ability to summarize lengthy prose papers, to resolve a problem by fitting specific facts to general regulations, to draw inferences from a simple table of social statistics, and to perform well in group discussions about problems of government.

Because bright civil service entrants lack specialized skills and need decades to reach the highest posts, socialization by senior civil servants is especially important. The process makes for continuity, since the head of the government's civil service usually started there as a young official under a head who had himself entered the civil service many decades before.

In the course of a career, civil servants become specialists in the difficult task of managing political ministers and government business. As the television series *Yes, Minister* shows, they are adept at saying "yes" to a Cabinet minister when they really mean "perhaps" and saying "up to a point" when they really mean "no." Increasingly, ministers have tended to discourage civil servants from pointing out obstacles in the way of what government wants to do; they look to "can do" advisors from outside the civil service.

Political Advisors

Most advisors are participants in party politics, for their job is to mobilize political support for the government and for the Cabinet minister for whom they work. Because their background is in party politics and the media, such advisors bring to Whitehall skills that civil servants often lack and that their ministers value. But because they have no prior experience with the civil service, they are often unaware of its conventions and legal obligations. The methods used by political appointees to put a desirable spin on what the government is doing can backfire and cause public controversy. For example, when the September 11 disaster dominated the news, a Whitehall advisor emailed colleagues that this was a good time to put out news that revealed departmental mistakes, since the media would bury it beneath stories from the United States.

In addition, experts in a given subject area, such as environmental pollution or cloning, can act as political advisors. Even if inexperienced in the ways of Whitehall, they can contribute specialized knowledge that is often lacking in government departments, and they can be supporters of the governing party, too. For example, Margaret Thatcher brought in a free market economics professor, Alan Walters, to give her advice from a different perspective than that of the advice she received from what she regarded as a "socialist" civil service.

Most leaders of institutions such as universities, banks, churches, and trade unions do not think of themselves as politicians and have not stood for public office. They are principally concerned with their own organization. But when government actions impinge on their work, they become involved in politics. For example, university heads lobby Whitehall for more money for higher education, while simultaneously demanding freedom from ministerial directions that they describe as "political" interference. Because the actions of government are directly or indirectly relevant to almost all major institutions of society, in effect their leaders intermittently must participate in political debates on public policy.

Selective Recruitment

Nothing could be more selective than an election that results in one person becoming prime minister of a country. Yet, nothing is more representative because an election is the one occasion when every adult can participate in politics with equal effect.

Traditionally, political leaders had high social status and wealth before gaining political office. Aristocrats, businesspeople, and trade union leaders can no longer expect to translate their high standing in other fields into an important political position. Today politics is a full-time occupation. As careers become more specialized, professional politicians become increasingly distant from other spheres of British life.

The greater the scope of activities defined as political, the greater the number of people actively involved in government. Government influence has forced company directors, television executives, and university heads to become involved in politics and public policy. Leadership in organizations outside Whitehall gives such individuals freedom to act independently of government, but the interdependence of public and private institutions, whether profit-making or nonprofit, is now so great that sooner or later they meet in discussions about the public interest.

ORGANIZING GROUP INTERESTS

Civil society institutions have existed in Britain for more than a century. Their leaders regularly discuss their views of public policy with government officials in the expectation that this will put pressure on government to do what they argue is in their groups' interest, as well as the public interest.

The scope of group demands varies enormously from the narrow concerns of an association for single parents to the encompassing economic policies of organizations representing business or trade unions.

Groups also differ in the nature of their interests: Some are concerned with material objectives, whereas others deal with single causes such as television violence or race relations.

The Confederation of British Industries is the chief representative organization of British business. As its name implies, its membership is large and varied. The Institute of Directors represents the highest-paid individuals at the top of large and small businesses. The largest British businesses usually have direct contacts with Whitehall and with ministers, whatever their party, because of the importance of these businesses' activities for the British economy and for its place in the international economy. For example, British Petroleum is one of the world's largest oil companies, and most of the oil it drills is found outside the United Kingdom. Government deems the success of such a company as important for national security, as well as for the national economy. The construction industry has access to government because home-building is important for the national economy, and Whitehall's tight control over land use influences where houses can be built.

The chief labor organization is the Trades Union Congress (TUC); its members are trade unions that represent many different types of workers, some white-collar and some blue-collar. Most member unions of the TUC are affiliated with the Labour Party, and some leading trade unionists have been Communists or Maoists. None has ever been a supporter of the Conservative Party.

Changes in employment patterns have eroded union membership; today only one-quarter of the labor force belongs to a trade union. Over the years the membership of trade unions has shifted from workers in such heavy industries as coal and railways to white-collar workers such as teachers and health service employees. Only one in six private-sector workers belongs to a trade union. By contrast, almost three-fifths of public-sector workers are union members. Elected representatives control their wages, and strikes or go-slow actions by teachers, hospital workers, or other public employees can cause political embarrassment to the government.

Britain has many voluntary and charitable associations, from clubs of football team supporters to the Automobile Association. It is also home to a number of internationally active nongovernmental organizations such as Oxfam, concerned with the problems of poor, developing countries, and Amnesty International, concerned with political prisoners. These nongovernmental organizations try to bring pressure not only on Westminster, but also on organizations such as the World Bank and on repressive governments around the world.

Unlike political parties, interest groups do not seek influence by contesting elections; they want to influence policies regardless of which party wins. Nonetheless, there are ties between interest groups and political parties. Trade unions have been institutionally part of the Labour Party since its foundation in 1900 and are the major source of party funds. The connection between business associations and the Conservatives is not formal, but the party's traditional commitment to private enterprise is congenial to business. Notwithstanding common interests, both trade unions and business groups demonstrate their autonomy by criticizing their party ally if it acts against the group's interest. Whichever party is in office, they seek to exercise influence.

Party politicians seek to distance themselves from interest groups. Conservatives know that they can win an election only by winning the votes of ordinary citizens, as well as prosperous businesspeople. Tony Blair sought to make the Labour government appear business friendly and reaped large cash donations from very wealthy businesspeople. However, this led union leaders to attack his government as unsympathetic, and a few small unions have left the Labour Party.

To lobby successfully, interest groups must be able to identify those officials most important in making public policy. They concentrate their efforts on Whitehall. When asked to rank the most influential offices and institutions, interest group officials named the prime minister first by a long distance; Cabinet ministers came second, the media third, and senior civil servants fourth (see Figure 5.5). Less than 1 percent thought MPs outside the ministerial ranks were of primary importance. However, interest groups do not expect to spend a lot of time at Downing Street. Most of their contacts are with officials within a government department concerned with issues of little public concern, but of immediate interest to the group.

What Interest Groups Want

Most interest groups pursue four goals:

1. Sympathetic administration of established policies
2. Information about government policies and changes in policies

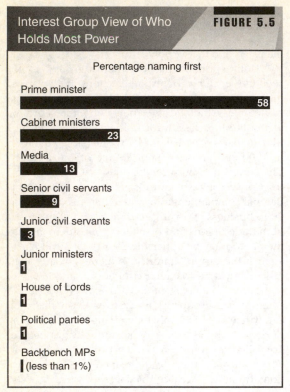

Source: Survey of officials of business, labor, and campaign groups, as reported in Rob Baggott, "The Measurement of Change in Pressure Group Politics," *Talking Points* 5, no. 1 (1992): 19.

3. Influence on policy making
4. Symbolic status, such as being given the prefix "Royal" in their title

Whitehall departments are happy to consult with interest groups insofar as they can provide government officials with reciprocal benefits:

1. Cooperation in administering and implementing policies
2. Information about what is happening in their field
3. Evaluation of the consequences of policies under consideration
4. Support for government initiatives

As long as the needs of Whitehall and interest groups are complementary, they can bargain as professionals sharing common concerns. Both sides are ready to arrive at a negotiated agreement.

Organizing for Political Action in Civil Society

The more committed members are to an interest group's goals, the more confidently leaders can speak for a united membership. Consumers are more difficult to organize because they have no social contacts with people who buy what they buy. Drivers of Ford cars are a category, rather than a social group. Changes in the economy, in class structure, and in the lifestyles of generations have resulted in a decline in the "dense" social capital networks of coal mining villages and textile mill towns. Individuals are now free to belong to a much wider range of institutions or to none.

Whitehall civil servants find it administratively convenient to deal with united interest groups that can implement agreements. But decades of attempts to plan the British economy demonstrate that business and union leaders cannot guarantee that their nominal followers will carry out bargains that leaders make. Group members who care about an issue can disagree, too, about what their leaders ought to do.

Individuals usually have a multiplicity of identities that are often in conflict—for example, as workers desiring higher wages and as consumers wanting lower prices. The spread of mass consumption and decline in trade union membership has altered the balance between these priorities. As a trade union leader has recognized, "Our members are consumers too."[30]

Even if a pressure or interest group is internally united, its demands may be counteracted by opposing demands from other groups. This is normally the case in economic policy, where interests are well defined, well organized, and competing. Ministers can play off producers against consumers or business against unions to increase their scope for choice and present their policies as "something for everybody" compromises.

The more a group's values are consistent with the cultural norms of society as a whole, the easier it is to equate its interest with the public interest. But in an open society such as Britain, the claims of one group to speak for the public interest can easily be challenged by competing groups. The centralization of authority in the British government means that interest groups must treat as given the political values and priorities of the governing party.

Insider pressure groups usually have values in harmony with every party. These groups are often noncontroversial, such as the Royal National Institute for the Blind. Insiders advance their case in quiet negotiations with Whitehall departments. Demands tend to be restricted to what is politically possible in the short term, given the values and commitments of the government of the day.[31]

Outsider pressure groups are unable to negotiate because their demands are inconsistent with the party in power. If their demands are inconsistent with the views of the Opposition as well, then outsider groups are completely marginalized. Outsider groups without any influence in Whitehall often campaign through the media. To television viewers their demonstrations appear as evidence of their importance; in fact, they are often signs of a lack of political influence. Green pressure groups face the dilemma of campaigning for fundamental change in hopes that eventually Whitehall departments will turn their way or of becoming insiders working within the system to improve the environment to some extent, but not as much as some ecologists would like.

Keeping Interest Groups at a Distance

For a generation after World War II, ministers endorsed the corporatist philosophy of bringing together business, trade unions, and political representatives in tripartite institutions to discuss such controversial issues as inflation, unemployment, and the restructuring of declining industries. Corporatist bargaining assumed that there was a consensus on political priorities and goals and that each group's leaders could deliver the cooperation of those they claimed to represent. In practice, neither Labour nor Conservative governments were able to maintain a consensus. Nor were interest group leaders able to deliver their nominal followers. By 1979 unemployment and inflation were both zooming upward out of control because government could not manage the national economy and trade union and business association leaders were unable to get their nominal followers to stick to agreements that their leaders had made with government.

The Thatcher administration demonstrated that a government firmly committed to distinctive values can ignore group demands and lay down its own pattern of policy. It did so by dealing at arm's length with both trade unions and business groups. Instead of consulting with interest groups, it practiced state-distancing, keeping the government out of everyday marketplace activities such as wage bargaining, pricing, and investment.

A state-distancing strategy concentrates on policies that government can implement without the agreement of interest groups. It emphasizes the use of legislation to achieve goals, since no interest group can defy an Act of Parliament. Laws have reduced the capacity of trade unions to frustrate government policies through industrial action. The sale of state-owned industries has removed government from immediate responsibility for the operation of major industries, and Labour Chancellor Gordon Brown transferred to the Bank of England responsibility for monetary policy.

State-distancing places less reliance on negotiations with interest groups and more on the authority of government. Business and labor are free to carry on as they like—but only within the pattern imposed by government legislation and policy. Most unions and some business leaders do not like being "outside the loop" when government makes decisions. Education and health service interest groups like it even less because they depend on government appropriations to fund their activities and cannot effectively turn to the market as an alternative source of revenue.

PARTY SYSTEM AND ELECTORAL CHOICE

British government is party government. A general election gives voters a choice of parties competing for the right to govern. Parties nominate parliamentary candidates and elect their leaders; one leader is the prime minister and the other leaders head Opposition parties.

A Multiplicity of Choices

A general election must occur at least once every five years; within that period the prime minister is free to call an election at any time. The most recent general election was held in May 2005; the next election is therefore due no later than Spring 2010. Although every prime minister tries to pick a date when victory is likely, often this aim is frustrated by events. The winner nationally is the party that gains the most MPs. In 1951 and in February 1974, the party winning the most votes nationally did not win the most seats; the runner-up party in the popular vote formed the government.

An election offers a voter a very simple choice between parliamentary candidates competing to represent a constituency in the House of Commons. Within each constituency the winner is the candidate who is first past the post—that is, the candidate who has a plurality (the largest number) of votes, even if this is less than half the vote.

If only two parties contest a constituency, the candidate with the most votes will have an absolute majority. But since at least three candidates now contest almost all of the 646 constituencies, a candidate can often win with less than half the vote, thanks to its division among multiple competitors. For example, in a hard-fought contest among four parties in Inverness in 1992, the Liberal Democrats won the seat with only 26 percent of the constituency vote.

Between 1945 and 1970, Britain had a two-party system; the Conservative and Labour parties together took an average of 91 percent of the popular vote and in 1951 as much as 97 percent (see Figure 5.6). The Liberals had difficulty fielding candidates to contest a majority of constituencies and even more difficulty winning votes and seats. Support for the two largest parties was evenly balanced; Labour won four elections and the Conservatives won four.

In a two-party system, the failure of one party tends to benefit its opponent. However, when both the largest parties are discredited, this gives other parties an opportunity to gain support. A **multiparty system** emerged in the elections of 1974. The Liberals won

nearly one-fifth of the vote, and nationalist parties did well in Scotland, Wales, and Northern Ireland. Together, the Conservative and Labour parties took only 75 percent of the vote. The Liberal Democratic and the nationalist parties have maintained their strength, as the results of the 2005 election show (see Table 5.5). The number of parties in the system today depends on the measure used.

1. The number of parties competing for votes varies from three to five in different parts of the United Kingdom. In England, three parties—the Labour, Conservative, and Liberal Democratic parties—compete for votes. In 2005 the United Kingdom Independence Party fought for a majority of seats, too, campaigning in opposition to the EU. In Scotland and Wales there are normally four parties, and the Scottish National and Plaid Cymru (Welsh Nationalist) parties elect MPs, too. In Northern Ireland at least five parties contest seats, two representing Unionist and Protestant voters, two Irish Republican and Catholic voters, and the weakest a cross-religious alliance of voters.

2. The two largest parties do not monopolize votes. Since 1974, the Conservative and Labour parties

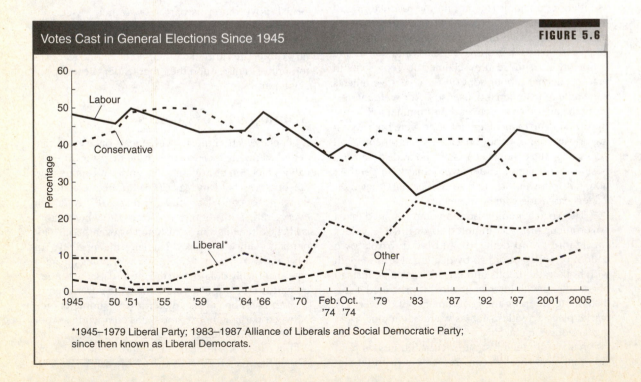

Votes Cast in General Elections Since 1945 FIGURE 5.6

*1945–1979 Liberal Party; 1983–1987 Alliance of Liberals and Social Democratic Party; since then known as Liberal Democrats.

The 2005 Election
Party vote percentages by nation in 2005

TABLE 5.5

	England	Scotland	Wales	Northern Ireland	United Kingdom
Labour	35.5	38.9	42.7	0	35.2
Conservative	35.7	15.8	21.4	0.1	32.4
Liberal Democratic	22.9	22.6	18.4	0	22.0
Nationalists*	0	17.7	12.6	93.3	4.6
Others	5.9	5.0	4.9	6.6	5.8

Source: *Colin Rallings and Michael Thrasher, ELECTION 2005: The Official Results. Plymouth LGC Elections Centre on behalf of the Electoral Commission, p. 178.* Official statistics.
*Scottish National Party; in Wales, Plaid Cymru; and in Northern Ireland, the Democratic Union and Ulster Unionist parties and the pro–Irish Republic Sinn Fein and Social Democratic and Labour Party.

together have won an average of three-quarters of the vote and in the 2005 election together gained just 67.6 percent of the total vote. No party has won half the popular vote since 1935.

3. The two largest parties in the House of Commons often are not the two leading parties at the constituency level. During the 2005 election in more than one-quarter of constituencies, one or both of the two front-running parties were neither Labour nor Conservative.

4. More than half a dozen parties consistently win seats in the House of Commons. In 2005 so-called third parties won 93 seats in the Commons.

5. Significant shifts in voting usually do not involve individuals moving between the Labour and Conservative parties, but in and out of the ranks of abstainers or between the Liberal Democrats and the two largest parties.

To win a substantial number of seats in the House of Commons, a party must either gain more than one-third of the popular vote nationally or concentrate its votes in a limited number of constituencies. For this reason the distribution of seats in the House of Commons is different from the distribution of the share of votes. In 2005 the Labour Party won more than 55 percent of the seats in the House of Commons with 35 percent of the popular vote (cf. Figures 5.6 and 5.7). The total vote for the Conservatives in England was actually higher than Labour's vote, but it won 92 fewer seats than Labour because more of its votes were where it finished second, whereas Labour candidates tended to come in either first or third.

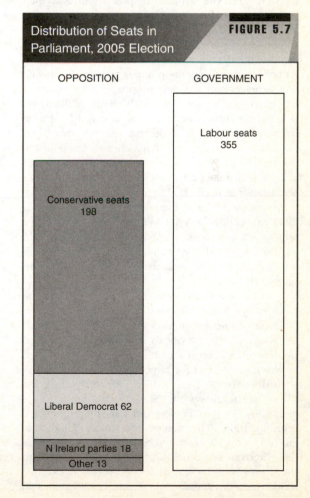

FIGURE 5.7

Distribution of Seats in Parliament, 2005 Election

OPPOSITION

GOVERNMENT

Labour seats
355

Conservative seats
198

Liberal Democrat 62

N Ireland parties 18

Other 13

Sitting in Opposition to the Labour government in the House of Commons are MPs whose parties have collectively won almost two-thirds of the popular vote. However, they have less than half the MPs because that vote is divided among more than eight different parties plus independents. Nationalist parties in Scotland, Wales, and Northern Ireland win seats because they concentrate their candidates in one part of the United Kingdom. Although the Liberal Democrats often win more than one-fifth of the popular vote, their support is spread relatively evenly across the country, making it far more likely that their candidates will finish second or third, rather than first.

The first-past-the-post electoral system manufactures a House of Commons majority for a party with two-fifths or less of the popular vote. Defenders of the British electoral system argue that proportionality is not a goal in itself. The first-past-the-post system is justified because it places responsibility for government in the hands of a single party. This justification is used in the United States, where the president can be described as representing all the people, whether he wins just over half or just under half the popular vote. In continental European countries, which use proportional representation, coalition or minority governments are the norm. When a coalition is necessary, a party finishing third in the popular vote can determine who governs by choosing the party that came in either second or first in the popular vote as its partner in creating a majority.

The strongest advocates of proportional representation are the Liberal Democrats. In a proportional representation system, the Liberal Democratic vote in 2005 would have given it 142 seats, more than twice what it actually received. A change is also supported by those who believe that a coalition government is a better government because it encourages a broad interparty consensus.

Successive British governments have altered the electoral system for contests that do not affect the composition of the Westminster Parliament.[32] All British Members of the European Parliament are elected by proportional representation, and it has been used in Northern Ireland for almost four decades. In the Scottish Parliament and the Welsh Assembly, there is a mixed electoral system: Some representatives are elected by first past the post and some by proportional representation. The mayor of Greater London is elected by the alternative vote, in which electors rank their candidates in order of preference and those with the fewest votes have their second preferences transferred to other candidates until one candidate has an absolute majority of preferences. The system for the Westminster Parliament remains unaltered because the decision about what kind of voting system to have is determined not by reasoning from abstract principles, but by the interests of the party that won power under the first-past-the-post system.

Political parties are often referred to as machines, but this description is very misleading, for parties cannot mechanically manufacture votes. Nor can they be commanded like an army. Parties are like universities; they are inherently decentralized, and people belong to them for a variety of reasons. Thus, party officials have to work hard to keep together three different parts of the party: those who vote for it, the minority active in its constituency associations, and the party in Parliament. If the party has a majority in Parliament, there is a fourth group, the party in government. Whether the party leader is the prime minister or the leader of the Opposition, he or she must maintain the confidence of all parts of the party or risk ejection as leader (see Box 5.5).

The headquarters of each party provides more or less routine organizational and publicity services to constituency parties and to the party in Parliament. Each party has an annual conference to debate policy and to vote on some policy resolutions. Constituency parties are nationally significant because each selects its own parliamentary candidate. The decentralization of the selection process has allowed the choice of parliamentary candidates with a wide variety of political outlooks and abilities. Under Tony Blair the Labour Party introduced more central direction in choosing candidates. It was justified on the grounds of promoting more women MPs by restricting the selection of the candidate in a safe Labour constituency to a short list consisting exclusively of women.

The Liberal Democrats have a small central organization; they have sought to build up the party's strength by winning council seats in local government elections. In parliamentary elections it targets seats where the party is strong locally. This strategy has paid off; it has more than tripled its number of MPs, from 20 in 1992 to 62 in 2005, while its share of the vote increased by only 0.5 percent. The candidates for leadership are nominated by Liberal MPs, and the leadership is determined by vote of the party's membership.

Party Images and Appeals

While the terminology of *left* and *right* is part of the language of elite politicians, it is rejected by the great majority of British voters. When asked to place themselves on a left-right scale, the median voter chooses

Electing and Ejecting a Party Leader

BOX 5.5

British voters decide which party has a majority in Parliament, while the majority party decides which of its MPs is its leader, and therefore prime minister. Opposition parties elect a leader in the hope that he or she will lead the party to election victory. The governing party wants its leader to win the next election, as well as the election that has given him or her office. If a party leader is unpopular and the party is trailing in opinion polls, MPs can try to eject their leader, even if he or she is prime minister.

A party leader is strongest when he or she is also prime minister. Constitutional principles and Cabinet patronage strengthen a prime minister's hand. Moreover, an open attack on a prime minister threatens electoral defeat as a result of conflict within the party. However, Margaret Thatcher lost the prime ministership by a vote of Conservative MPs in 1990. In 2006 Labour MPs were threatening to force a vote on Tony Blair's tenure if he did not leave office sooner rather than later. The following year Gordon Brown became unpopular and has faced demands to resign or be ejected after Labour began losing by-elections.

The Labour Party leadership is determined by an electoral college composed of three groups: Labour MPs, trade unions, and constituency party members. Each group has a very different number of members and method of deciding which candidate to back. In order to call a vote of confidence in a serving party leader, one-fifth of Labour MPs must sign a request for a vote on the leadership, and this must be endorsed by a party conference. This is difficult to achieve. If a vacancy results from the voluntary resignation of the leader or a resignation forced by Cabinet members calling for him or her to go, then there is an acting prime minister for several months while candidates compete for the party leadership.

Until 1965 the Conservative Party leader was not elected, but "emerged" as the result of consultation among senior MPs and members of the House of Lords. Since then the Conservatives have elected their leader in a two- or three-stage process. An election can be called if 15 percent of the party's MPs record their dissatisfaction in writing; their names are not supposed to be revealed. Alternatively, a leader can create a vacancy by resigning. Either way there is an initial ballot among Conservative MPs. The two MPs with the most votes are then voted on by the party membership at large, whose choice is decisive.

After Conservative Party members chose three leaders who were failures as vote-getters, it chose 39-year-old David Cameron in autumn 2005. They hoped that his youth would distance him from past Conservative defeats and his openness to change would appeal to middle-of-the-road voters needed for a Conservative election victory.

---

the central position, and only a tenth place themselves on the far left or far right. Consequently, parties that veer toward either extreme risk losing votes.

When public opinion is examined across a variety of issues, such as inflation, protecting the environment, spending money on the health service, and trade union legislation, a majority of Conservative, Labour, and Liberal Democratic voters tend to agree. Big divisions in contemporary British politics often cut across party lines; for example, attitudes toward the EU divide both Labour and Conservative MPs, and so has the Iraq War. Any attempt to impute a coherent ideology to a political party is doomed to failure, for institutions cannot think and are not organized to debate philosophy,

Instead of campaigning by promoting an ideology or by appealing to collectivist economic interests, increasingly parties stress consensual goals, such as promoting prosperity and fighting crime. They compete in terms of which party or party leader can best be trusted to do what people want or on the basis of whether it is time for a change because one party has been in office for a long time. The titles of election manifestos are virtually interchangeable between the Conservative and Labour parties. In 2005 one party's manifesto was entitled "It's Time for Action," and the other urged "Britain Forward not Back."[33]

In office the governing party has the votes to enact any parliamentary legislation it wishes, regardless of protests by the Opposition. However, most of the legislation introduced by the government is meant to be so popular, and often noncontroversial, that the Opposition dare not vote against the bill's principle. For every government bill that the Opposition votes against on principle in the House of Commons, three are adopted with interparty agreement.[34]

Most policies of government are not set out in party manifestos; they are inherited from predecessors of the same or a different party. When the Thatcher administration entered office in 1979, it inherited hundreds of programs enacted by preceding governments, including some on the statute books since 1760.[35] It repealed some programs inherited from its predecessors—and it repealed some of its own programs that were quickly recognized as mistakes. When Margaret Thatcher left office, two-thirds of the programs for which the government was responsible had been adopted before she had taken office 11 years earlier.

Prior to the 1997 general election, the Labour Party pledged that in its first term it would be prudent with public money, maintaining public expenditures at the same level as the Conservative government. Tony Blair initiated major measures to reform the delivery of public services in his second term. By the time Gordon Brown entered office in 2007, the legacy left behind by Blair—and by his own taxing and spending policies in a decade in the Treasury—made it difficult to come up with fresh policies.

The freedom of action of the governing party is limited by constraints embedded in the obligations of office. Once in office ministers find that all the laws enacted by their predecessors must be enforced, even if the government of the day would not have enacted them. A newly elected government also inherits many commitments to foreign countries and to the EU. As a former Conservative minister said of his Labour successors, "They inherited our problems and our remedies."[36]

CENTRALIZED AUTHORITY AND DECENTRALIZED DELIVERY OF GOVERNMENT POLICIES

In a unitary state, political authority is centralized. Decisions made by central government are binding on all public agencies through acts of Parliament and regulations prepared in Whitehall. In addition, Whitehall controls taxation and public expenditures to a degree unusual among other member states of the EU, where coalition government and federalism encourage decentralization.

For ordinary individuals the actions of government are tangible only when services are delivered locally at a school or a doctor's office or when rubbish is collected at their doorstep. However, Whitehall

departments usually do not deliver policies themselves. Most public goods and services are delivered by agencies headquartered outside Whitehall. Moreover, five-sixths of public employees work for non-Whitehall agencies.[37] Thus, making and delivering public policies involves *intra*governmental politics.

Whitehall

Running the *Whitehall obstacle race* is the first step in intragovernmental politics. Most new policies must take into account the effects of existing policies in a crowded policy "space." Before a bill can be put to Parliament, the Cabinet minister sponsoring it must determine with ministers in other departments how the new measure will affect existing programs and negotiate the terms of cooperation between departments to implement it. Such negotiations are time consuming. Often a department will begin work on a new initiative under one minister and complete it under another, or even under a different party in power.

The Treasury controls public expenditures. Before a bill can be put to Parliament, the Treasury must authorize the additional expenditure required because increased spending implies increased taxation. Ministers in charge of spending departments dislike constant Treasury reminders that there are strict limits on what they can spend. In the words of a veteran Treasury official, "the Treasury stands for reality."[38]

A minister anxious to gain attention by sponsoring a new policy must secure the approval of the prime minister's office before a bill can be put to Parliament. If the bill looks like it will produce favorable headlines and fit into Downing Street's overall strategy, it will be given a priority. Even if a measure is controversial, it can still go ahead as long as it will unite the governing party against attacks from Opposition parties and as long as public opinion will be on the government's side.

Once a bill becomes a law, there are many reasons why ministers do not want to be in charge of delivering services. Ministers may wish to avoid charges of political interference, allow for flexibility in the market, lend an aura of impartiality to quasi-judicial activities, allow qualified professionals to regulate technical matters, or remove controversial activities from Whitehall. The prime minister prefers to focus on the glamorous "high-level" politics of foreign affairs and economic management. However, since "low-level" services remain important to most voters' lives, ministers are under pressure to do something—or at least say something in response to media demands—when there is evidence of declining standards in schools, queues for hospital admission, or an increase of crime on the streets.

Local Government

Within England, *local government* is subordinate to central government. Westminster has the power to write or rewrite the laws that determine what locally elected governments do and spend—and even to abolish local authorities and create new units of government with different boundaries. Changes in local government boundaries have reflected a vain search to find a balance between efficiency (assumed to correlate with fewer councils delivering services to more people spread over a wider geographical area) and responsiveness (assumed to require more councils with a smaller territory and fewer people).

Local council elections are fought on party lines. In the days of the two-party system, many cities were solidly Labour for a generation or more, while leafy suburbs and agricultural counties were overwhelmingly Conservative. The Liberal Democrats now win many seats in local elections and, when no party has a majority, introduce coalition government into town halls. However, being a councillor is usually a part-time job.

The Blair government introduced the direct election of the mayor of Greater London, citing New York and Chicago as positive examples. However, it has refused to give London the independence in taxing and spending that large U.S. cities enjoy.[39] Nevertheless, the office is a political platform that attracts media attention. London's first mayor, a left-wing independent, and its second, a Conservative eccentric, used their legitimacy as elected officials to challenge the views of government at Westminster.

Local government is usually divided into two tiers of county and district councils, each with responsibility for some local services. The proliferation of public-private initiatives and special-purpose agencies has reduced the services for which local government is exclusively responsible. Today there is a jumble of more or less local institutions delivering such public services as education, police protection, refuse collection, housing, and cemeteries (see Box 5.6). Collectively, local institutions account for about a fifth of total public expenditures.

Delivering Public Services on the Doorstep   BOX 5.6

Government on the scale that the British people know it today could not exist if all its activities were concentrated in London, for five-sixths of the country's population lives elsewhere. As the demand for public services has increased, government has grown, chiefly through the multiplication of familiar institutions such as schools and hospitals. Devolution to Scotland and Wales has added to decentralization.

Education is an example of how different institutions relate. It is authorized by an Act of Parliament and principally financed by central government. Two Cabinet ministers divide responsibility: One is responsible for schools and another for universities. Both are Members of Parliament. However, the delivery of primary and secondary education is the responsibility of classroom teachers who are immediately accountable to the head of their school and not to Parliament. Dissatisfaction with the management of schools by local government has led Whitehall to establish city academies, secondary schools independent of local government, but dependent on Whitehall for funding.

Increasingly, central government seeks to monitor the performance of schools in nationwide examinations and set targets that teachers and pupils are expected to achieve. But since the Whitehall department responsible for schools employs only 1 percent of the people working in education, success depends on actions taken by others. Conservative Minister of Education Lord Hailsham contrasted his position with that of a defense minister: As the latter, "You say to one person 'come' and he cometh and another 'go' and he goeth"; with the former, "You say to one man 'come' and he cometh not, and another 'go' and he stays where he is."

Sources: *See Richard Rose, "The Growth of Government Organizations," in C. Campbell and B. G. Peters, eds., *Organizing Government, Governing Organizations* (Pittsburgh, PA: University of Pittsburgh Press, 1988), pp. 99–128. Lord Hailsham is quoted in Maurice Kogan, *The Politics of Education* (Harmondsworth: England: Penguin, 1971), p. 31.

Grants of money from the central government are the largest source of local government revenue. There is no local income tax, since the central government does not want to give local authorities the degree of fiscal independence that U.S. local governments have. The Thatcher government replaced the local property tax with a poll tax on every adult resident of a local authority, believing it would make voters more aware of the costs of local government and keep spending down. In practice, the tax produced a political backlash and was replaced by a community charge (tax) on housing, which the central government tends to control.[40] How to fund services that the local government delivers remains a contentious issue.

Centralization is justified in terms of **territorial justice**—that is, the same standards of public policy ought to apply everywhere in the country. For example, schools in inner cities and rural areas should have the same resources as schools in prosperous suburbs. This can be achieved only if tax revenues collected by the central government are redistributed from well-to-do to poorer parts of the country. In addition, ministers emphasize that they are accountable to a national electorate of tens of millions of people, whereas local councillors are accountable only to those who vote in their ward. Instead of small being beautiful, a big nationwide electorate is assumed to be better. The centralist bias of Westminster is illustrated by the statement of an activist law professor: "Local councillors are not necessarily political animals; we could manage without them."

Devolution to Scotland, Wales, and Northern Ireland is an extreme form of **decentralization.** Westminster delegates authority in different measures to elected assemblies. The Scottish government, accountable to a Parliament in Edinburgh, has the right to enact legislation on a broad range of social and public services of direct concern to individuals and communities, such as education, health, and roads. It is also responsible for determining spending priorities within the limits set by its block grant of money from the British Treasury. With the Scottish National Party in government, it has political incentives to challenge the authority of Westminster. The Welsh Assembly has administrative discretion, but no legislative or taxing powers. Northern Ireland is exceptional because the key service is police and security—and this is being kept under the control of British ministers until agreement is achieved under a power-sharing government that includes participants active in organizing its decades of civil war.

Nonelected Institutions

Executive agencies are headed by nonelected officials responsible for delivering many major public services. The largest, the National Health Service (NHS), is not one organization, but a multiplicity of separate institutions with separate budgets, such as hospitals and doctors' offices. Access to the NHS is free of charge to every citizen. But health care is not costless. Public money is allocated to hospitals and to doctors and dentists that must work to guidelines and targets established centrally. Because the central government picks up the bill, the Treasury, as the monopoly purchaser, regularly seeks to cut costs in providing increasingly expensive health care.

Public demand for more and better health care has increased with the aging of the population and the development of new forms of medical treatment. The government's rationing of the health care supply has led to lengthening queues, involving months of waiting before a person can see a medical specialist or have a hospital operation. British government has sought to deal with this problem through administrative changes intended to increase efficiency—that is, measures that will keep the total health care expenditure relatively constant by cutting the cost of individual services, while expanding the total number supplied. It has not adopted the practice common in most EU countries of asking patients to make a co-payment to cover part of the cost of seeing a doctor or getting hospital treatment.

British government sponsors more than a thousand **quasi-autonomous nongovernmental organizations (quangos)**. All are created by an Act of Parliament or by an executive decision; their heads are appointed by a Cabinet minister, and public money can be appropriated to finance their activities. Some quangos deliver services. When things go wrong, Parliament has difficulty assigning responsibility for decisions. Advisory committees draw on the expertise of individuals and organizations involved in programs for which Whitehall departments are nominally responsible. Ministry of Agriculture officials can turn to advisory committees for detailed information about farming practices; the department responsible for trade and industry can turn to business associations for information about a particular industry. Because they have no executive powers, advisory committees usually cost very little to run. Representatives of interest groups are glad to serve on such committees because this gives them privileged access to Whitehall and an opportunity to influence policies in which they are directly interested.

Administrative tribunals are quasi-judicial bodies that make expert judgments in such fields as medical negligence or handle small claims, such as disputes about whether the rent set for a rent-controlled flat is fair. Ministers may use tribunals to avoid involvement in politically controversial issues, such as decisions about deporting immigrants. Tribunals normally work much more quickly and cheaply than do the courts. However, the quasi-judicial role of tribunals has created a demand for independent auditing of their procedures to ensure that they are fair to all sides. The task of supervising some seventy tribunals is in the hands of a quango, the Council on Tribunals.

Turning to the Market

The 1945–1951 Labour government turned away from the market because its socialist leaders believed that government planning was better able to promote economic growth and full employment. It nationalized many basic industries, such as electricity, gas, coal, railways, and airlines. State ownership meant that industries did not have to run at a profit; some consistently made money, while others consistently lost money and required big subsidies. Government ownership politicized wage negotiations and investment decisions.

The Thatcher government promoted privatization by selling shares of nationalized industries on the stock market. Profit-making industries such as telephones, electricity, and gas were sold without difficulty. Selling council houses to tenants at prices well below their market value was popular with tenants. Industries that were losing money, such as British Airways, British Steel, and the coal mines, had to be reorganized, and unprofitable activities were shed to make them attractive to buyers. Industries needing large public subsidies to maintain public services, such as the railways, have continued to receive subsidies after privatization.

Privatization has been justified on grounds of economic efficiency (the market is better than civil servants at determining investment, production, and prices), political ideology (the power of government is reduced), service (private enterprise is more consumer oriented than are civil servants), and short-term financial gain (the sale of public assets can provide billions in revenue for government). Although the Labour Party initially opposed privatization, it quickly realized it would be electorally disastrous to take back privatized council houses and shares that people had bought at bargain prices.

Since many privatized industries affect the public interest, new regulatory agencies have been established to monitor telephones, gas, electricity, broadcasting, and water. Where there is a substantial element of monopoly in an industry, the government regulatory agency seeks to promote competition and often has the power to fix price increases at a lower rate than inflation. Even though it no longer owns an industry, government ministers cannot ignore things that go wrong. As an extreme example of government intervention, when several fatal accidents occurred on railway track maintained by a privatized transport company, the Blair government took it back into public ownership.

From Trust to Contract

Historically, the British civil service has relied on trust in delivering policies. British civil servants are much less rule bound than are their German counterparts and less threatened with being dragged into court than are U.S. officials. Intragovernmental relations between Whitehall departments and representatives of local authorities were characterized by consensual understandings upheld by all sides on the basis of trust as well as law. However, the Thatcher government preferred to constrain local government through its use of law and its control of finance and to promote competition by establishing new agencies or contracting for public services with private-sector companies. Since 1997 the Labour government has continued this practice and has intensified the use of targets that agencies receiving public money should meet.

Trust has been replaced by contracts with agencies delivering such everyday services as automobile licenses and patents. In addition, the government has sought to keep capital expenditures from visibly increasing public debt through private finance initiatives. Banks and other profit-making companies loan money to build facilities that will be leased by government agencies or even operated by profit-making companies. The theory is that government can obtain the greatest value for its money by buying services from the private sector, ranging from operating staff canteens in government offices to providing prison services. However, the government's experience with cost overruns and failure to meet targets for information technology services costing hundreds of millions of pounds indicates that government officials often lack the skills to negotiate procurement contracts for large purchases involving expensive technology.

Government by contract faces political limits because departmental ministers must answer to Parliament when something goes wrong. The Prison Service is a textbook example. It was established as an executive agency separate from Whitehall in 1993 to bring in private management to reduce unit costs in the face of a rising "demand" for prisons brought about by changes in crime rates and sentencing policies. However, when prisoners escaped and other problems erupted, the responsible Cabinet minister blamed the business executive brought in to head the Prison Service. The Prison Service head replied by attacking the minister's refusal to live up to the terms of the contract agreed to between them.

The proliferation of agencies, each with a distinctive and narrow responsibility for a limited number of policies, tends to fragment government. For example, parents may have to deal with half a dozen different agencies to secure all the public services to which they are entitled for their children. Tony Blair promoted "joined up" government, linking the provision of related services so that they could more easily be received by individual citizens. To many public agencies, this looked like a device to increase Downing Street's power. In fact, it had little effect and demonstrated the limits that result when a few dozen people at Downing Street determine what is done by millions of people delivering public services.

The Contingency of Influence

The theory of British government is centralist: All roads lead to Downing Street, where the prime minister and the chancellor of the Exchequer have their homes and offices. The Foreign Office and the Treasury are only a few steps away. In practice, policy making occurs in many buildings, some within Whitehall and others far from London. Those involved can be divided horizontally between ministries and executive agencies and vertically between central government and local authorities and other nondepartmental public bodies that deliver particular services.

Influence is contingent: It varies with the problem at hand. Decisions about war and peace are made at Downing Street by the highest-ranking political and military officials. With respect to the decision to support the Iraq War, the prime minister's media advisor was also heavily involved. By contrast, the decisions as to whether a particular piece of land should be used for housing is normally made by local authorities far from London.

Most political decisions involve two or more government agencies and therefore require discussion and bargaining before decisions can be implemented. The making of policy is constrained by disputes within government much more than by differences between the governing party and its opponents. Many tentacles of the octopus of government work against each other, as public agencies often differ in their definition of the public interest. For example, the Treasury wants to keep taxes down, while the Ministry of Defence wants more money for expensive equipment.

While the center of central government has been pressing harder on other public agencies, Whitehall itself has been losing influence because of its obligations in the EU. The Single Europe Act promotes British exports, but it also increases the potential for EU decisions to regulate the British economy. Whitehall has adopted a variety of strategies in its EU negotiations, including noncooperation and public dispute. Ironically, these are just the tactics that local government and executive agencies use when they disagree with Whitehall.

WHY PUBLIC POLICY MATTERS

However a citizen votes, she or he does not need to look far to see the outputs of government. If there is a school-age child or a pensioner in the house, the benefits to the family are continuous and visible. If a person is ill, the care provided by doctors and hospitals is an important output of public policy; so, too, are police protection and tight controls on land use that maintain green belts and reduce suburban sprawl around cities.

To produce the benefits of public policy, government relies on three major resources: laws, money, and personnel. Most policies involve a combination of these resources, but they do not do so equally. Policies regulating individual behavior, such as marriage and divorce, are law intensive; measures that pay benefits to millions of people, such as social security, are money intensive; and public services, such as health care, are labor intensive.

Laws are the unique resource of government, for private enterprises cannot enact binding laws and contracts are effective only if they can be enforced by courts. The British executive centralizes the power to draft laws and regulations that can be approved without substantial amendment by Parliament. Moreover, many laws give ministers significant discretion in administration. For example, an employer may be required to provide "reasonable" toilet facilities, rather than having all features of lavatories specified down to the size and height of a toilet seat.

Public employees are needed to administer laws and deliver major services. The number of people officially counted as civil servants and public employees has been reduced by privatization. Nonetheless, more than a fifth of the entire British labor force depends on public spending for their jobs. The largest public employer is the National Health Service. The top civil servants who work in Whitehall are few in number.

To meet the costs of public policy, British government collects almost two-fifths of the gross national product in taxation. Income tax accounts for 29 percent of tax revenue; the top rate of taxation is 40 percent. Social security taxes are paid by deductions from wages and additional contributions of employers; these account for an additional 19 percent of revenue. Since there are no state or local income taxes, a well-to-do British person can pay taxes on income at a lower total rate than does an American subject to federal, state, and local taxation in New York City.

Taxes on consumption are important, too. There is a value-added tax of 17.5 percent on the sale of almost all goods and services. Gasoline, cigarettes, and alcohol are taxed very heavily, too. Taxes on consumption in total account for one-quarter of all tax revenue. Since profits fluctuate from year to year, the government prefers businesses to pay taxes on their gross revenues through a value-added tax and on their total wages bill through the employer's contribution to social security. Taxes on the profits of corporations provide under a tenth of tax revenue. Additional revenue comes from "stealth" taxes that ordinary citizens rarely notice and from taxes that do cause complaints, such as the council tax on houses. The government also raises money by taking a big

cut from the National Lottery; more people play the lottery than vote in a general election.

Social security programs are the most costly government policies; they account for more than one-third of total public expenditures (Figure 5.8). They are also the most popular, transferring money from government to more than 10 million older people receiving pensions, plus millions of invalids, the unemployed, women on maternity leave, and poor people needing to supplement their limited incomes. Health and education are second and third, respectively, in their claims on the public purse. Together, these three social welfare programs account for two-thirds of total public expenditures. A classic commitment of government—providing defense and maintaining public order and safety through the police, fire service, courts, and prisons—is fourth in spending importance.

Since there is no item in the public budget labeled as "waste," any government wanting to make a big cut in public spending must squeeze existing programs—and big savings can be made only by squeezing popular programs. But doing so would go against public opinion. When Margaret Thatcher entered office in 1979, the public divided into three almost equal groups: those wanting to spend more and tax more, those wanting to cut taxes even if it meant a reduction in public services, and a large middle group wanting to leave things as they were. Thatcher's campaign to cut taxes and public spending initially produced a reaction in favor of increasing public expenditure. By the time she left office, a majority favored increased spending even if it meant increased taxes. However, since a Labour government took office in 1997, the pendulum has swung back to an almost equal division between those who want to cut taxes and spending and those who want to increase both, with the median group wanting to keep both as they are (Figure 5.9).

Policy Outcomes in Society

Public policies are meant to influence how people live, but only a totalitarian government would claim responsibility for everything that happens in society. In an open society such as Britain, social conditions reflect the interaction of public policies, the national and international economy, the not-for-profit institutions of civil society, and the choices that individuals and households make. Thus, the term *welfare state* is misleading to the extent that it implies that

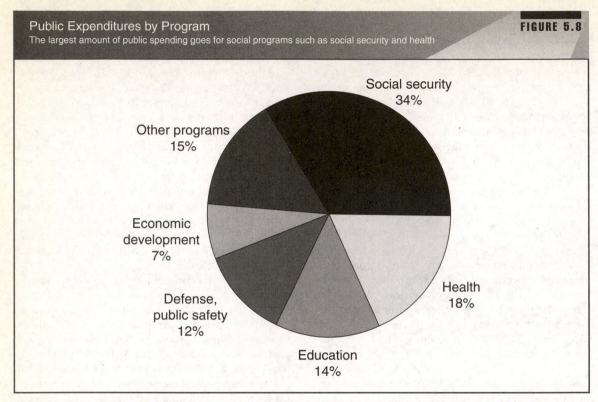

Public Expenditures by Program
The largest amount of public spending goes for social programs such as social security and health

FIGURE 5.8

Social security
34%

Other programs
15%

Economic
development
7%

Defense,
public safety
12%

Education
14%

Health
18%

Source: Her Majesty's Treasury, *Public Expenditure Statistical Analyses 2008*. London: Stationery Office, HC 489, Table 5.1.

the state is the exclusive supplier of welfare. Total welfare in society is the sum of a "welfare mix," combining actions of government, the market, and the nonmonetized production of welfare in the household.[41]

Although commentators on British society often bemoan the country's decline relative to the much more populous United States and to continental European countries that have experienced dynamic economies, ordinary people do not compare their lives with those of people in other countries. The most important comparison is with their own past. Evaluating change across time shows great improvements in the living conditions of most people, as compared with their parents or grandparents. The longer the time span, the greater the improvement. Furthermore, in the production of such political "goods" as freedom from the state, confidence in the honesty of public officials, and administrative flexibility, British government remains an international leader. The great majority of people are proud of the

achievements of Britain and would not want to be citizens of any other country.

Defending the population against threats to security at home and abroad is a unique responsibility of government. In an interdependent world, British government participates in international alliances. Since World War II it has been a founding member of the North Atlantic Treaty Organization and has fought alongside the United States from the Korean War to the Iraq War. Maintaining order within the United Kingdom is a unique responsibility of Westminster. In Northern Ireland Whitehall has created a power-sharing government after very lengthy negotiations with Irish Republicans about giving up the use of arms.[42]

Since terrorist attacks by jihadists in London in 2005, the British government has pursued a multiplicity of measures in an attempt to identify, isolate, and, as appropriate, arrest and jail those planning violence. One strategy has been to encourage moderate Muslim groups to engage in the "self-policing" of

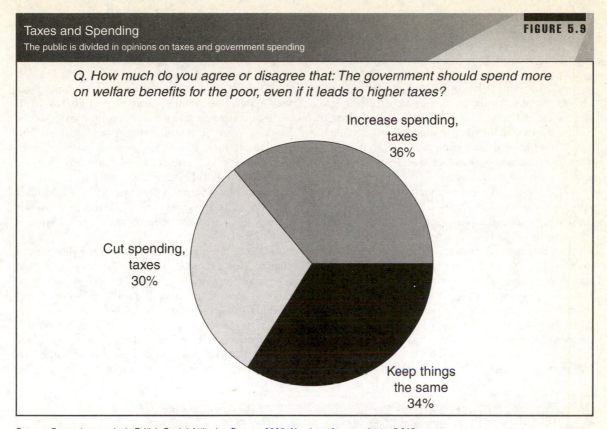

Taxes and Spending

FIGURE 5.9

The public is divided in opinions on taxes and government spending

Q. How much do you agree or disagree that: The government should spend more on welfare benefits for the poor, even if it leads to higher taxes?

- Increase spending, taxes 36%
- Keep things the same 34%
- Cut spending, taxes 30%

Source: Secondary analysis British Social Attitudes Survey, 2006. Number of respondents: 2,812.

their communities. Another has been to maintain surveillance on individuals and groups voicing fanatical opinions, including the endorsement of violence. A third has been to use extraordinary police powers to arrest and interrogate suspects.

Conservative as well as Labour governments accept responsibility for the economy. Most firms are profit-making, consumers can spend money as they like, and wages and prices are principally decided in the marketplace. Government influences the market through taxing and spending policies, interest rates, and policies on growth and unemployment. Increasingly, what happens to the British economy is also influenced by what happens elsewhere in the EU and on other continents, too, for British government cannot isolate the country from the global economy.

In each decade since World War II, the British economy has grown; compounding a small annual rate of growth over many decades results in a large rise in living standards. Per capita national income has more than tripled since 1945. Many consumer goods that were once thought of as luxuries—such as owning a car or a home or spending holidays abroad—are now mass-consumption goods. In addition, things unknown in 1945—such as color televisions, home computers, and mobile phones—are now commonplace. In the past decade the British economy has grown by one-third. Its growth rate has been higher than the average for the EU and for the G–7 nations.

Poverty can be found in Britain; the extent depends on the definition used. If poverty is defined in relative terms, such as having less than half the average wage, then about 10 percent of Britons are living in relative poverty. If poverty is defined as being trapped at a low income level for many years, then less than 4 percent are long-term poor.

Looking at all the major indicators of social well-being, the British people enjoy a higher standard of living today than they did a generation or two ago. Infant mortality has declined by more than four-fifths since 1951. Life expectancy for men and for women has risen by 12 years. A gender gap remains, as women on average live five years longer than men. The postwar expansion of schools has significantly raised the quantity of education available. Classes are smaller in size, and almost half of British youths go on to some form of further education, whether in universities or colleges, many of which did not exist in 1950. More than two-thirds of families now own their own home, and nine-tenths report satisfaction with their housing.

The outputs of public policy play a significant part in the everyday life of all Britons. Everyone makes major use of publicly financed health and education services. Children at school and patients seeing a doctor do not think of themselves as participating in politics. Yet, the services received are controlled and paid for by government. Social benefits such as free education, free health care, and the guarantee of an income in old age or during unemployment are so taken for granted today that most people see them as nonpolitical. People do not want a change in government after an election to result in radical changes in major social policies.

British people do not hold government responsible for what is most important in their lives; life satisfaction is evaluated very differently from public policy. When opinion polls annually ask what people think next year will be like for themselves and their family, nine-tenths of the time a majority say they expect the coming year to be all right for themselves, even when many expect economic difficulties for the country as a whole. When people are asked to evaluate their lives, they are most satisfied with their family, friends, home, and job and least satisfied with major political institutions of society.[43]

Satisfaction with the present goes along with acceptance of the principle of political change. However, even when a goal is agreed on, there are differences about the particular policy that can best achieve that goal. There are disagreements about the direction of change—for example, whether Westminster should take more responsibility for public services or devolve more responsibilities to regions and municipalities, and whether Britain should align itself more closely with the United States or with the EU. Politics in Britain is thus an ongoing debate about the direction, the means, and the tempo of adapting old institutions and inherited policies to the twenty-first century.

REVIEW QUESTIONS

- How would you describe the unwritten constitution of Britain?
- What are the similarities and differences between being a president and being a prime minister?
- How many nations are there in the United Kingdom, and what are they?
- What are the continents and countries with which Britain has the closest links?

- How would you describe the different parties that have seats in the House of Commons?
- What policies claim the largest portion of public expenditures and why?
- What will be the main challenges facing the winning government after the next general election?

KEY TERMS

Cabinet
centralization
class
collectivist theory of government
Conservative Party
core executive

Crown
decentralization
devolution
Downing Street
first-past-the-post electoral system
government

individualist theory
insider and outsider pressure groups
Irish Republican Army (IRA)
Labour Party
Liberal Democratic Party

multiparty system
New Labour Party
Northern Ireland
official secrecy
Parliament
prime minister
privatization

quasi-autonomous nongovernmental organization (quango)	territorial justice	United Kingdom	Westminster
	Thatcherism	unwritten constitution	Whitehall
	trusteeship theory of government	Wales	
Scotland			

SUGGESTED READINGS

Bache, Ian, and Andrew Jordan, eds. *The Europeanization of British Politics*. Basingstoke, England: Palgrave Macmillan, 2006.

Butler, D. E., and Geraint Butler. *British Political Facts Since 1979*. Basingstoke, England: Palgrave Macmillan, 2006.

_____. *Twentieth Century British Political Facts, 1900–2000*. 8th ed. Basingstoke, England: Macmillan, 2000.

Flinders, Matthew. *The Politics of Accountability in the Modern State*. Aldershot, England: Ashgate, 2001.

Hazell, Robert, ed. *The English Question*. London: Constitution Unit, 2006.

Ingle, Stephen. *The British Party System*. 4th ed. London: Routledge, 2008.

Jordan, Grant, and William A. Maloney. *Democracy and Interest Groups*. Basingstoke, England: Palgrave Macmillan, 2007.

Kavanagh, Dennis, and David Butler. *The British General Election of 2005*. Basingstoke, England: Palgrave Macmillan., 2005

McGarvey, Neil, and Paul Cairney. *Scottish Politics: An Introduction*. Basingstoke, England: Palgrave Macmillan, 2008.

Moran, Michael. *The British Regulatory State: High Modernism and Hyper-Innovation*. New York: Oxford University Press, 2003.

Norris, Pippa, and Joni Lovenduski. *Political Recruitment: Gender, Race, and Class in the British Parliament*. New York: Cambridge University Press, 1995.

Norris, Pippa, and Christopher Wlezien, eds. *Britain Votes 2005*. Oxford, England: Oxford University Press, 2005.

Oliver, Dawn. *Constitutional Reform in the United Kingdom*. New York: Oxford University Press, 2003.

Page, Edward C., and Bill Jenkins. *Policy Bureaucracy: Government with a Cast of Thousands*. Oxford, England: Oxford University Press, 2005.

Park, Alison, ed. *British Social Attitudes Survey: The 24th Report*. Thousand Oaks, CA: Sage, 2008.

Pattie, Charles, Patrick Seyd, and Paul Whitely. *Citizenship in Britain*. New York: Cambridge University Press, 2004.

Rallings, Colin, and Michael Thrasher. *British Electoral Facts, 1832–2006*. Aldershot, England: Ashgate, 2007.

Rose, Richard. *The Prime Minister in a Shrinking World*. Boston: Polity Press, 2001.

Rose, Richard, and Phillip L. Davies. *Inheritance in Public Policy: Change Without Choice in Britain*. New Haven, CT: Yale University Press, 1994.

Seldon, Anthony. *Blair*. New York: Free Press, 2004.

Seldon, Anthony, Peter Seldon, and Daniel Collings. *Blair Unbound*. New York: Simon & Schuster, 2007.

Smith, Martin J. *The Core Executive in Britain*. London: Macmillan, 1999.

Social Trends. London: Stationery Office, annual.

Whitaker's Almanack. London: J. Whitaker, annual.

Wilson, David, and Game, Chris. *Local Government in the United Kingdom*. 4th ed. Basingstoke, England: Palgrave Macmillan, 2007.

INTERNET RESOURCES

Site of British government departments. **www.gov.uk.**

Site of the House of Commons and of the House of Lords. **www.parliament.uk.**

Prime Minister's site. **www.pm.gov.uk.**

Comprehensive coverage of United Kingdom and global news. **www.news.bbc.co.uk.**

Commentaries on current proposals to reform government. **www.ucl.ac.uk/constitution-unit.**

Reports results of its frequent public opinion polls. **www.ipsos-mori.com/polls.**

Official site of the Political Studies Association, the professional body of British political scientists. **www.psa.ac.uk.**

ENDNOTES

1. See Richard Rose, *What Is Europe? A Dynamic Perspective* (New York: Addison Wesley Longman, 1996), ch. 3.

2. *Gallup Political and Economic Index* (London) no. 390 (February 1993): 42.

3. Quoted in Krishna Guha, "Labour Escapes from Its Bloody Tower," *Financial Times,* August 24, 2002.

4. Quoted in John Kampfner and David Wighton, "Reeling in Scotland to Bring England in Step," *Financial Times,* April 5, 1997.

5. See Richard Rose, "England: A Traditionally Modern Political Culture," in *Political Culture and Political Development,* ed. Lucian W. Pye and Sidney Verba (Princeton, NJ: Princeton University Press, 1965), pp. 83–129.

6. Quoted in Richard Rose, *Do Parties Make a Difference?* 2nd ed. (Chatham, NJ: Chatham House, 1984), p. xv.

7. Andrew Dilnot and Paul Johnson, eds., Election Briefing 1997 (Commentary 60) (London: Institute for Fiscal Studies, 1997), p. 2.

8. John Kampfner and David Wighton, "Blair Seals Labour's Switch to Low Tax Party," *Financial Times,* March 27, 1997.

9. Quoted in Peter Hennessy, "Raw Politics Decide Procedure in Whitehall," *New Statesman* (London), October 24, 1986, p. 10.

10. Winston Churchill, *Their Finest Hour* (London: Cassell, 1949), p. 14.

11. See Richard Rose, *The Prime Minister in a Shrinking World* (Boston: Polity Press, 2001), fig. 6.1.

12. Lord Butler of Brockwell, quoted in George Jones, "Blair Savaged on Spin," *Daily Telegraph* (London) December 11, 2004.

13. For transatlantic comparisons of presidents and prime ministers, see Richard Rose, "Giving Direction to Government in Comparative Perspective," in *The Executive Branch,* ed. Joel Aberbach and Mark A. Peterson (New York: Oxford University Press, 2005), pp. 72–99.

14. Walter Bagehot, *The English Constitution* (London: World's Classics, 1955), p. 9.

15. David Leppard and Robert Winnett, "Blair Blames Ministers for Policy Gaffes," *Sunday Times* (London), April 18, 2004.

16. Careers in the Civil Service. London: First Division Association, 1987, p. 12.

17. Quoted by David Leppard, "ID Cards Doomed, Say Officials," *Sunday Times* (London), July 9, 2006. See also an interview with Sir Robin Butler, "How Not to Run a Country," *Spectator* (London), December 11, 2004.

18. Quoted in "Whitehall Remains Closed to Outsiders and Needs Radical Change, Report Says," *Times* (London), August 7, 2006.

19. Eric Varley, quoted in A. Michie and S. Hoggart, *The Pact* (London: Quartet Books, 1978), p. 13.

20. Hugh Heclo and Aaron Wildavsky, *The Private Government of Public Money* (London: Macmillan, 1974).

21. Bernard Ingham, press secretary to Margaret Thatcher, quoted in Richard Rose, "British Government: The Job at the Top," in *Presidents and Prime Ministers,* ed. R. Rose and E. Suleiman (Washington, DC: American Enterprise Institute, 1980), p. 43.

22. See Samuel H. Beer, *Modern British Politics,* 3rd ed. (London: Faber and Faber, 1982).

23. House of Commons, *Hansard* (London: Her Majesty's Stationery Office), November 11, 1947, col. 206.

24. The words of former Conservative Prime Minister John Major, "The Threat to Liberty Is Graver than Terrorism," Times (London), June 6, 2008.

25. Colin Bennett, "From the Dark to the Light: The Open Government Debate in Britain," *Journal of Public Policy* 5, no. 2 (1985): 209.

26. Quoted in Sean O'Neill, "Too Sensitive to Reveal, Minister," *Times* (London), October 3, 2005.

27. See Richard Rose and Ian McAllister, *The Loyalties of Voters* (Newbury Park, CA: Sage, 1990), ch. 3.

28. Quoted in Maurice Kogan, *The Politics of Education* (Harmondsworth, England: Penguin, 1971), p. 135.

29. See the Fulton Committee, Report, vol. 1, pp. 27ff., and Appendix E, especially p. 162.

30. Sir Ken Jackson, quoted in Krishna Guha, "Engineers and Electricians Turn Away from Moderate Traditions," *Financial Times,* July 19, 2002.

31. See W. A. Maloney, G. Jordan, and A. M. McLaughlin, "Interest Groups and Public Policy: The Insider/Outsider Model Revisited," *Journal of Public Policy* 14, no. 1 (1994): 17–38.

32. See Ministry of Justice, *Review of Voting Systems* (Cm. 7304) (London: Stationery Office, 2008).

33. The Conservative Party used the first title and the Labour Party the second.

34. For details, see Denis Van Mechelen and Richard Rose, *Patterns of Parliamentary Legislation* (Aldershot, England: Gower, 1986), tab. 5.2, and more generally, Rose, *Do Parties Make a Difference?*

35. Richard Rose and Phillip L. Davies, *Inheritance in Public Policy: Change Without Choice in Britain* (New Haven, CT: Yale University Press, 1994), p. 28.

36. Reginald Maudling, quoted in David Butler and Michael Pinto-Duschinsky, *The British General Election of 1970* (London: Macmillan, 1971), p. 62.

37. See *Better Government Services: Executive Agencies in the 21st Century* (London: Office of Public Service Reforms and the Treasury, 2002).

38. Sir Leo Pliatzky, quoted in Peter Hennessy, "The Guilt of the Treasury 1000," *New Statesman* (London), January 23, 1987.

39. See Paul Peterson, "The American Mayor: Elections and Institutions," *Parliamentary Affairs* 53, no. 4 (2000): 667–679.

40. David Butler, Andrew Adonis, and Tony Travers, *Failure in British Government: The Politics of the Poll Tax* (Oxford, England: Oxford University Press, 1994).

41. See Richard Rose, "The Dynamics of the Welfare Mix in Britain," in *The Welfare State East and West,* ed. Richard Rose and Rei Shiratori (New York: Oxford University Press, 1986), pp. 80–106.

42. Jonathan Powell, *Great Hatred, Little Room: Making Peace in Northern Ireland* (London: Bodley Head, 2008).

43. Richard Rose, *Ordinary People in Public Policy: A Behavioural Analysis* (Newbury Park, CA: Sage, 1989), pp. 175ff.

POLITICS IN FRANCE

Martin A. Schain

Country Bio

Population
63.8 million

Territory
211,208 square miles

Year of Independence
486

Year of Current Constitution
1958

Head of State
President Nicolas Sarkozy

Head of Government
Prime Minister François Fillon

Language
French 100%, with rapidly declining regional dialects (Provença, Breton, Alsatian, Corsican, Catalan, Basque, Flemish)

Religion
Roman Catholic 89.5%, Muslim 7.5%, Protestant 2%, Jewish 1

FRANCE

Attracted by his dynamic image and promises of reform, a large majority of the French public elected Nicolas Sarkozy to the presidency of France in May 2007. A month later Sarkozy's party won a majority in the National Assembly, and he followed the election with a whirlwind of activities and initiatives. Two years later, however, as the economic crisis spread, Sarkozy's approval rating was as low as that of his predecessor, **Jacques Chirac**, and he was struggling to maintain the loyalty of his own majority.

The French electorate has been highly critical of those who have governed them under the **Fifth Republic.** In every legislative election between 1981 and 2007, they have favored the opposition. Nevertheless, French citizens now appear to have more confidence in the key institutions of the Republic than at any time in French history. Increasingly, however, they have little confidence in the politicians who are running them. The stability of the Republic

has surprised many of the French, as well as the outside world. By combining two models of democratic government, the presidential and the parliamentary, the Fifth Republic has succeeded in a constitutional experiment that now serves France well. For the first time since the French Revolution, there is no important political party or sector of public opinion that challenges the legitimacy of the regime.

CURRENT POLICY CHALLENGES

At a time in U.S. history when the party system is highly polarized around fundamental socioeconomic issues and the government is immersed in a war that has divided the country, French politics—at least most of the time—seems almost tranquil by comparison. The French have lived with divided government (*cohabitation*) for most of the period since 1986 without its impeding government effectiveness or undermining institutional legitimacy. At the same time, the French electorate is clearly concerned about many of the same issues that concern Americans.

In 2008 French citizens were most worried about the economy, unemployment, crime, and urban violence. These problems are often considered problems of the "suburbs," since impoverished neighborhoods, frequently with large immigrant populations, are often found in the old working-class suburbs surrounding large cities. In the fall of 2005, suburban youth rioted for three weeks, burning thousands of automobiles and some public buildings. A few months later mostly middle-class students in high schools and universities closed down much of the education system. In 2009, as the economic crisis deepened, vast strike movements, which once again centered on the education system, spread throughout the country.

Unemployment rates in France have recently averaged about a third higher than U.S. rates. Anxiety about unemployment is related to deep concern about the consequences of being a member of the **European Union (EU).** This, in part, explains the rejection of the European constitutional treaty in 2005. Finally, voters are increasingly disturbed by their relatively new president.

We should emphasize that many of the issues at the heart of contemporary American politics are of little concern to the French. French citizens are not much concerned about the size of the state. Recent conservative governments have tried to reduce the level of public spending, but there is little support for massive cuts in the welfare state programs. Such welfare programs have always been more extensive in France than in the United States. In fact, surveys show that French voters are willing to sacrifice a great deal to maintain these programs, as well as state-subsidized social security and long vacations. Although unemployment rates in France are a third higher than those of the United States, its poverty rate is among the lowest in the advanced industrial democracies and less than half that of the United States.

On the other hand, unlike their American counterparts, French voters are deeply concerned about the environmental and health consequences of genetically modified organisms. Far more than Americans, French citizens are willing to pay for efforts to reduce pollution. Gas prices are more than double those in the United States, and state subsidies for a growing public transportation network are not challenged by public opinion.

Multiculturalism related to integrating a large and growing Muslim population (the largest in Europe) is another important policy challenge. In an effort to promote civic integration, the government passed legislation in 2004 prohibiting students in public schools from wearing conspicuous religious symbols, including Islamic head scarves worn by women. Since the riots of 2005 and 2006, the government has promised reforms to address the special needs of immigrants. These promises have resulted in few concrete proposals, but they have renewed public debates on public policy toward immigrants.

Finally, although there was widespread sympathy for the United States just after the September 11, 2001, attacks on the World Trade Center and the Pentagon, there was a perceptible rise in anti-American sentiment and distrust of American policy in the wake of these events. This distrust generated a major transatlantic crisis when France took the lead in resisting the American-led military action against Iraq in the spring of 2003. A broad consensus of public opinion and political parties supported French opposition to the war. These tensions have moderated since Sarkozy became president, but the U.S.-French relationship will experience further change with the new American administration that entered office in 2009.

Nicolas Sarkozy was swept into office in June 2007 and gained considerable acclaim by appointing both minority women and Socialists to his Cabinet. During his first year in office, however, the government passed relatively little legislation to deal with the problems on which he focused during the presidential campaign. An example of the challenges that he faced was the government's difficulty in passing what were widely considered to be uncontroversial constitutional reforms, even though the opposition Socialists generally agreed with Sarkozy's proposed reforms (although they wanted them to go further). The reforms finally passed by a single vote in July 2008. By the end of 2008, the president's program was constrained even further by the emerging economic crisis, and by massive strikes in reaction to presidential proposals to reorganize the education system. Indeed France was the only major industrial society in which the reaction to the declining economy has been growing social unrest.

A HISTORICAL PERSPECTIVE

France is one of the oldest nation-states of Europe. The period of unstable revolutionary regimes that followed the storming of the Bastille in 1789 ended in the seizure of power by **Napoléon Bonaparte** a decade later. The French Revolution began with the establishment of a constitutional monarchy in 1791 (the First Republic), but the monarchy was overthrown the following year. Three more constitutions preceded Napoléon's seizure of power on the eighteenth day of the revolutionary month of Brumaire (November 10, 1799) and the establishment of the First Empire three years later. The other European powers formed an alliance and forced Napoléon's surrender, as well as the restoration of the Bourbon monarchy. Another revolution in 1830 drove the last Bourbon from the French throne and replaced him with Louis Philippe of the House of Orléans. He promised a more moderate rule bounded by a new constitution.

Growing dissatisfaction among the rising bourgeoisie and the urban population produced still another Paris revolution in 1848. With it came the proclamation of the Second Republic (1848–1852) and universal male suffrage. Conflict between its middle-class and lower-class components, however, kept the republican government ineffective. Out of the disorder rose another Napoléon, Louis Napoléon, nephew of the first emperor. He was crowned Napoléon III in 1852 and brought stability to France for more than a decade. However, his last years were marked by growing indecision and ill-conceived foreign ventures. His defeat and capture in the Franco-Prussian War (1870) began another turbulent period. France was occupied and forced into a humiliating armistice; radicals in Paris proclaimed the Paris Commune, which held out for two months in 1871, until crushed by the conservative government forces. In the commune's aftermath, the struggle between republicans and monarchists led to the establishment of a conservative Third Republic in 1871. The Third Republic was the longest regime in modern France, surviving World War I and lasting until France's defeat and occupation by Nazi Germany in 1940.

World War II deeply divided France. A defeated France was divided into a zone occupied by the Germans and a "free" Vichy zone in the southern half of France, where Marshall Pétain led a government sympathetic to the Germans. From July 1940 until August 1944, the government of France was a dictatorship. Slowly, a resistance movement emerged under the leadership of General **Charles de Gaulle**. It gained increased strength and support after the Allied invasion of North Africa and the German occupation of the Vichy zone at the end of 1942. When German forces were driven from occupied Paris in 1944, de Gaulle entered the city with the hope that sweeping reforms would give France the viable democracy it had long sought. After less than two years, he resigned as head of the Provisional Government, impatient with the country's return to traditional party politics.

In fact, the **Fourth Republic** (1946–1958) disappointed many hopes. Governments fell with disturbing regularity—twenty-four governments in twelve years. At the same time, because of the narrowness of government coalitions, the same parties and the same leaders tended to participate in most of these governments. Weak leadership had great difficulty coping with the tensions created first by the Cold War, then by the French war in Indochina, and finally by the anticolonialist uprising in Algeria.

When a threat of civil war arose over Algeria in 1958, a group of leaders invited de Gaulle to return to power and help the country establish stronger and more stable institutions. De Gaulle and his supporters formulated a new constitution for the Fifth Republic, which was enacted by a referendum in 1958. De Gaulle was the last prime minister of the Fourth Republic and then the first president of the newly established Fifth Republic.

ECONOMY AND SOCIETY

Geographically, France is at once Atlantic, Continental, and Mediterranean; hence, it occupies a unique place in Europe. In 2008 a total of 63.8 million people, about one-fourth as many as the population of the United States, lived in an area one-fifteenth the size of the United States. More than 3.6 million foreigners (noncitizens) live in France, more than half of whom come from outside of Europe, mostly from North Africa and Africa. In addition, nearly 2 million French citizens are foreign-born. Thus, almost 10 percent of the French population is foreign-born, slightly less than the proportion of foreign-born in the United States.

Urbanization has come slowly to France, but it is now highly urbanized. In 1936 only sixteen French cities had a population of more than 100,000; they now number thirty-six. Compared with European countries with similar population (Britain and

Germany), France has relatively few large cities; only Paris has more than a million people. Yet in 2002, 44 million people (three-quarters of the population) lived in urban areas, compared with half that number in 1936.

Almost one-quarter of the urban population—more than one-sixth of the entire nation and growing—lives in the metropolitan region of Paris. This concentration of people creates staggering problems. In a country with centuries-old traditions of administrative, economic, and cultural centralization, it has produced a dramatic gap in human and material resources between Paris and the rest of the country. The Paris region supports a per capita income almost 50 percent higher and unemployment substantially lower than the national average. The Paris region also has the highest concentration of foreigners in the country (twice the national percentage), and there are deep divisions between the wealthier and the poorer towns in the region.

Recent French economic development compares well with that of other advanced industrial countries. In per capita gross domestic product (GDP), France ranks among the wealthiest nations of the world, behind the Scandinavian countries, the United States, and Britain; it is ahead of Germany, Japan, and Italy and the average for the EU (see Chapter 1). During the period from 1996 to 2006, the French economy grew at about the EU average, but with an inflation rate at a little more than half the European average. Nevertheless, with estimates that the economy will contract by almost 3 percent by mid-2009, France now faces its greatest economic crisis since the Great Depression.[1]

Unemployment dipped after 1997 as the economy created new jobs, but it remains relatively high, compared with the averages of the EU and the United States. In 2008, with an unemployment rate of 7.8 percent, France was already experiencing some of the same problems as some of the poorer countries of Europe: long-term youth unemployment, homelessness, and a drain on social services. More than 40 percent of those unemployed in 2004 were the long-term unemployed (those without work for more than one year), a rate far higher than that of Britain, but less than those of Germany and Italy. Indeed, long-term unemployment rates have crept up, even though youth unemployment has declined significantly during the past fifteen years. All of these problems were projected to grow worse in 2009, as unemployment moved rapidly higher.

The labor force has changed drastically since the end of World War II, making France similar to other industrialized countries. During the 1990s the labor force grew by more than 1.6 million, continuing a growth trend that was greater than in most European countries. Most of these new workers were young people, and an increasing proportion consisted of women. For over a century, the proportion of employed women—mostly in agriculture, artisan shops, and factories—was higher in France than in most European countries. Today most women work in offices in the service sector of the economy. In 1954 women made up 35 percent of the labor force; today they make up 46 percent. The proportion of French women working (65 percent) is slightly lower than that of the United States, but one of the highest in Western Europe.

In 1938, 37 percent of French labor was employed in agriculture; this proportion was less than 3.5 percent in 2005. The percentage of the labor force employed in industry was down to about 24 percent, while employment in the service sector rose from 33 percent in 1938 to 71 percent today, slightly above the average for Western Europe.

By comparison with other advanced industrial countries, the agricultural sector of France remains important both economically and politically. France has more cultivated acreage than any other country in the EU. In spite of the sharp decline in the proportion of the population engaged in agriculture, agricultural production increased massively during the past quarter century.

Since 1945 there have been serious efforts to modernize agriculture, such as farm cooperatives, the consolidation of marginal farms, and improvements in technical education. Particularly after the development of the Common Agriculture Policy (CAP) in the European Community between 1962 and 1968, consolidation of farmland proceeded rapidly. By 1985 the average French farm was larger than that of any country in Europe except Britain, Denmark, and Luxembourg.

The EU has paid a large proportion of the bill for agricultural modernization, and subsidies have increased steadily. As a result, there are pressures (particularly from the British) to reduce CAP expenditures. With the enlargement of the EU in 2004 and the incorporation of more East European countries with large agricultural sectors, these pressures have increased. In addition to requiring the withdrawal of more land from production, major reforms in 1992,

1994, 1999, and 2003 at the European level have gradually moved subsidies away from price supports (that encourage greater production) and toward direct support of farm income. Nevertheless, total subsidies to French farmers through the CAP are greater than those provided to any other country.

French business is both highly dispersed and highly concentrated. Even after three decades of structural reorganization of business, about half of the 2.4 million industrial and commercial enterprises in France belong to individuals. In 1999, 54 percent of the salaried workers in the country worked in small enterprises with fewer than fifty workers. As in other advanced industrial societies, this proportion has been slowly increasing, primarily because of the movement of labor into the service sector.

From the perspective of production, some of the most advanced French industries are highly concentrated. The few firms at the top account for most of the employment and business sales. Even in some of the older sectors (such as automobile manufacture, ship construction, and rubber), half or more of the employment and sales are concentrated in the top four firms. The *Financial Times* reports that among the 500 largest industrial groups in the world in 2008, 31 were in France. France placed fifth in the number of firms on this list, behind the United States, Japan, the United Kingdom, and China, but ahead of all other European countries.

The organization of industry and commerce changed significantly during the 1990s. Privatization mandated by the EU has reduced the number of public enterprises by 24 percent and the number of those working in public enterprises by 31 percent. In 1997 among the top twenty enterprises in France, only four were public, compared with thirteen ten years before.

Despite a continuing process of privatization, relations between industry and the state remain close. In addition, more than 20 percent of the civilian labor force works in the civil service, which has grown about 10 percent during the past fifteen years.

CONSTITUTION AND GOVERNMENT STRUCTURE

The **Constitution of 1958** is the sixteenth since the fall of the Bastille in 1789. Past republican regimes, known less for their achievements than for their instability, were invariably based on the principle that Parliament could overturn a government that lacked a parliamentary majority. Such an arrangement can work satisfactorily, as it does in most of Western Europe, when the country (and the parliament) embraces two—or a few—well-organized parties. The party or the coalition that gains a majority at the polls forms the government and can count on the support of its members in parliament until the next elections. At that time it is either kept in power or replaced by an equally disciplined party or coalition of parties.

The Executive

De Gaulle's constitution for the Fifth Republic offered to remedy previous failings of French political parties and coalition politics. In preceding republics the president was little more than a figurehead. According to the new constitution, the **president of the Republic** is a visible head of state. He is to be placed "above the parties" to represent the unity of the national community. As guardian of the constitution, he is to be an arbiter who would rely on other powers—Parliament, the Cabinet, or the people—for the full weight of government action. He can appeal to the people in two ways. With the agreement of the government or Parliament, he can submit certain important legislation to the electorate as a referendum. In addition, after consulting with the prime minister and the parliamentary leaders, he can dissolve Parliament and call for new elections. In case of grave threat "to the institutions of the Republic," the president also has the option of invoking emergency powers.

Virtually all of the most powerful constitutional powers of the president—those that give the president formal power—have been used sparingly. Emergency powers were used only once by de Gaulle—in 1961 when the rebellion of the generals in Algiers clearly justified such use. De Gaulle dissolved Parliament twice (in 1962 and 1968), each time to strengthen the majority supporting presidential policies (see Figure 6.1).

Upon his election to the presidency in 1981, Socialist **François Mitterrand** dissolved the National Assembly. He did so again after his reelection seven years later in order have new parliamentary elections, expecting (correctly) that elections would provide him with a reliable majority. President Jacques Chirac dissolved the National Assembly in April 1997 in an attempt to extend the conservative majority into the next century and to gain political support for reduced public spending. The president lost his gamble.

French Presidents and Prime Ministers Since 1958	FIGURE 6.1	
PRIME MINISTER	YEAR	PRESIDENT
Michel Debré	1958	Charles de Gaulle
Georges Pompidou	1962	
Maurice Couve de Murville	1968	
Jacques Chaban-Delmas	1969	Georges Pompidou
Pierre Messmer	1972	
Jacques Chirac	1974	Valéry Giscard d'Estaing
Raymond Barre	1976	
Pierre Mauroy	1981	François Mitterrand
Laurent Fabius	1984	
Jacques Chirac	1986	
Michel Rocard	1988	
Edith Cresson	1991	
Pierre Bérégovoy	1992	
Edouard Balladur	1993	
Alain Juppé	1995	Jacques Chirac
Lionel Jospin	1997	
Jean-Pierre Raffarin	2002	
Dominique de Villepin	2005	
François Fillon	2007	Nicolas Sarkozy

Direct popular elections to the office have greatly augmented the legitimacy and political authority of the president. Instead of the indirect election called for by the 1958 constitution, a constitutional amendment approved by referendum in 1962 provided for the popular election of the president for a renewable term of seven years. In September 2000 the presidential term was reduced to five years—again by constitutional amendment—to coincide with the normal five-year legislative term. France is one of six countries in Western Europe to select its president by direct popular vote.

De Gaulle outlined his view of the office when he said that power "emanates directly from the people, which implies that the Head of State, elected by the nation, is the source and holder of this power." Every president who has succeeded de Gaulle has maintained the general's basic interpretation of the office. But, as we shall see, there have been some changes in the way the presidency has functioned. The **prime minister** is appointed by the president and has responsibility for the day-to-day running of the government. In fact, the division of responsibility within the executive, between the president and the prime minister, has varied not only with the personalities of those who hold both offices, but also with the conditions under which they serve.

The Legislature

The legislature is composed of two houses: the National Assembly and the Senate (see Figure 6.2). The **National Assembly** of 577 members is elected directly for five years by all citizens over age 18. The government may dissolve the legislature at any time, though not twice within one year. Experts have attributed the instability of previous regimes mostly to the constant meddling of Parliament with the activities of the executive. The 1958 constitution strove to end the subordination of government to Parliament. It imposed strict rules of behavior on each deputy and on Parliament as a body. These requirements, it was hoped, would ensure the needed equilibrium.

Under the 1958 rules, the government, rather than the legislature, controls proceedings in both houses and can require priority for bills it wishes to promote. The president, rather than the prime minister, generally chooses the Cabinet members, although this tends to be merely formal during periods of cohabitation. Parliament still enacts laws, but the

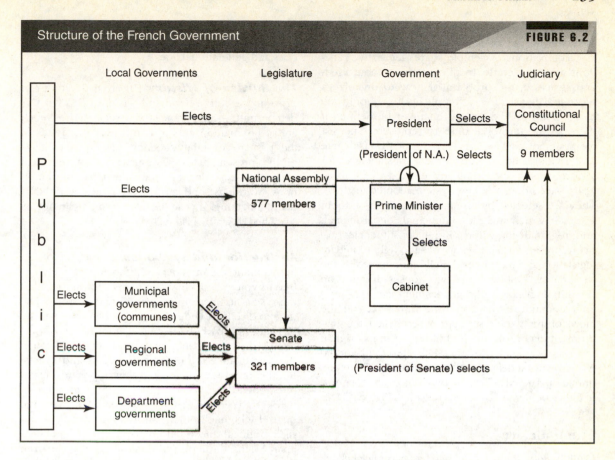

Structure of the French Government   FIGURE 6.2

domain of such laws is strictly defined. Many areas that in other democracies are regulated by laws debated and approved by Parliament are turned over to rulemaking by the executive in France.

The nineteen standing committees of the National Assembly under the Fourth Republic were reduced to six in 1958. The sizes of the committees were enlarged to 73 to 145 members. This prevents interaction among highly specialized deputies who could become effective rivals of the ministers. Each deputy is restricted to one committee, and party groups are represented in each committee in proportion to their size in the National Assembly.

It is not surprising that the new constitution detailed the conditions under which the National Assembly could overthrow a government. More than one-half of the actual members of the house must formulate and pass an explicit motion of censure. Even after a motion of censure is passed, the government may resist the pressure to resign: The president can

dissolve the National Assembly and call for new elections. During the first year after these elections, a new dissolution of the Assembly is prohibited by the constitution. The vote of censure is the only way Parliament can condemn the conduct of government, but no government has been censured since 1962. Since that time every government has had a working (if not always friendly) majority in the National Assembly.

Thus, the government maintains considerable control over the legislative agenda, the content of legislation, and the conditions under which Parliament can debate legislative proposals. However, amendments to the constitution passed in July 2008 shifted the balance in important ways to the majority party. The National Assembly now has the right to fix its own agenda (half the time), and in the future it may be easier for Parliament to amend legislation. The number of parliamentary committees has been increased from six to eight. The bills considered by Parliament will be those reported out and amended by these committees, rather than those presented by the government (with a few exceptions).

The National Assembly shares legislative functions with the **Senate**. In all countries without a federal structure, the problem of how to organize a bicameral legislature is complex. How should the membership of the second chamber be defined if there are no territorial units to represent? The 331 members of the Senate (the "upper house") are elected indirectly from department constituencies for a term of six years (half are elected every three years—according to a new system adopted in 2003). They are selected by an electoral college of about 150,000, which includes municipal, departmental, and regional councilors. Rural constituencies are overrepresented. The Senate has the right to initiate legislation and must consider all bills adopted by the National Assembly. If the two houses disagree on pending legislation, the government can appoint a joint committee to resolve the differences. If the views of the two houses are not reconciled, the government may resubmit the bill (either in its original form or as amended by the Senate) to the National Assembly for a definitive vote (Article 45). Therefore, unlike the United States, the two houses are not equal in either power or influence (see again Figure 6.2).

The Judiciary

Until the Fifth Republic, France had no judicial check on the constitutionality of the actions of its political authorities. The **Constitutional Council** was originally conceived primarily as a safeguard against any legislative erosion of the constraints that the constitution had placed on the prerogatives of Parliament.[2] Because of a constitutional amendment in 1974, however, the council now plays an important role in the legislative process. It is likely to play a more important judicial role as well because a constitutional amendment in 2008 gave the council appeal jurisdiction in cases in which the defendant claims that a law violates "rights and liberties" guaranteed by the constitution.

POLITICAL CULTURE

Themes of Political Culture

There are three ways that we understand political culture in France: history links present values to those of the past, abstraction and symbolism identify

a way of thinking about politics, and distrust of government represents a dominant value that crosses class and generational lines.

The Burden of History   Historical thinking can prove to be both a bond and—as the U.S. Civil War demonstrates—a hindrance to consensus. The French are so fascinated by their own history that feuds of the past are constantly superimposed on the conflicts of the present. This passionate use of historical memories—resulting in seemingly inflexible ambitions, warnings, and taboos—complicates political decisionmaking. In de Gaulle's words, France is "weighed down by history."

Abstraction and Symbolism   In the Age of Enlightenment, the monarchy left the educated classes free to voice their views on many topics, provided the discussion remained general and abstract. The urge to discuss a wide range of problems, even trivial ones, in broad philosophical terms has hardly diminished. The exaltation of the abstract is reflected in the significance attributed to symbols and rituals. Rural communities that fought on opposite sides in the French Revolution still pay homage to different heroes two centuries later. They seem to have no real quarrel with each other, but inherited symbols and their political and religious habits have kept them apart.[3] This tradition helps explain why a nation united by almost universal admiration for a common historical experience holds to conflicting interpretations of its meaning.

Distrust of Government and Politics   The French have long shared the widespread ambivalence of modern times that combines distrust of government with high expectations for it. The French citizens' simultaneous distrust of authority and craving for it feed on both individualism and a passion for equality. This attitude produces a self-reliant individual convinced that he is responsible to himself, and perhaps to his family, for what he was and might become. The outside world—the "they" who operate beyond the circle of the family, the family firm, and the village—creates obstacles in life. Most of the time, however, "they" are identified with the government.

Memories reaching back to the eighteenth century justify a state of mind that is potentially, if seldom overtly, insubordinate. A strong government is considered reactionary by nature, even if it pretends to be progressive. When citizens participate in public life, they hope to constrain government authority, rather than encouraging change, even when change is overdue. At times this individualism is tainted with anarchism. Yet, the French also accommodate themselves rather easily to bureaucratic rule. Since administrative rulings supposedly treat all situations with the same yardstick, they satisfy the sharp sense of equality possessed by a people who feels forever shortchanged by the government and by the privileges those in power bestow on others.

Although the Revolution of 1789 did not break with the past as completely as is commonly believed, it conditioned the general outlook on crisis and compromise and on continuity and change. Sudden change rather than gradual mutation, dramatic conflicts couched in the language of mutually exclusive, radical ideologies—these are the experiences that excite the French at historical moments when their minds are particularly malleable. In fact, what an outsider perceives as permanent instability is a fairly regular alternation between brief crises and prolonged periods of routine. The French are accustomed to thinking that no thorough change can ever occur except by a major upheaval (although this is not always true). Since the great Revolution, every French adult has experienced—usually more than once—occasions of political excitement followed by disappointment. This process has sometimes led to moral exhaustion and widespread skepticism about any possibility of change.

Whether they originated within the country or were brought about by international conflict, most of France's political crises have produced a constitutional crisis. Each time, the triumphant forces have codified their norms and philosophy, usually in a comprehensive document. This explains why constitutions have never played the role of fundamental charters. Prior to the Fifth Republic, their norms were satisfactory to only one segment of the polity and hotly contested by others.

In the years immediately following 1958, the reaction to the constitution of the Fifth Republic resembled the reaction to previous French constitutions. Support for its institutions was generally limited to voters who supported the governments of the day. This began to change after 1962, with the popular election of the president. The election of Mitterrand to the presidency in 1981 and the peaceful transfer of power from a right to a left majority in the National Assembly laid to rest the 200-year-old constitutional debate among French elites. It proved to be the capstone of acceptance of the institutions of the Fifth Republic among the masses of French citizens.

Confidence in the Fifth Republic's constitutional institutions has been strong. And despite growing disillusionment with politicians, it has grown stronger. Moreover, there is little significant variation in trust in institutions among voters by their party identity.[4] French people invariably give the highest confidence ratings to institutions closest to them: to local officials, rather than to political parties or national representatives (see Figure 6.3). In recent years distrust of government officials has been high, but expectations of government remain high as well.

Religious and Antireligious Traditions

France is at once a Catholic country—68 percent of the French population identified themselves as Catholic in 2002 (down from 87 percent in 1974)—and a country that the Church itself considers "dechristianized." Of those who describe themselves as Catholic, only 10 percent attend mass regularly (down from 21 percent in 1974), and 84 percent either never go to church or go only occasionally for ceremonies such as baptism or marriage.[5]

Until well into the twentieth century, the mutual hostility between the religious and the secular was one of the main features of the political culture. Since the Revolution, it has divided society and political life at all levels. Even now there are important differences between the political behavior of practicing Catholics and that of nonbelievers.

French Catholics historically viewed the Revolution of 1789 as the work of satanic men. Conversely, enemies of the Church became militant in their opposition to Catholic forms and symbols. This division continued through the nineteenth century. Differences between the political subcultures of Catholicism and anticlericalism deepened further with the creation of the Third Republic. After a few years, militant anticlericalism took firm control of the Republic. Parliament rescinded the centuries-old compact with the Vatican, expelled most Catholic orders, and severed all ties between church and state so that (in a phrase often used at the time) "the moral unity of the country could be reestablished." The Pope matched the militancy of the Republic's regime by excommunicating every deputy who voted for the separation laws in 1905. As in other European Catholic countries, the difference between the political right and

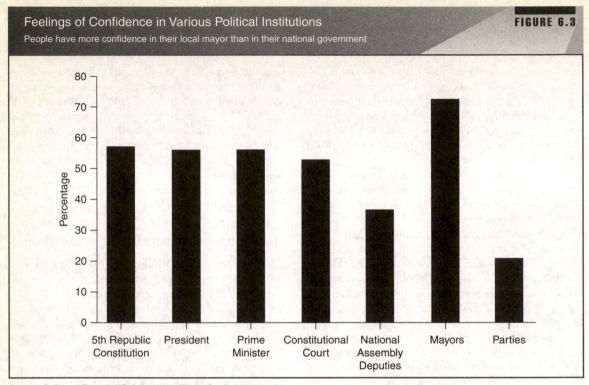

Feelings of Confidence in Various Political Institutions

People have more confidence in their local mayor than in their national government

FIGURE 6.3

Source: Sofres, *LEt at de l'Opinion 2001* (Paris: Seuil, 2001), p. 81.

left was largely determined by attitudes toward the Catholic Church.

The gap between Catholics and agnostics narrowed during the interwar period and after they found themselves working side by side in the resistance movement during World War II. Nevertheless, the depth of religious practice continues to be one of the best predictors of whether a voter will support an established party of the right.

Religious practice has been declining in France and many other industrialized countries since the 1950s. Less than 10 percent of the French population attends church regularly (once a week) today. Farmers are the most observant group, but their church attendance is only 23 percent. Blue-collar workers are the least observant: Now only 4 percent admit to attending church regularly.

In addition to secularization trends, important changes have occurred within the Catholic subculture. Today the vast majority of self-identified Catholics reject some of the most important teachings of the Church, including its positions on abortion, premarital

sex, and marriage of priests. Only 16 percent of identified Catholics perceive the role of the Church as important in political life, and Catholicism no longer functions as a well-integrated community with a common view of the world and common social values. In 2000 there were half the number of Catholic priests as in 1960 and a 75 percent decline of ordinations. Most private schools in France are nominally Catholic parochial schools, which the state subsidizes. The status of these schools (in a country in which state support for Catholic schools coexists with the separation of church and state) has never been fully settled. In 2008, 13 percent of primary schools and 31 percent of secondary schools were private.

French Jews (numbering about 600,000, or about 1 percent of the population) are sufficiently well integrated into French society that it is not possible to speak of a Jewish vote. One study demonstrates that, like other French voters, Jews tend to vote left or right, according to degree of religious practice. Anti-Semitic attitudes and behavior are not widespread in France. However, attacks against Jews and Jewish institutions—mostly by young Maghrebian men in mixed areas of large cities—increased dramatically in parallel with the emergence of the second intifada in the Middle East (2000–2002), but have since declined. These incidents were also related to emerging patterns of urban ethnic conflict in France.

Protestants (1.7 percent of the population and growing) have lived somewhat apart. There are heavy concentrations in Alsace, in Paris, and in some regions of central and southeastern France. About two-thirds of Protestants belong to the upper bourgeoisie. Protestants hold a large proportion of high public positions. Until recently, they usually voted more leftist than others in their socioeconomic position or in the same region. Although many Protestants are prominent in the Socialist Party, their electoral behavior, like their activities in cultural and economic associations, is determined by factors other than religion.

Islam is now France's second religion. There are 4 million to 4.5 million **Muslims** in France, two-thirds of whom are immigrants or their descendants from Muslim countries. The emergence of Islamic institutions in France is part of a larger phenomenon of integrating **new immigrants**. In the last decade, the affirmation of religious identification coincided with (and to some extent was a part of) the social and political mobilization of immigrants from Muslim countries.

There are now over a thousand mosques in France, as well as another thousand prayer rooms. In 2002 the government created the French Council of the Muslim Religion (CFCM) to represent Islam with public authorities (similar institutions exist for Jews and Catholics). A survey in 2005 notes that regular attendance of services at mosques is just above 20 percent—somewhat higher than average for the general population. More than 70 percent of those who identify as Muslims say that they attend services only occasionally.[6]

The growth of Muslim interests has challenged the traditional French view of the separation of church and state. Unlike Catholics and Jews, who maintain their own schools, or Protestants, who have supported the principle of secular state schools, some Muslim groups insist on the right both to attend state schools and to follow practices that education authorities consider contrary to the French tradition of secularism. Small numbers of Muslims have challenged dress codes, school curriculums, and school requirements and have more generally questioned stronger notions of *laïcité* (antireligious atheism).

In response to this challenge, the French Parliament passed legislation in 2004 that banned the wearing of "ostentatious" religious symbols in primary and secondary schools. Although the language is neutral about religion, the law is widely seen as an attempt to prevent the wearing of Islamic head scarves. The new law was widely debated, but it was also strongly supported by the French public. A sample of Muslim women surveyed two months before the law was passed also supported it.

Another response was the 2008 rejection by the administrative court (the Conseil d'Etat) of a citizenship application from a Moroccan woman who wore a burqua (a full-body covering), and was married to a man who was a French citizen. The court based the decision on what it termed practices "incompatible with essential values of the French community, notably with the principle of equality of the sexes."

Nevertheless, it is important to point out that surveys in 2006 indicated that French Muslims are better integrated than are those in other European countries (Britain and Germany, for example).[7] They have the strongest primary identity as French, rather than Muslim; the strongest commitment to "adopt national customs," rather than remaining distinct (78 percent); and the most favorable view of their fellow citizens who are Christian and Jewish.

Class and Status

Feelings about class differences shape a society's authority pattern and the style in which authority is exercised. The French, like the English, are conscious of living in a society divided into classes. But since equality is valued more highly in France than in England, deference toward the upper classes is far less developed, and resentful antagonism is widespread.

The number of citizens who are conscious of belonging to a social class is relatively high in France, particularly among workers. About two-thirds of workers in 2002 self-identified as working class.[8] There is some evidence that spontaneous class identity has been declining. However, a 1997 study showed an enduring and even a growing sense of class among white-collar workers and middle managers. In 2002 all social groups expressed a sentiment of belonging to a social class that was as high as or higher than that of workers.

Economic and social transformations have not eradicated subjective feelings about class differences and class antagonism. Indeed, periodic strike movements intensify class feelings and commitments to act. A survey in April 2006 revealed that half of those polled were prepared to participate in a demonstration to defend their ideas. In addition, as the number of immigrant workers among the least qualified workers has grown, traditional class differences are reinforced by a growing sense of racial and ethnic differences.

POLITICAL SOCIALIZATION

French political attitudes have been shaped through experience with the political system, as well as through some key institutions and agents. Some agents, such as political associations, act to socialize political values quite directly, while others, such as the family and the media, act in a more indirect manner.

In an old country like France, agents of political socialization change slowly, even when regimes change rapidly. Socializing agents are carriers of a broader cultural tradition. Like any other teaching process, political socialization passes on from one generation to the next "a mixture of attitudes developed in a mixture of historical periods." But "traditions, everyone agrees, do not form a constituted and fixed set of values, of knowledge and of representations; socialization never functions as a simple mechanism of identical reproduction [but rather as] an important instrument for the reorganization and the reinvention of tradition."[9]

Family

For those French who view their neighbors and fellow citizens with distrust and the institutions around them with cynicism, the family is a safe haven. Concern for stability, steady income, property, and continuity were common to bourgeois and peasant families, though not to urban or agricultural workers. The training of children in bourgeois and peasant families was often marked by close supervision, incessant correction, and strict sanctions.

Particularly during the last forty years, the life of the French family, the role of its members, and its relationship to outsiders have undergone fundamental, and sometimes contradictory, changes. Very few people condemn the idea of couples living together without being married. In 2001, 44 percent of all births were outside of marriage (compared with 6 percent in 1968), a percentage only slightly lower

than in the United States and higher than almost any other European country. The proportion of births outside of marriage is highest among women outside of the labor force and working-class women (with the notable exception of immigrant women). Very few of these children are in one-parent families, however. In virtually all cases, they are legally recognized by both parents before their first birthday. Nevertheless, 18 percent of young people below age 25 lived with only one of their natural parents in 2005, mostly due to divorce. The number of divorces was more than 40 percent of the number of marriages in 2000, and it has almost doubled since 1976, when new and more flexible divorce legislation came into effect.

Legislative changes have only gradually modified the legal restrictions on married women that existed in the Napoléonic legal codes. Not until 1970 did the law proclaim the absolute equality of the two parents in the exercise of parental authority and for the moral and material management of the family. Labor-saving devices for house and farm are described as the "secret agents of modernity" in the countryside.[10] Almost half of all women over age 15 are now employed, and 80 percent of French women between the ages of 25 and 49 are now working during their adult years.

The employment of more married women has affected the family's role as a vehicle of socialization. Working women differ from those who are not employed in regard to religious practice, political interest, electoral participation, party preference, and so on. In their attitudinal orientations, employed women are far closer to the men of the same milieu, class, or age group to which they belong than to women who are not employed.[11]

Although family structure, values, and behavior have changed, the family remains an important structure through which political values broadly conceived are transmitted from generation to generation. Several studies demonstrate a significant influence of parents over the religious socialization and the left-right political choices made by their children.[12]

There is perhaps no greater tribute to the continuing effectiveness of the French family than the results of a survey of French youth in 1994. With 25 percent of 18- to 24-year-olds unemployed, it was hardly surprising that 78 percent of young people had little confidence in the schools' ability to prepare them for the future. More surprising, more than 75 percent felt that their parents had confidence in them, that they were loved at home, and that their families had prepared them well for the future. In a survey taken in 1999, the family was ranked second only to school as a source of deep and durable friendship.

The effectiveness of the family in socializing general religious and ideological orientations does not mean that succeeding generations do not have formative experiences of their own or that there are no significant political differences by age. Therefore, political socialization is a product not only of the family experiences, but also of childhood experiences with peers, education, and the changing larger world. For instance, young people of Algerian origin, born in France, are somewhat more likely than their counterparts of French origin to practice their faith, but far less likely than their counterparts born in Algeria to practice their faith. Nevertheless, young people of Algerian origin were more likely to practice their religion in 2005 than they were in 1995.[13]

Associations and Socialization

The French bias against authority might have encouraged social groups and associations if the egalitarian thrust and the competition among individuals did not work in the opposite direction. The French ambivalence about participation in group life is not merely negativistic apathy, but also reflects a lack of belief in the value of cooperation. On the one hand, this cultural ambivalence is reinforced by legal restrictions on associational life, as well as by a strong republican tradition hostile to groups serving as intermediaries between the people and the state. On the other hand, the state and local governments traditionally subsidize numerous associations (including trade unions). Some associations (not always the same ones that were subsidized) receive privileged access to decisionmaking power.

After World War II, *overall* membership in associations in France was comparable to that in other European countries, but lower than in the United States. However, group membership in France was concentrated in politicized associations that reinforced existing social divisions and was less common for independent social and fraternal groups. Membership in key professional organizations, especially trade unions, was much lower in France than in other European countries.

The number of associations has sharply increased over the past two decades, while the overall percentage of membership among the adult population has remained relatively constant. In a 2002 survey, 36 percent claimed to belong to one or more associations. This percentage has increased during the last thirty years, but has remained about the same for the last decade.

The pattern of association membership, however, has changed considerably. The traditional advocacy and political groups, politicized unions, and professional associations suffered sharp declines in absolute (and proportional) membership. Sports associations, self-help groups, and newly established ethnic associations now attract larger numbers of people. As more middle-class people have joined associations, working-class people have dropped out.[14]

To some extent these changes reflect shifting attitudes about political commitment in France. Although associational life remains strong, *militantisme* (voluntary work, with its implication of deep and abiding commitment) has clearly diminished. Older advocacy and professional associations that were built on this kind of commitment have declined. Newer groups are built on different and often more limited commitment.

New legislation has also produced changes. A 1981 law made it possible for immigrant groups to form their own organizations. This encouraged the emergence of thousands of ethnic associations. Decentralization legislation passed a few years later encouraged municipalities to support the creation of local associations, some to perform municipal services.

Even with these changing patterns, there remain uncertainties about the role of associations, old and new, in the socialization process. Some observers seem to confirm that membership in French organizations involves less actual participation than in American or British organizations and hence has less impact on social and political attitudes. Cultural distrust is manifest less in lower overall membership than in the inability of organizational leaders to relate to their members and to mobilize them for action.

Education

One of the most important ways a community preserves and transmits its values is through education. Napoléon Bonaparte recognized the significance of education. Well into the second half of the twentieth century, the French educational system remained an imposing historical monument, in the unmistakable style of the First Empire. The edifice Napoléon erected combined education at all levels, from primary school to postgraduate professional training, into one centralized corporation: the imperial university. Its job was to teach the national doctrine through uniform programs at various levels.

As the strict military discipline of the Napoléonic model was loosened by succeeding regimes, each has discovered that the machinery created by Napoléon was a convenient and coherent instrument for transmitting the values—both changing and permanent—of French civilization. The centralized imperial university has therefore never been truly dismantled. The minister of education presides over a ministry that employs more than a million people and controls curriculums and teaching methods, the criteria for selection and advancement of pupils and teachers, and the content of examinations.

Making advancement at every step dependent on passing an examination is not peculiar to France (it is also found in Japan and other countries). What is distinctly French is an obsessive belief that everybody is equal before an examination. The idea that education is an effective weapon for emancipation and social betterment has had popular as well as official recognition. The **baccalauréat**—the certificate of completion of the academic secondary school, the lycée—remains almost the sole means of access to higher education. Such a system suits and profits best those self-motivated middle-class children for whom it was designed.

Nevertheless, during the Fifth Republic, the structure of the French educational system has undergone significant change. The secondary schools, which trained only 700,000 students as late as 1945, now provide instruction for 5.5 million. Between 1958 and 2007, the number of students in higher education rose from 170,000 to 2.3 million. By 2006 the proportion of 20- to 24-year-olds in higher education (40 percent) was comparable to that in any other European country.[15]

The introduction of a comprehensive middle school with a common core curriculum in 1963 basically altered the system of early academic selection. Other reforms eliminated rigid ability tracking. However, the implementation of reforms, whether passed by governments of the right or the left, has often faced difficult opposition from middle-class parents and from teachers' unions of the left.[16] Although more than 80 percent of the students who sat for the examination passed the baccalauréat in 2006 (more than double the proportion of 1980), education reforms have altered only slightly the vast differences in the success of children from different social backgrounds.

Because of the principle of open admission, every holder of the baccalauréat can gain entrance to a university. There is, as in some American state universities, a rather ruthless elimination at the end of the first year (particularly for students in such fields as medicine) and sometimes later. Students of lower-class backgrounds typically fare worse than the others. In addition, the number of students from such backgrounds is disproportionately large in fields in which diplomas have the lowest value in the professional market and in which unemployment is greatest.

The most ambitious attempt to reform the university system came in the wake of the student rebellion of 1968, followed by other reforms in the 1970s and 1980s. They strove to encourage the autonomy of each university; the participation of teachers, students, and staff in the running of the university; and the collaboration among different disciplines. The government subsequently withdrew some of the reforms. Others failed to be implemented because of widespread resistance by those concerned. Administrative autonomy has remained fragmentary, as the ministry has held the financial purse strings, as well as the right to grant degrees. Today the widely lamented crisis of the university system has hardly been alleviated, although the size of the student population appears to have stabilized.

Since 2003 the most important symbolic change in French higher education has been the introduction of affirmative action programs for students in "priority education zones"—schools in poor areas, generally in or near larger cities. Some of the elite institutions of higher education (Sciences-Po in Paris, for example) have created links to some of these schools and have established special conditions of admission for their best students. Although these programs involve only a handful of students, these experiments are important because they represent the first affirmative effort to integrate potential leaders from immigrant communities into the French system (which we will discuss later).

An additional characteristic of the French system of higher education is the parallel system of **grandes écoles**, a sector of higher education that functions outside of the network of universities under rules that permit a high degree of selectivity. As university enrollment has multiplied, the more prestigious grandes écoles have only modestly increased the number of students admitted upon strict entrance examinations.[17] For more than a century, the grandes écoles have been the training ground of highly specialized elites. These schools prepare students for careers in engineering, business management, and the top ranks of the civil service. Their different recruitment of students and of teaching staffs, as well as their teaching methods, influences the outlook and even the temperament of many of their graduates. In contrast to university graduates, virtually all graduates of the grandes écoles find employment and often assume positions of great responsibility.

Socialization and Communication

The political effectiveness of the mass media is often determined by the way in which people appraise the media's integrity and whether they believe that the media serve or disturb the functioning of the political system. In the past business firms, political parties, and governments (both French and foreign) often backed major newspapers. Today the press operates under the same conditions as it does in other Western democracies. Most newspapers and magazines are owned by business enterprises, many of them conglomerates that extend into fields other than periodical publications.

In spite of a growth in population, the number of daily newspapers and their circulation have declined since World War II. The decline in readership, a common phenomenon in most European democracies, is due to competition from other media, such as television, radio, and the Internet.

Television has replaced all other media as a primary source of political information in France and other Western democracies.[18] It is increasingly the primary mediator between political forces and individual citizens, and it has an impact on the organization and substance of politics. First, a personality that plays well on television (not just a unique personality such as Charles de Gaulle) is now an essential ingredient of politics. As in other countries, image and spectacle are important elements of politics. Second, television helps set the agenda of political issues by choosing among the great variety of themes, problems, and issues dealt with by political and social forces and by magnifying them for the public. Finally, television now provides the arena for national electoral campaigns, largely displacing mass rallies and meetings.

Confidence in various sources of political information varies among different groups. Young people and shopkeepers are most confident in radio and television information, while managers are more confident in the written press than television for political information.

Until 1982 all radio and television stations that originated programs on French territory were owned by the state and operated by personnel whom the state appointed and remunerated. Since then the system of state monopoly gradually has been dismantled. As a first and quite important step, the Socialist government authorized private radio stations. This move attempted to regularize and regulate more than a thousand existing pirate radio stations. Inevitably, this vast network of 1,600 stations was consolidated by private entrepreneurs who provide programming services and in some instances control of a large number of local stations.

The 1982 legislation also reorganized the public television system. It granted new rights of reply to government communications and allotted free time to all political parties during electoral campaigns. During the following years, however, even greater changes were produced by a process of gradual privatization and globalization of television broadcasting. Today as many as 900 television channels from throughout the world are available to French viewers (depending on the system that they choose), compared with 3 in 1980 and 30 in 1990.

RECRUITMENT AND STYLE OF ELITES

Until the Fifth Republic, Parliament provided the core of French decisionmakers. Besides members of Parliament, elected officers of municipalities or departments, some local party leaders, and a few journalists of national renown are counted among what is known in France as the **political class.** Altogether they comprise not more than 15,000 or 20,000 people. All gravitated toward the halls of the National Assembly or the Senate. From about 1879 on, professionals (lawyers, doctors, and journalists) dominated the Chamber of Deputies, now called the National Assembly. The vast majority were local notables, trained in law and experienced in local administration.

A substantial change in political recruitment occurred during the Fourth Republic, when the percentages of self-employed and farmers became a minority. The steadily diminishing share of blue- and white-collar workers during the Fifth Republic is due partially to the professionalization of parliamentary personnel, as well as to the decline of the Communist Party.

Strikingly, a large number of legislators now come from the public sector: almost half the deputies in the 1980s and 32 percent after the victory of the right in 2007. The number of top civil servants in the

National Assembly has risen constantly since 1958, and the left landslide of 1981 accentuated this process. Although the majority of high civil servants usually lean toward parties of the right, more than half of those who sat in the National Assembly elected in 2007 were part of the Socialist group.

Even more important than their number is the political weight that these deputy-bureaucrats carry in Parliament. Some of the civil servants who run for election to Parliament have previously held positions in the political executive, either as members of the ministerial staffs or as junior ministers. Not surprisingly, they are frequently candidates for a post in the Cabinet.

More than in any other Western democracy, the highest ranks of the civil service are the training and recruitment grounds for top positions in both politics and industry. Among the high civil servants, about 3,400 are members of the most important administrative agencies, the five **grands corps,** from which the vast majority of the roughly 500 administrators engaged in political decisionmaking are drawn.[19] The recruitment base of the highest levels of the civil service remains extremely narrow. The knowledge and capability required to pass the various examinations give clear advantages to the children of senior civil servants. As a result, the ranking bureaucracy forms something approaching a hereditary class. Past attempts to develop a system of more open recruitment into the higher civil service have been only marginally successful.

The **École Nationale d'Administration (ENA)** and the **École Polytechnique,** together with the other grandes écoles, play an essential role in the recruitment of administrative, political, and business elites. Virtually all the members of the grands corps are recruited directly from the graduating classes of the ENA and the Polytechnique. What differentiates the members of the grands corps from other ranking administrators is their general competence and mobility. At any one time, as many as two-thirds of the members of these corps might be on leave or on special missions to other administrative agencies or special assignments to positions of influence.

They might also be engaged in politics as members of Parliament (thirty-seven in the National Assembly elected in 2007), local government, or the executive. Twelve of the eighteen prime ministers who have served since 1959 were members of a grand corps and attended a grande école. The percentage of ministers in any given government who belong to the grands corps has varied between 10 and 60 percent. When Jean-Pierre Raffarin became prime minister in April 2002, he was widely described as an "outsider," in part because his political career had been primarily in the provinces and in part because he had *not* been a student at the ENA. One study calculates that 40 percent of those who graduated from the ENA between 1960 and 1990 served as ministerial advisors. Thus, the grandes écoles–grands corps group, though small in membership, produces a remarkable proportion of the country's political elite.

The same system is increasingly important in recruiting top-level business executives. Members of the grands corps can move from the public sector to the private sector because they can go on leave for years, while they retain their seniority, their pension rights, and the right to return to their job. (Few who leave do in fact return to serve as civil servants.)[20] In 2007, 75 percent of the members of the executive boards of the 40 largest companies in France were graduates of a grande école. In the early 1990s, 17 percent of all ENA graduates were working in French industry. Moreover, though the number of ENA graduates is small (about 170 a year), it is three times larger now than in the early 1960s.

The relationship between the grandes écoles and the grands corps, on the one hand, and politics and business, on the other hand, provides structure for an influential elite and survives changes in the political orientation of governments. While this system is not politically monolithic, the narrowness of its recruitment contributes to a persistent similarity of style and operation and to the fairly stable—at times rigid—value system of its operators.

For outsiders this tight network is difficult to penetrate. Even during the 1980s—the period when industrial restructuring and privatization of state-run enterprises encouraged a new breed of freewheeling businesspeople in the United States and in Britain—a similar process had a very limited impact on the recruitment of new elites in France.

The Importance of Gender

The representation of women among French political elites is almost the lowest in Western Europe. Women make up well over half the electorate, but were barely 18.5 percent of the deputies in the National Assembly in 2007 and only 18.2 percent of Senate members in 2008. Women fare better at the local level, where they made up 32 percent of the municipal councilors and 12 percent of the mayors elected in 2001, 50 percent more than six years before.

Political parties structure access to political representation far more in France than in the United States. The left has generally made a greater effort to recruit women than has the right. Thus, when the Socialists and Communists gained a substantial number of seats in the 1997 legislative elections, the proportion of women in the National Assembly almost doubled.

In contrast to the United States, political advancement in France generally requires a deep involvement in political parties, with a bias in favor of professional politicians and administrators. However, relatively few women have made this kind of long-term commitment to political life.

One woman who has is **Ségolène Royal.** A graduate of the ENA and a member of the Council of State (one of the five grands corps), she has also been a Socialist government minister, a deputy in the National Assembly, and president of one of the regions of France. She was the (defeated) Socialist candidate for the presidential elections in 2007. In addition, the present national secretary (and 2007 presidential candidate) of the French Communist Party is a woman, as is the president of the employers' confederation, the Mouvement des Enterprisès de France (MEDEF).

Periodically, governments and the political parties recognize this dearth of women in representative institutions, but little has been done about it. The Constitutional Council has rejected some remedies, and some proposed reforms have challenged accepted institutional norms. By the 1990s leaders of all political parties favored amending the constitution to permit positive discrimination to produce greater gender parity in representative institutions. Thus, with support of both the president of the Republic and the prime minister and without dissent, the National Assembly passed an amendment in December 1998 stipulating that "the law [and not the constitution] determines the conditions for the organization of equal access of men and women to electoral mandates and elective functions." Enforcement legislation requires greater gender parity, at least in the selection of candidates. This is a significant departure for the French political system, which has resisted the use of quotas in the name of equality. As a result of this parity legislation, the number of women in the 2007 National Assembly actually increased modestly, from 10.2 percent in 2000 to 18.5 in 2007.

Perhaps the most important change in the political behavior of French women is in the way they vote. During the Fourth Republic, a majority of women consistently voted for parties of the right. However, as church attendance among women has declined, their political orientation has moved from right to left. In every national election between 1986 and 1997, a clear majority of women voted for the left. By 2002, however, the pattern of voting among women changed. In both 2002 and 2007, women supported both Chirac and Sarkozy more than men, even though Sarkozy's opponent in 2007 was a woman. On the other hand, women have given far less support than men to the extreme right.[21]

INTEREST GROUPS

The Expression of Interests

As in many other European countries, the organization of French political life is largely defined within the historical cleavages of class and religious traditions. Interest groups have therefore frequently shared ideological commitments with the political parties with which they have organizational connections.

Actual memberships in most economic associations have varied considerably over time by sector, but they are generally much smaller than comparable groups in other industrialized countries. In 2005 no more than 8 percent of workers belonged to trade unions (the largest decline in Western Europe over the past twenty-five years). About 50 percent of French farmers and 75 percent of large industrial enterprises belong to their respective organizations.[22]

Historically, many of the important economic groups have experienced a surge of new members at dramatic moments in the country's social or political history. But membership then declines as conditions normalize, leaving some associations with a membership too small to justify their claims of representativeness.

Many groups lack the resources to employ a competent staff, or they depend on direct and indirect forms of state support. The modern interest group official is a fairly recent phenomenon that is found only in certain sectors of the group system, such as business associations.

Interest groups are also weakened by ideological division. Separate groups defending the interests of workers, farmers, veterans, schoolchildren, and consumers are divided by ideological preferences. The ideological division of representation forces each organization to compete for the same clientele in order to establish its representativeness. Consequently, even established French interest groups exhibit a radicalism in action and goals that is rare in other Western democracies. For groups that lack the means of using the information media, such tactics also become a way to put their case before the public at large. In such a setting, even the defense of purely economic, social, or cultural interests takes on a political color.

The Labor Movement

The French labor movement is divided into national confederations of differing political sympathies, although historical experiences have driven labor to avoid direct organizational ties with political parties.[23] Union membership has declined steeply since 1975, but there are indications that the decline has leveled off. Although union membership is declining in almost every industrialized country, it is now the lowest by far in France (see Figure 3.1 in Chapter 3). The youngest salaried workers virtually deserted the trade union movement in the 1990s. Although the decline in membership has slowed slightly in recent years, recruitment of young workers has lagged. In addition, after 1990, candidates supported by nonunion groups in various plant-level elections have attracted more votes than any of the established union organizations.[24] In fact, unions lost members and (electoral) support at the very time when the French trade union movement was becoming better institutionalized at the workplace and better protected by legislation.

Despite these clear weaknesses, workers still maintain considerable confidence in unions to defend their interests during periods of labor conflict. Support for collective action and confidence in unions and their leadership of strike movements remain strong. Indeed, during the massive strikes—strikes of truckers and taxi drivers in 2000 and strikes against changes in civil service pensions in 2003, youth contracts in 2006 and long strikes in education in 2009—public support for the strikers was far higher than confidence in the government against which the strikes were directed.[25] However, even though there are occasional massive strikes in France, strike levels have declined over the past thirty years.

French labor has had the most difficulty dealing with ideological fragmentation. Indeed, the decline in union membership has not encouraged consolidation; rather, it has produced more fragmentation (as we will see in the following discussion). Unlike workers in the United States, French workers in the same plant or firm may be represented by several union federations. As a result, there is constant competition among unions at every level for membership and support. Even during periods when the national unions agree to act together, animosities at the plant level sometimes prevent cooperation.

Moreover, the weakness of union organization at the plant level—which is where most lengthy strikes are called—means that unions are difficult bargaining partners. Unions at this level maintain only weak control over the strike weapon. Union militants are quite adept at sensitizing workers, producing the preconditions for strike action, and channeling strike movements once they begin. However, the unions have considerable difficulty in effectively calling strikes and ending them. Thus, unions depend heavily on the general environment, what they call the "social climate," in order to support their positions at the bargaining table. Because their ability to mobilize workers at any given moment is an essential criterion of their representativeness, union ability to represent workers is frequently in question.

The left government passed legislation in 1982–1983 (the Auroux laws) to strengthen the unions' position at the plant level. By creating an "obligation to negotiate" for management and by protecting the right of expression for workers, the government hoped to stimulate collective negotiations. In fact, this act brought about important changes in industrial relations and stimulated collective negotiations. However, given their increasing weakness, unions have not taken full advantage of the potential benefits of the legislation. This law refocused French industrial relations on the plant level without necessarily increasing the effectiveness of unions.

The oldest and the largest of the union confederations is the **Confédération Générale du Travail (CGT)** (General Confederation of Labor). Since World War II, the CGT has been identified closely with the Communist Party, with which it maintains a considerable overlap of leadership. Yet by tradition and by its relative effectiveness as a labor organization, it enrolls many non-Communists among its members. Its domination diminished in the 1990s, however, mostly because the CGT lost more members and support than all other unions.

The second largest labor organization in terms of membership is now the **Confédération Française Democratique du Travail (CFDT)** (French Democratic Confederation of Labor). In many ways the CFDT is the most original and the most interesting of all labor movements in Western Europe. An offshoot of a Catholic trade union movement, the CFDT's earlier calls for worker self-management (*autogestion*) were integrated into the Auroux laws. The leaders of the CFDT see the policy of the confederation as an alternative to the oppositional stance of the CGT. The CFDT now offers itself as a potential partner to modern capitalist management.

This movement to the right created splits within several CFDT public service unions and resulted in the establishment of a national rival, the *Solidaire Unitaire et Democratique (SUD)* (Solidarity United and Democratic), in 1989. The split was further accentuated by the CFDT's opposition to the massive public service strike of 1995. The SUD, in turn, was integrated into a larger group of twenty-seven militant autonomous civil service unions, **G-10** (le Groupe des dix), in 1998.

The third major labor confederation, **Force Ouvrière (FO)** (Workers' Force), was formed in 1948 in reaction to the Communist domination of the CGT. Although its membership is barely half that of the two other major confederations, the FO made gains in the 1990s. As the state moved to cut back benefits for civil servants, teachers, and railway workers, FO leadership adopted a more confrontational position with the state. During the strike movements of 1995 and 1996, FO leadership strongly supported the more radical elements of striking workers. Trotskyist elements of the left continue to hold considerable influence in the organization.

One of the most important and influential of the "autonomous" unions is the **Fédération de l'Education Nationale (FEN)** (Federation of National Education), the teachers' union. At the end of 1992, as a result of growing internal conflict and declining membership, the FEN split. The core FEN group continued. The rump of the FEN joined with other independent unions to form the *Union Nationale des Syndicats Autonomes (UNSA)* (National Union of Autonomous Unions). In October 1994 the UNSA was officially recognized by the government. In legal terms this means that the government placed the UNSA on the same level as the other national confederations. Nevertheless, by 1996 the FEN (and the UNSA) was substantially weakened when the rival *La Fédération Syndicale Unitaire (FSU)* (United Union Federation)— which is close to the Communist Party—gained greater support in social elections (elections for shop stewards, shop committees and union representatives), support that has been reaffirmed since then.

In addition to the fragmentation that results from differences within existing organizations, there are challenges from the outside. In 1995 the National Front organized several new unions. When the government and the courts blocked these initiatives, the extreme-right party began to penetrate existing unions.

Thus, at a time when strong opposition to government action seems to give union organizations an opportunity to increase both their organizational strength and their support, the trade union movement is more fragmented than ever. As in the past, massive strike movements have accentuated divisions and rivalries, rather than provoking unity.

Business Interests

Since the end of World War II, most trade associations and employers' organizations have kept within one dominant and exceptionally well staffed confederation, renamed in 1998 the **Mouvement des Entreprises de France (MEDEF)** (Movement of French Business). However, divergent interests, differing economic concepts, and conflicting ideologies frequently prevent the national organization from acting forcefully. At times this division hampers its representativeness in negotiations with government or trade unions. Nevertheless, the MEDEF weathered the difficult years of the **nationalization** introduced by the Socialists and the restructuring of social legislation and industrial relations without lessening its status as an influential interest group.

Since the MEDEF is dominated primarily by big business, shopkeepers and the owners of many small firms feel that they are better defended by more movement-oriented groups.[26] As a result, a succession of small business and shopkeeper movements has challenged the established organization and has evolved into organized associations in their own right.

Agricultural Interests

The defense of agricultural interests has a long record of internal strife. However, under the Fifth Republic, the **Fédération Nationale des Syndicats Agricoles (FNSEA)** (National Federation of Agricultural Unions) is the dominant group among several farm organizations. The FNSEA has also served as an effective instrument for modernizing French agriculture.

The rural reform legislation of the 1960s provided for the "collaboration of the professional agricultural organizations," and from the outset real collaboration was offered only to the FNSEA. From this privileged position, the federation gained both patronage and control over key institutions that were transforming agriculture. It used these instruments to organize a large proportion of French farmers. After establishing its domination over the farming sector with the support of the government, it then periodically demonstrated opposition to government policy with the support of the vast majority of a declining number of farmers.[27]

The principal challenges to the FNSEA in recent years are external, rather than internal. The agricultural sector has suffered from the fruits of its own productive success. Under pressure from the EU, France agreed in 1992 to major reforms of the Common Agricultural Policy (CAP) that took substantial amounts of land out of production and replaced some price supports with direct payments to farmers. That same year the EU reached an agreement with the United States that the EU would reduce subsidized grain exports and cut back cultivation of oilseed products. France is the largest exporter of these products in the EU. FNSEA protests (some of them violent) were joined by farm unions from throughout the EU. This ultimately resulted in a face-saving General Agreement on Tariffs and Trade (GATT) accord in 1994. The enlargement of the EU toward the East has heightened pressures to further reduce the budget of CAP. The substantial opposition in France (and other parts of Europe) to the importation of genetically modified agricultural products has increased the tensions within the World Trade Organization (WTO) (formerly GATT).

However, the more substantial issue for the WTO is agreement on the reduction of export subsidies for European and American agricultural products. Poorer countries have demanded the reduction of such subsidies for a long time. In 2007 and again in 2008, the Doha Round of trade negotiations broke down in part over this issue, the first time such multilateral trade negotiations have failed since World War II. The breakdown has been blamed on several factors, but specifically on the influence of agricultural groups in both France and the United States.

French organized interests are expressed through an impressive range of different kinds of organizations, from the weak and fragmented trade union movement to the well-organized FNSEA. Overall, what seems to differentiate French groups from those of other industrial countries is their style of expression and their forms of activity.

Means of Access and Styles of Action

In preceding regimes organized interests saw Parliament as the most convenient means of access to political power. During the Third and Fourth Republics, the highly specialized and powerful parliamentary committees often seemed to be little more than institutional facades for interest groups that frequently substituted bills of their own design for those submitted by the government.

Among the reasons given in 1958 for reforming and rationalizing Parliament was the desire to reduce the role of organized interests in the legislative process. By and large this has been accomplished. But interest groups have not lost all influence on rulemaking and policy formation. To be effective groups now use the channels that the best-equipped groups have long found most rewarding, channels that give them direct access to the administration. The indispensable collaboration between organized private interests and the state is institutionalized in advisory committees that are attached to most administrative agencies. These committees are composed mainly of civil servants and group representatives. Nonetheless, tendencies toward privileged access, sometimes called **neocorporatism** (democratic corporatism) (see Chapter 3), have, except in the areas of agriculture and big business, remained weak in France.

The weak organization of labor and small business means that these organizations are often regarded as unreliable partners. Organized interests also attempt to pressure the political executive. The ministerial staffs—those circles of personal collaborators who support every minister—are an important target. The strengthened position of the political executive enables both the prime minister and the president to function more effectively as arbiters between competing claims and to exercise stricter control over many agencies and ministries.

It is not surprising that some interests have easier access to government bureaus than others. An affinity of views between group representatives and public administrators might be based on common outlook, common social origin, or education. The official of an important trade association or its national association who sorts out the raw demands of constituents and submits them in rational fashion easily gets a more sympathetic hearing than the official of an organization that defends atomistic interests by mobilizing latent resentment.

High civil servants tend to distinguish between "professional organizations," which they consider serious enough to listen to, and "interest groups," which should be kept at a distance. The perspectives of interest representatives tend to reflect their own strength, as well as their experience in collaborating with different parts of the state and government. Trade union representatives acknowledge their reliance on the social climate (essentially the level of strike activity) to bargain effectively with the state. Representatives of business rely more on contacts with civil servants. Agricultural interests say that they rely more on contacts at the ministerial level.[28]

Central to the state interest group collaboration described as neocorporatism is the notion that the state plays a key role in both shaping and defining the legitimacy of the interest group universe. The state also establishes the rules by which the collaboration takes place. The French state, at various levels, strongly influences the relationship among groups and even their existence in key areas through official recognition and subsidies. Although representative organizations may exist with or without official recognition, this designation gives them access to consultative bodies, the right to sign collective agreements (especially important in the case of trade unions), and the right to obtain certain subsidies. Therefore, recognition is an important tool that both conservative and Socialist governments have used to influence the group universe.

The French state subsidizes interest groups, both indirectly and directly. By favoring some groups over others in these ways, the state seems to conform to neocorporatist criteria. However, in other ways the neocorporatist model is less applicable in France than in other European countries. Neocorporatist policy-making presumes close collaboration between the state administration and a dominant interest group (or coalition of groups) in major socioeconomic sectors. Yet, what stands out in the French case is the unevenness of this pattern of collaboration.[29]

If the neocorporatist pattern calls for interest group leaders to control organizational action and coordinate bargaining, the French interest groups' mass actions—such as street demonstrations, "wildcat" strikes, and attacks on government property—are often poorly controlled by group leadership. Indeed, it can be argued that group protest is more effective in France (at least negatively) than in other industrialized countries because it is part of a pattern of group-state relations.

Protests are limited in scope and intensity, but the government recognizes them as a valid expression of interest. In April 2006 half of those surveyed said that they were prepared to take part in such direct action. This explains why governments backed by a majority in Parliament frequently make concessions to weakly organized interest groups. In the spring of 2006, for example, legislation that created a new labor contract was passed by Parliament and signed by the president, but withdrawn after weeks of growing protests and occupations by students that threatened the stability of the government (see Box 6.1).[30]

POLITICAL PARTIES

The Traditional Party System

Some analysts of elections see a chronic and seemingly unalterable division of the French into two large political families, each motivated by a different mood or temperament and usually classified as the right and the left. If we view elections from this perspective, political alignments have remained surprisingly stable over long periods of history. As late as 1962, the opposition to de Gaulle was strongest in departments where republican traditions had a solid foundation for more than a century. The alignments in the presidential contest of 1974 and the parliamentary elections of 1978 mirrored the same divisions. Soon thereafter, however, the left's inroads into formerly conservative strongholds changed the traditional geographic distribution of votes. Majorities changed at each legislative election between 1981 and 2002, and few departments now remain solid bastions for either the right or the left.

The electoral system of the Fifth Republic favors a simplification of political alignments. In most constituencies runoff elections result in the confrontation of two candidates, each typically representing one of the two camps. A simple and stable division could have resulted long ago in a pattern of two parties or coalitions alternating in having power and being in opposition—and hence giving valid expression to the voters' opinions. Why has this not occurred?

Except for the Socialists and the Communists, and more recently the RPR (Rally for the Republic—now the UMP—see below), French political parties have mostly remained weakly organized. French parties developed in a mainly preindustrial and preurban environment, catering at first to upper-middle-class and

During the Socialist governments of the 1980s, more and more people—farmers, artisans, people in small businesses, truckers, doctors, medical students—took to the streets to protest impending legislation, often out of fear for their status. The demonstrations frequently led to violence and near riots. The same scenario took place later under conservative governments. Demonstrations by college and high school students forced the withdrawal of a planned university reform in 1987. A planned imposition of a "youth" minimum wage in 1994, ostensibly to encourage more employment of young people, was dropped when high school students opposed it in the streets of Paris and other large cities. After a month of public service strikes and massive demonstrations in 1995, the new Chirac government abandoned a plan to reorganize the nationalized railway system

and revised a plan to reorganize the civil service. A year later striking truckers won major concessions from a still weakened government. In the autumn of 2000, a protest led by truckers and taxi drivers (that spread to England) against the rising price of oil and gasoline forced the government to lower consumer taxes on fuel. Finally, in 2006 the government passed legislation to establish a work contract (one among many) meant to encourage employers to hire young people under the age of 25 by making it easier to fire them during the first two years of their employment. After a three-month struggle of street demonstrations and school occupations by many of the same young people who were supposed to be the beneficiaries of the law (which was supported by all of the major trade unions and the major parties of the left—at least initially), the law was withdrawn.

---

later to middle-class voters. Their foremost and sometimes only function was to provide a framework for selecting and electing candidates for local, departmental, and national offices. Even among the better organized parties, party organization has been both fragmentary at the national level and local in orientation, with only modest linkage between the two levels.

This form of representation and party organization survives largely because voters support it. An electorate that distrusts authority and wants protection against arbitrary government is likely to be suspicious of parties organized for political reform. For all their antagonism, the republican and antirepublican traditions have one thing in common: their aversion to well-established and strongly organized parties.

Party membership has always been low except during short and dramatic situations. As late as the 1960s, no more than 2 percent of registered voters were party members. In Britain and Germany, for example, some parties have had more than a million members, a membership level never achieved by any French political party. Organizational weakness contributes to the endurance of a multiparty system.

In a two- or three-party system, major parties normally move toward the political center in order to gain stability and cohesion. But where extreme party plurality prevails, the center is unable to become a political force. In France centrist coalitions were an

effective, if limited, means of maintaining a regime in the Third and Fourth Republics, but an ineffective means of developing coherent policy.

The Fifth Republic created a new political framework that has had a major, if gradual and mostly unforeseen, influence on all parties and on their relationships to each other. The emerging party system, in turn, influenced the way that political institutions actually worked.[31] The strengthening of parliamentary party discipline in the 1970s gave meaning to the strong executive leadership of president and prime minister and stabilized the political process. The main political parties also became the principal arenas in which to develop and debate alternative policies.

The main political parties still dominate the organization of parliamentary work and the selection of candidates, but they have become far less important as mass membership organizations. In 2002 at least seventy-nine parties or groups presented 8,424 candidates for 577 seats in the National Assembly, a record for the Fifth Republic. In 2007 the four main parties were supported by 78 percent of the electorate, with the National Front and the Greens attracting an additional 15 percent. If we include the National Front and the Greens, less than 10 percent of the electorate supported an array of issue-based and personality-based parties in 2007, a sharp decline compared with 2002. Nine parties are represented in the National

Assembly in four parliamentary groups, two in the right majority, two allied in the left opposition.

The Main Parties: The Right and Center

Union for a Popular Movement The **Union for a Popular Movement (UMP)** is the most recent direct lineal descendant of the Gaullist party. The original Gaullist party was hastily thrown together after de Gaulle's return to power in 1958. Only weeks after its birth, it won almost 18 percent of the vote and about 38 percent of the seats in the first Parliament of the new Republic in 1958 (see Table 6.1).

In several respects the new Gaullist party differed from the traditional conservative parties of the right. It appealed directly to a broad coalition of groups and classes, including a part of the working class. The party's leadership successfully built a membership that at one time reached several hundred thousand. Yet the membership's role was generally limited to appearing at mass meetings and assisting in propaganda efforts at election time. An important novelty was that the party's representatives in Parliament followed strict discipline in voting on policy. Electoral success increased with each contest until the landslide election—held after the massive strikes and student **demonstrations of May–June 1968**—enabled the Gaullists to hold a majority in the National Assembly. This achievement was never before attained under a republican regime in France.

For sixteen years (from 1958 to 1974) both the presidency and the prime ministership were in Gaullist hands. In 1974, after the death of both Charles de Gaulle and Georges Pompidou, Valéry Giscard-d'Estaing was elected president. He was a prominent conservative who was not a Gaullist; thus, the Gaullist party's status deteriorated and electoral support declined.

For a time Jacques Chirac reversed the party's decline by restructuring it and renaming it the **Rally for the Republic (RPR)**. In fact, the RPR was quite different from its Gaullist predecessors. Although Chirac frequently invoked Gaullism as his inspiration, he avoided the populist language that had served the movement at its beginnings. The RPR appealed to a restricted, well-defined constituency of the right, similar to the classic conservative clientele. Its electorate overrepresented older, wealthier voters, as well as farmers (now included as the dominant part of the UMP electorate in Table 6.2). Its voters were most likely to define themselves as being on the right, antileft, positive

toward business and parochial schools, more likely to vote for personality than for ideas, and least supportive of a woman's right to abortion. After presiding over a government that dubbed itself neoliberal and that engaged in a round of privatization of previously nationalized industries between 1986 and 1988, Chirac set out to assure those who feared change.

The party's electoral level remained more or less stagnant in the 1980s. Even in the massive electoral victory for the right in 1993, when the conservative coalition gained 80 percent of the parliamentary seats, the RPR just edged out its conservative rivals with less than 20 percent of the vote in the first round of the elections. In 1997 its vote declined to 16.8 percent, less than 2 percentage points more than the National Front. Nevertheless, with an estimated 100,000 members in 1997 (relatively low by European standards), the RPR was the largest party in France.[32]

By 2002 the RPR was a long way from the party once dominated with a firm hand by Gaullist "barons" and defined by the organizing discourse of Gaullism. Jacques Chirac's victory in the 1995 presidential elections should have given him an opportunity to rebuild the RPR as a party of government. However, a seemingly unending series of political crises after the summer of 1995 and the disastrous losses in the June 1997 legislative elections only intensified the divisions within the party and with its partners. In 1999 Chirac (still president of the Republic) lost control over the party when his chosen candidate was defeated in an election for party president.

In the fall of 2000, Chirac's candidacy for reelection in 2002 seemed to be undermined by dramatic new evidence of massive corruption in the Paris party machine that directly implicated the president (and former mayor of Paris). However, the unexpected match against Jean-Marie Le Pen (leader of the National Front—see below) in the presidential race of 2002 gave both Chirac and the party a new lease on life.

Chirac's massive victory in the second round of the 2002 presidential election created the basis for the organization of the UMP, a new successor to the RPR. (The UMP was originally called the Union for a Presidential Majority in 2002.) The party included deputies from the RPR, some from the **Union for French Democracy (UDF)**, and some from other small parties of the right. With more than 60 percent of the new National Assembly, the UMP united the

Parliamentary Elections in the Fifth Republic

TABLE 6.1

Shifting party vote shares and parliamentary seats since 1981—percentage of votes cast, first ballot

	1981		1986[a]		1988		1993		1997		2002		2007	
Registered voters (in millions)	35.5		36.6		37.9		37.0		39.2		41.0		43.9	
Abstentions (%)	29.1		21.5		34.3		31.0		32.0		35.6		39.6	
Party Seats	**%**	**Seats**	**%**	**Seats**	**%**	**Seats**	**%**	**Seats**	**%**	**Seats**	**%**	**Seats**	**%**	**Seats**
Communists (PCF)	16.2	44	9.7	35	11.3	27	9.1	24	10.0	37	4.8	21	4.6	18[h]
Socialists (PS)	37.6	267	31.6	208	34.8	274	19.2	61	23.7	245	25.3	141	27.7	201[h]
*Left Radicals	—	14	3.0	2	1.1	2	—	8	1.5	13	—	8	—	7
Majority (UMP)	—	—	—	—	—	—	—	—	—	—	33.3[f]	362[f]	45.5	335[h]
*UDF (RI and other centrists)	19.2	63	—	129	18.5	130	18.8	207	14.8	109	4.9	22	7.7	4
Gaullists (RPR)	20.8	87	42.0	145	19.2	128	19.7	242	16.8	140	—	—	—	—
National Front (FN)	—	—	9.9	35	9.8	1	12.7	0	15.1	1	11.3	—	4.7	—
Others	6.2	16	6.6	23	5.3	15	20.5[b]	37[c]	18.7[d]	32[e]	16.3[g]	13	6.3	12[g]

*Votes for the Left Radicals in 1981, 1993, 2002, and 2007 are included with those of the Socialists; votes for the UDF in 1986 are included with those of the Gaullists.

[a] The 1986 election was by proportional representation.

[b] Includes the three Green parties, which received 10.9 percent of the vote.

[c] Includes 36 unaffiliated deputies of the right.

[d] Includes the Green parties' vote of 6.3 percent, as well as votes for smaller movements of the right and the left.

[e] Includes eight ecologists (Greens), seven dissident Socialists, and other unaffiliated deputies.

[f] UMP (Union of the Presidential Majority—new center-right party organized for the 2002 legislative election).

[g] Includes ecologists (Greens) and dissidents of the right and left, as well as the extreme right party (MNR) in 2002.

[h] Includes affiliated independent deputies.

Source: Official results from the Ministry of the Interior, found on www.assemblee-nationale.fr/elections.

TABLE 6.2

Voting Patterns in the 2007 Legislative Elections

Leftist parties disproportionately gain support from the young and white-collar
employees, while UMP/UDF draw more votes from older voters and the bourgeoisie

	PS/PC/Greens + Other Left	UMP/UDF + Other Right	Extreme Right FN/MNR
Sex			
Men	36%	50%	7%
Women	38	56	2
Age			
18–29	43	49	1
30–49	39	52	5
50+	32	56	6
Profession			
Shopkeepers, craftsmen, and businesspeople	21	62	1
Executives, professionals, and intellectuals	41	44	1
Middle management	45	47	1
White-collar	39	49	6
Workers	32	48	16
Unemployed	43	40	15
Level of Education			
No degree	34	52	9
Vocational degree	36	55	6
High School (academic)	45	49	3
Higher education	38	55	2
All Voters	37	53	4

Source: CSA–CISCO, *Les Elections Legislatives: Explication du Vote et Perspectives Politiques, Sondage Jour du vote*, June 2007, p. 10.

fragmented groups of the right behind the victorious president. By 2006 Chirac's detested rival within the party, **Nicolas Sarkozy**, had become party leader, minister of the interior, and virtually unchallenged party candidate for the presidency in 2007.

Union for French Democracy (UDF) Valéry Giscard d'Estaing's foremost concern was to prevent the center's exclusion from power in the Gaullist Republic. His small party, the Independent Republican Party (RI), was the typical party, or rather nonparty, of French conservatism. It came into existence in 1962, when Giscard and a few other conservative deputies opposed de Gaulle's strictures against European unity and his referendum on direct elections for the presidency.

From that time on, the group provided a small complement for the conservative majority in Parliament.

Giscard himself, a scion of families long prominent in business, banking, and public service, was finance minister under both de Gaulle and Pompidou before his election to the presidency in 1974. His party derived its political strength from its representatives in Parliament, many of whom held Cabinet posts, and from local leaders who occupied important posts in municipal and departmental councils.

To increase the weight of the party (the name was changed to the Parti Républicain [PR] in 1977), President Giscard chose the path that parties of the right and center have always found opportune: a heterogeneous alliance among groups and personalities organized to support the president in the 1978 legislative elections. The result was the Union for French Democracy (UDF). In addition to Giscard's Republicans, it included remnants of a Catholic party (CDS), the once militant anti-Catholic radicals, and some former Socialists. It is estimated that all of the parties of the UDF combined had no more than 38,000 members as the party moved into the 2002 elections.

After 1981 the UDF and the RPR generally cooperated in elections. As the National Front gained in electoral support after 1983, the UDF and the RPR presented more joint candidates in the first round of parliamentary elections to avoid being defeated by the National Front. Nevertheless, even combined, they were incapable of increasing their vote percentage beyond 45 percent. Still, they won majorities in Parliament in 1986, 1993, and 2002 (see Figure 6.4). The two governments organized after Chirac's election in 1995 under Prime Minister **Alain Juppé** were double coalitions: first, coalitions of factions within the RPR and the UDF and, second, coalitions between the RPR and the UDF. Thus, the representatives of the UDF exercised considerable influence over the policymaking process, both as members of the Cabinet and as chairs of three of the six permanent committees of the National Assembly. The government in 2002 was also a double coalition. Prime Minister Jean-Pierre Raffarin (who served until 2005) was a longtime member of the UDF. With the integration of most of the UDF deputies into the UMP, the UDF as a party lost most of its independent influence.

National Front Divisions within the right result in part from different reactions to the electoral rise of the **National Front (FN). Jean-Marie Le Pen** founded the FN in 1972. Until the 1980s it was a relatively obscure party of the far right. In none of the elections before 1983 did the FN attract more than 1 percent of the national vote. In the 1984 European Parliament elections, the FN built on support in local elections and attracted almost 10 percent of the vote, to the consternation of the established parties of the right and the left.

Then, in the parliamentary elections of 1986, the FN won almost 10 percent of the vote (about 2.7 million votes—and in metropolitan France, more votes than the Communists). This established it as a substantial political force. Two-thirds of the FN's votes came from voters who previously supported established parties of the right, but the remainder came from some former left voters (mostly Socialists) or from new voters and former abstainers.

Profiting from the change to proportional representation elections in 1986, thirty-five FN deputies entered Parliament. In the 1993 legislative elections, FN candidates attracted almost 13 percent of the vote in the first round. Because the electoral system was once again based on single-member districts, the party elected no deputies. With over 15 percent of the vote in the first round of the 1997 legislative elections, the FN sent a record number of candidates into the second round. However, only one of these candidates was elected.

Nevertheless, the FN seemed well on its way to developing a network of local bases. In 1992 the right depended on the party for its majority in fourteen out of twenty-two regions. In 1998 this dependency was translated into a political breakthrough when five

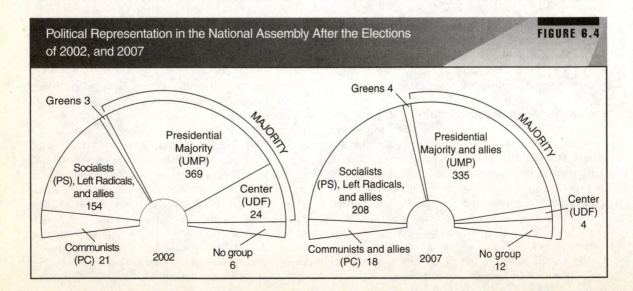

Political Representation in the National Assembly After the Elections of 2002, and 2007   FIGURE 6.4

Greens 3

Presidential Majority (UMP) 369

MAJORITY

Socialists (PS), Left Radicals, and allies 154

Center (UDF) 24

Communists (PC) 21   2002   No group 6

Greens 4

Presidential Majority and allies (UMP) 335

MAJORITY

Socialists (PS), Left Radicals, and allies 208

Center (UDF) 4

Communists and allies (PC) 18   2007   No group 12

UDF regional leaders formally accepted FN support to maintain their regional presidencies. In 1995, for the first time, the FN won municipal elections in three cities and gained some representation in almost half of the larger towns in France. It gained one additional city in a special election in 1997.

The ability of Le Pen to come in second—with 17 percent of the vote in the first round of the presidential elections of 2002—was a considerable shock to the political system. The FN results in the legislative elections two months later (11 percent) were far lower, but a confirmation that the party—and not simply Le Pen—remained a political force.

The National Front is often compared to the shopkeeper movement (the Poujadist movement), which attracted 2.5 million votes in the 1956 legislative elections and then faded from the scene.[33] But the FN draws its electoral and organizational support from big-city, rather than small-town, voters. Its supporters come more from transfers from the right than did those of Poujade. In addition, the FN has been far more successful than the Poujadist movement in building a strong organizational network.

Because of the electoral system, the FN never had more than one deputy in the National Assembly after 1988. But it has hundreds of elected representatives on the regional, departmental, and local levels (as well as in the European Parliament). By 1998 it was estimated that the FN had 50,000 members (compared with 10,000 in 1985).

The National Front was seemingly given new life by Le Pen's success in 2002, success that was generally confirmed by the results of the regional and European parliamentary elections in 2004. In addition, the process of party development has affected voters of all parties, especially those who would normally vote for the right and young workers who had formerly been mobilized by the Communist Party.

Approval of the FN's issues increased dramatically among *all* voters in the 1980s and, after mid-1999, increased again. Moreover, the dynamics of party competition have forced other political parties to place FN issues high on their political agenda. Thus, Nicolas Sarkozy, in an attempt to attract FN supporters, used his position as minister of the interior to confront illegal immigration and deal with issues of law and order.

Although this strategy had been tried before, Sarkozy's efforts showed some indications of success. In fact, it proved to be remarkably successful in the presidential elections of 2007. Jean-Marie Le Pen received 800,000 fewer votes than in 2002, and almost all of them went to Sarkozy. This stunning loss weakened the party, as confirmed by the local election results in March 2008.

The Left

Socialist Party In comparison with the solid social-democratic parties in other European countries, the French **Socialist Party (PS)** lacked muscle almost since its beginnings in 1905. Slow and uneven industrialization and reluctance to organize not only blocked the development of labor unions, but also deprived the PS of the working-class strength that other European labor parties gained from their trade union affiliations.

Unlike the British Labour Party, the early PS also failed to absorb middle-class radicals, the equivalent of the Liberals in England. The Socialist program, formulated in terms of doctrinaire Marxism, prevented inroads into the electorate of the left-of-center middle-class parties for a long time. The pre–Fifth Republic party was never strong enough to assume control of the government by itself. Its weakness reduced it to being, at best, one of several partners in the unstable coalition governments of the Third and Fourth Republics.

The emergence of the French Communist Party in 1920 effectively deprived the Socialists of core working-class support. Most of the Socialists' working-class following was concentrated in a few regions of traditional strength, such as the industrial north and urban agglomeration in the center. However, the party had some strongholds elsewhere—among the winegrowers of the south, devotees of republican ideals of anticlericalism, and producers' cooperatives. The proportion of civil servants, especially teachers, and people living on fixed incomes has been far higher among Socialist voters than in the population at large.

The party encountered considerable difficulties under the changed conditions in the Fifth Republic. After several false starts, the old party dissolved, and a new Socialist Party emerged in 1969. The new party successfully attracted new members and reversed its electoral decline. Incipient public disenchantment with conservative governments combined with the strong party leadership of François Mitterrand brought about this reversal in party fortunes. Compared with the past, the party membership reached respectable heights in the 1980s (about 180,000 by 1983), though it was still not comparable to the large labor parties of Britain and the Continent.

The new members came predominantly from the salaried middle classes, the professions, the civil service, and especially the teaching profession. Workers rallied to the PS in large numbers in the 1970s, but they were still sparsely represented in the party's leadership. In the 1970s the PS did what other European Socialist parties were unable to do: It attracted leaders of some of the new social movements of the late 1960s—among them, ecologists and regionalists, as well as leaders of small parties of the non-Communist left.[34]

Mitterrand reaped the benefits of the elections of 1981. With Mitterrand as president of the Republic and a Socialist majority in Parliament (but also supported by the Communists), the PS found itself in a situation it had never known—and for which it was ill-prepared. The following years of undivided power affected the party's image and outlook. The years in office between 1981 and 1986 were an intense, and painful, learning experience for the PS at all levels. Under pressure from Mitterrand and a succession of Socialist governments, the classical socialist ideology was dismantled. What the German Social Democrats had done by adopting a new program at Bad Godesberg in 1959 the French PS did in the early 1980s by its daily practice.

Indeed, by most measures the Socialist Party was to the 1980s what Gaullists were to the 1960s: a party of government with broad support among most social groups throughout the country. When reelected for a second seven-year term in 1988, Mitterrand carried seventy-seven of the ninety-six departments of metropolitan France. The Socialists made inroads in the traditionally conservative western and eastern areas of the country. However, this nationalization of Socialist electoral strength meant that the party's legislative majority depended on constituencies where voter support was far more conditional. In the legislative elections of 1993, the PS lost a third of its electorate, compared with 1988, but far more than that in areas outside of its traditional bastions.

Social trends favored the left for a time. The decline of religious observance, urbanization, the growth of the salaried middle classes (technicians, middle management, etc.) and the service sector of the economy, and the massive entry of women into the labor market all weakened the groups that provided the right's stable strength. This included farmers, people in small businesses, the traditional bourgeoisie, and the nonemployed housewives.

However, the party loyalty of large numbers of voters, especially younger voters, was evolving during the 1980s. Voter loyalty became more related to individual attitudes toward specific issues than to collective loyalties based on group or class. Thus, rising unemployment rates, the growing sense among even Socialist voters that the party leadership was worn out, and the mobilization of large numbers of traditional Socialist voters against the government during the campaign for the Maastricht referendum all undermined Socialist support between 1992 and 1994.

During ten years as a governing party (broken by two years of opposition from 1986 to 1988), Socialist leadership cohesion depended on the prerogatives of power. If the Fifth Republic became normalized during the 1980s—in the sense that the left and the right alternated in government with each legislative election—the PS became like other governing parties in its dependence on governing power. One index of this normalization was the increased incidence of political corruption within the party. Accusations, investigations, and convictions for corruption swept all parties beginning in the late 1980s. For the Socialists, however, this corruption undermined the party's image and contributed to the voters' desertion of the party. Estimated membership dropped to about 100,000 by 1995.

Under these circumstances PS leader **Lionel Jospin** was a remarkably effective presidential candidate in 1995, winning the first round before being defeated in the second round by Chirac. After the elections the PS gained in the municipal elections, performed well in by-elections, and made significant gains in the (indirect) 1995 Senate elections. The real test for Socialist leadership came when President Chirac called surprise legislative elections in April 1997.

Although Jospin and his colleagues were clearly unprepared for the short campaign, they benefited from Chirac's rapidly deteriorating popularity and the lack of efficacy of his majority, as well as from the electorate's tendency to vote against the majority in power. Jospin put together a thirty-one-seat majority (called the *plural left*), became prime minister, and formed the first cohabitation government of the left in June 1997.

The government passed a set of important, but controversial reforms, including a thirty-five–hour workweek, domestic partnership legislation, and a constitutional amendment requiring parity for women candidacies for elective office. Finally, there were major structural reforms: The presidential term was reduced to five years (with the agreement of the president), and a process began to radically alter the relationship between Corsica and the French state.

Although the government's popularity had been declining, the elimination of Jospin in the first round of the 2002 presidential elections (by less than 1 percent) was entirely unexpected. It largely resulted from the defection of PS voters to marginal candidates of the left alliance. Jospin quickly resigned as party leader, leaving the PS without effective leadership. This resulted in the left's defeat in the legislative elections that followed, as PS representation was cut in half.

Following a well-established rhythm, the Socialists —together with their allies on the left—rebounded two years later and swept the regional elections in 2004. They won control of all but one of the twenty-two regional governments in France. They accomplished this impressive victory without strong leadership at the national level. The victory represented profound public disappointment with—and opposition to—the right, which had used the majority it had gained in 2002 to push through cuts in welfare state benefits.

Without strong leadership, however, the PS appeared engaged in a self-destructive struggle to choose a presidential candidate for the elections of 2007. In this environment Ségolène Royal initiated a well-orchestrated and well-financed campaign for the nomination a full year and a half before the elections. The campaign was to convince members of the party—who would select her by a large majority in the fall of 2006—that her candidacy was a *fait accompli*. What made her campaign interesting is that it was directed toward the voters, rather than the party members who vote for the nominee.

Royal, the first woman candidate for a major political party, was a well-established political leader of the Socialist Party. A graduate of the ENA, she rose through the party ranks, first as a deputy, then with various ministerial posts, and then as president of the Poitou-Charentes region. Her campaign substantially increased the membership of the PS. With a claimed membership of 133,000 in December 2005, the PS's paid membership increased by 54,000 in three months; membership in Paris alone doubled during this period. Therefore, it was even more disappointing when Royal lost the election to Nicolas Sarkozy in May 2007, once again leaving the party without leadership.

French Communist Party Until the late 1970s, the **French Communist Party (PCF)** was a major force in French politics. This was so despite the fact that, except for a short interlude after World War II (1944–1947), the party was rejected as a coalition partner in national government until 1981.

During most of the Fourth Republic, the PCF received more electoral support than any other single party (with an average of just over 25 percent of the electorate). During the Fifth Republic, the party remained, until 1978, electorally dominant on the left, although it trailed the Gaullists on the right. In addition to its successes in national elections, the party commanded significant strength at the local level until the early 1980s. Between 1977 and 1983, Communist mayors governed in about 1,500 towns in France, with a total population of about 10 million people.

Over several decades the party's very existence constantly impinged nationally, as well as locally, on the rules of the political game and thereby on the system itself. The seemingly impressive edifice of the Communists and of its numerous organizations of sympathizers was badly shaken, however—first by the rejuvenation of the PS under Mitterrand's leadership in the 1970s and then by the collapse of international communism and the Soviet Union in the 1980s.

The PCF fielded its leader, **Georges Marchais,** as a candidate in the first ballot of the presidential election of 1981 with disastrous results: With 15 percent of the vote, the PCF lost one-fourth of its electorate. In the parliamentary elections that followed, the number of its deputies was cut in half. The party's defeats in 1981 were only the beginning of a tailspin of electoral decline.[35] The voters who left the party in 1981 never came back.

By 2007 its presidential candidate attracted a mere 2 percent of the vote (about half that of far-left candidate Olivier Besancenot) and just 2 percent of the working-class vote. In the legislative elections that followed, the PCF was clearly marginal to the left. To win elections, it has grown increasingly dependent on continued (and often difficult) cooperation with the Socialists, as well as on the personal popularity of some of its long-established mayors. Nineteen of the twenty-four Communist deputies, and those associated with them, elected in 2007 were municipal council members. In 2003 the party selected **Marie-George Buffet** as its national secretary.

Although the party's claimed membership remains large by French standards, more than 200,000— but certainly less—its organization is increasingly divided, ineffective, and challenged by successive waves of dissidence from within.

What does the marginalization of the PCF mean for the French party system? It has healed the division that had enfeebled the left since the split of the Socialist Party in 1920, in the wake of the Bolshevik seizure of power in Russia. But a price has been paid: This has weakened political representation of the French working class. Although the fortunes of the PCF have fallen in inverse relation to the PS's rising electoral strength, the proportion of workers actually voting for both parties combined has declined by 30 percent since the 1970s. Perhaps most important, it appears that many young workers, who previously would have been mobilized by Communist militants, are now being mobilized to vote for the National Front.

PATTERNS OF VOTING

Although France is a unitary state, elections are held with considerable frequency at every territorial level. Councilors are elected for each of the more than 36,000 **communes** in France, for each of the 100 departments (counties), and for each of the twenty-two regions. Deputies to the National Assembly are elected at least once every five years, and the president of the Republic is elected (or reelected) every five years (since 2002—every seven years before that). In addition, France elects representatives to the European Parliament every five years.

France was the first European country to enfranchise a mass electorate, and France was also the first European country to demonstrate that a mass electorate does not preclude the possibility of authoritarian government. The electoral law of 1848 enfranchised all male citizens over age 21. However, within five years this same mass electorate had ratified Louis Napoléon's *coup d'état* and his establishment of the Second Empire. Rather than restricting the electorate, Napoléon perfected modern techniques for manipulating it by gerrymandering districts, skillfully using public works as patronage for official candidates, and exerting pressure through the administrative hierarchy.

From the Second Empire to the end of World War II, the size of the electorate remained more or less stable. It suddenly more than doubled when women age 21 and older were granted the vote in 1944. After the voting age was lowered to 18 in 1974, 2.5 million voters were added to the rolls. By 2007 there were more than 42 million voters in France.

Electoral Participation and Abstention

Voting participation in elections of the Fifth Republic has undergone a significant change and fluctuates far more than during previous republics. Abstention tends to be highest in referendums and European elections and lowest in presidential contests, with other elections falling somewhere in between (see Table 6.1). In the presidential election of 2007, a

trend toward growing abstention was broken when 84 percent of registered voters voted in the first round.[36] The elections for the European Parliament always attract relatively few voters, but in 2004 more than 57 percent of the registered voters stayed home (slightly more than in 1999). For referendums a new record was set in 2000: Almost 70 percent of the registered voters chose not to vote in a (successful) referendum to reduce the presidential term from seven to five years (after the elections of 2002).

Rising abstention seems linked to a larger phenomenon of change in the party system. Since the late 1970s, voters' confidence in all parties has declined, and the highest abstention rates are usually among those voters who express no preference between parties of the right and left. Nevertheless, in contrast with the United States, among the 90 percent of the electorate that is registered to vote, individual abstention appears to be cyclical and there are few permanent abstainers.[37] In this sense it is possible to see abstention in an election as a political choice (42 percent of them in 2002 said that they abstained because they had no confidence in politicians).[38] Nevertheless, as in other countries, the least educated, the lowest income groups, and the youngest and oldest age groups vote less frequently.

Voting in Parliamentary Elections

France has experimented with a great number of electoral systems and devices without obtaining more satisfactory results in terms of government coherence. The stability of the Fifth Republic cannot be attributed to the method of electing National Assembly deputies, for the system is essentially the same one used during the most troubled years of the Third Republic.

As in the United States, electoral districts (577) are represented by a single deputy who is selected through two rounds of elections. On the first election day, candidates who obtain a majority of all votes cast are elected to Parliament. This is a relatively rare occurrence (less than 20 percent in 2007) because of the abundance of candidates. Candidates who obtain support of less than 12.5 percent of the registered voters are dropped from the "second round" a week later. Other candidates voluntarily withdraw in favor of a better-placed candidate close to their party on the political spectrum. For instance, preelection agreements between Communists and Socialists (and, more recently, the Greens) usually lead to the withdrawal of the weaker candidate(s) after the first round. Similar arrangements have existed between the UMP and other parties of the center-right. As a result, generally three (or at most four) candidates face each other in the second round, in which a plurality of votes ensures election.

This means that the first round is similar to American primary elections except that in the French case the primary is among candidates of parties allied in coalitions of the left or center-right. There is considerable pressure on political parties to develop electoral alliances, since those that do not are at a strong disadvantage in terms of representation.

The National Front has been more or less isolated from coalition arrangements with the parties of the center-right in national elections (though less so at the subnational level). Consequently, in 2007, with electoral support of 4.4 percent, none of the FN candidates

was elected. In comparison, the Communist Party benefited from an electoral agreement with the Socialists: With the same 4.4 percent of the vote, fifteen of their candidates were elected. Not surprisingly, the leading party (or coalition of parties) generally ends up with a considerably larger number of seats than is justified by its share in the popular vote.

Voting in Referendums

Between 1958 and 1969, the French electorate voted five times on referendums (see Table 6.3). In 1958 a vote against the new constitution might have involved the country in a civil war, which it had narrowly escaped a few months earlier. The two **referendums** that followed endorsed the peace settlement in the Algerian War. In 1962, hardly four

Election Results
French Presidential Elections (second round) and Referendums

TABLE 6.3

Date	Abstained (%)	Winner (%)	Voted for: Winning Candidate	Voted for: Losing Candidate
Presidential Elections				
12/19/65	15.4	54.5	de Gaulle	Mitterrand
6/15/69	30.9	57.5	Pompidou	Poher
5/19/74	12.1	50.7	Giscard d'Estaing	Mitterrand
5/10/81	13.6	52.2	Mitterrand	Giscard d'Estaing
5/8/88	15.9	54.0	Mitterrand	Chirac
5/7/95	20.1	52.6	Chirac	Jospin
6/5/02	20.3	82.2	Chirac	Le Pen
5/10/07	16.0	53.1	Sarkozy	Royal

Abstained	% Voted	Yes	Outcome
Referendums			
9/28/58	15.1	79.2	Constitution passed
1/8/61	23.5	75.3	Algeria settlement
4/8/62	24.4	90.7	Algeria settlement
10/28/62	22.7	61.7	Direct election of president
4/18/69	19.6	46.7	Defeat reform package
4/23/72	39.5	67.7	Britain joins Common Market
11/6/88	63.0	80.0	New Caledonia agreement
9/20/92	28.9	50.8	Maastricht Treaty
9/24/00	69.7	73.2	Reduction of presidential term
5/29/05	30.7	45.3	Defeat EU Constitution

Source: Official results from the Ministry of the Interior for each election and referendum:
http://www.interieur.gouv.fr/misill/sections/a_votre_service/elections/resultats/accueil-resultats/view

The loss of the referendum on the European Constitutional Treaty in 2005 was in many ways a repeat of what had happened in 1992, but with a key difference. In 1992 the president of the Republic, the leaders of the Socialist Party, most (but not all) of the leaders of the conservative opposition, and (before the summer) two-thirds of the electorate supported the referendum. It would establish the European Union, with European citizenship and (within a decade) a single European currency. It was expected to achieve an impressive majority and give a boost of support for the Socialist president and government in anticipation of the 1993 legislative elections. The results were far different. The proposed treaty split the electorates of each of the major political parties in unanticipated ways, and the summer campaign proved particularly bitter. The Gaullist opposition to the treaty was partly a revolt against the leadership of Jacques Chirac, and it was supported by a majority of RPR deputies and voters. Within the left the Communists were

weak, but bitter opponents to the approval of the treaty, and Socialist leaders were less than enthusiastic proponents. The National Front was united in its opposition. In the end the treaty was approved by a slim majority of the voters, but the results were a political disaster for those who won. For each of the major parties, their "natural" electorates split badly, and the results—in which opposition to the treaty was concentrated among the less privileged voters and in the poorest regions of the country—were widely viewed as a broad rejection of established political leadership, particularly that of the governing coalition. In 1992, with the exception of the Communists, the voters of the left strongly supported the "yes" vote, while the voters of the right generally voted "no." In 2005 the French electorate rejected the proposed new European "constitution." This time, however, the pattern was the reverse—voters of the right strongly voted "yes," while those of the left generally voted "no."

---

years after he had enacted by referendum his "own" constitution, General de Gaulle asked the electorate to endorse a constitutional amendment of great significance: to elect the president of the Republic by direct popular suffrage. Favorable attitudes toward the referendum and the popular election of the president, however, did not prevent the electorate from voting down another proposal submitted by de Gaulle in 1969, thereby provoking his resignation.

Since 1969 there have been only five referendums (see Table 6.3). President Georges Pompidou called a referendum for the admission of Britain to the Common Market. The first referendum during the Mitterrand period, in 1988, dealt with approval for an accord between warring parties on the future of New Caledonia; the referendum was a condition of the agreement. Sixty-three percent of the voters stayed home, but the accord was approved. The electorate was far more extensively mobilized when the question of ratifying the **Maastricht Treaty** on the European Union was submitted to referendum in 1992. The results were far more significant for the future of French political life (see Box 6.2). The 2000 referendum—on the reduction of the presidential term from seven to five years—was

overwhelmingly approved (by 73 percent of those who voted), but the referendum was most notable for the record number of abstentions—almost 70 percent.

In contrast, the most recent referendum, in 2005 on a European constitutional treaty, attracted far more voter interest. As in a similar referendum in 1992 on the Maastricht Treaty, the campaign deeply divided both the right and the left (although the largest parties of both supported the "yes" vote), and abstention was relatively low. In contrast with 1992, however, the government decisively lost its gamble, and the majority voted no. When the Netherlands also rejected the document a few days later, the treaty was effectively killed.

Public opinion polls indicate that the electorate is positive toward the referendum as a form of public participation. It ranked just behind the popularly elected presidency and the Constitutional Council, among the most highly approved institutional innovations of the Fifth Republic. In one of its first moves, the new government under President Jacques Chirac in 1995 passed a constitutional amendment that expanded the use of the referendum in the areas of social and economic policy.

Voting in Presidential Elections

Presidential elections are for French voters the most important expressions of the general will. After the presidential elections of 1965, it was evident that French voters got great satisfaction from knowing that, unlike in past parliamentary elections, national and not parochial alignments were at stake and that they could pronounce themselves on such issues. The traditional and once deeply rooted attitude that the only useful vote was against the government no longer made sense when people knew that the task was to elect an executive endowed with strong powers. Accordingly, turnout in presidential elections, with one exception, has been the highest of all elections (84 percent in 2007).

The nomination procedures for presidential candidates make it very easy to put a candidate on the first ballot, far easier than in presidential primaries in the United States. So far, however, no presidential candidate, not even de Gaulle in 1965, has obtained the absolute majority needed to ensure election on the first ballot. In runoffs, held two weeks after the first ballot, only the two most successful candidates face each other. All serious candidates are backed by a party or a coalition of parties.. Nevertheless, with a record number of candidates in 2002 (sixteen—twelve in 2007), this proposition was stretched to the limit.

Because the formal campaigns are short and concentrated, radio, television, and newspapers grant candidates, commentators, and forecasters considerable time and space. The televised duels between the presidential candidates in the last four elections—patterned after debates between presidential candidates in the United States, but longer and of far higher quality—were viewed by at least half of the population.

Informal campaigns, however, are long and arduous. The fixed term of the French presidency means that, unless the president dies or resigns, there are no snap elections for the chief executive. As a result, even in the absence of primaries, the informal campaign gets quite intense years before the election. In many ways the presidential campaign of 2007 began soon after the elections of 2002.

Just as in the United States, coalitions that elect a president are different from those that secure a legislative majority for a government. This means that any candidate for the presidency who owes his nomination to his position as party leader must appeal to an audience broader than a single party. Once elected, the candidate seeks to establish political distance from his party origins. François Mitterrand was the first president in the history of the Fifth Republic to have been elected twice in popular elections. Jacques Chirac accomplished this same achievement, but served two years less because of

---

The Accidental President

BOX 6.3

On May 5, 2002, Jacques Chirac was reelected president of France by the largest majority ever obtained by a presidential candidate in a popular election during the Fifth Republic. Yet, when the results of the first round of the presidential elections were tabulated two weeks before, this victory was wholly unexpected. Chirac's first term was marked by the largest strike movement since 1968 and then by an ill-conceived decision to call early legislative elections in 1997, which were won by the left. After 1997 his leadership of the RPR was challenged by fragmentation and then by loss of control of the party machine (eventually to his rival, Nicolas Sarkozy). This was followed by revelations of dramatic new evidence of massive corruption in the Paris party machine that directly implicated the president (the former mayor of Paris). He appeared to be headed for likely defeat in 2002.

Then came the "divine surprise" of April 2002. With the worst result of any outgoing president in the first round (less than 20 percent of the vote), Chirac edged out his Socialist rival, Lionel Jospin. But Jospin himself was edged out by the resurgent candidate of the extreme right, Jean-Marie Le Pen. With sixteen candidates in the first round, Le Pen's considerable achievement was due in part to an accident of the electoral system and in part to the inability of leftist voters to anticipate the consequences of their dispersed votes. As a result, the shocked and leaderless left rallied to the support of Chirac to block Le Pen. Confronted with an unhappy choice between a candidate who had been accused of corruption and a candidate of the extreme right, more than 82 percent of the electorate voted for the former.

the reduction in the length of the presidential term. (See Box 6.3.)

Although the 2002 presidential election deeply divided all of the major parties, the process of coalition-building around presidential elections has probably been the key element in political party consolidation and in the development of party coalitions since 1968. The prize of the presidency is so significant that it has preoccupied the parties of both the right and the left. It influences their organization, their tactics, and their relations with one another.

POLICY PROCESSES

The Executive

As we have seen, the French constitution has a two-headed executive. As in other parliamentary regimes, the prime minister presides over the government. But unlike in other parliamentary regimes, the president is far from being a figurehead. It was widely predicted that such an arrangement would necessarily lead to frequent political crises. Each of the four presidents of the Fifth Republic, and each of the prime ministers who have served under them, left no doubt that the executive has only one head: the president.

The exercise of presidential powers in all their fullness was made possible not so much by the constitutional text as by a political fact: Between 1958 and 1981, the president and the prime minister derived their legitimacy from the same Gaullist majority in the electorate—the president by direct popular elections, the prime minister by the majority support in the National Assembly. In 1981 the electorate shifted its allegiance from the right to the left, yet for the ensuing five years, the president and Parliament were still on the same side of the political divide.

The long years of political affinity between the holders of the two offices solidified and amplified presidential powers and shaped constitutional practices in ways that appear to have a lasting impact. From the very beginning of the Fifth Republic, the president not only *formally appointed* to Parliament the prime minister proposed to him (as the presidents of the previous republics had done, and as the queen of England does), but also *chose* the prime minister and the other **Cabinet** ministers. In some cases the president also dismissed a prime minister who clearly enjoyed the confidence of a majority in Parliament.

Hence, the rather frequent reshuffling of Cabinet posts and personnel in the Fifth Republic is different from similar happenings in the Third and Fourth Republics. In those systems the changes occurred in response to shifts in parliamentary support and frequently in order to forestall, at least for a short time, the government's fall from power. In the present system, the president or the prime minister—depending on the circumstances—may decide to appoint, move, or dismiss a Cabinet officer on the basis of his or her own appreciation of the member's worth (or lack of it). This does not mean that considerations of the executive are merely technical. They may be highly political, but they are exclusively those of the executive.

Since all powers proceeded from the president, the government headed by the prime minister became essentially an administrative body until 1986, despite constitutional stipulations to the contrary. The prime minister's chief function was to provide whatever direction or resources were needed to implement the policies conceived by the president. The primary task of the government was to develop legislative proposals and present an executive budget. In many respects the government's position resembled that of the Cabinet in a presidential regime such as the United States, rather than that of a government in a parliamentary system such as Britain and the earlier French republics.

Regardless of the political circumstances, weekly meetings of the Cabinet are chaired by the president and are officially called the **Council of Ministers.** They are not generally a forum for deliberation and confrontation. Although Cabinet decisions and decrees officially emanate from the council, in fact real decisions are made elsewhere.

The prime minister is more than first among equals in relation to Cabinet colleagues. Among the prime minister's many functions is the harnessing of a parliamentary majority for presidential policies, since according to the constitution, the government must resign when a majority in Parliament adopts a motion of censure or rejects the government program. This provision distinguishes France from a truly presidential regime, such as the United States or Mexico.

The relationship between president and the prime minister, however, has operated quite differently during the periods of so-called cohabitation. From 1986 to 1988 and from 1993 to 1995, a conservative majority controlled Parliament, and the president was a Socialist. From 1997 to 2002, the left held a parliamentary majority, and the president was from a conservative party. Without claiming any domain exclusively as his own, the president (Mitterrand in the first two cases and Chirac from 1997 to 2002) continued to occupy the foreground in foreign and military affairs, in accordance with his interpretation of his mandate under the constitution. The prime minister became the effective leader of the executive and pursued government objectives, but avoided interfering with presidential prerogatives.

In part because of the experiences of cohabitation, the president's role is now less imposing than it had been before 1986. Even during the interlude of Socialist government between 1988 and 1993, the Socialist prime minister was largely responsible for the main options for government action, with the president setting the limits and the tone. The relationship between President Sarkozy and his prime minister, François Fillion, indicates a reassertion of presidential prerogatives.

Another limit to executive power became clear in the spring of 2006. The effective authority of both the president and the prime minister was diminished by important policy failures (the loss of the referendum in May 2005, the urban riots the following fall, and strikes in the spring of 2006). Support for the government within the large parliamentary majority began to fray. The minister of the interior, Nicolas Sarkozy, introduced policy proposals often opposed by President Chirac and Prime Minister de Villepin, but sometimes supported by parliamentary leaders.

Thus, after the 1990s the relationship between the president and the prime minister was more complicated than during the earlier period of the Fifth Republic and varied according to the political circumstances in which each had assumed office. By 2006 the relationship between the executive and the parliamentary majority showed signs of changing as well.

Since the early days of the de Gaulle administration, the office of the chief of state has been organized to maximize the ability of the president to initiate, elaborate, and frequently execute policy. In terms of function, the staff at the Elysée Palace, the French White House, composed of a general secretariat and the presidential staff, is somewhat similar to the Executive Office staff of the U.S. president. Yet it is much smaller, comprising only forty to fifty people, with an additional support staff of several hundred people.

As the president's eyes and ears, his staff members are indispensable for the exercise of presidential powers. They are in constant contact not only with the prime minister's collaborators, but also directly with individual ministries. Through these contacts the president can initiate, impede, interfere, and assure himself that presidential policies are followed.

The prime minister has a parallel network for developing and implementing policy decisions. The most important method is the so-called interministerial meetings, regular gatherings of high civil servants attached to various ministries. The frequency of these sessions, chaired by a member of the prime minister's personal staff, reflects the growing centralization of administrative and decisionmaking authority within the office of the prime minister and the growing importance of the prime minister's policy network in everyday policymaking within the executive.

As we have seen, two different patterns exist for the sharing of executive power. When the presidential and parliamentary majorities are identical (as has been the case since 2008), the prime minister is clearly subordinate to the president.[39] Even in this case, however, the president's power is limited because he does not control the administrative machinery directly and must work through the prime minister's office and the ministries. Cooperation between the two is thus essential for effective government.

Parliament

The constitution severely and intentionally curtails the powers of Parliament both as a source of legislation and as an organ of control over the executive. The fact that both houses of Parliament were initially confined to sessions of no more than six months in a calendar year severely reduced effectiveness. In 1995 maximum sessions were increased to nine months, opening new possibilities for parliamentary leadership to exercise initiative and control.

Despite restrictions on parliamentary activity, the legislative output of the Parliament in the Fifth Republic has been quite respectable. The average of only 98 laws per year enacted during the years of the Fifth Republic (125 per year during the reform period between 1981 and 1986) is much lower than that during the Fourth Republic. However, it is double the British average for the same period. Although either the government or Parliament may propose bills, almost all legislation is proposed by the government. The government effectively controls the proceedings in both houses and can require priority for those bills that it wishes to see adopted (see Figure 6.5). Article 44 of the Constitution empowers the government to force Parliament by the so-called **blocked vote** to accept a bill in its entirety with only the amendments agreed to

How a Bill Becomes a Law

FIGURE 6.5

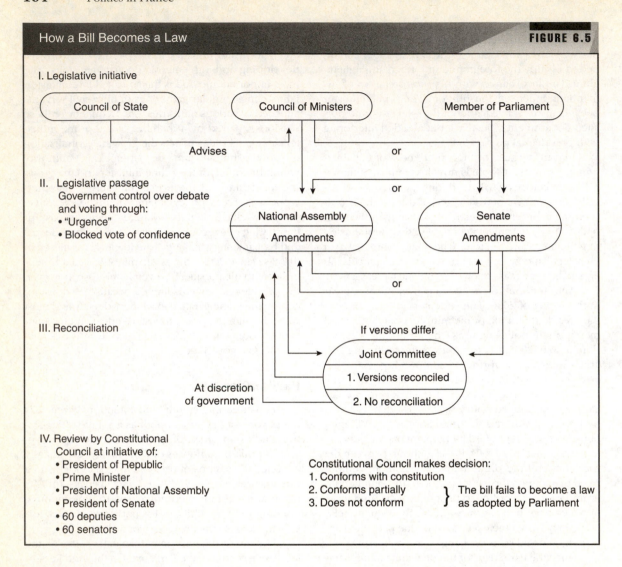

I. Legislative initiative

| Council of State | Council of Ministers | Member of Parliament |

Advises   or

II. Legislative passage
Government control over debate and voting through:
• "Urgence"
• Blocked vote of confidence

or

National Assembly — Amendments   Senate — Amendments

or

III. Reconciliation

If versions differ

Joint Committee
1. Versions reconciled
2. No reconciliation

At discretion of government

IV. Review by Constitutional Council at initiative of:
• President of Republic
• Prime Minister
• President of National Assembly
• President of Senate
• 60 deputies
• 60 senators

Constitutional Council makes decision:
1. Conforms with constitution
2. Conforms partially   } The bill fails to become a law
3. Does not conform   as adopted by Parliament

by the government. In recent years the government has used the blocked vote to maintain discipline within the majority, rather than to impose the will of the executive over a chaotic Parliament. Its use has become an index of conflict within the governing party or coalition.[40] Now the amendments of 2008 have constrained the use of the blocked vote, and its use has been linked to the parliamentary majority.

Article 38 invites Parliament to abandon "for a limited time" its legislative function to the government if the government wishes to act as legislator "for the implementation of its program." Once Parliament votes a broad enabling law, the government enacts

legislation by way of so-called **ordinances**. The government used this possibility of executive lawmaking twenty-two times between 1958 and 1986—often for important legislation and sometimes simply to expedite the legislative process. Decisions of the Constitutional Council have limited the use of enabling laws, requiring that the enabling act spell out the limits of executive lawmaking with some precision.

Another constitutional provision gives the government a unique tool to ensure parliamentary support for any bill that it introduces. According to Article 49, Section 3, the prime minister may pledge the "government's responsibility" on any bill (or section of a bill) submitted to the National Assembly. In such a case, the bill is automatically "considered as adopted," without further vote, unless the deputies succeed in a **motion of censure** against the government according to the strict requirements discussed earlier. The success of this motion would likely result in new elections. So far, however, the threat of having to face new elections has always put sufficient pressure on the incumbent deputies not to support a motion of censure. As a consequence, whenever the government pledges its responsibility to a bill it has introduced, the bill has become law without any parliamentary vote.

Earlier in the Fifth Republic, little use was made of this provision. Between 1981 and 1986, the governments of the left used it for reasons of expediency. It permitted them to enact important legislation quickly, without laying bare conflicts within the ranks of the governing majority. After 1986 governments of both the right and the left resorted to this procedure with considerable frequency when they needed to overcome the precariousness of their majorities in Parliament. During the five years between 1988 and 1993, prime ministers engaged the responsibility of their governments thirty-nine times, nine times each year in 1990 and 1991 alone. Between June 1997 and the election of a new parliament in 2002, this procedure was not used, but it was used three times between 2002 and 2007. The 2008 amendments to finance laws have now limited its use.

Other devices for enhancing the role of Parliament have become somewhat more effective over the years, even before the 2008 amendments. In the 1970s the National Assembly instituted a weekly question period that is similar to the British (and German) version. Two days a week the party groups submit a dozen or more written questions an hour in advance, in rough proportion to the membership of each group, and then the relevant minister answers them. This process has been expanded by the amendments of 2008. The presence of television cameras in the chamber (since 1974) creates additional public interest and records the dialogue between the government representatives and the deputies.

By using its power to amend, Parliament has vastly expanded its role in the legislative process during the past decades. During the 1980s proposed amendments averaged almost 5,000 a year. Since 1990 this average has more than doubled, which coincides with the doubling of hours devoted to legislative debate each year. About two-thirds of the amendments that are eventually adopted (33 percent of those proposed in 1997–2002) are proposed by parliamentary committees

working with the government. Thus, committees help shape legislation, and governments have all but abandoned their constitutionally guaranteed prerogative to declare amendments out of order.[41] The long parliamentary session introduced in 1995 has enhanced the role of committee leaders in the legislative process. The amendments passed in 2008 bring parliamentary committees directly into the legislative process by making the legislation reported out of committees the basis for parliamentary approval.

Finally, the role of Parliament is strengthened by the general support that French citizens give their elected deputies. Better organized parties both add to the deputy's role as part of a group and somewhat diminish his or her role as an independent actor, capable of influencing the legislative process merely for narrow parochial interests. Nevertheless, individual deputies still command a considerable following within their constituencies. This pattern is enhanced because more than 87 percent of the deputies in the National Assembly in 2008 held local office, most of them municipal councilors or mayors. Large numbers were also on departmental or regional councils, and some were both municipal and departmental or regional councilors.[42] In 2001, when confidence in political parties was at 24 percent, confidence stood at 36 percent for deputies and 70 percent for mayors (see again Figure 6.3).

Because the electoral college that elects the members of the Senate is composed almost entirely of people selected by small-town elected officials, the parties of the center that are most influential in small towns are best represented in the upper house. Not surprisingly, 61 percent of senators also held local office in 2008. In 2008 the Senate was dominated by the governing majority party, the UMP, which is dependent, however, on the UDF for its majority. The Socialists are the second largest group, a result of the PS's strong roots at the local level. The Communists continue to be well represented for the same reason. Although the right remains dominant in the upper house, the Senate has not always been on the right of the political spectrum. Its hostility to social and economic change is balanced by a forthright defense of traditional republican liberties and by a stand against demagogic appeals to latent antiparliamentary feelings.

The Senate, in the normal legislative process, can do little more than delay legislation approved by the government and passed by the National Assembly. However, there are several situations in which the accord of the Senate is necessary. The most important is that any constitutional amendment needs the approval of either a simple or a three-fifths majority of senators (Article 89). In 2000 lack of support in the Senate forced the president (and prime minister) to withdraw an amendment to create an independent judiciary and to modify the amendment on parity for women (that was passed).

Some legislation of great importance—such as the nuclear strike force, the organization of military tribunals in cases involving high treason, the reorganization of local government in Corsica, and the change in the system of departmental representation—was enacted in spite of senatorial dissent. Nonetheless, until 1981 relations between the Senate and the National Assembly were relatively harmonious. The real clash with the Senate over legislation came during the years of Socialist government between 1981 and 1986, when many key bills were passed over the objections of the Senate. However, leftist government bills that dismantled some of the "law and order" measures enacted under de Gaulle, Pompidou, and Giscard were supported by the Senate. The upper house also played an active role when it modified the comprehensive decentralization statute passed by the Socialist majority in the Assembly. Most of the changes were accepted in joint committee.

Criticism of the Senate as an unrepresentative body and proposals for its reform have come from Gaullists and Socialists alike (most recently in 2008). All of these proposals for reforming the Senate have failed, though some minor modifications in its composition and mode of election have been passed.

Checks and Balances

France has no tradition of judicial review. As in other countries with civil law systems, the sovereignty of Parliament has meant that the legislature has the last word. A law enacted in a constitutionally prescribed form is not subject to further scrutiny.

This principle seemed to be infringed upon when the Constitution of 1958 brought forth an institutional novelty, the Constitutional Council. The council in certain cases must, and in other cases may upon request, examine legislation and decide whether it conforms to the constitution. A legal provision declared unconstitutional may not be promulgated.

The presidents of the National Assembly and Senate each choose three of the council's members, and the president of the Republic chooses another three for a (nonrenewable) nine-year term. Those who nominate the council's members were, until 1974, together with the prime minister, the only ones

entitled to apply to the council for constitutional scrutiny. In 1974 an amendment to the constitution made it possible for sixty deputies or sixty senators to submit cases to the Constitutional Council. Since then, appeals to the council by the opposition, and at times by members of the majority, have become a regular feature of the French legislative process.

Whichever side is in opposition, conservative or Socialist, routinely refers all major (sometimes minor) pieces of legislation to the council. In a given year, as many as 28 percent of laws passed by Parliament have been submitted for review. A surprisingly high percentage of appeals lead to a declaration of unconstitutionality. Few decisions declare entire statutes unconstitutional, and those that declare parts of legislation unconstitutional (sometimes trivial parts) effectively invite Parliament to rewrite the text in an acceptable way.

The Constitutional Council's decisions have considerable impact and have sometimes modified short-term, and occasionally long-term, objectives of governments. The council assumes the role of a constitutional court. By doing so, it places itself at the juncture of law and politics, in a way similar to the U.S. Supreme Court when it reviews the constitutionality of legislation.

In a landmark decision rendered in 1971, the council declared unconstitutional a statute adopted by a large majority in Parliament that authorized the prefects to refuse authorization to any association that they thought might engage in illegal activities. According to the decision, to require any advance authorization violated the freedom of association, one of "the fundamental principles recognized by the laws of the Republic and solemnly reaffirmed in the preamble of the Constitution." The invocation of the preamble greatly expanded the scope of constitutional law, since the preamble incorporated in its wording broad "principles of national sovereignty," the "attachment to The Declaration of Rights of Man," and an extensive bill of rights from the Fourth Republic constitution. For introducing a broad view of judicial review into constitutional law, the decision was greeted as the French equivalent of the U.S. Supreme Court decision in *Marbury v. Madison*.

Some of the Constitutional Council's most important decisions—such as those on the nationalization of private enterprises (under the Socialists), on the privatization of parts of the public sector (under the conservatives), and on government control over the media (under both)—conform to an attitude that in

BOX 6.4

Judicial Review in France and the United States

Judicial review has become part of the French legislative process, but in a way it is still quite different from judicial review in of the United States. Direct access is limited, although citizens will have the right to bring appeals based on some constitutional issues before the Constitutional Council after 2008. The council, unlike the U.S. Supreme Court, considers legislation before it is promulgated. Since 1981 virtually all constitutional challenges have been initiated by legislative petition, a process that does not exist in the United States. A time element precludes the possibility of extensive deliberation: Rulings must be made within a month and, in emergency situations, within eight days. This is surely speedy justice, but the verdicts cannot be as explanatory as those rendered by constitutional courts in other countries. Dissenting opinions are never made public.

---

the United States is called judicial restraint. A few decisions can be qualified as activist, since they directly alter the intent of the law. But as a nonelected body, the council generally avoids interference with the major political choices of the government majority. In recent years the council has nevertheless reviewed 10 percent or more of legislation that is passed each year. On average it has found 50 percent of this legislation at least partially violates the constitution. In 2007 almost 80 percent of the laws that came before the council were declared unconstitutional in part.

In a period in which alternation of governments has often resulted in sharp policy changes, the council decisions have helped to define an emerging consensus. By smoothing out the raw edges of new legislation in judicial language, it often makes changes ultimately more acceptable (see Box 6.4).

The approval of the council's activities by a large sector of public opinion (52 percent in 2001, as shown in Figure 6.3) has encouraged the council to enlarge its powers. These efforts were partially successful in 2008, as an amendment gave the council a role in the judicial system. Cases in which the defendant claims that a law violates "rights and liberties" guaranteed by the constitution can now be appealed to the Constitutional Council, once the appeal is vetted by either the appeals court or the Conseil d'Etat.

Thus, the judicial appeal and the development of a judicial check on policymaking enhance the role of the much older **Council of State**, which in its present form dates back to 1799. The government now consults this council more extensively on all bills before they are submitted to Parliament and, as it has always done, on all government decrees and regulations before they are enacted. The council also gives advice on the interpretation of constitutional texts. While its advice is never binding, its prestige is so high that its recommendations are seldom ignored.

Unlike the Constitutional Council, the Council of State provides recourse to individual citizens and organized groups who have claims against the administration. The judicial section of the Council of State, acting either as a court of appeal or as the court of first instance, is the apex of a hierarchy of administrative courts. Whenever the council finds official acts to be devoid of a legal basis, whether those of a Cabinet minister or a village mayor, the council will annul them and grant damages to the aggrieved plaintiff.

THE STATE AND TERRITORIAL RELATIONS

Since the First Republic in the eighteenth century, when the Jacobins controlled the revolutionary National Assembly, the French state has been characterized by a high degree of centralized political and administrative authority. Although there have always been forces that have advocated *decentralization* of political authority, as well as deconcentration of administrative authority, the French unitary state remained (formally) "one and indivisible."[43] Essentially, this meant that subnational territorial units (communes, departments, and regions) had little formal decisionmaking autonomy. They were dominated by political and administrative decisions made in Paris. Both state action and territorial organization in France depended on a well-structured administration, which during long periods of political instability and unrest kept the machinery of the state functioning.

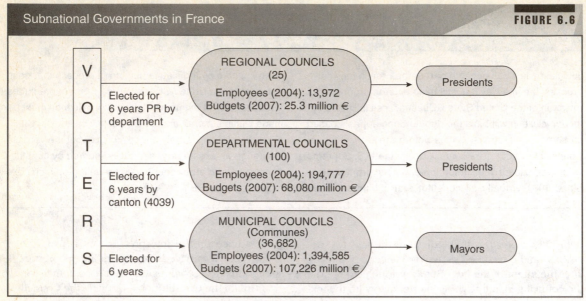

Subnational Governments in France **FIGURE 6.6**

REGIONAL COUNCILS (25) Employees (2004): 13,972 Budgets (2007): 25.3 million €	→	Presidents

V O T E R S

Elected for 6 years PR by department

Elected for 6 years by canton (4039)

Elected for 6 years

REGIONAL COUNCILS
(25)
Employees (2004): 13,972
Budgets (2007): 25.3 million € → Presidents

DEPARTMENTAL COUNCILS
(100)
Employees (2004): 194,777
Budgets (2007): 68,080 million € → Presidents

MUNICIPAL COUNCILS
(Communes)
(36,682)
Employees (2004): 1,394,585
Budgets (2007): 107,226 million € → Mayors

Source: Ministère de l'Intérieur, DGCL: http://www.dgcl.interieur.gouv.fr/

France is divided into 100 **departments** (including four overseas departments), each about the size of an American county. Each is under the administrative responsibility of a **prefect** and has a directly elected general council. Since 1955 departments have been grouped into twenty-two **regions**, each with its own appointed prefect (in addition to the departmental prefects). Since 1986, each region has an elected assembly and president as well as a prefect (see Figure 6.6).

Centralization has always been more impressive in its formal and legal aspects than it has been in practice. The practical and political reality has always been more complex. Although France is renowned for its centralized state, what is often ignored is that political localism dilutes centralized decisionmaking (see Box 6.5).

The process of decentralization initiated by the government of the left between 1982 and 1986 was undoubtedly the most important and effective reform passed during that period. The reform built on the long-established system of interlocking relationships between central and local authorities, as well as on the previous patterns of change. The reform altered the formal roles of all the local actors, but the greatest change was that it formalized the previously informal power of these actors.[44]

The Political Durability of Local Governments **BOX 6.5**

One manifestation of the political importance of local government in France has been the ability of local units to endure. It is no accident that even after recent consolidations there are still 36,551 communes (the basic area of local administration), each with a mayor and council, or about as many as in the original six Common Market countries and Britain together. Almost 33,000 French communes have fewer than 2,000 inhabitants, and of these more than 22,000 have fewer than 500. What is most remarkable, however, is that since 1851 the number of communes in France has been reduced by only 400. Thus, unlike every other industrialized country, the consolidation of population in urban areas has resulted in almost no consolidation of towns and villages.

These powers are based on a system of mutual dependency between local actors and the prefects, as well as field services of the national ministries. The administrators of the national ministries had the formal power to implement laws, rules, and regulations at the local level. However, they needed the cooperation of local officials, who had the confidence of their constituents, to facilitate the acceptance of the authority of the central state and to provide information to operate the administration effectively at the local level. Local officials, in turn, needed the resources and aid of the administration to help their constituents and keep their political promises.[45] As in any relationship based on permanent interaction and on cross-functioning controls, it was not always clear who controlled whom. Both the autonomy and the relational power of municipalities were conditioned by the extent of the mayor's contacts within the political and administrative network. These contacts were reinforced by the linkage to national decision-making that mayors had established through **cumul des mandats**—the ability to hold several electoral offices at the same time (since 2000 deputies are prohibited from holding a local executive office, including mayor of a larger city).

The decentralization legislation transferred most of the formal powers of the departmental and regional prefects to the elected presidents of the departmental and regional councils. In March 1986 *regional councils* were elected for the first time (by a system of proportional representation). In one stroke the remnants of formal prefectural authorization of local government decisions were abandoned in favor of the decisions of local officials. The department presidents, elected by their department councils, are now the chief departmental executive officers, and they, rather than the prefects, control the department bureaucracy.[46]

What then is left of the role of the central bureaucracy in controlling the periphery? The greatest loss of authority has probably been that of the prefects. Their role now seems limited to security (law and order) matters, to the promotion of the government's industrial policies, and to the coordination of the state bureaucracy at the departmental level.

In matters of financing, the principal mechanisms through which the state influences local government decisions (financial dependency and standards) have been weakened, but have not been abandoned. There is still overall financial dependence of subnational governments on the state. Particularly at the commune level, local taxes provide only 40 percent of the annual budget (collected by the state). The price for financial assistance from above is enforced compliance with standards set by the state. In areas in which the state retains decision-making power—police, education, a large area of welfare, and social security, as well as a great deal of construction—administrative discretion and central control remain important.

Decentralization in the 1980s, combined with the system of *cumul des mandats,* gave a new impetus to local officials to expand what they previously had done in a more limited way: to trade influence for private money, to direct kickbacks into party funding operations, and to use their public office for private advantage. The pressures that led to corruption also led to more expensive political campaigns and an often poorly demarcated frontier between the public and private arenas in a country in which people who emerge from the grandes écoles–grands corps system move easily between the two.

PERFORMANCE AND PROSPECTS

A Welfare State

The overall performance of democracies can be measured by their commitment and ability to distribute the benefits of economic growth. France has a mediocre record for spreading the benefits of the postwar boom and prosperity among all its citizens. In terms of income and of wealth, discrepancies between the rich and the poor remain somewhat less in France than in other countries in Europe (see also Table 1.2 in Chapter 1). In 2001 the percentage of income earners in the top 10 percent of incomes (25 percent) was higher than in Sweden, but lower than in Germany, the United Kingdom, or the United States.[47] The percentage in the lowest 10 percent of incomes was lower than in Germany or Sweden, but slightly higher than in the United Kingdom or the United States. The income gap narrowed significantly between 1976 and 1981, and then even more during the first year of Socialist government. Yet, subsequent austerity measures, especially the government's successful effort to hold down wages, have widened the gap again.

The emergence of long-term unemployment (about 40 percent of those unemployed in 2004) has increased the number of the new poor, who are concentrated among those who are poorly trained for a rapidly evolving employment market. As opposed to the past, the majority of the lowest income group is no longer the elderly and retired and the heads of households with marginal jobs. Particularly since 1990, the unemployed are younger people, many of them long-term unemployed, especially younger single parents. Although youth unemployment rates have come down during the past decade, they remain double the national average.

Since large incomes permit the accumulation of wealth, the concentration of wealth is even more conspicuous than the steepness of the income pyramid. In the 1970s the richest 10 percent controlled between 35 and 50 percent of all wealth in France; the poorest 10 percent owned not more than 5 percent. In the 1990s it is estimated that the richest 10 percent of the families in the country owned 50 percent of the wealth, while the richest 20 percent owned 67 percent.[48]

In spite of some assertions to the contrary, it is not true that the French economy is burdened with higher taxes than other countries of similar development. Overall tax rates in 2008 were higher than those in the United Kingdom or the United States, but lower than those in Sweden or Germany. What is special about France is the distribution of its taxes. The share of indirect taxes—such as the value-added tax (VAT) and excise taxes—remains far higher in France than in other industrialized countries. Indirect taxes not only drive up prices, but also weigh most heavily on the poor. The percentage of revenue collected through regressive indirect taxation was the same in 1986, after five years of Socialist government, as it had been in 1980, and remains about the same now (77 percent in 2004).

The French welfare state is most effective in the area of social transfers. These transfers are at about the same level as in Germany and Denmark, but ahead of most other European democracies, and far ahead of the United States. A comprehensive health and social security system, established after World War II and extended since then, and a variety of programs assisting the aged, large families, persons with disabilities, and other such groups, disburses substantial benefits (Figure 6.7). When unemployment benefits, the cost of job-training programs, and housing subsidies are added in, total costs are as high as the remainder of the public budget, with three-fourths of them borne by employers and employees.

The effectiveness of the French welfare state is most evident in the relatively low poverty rates—slightly higher than in Sweden, but lower than in Germany, and far lower than in the United Kingdom and the United States. France has also maintained a high level of quality medical services and public services. High spending for welfare programs has also cushioned the worst impact of the economic crisis in 2008-2009. Much of the ad hoc stimulus spending in the United States is already built into the way the welfare state functions in France.

In contrast with the United States, there have been fewer cutbacks in welfare state programs in France in recent years—even after the cutbacks of pension benefits in 2003. Indeed, the population covered by health insurance has expanded, but financing for these programs has been at the heart of government concerns since 1995 (see Table 6.4). Although spending on social programs has remained stable as a percentage of the gross national product (GNP) since 1984, the government cut public spending to reduce its

The French Budget, 2007 — FIGURE 6.7

- Government Operations 8%
- The Economy and Economic Development 3.80%
- Social, Cultural, and Environmental Programs 13.80%
- Intergovernmental and Police Activities 5.10%
- National Defense and Foreign Policy 12.10%
- Education 23%
- Debt Service and Tax Reimbursement 33.80%

Source: Ministry of Finance, Projet de loi de finances, 2008, *Tableau de comparaison, à structure 2008, par mission et programme, des crédits proposés pour 2008 à* ceux votés pour 2007`.

Welfare State Spending

France ranks relatively high in government spending as a share of the GDP and social service programs

TABLE 6.4

	General Government Expenditure as Percentage of GDP 2006	Government Employment as Percentage of Total Employment 1996–2000	State Contributions to Protection Programs as Percentage of GDP 2001	State Health Expenses as Percentage of GDP	
				1994–1995	2005–2006
Britain	45.0	18.7	27.2	5.2	8.4
France	53.4	20.1	30.0	6.6	11.1
Germany	45.7	12.3	29.8	6.3	10.6
Italy	50.1	20.5	25.6	5.3	8.9
Spain	38.5	11.6	20.6	4.7	8.2
Sweden	55.5	6.6	31.3	8.1	9.1
United States	36.6	15.6	16.0	13.3	15.3

Source: OECD 2008 (www.oecd.org), French Ministry of Finance, 2004 (www.finances.gouv.fr), Eurostat, 2004 (http://epp.eurostat.ec.europa.eu/portal/), OECD Public Sector Pay and Employment Database (www.oecd.org).

budget deficit in a successful effort to conform to criteria for the common European currency.

In addition, some important gaps in benefits remain. As in other systems where outcomes have been compared with socioeconomic status, studies of the French system indicate that there are important inequalities in France in access to services and in health outcomes. These disparities have grown since 1980, even as financial barriers to health care have diminished.[49] High levels of unemployment, social problems, and problems of homelessness create pressures to expand social programs, while diminishing the revenue base that finances them. Since 1998 the French government has confronted many of the same social service problems facing the United States, but resistance to the American-type solutions is widespread. In 1999, for example, as part of the campaign to fight "social exclusion" in France, the Socialist government passed legislation instituting universal medical coverage. This means-tested, tax-financed, and targeted health insurance program represents a departure from the tradition of social insurance in France.

In reaction to the riots of November 2005 in the "suburbs" of large French cities (the equivalent of inner-city neighborhoods), the government vowed to increase social spending in these areas and to increase employment and educational opportunities for youth. These promises were placed on hold, however, until after the presidential and legislative elections of 2007, and several years later still remain on hold.

Nationalization and Regulation

Government-operated business enterprises have long existed in France in fields that are under private ownership in other Western European countries. After several waves of nationalization in the 1930s and after the end of World War II, the government owned and operated all or part of the following: railroads, energy production (mining, electricity, nuclear energy), telecommunication (radio and television), air and maritime transport, the aeronautic industry, 85 percent of bank deposits, 40 percent of insurance premiums, one-third of the automobile industry, and one-third of the housing industry. All this was in addition to the old state monopolies of mail services, telephone, telegraph, tobacco, match manufacture, and various less important activities.

By the 1970s public enterprises accounted for about 11 percent of the GNP. Fifteen percent of the total active population, or 27 percent of all salary and wage earners (excluding agricultural labor), were paid directly by the state as civil servants, either as salaried workers or on a contractual basis. Their income came close to one-third of the total sum of wages and salaries.

Legislation enacted during the first governments of the left in 1981–1982 completed the nationalization of the banking sector and expanded state ownership to thirteen of the twenty largest firms in France and controlling interest in many other firms in such fields as machine tools, chemistry (including pharmaceutical products), glass, metals, and electrical power. In addition, the government obtained majority control of two important armaments firms and several ailing steel companies.

The conservative government that held power in 1986–1988 substantially altered the structure of the nationalized sector in France, accelerating a trend of partial privatization begun during the previous government of the left. Its ambitious plans for **privatization** were halted (40 percent completed) only a year after their implementation began, partially because of the stock market collapse in 1987.[50] Thus some, but not all, of the companies that were nationalized by the Socialist government in 1982 were returned to private stockholders. The conservative government also privatized some companies that the state had long controlled. However, both the companies that were privatized and those that remained in the hands of the state were quite different from what they had been a few years before. Recapitalized, restructured, and modernized, for the most part, they were, in 1988, the leading edge of the French industrial machine.[51]

After the wave of privatization, the percentage of salary and wage earners receiving their checks directly or indirectly from the French state was reduced to about 22 percent in 1997. While this was high compared with the U.S. percentage, it was not out of line with other European countries. If one out of five French citizens depended on the state for his or her paychecks in the 1990s, so did about the same proportion of British and Italian citizens (see again Table 6.4). Moreover, under pressure of EU directives on competition and globalization trends, privatization is a continuing process, which is most controversial in the service sector. The state maintains only small minority interests in France Télécom and Air France, and discussions continue about selling off the few remaining state monopolies (notably the railroads and gas and electricity).

For the actual operation of French business, the move toward deregulation of the economy begun by the Socialists and continued by conservative governments was probably more important than privatization. The deregulation of the stock market, the banking system, telecommunications, and prices fundamentally changed the way business is conducted in both the private and public sectors.[52] The combination of budgetary rigor, pressures from the EU, and state disengagement meant a real reduction of aid to industry. Sectors in difficulty—including steel, chemicals, shipbuilding, and automobile manufacturing—were therefore forced to accelerate their rationalization plans and their cutbacks in workers.

As a result, the interventionist and regulatory weight of the state in industry is less important now than it was before the Socialists came to power in 1981. The old issue of nationalization and ownership has been bypassed and replaced by more subtle issues of control and regulation in the context of global competition.

In other areas, the regulatory weight of the state has not diminished, but has changed during the past twenty-five years. During the 1970s France expanded individual rights by fully establishing the rights to divorce and abortion. Under the Socialist governments of the 1980s, capital punishment was abolished, the rights of those accused of crimes were strengthened, and detention without trial was checked by new procedures. After much wrangling, in 1994 the Parliament replaced the obsolete Criminal Code dating from the time of Napoléon. The new code is generally hailed as expressing a consensus across the political spectrum on questions of crime and punishment. Moreover, individual rights in France must now conform to the decisions of the European courts under the general umbrella of the EU. Finally, in conformity with the Maastricht Treaty, citizenship rights of EU residents in France have increased during the 1990s, and in 2006 a right to the presumption of innocence in criminal cases was created under French law.

Finally, in still other areas, the regulatory weight of the state has increased. One of the most obvious is environmental controls. Beginning in the 1990s, the French state made its first significant efforts to regulate individual behavior that has an impact on the environment. The first limitations on smoking, for example, came into effect in the late 1980s and expanded after that. In February 2007 smoking was banned in most public spaces and was extended to restaurants and bars in December 2007.

In an effort to deal with the politics of immigration, particularly after 1993, the state increased the regulation of all residents of foreign origin in ways that have diminished individual rights. In 2004 France moved to regulate "ostentatious" religious symbols worn by students in public schools in response to the wearing of Islamic head scarves.

The "war on terror" had begun in France more than a decade before the September 11, 2001, attacks in the United States. However, a group of investigating judges controls the process. Although actions by the police are therefore scrutinized by judges and are undertaken under law, the challenge to civil liberties remains important nevertheless.

Outlook: France and the New Architecture of Europe

The main concerns that dominate French politics have changed dramatically from three decades ago. In the 1980s, a coalition of Socialists and Communists was promising a "rupture" with capitalism, and the ideological distance between left and right appeared to be enormous. Today none of the major parties—including the National Front—is proposing dramatic change in society or the political system. As in the United States, political parties are making their commitments as vague and as flexible as possible (with the exception of the National Front). After an experiment with socialism, followed by a reaction of conservative neoliberalism, political parties appear to lack fresh ideas on how to deal with the major problems of the French economy and society. The transition away from a smokestack economy has been difficult and painful, and the resulting unemployment continues to dominate public concerns.

Political cleavages based on new conflicts are emerging, even if their outlines are still unclear. Indeed, the issues of the first decade of the twenty-first century may very well be more profound and untenable than those of the past. The political stakes have moved away from questioning the nature of the regime: They are focused much more intensely on the nature of the political community. Between 1986 and the present, this has become evident in a variety of ways.

Immigration has given way to ethnic consciousness, particularly among the children of immigrants from North Africa. Unlike most of the immigrant communities in the past, those of today are more reluctant to assume French cultural values as their own. This, in turn, leads to questioning the rules of naturalization for citizenship, integration into French society, and (in the end) what it means to be French.[53] During the 1980s, the National Front gave a political voice to growing ethnic tensions, which mobilized voters and solidified support based on racist appeals. In part because of the growing role of the FN, ethnic consciousness and diversity have grown in France and altered the context of French politics.

Twenty years ago the Cold War and the division of Europe were the basis for much of French foreign, defense, and, to some extent, domestic policy. The Cold War is long over. As a result, Eastern European ethnic consciousness and conflicts previously held in check by Soviet power, and in any case insulated from Western Europe by the Iron Curtain, now have been suddenly liberated. The disintegration of the Soviet Communist experiment (and the Soviet Union) has also undermined the legitimacy of classic socialism and has thus removed from French (and European) politics many of the issues that have long separated left from right. Parties of the right have lost the anti-Communist glue that contributed to their cohesiveness, but parties of the left have lost much of their purpose.

Coincidentally, the disintegration of the Communist bloc has occurred at the same time that the countries of the European Union have reinvigorated the process of European enlargement and integration, with France in the lead. Membership in the EU shapes almost every aspect of policy and provides the context for the expansion and restructuring of the economy during the Fifth Republic.[54]

At the beginning of his presidency in the early 1980s, François Mitterrand expressed his satisfaction with the existing structures of the Common Market. Having experienced their weakness, however, he increasingly felt that some form of federalism—a federalist finality—was necessary to enable Western Europe to use its considerable resources more effectively. Thus, during the Mitterrand presidency, France supported a larger and a more tightly integrated Europe. This included efforts to increase the powers of European institutions and the establishment of a European monetary and political union as outlined in the Maastricht Treaty, approved somewhat reluctantly in 1992. French commitment to a common European currency generated plans to cut public spending, plans that many French citizens ferociously resisted. Nevertheless, in 1998 France met all key requirements for and is now firmly part of the European Monetary Union.

The opening of French borders, not only to the products of other countries, but increasingly to their people and values (all citizens of the EU had the right to vote and run for office in the French local elections in 2001), feeds into the more general uneasiness about French national identity.

The integration of French economic and social institutions with those of its neighbors will progressively remove key decisions from the French government acting alone. In the past the French economy reacted to joint decisions made in Brussels. In the future, a broader range of institutions will be forced to do the same. Rumblings of resistance are no longer limited to the fringe parties (the parties of the extreme right and the Communists). Opposition exists within all of the major political parties, especially the UMP. Here, too, there is considerable potential for new political divisions.

The rejection of the European Constitutional Treaty in 2005 was what one scholar has called "an event waiting to happen." It reflected a deep questioning of two aspects of European development. First, the enlargement of Europe, particularly the candidacy of Turkey, has raised questions of both French and European identity, particularly among voters of the center-right. Second, the rapidly growing regulatory power of the EU and its liberal use of this power have deeply troubled voters of the left.

The divisions evoked by the referendum of 2005 were not new, but reflected the same ones revealed in the 1992 Maastricht referendum.

Nevertheless, this chapter, completed at the end of the first year of the presidency of Nicolas Sarkozy, presents a story of a strong and stable political system with an increasingly volatile and unstable party system. The forces destabilizing the party system are the major challenges now confronting all of the members of the European Union: the problem of identity in an expanding European Union and an independent world; the problem of democratic legitimacy among voters who are less ideologically committed, and an increasing skepticism of government and politicians, by those who expect more from government.

KEY TERMS

baccalauréat
blocked vote
Bonaparte, Napoléon
Buffet, Marie-George
Cabinet
Chirac, Jacques
communes
Confédération Française Democratique du Travail (CFDT)
Confédération Générale du Travail (CGT)
Constitution of 1958
Constitutional Council
Council of Ministers
Council of State
cumul des mandats (accumulation of electoral offices)
de Gaulle, Charles

departments
demonstrations of May–June 1968
Ecole Nationale d'Administration (ENA)
Ecole Polytechnique
European Union (EU) (European Community before 1992)
Fédération de' l'Education Nationale (FEN)
Fédération Nationale des Syndicats Agricoles (FNSEA)
Fifth Republic
Force Ouvrière (FO)
Fourth Republic
French Communist Party (PCF)

G-10
grands corps
grandes écoles
Jospin, Lionel
Juppé, Alain
Le Pen, Jean-Marie
Maastricht Treaty
Marchais, Georges
Mitterrand, François
motion of censure
Mouvement des Entreprises de France (MEDEF)
Muslims
National Assembly
National Front (FN)
nationalization
neocorporatism
new immigrants

political class
prefect
president of the Republic
prime minister
privatization
Rally for the Republic (RPR)
referendums
regions
Royal, Ségolène
Sarkozy, Nicolas
Senate
Socialist Party (PS)
Union for French Democracy (UDF)
Union for a Popular Movement (UMP)

SUGGESTED READINGS

Ambler, John, ed. *The Welfare State in France.* New York: New York University Press, 1991.

Baumgartner, Frank R. *Conflict and Rhetoric in French Policymaking.* Pittsburgh, PA: University of Pittsburgh Press, 1989.

Bleich, Erik. *Race Politics in Britain and France: Ideas and Policymaking Since the 1960s.* Cambridge, England: Cambridge University Press, 2003.

Bowen, John. *Why the French Don't Like Headscarves: Islam, the State and Public Space.* Princeton, NJ: Princeton University Press, 2007.

Chapman, Herrick, Mark Kesselman, and Martin Schain. *A Century of Organized Labor in France.* New York: St. Martin's Press, 1998.

Culpepper, Pepper D., Peter Hall, and Bruno Palier. *Changing France: The Politics That Markets Make.* Basingstoke, England: Palgrave, 2006.

Gordon, Philip, and Sophie Meunier. *The French Challenge.* Washington, DC: Brookings Institution Press, 2001.

Hollifield, James. *Immigrants, Markets, and States: The Political Economy of Postwar Europe.* Cambridge: Harvard University Press, 1992.

Keeler, John T. S. *The Politics of Neocorporatism in France.* New York: Oxford University Press, 1987.

Keeler, John T. S., and Martin A. Schain, eds. *Chirac's Challenge: Liberation, Europeanization, and Malaise in France.* New York: St. Martin's Press, 1996.

Lewis-Beck, Michael. *The French Voter Before and After the 2002 Elections.* Basingstoke, England: Palgrave 2004.

Perrineau, Pascal, ed. *Le Vote Européen, de l'Élargissement au Référendum Français.* Paris: Presses de Sciences-Po, 2005.

Schain, Martin. *The Politics of Immigration in France, Britain and the United States: A Comparative Analysis.* New York: Palgrave-Macmillan, 2008.

Schmidt, Vivien A. *From State to Market: The Transformation of Business and Government.* New York: Cambridge University Press, 1996.

Smith, Rand W. *Crisis in the French Labor Movement: A Grassroots Perspective.* New York: St. Martin's Press, 1988.

Stone, Alec. *The Birth of Judicial Politics in France: The Constitutional Council in Comparative Perspective.* New York: Oxford University Press, 1992.

Suleiman, Ezra. *Elites in French Society.* Princeton, NJ: Princeton University Press, 1978.

———. *Private Power and Centralization in France.* Princeton, NJ: Princeton University Press, 1987.

Wilson, Frank L. *Interest Group Politics in France.* New York: Cambridge University Press, 1987.

INTERNET RESOURCES

Office of the President: **www.elysee.fr/ang/index.shtm**

National Assembly: **www.assemblee-nat.fr**

Senate: **www.senat.fr**

Collection of websites to French institutions: **www.assemblee-nationale.fr/liens.asp**

Embassy of France in the United States: **www.info-france-usa.org**

ENDNOTES

1. Claire Guéland, "La France s'enfonce dans une recession d'une ampleur jamais vue," *Le Monde*, March 21, 2009, p. 12.

2. The best book in English on the Constitutional Council is Alec Stone, *The Birth of Judicial Politics in France* (New York: Oxford University Press, 1992).

3. Laurence Wylie, "Social Change at the Grass Roots," in *In Search of France*, ed. Stanley Hoffmann, Charles Kindleberger, Laurence Wylie, Jesse R. Pitts, Jean-Baptiste Duroselle and François Goguel (Cambridge: Harvard University Press, 1963), p. 230.

4. See Olivier Duhamel, "Confance institutionnelle et *défiance* politique: *la démocratic* française," in Sofres, *L'État de l'opinion 2001* (Paris: Seuil, 2001), p. 75.

5. Interesting data on religious practice can be found in Sofres, *L'Etat de l'opinion 1994* (Paris: Seuil, 1994), pp. 179–199. These data are taken from an unpublished exit poll dated 26 May 1997.

6. See Sylvain Brouard and Vincent Tiberj, *Français comme les autres? Enquête sur les citoyens d'origine maghrébine, africaine et turque* (Paris: Presses de Sciences-Po, 2006).

7. See the Pew Global Attitudes Project, 6 July 2006. Retrieved July, 2006 from pewglobal.org/reports.

8. One important study found greater spontaneous class consciousness among French workers in the 1970s than among comparable groups of British workers. Duncan Gallie, *Social Inequality and Class Radicalism*

in France and Britain (London: Cambridge University Press, 1983), p. 34.

9. Annick Percheron, "Socialization et tradition: transmission et invention du politique," *Pouvoirs* 42 (1988): 43.

10. Edgar Morin, *The Red and the White* (New York: Pantheon Books, 1970), discusses the noisy revolution of the teenagers and the silent one of women.

11. See Janine Mossuz-Lavau and Mariette Sineau, *Les Femmes françaises en 1978: Insertion sociale, Insertion politique* (Paris: Centre de Documentation Sciences Humaine de CNRS, 1980). The authors also found that women who were previously employed were likely to express opinions closer to those of working women than of nonworking women.

12. Annick Percheron and M. Kent Jennings, "Political Continuities in French Families: A New Perspective on an Old Controversy," *Comparative Politics* 13, no. 4 (July 1981): 421–436.

13. Ronald Inglehart, *Culture Shift* (Princeton, NJ: Princeton University Press, 1990), chs. 1–3 and tab. 2.4; Michele Tribalat, *Faire France* (Paris: La Découverte, 1995), pp. 93–98; Sylvain Brouard and Vincent Tiberj, *Français com les autres? Enquête sur les citoyens d'origine maghrébine, africaine, et turque* (Paris: Presses de Sciences-Po, 2006), pp. 30–32.

14. See Laurence Haeusler, "Le monde associatif de 1978–1986," in *Données Sociales 1990*, ed. INSEE (Paris: INSEE, 1990), pp. 369–370. See also Henry Ehrmann and Martin Schain, *Politics in France*, 5th ed. (New York: HarperCollins, 1992), tab. 3.6.

15. Institut national de la statistique et des études économiques, *Tableaux de l'économie française* (Paris: INSEE, 2008).

16. John Ambler, "Constraints on Policy Innovation in Education: Thatcher's Britain and Mitterrand's France," *Comparative Politics* 20, no. 1 (October 1987): 85–105. See also John Ambler, "Conflict and Consensus in French Education," in *Chirac's Challenge: Liberalization, Europeanization, and Malaise in France*, ed. John T. S. Keeler and Martin A. Schain (New York: St. Martins Press, 1996).

17. The restrictive recruitment of the grandes écoles is confirmed by a study: "Le recruitment social de l élite scolaire depuis quarante ans," *Education et Formations* 41 (June 1995). Which institutions qualify as grandes écoles is controversial. But among the 140 or so designated as such in some estimates, only 15 or 20, with an enrollment of 2,000 to 2,500, are considered important, prestige schools. The number of private engineering and business schools that are generally considered to be grandes écoles has increased in recent years. Therefore, the total enrollment of all these schools has increased significantly to well over 100,000.

18. These results are taken from Russell J. Dalton, *Citizen Politics in Western Democracies*, 5th ed. (Washington, DC: CQ Press, 2008), ch. 2. See Sofres, *L'Etat de l'opinion 1994*, p. 232.

19. There is no legal definition for a grande école, although it is widely alluded to by citizens, journalists, and scholars. On these issues, see J.-T. Bodiguel and J.-L. Quermonne. *La Haute fonction publique sous la Ve République* (Paris: PUF, 1983), pp. 12–25, 83–94. The figures given here for grands corps (the elite administrative agencies) are approximations, based on a series of articles in *Les Echos,* 20–22 June 2006.

20. See *le Figaro*, March 25, 2008.

21. Janine Mossuz-Levau, "Les Femmes," in *Presidentielle 2007: Atlas électoral,* ed. Pascal Perrineau (Paris: Presses de Sciences Po, 2007), pp. 75–78.

22. These percentages are only approximations, since interest groups in France either refuse to publish membership figures or publish figures that are universally viewed as highly questionable. For estimates of interest group memberships, see Peter Hall, "Pluralism and Pressure Politics," in *Developments in French Politics,* rev. ed. Peter Hall, Jack Hayward, and Howard Machin (London: Macmillan, 1994). For recent estimates of trade union membership, see Antoine Bevort, "Les effectifs syndiqués à la CGT et à la CFDT 1945–1990," *Communisme* 35–37 (1994): 87–90. See also the recent study by Dominique Andolfatto and Dominique Labbé, *Histoire des Syndicats* (Paris: Seuil, 2006).

23. Herrick Chapman, Mark Kesselman, and Martin Schain, *A Century of Organized Labor in France* (New York: St. Martin's Press, 1998).

24. Mark Kesselman, "Does the French Labor Movement Have a Future?" in *Chirac's Challenge,* ed. Keeler and Schain. The reports of the congresses of the two largest union confederations in 2006 confirm that less than 5 percent of their members are under age 30. See *Le Monde,* 12 June 2006.

25. See Martin A. Schain, "French Unions: Myths and Realities," *Dissent* (Summer 2008), pp. 11–15.

26. The most interesting recent study is Sylvie Guillaume, *Le Petit et moyen patronat dans la nation française, de Pinay a Rafferin, 1944–2004* (Pessac, France: Presses Universitaires de Bordeaux, 2004). An earlier study by Henry W. Ehrmann. *Organized Business in France* (Princeton, NJ: Princeton University Press, 1957), presents case studies about the contacts between the administration and the employers' organizations, but it is now dated.

27. John Keeler, *The Politics of Neocorporatism in France* (New York: Oxford University Press, 1987).

28. Frank Wilson, *Interest-Group Politics in France* (New York: Cambridge University Press, 1987), pp. 151, 153, 162, and 164.

29. John T. S. Keeler, "Situating France on the Pluralism-Corporatism Continuum," *Comparative Politics* 17 (January 1985): 229–249. On subsidies, see "Patronat et organizations syndicales: un système a bout de soufflé," dossier special, *Le Monde*, 30 October 2007.

30. See the articles by John Ambler, Frank Baumgartner, Martin Schain, and Frank Wilson in *French Politics and Society* 12 (Spring/Summer 1994).

31. For a good survey of party developments between 1958 and 1981, see Frank L. Wilson, *French Political Parties Under the Fifth Republic* (New York: Praeger, 1982).

32. See Colette Ysmal, "Transformations du militantisme et déclin des partis," in *L'Engagement Politique, déclin ou mutation?* ed. Pascal Perrineau (Paris: Presses de la FNSP, 1994), p. 48. See also *L'Etat de la France* (Paris: La Découverte, 1997), pp. 521–526.

33. Stanley Hoffmann, *Le Mouvement Poujade* (Paris: A. Colin, 1956).

34. D. S. Bell and Byron Criddle, *The French Socialist Party: The Emergence of a Party of Government,* 2nd ed. (Oxford, England: Clarendon, 1988).

35. For an analysis of the decline of the Communist vote, see Martin Schain, "The French Communist Party: The Seeds of Its Own Decline," in *Comparative Theory and Political Experience,* ed. Peter Katzenstein, Theodore Lowi, and Sidney Tarrow (Ithaca, NY: Cornell University Press, 1990). Also see Jane Jenson and George Ross, *View from the Inside: A French Communist Cell in Crisis* (Berkeley: University of California Press, 1984), p. 5.

36. It must be noted—and this is true for all figures on electoral participation throughout this chapter—that French statistics calculate electoral participation based on registered voters, while American statistics take as a basis the total number of people of voting age. About 9 percent of French citizens entitled to vote are not registered. This percentage must therefore be added to the published figures when one wishes to estimate the true rate of abstention and to compare it with the American record.

37. See Françoise Subileau and Marie-France Toinet, *Les chemins de l'abstention* (Paris: La Découverte, 1993), and Marie-France Toinet, "The Limits of Malaise in France," in *Chirac's Challenge,* ed. Keeler and Schain, pp. 289–91.

38. *Le Monde,* 15 June 2002, p. 8.

39. John T. S. Keeler and Martin A. Schain, "Presidents, Premiers and Models of Democracy in France," in *Chirac's Challenge,* ed. Keeler and Schain.

40. One of the very few analyses of the use of the blocked vote, as well as the use by the government of Article 49.3, is found in John Huber, "Restrictive Legislative Procedures in France and the United States," *American Political Science Review* 86, no. 3 (September 1992): 675–687. Huber also compares such tools with similar procedures in the U.S. Congress.

41. Didier Maus, "Parliament in the Fifth Republic: 1958–1988," in *Policy-Making in France.* ed. Paul Godt (New York: Pinter, 1989), 17; Didier Maus, *Les grands textes de la pratique institutionelle de la Ve République* (Paris: La Documentation Française, 1992).

42. These figures are taken from *cumul des mandates* presented by a committee of the French National Assembly: "Rapport fait au nom de la Commissions des lois constitutionnelles, de la legislation et de l'administration générale de la République sur le projet de loi organiques (no. 827) *limitant le* cumul *des* mandats électoraux *et* fonctions électives,*" par M. Bernard Roman. 2008 figures were retrieved 3 January 2009 from www. assemblée-nationale.

43. This description refers to the first article of the Constitution of 1793, which proclaims: "The French Republic is one and indivisible." The Constitution of the Fifth Republic repeats it.

44. Vivien A. Schmidt, *Democratizing France* (New York: Cambridge University Press, 1990).

45. The now classic statement of this relationship was written by Jean-Pierre Worms, who years later had major responsibilities for developing the decentralization reforms for the government of the left. See "Le Préfet et ses notables," *Sociologie du Travail* 8, no. 3 (1966): 249–275.

46. Mark Kesselman, "The Tranquil Revolution at Clochemerle: Socialist Decentralization in France," in *Socialism, the State, and Public Policy in France,* ed. Philip G. Cerny and Martin A. Schain (New York: St. Martin's Press, 1985), p. 176.

47. *OECD Factbook 2008* (Washington, DC: OECD, 2008), pp. 248–249.

48. See *Le Monde,* 7 October 1999, p. 6.

49. Victor Rodwin and Contributors, *Universal Health Insurance in France: How Sustainable?* (Washington, DC: Embassy of France, 2006), p. 187.

50. As a result, the number of workers paid indirectly by the state declined. Nevertheless, the proportion of the workforce paid directly by the state (government employment) remained stable at about 23 percent, about a third higher than in the United States, Germany, and Italy, but lower than in the Scandinavian countries. See Vincent Wright, "Reshaping the State: The Implications for Public Administration," *West European Politics* 17, no. 3 (July 1994).

51. They were also controlled by the same people as when they were nationalized. None of the newly privatized firms changed managing directors. See Michel Bauer, "The Politics of State-Directed Privatization: The Case of France 1986–1988," *West European Politics* 11, no. 4 (October 1988): 59.

52. Philip G. Cerny, "The 'Little Big Bang' in Paris," *European Journal of Political Research* 17, no. 2 (1989).

53. Martin A. Schain, *The Politics of Immigration in France, Britain and the United States: A Comparative Study* (New York: Palgrave-Macmillan, 2008).

54. See Alain Gayomarch, Howard Machin, and Ella Ritchie, *France and the European Union* (New York: St. Martin's Press, 1998).

POLITICS IN GERMANY

Russell J. Dalton

Country Bio

GERMANY

Population
82.4 million

Territory
137,803 square miles

Year of Independence
1871

Year of Current Constitution
1949

Head of State
President Horst Köhler

Head of Government
Chancellor Angela Merkel

Language
German

Religion
Protestant 34%, Roman Catholic 34%, Muslim 4%, unaffiliated or other 28%

The unusual outcome of the 2005 elections has shaped contemporary German politics. The election results were so close that even the next day it was unclear who "won" the election. This began a protracted process of coalition-building. Neither of the largest two parties had a majority of votes, and in such cases, one party normally forms a coalition with a smaller party. But after weeks of negotiation and false starts, a new solution appeared. The two major parties—Christian Democrats and Social Democrats—would form a Grand Coalition with **Angela Merkel** becoming Germany's newest chancellor.

This result is unusual because these two parties were rivals in the just-completed election. It was as if the Democratic Party and the Republican Party in the United States decided to govern as partners despite their policy differences. The logic was that the two German parties could unite to address some of the nation's political problems that required a broad political agreement. But this meant the parties forming the government held three-quarters of the seats in the parliament and the opposition held only a quarter of the seats.

At another level Merkel's selection as chancellor was an important result. She had never held a major elective office. Having grown up in East Germany, she had been a member of the Communist Youth League. Instead of seeking a political career, she worked as a chemist until the collapse of the Berlin Wall. Further, she was a woman in a society that had always been governed by men. Merkel's election represents how much Germany has changed. Communism now seems like a memory from the distant past, and traditional social norms that shaped gender roles and political roles have changed.

The major achievement of contemporary German politics is the creation of a unified, free, and democratic nation in the short period since the unification of West Germany—the **Federal Republic of Germany (FRG)**—and East Germany—the **German Democratic Republic (GDR)**—occurred in 1990. A unified, democratic Germany has contributed to the political stability of Europe and has given millions of Eastern Germans their freedom and new opportunities. Now the challenge facing the government is to maintain the social and economic vitality of the nation, to enact reforms to ensure that the German economy and political system continue to function effectively, and to build a policy consensus on the reforms to achieve these goals.

CURRENT POLICY CHALLENGES

What political problems do Germans typically read about when they open the daily newspaper or watch their favorite television newscast—and what political problems preoccupy policymakers in Berlin? Often the answer is the same as in most other industrial democracies. News reports analyze the state of the economy, report on crime, and generally track the social and economic health of the nation.

Economic issues are a recurring source of political debate. Germany still faces a series of economic and social problems that emerged from unification. Because the economic infrastructure of the East lagged far behind that of the West, the Eastern economy has struggled to compete in the globalized economic system. Eastern plants lacked the technology and management of Western firms, Eastern workers lacked the training and experience of their Western counterparts, and the economic infrastructure of the East was crumbling under the Communist regime. Consequently, government agencies and the **European Union (EU)** have invested more than 1,000 billion euros (€) in the East since unification—raising taxes for all Germans in the process. Still, the nightly news routinely chronicles the continuing economic difficulties in the East, which still affect the entire nation (see Box 7.1).

The economic challenges have worsened with the worldwide recession that began in late 2008. In the mid 2000s, Germany's export-oriented economy benefited from global economic expansion and domestic economic reforms. However, when the recession decreased international trade and consumption within Europe, this created new economic strains. Merkel's government has moved very cautiously, enacting two modest stimulus bills in early 2009. The recession (and a looming election in 2009) ended plans for broad structural reforms of the economic system and social programs. The Federal Republic faces greater economic uncertainty than perhaps at any other time in its history. Germany has joined with other EU member states to strengthen the banking and credit system and now faces economic slowdown with an unreformed economic system. This will be a major challenge for the new government elected in 2009.

Social services represent another source of policy debate. Health, pension, and other social welfare costs have spiraled upward, but there is little agreement on how to manage these costs. As the German population ages, the demands being placed on the social welfare system are predictably increasing. Few economists believe that the present system of social benefits is sustainable in the future, especially as Germany competes in a global economic system and works to improve conditions in the East. As the federal elections approach in fall 2009, it is likely that partisan differences on economic or social services policy will widen between the governing partners and little policy reform will occur.

| The Curse of Unification? | **BOX 7.1** |

Germany's attempt to rebuild its once Communist East has been an unmitigated disaster, and the massive financial transfers from the West endanger the entire nation's economy, according to a government-commissioned report.

A panel of thirteen experts, headed by former Hamburg Mayor Klaus von Dohnanyi, was charged with examining the reconstruction of Germany's eastern states. The panel concluded that the estimated €1.25 trillion ($1.54 trillion) in aid has done little to help the economically depressed region.

Perhaps even more worrying, the experts fear the €90 billion spent by the government each year is slowly destroying the economy of western Germany, as growth stagnates and the eastern states fail to revive fourteen years after German reunification.

Source: *The Deutsche Welle Report,* April 4, 2004, p. 62.

The challenges of becoming a multicultural nation create another new source of political tension. Germany already had a sizeable foreign-born population because of its foreign worker programs of the 1960s and 1970s. During the 1990s there was a large influx of refugees from the Balkan conflict, asylum seekers, and ethnic Germans from East Europe. Some people argue that "the boat is full" and new immigration should be limited, while others claim that immigration is essential for the nation's future. Policy reforms in the 1990s restricted further immigration, and the government changed citizenship laws in 2000 and reformed immigration legislation in 2002. However, the public is divided on the appropriate policies. Like much of the rest of Europe, Germany now struggles to address these issues, which are particularly difficult because of the legacy of Germany's past.

Finally, foreign policies are another source of public debate. The EU is an increasingly visible part of political reporting, and Germans are trying to determine their desired role in an expanding EU (see Chapter 12). Germany has been a prime advocate of the expansion of EU membership to include Eastern Europe, even though this may dilute Germany's influence within the EU. However, EU policies, such as monetary union and the development of a European currency, are creating internal divisions over the nation's relationship to the EU. The economic downturn in 2008 was exceptionally hard in Eastern Europe, prompting calls for Germany and other affluent western economies to support the new EU members in the East. This creates a joint economic and foreign policy challenge.

In addition, Germany is trying to define its role in the post–Cold War world. For the first time since World War II, German troops took part in a military action outside of German territory: in Kosovo in 1999 and in Afghanistan in 2001. However, Germany actively opposed the U.S. invasion of Iraq in 2003, and the current government remains critical of the U.S. actions in Iraq. Merkel, however, has worked to strengthen Germany's ties to the United States through the North Atlantic Treaty Organization (NATO) military alliance and other foreign policy activities.

The Federal Republic is one of the most successful and vibrant democracies in the world today. It has made substantial progress in improving the quality of life of its citizens, strengthening democracy, and developing a secure nation, and it has become an important member of the international community. But the continuing burdens of German unification and the lack of consensus on future policy directions mean that the current government has managed the current policy challenges, but has not taken decisive action to fully address them. These policy challenges will thus carry over to the new government elected in 2009.

THE HISTORICAL LEGACY

The German historical experience differs considerably from that of most other European democracies. The social and political forces that modernized the rest of Europe came much later in Germany and had a less certain effect. By the nineteenth century, when most nations had defined their borders, German territory was still divided among dozens of political units. Although most European states had developed a dominant national culture, Germany was split by sharp religious, regional, and economic divisions. Industrialization generally was the driving force behind the modernization of Europe, but German industrialization came late and did not overturn the old feudal and aristocratic order. German history, even to the present, represents a difficult and protracted process of nation-building.

The Second German Empire

Through a combination of military and diplomatic victories, Otto von Bismarck, the Prussian chancellor, enlarged the territory of Prussia and established a unified Second German Empire in 1871.[1] The empire was an authoritarian state, with only the superficial trappings of a democracy. Political power flowed from the monarch—the **Kaiser**—and the government at times bitterly suppressed potential opposition groups, especially the Roman Catholic Church and the Social Democratic party. The government expected little of its citizens: They were to pay their taxes, serve in the army, and keep their mouths shut.

The central government encouraged national development during this period. Industrialization finally occurred, and German influence in international affairs grew steadily. The force of industrialization was not sufficient to modernize and liberalize society and the political system, however. Economic and political power remained concentrated in the hands of the bureaucracy and traditional aristocratic elites. The authoritarian state was strong enough to resist the democratic demands of a weak middle class. The state was supreme: Its needs took precedence over those of individuals and society.

Failures of government leadership, coupled with a blindly obedient public, led Germany into World War I (1914–1918). The war devastated the nation. Almost 3 million German soldiers and civilians lost their lives, the economy was strained beyond the breaking point, and the government of the empire collapsed under the weight of its own incapacity to govern. The war ended with Germany a defeated and exhausted nation.

The Weimar Republic

In 1919 a popularly elected constitutional assembly established the new democratic system of the **Weimar Republic**. The constitution granted all citizens the right to vote and guaranteed basic human rights. A directly elected parliament and president held political power, and political parties became legitimate political actors. Belatedly, the Germans had their first real experience with democracy.

From the outset, however, severe problems plagued the Weimar government. In the Versailles peace treaty ending World War I, Germany lost all its overseas colonies and a large amount of its European territory. The treaty further burdened Germany with the moral guilt for the war and the financial cost of postwar reparations to the victorious Allies. A series of radical uprisings threatened the political system. Wartime destruction and the reparations produced continuing economic problems that finally led to an economic catastrophe in 1923. In less than a year, the inflation rate was an unimaginable 26 billion percent! Ironically, the Kaiser's government, which had produced these problems, was not blamed for these developments. Instead, many people criticized the empire's democratic successor—the Weimar Republic.

The fatal blow came with the Great Depression in 1929. The Depression struck Germany harder than most other European nations or the United States. Almost a third of the labor force became unemployed, and people were frustrated by the government's inability to deal with the crisis. Political tensions increased, and parliamentary democracy began to fail. **Adolf Hitler** and his **National Socialist German Workers' Party (the Nazis)** were the major beneficiaries. Their vote share grew from a mere 2 percent in 1928 to 18 percent in 1930 and 33 percent in November 1932.

Increasingly, the machinery of the democratic system malfunctioned or was bypassed. In a final attempt to restore political order, President Paul von Hindenburg appointed Hitler chancellor of the Weimar Republic in January 1933. This was democracy's death knell.

Weimar's failure resulted from a mix of factors.[2] The lack of support from political elites and the public was a basic weakness of Weimar. Democracy depended on an administrative and military elite that often longed for the old authoritarian political system. Elite criticism of Weimar encouraged similar sentiments among the public. Many Germans were not committed to democratic principles. The fledgling state then faced a series of severe economic and political crises. Such strains might have overloaded the ability of any system to govern effectively. These crises further eroded public support for Weimar and opened the door to Hitler's authoritarian and nationalistic appeals. The institutional weaknesses of the political system contributed to Weimar's political vulnerability. Finally, most Germans drastically underestimated Hitler's ambitions, intentions, and political abilities. This underestimation, perhaps, was Weimar's greatest failure.

The Third Reich

The Nazis' rise to power reflected a bizarre mixture of ruthless behavior and concern for legal procedures. Hitler called for a new election in March 1933 and then suppressed the opposition parties. Although the Nazis failed to capture an absolute majority of the votes, they used their domination of the parliament to enact legislation granting Hitler dictatorial powers. Democracy was replaced by the new authoritarian "leader state" of the **Third Reich**.

Once entrenched in power, Hitler pursued extremist policies. Social and political groups that might challenge the government were destroyed, taken over by Nazi agents, or coopted into accepting the Nazi regime. The powers of the police state grew and choked off opposition. Attacks on Jews and other minorities steadily became more violent. Massive public works projects lessened unemployment, but also built the infrastructure for a wartime economy. The government enlarged and rearmed the military in violation of the Versailles treaty. The Reich's expansionist foreign policy challenged the international peace.

Hitler's unrestrained political ambitions finally plunged Europe into World War II in 1939. After initial victories a series of military defeats beginning in 1942 led to the total collapse of the Third Reich in May 1945. A total of 60 million lives were lost worldwide in the war, including 6 million European Jews who were murdered in a Nazi campaign of systematic genocide.[3]

Germany lay in ruins: Its industry and transportation systems were destroyed, its cities were rubble, millions were homeless, and even food was scarce. Hitler's grand design for a new German Reich had instead destroyed the nation in a Wagnerian *Götterdämmerung*.

The Occupation Period

The political division of postwar Germany began as foreign troops advanced onto German soil. At the end of the war, the Western Allies—the United States, Britain, and France—controlled Germany's Western zone, and the Soviet Union occupied the Eastern zone. This was to be an interim division, but growing frictions between Western and Soviet leaders increased tensions between the regions.

In the Western zone, the Allied military government began a denazification program to remove Nazi officials and sympathizers from the economic, military, and political systems. The occupation authorities licensed new political parties, and democratic political institutions began to develop. These authorities also reorganized the economic system along capitalist lines. Currency and market economy reforms in 1948 revitalized the economic system of the Western zone, but also deepened divisions between the Eastern and Western zones.

Political change followed a much different course in the Eastern zone. The new **Socialist Unity Party (SED)** was a mechanism for the Soviets to control the political process. Since they saw capitalism as responsible for the Third Reich, the Soviets tried to destroy the capitalist system and construct a new socialist order in its place. By 1948 the Eastern zone was essentially a copy of the Soviet political and economic systems.

As the political distance between occupation zones widened, the Western allies favored creation of a separate German state in the West. In Bonn, a small university town along the banks of the Rhine, the Germans began to create a new democratic system. In 1948 a parliamentary council drafted an interim constitution that was to last until the entire nation was reunited. In May 1949 the state governments in the Western zone agreed on the **Basic Law (Grundgesetz)** that created the FRG, or West Germany.

These developments greatly worried the Soviets. The Soviet blockade of Berlin in 1948, for example, partially sought to halt the formation of a separate West German state—though it actually strengthened Western resolve. Once it became apparent that West Germany would follow its own course, preparations began for a separate East German state. A week after the formation

of the FRG, the People's Congress in the East approved a draft constitution. On October 7, 1949, the GDR, or East Germany, was formed. As in earlier periods of German history, a divided nation was following different paths (see Figure 7.1). It would be more than forty years before these paths would converge.

FOLLOWING TWO PATHS

Although they had chosen different paths (or had these paths chosen for them), the two German states faced many of the same challenges in their initial years. The economic picture was bleak on both sides of the border. Unemployment remained high in West Germany, and the average wages were minimal. In 1950 almost two-thirds of the West German public felt they had been better off before the war, and severe economic hardships were still common. The situation was even worse in East Germany.

West Germany was phenomenally successful in meeting this economic challenge.[4] Relying on a free enterprise system championed by the **Christian Democratic Union (CDU)**, the country experienced sustained and unprecedented economic growth. By the early 1950s, incomes had reached the prewar level, and growth had just begun. Over the next two decades, per capita wealth nearly tripled, average hourly industrial wages increased nearly fivefold, and average incomes grew nearly sevenfold. By most economic indicators, the West German public in 1970 was several times more affluent than at any time in its pre–World War II history. This phenomenal economic growth is known as West Germany's **Economic Miracle (Wirtschaftswunder)**.

East Germany's postwar economic miracle was almost as impressive. Its economic system was based on collectivized agriculture, nationalized industry, and centralized planning.[5] From 1950 until 1970, industrial production and per capita national income increased nearly fivefold. Although still lagging behind its more affluent relatives in the West, the GDR was the model of prosperity among socialist states.

The problem of nation-building posed another challenge. The FRG initially was viewed as a provisional state until both Germanies could be reunited. The GDR struggled to develop its own identity in the shadow of West Germany, while expressing a commitment to eventual reunification. In addition, the occupation authorities retained the right to intervene in the two Germanies even after 1949. Thus, both

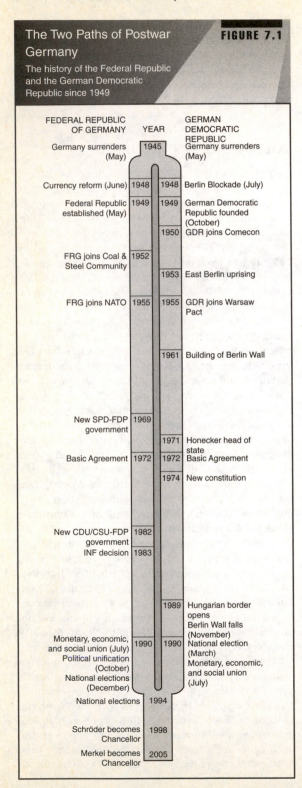

The Two Paths of Postwar Germany   FIGURE 7.1

The history of the Federal Republic and the German Democratic Republic since 1949

FEDERAL REPUBLIC OF GERMANY	YEAR	GERMAN DEMOCRATIC REPUBLIC
Germany surrenders (May)	1945	Germany surrenders (May)
Currency reform (June)	1948	Berlin Blockade (July)
Federal Republic established (May)	1949	German Democratic Republic founded (October)
	1950	GDR joins Comecon
FRG joins Coal & Steel Community	1952	
	1953	East Berlin uprising
FRG joins NATO	1955	GDR joins Warsaw Pact
	1961	Building of Berlin Wall
New SPD-FDP government	1969	
	1971	Honecker head of state
Basic Agreement	1972	Basic Agreement
	1974	New constitution
New CDU/CSU-FDP government	1982	
INF decision	1983	
	1989	Hungarian border opens Berlin Wall falls (November)
Monetary, economic, and social union (July) Political unification (October) National elections (December)	1990	1990 National election (March) Monetary, economic, and social union (July)
National elections	1994	
Schröder becomes Chancellor	1998	
Merkel becomes Chancellor	2005	

states faced the challenge of defining their identity—as separate states or as parts of a larger Germany—and regaining national sovereignty.

West Germany's first chancellor, **Konrad Adenauer**, steered a course toward gaining national sovereignty by integrating the FRG into the Western alliance. The Western Allies would grant greater autonomy to West Germany if it was exercised within the framework of an international body. For example, economic redevelopment was channeled through the European Coal and Steel Community and the European Economic Community. West Germany's military rearmament occurred within NATO.

The Communist regime in the GDR countered the FRG's integration into the Western alliance with calls for German unification. And yet, the GDR was simultaneously establishing itself as a separate German state. In 1952 the GDR transformed the boundary between East and West Germany into a fortified border; this restricted Western access to the East and limited Easterners' ability to go to the West. The GDR integrated its economy into the Soviet bloc through membership in the Council for Mutual Economic Assistance (COMECON), and it was a charter member of the Warsaw Pact military alliance. The Soviet Union recognized the sovereignty of the GDR in 1954. The practical and symbolic division of Germany became official with the GDR's construction of the Berlin Wall in August 1961. More than a physical barrier between East and West, it marked the formal existence of two separate German states.

Intra-German relations took a dramatically different course after the **Social Democratic Party (SPD)** won control of West Germany's government after the 1969 elections. The new SPD chancellor, Willy Brandt, followed a policy toward the East (**Ostpolitik**) that accepted the postwar political situation and sought reconciliation with Eastern European nations, including the GDR. West Germany signed treaties with the Soviet Union and Poland to resolve disagreements dating back to World War II and to establish new economic and political ties. In 1971 Brandt received the Nobel Peace Prize for his actions. The following year the two Germanies adopted the Basic Agreement, which formalized their relationship as two states within one nation. To the East German regime, *Ostpolitik* was a mixed blessing. On the one hand, it legitimized the GDR through its recognition by the FRG and the normalization of East-West relations. On the other hand, economic and social exchanges increased East Germans' exposure to Western values and ideas, which many GDR politicians worried would undermine their closed system. The eventual revolution of 1989 seemingly confirmed their fears.

After reconciliation between the two German states, both spent most of the next two decades addressing their internal needs. SPD policy reforms in the West expanded social services and equalized access to the benefits of the Economic Miracle. Total social spending nearly doubled between 1969 and 1975. As global economic problems grew in the mid-1970s, Helmut Schmidt of the SPD became chancellor and slowed the pace of reform and government spending.

The problems of unrealized reforms and renewed economic difficulties continued into the 1980s. In 1982 the CDU enticed the **Free Democratic Party (FDP)** to form a new government under the leadership of **Helmut Kohl**, head of the Christian Democratic Union. The new government wanted to restore the FRG's economy, while still providing for social needs. Kohl presided over a dramatic improvement in economic conditions. The government also demonstrated its commitment to the Western defense alliance by accepting new NATO nuclear missiles. The public returned Kohl's coalition to office in the 1987 elections.

Worldwide economic recession also buffeted the GDR's economy starting in the late 1970s. The cost competitiveness of East German products diminished in international markets, and trade deficits with the West grew steadily. Moreover, long-delayed investment in the country's infrastructure began to show in a deteriorating highway system, an aging housing stock, and an outdated communications system. Although East Germans heard frequent government reports about the nation's economic success, their living standards evidenced a widening gap between official pronouncements and reality.

In the late 1980s, East German government officials were concerned with the winds of change rising in the East. Soviet President Mikhail Gorbachev's reformist policies of *perestroika* and *glasnost* seemed to undermine the pillars supporting the East German system (see Chapter 10). At one point an official GDR newspaper even censored news from the Soviet Union in order to downplay Gorbachev's reforms. Indeed, the stimulus for political change in East Germany came not from within, but from the events sweeping across the rest of Eastern Europe.

In early 1989 the first cracks in the Communist monolith appeared. Poland's Communist government accepted a series of democratic reforms, and the Hungarian Communist Party endorsed democratic and market reforms. When Hungary opened its border with neutral Austria, a stream of East Germans vacationing in Hungary started leaving for the West. East Germans were voting with their feet. Almost 2 percent of the East German population emigrated to the FRG over the next six months. The exodus also stimulated mass public demonstrations against the regime within East Germany.

Gorbachev played a crucial role in directing the flow of events in Germany. He encouraged the GDR leadership to undertake internal reforms with the cautious advice that "life itself punishes those who delay." Without Soviet military and ideological support, the end of the old GDR system was inevitable. Rapidly growing public protests increased the pressure on the government, and the continuing exodus to the West brought the East's economy to a near standstill. The government did not govern; it barely existed, struggling from crisis to crisis. In early November the government and the SED Politburo resigned. On the evening of November 9, 1989, a GDR official announced the opening of the border between East and West Berlin. In the former no-man's-land of the Berlin Wall, Berliners from East and West joyously celebrated together.

Once the euphoria of the Berlin Wall's opening had passed, East Germany had to address the question of "What next?" The GDR government initially tried a strategy of damage control, appointing new leaders and attempting to court public support. However, the power of the state and the vitality of the economy had already suffered mortal wounds. Protesters who had chanted "We are the people" when opposing the Communist government in October took up the call for unification with a new refrain: "We are one people." The only apparent source of stability was unification with the FRG, and the rush toward German unity began.

In March 1990 the GDR had its first truly free elections since 1932. The Alliance for Germany, which included the eastern branch of the Christian Democrats, won control of the government. Helmut Kohl and Lothar de Maiziere, the new GDR leader, both forcefully moved toward unification. On July 1 an intra-German treaty gave the two nations one currency and essentially one economy. Soviet concessions on the terms of union opened the road to complete unification. On October 3, 1990, after more than four decades of separation, the two German paths again converged.

Unification largely occurred on Western terms. In fact, Easterners sarcastically claim that the only trace of the old regime is one law kept from the

GDR: Automobiles can turn right on a red light in the East. Otherwise, the Western political structures, Western interest groups, Western political parties, and Western economic and social systems were simply exported to the East.

Unification was supposed to be the answer to a dream, but during the next few years, it must have occasionally seemed like a nightmare. The Eastern economy collapsed with the end of the GDR; at times unemployment rates in the East exceeded the worst years of the Great Depression. The burden of unification led to inflation and tax increases in the West and weakened the Western economy. The social strains of unification stimulated violent attacks against foreigners in both halves of Germany. At the end of 1994, Kohl's coalition won a razor-thin majority in national elections.

Tremendous progress had been made by 1998, but the economy still struggled and necessary changes in tax laws and social programs languished. When the Germans went to the polls in 1998, they voted for a change and elected a new government headed by **Gerhard Schröder** and the Social Democrats in alliance with The Greens (*Die Grünen*). The new governing coalition made some progress on addressing the nation's major policy challenges—such as a major reform of the tax system and continued investments in the East—but not enough progress. The coalition won the 2002 election, but with a reduced margin.

After cumulative losses in state elections and deepening dissatisfaction with the government, Schröder called for early elections in 2005. After an intense campaign, both the SPD and the Christian Democratic Union/Christian Social Union (CDU/CSU) gained the same share of the vote. The closeness of the vote showed the divisions on how the nation should deal with its current policy challenges. Merkel eventually convinced a Schröder-less SPD to join the CDU/CSU in forming a Grand Coalition. Analysts hoped that this alliance could enact significant economic and policy reforms, but the divisions within the coalition have led to a cautious style of government with little major policy change.

SOCIAL FORCES

The new unified Germany is the largest state in the European Union. It has about 82 million people, 68 million in the West and 14 million in the East, located in Europe's heartland. The total German economy is also Europe's largest. The combined territory of the new Germany is also large by European standards, although it is small in comparison to the United States—a bit smaller than Montana.

The merger of two nations is more complex than the simple addition of two columns of numbers on a balance sheet, however. Unification created new strengths, but it also redefined and potentially strains the social system that underlies German society and politics. The merger of East and West holds the potential for reviving some of Germany's traditional social divisions.

Economics

Postwar economic growth occurred at different rates in the West and East and followed different paths. In the FRG, the service and technology sectors grew substantially, and government employment more than doubled during the later twentieth century. Although we often think of Germany as an industrial society, barely a quarter of those in the labor force describe themselves as blue-collar workers; two-thirds say they have a white-collar occupation. In contrast, the GDR's economic expansion was concentrated in heavy industry and manufacturing. In the mid-1980s about half of the Eastern labor force worked in these two areas, and the service-technology sector was a small share of the economy.

By the mid-1980s the FRG's standard of living ranked among the highest in the world. By comparison, the average East German's living standard was barely half that of a Westerner. Basic staples were inexpensively priced in the East, but most consumer goods were more expensive, and so-called luxury items (color televisions, washing machines, and automobiles) were beyond the reach of the average family. In 1985 about a third of the dwellings in East Germany lacked their own bathroom. GDR residents lived a comfortable life by East European standards, although far short of Western standards.

German unification meant the merger of these two different economies: the affluent Westerners and their poor cousins from the East; the sophisticated and technologically advanced industries of the FRG and the aging rust-belt factories of the GDR. At least in the short run, unification worsened the economic problems of the East. By some accounts, Eastern industrial production fell by two-thirds between 1989 and 1992—worse than the decline during the Great Depression. The government sold Eastern firms, and often the new owners began by reducing the labor force. Even by mid-2008, a sixth of the Eastern labor force was still unemployed.

During the unification process, politicians claimed that the East would enjoy a new economic miracle in a few years. This claim was overly optimistic. The government assumed a major long-term role in rebuilding the East's economic infrastructure and encouraging investment in the East. Only massive social payments by the FRG initially maintained the living standards in the East. And many young Easterners moved to the West to find a job. While economic conditions have improved in the East, many Easterners remain skeptical about their economic future. The persisting economic gap between East and West creates a basis for social and political division in the new Germany. Even after significant economic growth in recent years, in 2008 Germans felt they have benefited little from this growth and worried that inflation is eroding their living standard.[6]

Religion

The postwar FRG experienced a moderation of religious differences, partly because there were equal numbers of Catholics and Protestants and partly because elites made a conscious effort to avoid the religious conflicts of the past. Secularization also gradually reduced the public's religious involvement. In the East the Communist government sharply limited the political and social roles of the churches.

German unification has shifted the religious balance in the new Federal Republic. Catholics make up two-fifths of Westerners, but less than a tenth of Easterners. Thus, Protestants now slightly outnumber Catholics in unified Germany. There is also a small Muslim community that accounts for about 4 percent of the population. Even more dramatic, most Easterners claim to be nonreligious, which may decrease support for policies that benefit religious interests. A more Protestant and secular electorate should change the policy preferences of the German public on religiously based issues, such as abortion, and may potentially reshape electoral alliances.

Gender

Gender roles are another source of social differentiation. In the past the three K's—*Kinder* (children), *Kirche* (church), and *Küche* (kitchen)—defined the woman's role, while politics and work were male matters. Attempts to lessen role differences have met with mixed success. The FRG's Basic Law guarantees the equality of the sexes, but the specific legislation to support this guarantee has been lacking. Cultural norms changed only slowly; cross-national surveys show that males in the West are more chauvinist than the average European and that women in the West feel less liberated than other European women.[7]

The GDR constitution also guaranteed the equality of the sexes, and the government aggressively protected this guarantee. However, East German women were one of the first groups to suffer from the unification process. Eastern women lost rights and benefits that they had held under East German law. For instance, in 1993 the Constitutional Court resolved conflicting versions of the FRG and GDR abortion laws and essentially ruled for the FRG's more restrictive standards. The GDR provided childcare benefits for working mothers that the FRG did not. The greater expectations of Eastern women moved gender issues higher on the FRG's political agenda after unification. The government passed new legislation on job discrimination and women's rights in 1994. Most Eastern women feel they are better off today than under the old regime because they have gained new rights and new freedoms that were lacking under the GDR. Merkel's selection as chancellor in 2005 is stimulating further changes in gender norms and policies in Germany.

Minorities

A new social cleavage involves Germany's growing minority of foreigners.[8] When the FRG faced a severe labor shortage in the 1960s, it recruited millions of workers from Turkey, Yugoslavia, Italy, Spain, Greece, and other less developed countries. German politicians and the public considered this a temporary situation, and the foreigners were called **guest workers (Gastarbeiter)**. Most of these guest workers worked long enough to acquire skills and some personal savings, and then they returned home.

A strange thing happened, however. Germany asked only for workers, but they got human beings. Cultural centers for foreign workers emerged in many cities. Some foreign workers chose to remain in the FRG, and they eventually brought their families to join them. Foreigners brought new ways of life, as well as new hands for factory assembly lines.

From the beginning the foreign worker population has faced several problems. They are concentrated on the low rung of the economic ladder. Foreigners—especially those from Turkey and other non-European nations—are culturally, socially, and linguistically isolated from mainstream society. The problems of social and cultural isolation are especially difficult for the children of foreigners. Foreigners also were a target for violence in reaction to the strains of unification, and there is opposition to further immigration.

The nation has struggled with the problem of becoming a multicultural society, but the solutions are still uncertain. The Federal Republic revised the Basic Law's asylum clause in 1993 (making it closer to U.S. immigration policy), took more decisive action in combating violence, and mobilized the tolerant majority in German society. The government changed the citizenship laws in 2000 to better integrate foreign-born residents into German society. However, the gap between native Germans and Muslim immigrants seems to be widening. Attempts to liberalize naturalization of citizenship are linked to programs to educate the new citizens about German language, culture, and political norms. Addressing the issues associated with permanent racial/ethnic minorities (roughly 6 percent of the population) will be a continuing feature of German politics.

Regionalism

Regionalism is another potential social and political division. Germany is divided into sixteen states (*Länder*), ten states in the West and six new states created in the East, including the city-state of Berlin. Many of the *Länder* have their own distinct historical traditions and social structure. The language and idioms of speech differentiate residents from the Eastern and Western halves of the nation. No one would mistake a northern German for a Bavarian from the south—their manners and dialects are too distinct.

Unification greatly increased the cultural, economic, and political variations among the states because of differences between West and East. It is common to hear of "a wall in the mind" that separates *Wessies* (Westerners) and *Ossies* (Easterners). Easterners still draw on their separate traditions and experiences when making political decisions, just as Westerners do. Regional considerations thus are an important factor in society and politics.

The decentralized nature of society and the economy reinforces these regional differences. Economic and cultural centers are dispersed throughout the country, rather than being concentrated in a single national center. There are more than a dozen regional economic centers, such as Frankfurt, Cologne, Dresden, Düsseldorf, Munich, Leipzig, and Hamburg. The mass media are organized around regional markets, and there are even several competing "national" theaters.

These various social characteristics—economic, religious, gender, ethnicity, and regionalism—are politically relevant for many reasons. They define differing social interests, such as the economic needs of the working class versus those of the middle class, that are often expressed in policy debates. Social groups also are a source of political and social identity that links individuals to interest groups and political parties. Voting patterns, for instance, typically show clear group differences in party support. Thus, identifying the important group differences in German society provides a foundation for understanding parts of the political process.

THE INSTITUTIONS AND STRUCTURE OF GOVERNMENT

When the Parliamentary Council met in Bonn in 1948–1949, its members faced a daunting task. They were supposed to design a new political structure for a new democratic Germany that would avoid the problems that led to the collapse of the Weimar Republic.[9] If they failed, the consequences might be as dire as the last collapse of German democracy.

The Basic Law they crafted is an exceptional example of political engineering—the construction of a political system to achieve specific goals:

- Develop a stable and democratic political system,
- Maintain some historical continuity in political institutions (which, for Germany, meant a parliamentary system of government),
- Re-create a federal structure of government,
- Avoid the institutional weaknesses that contributed to the collapse of Weimar democracy, and
- Establish institutional limits on extremist and antisystem forces.

The framers wanted to establish clearer lines of political authority and to create a system with extensive checks and balances in order to prevent the usurpation of power that occurred during the Third Reich. The new system created a parliamentary democracy that involves the public, encourages elite political responsibility, disperses political power, and limits the influence of extremists.

The Basic Law was supposedly temporary until both halves of Germany were united. In actuality, the GDR's rapid collapse in 1990 led to its incorporation into the existing constitutional and economic systems of the Federal Republic. In September 1990 the FRG and the GDR signed a treaty to unify their two states, and the government amended the Basic Law to include the states in the East. Thus, the political system of the unified Germany functions according to the Basic Law. This section describes the key institutions and procedures of this democratic system.

A Federal System

One way to distribute political power and to build checks and balances into a political system is through a federal system of government. The Basic Law created one of the few federal political systems in Europe (see Figure 7.2). Germany is organized into sixteen states (*Länder*). Political power is divided between the federal government (*Bund*) and the state governments. The federal government has primary policy responsibility in most policy areas. The states, however, have jurisdiction in education, culture, law enforcement, and regional planning. In several other policy areas, the federal government and the states share responsibility, although federal law takes priority. Furthermore, the states can legislate in areas that the Basic Law does not explicitly assign to the federal government.

The state governments have a unicameral legislature, normally called a *Landtag*, which is directly elected by popular vote. The party or coalition that controls the legislature selects a minister president to head the state government. Next to the federal chancellor, the minister presidents are among the most powerful political officials in the Federal Republic.

The federal government is the major force in the legislation of policy, and the states are primarily responsible for policy administration. The states enforce most of the domestic legislation enacted by the federal government, as well as their own regulations. The state governments also oversee the operation of the local governments.

One house of the bicameral federal legislature, the Bundesrat, is comprised solely of representatives

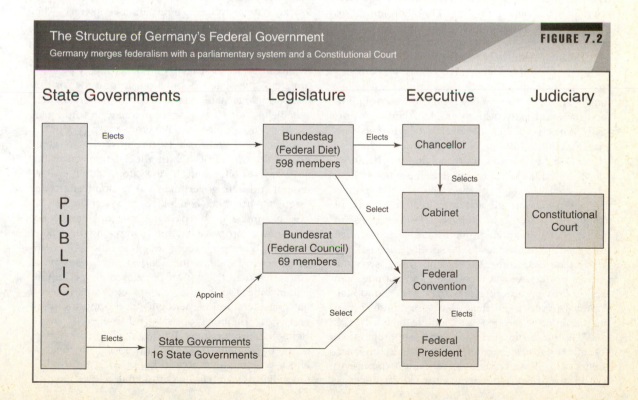

The Structure of Germany's Federal Government

Germany merges federalism with a parliamentary system and a Constitutional Court

FIGURE 7.2

State Governments | Legislature | Executive | Judiciary

PUBLIC

Elects → Bundestag (Federal Diet) 598 members → Elects → Chancellor → Selects → Cabinet

Bundestag Select →

Bundesrat (Federal Council) 69 members

State Governments — Appoint → Bundesrat

Public Elects → State Governments 16 State Governments

Select → Federal Convention → Elects → Federal President

Constitutional Court

appointed by the state governments. State government officials also participate in selecting the federal president and the justices of the major federal courts. This federal system thus decentralizes political power by balancing the power of the state governments against the power of the federal government.

Parliamentary Government

The central institution of the federal government is the parliament, which is bicameral: The popularly elected Bundestag is the primary legislative body; the Bundesrat represents the state governments at the federal level.

The Bundestag The 598 deputies of the **Bundestag (Federal Diet)** are the only national government officials who are directly elected by the German public.[10] Elections to select parliamentary deputies normally occur every four years.

The Bundestag's major function is to enact legislation; all federal laws must receive its approval. The initiative for most legislation, however, lies in the executive branch. Like other modern parliaments, the Bundestag primarily evaluates and amends the government's legislative program. Another important function of the Bundestag is to elect the federal chancellor, who heads the executive branch.

Through a variety of mechanisms, the Bundestag is a forum for public debate. Its plenary sessions discuss the legislation before the chamber. Debating time is allocated to all party groupings according to their size; both party leaders and backbenchers normally participate. The Bundestag televises its sessions, including live broadcasts on the Internet, to expand the public audience for its policy debates.[11]

The Bundestag also scrutinizes the actions of the government. The most common method of oversight is the "question hour" adopted from the British House of Commons. An individual deputy can submit a written question to a government minister: Questions range from broad policy issues to the specific needs of one constituent. Government representatives answer the queries during the question hour, and deputies can raise follow-up questions at that time. Bundestag deputies posed more than 15,000 oral and written questions during the 1998–2002 term of the Bundestag.

The Bundestag boasts a strong set of legislative committees that strengthen its legislative and oversight roles. These committees provide expertise to balance the policy experience of the federal agencies;

the committees also conduct investigative hearings in their area of specialization. Their oversight function is further strengthened because opposition parties chair a proportionate share of these committees, a very unusual pattern for democratic legislatures.

The opposition parties normally make greatest use of these oversight opportunities; about two-thirds of the questions posed during the 1994–1998 term came from the opposition parties. Rank-and-file members of the governing parties also use these devices to make their own views known.

Overall, the Bundestag's oversight powers are considerable, especially for a legislature in a parliamentary system. Legislative committees can collect the information needed to understand and question government policymakers. Bundestag members can use the question hour and other methods to bring attention to political issues and challenge the government. And through its votes, the Bundestag often prompts the government to revise its legislative proposals to gain passage.

The Bundesrat The second chamber of the parliament, the **Bundesrat (Federal Council)**, reflects Germany's federal system. The state governments appoint its sixty-nine members to represent their interests. The states normally appoint members of the state cabinet to serve jointly in the Bundesrat; the chamber thus acts as a permanent conference of state officials. Each state receives Bundesrat seats in numbers roughly proportionate to the state's population, from three for the least populous states to six seats for the most. Each state delegation casts its votes in a bloc, according to the instructions of the state government.

The Bundesrat's role is to represent state interests. It does this in evaluating legislation, debating government policy, and sharing information between federal and state governments. The Bundesrat is an essential part of the German federal system.

In summary, the parliament mainly reacts to government proposals, rather than taking the policy initiative. However, in comparison to other European parliamentary systems, the Bundestag exercises more autonomy than the typical parliament. Especially if one includes the Bundesrat, the German parliament has considerable independence and opportunity to revise government proposals and to exercise oversight on the government. By strengthening the power of the parliament, the Basic Law sought to create a check on executive power. Experience shows that the political system has met this goal.

The Federal Chancellor and Cabinet

A weakness of the Weimar system was the division of executive authority between the president and the chancellor. The Federal Republic still has a dual executive, but the Basic Law substantially strengthened the formal powers of the **federal chancellor (Bundeskanzler)** as the chief executive office. Moreover, the incumbents of this office have dominated the political process and symbolized the federal government by their personalization of power. The chancellor plays such a central role in the political system that some observers describe the German system as a "chancellor democracy."

The Bundestag elects the chancellor, who is responsible for the conduct of the federal government. The chancellor wields substantial power. She represents a majority of the Bundestag and normally can count on their support for the government's legislative proposals. The chancellors usually have led their own party, directing party strategy and leading the party at elections. Each chancellor also brings a distinct personality to the office. Schröder was a doer who governed with a strong personality; Merkel prefers a more consultative and cooperative decisionmaking style, while still shaping the course of her government.

Another source of the chancellor's authority is her control over the Cabinet. The federal government now consists of fourteen departments, each headed by a minister. The Cabinet ministers are formally appointed, or dismissed, by the federal president on the recommendation of the chancellor (Bundestag approval is not necessary). The Basic Law also grants the chancellor the power to decide the number of Cabinet ministers and their duties.

The federal government functions in terms of three principles described in the Basic Law. First, the *chancellor principle* says that the chancellor defines government policy. The formal policy directives issued by the chancellor are legally binding on the Cabinet and the ministries. Thus, in contrast to the British system of shared Cabinet responsibility, the German Cabinet is formally subordinate to the chancellor in policymaking.

The second principle, *ministerial autonomy,* gives each minister the authority to direct the ministry's internal workings without Cabinet intervention as long as the policies conform to the government's guidelines. Ministers are responsible for supervising the activities of their departments, guiding their policy planning, and overseeing the administration of policy within their jurisdiction.

The *cabinet principle* holds that when conflicts arise between departments over jurisdictional or budgetary matters, the Basic Law calls for the Cabinet to resolve them.

The actual working of the federal government is more fluid than the formal procedures listed in the Basic Law. The number and choice of ministries for each party are major issues in building a multiparty government coalition after each election. Cabinet members also display great independence on policy despite the formal restrictions of the Basic Law. Ministers are appointed because of their expertise in a policy area. In practice, ministers often identify more with their role as department head than with their role as agent of the chancellor; their political success is judged by their representation of department interests.

The Cabinet thus serves as a clearinghouse for the business of the federal government. Specific ministers present policy proposals originating in their departments in the hope of gaining government endorsement. The chancellor defines a government program that reflects a consensus of the Cabinet and relies on negotiations and compromise within the Cabinet to maintain this consensus.

The Federal President

Because of the problems associated with the Weimar Republic's divided executive, the Basic Law changed the office of **federal president (Bundespräsident)** into a mostly ceremonial post. The president's official duties involve greeting visiting heads of state, attending official government functions, visiting foreign nations, and carrying out similar tasks.[12] To insulate the office from electoral politics, the president is selected by the Federal Convention, composed of all Bundestag deputies and an equal number of representatives chosen by the state legislatures. The president is supposed to remain above partisan politics once elected.

The reduction in the president's formal political role does not mean that an incumbent is uninvolved in the policy process. The Basic Law assigns several legal functions to the president, who appoints government and military officials, signs treaties and laws, and has the power of pardon. In these instances, however, the chancellor must countersign the actions. The president also nominates a chancellor to the Bundestag and can dissolve parliament if a government bill loses a no-confidence vote. In both instances the Basic Law limits the president's ability to act independently.

Potentially more significant is the constitutional ambiguity over whether the president must honor certain government requests. The legal precedent is unclear on whether the president has the constitutional right to veto legislation, to refuse the chancellor's recommendation for Cabinet appointments, or even to reject a request to dissolve the Bundestag. Analysts see these ambiguities as another safety valve built into the Basic Law's elaborate system of checks and balances.

The office of the federal president also has political importance that goes beyond the articles of the Basic Law. An active, dynamic president can influence the political climate through his speeches and public activities. The president is the one political figure who can rightly claim to be above politics and who can work to extend the vision of the nation beyond its everyday concerns. Horst Köhler was elected president in 2004 after serving as director of the International Monetary Fund.

The Judicial System

The ordinary courts, which hear criminal cases and most legal disputes, are integrated into a unitary system. The states administer the courts at the local and state levels. The highest ordinary court, the Federal Court of Justice, is at the national level. All courts apply the same national legal codes.

A second set of administrative courts hear cases in specialized areas. One court deals with administrative complaints against government agencies, one handles tax matters, another resolves claims involving social programs, and one deals with labor-management disputes. Like the rest of the judicial system, these specialized courts exist at both the state and the federal levels.

The Basic Law created a third element of the judiciary: the independent **Constitutional Court**. This court reviews the constitutionality of legislation, mediates disputes between levels of government, and protects the constitutional and democratic order.[13] This is an innovation for the German legal system because it places one law, the Basic Law, above all others. This also implies limits on the decisionmaking power of the parliament and the judicial interpretations of lower court judges. Because of the importance of the Constitutional Court, its sixteen members are selected in equal numbers by the Bundestag and Bundesrat and can be removed only for abuse of the office.

The creation of a body to conduct constitutional review is another successful institutional innovation of the Federal Republic. The Constitutional Court provides another check on the potential excesses of government and gives citizens additional protection for their human rights. It has become a third pillar of contemporary German democracy.

The Separation of Powers

One of the Basic Law's secret strengths is avoiding the concentration of power in the hands of any one actor or institution. The framers wanted to disperse political power so that extremists or antidemocrats could not overturn the system; democracy would require a consensus-building process. Each institution of government has strong powers within its own domain, but a limited ability to force its will on other institutions.

For instance, the chancellor lacks the authority to dissolve the legislature and call for new elections, something that normally exists in parliamentary systems. Equally important, the Basic Law limits the legislature's control over the chancellor. In a parliamentary system, the legislature typically can remove a chief executive from office by a simple majority vote. During the Weimar Republic, however, extremist parties used this device to destabilize the democratic system by opposing incumbent chancellors. To address situations where parliament might desire to remove the chancellor, the Basic Law created a **constructive no-confidence vote**.[14] In order for the Bundestag to remove a chancellor, it simultaneously must agree on a successor. This ensures continuity in government and an initial majority in support of a new chancellor. It also makes it more difficult to remove an incumbent; opponents cannot simply disagree with the government—a majority must agree on an alternative. The constructive no-confidence vote has been attempted only twice—and has succeeded only once. In 1982 a majority replaced Chancellor Schmidt with a new chancellor, Helmut Kohl.

The Constitutional Court is another check on government actions, and it has assumed an important role as the guarantor of citizen rights and the protector of the constitution. The distribution of power and policy responsibilities between the federal and state governments is another moderating force in the political process. Even the strong bicameral legislature ensures that multiple interests must agree before making public policy.

This structure complicates the governing process —compared with a unified system, such as that in Britain, the Netherlands, or Sweden. However, democracy is often a complicated process. This system of shared powers and of checks and balances has enabled German democracy to grow and flourish. This is a very successful example of how constitutional engineering helped democratize the nation.

REMAKING POLITICAL CULTURES

Consider for a minute what the average German must have thought about politics as World War II was ending. Germany's political history was hardly conducive to good democratic citizenship. Under the Kaiser the government expected people to be subjects, not active participants in the political process; this style nurtured feelings of political intolerance. The interlude of the Weimar Republic did little to change these values. The polarization, fragmentation, and outright violence of the Weimar Republic taught people to avoid politics, not to be active participants. Moreover, democracy eventually failed, and national socialism arose in its place. The Third Reich then raised another generation under an intolerant, authoritarian system.

Because of this historical legacy, the Federal Republic's development was closely linked to the question of whether its political culture was congruent with its democratic system. Initially, there were widespread fears that West Germany lacked a democratic political culture, thereby making it vulnerable to the same problems that undermined the Weimar Republic. Postwar opinion polls in the West presented a negative image of public opinion that was probably equally applicable to the East.[15] West Germans were politically detached, accepting of authority, and intolerant in their political views. A significant minority of them were unrepentant Nazis, sympathy for many elements of the Nazi ideology was widespread, and anti-Semitic feelings remained commonplace.

Perhaps even more amazing than the Economic Miracle was the transformation of West Germany's political culture in little more than a generation. Confronted by an uncertain public commitment to democracy, the government undertook a massive political reeducation program. The schools, the media, and political organizations were mobilized behind the effort. The citizenry itself also was changing—older generations raised under authoritarian regimes were gradually being replaced by younger generations socialized during the postwar democratic era. The successes of a growing economy and a relatively smoothly functioning political system also changed public perceptions. These efforts created a new political culture more consistent with the democratic institutions and process of the Federal Republic.

With unification Germany confronted another serious cultural question. The Communists had tried to create a rival culture in the GDR that would support their state and its socialist economic system. Indeed, the efforts at political education in the East were intense and extensive; they aimed at creating a broad "socialist personality" that included nonpolitical attitudes and behavior.[16] Young people were taught a collective identity with their peers, a love for the GDR and its socialist brethren, acceptance of the Socialist Unity Party, and a Marxist-Leninist understanding of history and society.

German unification meant the blending of these two different political cultures, and at first the consequences of this mixture were uncertain. Without scientific social science research in the GDR, it was unclear if Easterners had internalized the government's propaganda. At the same time, the revolutionary political events leading to German unification may have reshaped even long-held political beliefs. What does a Communist think after attending communism's funeral?

Unification thus created a new question: Could the FRG assimilate 16 million new citizens with potentially different beliefs about how politics and society should function? The following sections discuss the key elements of German political culture and how they have changed over time.

Orientations Toward the Political Community

A common history, culture, territory, and language created a sense of a single German community long before Germany was politically united. Germany was the land of Schiller, Goethe, Beethoven, and Wagner, even if the Germans disagreed on political boundaries. The imagery of a single *Volk* binds Germans together despite their social and political differences.

Previous regimes had failed, however, to develop a common political identity to match the German social identity. Succeeding political systems were short lived and did not develop a popular consensus on the nature and goals of German politics. Postwar West Germany faced a similar challenge: building a political community in a divided and defeated nation.

In the early 1950s, large sectors of the West German public identified with the symbols and personalities of previous regimes.[17] Most people felt that the Second Empire or Hitler's prewar Reich represented the best times in German history. Substantial minorities favored a restoration of the monarchy or a one-party state. Almost half the population believed that if it had not been for World War II, Hitler would have been one of Germany's greatest statesmen.

Over the next two decades, these ties to earlier regimes gradually weakened, and the bonds to the new institutions and leaders of the Federal Republic steadily grew stronger (see Figure 7.3). The number of citizens who believed that Bundestag deputies represent the public interest doubled between 1951 and 1964; public respect shifted from the personalities of prior regimes to the chancellors of the Federal Republic. By the 1970s an overwhelming majority of the public felt that the present was the best time in German history. West Germans became more politically tolerant, and feelings of anti-Semitism declined sharply. The public displayed a growing esteem for the new political system.[18]

Even while Westerners developed a new acceptance of the institutions and symbols of the Federal Republic, something was missing, something that touched the spirit of their political feelings. The FRG was a provisional entity, and "Germany" meant a unified nation. Were citizens of West Germany to think of themselves as Germans, West Germans, or some mix of both? In addition, the trauma of the Third Reich burned a deep scar in the Western psyche, making citizens hesitant to express pride in their nation or a sense of German national identity. Because of this political stigma, the FRG avoided many of the emotional national symbols that are common in other nations. There were few political holidays or memorials, one seldom heard the national anthem, and even the anniversary of the founding of the FRG received little public attention. This legacy means that even today Germans are hesitant to openly express pride in the nation (see Box 7.2).

The quest for a national identity also occurred in the East. The GDR claimed to represent the "pure" elements of German history; it portrayed the FRG as the successor to the Third Reich. Most analysts believe that the GDR had created at least a sense of resigned loyalty to the regime because of its political and social accomplishments. Thus, a 1990 study found that Eastern youth most admired Karl Marx (followed by the first president of the GDR), while Western youth were most likely to name Konrad Adenauer, the first chancellor of the FRG.[19] Once socialism failed, however, the basis for a separate East German political identity also evaporated.

Unification began a process by which the German search for a national political identity could finally be resolved. The opening of the Berlin Wall created positive political emotions that were previously lacking. The celebration of unification, and the designation of October 3 as a national holiday, finally gives Germans a positive political experience to celebrate. Citizens in East and West remain somewhat hesitant to embrace an emotional attachment to the nation, and Easterners retain a lingering tie to their

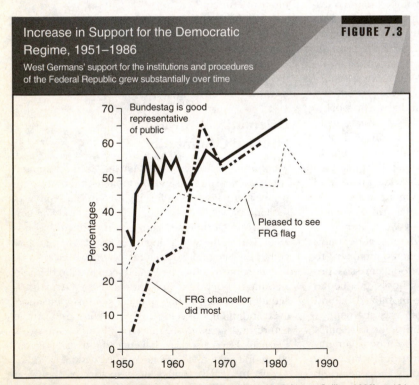

Increase in Support for the Democratic Regime, 1951–1986

FIGURE 7.3

West Germans' support for the institutions and procedures of the Federal Republic grew substantially over time

Source: Russell J. Dalton, *Politics in Germany,* 2nd ed. (New York: HarperCollins, 1993), p. 121.

BOX 7.2

Can One Be Proud and German?

Could anyone imagine a French president or a British prime minister or indeed just about any other world leader refusing to say he was proud of his nationality? Yet, this is a contentious statement in Germany because expressions of nationalism are still linked by some to the excessive nationalism of the Third Reich. Thus, when in 2001 the general secretary of the Christian Democratic Union declared: "I am proud to be German," he set off an intense national debate. A Green member of the Social Democratic Party–Green Cabinet replied that this statement demonstrated the mentality of a right-wing skinhead. President Rau tried to sidestep the issue by declaring that one could be "glad" or "grateful" for being German, but not "proud." Then Chancellor Schröder entered the fray: "I am proud of what people have achieved and our democratic culture. . . . In that sense, I am a German patriot who is proud of his country." It is difficult to imagine such exchanges occurring in Washington, D.C., or Paris.

Source: *The Economist*, March 24, 2001, p. 62.

---

separate past. Yet, the basic situation has changed. For the first time in over a century, nearly all Germans agree where their borders begin and end. Germany is now a single nation—democratic, free, and looking toward the future.

Orientations Toward the Democratic Process

A second important element of the political culture involves citizen attitudes toward the political process and system of government. In the early years of West Germany, the rules of democratic politics—majority rule, minority rights, individual liberties, and pluralistic debate—did not fit citizens' experiences. To break this pattern, political leaders constructed a system that formalized democratic procedures. Citizen participation was encouraged and expected, policymaking became open, and the public gradually learned democratic norms by continued exposure to the new political system. Political leadership provided a generally positive example of competition in a democratic setting. Consequently, a popular consensus slowly developed in support of the democratic political system. By the mid-1960s there was nearly unanimous agreement that democracy was the best form of government. More important, the Western public displayed a growing commitment to democratic procedures—a multiparty system, conflict management, minority rights, and representative government.[20]

Political events occasionally have tested popular commitment to democratic values in West Germany. For instance, during the 1970s a small group of extremists attempted to topple the system through a terrorist campaign.[21] In the early 1980s, the Kohl government faced a series of violent actions by anarchic and radical ecology groups. In recent years new threats from international terrorists and jihadist extremists have threatened the nation. In these instances, however, the basic conclusion was that the political system could face the onslaughts of political extremists and survive with its basic procedures intact—and without the public losing faith in the democratic process.

The propaganda of the East German government also stressed a democratic creed. In reality, however, the regime tried to create a political culture that was compatible with a communist state and a socialist economy. The culture drew on traditional Prussian values of obedience, duty, and loyalty: The government again told people that obedience was the responsibility of a good citizen and that support of the state (and the party) was an end in itself. Periodically, political events—the 1953 East Berlin uprising, the construction of the Berlin Wall, and the expulsions of political dissidents—reminded East Germans of the gap between the democratic rhetoric of the regime and reality.

One reason the popular revolt may have grown so rapidly in 1989 was that citizens no longer supported the principles of the regime, even if they might be hesitant to publicly express such sentiments under a Stasi police state. For instance, studies of young Easterners found that identification with Marxism-Leninism and belief in the inevitable victory of socialism dropped off dramatically during the mid-1980s.[22] At the least, the revolutionary changes that swept through East Germany as the Berlin Wall fell nurtured a belief in democracy as the road to political reform. A 1990 public opinion survey found nearly universal support for basic tenets of democracy among both West and East Germans.[23]

The true test of democracy, of course, occurs in the real world. Some studies suggest that Easterners' initial understanding of democracy was limited, or at least different from that of Westerners.[24] Yet, Easterners in 1989 were markedly more supportive of democracy than were Germans in 1945. Rather than remaking this aspect of the East German culture, the greater need was to transform Eastern support for democracy into a deeper and richer understanding of the workings of the process and its pragmatic strengths and weaknesses. And now, almost two decades after unification, with an Easterner as the chancellor, the principles of democracy are becoming engrained in the political culture—both West and East.

Social Values and the New Politics

Another area of cultural change in West Germany involves a shift in public values produced by the social and economic accomplishments of the nation. Once West Germany addressed traditional social and economic needs, the public broadened its concerns to include a new set of societal goals. New issues—such as the environment, women's rights, and increasing citizen participation—attracted public attention.

Ronald Inglehart explained these political developments in terms of the changing value orientations of Westerners.[25] He maintains that a person's value priorities reflect the family and societal conditions that prevail early in life. Older generations, socialized before the post–World War II transformation, have experienced uncertain economic and political conditions, which lead them to still emphasize economic security, law and order, religious values, and a strong national defense—despite the economic and political advances of the past half century. In contrast, because younger generations grew up in a democratic and affluent nation, they were shifting their attention toward **New Politics** values. These new values emphasize self-expression, personal freedom, social equality, self-fulfillment, and quality of life.

Although only a minority of Westerners hold these new values, they represent a "second culture" embedded within the dominant culture of FRG society. These values are less developed among Easterners. Still, the evidence of political change is apparent. Public interest in New Politics issues has gradually spread beyond its youthful supporters and developed a broader base. Even in the East, many of the early demonstrations for democracy had supporters calling for *"Freiheit und Umwelt"* (freedom and the environment).

Two Peoples in One Nation?

Citizens in the East and West share a common German heritage, but forty years of separation created cultural differences that now are blended into a single national culture.

Because of these different experiences, the broad similarities in many of the political beliefs of Westerners and Easterners are surprising. Easterners and Westerners both espouse support for the democratic system and its norms and institutions. There is also broad acceptance of the principles of Germany's social market economy. Thus, the Federal Republic's second transition to democracy features an agreement on basic political and economic values that is markedly different from the situation after World War II.

Yet, other aspects of cultural norms do differ between regions. For instance, although residents in both the West and the East endorse the tenets of democracy, it is harder to reach agreement on how these ideals translate into practical politics. The open, sometimes confrontational style of Western politics is a major adjustment for citizens raised under the closed system of the GDR. In addition, Easterners endorse a broader role for government in providing social services and guiding social development than is found among Westerners.[26]

There are also signs of a persisting gap in regional identities between East and West. The passage of time and harsh postunification adjustments created a nostalgia for some aspects of the GDR among its former residents. Easterners do not want a return to communism or socialism, but many miss the slower and more predictable style of their former lives. Even while expressing support for Western capitalism, many Easterners have difficulty adjusting to the idea of unemployment and to the competitive pressures of a market-based economy. There is a nostalgic yearning for symbols of these times, ranging from the Trabant automobile to consumer products bearing Eastern labels. The popularity of the 2003 movie *Goodbye Lenin!* is an indication of these sentiments—and a good film for students interested in this phase of German history. In fact, Easterners have developed a regional identity that is similar to the feelings of Southerners in the United States.

Moreover, even though Easterners favor democracy, only 41 percent in 2007 were satisfied with how it functions in the Federal Republic, compared with more than two-thirds among Westerners.[27] Easterners still feel that the political system overlooks their needs.

Unification may have also heightened New Politics conflicts within German society. The GDR had struggled to become a materialist success, while the West enjoyed its postmaterial abundance. Consequently, Easterners give greater weight to such goals as higher living standards, security, hard work, and better living conditions. Most Easterners want first to share in the affluence and consumer society of the West before they begin to fear the consequences of this affluence. The clash of values within West German society is now joined by East-West differences.

Germans share a common language, culture, and history—and a common set of ultimate political goals—although the strains of unification may magnify and politicize the differences. The nation's progress in blending these two cultures successfully will strongly affect the course of the new Germany.

POLITICAL LEARNING AND POLITICAL COMMUNICATION

If a congruent political culture helps a political system to endure, as many political experts maintain, then one of the basic functions of the political process is to create and perpetuate these attitudes. This process is known as *political socialization*. Researchers normally view political socialization as a source of continuity in a political system, with one generation transmitting the prevailing political norms to the next. In Germany, however, the socialization challenges for the past half century have been to change the culture inherited from the Third Reich and then to change the culture inherited from the GDR.

Family Influences

During their early years, children have few sources of learning comparable to their parents—normally the major influence in forming basic values. Family discussions can be a rich source of political information and one of the many ways that children internalize their parents' attitudes. Basic values acquired during childhood often persist into adulthood.

In the early postwar years, family socialization did not function smoothly on either side of the German border. Many parents did not discuss politics with their children for fear that the child would ask, "What did you do under Hitler, Daddy?" The potential for parental socialization grew steadily as the political system of the FRG began to take root, however.[28] The frequency of political discussion increased in the West, and family conversations about politics became commonplace. Moreover, young new parents raised under the system of the FRG could pass on democratic norms held for a lifetime.

The family also played an important role in the socialization process of the GDR. Family ties were especially close in the East, and most young people claimed to share their parents' political opinions. The family was one of the few settings where people could openly discuss their beliefs, a private sphere where individuals could be free of the watchful eyes of others. Here one could express praise for—or doubt about—the state.

Despite the growing socialization role of the family, there is often a generation gap in political values in both West and East. Youth in the West are more liberal than their parents, more oriented toward noneconomic goals, more positive about their role in the political process, and more likely to challenge prevailing social norms.[29] Eastern youth are also a product of their times, now being raised under the new democratic and capitalist systems of the Federal Republic. Under the GDR, conformity was mandated; imagine what Eastern parents think when their teenagers adopt hiphop or punk lifestyles. Clearly, young people's values and goals are changing, often putting them in conflict with their elders.

Education

The educational system was a major factor in the creation of a democratic political culture in the FRG. As public support for the FRG's political system increased, this decreased the need for formal instruction in the principles of democracy and the new institutions of the political system. The content of civics instruction changed to emphasize an understanding of the dynamics of the democratic process—interest representation, conflict resolution, minority rights, and the methods of citizen influence. The present system tries to prepare students for their adult roles as political participants.

In the East the school system also played an essential role in political education, although the content was very different. The schools tried to create a socialist personality that encompassed a devotion to communist principles, a love of the GDR, and participation in state-sponsored activities. Yet, again, the rhetoric of education conflicted with reality. The textbooks told students that the GDR endorsed personal freedom, but then they stared from their school buses at the barbed wire strung along the border. Many young people accepted the rhetoric of the regime, but the education efforts remained incomplete.

Another cornerstone of the GDR's socialization efforts was a system of government-supervised youth groups. Nearly all primary school students enrolled in the Pioneers, a youth organization that combined normal social activities—similar to those in the Boy Scouts or Girl Scouts in the United States—with a heavy dose of political education. At age 14 about three-fourths of the young joined the Free German Youth (FDJ) group, which was a training and recruiting ground for the future leadership of East Germany. Like other communist states, the GDR staged mass sporting events that included an opportunity for political indoctrination and used the Olympic medal count as a measure of the nation's international status. In short, from a school's selection of texts for first-grade readers to the speeches at a sports awards banquet, the values of the GDR regime touched everyday life. This changed, of course, with German unification, so that the schools teach about common values across the nation.

Social Stratification Another important effect of education involves its consequences for the social stratification of society. The secondary school system in the Federal Republic has three distinct tracks. One track provides a general education that normally leads to vocational training and working-class occupations. A second track mixes vocational and academic training. Most graduates from this program are employed in lower middle-class occupations. A third track focuses on academic training at a Gymnasium (an academic high school) in preparation for university education.

In selecting students for different careers, these educational tracks reinforce social status differences within society. The schools direct students into one track after only four to six years of primary schooling, based on their school record, parental preferences, and teacher evaluations. At this early age, family influences are still a major factor in the child's development—your future career choices are largely determined

at age 10. This means that most children in the academic track come from middle-class families, and most students in the vocational track are from working-class families. Sharp distinctions separate the three tracks. Students attend different schools, so that social contact across tracks is minimized. The curriculums of the three tracks are so different that once a student is assigned, he or she would find it difficult to transfer. The Gymnasia are more generously financed and recruit the best-qualified teachers. Every student who graduates from a Gymnasium is guaranteed admission to a university, where tuition is free.

Reformers have made numerous attempts to lessen the class bias of the educational system. There is a clear tendency for middle-class children to benefit under the tracked educational system. Some states have a single, comprehensive secondary school that all students may attend, but only about 10 percent of Western secondary school students are enrolled in these schools. Reformers have been more successful in expanding access to the universities. In the early 1950s, only 6 percent of college-aged youths pursued higher education; today this figure is over 30 percent. The Federal Republic's educational system retains an elitist accent, though it is now less obvious.

The socialist ideology of the GDR led to a different educational structure. Students from different social backgrounds and with different academic abilities attended the same school—much like the structure of public education in the United States. The schools emphasized practical career training, with a heavy dose of technical and applied courses in the later years. Those with special academic abilities could apply to the extended secondary school during their twelfth year, which led to a university education. Ironically, the Eastern system provided more opportunities for mobility than did the educational system in the FRG.

At first, the Eastern states attempted to keep their system of comprehensive schools after German union. However, unification has generally led to the expansion of the West's highly tracked educational system to the East, rather than to reforms to liberalize the German system of secondary education to lessen social biases and grant greater opportunity to all.

Mass Media

The mass media have a long history in Germany: The world's first newspaper and first television service both appeared on German soil. Under previous regimes, however, political authorities frequently censored or manipulated the media. National socialism showed what a potent socialization force the media could be, especially when placed in the wrong hands.

The mass media of the Federal Republic were developed with the goal of avoiding the experience of Nazi propaganda and contributing to a new democratic political culture.[30] The Federal Republic began with a new journalistic tradition, committed to democratic norms, objectivity, and political neutrality.

The German media are also highly regionalized. The Federal Republic lacks an established national press like that of Britain or France. Instead, each region or large city has one or more newspapers that circulate primarily within that locale. Of the several hundred daily newspapers, only a few—such as the *Frankfurter Allgemeine Zeitung, Welt, Süddeutsche Zeitung,* and *Frankfurter Rundschau*—have a national following.

The electronic media in the Federal Republic are also regionally decentralized. Public corporations organized at the state or regional level manage the public television and radio networks. These public broadcasting networks still are the major German television channels. To ensure independence from commercial pressures, the public media are financed mostly by taxes assessed on owners of radios and television sets. But new technologies of cable and satellite television have undercut the government's media monopoly. These new media have eroded the government's control of the information flow and increased pressures to cater to consumer preferences. Many analysts see these new media offerings as expanding the citizens' choice and the diversity of information, but others worry that the quality of German broadcasting has suffered as a result. Once one could not even watch soccer matches on television because government planners considered it inappropriate. Now cable subscribers can watch a previously unimaginable range of social, cultural, political, and sports programming.

The mass media are a primary source of information for the public and a communications link between elites and the public. The higher-quality newspapers devote substantial attention to domestic and international reporting, although the largest circulation newspaper, *Bild Zeitung,* sells papers through sensationalist stories. The public television networks are also strongly committed to political programming; about one-third of their programs deal with social or political issues.

Public opinion surveys show that Germans have a voracious appetite for the political information provided by the mass media. A 2005 survey found that 52 percent of the public claimed to read news in the newspaper on a daily basis, 56 percent listened to news on the radio daily, and 70 percent said they watched television news programs daily.[31] These high levels of media usage indicate that Germans are attentive media users and well informed on the flow of political events.

CITIZEN PARTICIPATION

In the 1950s the Western public did not participate in the new political process; they acted like political spectators who were following a soccer match from the grandstand. Previous German history certainly had not been conducive to developing widespread public involvement in politics. The final step in remaking the political culture was to involve citizens in the process—to have them come onto the field and participate.

From the start both German states encouraged their citizens to be politically active, but with different expectations about what was appropriate. The democratic procedures of West Germany induced many people to at least vote in elections. Turnout reached up to 90 percent for some national elections. Westerners became well informed about the political system and developed an interest in political matters. After continued democratic experience, people began to internalize their role as participants. Most Westerners think their participation can influence the political process—people believe that democracy works.

The public's changing political norms led to a dramatic increase in involvement. In the 1950s almost two-thirds of the West German public never discussed politics; today about three-quarters claim they talk about politics regularly. Expanding citizen interest created a participatory revolution in the FRG as involvement in campaigns and political organizations increased. Perhaps the most dramatic example of rising participation levels was the growth of **citizen action groups (Bürgerinitiativen)**. Citizens interested in a specific issue form a group to articulate their political demands and influence decisionmakers. Parents organize for school reform, homeowners become involved in urban redevelopment projects, taxpayers complain about the delivery of government services, or residents protest the environmental conditions in their locale. These groups expanded citizen influence significantly beyond the infrequent and indirect methods of campaigns and elections.

The GDR system also encouraged political involvement, but people could be active only in ways that reinforced their allegiance to the state. For example, elections offered the Communist leadership an opportunity to educate the public politically. More than 90 percent of the electorate cast ballots, and the government parties always won nearly all the votes. People were expected to participate in government-approved unions, social groups (such as the Free German Youth or the German Women's Union), and quasi-public bodies, such as parent-teacher organizations. However, participation was a method not for citizens to influence the government, but for the government to influence its citizens.

Although they draw on much different experiences, Germans from both the East and the West have been socialized into a pattern of high political involvement (see Figure 7.4).[32] Voting levels in national

elections are among the highest of any European democracy. Almost 80 percent of Westerners and almost 75 percent of Easterners turned out at the polls in the 2005 Bundestag elections. This turnout level is very high by U.S. standards, but it has declined from nearly 90 percent in FRG elections of the 1980s. High turnout partially reflects the belief that voting is part of a citizen's duty. In addition, the electoral system encourages turnout: Elections are held on Sunday when everyone is free to vote, voter registration lists are constantly updated by the government, and the ballot is always simple—there are at most two votes to cast.

Beyond the act of voting, many Germans participate in other ways. A survey conducted after the 2004 European election illustrates the participation patterns of Easterners and Westerners (see again Figure 7.4). Almost a third of the public in West and East had signed a petition in the previous year, and a fifth had boycotted some product on political grounds. These are high levels by cross-national standards.

The pattern of working with political parties and citizen action groups is also interesting. A significant proportion of Westerners (3 percent) and Easterners

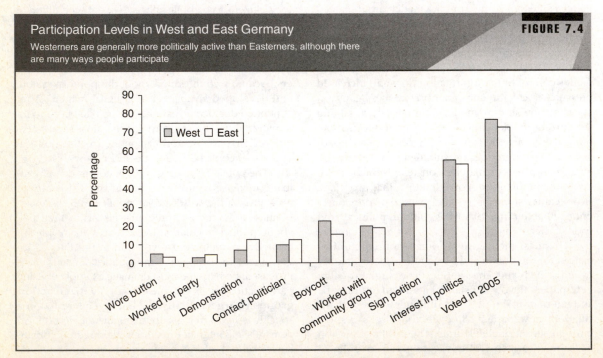

Participation Levels in West and East Germany   **FIGURE 7.4**

Westerners are generally more politically active than Easterners, although there are many ways people participate

Source: 2004 European Social Survey (ess.nsd.uib.no); voter turnout is from government statistics for the 2005 election.

(4 percent) said they had worked for a political party during the 2004 election, and about the same percentages said they had displayed a campaign sticker or button. Yet, participating in a legal demonstration or working with others on a community problem was much more common than campaign activity in both regions. A substantial proportion of the public had also written or contacted a politician during the past year. This indicates the expansion of political involvement to new modes of action.

Thus, Germans on both sides of the former border are now actively involved in politics. Moreover, participation extends beyond the traditional role of voting in elections to include a wide range of political activities. The spectators have become participants.

POLITICS AT THE ELITE LEVEL[33]

The Federal Republic is a representative democracy. This means that above the populace is a group of a few thousand political elite who manage the actual workings of the political system. Elite members, such as party leaders and parliamentary deputies, are directly responsible to the public through elections. Civil servants and judges are appointed, and they are at least indirectly responsible to the citizenry. Leaders of interest groups and political associations participate as representatives of their specific clientele groups. Although the group of politically influential elites is readily identifiable, it is not a homogeneous power elite. Rather, elites in the Federal Republic represent the diverse interests in German society. Often there is as much heterogeneity in policy preferences among the political elites as there is among the public.

Individuals may take numerous pathways to elite positions. Party elites may have exceptional political abilities; administrative elites are initially recruited because of their formal training and bureaucratic skills; interest group leaders are selected for their ability to represent their group.

One feature of elite recruitment that differs from American politics is the long apprenticeship period before one enters the top elite stratum. Candidates for national or even state political office normally have a long background of party work and office-holding at the local level. Similarly, senior civil servants spend nearly all their adult lives working for the government. Chancellor Merkel's biography is an unusual example because she did not follow the typical model of a long career or party and political positions (see Box 7.3).

A long apprenticeship means that political elites have extensive experience before attaining a position of greatest power; elites also share a common basis of experience built up from interacting over many years. National politicians know each other from working together at the state or local level; the paths of civil servants frequently cross during their long careers. These experiences develop a sense

---

The Atypical Chancellor   **BOX 7.3**

Angela Merkel has the most unlikely biography for a German chancellor. She was born in West Germany in 1954, and when she was a year old, her father, a left-leaning Protestant minister, chose to move his family to East Germany. Like many young East Germans, she became a member of the Communist youth league, the Free German Youth group. She eventually earned a Ph.D. in chemistry from the East Berlin Academy of Sciences in 1989. Merkel pursued a career as a research scientist until the German Democratic Republic (GDR) began to collapse in 1989. She first joined the Democratic Awakening and then the Christian Democratic Union (CDU) and was elected to the Bundestag as a CDU deputy in 1990. She rose quickly through the ranks of CDU leaders, serving as minister for women and youth from 1991 to 1994 and as environment minister from 1994 to 1998. In 2000 Merkel became the national chair of the CDU. With her election in 2005, she became the first woman, and the first former citizen of the GDR, to head the German federal government. In 2008 *Forbes* magazine ranked Chancellor Merkel as number 1 on their list of the 100 most powerful women in the world.

of trust and responsibility in elite interactions. For instance, members of a chancellor's Cabinet are normally drawn from party elites with extensive experience in state or federal government. Until Merkel was elected, chancellors since the 1960s had previously served as the minister president of their state. Seldom can top business leaders or popular personalities use their outside success to attain a position of political power quickly. This also contributes to the cohesion of elite politics.

Because they represent different political constituencies, elites differ in many of their policy priorities. For instance, SPD elites and officials from labor unions are more likely to emphasize the need for greater social and economic equality, social security, and the integration of foreigners.[34] Church officials stress moral and religious principles, while CDU/CSU and business representatives typically have a distinct economic position. Green activists have their own distinct alternative agenda. This method of representation gives citizens a voice in the decisions made by elites, and the clearer the link, the more direct the voice.

INTEREST GROUPS

Interest groups are an integral part of the German political process, even more so than in the United States. Some specific interests may be favored more than others, but interest groups are generally welcomed as necessary participants in the political process.

German interest groups are connected to the government more closely than are such groups in the United States. Doctors, lawyers, and other self-employed professionals belong to professional associations that are established by law and receive government authorization of their activities, making them quasi-public bodies. These associations, which date back to the medieval guilds, enforce professional rules of conduct.

Interest groups also participate in a variety of governmental commissions and bodies, such as that managing public radio and television. Some groups receive financial or administrative support from the government to assist them in carrying out policy-related activities, such as the administration of a hospital or the monitoring of environmental conditions. Federal administrative law requires that ministry officials contact the relevant interest groups when formulating new policies that may affect them. These consultations ensure that the government can benefit from the groups' expertise.

In some instances the pattern of interest group activity approaches the act of governance. For example, when the government sought structural reform in the steel industry, it assembled interest group representatives from the affected sectors to discuss and negotiate a common plan. Group officials attempted to reach a consensus on the necessary changes and then implemented the agreements, sometimes with the official sanction of the government. Similar activities have occurred in other policy sectors.

This cooperation between government and interest groups is described as **neocorporatism**, a general pattern having the following characteristics:[35]

- Social interests are organized into virtually compulsory organizations.
- A single association represents each social sector.
- Associations are hierarchically structured.
- Associations are accepted as formal representatives by the government.
- Associations may participate directly in the policy process.

Policy decisions are reached in discussions and negotiations between the relevant association and the government—then the agreements are implemented by government action.

This neocorporatist pattern solidifies the role of interest groups in the policy process. Governments feel that they are responding to public demands when they consult with these groups, and the members of these interest groups depend on the organization to have their views heard. Thus, representatives of the major interest groups are important actors in the policy process. Neocorporatist relations also lessen political conflict; for instance, strike levels and political strife tend to be lower in neocorporatist systems.

Another advantage of neocorporatism is that it makes for efficient government; the involved interest groups can negotiate on policy without the pressures of public debate and partisan conflict. However, efficient government is not necessarily the best government, especially in a democracy. Decisions are reached in conference groups or advisory commissions, outside of the representative institutions of government decisionmaking. The "relevant" interest groups are involved, but this assumes that all relevant interests are organized and that only organized interests are relevant. Decisions affecting the entire public are often made through private negotiations, as democratically elected representative institutions—state governments and the Bundestag—are sidestepped and interest groups deal directly with government agencies. Consequently, interest groups play a less active role in electoral politics, as they concentrate their efforts on direct contact with government agencies.

Interest groups come in many shapes and sizes. This section describes the large associations that represent the major socioeconomic forces in society. These associations normally have a national organization, a so-called **peak association**, that speaks for its members.

Business

Two major organizations represent business and industrial interests. The **Federation of German Industry (BDI)** is the peak association for thirty-five separate industrial groupings. The BDI-affiliated associations represent nearly every major industrial firm, forming a united front that speaks with authority on matters affecting their interests.

The **Confederation of German Employers' Associations (BDA)** includes even more business organizations. Virtually every large- or medium-sized employer in the nation is affiliated with one of the sixty-eight employer and professional associations of the BDA.

The two organizations have overlapping membership, but they have different roles in the political process. The BDI represents business on national political matters. Its officials participate in government advisory committees and planning groups, presenting the view of business to government officials and members of parliament. In contrast, the BDA represents business on labor and social issues. The individual employer associations negotiate with the labor unions over employment contracts. At the national level, the BDA represents business on legislation dealing with social security, labor legislation, and social services. It also nominates business representatives for a variety of government committees, ranging from the media supervisory boards to social security committees.

Business interests have a long history of close relations with the Christian Democrats and conservative politicians. Companies and their top management provide significant financial support for the Christian Democrats, and many Bundestag deputies have strong ties to business. Yet both the Social Democrats and the Christian Democrats readily accept the legitimate role of business interests within the policy process.

Labor

The **German Federation of Trade Unions (DGB)** is the peak association that incorporates eight separate unions—ranging from the metalworking and building trades to the chemical industry and the postal system—into a single organizational structure.[36] The DGB represents more than 7 million workers. Union membership has declined, however, and today barely a third of the labor force belongs to a union. The membership includes many industrial workers and an even larger percentage of government employees.

As a political organization, the DGB has close ties to the Social Democratic Party, although there is no formal institutional bond between the two. Most SPD deputies in the Bundestag are members of a union, and about one-tenth are former labor union officials. The DGB represents the interests of labor in government conference groups and Bundestag committees. The large mass membership of the DGB also makes union campaign support and the union vote essential parts of the SPD's electoral base.

In spite of their differing interests, business and unions have shown an unusual ability to work together. The Economic Miracle was possible because labor and management implicitly agreed that the first priority was economic growth, from which both sides would prosper. Work time lost through strikes and work stoppages has been consistently lower in the Federal Republic than in most other Western European nations.

This cooperation is encouraged by joint participation of business and union representatives in government committees and planning groups. Cooperation also extends into industrial decisionmaking through **codetermination (Mitbestimmung)**, a federal policy requiring that employees elect half of the board of directors in large companies. The system was first applied to the coal, iron, and steel industries in 1951, and in 1976 it was extended a modified form to large corporations in other fields. Initially, there were dire forecasts that codetermination would destroy German industry. The system generally has been successful, however, in fostering better labor-management relations and thereby strengthening the economy. The Social Democrats also favor codetermination because it introduces democratic principles into the economic system.

Religious Interests

Religious associations are the third major organized interest. Rather than being separated from politics, as in the United States, church and state are closely related. The churches are subject to the rules of the state, and in return they receive formal representation and support from the government.

The churches are financed mainly through a church tax collected by the government. The government adds a surcharge (about 10 percent) to an employee's income tax, and the government transfers this amount to the employee's church. A taxpayer can officially decline to pay that tax, but social norms discourage this. Catholic primary schools in several states receive government funding, and the churches accept government subsidies to support their social programs and aid to the needy.

The churches are often directly involved in the policy process. Church appointees regularly sit on government planning committees that deal with education, social services, and family affairs. By law the churches participate on the supervisory boards of the public radio and television networks. Members of the Protestant and Catholic clergy occasionally serve in political offices, as Bundestag deputies or as state government officials.

The Catholic and Protestant churches receive the same formal representation by the government, but the two churches differ in their political styles. The Catholic Church has close ties to the Christian Democrats and at least implicitly encourages its members to support this party and its conservative policies. The Catholic hierarchy is not hesitant to lobby the government on legislation dealing with social or moral issues and often wields an influential role in policy-making.

The Protestant community is a loose association of mostly Lutheran churches spread across Germany. Church involvement in politics varies with the preferences of local pastors, bishops, and their respective congregations. In the West the Protestant churches are not very involved in partisan politics, although they are seen as favoring the Social Democrats. Protestant groups also work through their formal representation on government committees or function as individual lobbying organizations.

Protestant churches played a more significant political role in the GDR because they were one of the few organizations that was autonomous from the state. Churches were places where people could freely discuss the social and moral aspects of contemporary issues. As the East German revolution gathered force in 1989, many churches acted as rallying points for opposition to the regime. Religion was not the opiate of the people, as Marx had feared, but one of the forces that swept the Communists from power.

Declining church attendance in both West and East marks a steady secularization of German society. About one-tenth of Westerners claim to be nonreligious, as are nearly half the residents in the East. The gradual secularization of German society suggests that the churches' popular base will continue its slow erosion.

Germany's growing Muslim community represents a new aspect of religious interests. These communities have built mosques across Germany, often facing resistance from the local population. The mosques then receive tax support, just like the Catholic and Protestant churches. Some activists have demanded that schools teach the Koran and that they provide instruction in languages other than German. As more foreign residents become German citizens, this community is likely to become a more vocal participant in the political process.

New Politics Movement

During the late twentieth century, new citizen groups emerged as part of the New Politics movement. Challenging business, labor, religion, agriculture, and other established socioeconomic interests, these new organizations have focused their efforts on the lifestyle and quality-of-life issues facing Germany.[37] Environmental groups are the most visible part of the movement. Following the flowering of environmental interests in the 1970s, antinuclear groups popped up like mushrooms around nuclear power facilities, local environmental action groups proliferated, and new national organizations formed. The women's movement is another part of the New Politics network. That movement developed a dualistic strategy for improving the status of women: changing the consciousness of women and reforming the laws. A variety of associations and self-help groups at the local level nurture the personal development of women, while other organizations focus on national policymaking.

Different New Politics groups have distinct issue interests and their own organizations, but they are also part of a common movement unified by their shared interest in the quality of life for individuals, including the quality of the environment, the protection of human rights, and peace in an uncertain world. They draw their members from the same social base: young, better educated, and middle-class citizens. These groups also are more likely to use unconventional political tactics, such as protests and demonstrations.

New Politics groups do not wield the influence of the established interest groups, although their combined membership now exceeds the formal membership in the political parties. These groups are important and contentious actors in the political process. Moreover, the reconciliation of women's legislation in the united Germany and the resolution of the East's environmental problems are likely to keep these concerns near the top of the political agenda.

THE PARTY SYSTEM

Political parties are an essential part of a democratic government, and they perform a variety of functions within the political process. Moreover, political parties in Germany play a larger and more active role than do political parties in the United States. Germany is often described as a system of party government.

Following World War II, the Western Allies created a new democratic, competitive party system in the West. The Allies licensed a diverse set of parties that were free of Nazi ties and committed to democratic procedures. The Basic Law requires that parties support the constitutional order and democratic methods of the FRG. Because of these provisions, the FRG developed a strong system of competitive party politics that is a mainstay of the democratic order. Elections focused on the competition between the conservative Christian Democrats and the leftist Social Democrats, with the smaller parties typically holding the balance of power. When New Politics issues entered the political agenda in the 1980s, a new political party, the Greens, formed to represent these concerns. A small extreme-right party, the **Republikaner (REP)**, formed in the late 1980s as an advocate of nationalist policies and antiforeigner propaganda.[38]

The GDR supposedly had a multiparty system and elections, but this presented only the illusion of democracy—the Socialist Unity Party (SED) firmly held political power. When the GDR collapsed, the SED and other Communist front parties also collapsed. Support for the SED plummeted, and the party remade itself by changing its name to the **Party of Democratic Socialism (PDS)**. Although many opposition groups competed in the 1990 democratic

elections in the East, the West German parties largely controlled the electoral process, taking over the financing, tactics, organization, and substance of the campaign. Today the party system of unified Germany largely represents an extension of the Western system to the East.

Christian Democrats

The creation of the **Christian Democratic Union (CDU)** in postwar West Germany signified a sharp break with the tradition of German political parties. The CDU was founded by a mixed group of Catholics and Protestants, businesspeople and trade unionists, conservatives and liberals. Rather than representing narrow special interests, the party wanted to appeal to a broad segment of society in order to gain government power. The party sought to reconstruct West Germany along Christian and humanitarian lines. Konrad Adenauer, the party leader, developed the CDU into a conservative-oriented catchall party (*Volkspartei*)—a sharp contrast to the fragmented ideological parties of Weimar. This strategy succeeded; within a single decade, the CDU emerged as the largest party, capturing 40 to 50 percent of the popular vote (see Figure 7.5).

The CDU operates in all states except Bavaria, where it allies itself with the Bavarian **Christian Social Union (CSU)**, whose political philosophy is more conservative than that of the CDU. These two parties generally function as one (CDU/CSU) in national politics, forming a single parliamentary group in the Bundestag and campaigning together in national elections.

The CDU/CSU's early voting strength allowed the party to control the government, first under Adenauer (1949–1963) and then under Ludwig Erhard (1963–1966), as shown in Table 7.1. In 1966, however, the party lost the support of its coalition partner, the Free Democrats, and formed a Grand Coalition with the Social Democrats. Following the 1969 election, the Social Democrats and Free Democrats formed a new government coalition; for the first time in the history of the FRG, the CDU/CSU was the opposition party.

In the early 1980s, a weakening economic situation increased public support for the party and its conservative policies. In 1982 the Christian Democrats and the Free Democrats formed a new conservative government through the first successful constructive no-confidence vote, which elected Helmut Kohl as

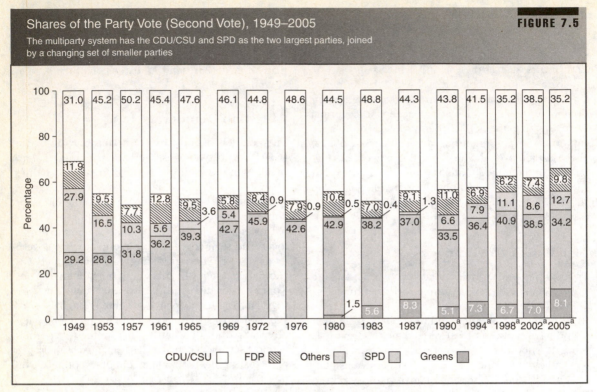

Shares of the Party Vote (Second Vote), 1949–2005

The multiparty system has the CDU/CSU and SPD as the two largest parties, joined by a changing set of smaller parties

FIGURE 7.5

[a]1990–2005 percentages combine results from western and eastern Germany.

chancellor. Public support for Kohl's policies returned the governing coalition to power following the 1983 and 1987 elections.

The collapse of the GDR in 1989 provided a historic opportunity for the CDU and Kohl. While others looked on the events with wonder or uncertainty, Kohl embraced the idea of closer ties between the two Germanies. Thus, when the March 1990 GDR election became a referendum in support of German unification, the Christian Democrats were assured of victory because of the party's early commitment to German union. Kohl emerged victorious from the 1990 Bundestag elections, but his government struggled with the policy challenges produced by German unification. The governing coalition lost seats in the 1994 elections, but Kohl retained a slim majority. By the 1998 elections, the accumulation of sixteen years of governing and the special challenges of unification had taken their toll on the party and Helmut Kohl. Many Germans looked for a change. The CDU/CSU fared poorly in the election, especially in the Eastern

Länder, which were frustrated by their persisting second-class status. The CDU's poor showing in the election was a rebuke to Kohl, and he resigned the party leadership.

The CDU made some gains after the election and seemed poised to win several state elections in 1999 and 2000—and then lightning struck. Investigations showed that Kohl had accepted illegal campaign contributions while he was chancellor. Kohl's allies within the CDU were forced to resign, and the party's electoral fortunes suffered. To change its popular image, in 1999 the CDU selected a party leader who was nearly the opposite of Kohl: Angela Merkel.

The CDU/CSU chose Edmund Stoiber, the head of the Christian Social Union, as its chancellor candidate in 2002. Stoiber's campaign stressed the struggling German economy, and the CDU/CSU gained the same vote share as the Social Democrats and nearly as many seats in the Bundestag (see Figure 7.6). However, an SPD-led coalition retained control of the government.

Composition of Coalition Governments

A listing of government parties and chancellors of the Federal Republic

TABLE 7.1

Date Formed	Source of Change	Coalition Partners[a]	Chancellor
September 1949	Election	CDU/CSU, FDP, DP	Adenauer (CDU)
October 1953	Election	CDU/CSU, FDP, DP, G	Adenauer (CDU)
October 1957	Election	CDU/CSU, DP	Adenauer (CDU)
November 1961	Election	CDU/CSU, FDP	Adenauer (CDU)
October 1963	Chancellor retirement	CDU/CSU, FDP	Erhard (CDU)
October 1965	Election	CDU/CSU, FDP	Erhard (CDU)
December 1966	Coalition change	CDU/CSU, SPD	Kiesinger (CDU)
October 1969	Election	SPD, FDP	Brandt (SPD)
December 1972	Election	SPD, FDP	Brandt (SPD)
May 1974	Chancellor retirement	SPD, FDP	Schmidt (SPD)
December 1976	Election	SPD, FDP	Schmidt (SPD)
November 1980	Election	SPD, FDP	Schmidt (SPD)
October 1982	Constructive no-confidence vote	CDU/CSU, FDP	Kohl (CDU)
March 1983	Election	CDU/CSU, FDP	Kohl (CDU)
January 1987	Election	CDU/CSU, FDP	Kohl (CDU)
December 1990	Election	CDU/CSU, FDP	Kohl (CDU)
October 1994	Election	CDU/CSU, FDP	Kohl (CDU)
September 1998	Election	SPD, Greens	Schröder (SPD)
September 2002	Election	SPD, Greens	Schröder (SPD)
September 2005	Election	CDU/CSU, SPD	Merkel (CDU/CSU)

CDU: Christian Democratic Union; CSU: Christian Social Union; DP: German Party; FDP: Free Democratic Party; G: All-German Bloc Federation of Expellees and Displaced Persons; SPD: Social Democratic Party.

When early elections were called in 2005, the CDU/CSU selected Merkel as its chancellor candidate. Merkel and the party ran ahead of the SPD throughout the campaign, and most observers expected a CDU victory. But the party, and Merkel, faltered late in the campaign. The election ended as a dead heat between the CDU/CSU and the SPD—and both Merkel and Schröder declared victory. After weeks of negotiation and the exploration of potential coalitions, the CDU/CSU and a Schröder-less SPD agreed to form a Grand Coalition, which was similar to the U.S. Democrats and Republicans sharing control of the government. Government positions, including Cabinet posts, were split between the two parties. It was hoped that this collaboration between the two large parties would enable the government to undertake the difficult reforms needed to reenergize the economy and society. In actuality, the differences in political philosophies between the two large parties led to limited policy change. Merkel's style of modernization and compromise kept the coalition together, but little more. Thus, many of the challenges the government faced in 2005 will still face the new government elected in 2009.

Social Democrats

The postwar **Social Democratic Party (SPD)** in West Germany was constructed along the lines of the SPD in the Weimar Republic—an ideological party, primarily representing the interests of unions and the working class.[39] In the early postwar years, the Social Democrats espoused strict Marxist doctrine and consistently opposed Adenauer's Western-oriented foreign policy. The SPD's image of the nation's future was radically different from that of Adenauer and the Christian Democrats.

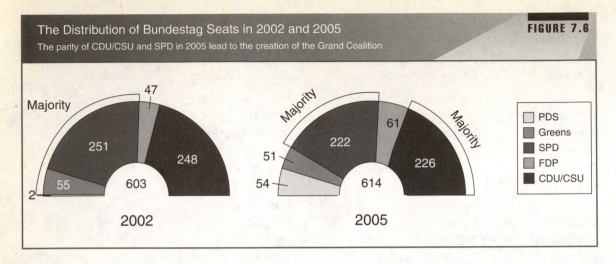

FIGURE 7.6

The Distribution of Bundestag Seats in 2002 and 2005

The parity of CDU/CSU and SPD in 2005 lead to the creation of the Grand Coalition

The SPD's poor performance in early elections (see again Figure 7.5) generated internal pressures for the party to broaden its electoral appeal. At the 1959 Godesberg party conference, the party renounced its Marxist economic policies and generally moved toward the center on domestic and foreign policies. The party continued to represent working-class interests, but by shedding its ideological banner, the SPD hoped to attract new support from the middle class. The SPD transformed itself into a progressive catchall party that could compete with the Christian Democrats.

An SPD breakthrough finally came in 1966 with the formation of the Grand Coalition (see again Table 7.1). By sharing government control with the CDU/CSU, the SPD decreased public uneasiness about the party's integrity and ability to govern. Political support for the party also grew as the SPD played an active part in resolving the nation's problems.

Following the 1969 election, a new SDP–FDP government formed with Willy Brandt (SPD) as chancellor. After enacting an ambitious range of new policies, a period of economic recession let to Brandt's replacement by Helmut Schmidt in 1974 and a new focus on the faltering economy. The SPD retained government control in the 1976 and 1980 elections, but these were trying times for the party. The SPD and the FDP frequently disagreed on economic policy, and political divisions developed within the SPD.

These policy tensions eventually led to the breakup of the SPD-led government in 1982. Once again in opposition, the SPD faced an identity crisis. In one election it tried to appeal to centrist voters and in the next election to leftist/Green voters—but neither strategy succeeded. In 1990 the SPD campaign was overtaken by events in the East.

Perhaps no one (except perhaps the Communists) was more surprised than the SPD by the course of events in the GDR in 1989–1990. The SPD had been normalizing relations with the SED as a basis of intra-German cooperation, only to see the SED ousted by the citizenry. The SDP stood by quietly as Kohl spoke of a single German *Vaterland* to crowds of applauding East Germans. The party's poor performance in the 1990 national elections reflected its inability either to lead or to follow the course of the unification process. Germans were frustrated by the nation's policy course after unification; they came to the brink of voting the SPD into office in 1994—and then pulled back.

In 1998 the Social Democrats selected the moderate Gerhard Schröder to be their chancellor candidate. Schröder attracted former CDU/CSU and Free Democratic voters who were dissatisfied with the government's performance. The SPD vote share increased in 1998, and the party formed a new coalition government with the Green Party. Schröder pursued a middle course, balancing the centrist and leftist views existing within the governing coalition. For instance, the government allowed German troops to play an active role in Kosovo and Afghanistan, while mandating the phasing out of nuclear power.

During the 2002 election, Schröder vocally opposed U.S. policy toward Iraq to win support from leftist voters. This strategy succeeded, and the SPD-Green government returned to office with a narrow majority, but this strained relations between Germany and the United States.

The SPD-Green government was criticized by some for doing too much to reform the economy and by others for not doing enough. As the economy stagnated, the party lost important state elections, and its popularity declined further. Schröder was a gambler, and instead of struggling on until the next election, in early 2005 he called for early elections. At first, few gave him a chance to win—but by the end of the campaign, he had matched Merkel in the final vote tally. This was Schröder's last hurrah, and he left the party to new faces.

The SPD now shares governing responsibilities with the CDU/CSU, with Frank-Walter Steinmeier of the SPD serving as vice chancellor and foreign minister. In 2008 the party selected Steinmeier as its chancellor candidate for 2009. His election would return Germany to many of the policies of the Schröder era, although winning a majority in the election appears to be very difficult. Certainly, he and Merkel would offer distinctly different choices for Germany's future in the election.

Free Democratic Party

Although the **Free Democratic Party (FDP)** is far smaller than the CDU/CSU or the SPD, it has often held enough seats to have a pivotal role in forming a government coalition. This has given the FDP a larger political role than its small size would suggest.

The FDP was initially a strong advocate of private enterprise and drew its support from the Protestant middle class and farmers. Its economic policies made the FDP a natural ally of the CDU/CSU in difficult economic times (see again Table 7.1). Its liberal foreign and social programs have opened the way for coalition with the SPD when the these issues dominate the agenda. This led to a coalition with the SPD from 1969 until 1982.

The FDP has generally been a moderating political influence, limiting the leftist leanings of the SPD and the conservative tendencies of the CDU/CSU. This places the party in a precarious position, however, because if it allies itself too closely with either major party, it may lose its political identity. The party struggled with this problem for the past several elections.

In January 2001 Guido Westerwelle became party leader. The party fared poorly in 2002 because of internal divisions, which kept the conservative CDU/CSU–FDP coalition from winning a majority.

After 2005 it became the largest party on the opposition benches. The party's hope is that it will hold the balance of power after the 2009 election and reenter the government to pursue its mix of economic conservatism and social liberalism.

The Greens

The Greens *(Die Grünen)* are literally a party of a different color.[40] The party addresses a broad range of New Politics issues: opposition to nuclear energy and Germany's military policies, commitment to environmental protection, support for women's rights, and further democratization of society. The party also was synonymous with an unconventional political style. The Greens initially differed so markedly from the established parties that one Green leader described them as the "antiparty party."

The party won its first Bundestag seats in 1983, becoming the first new party to enter parliament since the 1950s. Using this political forum, the Greens campaigned vigorously for an alternative view of politics, such as stronger measures to protect the environment, gender equality, and staunch opposition to nuclear power. The Greens also added a bit of color and spontaneity to the normally staid procedures of the political system. The typical dress for Green deputies was jeans and a sweater, rather than the traditional business attire of the established parties; their desks in parliament often sprouted flowers, rather than folders of official-looking documents. The party's loose and open internal structure stood in sharp contrast to the hierarchic and bureaucratized structure of the established parties. Despite initial concerns about the Greens' impact on the political system, most analysts now agree that the party brought necessary attention to political viewpoints that previously were overlooked.

German unification caught the Greens unprepared. To stress their opposition of Western hegemony, the Western Greens refused to form an electoral alliance with the Eastern Greens in the 1990 elections. The Eastern Greens/Alliance '90 won enough votes to enter the new Bundestag, but the Western Greens fell short of the 5 percent hurdle and won no seats. The Greens' unconventional politics had caught up with them. After this loss the Greens charted a more moderate course for the party. They remained committed to the environment and an alternative agenda, but they tempered the unconventional style and structure of the party. The party reentered the Bundestag in 1994.

By 1998 moderates controlling the Green Party asked voters to support a new Red-Green coalition of SPD and the Greens. This Red-Green coalition received a majority in the election, and for the first time, the Greens became part of the national government. It is difficult to be an outsider when one is inside the establishment, however. The antiparty party struggled to balance its unconventional policies with the new responsibilities of governing—and steadily gave up its unconventional style. For instance, the party supported military intervention into Kosovo, despite its pacifist traditions; it supported tax reform that lowered the highest rates in exchange for a new environmental tax. It pressed for the abolition of nuclear power, but agreed to wait thirty years for this to happen. The Greens ran a 2002 campaign heavily based on the personal appeal of their leader, Joschka Fischer, and their success returned the SPD-Green government to power.

The Greens faired well in 2005, but the coalition math did not include them in the government. And with a new strong rival in the *Die Linke,* their future identity and electoral fortunes have blurred. The Greens have become a conventional party in terms of their style, now pursuing unconventional and reformist policies as a critique of the CDU/CSU–SPD alliance.

Communists to *Die Linke*

The Communist Party was one of the first parties to form in postwar Germany, and its history reflects Germany's two postwar paths. In the West the Communist Party (KPD) suffered because of its identification with the Soviet Union and the GDR. The party garnered a shrinking sliver of the vote in the early elections, and then in 1956 the Constitutional Court banned the KPD because of its undemocratic principles. A reconstituted party began contesting elections again in 1969, but never attracted a significant following.

The situation was obviously different in the East. As World War II was ending, Walter Ulbricht returned to Berlin from exile in Moscow to reorganize the Communist Party in the Soviet military zone. In 1946 the Soviets forced a merger of the Eastern KPD and SPD into a new Socialist Unity Party of Germany (SED), which became the ruling institution in the East. The SED controlled the government apparatus and the electoral process, party agents were integrated into the military command structure, the party supervised the infamous state security police (*Stasi*), and party membership was a prerequisite to positions of authority and influence. The state controlled East German society, and the SED controlled the state.

The SED's power collapsed in 1989 along with the East German regime. Party membership plummeted, and local party units abolished themselves. The omnipotent party suddenly seemed impotent. To save the party from complete dissolution and to compete in the upcoming democratic elections, the party changed its name to the Party of Democratic Socialism (PDS). The old party guard was ousted from positions of authority, and new moderates took over the leadership.

The PDS has campaigned as the representative of those who opposed the economic and social course of German unity. In the 1990 Bundestag elections, the PDS won 11 percent of the Eastern vote, but captured only 2 percent of the national vote. The PDS was successful in winning Bundestag seats in the 1994 and 1998 elections, but failed to surmount the electoral threshold in 2002.

The PDS suffered in 2002 partly because of internal party divisions and partly because the SPD consciously sought support from former PDS voters. The party's popular leadership was also aging, and the PDS seemed destined to be a regional party of the East. Then the early elections in 2005 prompted a change in party history. Oscar Lafontaine, a former SPD chancellor candidate, orchestrated a coalition of leftist interests in the West, *Die Linke,* and the PDS in the East. This new party drew the support of Western leftists who were disenchanted by Schröder's government and PDS voters from the East. They nearly doubled the PDS vote over the previous election and gained more than fifty Bundestag seats. The party's success precluded the formation of either an SPD-Green or a CDU/CSU–FDP government.

In 2007 the two parties formally merged, and now will compete under the label **Die Linke**.[41] This is likely to inject new ideological debate into the political process and make it more complicated to form a majority coalition in national and state governments.

THE ROLE OF ELECTIONS

The framers of the Basic Law had two goals in mind when they designed the electoral system. One was to create a **proportional representation (PR)** system that allocates legislative seats based on a party's percentage of the popular vote. If a party receives 10 percent of the popular vote, it should receive 10 percent of the Bundestag seats. Other individuals saw advantages in the system of single-member districts used in Britain and the United States. They thought that this system would avoid the fragmentation of the Weimar party system and ensure some accountability between an electoral district and its representative.

To satisfy both objectives, the FRG created a mixed electoral system. On one part of the ballot, citizens vote for a candidate to represent their district. The candidate with the most votes in each district is elected to parliament.

On a second part of the ballot, voters select a party. These second votes are added nationwide to determine each party's share of the popular vote. A party's proportion of the second vote determines its total representation in the Bundestag. Each party receives additional seats so that its percentage of the combined candidate and party seats equals its percentage of the second votes. These additional seats are distributed to party representatives according to lists prepared by the state parties before the election. Half of the Bundestag members are elected as district representatives and half as party representatives.[42]

An exception to this PR system is the 5-percent clause, which requires that a party win at least 5 percent of the national vote (or three district seats) to share in the distribution of party-list seats.[43] The law aims to withhold representation from the type of small extremist parties that plagued the Weimar Republic. In practice, however, the 5-percent clause handicaps all minor parties and lessens the number of parties represented in the Bundestag.

This mixed system has several consequences for electoral politics. The party-list system gives party leaders substantial influence on who will be elected to parliament by the placement of people on the list. The PR system also ensures fair representation for the smaller parties. The FDP, for example, has won only one direct candidate mandate since 1957 and yet it receives Bundestag seats based on its national share of the vote. In contrast, Britain's district-only system discriminates against small parties; in 2005 the British Liberal Democrats won 22.1 percent of the national vote but less than 10 percent of the parliamentary seats. The German two-vote system also affects campaign strategies. Although most voters cast both their ballots for the same party, the smaller parties encourage supporters of the larger parties to "lend" their second votes to the smaller party. Because of its mixed features, the German system is sometimes described as the ideal compromise in building an electoral system.[44]

The Electoral Connection

Democratic elections are about making policy choices in the form of a future government, and Germans have a rich set of parties and policy programs from which to choose. Think of how the United States would be different if there were some communists and environmentalists elected to the House of Representatives, as well as the two major parties and a traditional European liberal party. One of the essential functions of political parties in a democracy is interest representation, and this is especially clear in the case of Germany elections.

The voting patterns of social groups reflect the ideological and policy differences among parties. Although social differences in voting have gradually narrowed, voting patterns in 2005 reflect the traditional social divisions in German society and politics (see Table 7.2).[45]

The CDU/CSU's electoral coalition draws more voters from the conservative sectors of society, with greater support from seniors, residents of rural areas and small towns, and the middle class. Catholics and those who attend church frequently also give disproportionate support to the party.

The SPD now forms a coalition with the CDU/CSU in the government, but its voter base contrasts with that of the CDU/CSU: A large share of SPD votes comes from nonreligious voters and blue-collar workers, although the middle class provides most of the party's voters. In some ways the SPD has suffered because its traditional voter base—blue-collar workers—has declined in size and it has not established a new political identity that draws a distinct voter clientele.

The Greens' electoral base is heavily drawn from groups that support New Politics movements: the new middle class, the better educated, the nonreligious, and urban voters. A large proportion of Green voters (42.5 percent) are under age 40. However, this youth vote has steadily declined over time, partially because the party and its leadership are aging.

The FDP's voter base in 2005 illustrates the party's ambiguous electoral appeal. The FDP voters still include a high percentage of the self-employed, but for many other characteristics, it mirrors the general population. It no longer clearly appeals to the better educated, Protestants, and urban voters, which were its traditional voter base.

Perhaps the most distinct voter bloc is the Linke/PDS. This is first an East-oriented party, with 46.9

Electoral Coalitions in 2005

Voting patterns show the conservative social base of the CDU/CSU and the liberal base of the SPD, Greens, and Linke

TABLE 7.2

	CDU/CSU	SPD	Greens	FDP	Linke/PDS	Total Public
Region						
West	78.3%	82.3%	84.0%	81.6%	53.2%	81.1%
East	21.7	17.7	16.0	18.4	46.9	18.9
Occupation						
Worker	20.1%	23.8%	19.3%	16.8%	29.7%	22.0%
Self-employed	13.7	4.9	16.1	17.8	9.5	10.7
White-collar/government	66.3	71.3	64.6	65.4	60.8	67.4
Education						
Basic	49.5%	45.0%	28.9%	34.0%	33.3%	42.5%
Medium	30.5	31.4	26.0	43.2	44.9	33.5
Advanced	20.0	23.6	45.3	22.8	21.8	24.0
Religion						
Catholic	44.2%	34.0%	20.4%	35.3%	12.8%	35.3%
Protestant	39.5	45.3	45.3	40.3	32.1	41.4
Other, none	16.3	20.7	34.3	24.3	55.1	24.0
Church Attendance						
Never	24.2%	39.2%	43.6%	35.4%	60.3%	36.2%
Occasionally	53.8	50.1	47.0	51.9	33.3	49.8
Frequently	22.0	10.7	9.4	12.6	6.4	14.0
Size of town						
Less than 50,000	30.0%	21.3%	13.7%	21.8%	26.4%	24.0%
50,001–100,000	24.1	23.7	29.7	23.3	23.7	24.2
100,001–500,000	24.8	24.8	26.4	30.6	25.0	25.9
More than 500,000	21.1	20.1	30.2	24.3	25.0	26.0
Age						
Under 40	28.4%	34.3%	42.5%	37.9%	29.5%	33.4%
40–59	32.9	32.9	36.9	34.5	47.4	34.5
60 and over	38.8	32.7	21.0	27.7	23.1	32.2
Gender						
Male	46.7%	46.8%	47.0%	54.9%	57.1%	47.9%
Female	53.3	53.2	53.0	45.1	42.9	52.3

Note: Some percentages may not total 100 because of rounding.

Source: Comparative Study of Electoral Systems Survey, Germany, Postelection September 2005 conducted by the Bernhard Wessels, Wissenschaftszentrum Berlin für Sozialforschung (weighted N = 2,018).

percent of its vote coming from the East. The PDS's Communist roots also appear in its appeal to blue-collar workers and the nonreligious. The Linke/PDS has the most distinctly male electorate. It is a party for those frustrated with the economic and political path Germany has followed since unification.

In recent elections these social group differences have generally narrowed, as fewer voters make their decisions based on class, religious, or other cues. Instead, more voters are deciding based on their issue opinions or evaluations of the candidates. Yet, the ideology and clientele networks of the parties still reflect these traditional group bases, so they have a persisting influence on the parties.

PARTY GOVERNMENT

Political parties in Germany deserve special emphasis because they are such important actors in the political process, perhaps even more important than in most other European democracies. Some observers describe the political system as government for the parties, by the parties, and of the parties.

The Basic Law is unusual because it specifically refers to political parties (the U.S. Constitution does not). Because the German Empire and the Third Reich suppressed political parties, the Basic Law guarantees their legitimacy and their right to exist if they accept the principles of democratic government. Parties are also designated as the primary institutions of representative democracy. They act as intermediaries between the public and the government and function as a means for citizen input on policy preferences. The Basic Law takes the additional step of assigning an educational function to the parties, directing them to "take part in forming the political will of the people." In other words, the parties should take the lead and not just respond to public opinion.

The parties' centrality in the political process appears in several ways. There are no direct primaries that would allow the public to select party representatives in Bundestag elections. Instead, a small group of official party members or a committee appointed by the membership nominates the district candidates. State party conventions select the party-list candidates. Thus, the leadership can select list candidates and order them on the list. This power can be used to reward faithful party supporters and discipline party mavericks; placement near the top of a party list virtually ensures election, and low placement carries little chance of a Bundestag seat.

Political parties also dominate the election process. Most voters view the candidates merely as party representatives, rather than as autonomous political figures. Even the district candidates are elected primarily because of their party ties. Bundestag, state, and European election campaigns are financed by the government; the parties receive public funds for each vote they get. The government provides free television time for a limited number of campaign advertisements, and these are allocated to the parties, not the individual candidates. Government funding

for the parties also continues between elections, to help them perform their informational and educational functions as prescribed in the Basic Law.

Once an election is completed, the parties then shift to forming a government. Since no party has a majority, a group of parties with a majority of the votes must agree to form a coalition government. Often such agreements are made before the election, but sometimes they wait until the votes are counted. Because of the closeness of the vote in 2005, it took months for the eventual governing parties to agree on a coalition and the program that the new CDU/CSU–SPD government would follow.

Within the Bundestag, the parties are also central actors. The Bundestag is organized around party groups (*Fraktionen*), rather than individual deputies. The important legislative posts and committee assignments are restricted to members of a party Fraktion. The size of a Fraktion determines its representation on legislative committees, its share of committee chairs, and its participation in the executive bodies of the legislature. Government funds for legislative and administrative support are distributed to the Fraktion, not to the deputies.

Because of these factors, the cohesion of parties within the Bundestag is exceptionally high. Parties caucus before major legislation to decide the party position, and most legislative votes follow strict party lines. This is partially a consequence of a parliamentary system and partially a sign of the pervasive influence parties have throughout the political process.

As a result of these many factors, political parties play a larger role in structuring the political process in Germany (and many other parliamentary systems) than they do in the United States. Parties are more distinctive in their policy positions, more unified in their views, and more decisive in their actions. Representative democracy works largely through and by political parties as the means to connect voters to the decisions of government.

THE POLICYMAKING PROCESS

The policymaking process may begin with any part of society—an interest group, a political leader, an individual citizen, or a government official. These elements interact in making public policy. This makes it difficult to trace the true genesis of any policy idea. Moreover, once a new policy is proposed, other interest groups and political actors are active in amending, supporting, or opposing the policy.

The pattern of interaction among policy actors varies with time and policy issues. One set of groups is most active on labor issues, and these groups use the methods of influence that are most successful for their cause. A very different set of interests may attempt to affect defense policy and use far different methods of influence. This variety makes it difficult to describe policymaking as a single process, although the institutional framework for enacting policy is relatively uniform in all policy areas.

The growing importance of the European Union has also changed the policymaking process for its member states.[46] Now, policies made in Brussels often take precedence over German legislation. Laws passed by the German government must conform to EU standards in many areas. The European Court of Justice also has the power to overturn laws passed by the German government. Thus, policymaking is no longer a solely national process.

This section describes the various stages of the policy process and clarifies the balance of power among the institutions of the German government.

Policy Initiation

Most issues reach the policy agenda through the executive branch. One reason for this predominance is that the Cabinet and the ministries manage the affairs of government. They are responsible for preparing the budget, formulating revenue proposals, administering existing policies, and conducting the other routine activities of government. The nature of a parliamentary democracy further strengthens the policymaking influence of the chancellor and the Cabinet. The chancellor is the primary policy spokesperson for the government and for a majority of the Bundestag deputies. In speeches, interviews, and formal policy declarations, she sets the policy agenda for the government. It is the responsibility of the chancellor and Cabinet to propose new legislation to implement the government's policy promises. Interest groups realize the importance of the executive branch, and they generally work with the federal ministries—rather than Bundestag deputies—when they seek new legislation.

The executive branch's predominance means that the Cabinet proposes about two-thirds of the legislation considered by the Bundestag. Thirty members of the Bundestag may jointly introduce a bill, but only about 20 percent of legislative proposals

begin in this manner. Most of the Bundestag's own proposals involve private-member bills or minor issues. State governments also can propose legislation in the Bundesrat, but they do so infrequently.

The Cabinet generally follows a consensual decisionmaking style in setting the government's policy program. Ministers seldom propose legislation that is not expected to receive Cabinet support. The chancellor has a crucial part in ensuring this consensus. The chancellor's office coordinates the legislative proposals drafted by the various ministries. If the chancellor feels that a bill conflicts with the government's stated objectives, she may ask that the proposal be withdrawn or returned to the ministry for restudy and redrafting. If a conflict on policy arises between two ministries, the chancellor may mediate the dispute. Alternatively, interministerial negotiations may resolve the differences. Only in extreme cases is the chancellor unable to resolve such problems; when such stalemates occur, policy conflicts are referred to the full Cabinet.

The chancellor also plays a major role in Cabinet deliberations. The chancellor is a fulcrum, balancing conflicting interests to reach a compromise that the government as a whole can support. This leadership position gives the chancellor substantial influence as she negotiates with Cabinet members. Very seldom does a majority of the Cabinet oppose the chancellor. When the chancellor and Cabinet agree on a legislative proposal, they have a dominant position in the legislative process. Because the Cabinet also represents the majority in the Bundestag, most of its initiatives are eventually enacted into law. In the fifteenth Bundestag (2002–2005), almost 90 percent of the government's proposals became law; in contrast, about 40 percent of the proposals introduced by Bundestag members became law. The government's legislative position is further strengthened by provisions in the Basic Law that limit the Bundestag's authority in fiscal matters. The parliament can revise or amend most legislative proposals. However, it cannot alter the spending or taxation levels of legislation proposed by the Cabinet. Parliament cannot even reallocate expenditures in the budget without the approval of the finance minister and the Cabinet.

Legislating Policy

When the Cabinet approves a legislative proposal, the government sends it to the Bundesrat for review (see Figure 7.7). After receiving the Bundesrat's comments,

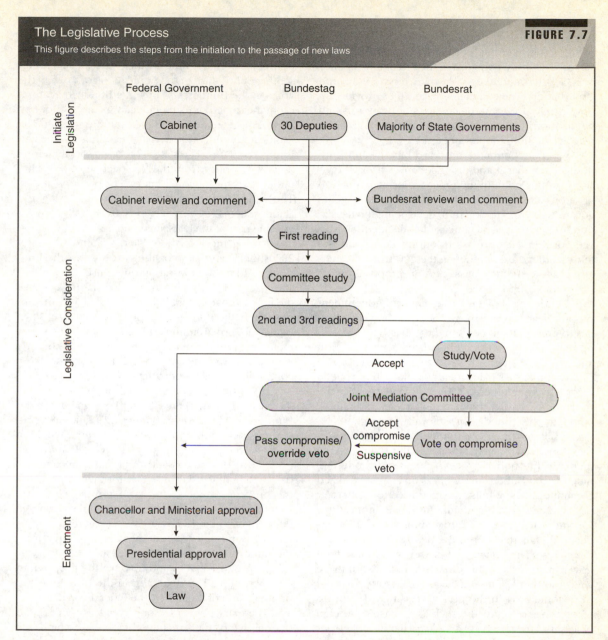

The Legislative Process

This figure describes the steps from the initiation to the passage of new laws

FIGURE 7.7

Initiate Legislation

Legislative Consideration

Enactment

Federal Government — Bundestag — Bundesrat

Cabinet | 30 Deputies | Majority of State Governments

Cabinet review and comment | Bundesrat review and comment

First reading

Committee study

2nd and 3rd readings

Study/Vote

Accept

Joint Mediation Committee

Pass compromise/override veto | Vote on compromise

Accept compromise

Suspensive veto

Chancellor and Ministerial approval

Presidential approval

Law

the Cabinet formally transmits the government's proposal to the Bundestag. The bill receives a first reading, which places it on the agenda of the chamber, and it is assigned to the appropriate committee.

Much of the Bundestag's work takes place in these specialized committees. The committee structure generally follows the divisions of the federal ministries, such as transportation, defense, labor, or agriculture. Because bills are referred to the committee early in the legislative process, committees have real potential for reviewing and amending their content. Committees evaluate proposals, consult with interest groups, and then submit a revised proposal to the full Bundestag. Research staffs are small, but committees also use investigative hearings. Government and interest group representatives testify on pending legislation, and committee members themselves often have expertise in their designated policy area. Most committees hold their meetings behind closed doors. The committee system thus provides an opportunity for frank discussions of proposals and negotiations among the parties before legislation reaches the floor of the Bundestag.

When a committee reports a bill, the full Bundestag examines it and discusses any proposed revisions. At this point in the process, however, political positions already are well established. Leaders in the governing parties took part in developing the legislation. The parties have caucused to decide their official position. Major revisions during the second and third readings are infrequent; the government generally is assured of the passage of its proposals as reported out of committee.

Bundestag debate on the merits of government proposals is thus mostly symbolic. It allows the parties to present their views to the public. The successful parties explain the merits of the new legislation and advertise their efforts to their supporters. The opposition parties place their objections in the public record. Although these debates seldom influence the outcome of a vote, they are nevertheless an important part of the Bundestag's information function.

A bill that passes the Bundestag is transmitted to the Bundesrat, which represents the state governments in the policy process. As in the Bundestag, much of the Bundesrat's work is done in specialized committees where bills are scrutinized for both their policy content and their administrative implications for the states. The legislative authority of the Bundesrat equals that of the Bundestag in areas where the states share concurrent powers with the federal government or administer federal policies. In these areas the Bundesrat's approval is necessary for a bill to become law. In the policy areas that do not involve the states directly, such as defense or foreign affairs, Bundesrat approval of legislation is not essential. Historically, about two-thirds of legislative proposals required Bundesrat approval.[47]

The sharing of legislative power between the state and federal governments has mixed political consequences. State leaders can adapt legislation to local and regional needs through their influence on policymaking. This division of power also provides another check in the system of checks and balances. With strong state governments, it is less likely that one leader or group could control the political process by usurping the national government.

The Bundesrat's voting procedures give disproportionate weight to the smaller states; states representing only a third of the population control half the votes in the Bundesrat. Thus, the Bundesrat cannot claim the same popular legitimacy as the proportionally represented and directly elected Bundestag. The Bundesrat voting system may encourage parochialism by the states. The states vote as a bloc; therefore, they view policy from the perspective of the state, rather than the national interest or party positions. The different electoral bases of the Bundestag and Bundesrat make such tensions over policy an inevitable part of the legislative process.

During most of the 1990s and into the early 2000s, different party coalitions controlled the Bundestag and the Bundesrat. In one sense this division strengthened the power of the legislature because the federal government had to negotiate with the opposition in the Bundesrat, especially on the sensitive issues of German union. However, divided government also prevented necessary new legislation in a variety of areas. The current CDU/CSU–SPD coalition controls both houses of parliament.

If the Bundesrat approves of a bill, it transmits the measure to the chancellor for her signature. If the Bundesrat objects to the Bundestag's bill, the representatives of both bodies meet in a joint mediation committee and attempt to resolve their differences.

The mediation committee submits its recommendation to both legislative bodies for their approval. If the proposal involves the state governments, the Bundesrat may cast an absolute veto and prevent the bill from becoming a law. In the remaining policy areas, the Bundesrat can cast only a suspensive veto. If the Bundestag approves of a measure, it may override a suspensive veto and forward the proposal to the chancellor. The final step in the process is the promulgation of the law by the federal president.

There are several lessons from this process. On the one hand, the executive branch is omnipresent throughout the legislative process. After transmitting the government's proposal to the Bundestag, the federal ministers work in support of the bill. Ministry representatives testify before Bundestag and Bundesrat committees to present their position. Cabinet ministers lobby committee members and influential members of parliament. Ministers may propose amendments or negotiate policy compromises to resolve issues that arise during parliamentary deliberations. Government representatives may also attend meetings of the joint mediation committee between the Bundestag and Bundesrat; no other nonparliamentary participants are allowed. The importance of the executive branch is common with most parliamentary systems.

On the other hand, despite this large role played by the executive, the German parliament has greater autonomy than most parliamentary legislatures. The government frequently makes compromises and accepts amendments proposed in the legislature. The two houses of parliament often reflect different party coalitions and different political interests, so the government must take these into account. This is especially important for state interests advocated in the Bundesrat.

Thus, the process reflects the autonomy of both branches and the checks and balances that the framers had sought in designing the Federal Republic's institutions. Compared to other parliamentary systems in Europe, the German system gives more voice to competing interests and is more likely to require compromise to enact new legislation.

Policy Administration

In another attempt to diffuse political power, the Basic Law assigned the administrative responsibility for most domestic policies to the state governments. As evidence of the states' administrative role, the states employ more civil servants than the federal and local governments combined.

Because of the delegation of administrative duties, federal legislation normally is fairly detailed to ensure that the actual application of a law matches the government's intent. Federal agencies may also supervise state agencies, and in cases of dispute, they may apply sanctions or seek judicial review.

Despite this oversight by the federal government, the states retain discretion in applying most federal legislation. This is partially because the federal government lacks the resources to follow state actions closely. Federal control of the states also requires Bundesrat support, where claims for states' rights receive a sympathetic hearing. This decentralization of political authority provides additional flexibility for the political system.

Judicial Review

As in the United States, legislation in Germany is subject to judicial review. The Constitutional Court can evaluate the constitutionality of legislation and void laws that violate the provisions of the Basic Law.[48]

Constitutional issues are brought before the court by one of three methods. The most common involves constitutional complaints filed by individual citizens. Individuals may appeal directly to the court when they feel that a government action violates their constitutional rights. More than 90 percent of the cases presented to the court arise from citizens' complaints. Moreover, cases can be filed without paying court costs and without a lawyer. The court is thus like an ombudsman, assuring the average citizen that his or her fundamental rights are protected by the Basic Law and the court.

The Constitutional Court also hears cases based on "concrete" and "abstract" principles of judicial review. Concrete review involves actual court cases that raise constitutional issues and are referred by a lower court to the Constitutional Court. In an abstract review, the court rules on legislation as a legal principle, without reference to an actual case. The federal government, a state government, or one-third of the Bundestag deputies can request review of a law. Groups that fail to block a bill during the legislative process sometimes use this legal procedure. In recent years various groups have challenged the constitutionality of the unification treaty with the GDR (upheld), the abortion reform law (overturned), the involvement of German troops in United Nations peacekeeping roles (upheld), the new citizenship law (upheld), and several other important pieces of legislation. Over the last two decades, the court received an average of two or three such referrals a year.[49] Judicial review in the abstract expands the constitutional protection of the Basic Law. This directly involves the court in the policy process and may politicize the court as another agent of policymaking.

In recent years the judicial review by the European Court of Justice (ECJ) has added a new dimension to policymaking in Germany and the other EU states.[50] Petitioners can challenge German legislation that they believe violates provisions of certain EU policies. Hundreds of German laws are reviewed each year, and anticipation of ECJ review also now influences the legislative process of the parliament.

POLICY PERFORMANCE

By most standards, the two Germanies could both boast of their positive records of government performance since their formation. The FRG's economic advances in the 1950s and early 1960s were truly phenomenal, and the progress in the GDR was nearly as remarkable. By the 1980s the FRG had one of the strongest economies in the world, and other policies improved the education system, increased workers' participation in industrial management, extended social services, and improved environmental quality.

The GDR had its own impressive record of policy accomplishments, even though it lagged behind the West. It developed a network of social programs, some of which were even more extensive than in the West. The GDR was the economic miracle of the Eastern bloc and the strongest economy in COMECON. Unification created new challenges of maintaining the advances in the West and improving conditions in the East.

The integration of two different social and political systems created strains that are still one of Germany's major policy challenges. In addition, the nation faces many of the same policy issues as other European democracies: competing in a global economic system, dealing with the new issues of multiculturalism, and charting a foreign policy course in a changing world. This section describes the present policy programs and outputs of the Federal Republic. Then we discuss the policy challenges currently facing the nation.

The Federal Republic's Policy Record

For Americans who hear politicians rail against "big government" in the United States, the size of the German government gives greater meaning to this term. Over the past half century, the scope of German government has increased both in total public spending and in new policy responsibilities. Today government spending accounts for almost half of the total economy, and government regulations touch many areas of the economy and society. Germans are much more likely than Americans to consider the state responsible for addressing social needs and to support government policy activity. In summary, total public expenditures— federal, state, local, and the social security system—have increased from less than €15 billion in 1950 to €269 billion in 1975 and over €1 trillion for a united Germany in 2006, which is nearly 50 percent of the gross domestic product. That is big government.

Public spending in Germany flows from many different sources. Social security programs are the largest part of public expenditures; however, they are managed in insurance programs that are separate from the government's normal budget.

In addition, the Basic Law distributes policy responsibilities among the three levels of government. Local authorities provide utilities (electricity, gas, and water), operate the hospitals and public recreation facilities, and administer youth and social assistance programs. The states manage education and cultural policies. They also hold primary responsibility for public security and the administration of justice. The federal government's responsibilities include foreign policy and defense, transportation, and communications. Consequently, public expenditures are distributed fairly evenly over the three levels of government. In 2006 the federal budget's share was 28.3 percent, the state governments spent 25.9 percent, and the local governments spent 15.6 percent (plus the social insurance spending and other miscellaneous programs).

Figure 7.8 describes the activities of government, combining public spending by local, state, and federal governments, as well as the expenditures of the social insurance systems in 2002. Public spending on social programs alone amounted to €555.3 billion, more than was spent on all other government programs combined. Because of these extensive social programs, analysts often describe the Federal Republic as a welfare state—or more precisely, a social services state. A compulsory social insurance system includes nationwide health care, accident insurance, unemployment compensation, and retirement benefits. Other programs provide financial assistance for the needy and individuals who cannot support themselves. Finally, additional programs spread the benefits of the Economic Miracle regardless of need. For instance, the government provides financial assistance to all families with children and has special tax-free savings plans and other savings incentives for the average wage earner. The unemployment program is a typical example of the range of benefits available (see Box 7.4). For much of the FRG's early history, politicians competed to expand the coverage and benefits of such programs. Since the 1980s the government has tried to scale back social programs, but the basic structure of the welfare state has endured.

Unification has put this system (and the federal budget) to an additional test. Unemployment, welfare, and health benefits provided for basic social needs in the East during the difficult economic times following

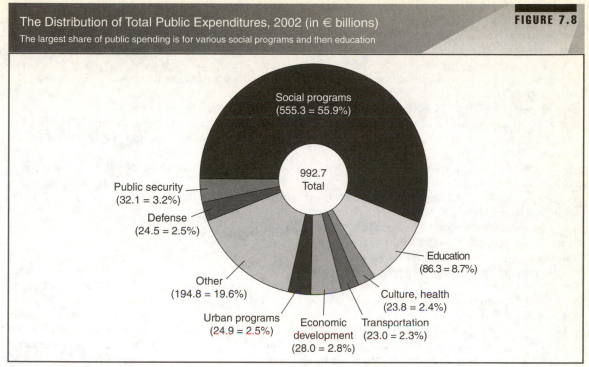

FIGURE 7.8

The Distribution of Total Public Expenditures, 2002 (in € billions)

The largest share of public spending is for various social programs and then education

Social programs
(555.3 = 55.9%)

992.7
Total

Public security
(32.1 = 3.2%)

Defense
(24.5 = 2.5%)

Education
(86.3 = 8.7%)

Other
(194.8 = 19.6%)

Culture, health
(23.8 = 2.4%)

Urban programs
(24.9 = 2.5%)

Economic
development
(28.0 = 2.8%)

Transportation
(23.0 = 2.3%)

Source: *Statistisches Jahrbuch für die Bundesrepublik Deutschland* (Berlin: Statistiches Bundesamt, 2005), p. 565.

unification. However, this effort cost several hundred billion Deutschmarks (DM; now euros) and placed new strains on the political consensus in support of these social programs, as well as the government's ability to provide these benefits (as discussed in the following section).

The federal government is also involved in a range of other policy activities. Education, for example, is an important concern of all three levels of government, accounting for about one-tenth of all public spending (see again Figure 7.8). The federal government is deeply involved in communications and transportation; it manages public television and radio, as well as owning the railway system.

In recent years the policy agenda has expanded to include new issues; environmental protection is

BOX 7.4

German Unemployment Benefits

An unemployed worker receives insurance payments that provide up to 67 percent of normal pay (60 percent for unmarried workers and those without children) for up to two years. After that, unemployment assistance continues at a reduced rate for a period that depends on one's age. The government pays the social insurance contributions of individuals who are unemployed, and government labor offices help the unemployed worker find new employment or obtain retraining for a new job. If the worker locates a job in another city, the program partially reimburses travel and moving expenses. These benefits are much more generous than those typically found in the United States and may be a factor in the higher unemployment rate in Germany.

the most visible example. Several indicators of air and water quality show real improvements in recent decades, and Germany has a very ambitious recycling program. The Green Dot system recycles about 80 percent of bottles used in commercial packaging, compared to about 20 percent in the United States. The SPD-Green government developed stronger policies for environmental protection, such as phasing out nuclear power, encouraging renewable energy, and initiating programs to limit global warming.

Defense and foreign relations are also important activities of government. More than for most other European nations, the FRG's economy and security system are based on international interdependence. The Federal Republic's economy depends heavily on exports and foreign trade; in the mid-1990s over one-fourth of the Western labor force produced goods for export, a higher percentage than for most other industrial economies.

The FRG's international economic orientation makes the nation's membership in the European Union (EU) a cornerstone of its economic policy. The FRG was an initial advocate of the EU and has benefited considerably from its EU membership. Free access to a large European market was essential to the success of the Economic Miracle, and it still benefits the FRG's export-oriented economy. Germany's integration into the EU has gradually grown over recent decades, as illustrated by the currency shift from the DM to the euro in 2002. The Federal Republic has also strongly advocated expanding the policy responsibilities and membership of the EU. At the same time, participation in EU decisionmaking gives the Federal Republic an opportunity to influence the course of European politics on a transnational scale.

The Federal Republic is also integrated into the Western military alliance through its membership in the North Atlantic Treaty Organization (NATO). Among the Europeans the Federal Republic makes the largest personnel and financial contributions to NATO forces, and the German public supports the NATO alliance. In the post–Cold War world, however, the threats to Germany's national security no longer come from the Warsaw Pact in the East. This has led to a reduction in overall defense spending to less than 3 percent of total public spending.

Public expenditures show the policy efforts of the government, but the actual results of this spending are more difficult to assess. Most indicators of policy performance suggest that the Federal Republic is relatively successful in achieving its policy goals. Standards of living have improved dramatically, and health statistics show similar improvement. Even in new policy areas such as energy and the environment, the government has made real progress. The opinions of the public reflect these policy advances (see Figure 7.9). In 2004 most Westerners were satisfied with most aspects of life that might be linked to government performance: housing, living standards, work, income, and education. Eastern evaluations of their lives lag behind those of the West, but still represent a marked improvement from the years immediately after unification.

Paying the Costs

The generous benefits of government programs are not, of course, due to government largesse. Individual and corporate taxes and financial contributions provide the funds for these programs. Therefore, large government outlays inevitably mean an equally large collection of revenues by the government. These revenues are the real source of government programs.

Three different types of revenue provide the bulk of the resources for public policy programs.[51] Contributions to the social security system represent the largest source of public revenues (see Figure 7.10). The health, unemployment, disability, retirement, and other social security funds are primarily self-financed by employer and employee contributions. For example, contributions to the pension plan amount to about 20 percent of a worker's gross monthly wages; health insurance is about 13 percent of wages; and unemployment is 6.5 percent. The various insurance contributions are divided between contributions from the worker and from the employer.

The next most important source of public revenues is direct taxes—that is, taxes that are directly assessed by the government and paid to a government office. One of the largest portions of public revenues comes from a personal income tax that the federal, state, and local governments share. The rate of personal taxation rises with income level, from a base of 15 percent to a maximum of 45 percent for high-income taxpayers (plus a solidarity surcharge to benefit the East). Even after the recent reforms of the tax rates, the German rates are still significantly higher than those in the United States. Corporate profits are taxed at a lower rate than personal income

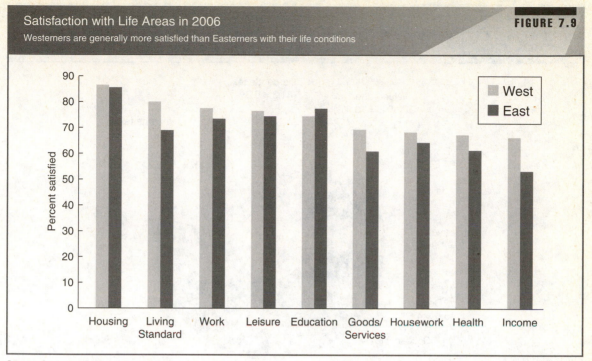

Satisfaction with Life Areas in 2006

Westerners are generally more satisfied than Easterners with their life conditions

FIGURE 7.9

Source: Statistisches Bundesamt, ed., *Datenreport 2006* (Berlin: Bundeszentrale für politische Bildung, 2006), pp. 443–444.

to encourage businesses to reinvest their profits in further growth.

The third major source of government revenues is indirect taxes. Like sales and excise taxes, indirect taxes are based on the use of income, rather than on wages and profits. The most common and lucrative indirect tax is the **value-added tax (VAT)**—a charge that is added at every stage in the manufacturing process and increases the value of a product. The standard VAT is 19 percent for most goods and 7 percent for basic commodities such as food. Other indirect taxes include customs duties and liquor and tobacco taxes. In 1999 the government introduced a new energy tax on the use of energy to create incentives for conservation and to provide additional government revenue. Altogether, indirect taxes account for about two-fifths of all public revenues. Indirect taxes—one of the secrets to the dramatic growth of government revenues—are normally "hidden" in the price of an item, rather than explicitly listed as a tax. In this way people are not reminded that they are paying taxes every time they purchase a product; it is also easier for policymakers to raise

indirect taxes without evoking public awareness and opposition. Indirect taxes are regressive, however; they weigh more heavily on low-income families because a larger share of their income goes for consumer goods.

The average German obviously has deep pockets to fund the extensive variety of public policy programs; U.S. taxation levels look quite modest by comparison. On average German workers pay about half of their income for taxes and social security contributions, compared with a rate of about 40 percent in the United States.

Even with these various revenue sources, public expenditures repeatedly have exceeded public revenues in recent years. To finance this deficit, the government draws on another source of "revenue"—loans and public borrowing—to maintain the level of government services. The costs of unification inevitably increased the flow of red ink. A full accounting of public spending would show deficits averaging more than €50 billion a year since union.

The German taxpayer seems to contribute an excessive amount to the public coffers, and Germans are

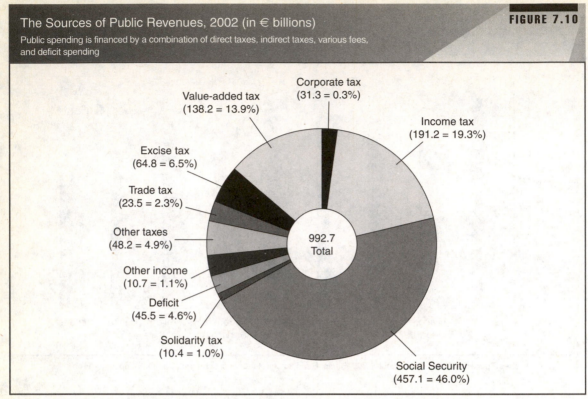

FIGURE 7.10

The Sources of Public Revenues, 2002 (in € billions)

Public spending is financed by a combination of direct taxes, indirect taxes, various fees, and deficit spending

Corporate tax
(31.3 = 0.3%)

Value-added tax
(138.2 = 13.9%)

Income tax
(191.2 = 19.3%)

Excise tax
(64.8 = 6.5%)

Trade tax
(23.5 = 2.3%)

Other taxes
(48.2 = 4.9%)

992.7
Total

Other income
(10.7 = 1.1%)

Deficit
(45.5 = 4.6%)

Solidarity tax
(10.4 = 1.0%)

Social Security
(457.1 = 46.0%)

Source: *Statistisches Jahrbuch für die Bundesrepublik Deutschland* (Berlin: Statistiches Bundesamt, 2005), p. 571.

no more eager than other nationalities to pay taxes. Yet, the current CDU/CSU–SPD government has further decreased corporate taxes, while raising income taxes on the highest earners. Still, the question is not how much citizens pay, but how much value is returned for their payments. In addition to normal government activities, Germans are protected against sickness, unemployment, and disability; government pension plans furnish livable retirement incomes. Moreover, the majority of the public expects the government to take an active role in providing for the needs of society and its citizens.

ADDRESSING THE POLICY CHALLENGES

The last decade has been a time of tremendous policy change and innovation for the Federal Republic as it has adjusted to its new domestic and foreign policy circumstances. While a government faces policy needs in

many areas, we discuss three prominent issues. The first is to accommodate the remaining problems flowing from German unification. The second is to reform the German economic and social systems. And the third is to define a new international role for Germany.

The Problems of Unification

Some of the major policy challenges facing contemporary Germany flow from the unification of East and West. Most observers were surprised by the sudden and dramatic collapse of the East German economic and social systems in the wake of the November 1989 revolution. During the first half of 1990, for instance, the gross domestic product of the GDR decreased by nearly 5 percent, unemployment skyrocketed, and industrial production fell off by nearly 60 percent.[52]

The most immediate economic challenge after unification was the need to rebuild the economy of the East, integrating Eastern workers and companies into the West's social market economy. The GDR's impressive growth statistics and production figures often papered over a decaying economic infrastructure and outdated manufacturing facilities. Similarly, the GDR was heavily dependent on trade with other COMECON nations. When COMECON ended with the collapse of communism in Eastern Europe, a major portion of the GDR's economy was destroyed.

The Currency Union in July 1990 was an experience in "cold turkey capitalism"—overnight the Eastern economy had to accept the economic standards of the Federal Republic. Even with salaries one-third lower in the East, productivity was still out of balance. Matching the Western economy against that of the East was like racing a Porsche against the GDR's antiquated two-cylinder Trabant—a race in which the outcome is foreordained.

The Federal Republic took several steps to rebuild the economy of the East and then raise it to Western standards. The government-directed Trust Agency (*Treuhandanstalt*) privatized the 8,000 plus firms that the GDR government had owned. All of these firms were sold off or closed by 1994, when the Treuhand itself was disbanded. However, privatization did not generate capital for investment as had been planned, and disputes about property ownership further slowed the pace of development. The sale of the GDR's economic infrastructure generated a net loss for the nation.

German unification had multiple economic by-products. The high levels of unemployment placed great demands on the Federal Republic's social welfare programs. Unemployed Eastern workers drew unemployment compensation, retraining benefits, and relocation allowances—without having made prior contributions to these social insurance systems. The FRG also took over the pensions and health insurance benefits of Easterners. The government spent massive amounts: from rebuilding the highway and railway systems of the East, to upgrading the telephone system, to moving the capital from Bonn to Berlin. In 1991, for example, the combined payments to the new Länder from official sources amounted to DM 113 billion (almost DM 7,000 per capita); this was more than twice Poland's per capita disposable income for the same year.[53] Even today, roughly 4 percent of the gross domestic product is transferred to the East.

Economic progress is being made. Recent economic growth rates in the East often exceed those in the Western states by a comfortable margin. However, the East-West gap is still wide. Unemployment rates in the East are still more than double the rates in the West, and even after years of investment, productivity in the East still lags markedly behind that of the West. Although standards of living in the East have rapidly improved since the early 1990s, they remain significantly below Western standards. Furthermore, even if the Eastern economy grows at double the rate of the West, it will take decades to reach full equality.

German unification also creates new noneconomic challenges. For example, the GDR had model environmental laws, but these laws were not enforced. Consequently, many areas of the East resembled an environmentalist's nightmare: Untreated toxic wastes from industry were dumped into rivers, emissions from power plants poisoned the air, and many cities lacked sewage treatment plants. The unification treaty called for raising the environmental quality of the East to Western standards. The cost of correcting the GDR's environmental legacy competes against economic development projects for government funding. Thus, unification intensified the political debate on the trade-offs between economic development and environmental protection.

Thus, despite the real progress that has been made since 1990, a real policy gap still exists between West and East. At the same time, Germans still pay an extra "solidarity surcharge" on their income tax that funds part of the Eastern reconstruction. Equalizing living conditions across regions remains a national goal, but it is a goal that will demand continuing resources and take decades more to accomplish.

Reforming the Welfare State

The *Wirtschaftswunder* (Economic Miracle) is a central part of the Federal Republic's modern history—but these miraculous times are now in the distant past. Contemporary Germany faces a series of new problems as its economy and social programs strain to adjust to a new global economic system.

For instance, business interests repeatedly criticize the uncompetitiveness of the German economy in a global economy. Labor costs are higher than in many other European nations and dramatically higher than labor costs in Eastern Europe and other regions. The generous benefits from liberal social services programs come at a cost in terms of employee and employer contributions. Other regulations impede the creation of new jobs or temporary employment. A recent report claimed that some German firms are mired in a spider web of government bureaucracy; they must provide sixty-two different datasets to government offices, file seventy-eight reports for social insurance, supply another sixty forms for tax purposes, and complete no less than 111 more to comply with labor laws. Thus, German unemployment remains relatively high, productivity has not grown as rapidly as experts might expect, and Germany faces pressures to change these public policies.

A related issue is the economic viability of Germany's social service programs. A rapidly aging population means that the demand for health care and pension benefits will steadily increase over time, but there are fewer employed workers to contribute to social insurance programs. For instance, in the 1950s there were roughly four employees for every person receiving a pension; by 2010 there will be fewer than two employees for every pensioner. Similar demographic issues face Germany's other social programs. As the population ages, health care costs have also increased.

The Schröder government commissioned a series of studies and blue-ribbon commissions to formulate policy reforms. In 2004 the government enacted a new reform program known as Agenda 2010. One set of measures reformed the labor market by easing employment rules, reducing the nonwage labor costs, and reforming the unemployment system. A second set of reforms reduced benefits in the pension and health care systems. The third set of reforms was to restructure the tax system.

While these reforms moved in a positive direction, many experts claimed that more was needed. The economy stagnated during Schröder's second term, which contributed to the government's loss in the 2005 elections. The economy began to grow in 2005, partially as a result of earlier reforms. The gross domestic product increased by 10 percent from 2005 to 2008, and unemployment edged downward.

Many analysts hoped the Grand Coalition of CDU/CSU and SPD would undertake a new round of reforms that would be even more far-reaching and reap even greater returns. However, Merkel has pursued a cautious course. Modest economic and social services reforms changed policies at the margins without dealing with the fundamental policy challenges. Then the German economy suffered as part of the global recession that began in 2008. The immediate economic priorities took precedence over longer term economic reforms. In addition, the citizens and the elites lack a political consensus on what policies are most desirable. Thus, these policy challenges will still face the new German government that forms after the 2009 Bundestag elections.

A New World Role

Paralleling its domestic policy challenges, the new Germany is redefining its international identity and its foreign policy goals. The Federal Republic's role in international politics is linked to its participation in the NATO alliance and the European Union. Both relationships are changing because of German unity.

In mid-1990 Russia agreed to continued German membership in NATO in return for concessions on the reduction of combined German troop levels; the definition of the GDR territory as a nuclear-free zone; and Germany's continued abstention from the development or use of atomic, biological, and chemical weapons. With unification, Germany became a fully sovereign nation and now seeks its own role in international affairs.

The new Germany will likely play a different military and strategic role because of these agreements and the changing international context. NATO existed as a bulwark of the Western defense against the Soviet threat; the decline of this threat will lessen the military role of the alliance. Moreover, Germany wants to be an active advocate for peace within Europe, developing its role as a bridge between East and West. The Federal Republic thus was among the strongest proponents of the recent expansion of EU membership to several East European nations.

The new Germany is also assuming a larger responsibility in international disputes outside the NATO region. In 1993 the Constitutional Court interpreted the Basic Law to allow German troops to serve outside of Europe as part of international peacekeeping activities. In 1998 Schröder survived a no-confidence vote on sending German soldiers into former Yugoslavia, which changed the course of German foreign policy. In mid-2008 German troops served in twelve nations as part of international peacekeeping efforts.

After Schröder's disagreements with the United States over the Iraq war, Merkel worked to restore Germany's relationship with the United States. Even in the case of Iraq, Germany assists the reconstruction through training and support programs that do not require a military presence in Iraq. There may be more disagreements between Merkel and her

SPD foreign minister Frank-Walter Steinmeier than between her and American foreign policy. But regardless of the outcome of the 2009 election, the Federal Republic will likely exercise a more independent foreign policy, within a framework of partnership with its allies.

Unification is also reshaping the Federal Republic's relationship to the European Union.[54] The new Germany outweighs the other EU members in both its population and its gross national product; thus, the parity that underlies the consensual nature of the EU will change. Germany has been a strong advocate of the EU, but this has sometimes made other Western members uneasy. For instance, Germany had pushed for the eastward expansion of the EU and strongly supported the euro, while other nations favor a slower course. And now with the new EU constitution on hold and difficult issues of further expansion of EU membership on the table, the debates on the future of the EU will intensify. At the least, it is clear that a united Germany will approach the process of European integration based on a different calculus than that which guided its actions for the previous forty years.

AFTER THE REVOLUTION

Revolutions are unsettling, both to the participants and to the spectators. Such is the case with the German revolution of 1989. Easterners realized their hopes for freedom, but they also have seen their everyday lives change before their eyes, sometimes in distressing ways. Westerners saw their hopes for German union

and a new peace in Europe a[...] stantial political and economi[...] Federal Republic is now forgi[...] litical identity that will shape i[...] tional policies. Many Germa[...] former border are hopeful ab[...] what the future holds for thei[...] public's neighbors wonder what role the [...] many will play in European and international affairs. Addressing these questions will test the strength of the Federal Republic and its new residents in the East.

Unification has clearly presented new social, political, and economic challenges for the nation. One cannot merge two such different systems without experiencing problems. However, these strains were magnified by the inability or unwillingness of elites to state the problems honestly and to deal with them in a forthright manner. As seen in the 2005 elections, Germans are divided on the direction they want the government to follow. To make further progress, Germany must reforge the social and political consensus that was a foundation for the Federal Republic's past accomplishments.

Unification has created a new German state linked to Western political values and social norms. Equally important, unity was achieved through a peaceful revolution (and the power of the DM), not blood and iron. The trials of the unification process are testing the public's commitment to these values. The government's ability to show citizens in the East that democracy and the social market economy can improve the quality of their lives is the best way to consolidate the political gains of unification and to move the nation's social development forward.

KEY TERMS

Adenauer, Konrad

Basic Law
   (*Grundgesetz*)

Bundesrat (Federal
   Council)

Bundestag (Federal
   Diet)

Christian Democratic
   Union (CDU)

Christian Social Union
   (CSU)

citizen action groups
   (*Bürgerinitiativen*)

codetermination
   (*Mitbestimmung*)

Confederation of
   German Employers'
   Associations (BDA)

Constitutional Court

constructive
   no-confidence vote

Economic Miracle
   (*Wirtschaftswunder*)

European Union (EU)

federal chancellor
   (*Bundeskanzler*)

federal president
   (*Bundespräsident*)

Federal Republic of
   Germany (FRG)

Federation of German
   Industry (BDI)

Free Democratic Party
   (FDP)

German Democratic
Republic (GDR)
German Federation of
Trade Unions (DGB)
The Greens
guest workers
(*Gastarbeiter*)
Hitler, Adolf

Kaiser
Kohl, Helmut
Die Linke
Merkel, Angela
National Socialist
German Workers'
Party (the Nazis)
neocorporatism

New Politics
Ostpolitik
Party of Democratic
Socialism (PDS)
peak association
proportional
representation (PR)
Republikaner (REP)

Schröder, Gerhard
Social Democratic Party
(SPD)
Socialist Unity Party
(SED)
Third Reich
value-added tax (VAT)
Weimar Republic

SUGGESTED READINGS

Anderson, Christopher, and Karsten Zelle, eds. *Stability and Change in German Elections: How Electorates Merge, Converge, or Collide*. Westport, CT: Praeger, 1998.

Ash, Timothy Garton. *In Europe's Name: Germany in a Divided Continent*. New York: Random House, 1993.

Bark, Dennis, and David Gress. *A History of West Germany*. 2 vols. 2nd ed. London: Blackwell, 1993.

Childers, Thomas, and Jane Caplan, eds. *Reevaluating the Third Reich*. New York: Holmes and Meier, 1993.

Fulbrook, Mary. *Anatomy of a Dictatorship: Inside the GDR, 1949–1989*. New York: Oxford University Press, 1995.

———. *History of Germany, 1918–2000*. Oxford, England: Blackwell, 2002.

Gellner, Winand, and John Robertson, eds. "The Berlin Republic: German Unification and a Decade of Changes," special issue of *German Politics* 11, no. 3 (December 2002).

Kershaw, Ian. *Hitler: A Biography*. New York: Norton, 2008.

Kolinsky, Eva. *Women in Contemporary Germany*. New York: Berg, 1993.

Kopstein, Jeffrey. *The Politics of Economic Decline in East Germany, 1945–1989*. Chapel Hill: University of North Carolina Press, 1997.

Krisch, Henry. *The German Democratic Republic: The Search for Identity*. Boulder, CO: Westview Press, 1985.

Langenbocher, Eric. *Launching the Grand Coalition: The 2005 Election and the Future of German Politics*. New York: Berghahn Books, 2006.

McAdams, James. *Germany Divided: From the Wall to Unification*. Princeton, NJ: Princeton University Press, 1993.

———. *Judging the Past in Unified Germany*. New York: Cambridge University Press, 2001.

Merkl, Peter, ed. *The Federal Republic at Fifty: The End of a Century of Turmoil*. New York: New York University Press, 1999.

Orlow, Dietrich. *A History of Modern Germany*. 5th ed. Englewood Cliffs, NJ: Prentice Hall, 2001.

Padgett, Stephen. *Organizing Democracy in Eastern Germany*. Cambridge, England: Cambridge University Press, 2000.

Padgett, Stephen, William Patterson, and Gordon Smith, eds. *Developments in German Politics 3*. London: Palgrave, 2003.

Rohrschneider, Robert. *Learning Democracy: Democratic and Economic Values in Unified Germany*. New York: Oxford University Press, 1999.

Sheehan, James. *German History 1770–1866*. New York: Oxford University Press, 1989.

Sinn, Gerlinde, and Hans-Werner Sinn. *Jumpstart: The Economic Unification of Germany*. Cambridge, MA: MIT Press, 1992.

Sinn, Hans-Werner. *Can Germany Be Saved? The Malaise of the World's First Welfare State*. Cambridge, MA: MIT Press, 2007.

Spielvogel, Jackson. *Hitler and Nazi Germany: A History*. 5th ed. Englewood Cliffs, NJ: Prentice Hall, 2005.

Turner, Henry. *Germany from Partition to Unification*. New Haven, CT: Yale University Press, 1992.

Vanberg, Georg. *The Politics of Constitutional Review in Germany*. New York: Cambridge University Press, 2005.

INTERNET RESOURCES

Bundestag: **www.bundestag.de**

Federal government: **www.bundesregierung.de**

German Information Center: **www.germany-info.org**

Politics in Germany (online textbook edition): **www.socsci.uci.edu/~rdalton/Pgermany.htm**

ENDNOTES

1. The First German Empire was formed in the ninth century through the partitioning of Charlemagne's empire. See Kurt Reinhardt, *Germany: 2000 Years,* vol. 1 (New York: Ungar, 1986).

2. Karl Dietrich Bracher, *The German Dictatorship* (New York: Praeger, 1970); Martin Broszat, *Hitler and the Collapse of Weimar Germany* (New York: St. Martin's Press, 1987).

3. Raul Hilberg, *The Destruction of the European Jews,* 3rd. ed. (New York: Holmes and Meier, 2003); Deborah Dwork and Robert Jan van Pelt, *Holocaust: A History* (New York: Norton, 2002).

4. Karl Hardach, *The Political Economy of Germany in the Twentieth Century* (Berkeley: University of California Press, 1980); Eric Owen Smith, *The German Economy* (London: Routledge, 1994).

5. Gregory Sandford, *From Hitler to Ulbricht: The Communist Reconstruction of East Germany, 1945–1946* (Princeton, NJ: Princeton University Press, 1983).

6. Forschungsgruppe Wahlen, *Politbarometer, June 2008* (Mannheim, Germany: Forschungsgruppe Wahlen, 2008).

7. Eva Kolinsky, *Women in Contemporary Germany* (New York: Berg, 1993); Pippa Norris and Ronald Inglehart, *A Rising Tide* (New York: Cambridge University Press, 2003); Russell Dalton, *Citizen Politics, 5th ed.* (Washington, DC: CQ Press, 2008), ch. 6.

8. Ruud Koopmans, Paul Statham, Marco Giugni, and Florence Passy, *Contested Citizenship: Immigration and Cultural Diversity in Europe* (Minneapolis: University of Minnesota Press, 2005); Richard Alba, Peter Schmidt, and Martina Wasmer, eds., *Germans or Foreigners? Attitudes Toward Ethnic Minorities in Post-reunification Germany* (New York: Palgrave Macmillan, 2003).

9. The Allied occupation authorities oversaw the drafting of the Basic Law and held veto power over the final document. See Peter Merkl, *The Origins of the West German Republic* (New York: Oxford University Press, 1965).

10. In 2002 the membership of the Bundestag was reduced from its previous size of 656. This resulted from redistricting to equalize the number of voters in each district.

11. The URL for the Bundestag is: www.bundestag.de.

12. Ludger Helms, "Keeping Weimar at Bay: The German Federal Presidency Since 1949," *German Politics and Society* 16 (Summer 1998): 50–68.

13. Donald Kommers, *Constitutional Jurisprudence of the Federal Republic* (Durham, NC: Duke University Press, 1989); Donald Kommers, "The Federal Constitutional Court in the German Political System," *Comparative Political Studies* 26 (1994): 470–491.

14. A second type of no-confidence vote allows the chancellor to attach a no-confidence provision to a government legislative proposal. If the Bundestag defeats the proposal, the chancellor may ask the federal president to call for new Bundestag elections. This tool was used by Kohl in 1983 and Schröder in 2005 to call for early elections.

15. Anna Merritt and Richard Merritt, *Public Opinion in Occupied Germany* (Urbana: University of Illinois Press, 1970); Ralf Dahrendorf, *Society and Democracy in Germany* (New York: Doubleday, 1967).

16. Christiane Lemke, "Political Socialization and the 'Micromilieu,'" in *The Quality of Life in the German Democratic Republic,* ed. Marilyn Rueschemeyer and Christiane Lemke (New York: M. E. Scharpe, 1989).

17. Gabriel Almond and Sidney Verba, *The Civic Culture* (Princeton, NJ: Princeton University Press, 1963); David Conradt, "Changing German Political Culture," in *The Civic Culture Revisited,* ed. Gabriel Almond and Sidney Verba (Boston: Little Brown, 1980).

18. Conradt, "Changing German Political Culture," pp. 229–231; Kendall Baker, Russell J. Dalton, and Kai Hildebrandt, *Germany Transformed: Political Culture and the New Politics* (Cambridge: Harvard University Press, 1981).

19. Deutsches Jugendinstitut, *Deutsche Schüler im Sommer 1990* (Munich: Deutsches Jugendinstitut, 1990).

20. Conradt, "Changing German Political Culture."

21. Gerald Braunthal, *Political Loyalty and Public Service in West Germany* (Amherst: University of Massachusetts Press, 1990).

22. Walter Friedrich and Hartmut Griese, *Jugend und Jugend forschung in der DDR* (Opladen, Germany: Westdeutscher Verlag, 1990).

23. Russell Dalton, "Communists and Democrats: Democratic Attitudes in the Two Germanies," *British Journal of Political Science* 24 (1994): 469–493; Frederick Weil, "The Development of Democratic Attitudes in Eastern and Western Germany in a Comparative Perspective," in *Democratization in Eastern and Western Europe,* ed. Frederick Weil (Greenwich, CT: JAI Press, 1993).

24. Richard Hofferbert and Hans-Dieter Klingemann, "Democracy and Its Discontents in Post-wall Germany," *International Political Science Review* 22 (2001): 363–378; Robert Rohrschneider, *Learning Democracy: Democratic and Economic Values in Unified Germany* (New York: Oxford University Press, 1999).

25. Ronald Inglehart, *Modernization and Postmodernization* (Princeton, NJ: Princeton University Press, 1997); Ronald Inglehart, *Culture Shift in Advanced Industrial Society* (Princeton, NJ: Princeton University Press, 1990).

26. See Chapter 3; Dalton, *Citizen Politics*, ch. 6.

27. Commission of the European Union, *Eurobarometer 67* (Brussels: European Union, 2007).

28. Christiane Lemke, "Political Socialization and the 'Micromilieu.'"

29. Meredith Watts et al., *Contemporary German Youth and Their Elders* (New York: Greenwood, 1989); Elizabeth Noelle-Neumann and Renate Köcher, *Die verletze Nation* (Stuttgart: Deutsche Verlag, 1987); Deutsches Jugendinstitut, *Deutsche Schüler im Sommer* 1990.

30. Peter Humphreys, *Media and Media Policy in Germany: The Press and Broadcasting Since 1945*, rev. ed. (New York: Berg, 1994).

31. Commission of the European Union, *Eurobarometer 63.4.*

32. Achim Koch, Martina Wasmer, and Peter Schmidt, eds., *Politische Partizipation in der Bundesrepublik Deutschland: Empirische Befunde und theoretische Erklärungen.* (Opladen, Germany: Leske and Budrich, 2001).

33. Wilhelm Bürklin, Hilke Rebenstorf, et al. *Eliten in Deutschland: Rekutierung und Integration* (Opladen, Germany: Leske and Budrich, 1997); Dietrich Herzog, Hilke Rebensstorf, and Bernhard Wessels, eds., *Parliament und Gessellschaft:* (Opladen, Germany: Westdeutscher Verlag, 1993).

34. Wilhelm Bürklin, "Einstellungen und Wertorientierungen ost-und westdeutscher Eliten 1995," in *Einstellungen und politisches Verhalten in Transformationsprozess*, ed. Oskar Gabriel (Opladen, Germany: Leske and Budrich, 1996); Rohrschneider, *Learning Democracy.*

35. Also see Chapter 4; Volker Berghahn and Detlev Karsten, *Industrial Relations in West Germany* (New York: Berg, 1989); Claus Offe, "The Attribution of Political Status to Interest Groups," in *Organizing Interests in Western Europe*, ed. Suzanne Berger (New York: Cambridge University Press, 1981), pp. 123–158.

36. Kathleen Thelen, *Union in Parts: Labor Politics in Postwar Germany* (Ithaca, NY: Cornell University Press, 1991).

37. Ruud Koopmans, *Democracy from Below: New Social Movements and the Political System in West Germany* (Boulder, CO: Westview Press, 1995).

38. The Republikaner and other small right-wing parties have not won Bundestag seats, but they have won seats at the state and local levels. See Hans-Joachim Veen, Norbert Lepszy, and Peter Mnich, *Die Republikaner Party in Germany: Right-Wing Menace or Protest Catchall?* (Westport, CT: Praeger, 1993); and Pietro Ignazi, *Extreme Right Parties in Western Europe* (Oxford, England: Oxford University Press, 2006).

39. Gerard Braunthal, *The German Social Democrats Since 1969,* 2nd ed. (Boulder, CO: Westview Press, 1994).

40. Thomas Poguntke, *Alternative Politics: The German Green Party* (Edinburgh: University of Edinburgh Press, 1993); Margit Mayer and John Ely, eds., *The German Greens: Paradox Between Movement and Party* (Philadelphia: Temple University Press, 1998).

41. Dan Hough, Michael Koss, and Jonathan Olsen, *The Left Party in Contemporary German Politics* (London: Palgrave, 2007).

42. If a party wins more district seats in a state than it should have based on its proportion of the second vote, the party is allowed to keep the additional seats and the size of the Bundestag is increased. In 2005 the actual Bundestag membership was 614.

43. A party that wins at least three district seats also shares in the PR distribution of seats. In 1994 and 1998, the PDS won four district seats in East Berlin, which earned it additional seats through the PR distribution. In 2002 the PDS won only two district seats.

44. Matthew Shugart and Martin Wattenberg, eds., *Mixed-Member Electoral Systems: The Best of Both Worlds?* (Oxford, England: Oxford University Press, 2001). Also see Chapter 4.

45. For voting patterns in prior elections, see Christopher Anderson and Karsten Zelle, eds., *Stability and Change in German Elections: How Electorates Merge, Converge, or Collide* (Westport, CT: Praeger, 1998); and Russell Dalton, "Voter Choice and Electoral Politics" in *Developments in German Politics* 3, Stephen Padgett, William Patterson, and Gordon Smith, eds. (London: Palgrave, 2003).

46. Vivien Schmitt, *The Futures of European Capitalism* (Oxford, England: Oxford University Press, 2002); Alec Stone Sweet, Wayne Sandholtz, and Neil Fligstein, eds., *The Institutionalization of Europe* (Oxford, England: Oxford University Press, 2001).

47. A constitutional reform in 2006 has changed the Bundesrat's legislative role. In exchange for greater state

autonomy in several policy areas, the Bundesrat's approval is no longer required for the passage of various administrative proposals. Analysts predict that under the new system only 30–40 percent of legislation will now require Bundesrat approval.

48. The European Court of Justice also has the power to evaluate German legislation against the standards of the EU agreements.

49. Alec Stone, "Governing with Judges: The New Constitutionalism," in *Governing the New Europe*, ed. Jack Hayward and Edward Page (Oxford, England: Polity Press, 1995).

50. Karen Alter, *Establishing the Supremacy of European Law: The Making of an International Rule of Law in Europe* (Oxford, England: Oxford University Press, 2001).

51. Arnold Heidenheimer, Hugh Heclo, and Carolyn Adams, *Comparative Public Policy*, 3rd ed. (New York: St. Martin's Press, 1990), ch. 6.

52. Gerlinde Sinn and Hans-Werner Sinn, Jumpstart: *The Economic Unification of Germany* (Cambridge, MA: MIT Press, 1992).

53. Sinn and Sinn, *Jumpstart*, pp. 24–25.

54. Maria Cowles, Thomas Risse, and James Caporaso, eds., *Transforming Europe* (Ithaca, NY: Cornell University Press, 2001); Desmond Dinan, *Ever Closer Union? An Introduction to the European Community*, 2nd ed. (Boulder, CO: Lynne Rienner, 1999).

ATLANTIC OCEAN

Bay of Biscay

GALICIA

ASTURIAS
CANTABRIA
BASQUE COUNTRY
Bilbao

NAVARRA
CASTILE y LEÓN
LA RIOJA

CASTILE-LEÓN

Duero

FRANCE

ANDORRA

Ebro
Saragossa

ARAGÓN

CATALONIA

Barcelona

MADRID

Madrid ⊛

Tagus

PORTUGAL

Lisbon ⊛

ESTREMADURA

Guadiana

CASTILE-LA MANCHA

VALENCIA

Valencia

Balearic Sea

Minorca

Majorca

Ibiza

Formentera

BALEARIC ISLANDS

MEDITERRANEAN SEA

Córdoba

Guadalquivir

Murcia

MURCIA

Sevilla

ANDALUSIA

Málaga

Strait of Gibraltar

N

CANARY ISLANDS
La Palma
Gomera
Hierra
Tenerife
Lanzarote
Fuerteventura
Gran Canaria

MOROCCO

ALGERIA

POLITICS IN SPAIN

Donald Share

Country Bio

SPAIN

Population
45.2 million

Territory
194,896 square miles

Year of Independence
1492

Year of Current Constitution
1978

Chief of State
King Juan Carlos

Head of Government
José Luís Rodríguez Zapatero

Language(s)
Castilian Spanish 74%, Catalan 17%,
Galician 7%, Basque 2%

Religion
Roman Catholic 94%, other 6%

Spain has largely overcome the legacy of forty years of authoritarian rule. It was one of the first nations in the Third Wave of democratization beginning in the 1970s, and its political future was initially uncertain. Today democracy is flourishing in Spain and is arguably as healthy there as in any European political system. This chapter analyzes Spain's development over this period and the challenges that remain.

CURRENT POLICY CHALLENGES

Early in the twenty-first century, Spanish democracy faces three serious policy challenges—terrorism, chronic unemployment, and immigration—and the first two are at least partly related to its legacy of authoritarian rule.[1]

Three decades after its transition to democracy, Spain continues to suffer from violence perpetrated by ETA, the pro-independence Basque terrorist organization that has killed over 800 Spaniards since

1975. Basque terrorism has its roots in the particular brutality with which Francisco Franco treated the Basque Country, a wealthy region of northern Spain, during his dictatorship (1939–1975). It has been sustained by a deeply polarized political environment within the Basque Country and the electoral success of Basque parties who support the goals (including an independent Basque Country), if not the tactics, of ETA. Spanish governments of the left and the right have failed to persuade ETA to abandon its armed struggle. Most recently, Prime Minister José Luis Rodríguez Zapatero's attempt to negotiate with ETA was foiled by the December 2006 terrorist attack on Madrid's airport. Efforts to defeat ETA militarily have had increasing success over the past decade, but Basque terrorism remains a serious challenge.

The single worst terrorist attack in Spain, the railway bombings of March 2004, killed almost 200 and injured about 1,400 people in Madrid. It highlighted a second challenge facing Spain: the dramatic growth of

Spain's immigrant population. Franco's isolated dictatorship severely limited immigration. Since Spain's entry into the European Union (EU) in 1986, there has been a rapid increase in immigration, mostly from Africa, Latin America, and Eastern Europe. In 1996 immigrants made up about 1 percent of the population, but by 2007 that figure had risen to almost 10 percent.[2] Spain's Muslim population has grown rapidly as large numbers of illegal immigrants have crossed the thirteen-mile Strait of Gibraltar in search of employment. Moroccans now make up about a quarter of all Spanish immigrants. They played a crucial role in Spain's recent economic boom, but also pose new challenges to Spanish society.

A network of mostly Moroccan Islamic terrorists carried out the 2004 bombing, and many of the terrorists were residents of Spain. To date Spain has not seen the emergence of the type of anti-immigrant political parties that have arisen in other European societies. Although some acts of violence have been aimed at immigrants, Spaniards have generally reacted with tolerance. However, polling data reveal a growing hostility toward immigrants that could be a source of future concern, and immigration has become a bitterly contested issue in domestic politics.[3]

A third problem facing Spanish policymakers is an unemployment level that stubbornly remains well above the European average. In large part this is the result of Spain's transition from a highly protected economy to an increasingly global one. Franco had achieved labor quiescence and near-full employment through repression, laws that prevented layoffs of workers, protectionism, and massive emigration. With Spain's democratization and integration into the EU, governments of the right and left have cautiously (some argue too cautiously) liberalized the economy, reducing the state role, making labor laws more flexible, and ending subsidies to Spain's many inefficient industries. Despite these efforts, by 2000 Spanish labor laws were still among the most restrictive in Europe, and vestiges of Franco's statist economy were still evident. The results were predictable: Unemployment rose from 4.5 percent on the eve of the transition to 20.8 percent ten years later and remained in double digits until quite recently. Only in the late 1990s did Spain start to create new jobs at a pace sufficient to reduce unemployment. The unemployment rate (near 17 percent in 2009) is among the highest in Europe and poses a formidable challenge to Spanish policymakers. In monthly polls unemployment is regularly named as one of Spain's most pressing problems.

THE HISTORICAL LEGACY

All U.S. schoolchildren learn the significance of 1492 in American history. That date is even more significant for Spain. In the events of that year, we can observe the major themes that dominated Spanish history from the fifteenth century to the present (Figure 8.1).

First and foremost, the date represents the victory of the **Reconquista**, the Catholic reconquest of the Iberian Peninsula from the Moors. The Moors were nomadic African Muslims who crossed the Strait of Gibraltar in 711 and occupied most of the peninsula for more than seven centuries. Their presence added immeasurably to Spanish culture and society. The Moorish influence on architecture, music, cuisine, and language is still evident 500 years after their forced expulsion (along with Spain's Jews) in 1492. Spain's long isolation from the rest of Christian Europe led many Spaniards (including Francisco Franco) to argue that Spain was (and should remain) fundamentally distinct from its European neighbors. This legacy also frames the current debate over how Spain should view its growing Muslim minority.

Second, the expulsion of the Moors was made possible by the political unification and centralization of a previously fragmented Iberian Peninsula. Ferdinand and Isabel, the monarchs of Spain's most important independent kingdoms, were married in 1492, uniting much of the peninsula in a single, centralized state. This unification is often credited with facilitating the building of Spain's vast global empire from the fifteenth to the nineteenth centuries. However, some Spaniards never completely accepted a centralized Spain. Many formerly independent peoples, including the Basques and the Catalans, stubbornly resisted centralization and maintained separate languages, cultural identities, and even some political institutions. The struggle between center and periphery in Spanish politics continues to this day.

Third, the fierce military struggle by Catholics to unify Spain and expel the Moors set a precedent for repressive authoritarian rule. The victorious Catholic monarchs expelled all religious minorities from Spain and established the notorious **Spanish Inquisition**, a tribunal used to enforce strict moral, religious, and political uniformity throughout Spain's empire. The dominant role given military leaders in the Reconquista and in the creation of Spain's vast American empire set the stage for numerous *pronunciamientos* (military uprisings) during the nineteenth and twentieth centuries.

Timeline of Major Events in Spanish Political History

FIGURE 8.1

1492	Reconquest of Spain by Catholic monarchs and expulsion of Moors
1812	Short-lived Liberal Constitution proclaimed
1898	Loss of last major pieces of Spanish empire (Cuba and Philippines)
1931–1936	Spanish Second Republic
1936–1939	Spanish Civil War
1939–1975	Authoritarian regime of Francisco Franco
1975	Death of Francisco Franco and the beginning of transition to democracy
1977	Restoration of democratic elections
1978	Democratic constitution approved in a referendum
1982	First alternation in power as Socialists win elections
1986	Spain joins the European Union
1996	Conservative Popular Party under José María Aznar wins election, ending fourteen years of Socialist government
2004	Election of Socialists under José Luis Rodríguez Zapatero

Finally, Columbus arrived in the New World in 1492, marking the start of Spain's imperial experience. The immensity and wealth of Spain's empire gave rise to a national pride (some would say arrogance) that rivaled British nationalism. When the rigidly centralized and overly bureaucratized empire began a slow and painful decline in the eighteenth century, many Spaniards were unable to accept that reality. The loss of Spain's last colonies, Cuba and the Philippines, in 1898 marked the end of the Spanish Empire. By then Spain had become an impoverished and peripheral European nation, but many Spaniards continued to wallow in Spain's past glory, rather than accepting the need for political and economic change. Some Spaniards blamed the forces of modernity for having accelerated the loss of empire and the subsequent economic decline. Others argued that the backwardness of Spain's economy and the rigidity of its political structures were responsible for Spain's demise. They called for economic reform and democratization. This dispute between what have been dubbed the **two Spains** partly explains the political chaos of the nineteenth century, during which liberals (who tended to favor republican forms of government) and conservatives (who tended to favor authoritarian monarchies) repeatedly dislodged each other from power. The Constitution of 1812, for example, was one of Europe's earliest constitutions, and it embodied ideas that were very liberal and democratic for its time. It was short lived, however, as Ferdinand VII abolished it in 1814. Between 1812 and 1931, Spain had seven different constitutions, four of which were liberal and three conservative.

During the **Spanish Second Republic (1931–1936)**, the forces of the two Spains met head on.[4] Antimonarchical liberals and socialists founded the Republic, and its constitution contained protections for democracy, regional decentralization, and secularism. Conservative forces immediately felt threatened by the rapid political changes, especially measures that weakened the Catholic Church and the central state. The left controlled government from 1931 to 1933, while the right governed from 1934 to 1935. When a leftist coalition won the 1936 elections, forces of the right, led by a conservative sector of the Spanish military, launched a rebellion against the Republic.

The **Spanish Civil War (1936–1939)** was the defining event of twentieth-century Spanish history, and the brutality of that conflict traumatized an entire generation of Spaniards. When the rebels under the leadership of **Francisco Franco** declared victory, they set out to destroy democracy and its supporters in Spain once and for all. Franco was particularly vindictive toward the losers of the war. He imposed laws that made it a crime to have supported the Republic, and his regime executed thousands of the Republic's supporters and exiled hundreds of thousands more. The government banned political parties and independent trade unions and imposed strict censorship on the press. The regime centralized all political power in Madrid; fused executive, legislative, and judicial power; and made Franco dictator for life. The Catholic Church's official status and privileges were restored, and manifestations of regional culture, including the speaking of regional languages, were banned. The severe repression during the first three decades of Francoist rule quashed the democratic opposition. Franco eased the repression in the 1960s, and protest activity increased, but rapid economic growth during that period helped preserve the regime's strength.

Many feared that the death of Franco in 1975 would rekindle a conflict between the two Spains. Instead, Spain's transition to democracy between 1975 and 1978, after four decades of authoritarianism, has been hailed as a model of peaceful regime change. The transition to democracy was not only peaceful, but also appears to have resolved two of the historical cleavages, regime type and church and state, that formed the basis of the struggle between the two Spains. The center-periphery cleavage persists, but no longer directly threatens democratic rule.

DEMOCRACY AND SPAIN'S HISTORICAL CLEAVAGES

Monarchy Versus Republic—or Both?

The transition to democracy was accomplished peacefully for several reasons. First, members of the Franco regime, not the democratic opposition, initiated it. Opposition to Franco was strong and growing, but it alone could not force the regime to democratize. The transition to democracy was stewarded by **King Juan Carlos**, Franco's handpicked successor as head of state, and **Adolfo Suárez**, a former Francoist bureaucrat and Juan Carlos's second prime minister. Second, the transition to democracy was carried out within the existing laws of the Franco regime. The laws that called for the first democratic elections and the dissolution of the Francoist legislature, for example, were passed according to the Francoist legal

process. Third, key leaders of the transition not only promoted democratic change, but also assumed a leading role in the early years of the new democracy. Adolfo Suárez, the last authoritarian prime minister, became the first democratically elected prime minister. The last authoritarian head of state, Juan Carlos, became the first head of state under the democratic Constitution of 1978.

Finally, many aspects of the transition to democracy were negotiated between the Francoist reformers and the democratic opposition.[5] The negotiated nature of the transition helps explain why the Constitution of 1978 was purposely vague on a number of key issues, including regional devolution. Moreover, the negotiated transition meant that there were never any purges or prosecutions of Francoist officials for human rights abuses or corruption, nor until very recently were there any official attempts to condemn the Francoist past or to erase the symbols of Franco's regime. Herein lies what may be the chief asset of Spain's transition to democracy. The historical enmity between advocates of different types of political regimes was virtually eliminated by Spain's transition. Francoist loyalists were assured that the Franco regime implemented (indeed legislated) the transition to democracy and were assuaged by the continued presence of Franco's handpicked successor in the role of head of state. Today democrats can take comfort from the fact that Spain's democracy is fully established and widely supported, even by the historically antidemocratic Spanish right. Both sides can be relieved that the change of regimes took place without much bloodshed, in marked contrast to the bitter precedent set during the Spanish Civil War.

Church and State: Bridging the Religious Divide

The feud over the proper role of the Catholic Church in Spanish society has been explosive. Maintaining a key role in Spain's history, the Church was a central actor in the counterreformation, and the Spanish Inquisition, an institution run by the Spanish Church that epitomized religious intolerance, was not abolished until the 1830s. Many liberals and leftists viewed Spain's decline as the result of its cultural and economic backwardness, and the dominant historical role of the Church was seen as a chief culprit. Church supporters rallied to defend their privileges and blamed the forces of secularism for Spain's problems. From the Napoleonic Wars of the early nineteenth century to the 1930s, Spain experienced a protracted and often violent struggle between the Church and liberal opponents. During this period the Church begrudgingly accepted the end of the old regime and a loss of much of its power, but it was able to secure generous state financial support from weak liberal regimes and dominated important institutions, like education. The religious cleavage exploded during the Spanish Second Republic when a republican regime attempted to secularize Spain and limit the Church's role in Spanish politics. Secular forces, angered over the Church's historical support for authoritarian rule and convinced of the need to modernize Spain, advanced an antagonistic anticlerical agenda that was deeply offensive to many Spaniards and turned many against democracy. Repression of the Church (including expulsion of religious orders and attacks on clergy) during the Republic quickly turned the Church into one of Franco's major supporters.

Church support for Franco paid off handsomely. A thoroughly united Church emerged triumphant from the Spanish Civil War, and it no longer needed to seek compromises with liberal regimes. The Franco regime was unabashedly Catholic from the start, and all other religions were initially banned and repressed. The Church was given control over marriage, was allowed to run about half of all Spanish schools, and was handed the reins of state censorship. The Francoist state lavished the Church with generous economic benefits.

The Church was a pillar of Franco's regime, but by the mid-1950s some within the Church began to distance themselves from authoritarian rule. Reformist currents of thought in Rome began to influence the Spanish Church, and in the 1960s sectors of the Church represented one of the most serious sources of opposition to Franco. The Church was thus divided on the eve of Spain's transition to democracy. Some conservative Catholic organizations (like the secretive lay society, the Opus Dei) advocated the continuation of authoritarian rule, while other sectors of the Church wholeheartedly endorsed democratization. Given the historical intensity of the religious cleavage, many observers were surprised by the relatively neutral role the Church assumed during the transition to democracy. However, as noted later in this chapter, there is lingering evidence of religious controversy in Spanish politics.

Resolving the Center-Periphery Cleavage

Another historical trademark of Spanish politics has been the center-periphery cleavage. Many readers may think of Spain as a single nation with a single language. However, most residents of Barcelona, Bilbao, and Valencia, for example, would take issue with this characterization. They would note that Spain currently contains many regional ethnic identities (**Basques**, **Catalans**, **Galicians**, **Castilians**, etc.) and that there are many Spanish languages (Basque, Catalan, Galician, etc.) in addition to Castilian, what most foreigners inaccurately call "Spanish." An ardent advocate of centralism would reject this characterization of Spain.

There has been much speculation about the causes of Spain's intense regionalism. For centuries Spaniards have been more loyal to their families, towns, and regions than to the central state. Spain is one of Europe's largest countries, and its mountainous terrain and poor infrastructure historically isolated communities from one another. Until the late 1970s, car travel between Madrid and Barcelona (about 300 miles), Spain's two largest cities, took nine hours. There may also be historical reasons for the intensity of Spanish regionalism. The invasion of the Moors from North Africa in 711 shattered a budding national identity and forced the retreating Christians into isolated "statelets." During much of the long struggle to retake the Iberian Peninsula from Muslim forces, these isolated regions retained significant autonomy. Attempts to unify Spain under a centralized monarchy were far from complete. The image of a unified Catholic Spain that built a vast global empire obscures the reality of persistent regional identity.

Another foreign invasion, this time by Napoleon at the start of the nineteenth century, was also unable to extinguish regionalism despite the Napoleonic penchant for centralization. Attempts to abolish the historical privileges of the Basque Country, for example, gave rise to a fierce, politically conservative Basque nationalism, known as Carlism. Two bitter and protracted wars waged by Carlist forces (in 1841 and 1876) were unable to restore regional privileges in the Basque Country, but they helped intensify the center-periphery cleavage. By the end of the nineteenth century, there was considerable popular support in the Basque Country and Catalonia, two of the wealthiest and most industrialized regions of Spain, for greater political autonomy from Madrid.

During the Spanish Second Republic, the center-periphery cleavage intensified. Republican leaders actively supported autonomy for the Basque Country and Catalonia. These moves, and calls by radical nationalists in both regions for outright independence, frightened the Spanish right and helped precipitate the Civil War. Basques and Catalans were cruelly punished for their support of the Republic, and both regions experienced some of the harshest repression during and after the Civil War. Perhaps the most famous symbol of this repression is Pablo Picasso's *Guernica,* a painting depicting the aerial bombardment of a Basque town in 1937. Franco immediately revoked political and economic autonomy and harshly circumscribed the use of regional languages—street names were "Castilianized"—and cultural practices. This repression, particularly ruthless in the Basque Country, gave rise in the 1950s to new Basque separatist and terrorist movements, which constituted the single greatest threat to the Franco regime.

The regional cleavage remained potentially explosive on the eve of Spain's transition to democracy. Strong regional movements existed in Catalonia and the Basque Country. Spain's military and much of the Spanish right vehemently objected to any kind of federalism, and they steadfastly opposed threats to the "unity of Spain." As described later, the Constitution of 1978 struck some unusual and not completely successful compromises in an attempt to resolve the regional question in Spanish politics.

Economics and the Weakening of Historical Cleavages

To a remarkable extent, Spain's transition to democracy overcame the cleavages of regime type, church and state, and center-periphery. By Franco's death in 1975, however, economic growth and the concomitant social and cultural changes had already done much to erode the passions these schisms aroused. In comparative perspective Spain stands out because its transformation from an underdeveloped, largely agrarian country to a modern urban country occurred in a very short time. At the turn of the twentieth century, most of the population lived in villages and small towns. By the 1960s an economic "miracle" turned Spain into a largely urban country; today about 80 percent of Spaniards live in urban settings. The economic boom also contributed to a more secular and less isolationist culture. During the 1960s

unemployment led to a massive emigration of labor. Simultaneously, hordes of foreign tourists began to discover Spain's beaches. Tourist development, combined with industrialization and economic growth, thus created a new politically and socially tolerant middle class.

STRUCTURE AND PROCESS OF THE POLITICAL SYSTEM

The Constitution of 1978: The Constitution of Consensus

After Franco's death the new democratic regime, embodied in the Constitution of 1978, resulted from a set of complex negotiations between the left and the right. The Constitution gained considerable legitimacy in a November 1978 referendum, when 87.8 percent of the voters approved it, and it became law on December 27, 1978.

The Constitution borrows heavily from other European countries. It is the longest and most complex constitution in Spanish history, and some aspects of it are imprecise and vague, in part due to compromises required by Spain's unusual transition. Figure 8.2 provides an overview of the institutions of Spanish government as established by the Constitution.

Spain's Constitution establishes a parliamentary system in which voters elect the lower house of the legislature (parliament), whose members then select the prime minister from among its members (normally the leader of the largest party in the lower house). The main components of Spain's parliamentary system are described below.

The Monarchy

The Constitution defines Spain as a constitutional monarchy, which initially drew strong opposition from the Spanish left. In principle the creation of a monarchy in the 1970s was anathema to the left not only because it was an unabashedly elitist institution, but also because it installed Juan Carlos de Borbón, Franco's handpicked successor, as king. Worse, Juan Carlos was not even the legitimate Bourbon heir to the throne. He was the grandson of Alfonso XIII, the last reigning Bourbon monarch, and the son of the legitimate heir, Don Juan de Borbón. During the Franco regime, Don Juan lived in exile and openly opposed the dictator. Curiously, he allowed his son

FIGURE 8.2

Structure of the Spanish Government

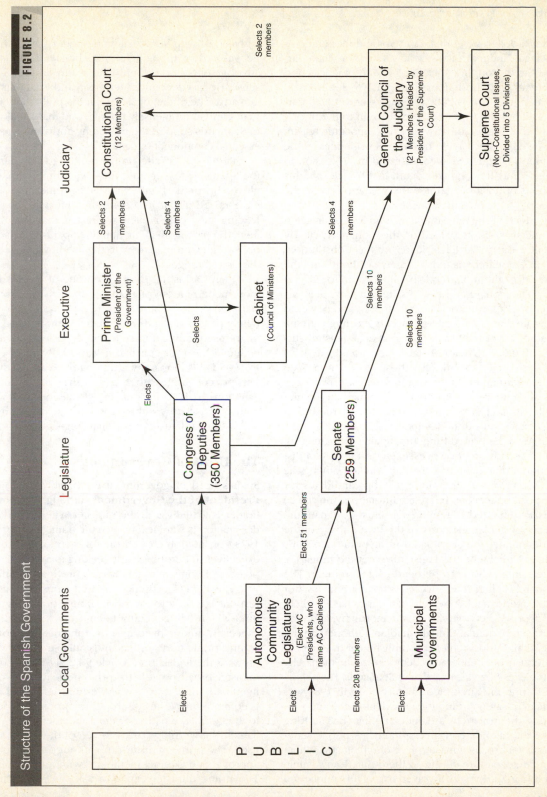

Juan Carlos to be educated in Spain under Franco's tutelage. Under Franco's close supervision, Juan Carlos was thoroughly socialized in the practices and protocol of authoritarian Spain. In 1969 Franco designated Juan Carlos to be his successor, yet Juan Carlos's father did not renounce his right to the throne until after Franco died, when the democratic reform was well under way. Juan Carlos's willingness to be Franco's designated successor and his accession to the throne after Franco's death in 1975 (despite his father's opposition) tainted the young prince in the eyes of the democratic opposition.

Much of the left's initial resistance was mitigated by the strict limits placed on the monarchy, clearly spelled out in Articles 56–65 of the Constitution. Spain's monarchy is today largely symbolic, and the powers of the monarch leave little room for discretion. The monarch is head of state, but more of an arbiter than a key actor. The monarch has no power to legislate, but is entitled to a weekly meeting with the head of government in order to keep abreast of current affairs. The head of state does promulgate laws and issue decrees, but only those already approved by the parliament. One of the greatest powers enjoyed by the monarch is that of commander in chief of the armed forces, a power that proved crucial during Spain's transition to democracy.

As in the United Kingdom, Spain's monarch can, under certain circumstances, exercise a degree of discretion. The monarch is charged with appointing the prime minister from among the top candidates for the post, but except in rare circumstances, the choice is strictly limited. The monarch must designate the leader of the largest party in the lower house of the parliament as the candidate for the prime minister's office. Ultimately, the legislature, not the monarch, determines who is to be head of government. The monarch's chief role is to act as Spain's ambassador to the world, a job in which Juan Carlos has excelled.

For a variety of reasons, the monarchy, and Juan Carlos in particular, initially had an authoritarian image. Juan Carlos's chief accomplishment has been to cautiously but deliberately democratize the monarchy in the eyes of a vast majority of Spaniards. His behavior during the attempted military coup in 1981 was crucial in safeguarding the new democracy and validating the monarchy's democratic image. The King generally avoids controversy, and his public statements are usually a masterpiece of diplomacy. When, in a rare departure during an Ibero-American summit, King Juan Carlos was involved in a highly publicized verbal joust with Venezuelan president Hugo Chávez, he was widely applauded for his behavior. He is an advocate of political compromise, calm, and common sense. He has denounced terrorism and is an outspoken advocate of democracy. Opinion polls show that Juan Carlos is immensely popular and that a majority of Spaniards support the monarchy and view it as an essential component of democracy.

Perhaps as a reflection of the King's popularity, the Spanish press treated the royal family with kid gloves up until about 1990, when some questions were raised about its "jet-setting" lifestyle. Spain's leading newspaper even suggested that the King might be having an affair. Still, the Spanish press has not savaged the monarchy to the extent witnessed in the United Kingdom.

Juan Carlos has established one of the world's most modern, least ostentatious, and least controversial monarchies. There is no royal court. The royal family pays taxes and lives relatively modestly, having refused to live in the Palacio de Oriente, a huge eighteenth-century palace in Madrid. By some estimates Spain's monarchy is among the least costly in Europe, costing less than half of that of the United Kingdom. Juan Carlos is a very visible monarch who regularly visits towns throughout Spain, occasionally addressing audiences in regional languages.

The Head of Government

Spain's head of government is officially called the **President of the Government**, although the office-holder is actually a prime minister. The "President" designation is significant, since the framers of Spain's 1978 Constitution created one of the most powerful executives in Europe, clearly seeking to avoid the impotence of prime ministers of both previous republics.

The 1978 Constitution created a prime minister responsible only to the lower house of the legislature, which has generally been a meek institution, especially under majority governments. Moreover, Spain's prime minister has unusually strong powers vis-à-vis the legislature. Article 98.2 gives the prime minister broad powers to form and lead a government and, in contrast to the Westminster model that is common in Western Europe, to appoint anybody to the Cabinet, whether or not a member of the parliament's governing party or even of the parliament itself. The prime minister can without parliamentary approval add Cabinet members "without portfolio." The prime minister can also ask the monarch to dissolve the legislature (though only once per year and not while a motion of censure against the government is being considered).

After parliamentary elections the monarch selects a prime minister–designate who must then win a vote of investiture in the lower house. Once elected, the prime minister may serve for a maximum of four years, but there are no limits to the number of times that a prime minister may be reelected. The prime minister can request a vote of confidence at any time during his or her term of office. **Felipe González**, prime minister between 1982 and 1996, called and won such a vote in April 1990. The prime minister may be ousted by the legislature only if legislators can agree on a replacement (Article 113). The legislature cannot, however, remove an unpopular prime minister alone: The entire government falls whenever a head of government is ousted, making the constructive vote of no confidence (also known as censure) a measure that is likely to be employed rarely.

Table 8.1 lists the thirteen governments and six prime ministers since the death of Franco. Three heads of government, Adolfo Suárez, Felipe González, and José María Aznar, have dominated the office and shaped its powers. Adolfo Suárez (1976–1981), despite having immense prestige associated with his stewardship of the transition to democracy, was a very weak

head of government beholden to the leaders of his coalition's factions. The minority status of both of his governments exacerbated his dependence on his squabbling coalition partners. Suárez's more conservative successor, Leopoldo Calvo Sotelo (1981–1982), was equally weak due to his lack of charisma, his coalition's rapid disintegration, and the continuing minority status of his government.

Felipe González, a Socialist, was elected in 1982 in the first alternation of power in the young democracy. From 1982 to 1989, he presided over the first single-party majority government in Spanish history and was thus in a perfect position to enhance the powers of his office. Moreover, during much of that time he faced a disorganized and demoralized political opposition. Beginning with the elections of 1989, González's strength slowly began to erode and from 1993 to 1996 he presided over a minority government. Many observers argued that the immense powers granted to the government, the timid legislature, and the Socialists' long tenure in power had created the conditions under which corruption thrived. Indeed, the corruption scandals that plagued Socialist administrations in the 1990s were largely responsible for their fall from power.

The conservative José María Aznar (1996–2004) was first elected in 1996, but his Popular Party (PP)

Spanish Heads of Government, 1974–2008				**TABLE 8.1**
Head of Government	**Term**	**Party**	**Elected by Cortes After General Elections?**	**Minority, Coalition, or Majority Government?**
Carlos Arias Navarro	1974–1975	Appointed by Franco		n/a
Carlos Arias Navarro	1976–1976	Appointed by King		n/a
Adolfo Suárez	1976–1977	Appointed by King		n/a
Adolfo Suárez	1977–1979	UCD	yes	Minority
Adolfo Suárez	1979–1981	UCD	yes	Minority
Leopoldo Calvo Sotelo	1981–1982	UCD	no	Minority
Felipe González	1982–1986	PSOE	yes	Majority
Felipe González	1986–1989	PSOE	yes	Majority
Felipe González	1989–1993	PSOE	yes	Minority
Felipe González	1993–1996	PSOE	yes	Minority
José María Aznar	1996–2000	PP	yes	Minority
José María Aznar	2000–2004	PP	yes	Majority
José Rodríguez Zapatero	2004–2008	PSOE	yes	Minority
José Rodríguez Zapatero	2008–	PSOE	yes	Minority

Source: Adapted from Paul Heywood, "Governing a New Democracy: The Power of the Prime Minister in Spain," *West European Politics* 14, no. 2 (April 1991): 98.

lacked a parliamentary majority. He was forced to work with regional parties in order to maintain a parliamentary majority until his party obtained an absolute majority in the March 2000 elections. Aznar was the first post–Franco era conservative to govern Spain. He clearly established the democratic credentials of a modern conservative party. He presided over an extraordinary economic boom, but his foreign policy was extremely controversial, especially his support of the Iraq War. Aznar set an important precedent by deciding not to seek a third term in office, choosing to leave the party in the hands of his handpicked successor.

Spanish heads of government are strongest when their parties are unified. Indeed, given the constitutional advantages enjoyed by prime ministers, it is fair to say that the most significant limits to their power come from within their own parties. Thus, from 1982 to 1990, the Socialists maintained iron (some would say quasi-authoritarian) internal party discipline, and this greatly enhanced the power of Felipe González.[6] After 1990, due to a series of corruption scandals, internal party dissent increased, there were calls for an internal democratization of the party, and González lost some power. José María Aznar was an even more successful party manager, and he maintained strong discipline within his ranks during both of his terms.

It is still too early to tell whether Spain's current prime minister, José Luis Rodríguez Zapatero, deserves to be considered a particularly influential prime minister. His first term accomplished a great deal of social reform, and he led the Socialists to a second term in government in the 2008 elections.

Two prime ministers, Adolfo Suárez and Felipe González, used their immense personal charm and charisma to enhance their power in office. Unlike in some parliamentary systems, Spain's prime ministers have generally remained aloof vis-à-vis the legislature and their own party. González, for example, went long periods without appearing in the parliament (there is no constitutional requirement for the prime minister to appear before the legislature). Near the end of his stint in power, he was clearly much more interested in foreign than domestic affairs.

Even though the parliament does not exercise much control over the head of government, it would be a mistake to argue that Spain's prime minister has limitless power. During the first two decades of Spain's democracy, prime ministers often appeared to make decisions that represented compromises with entrenched political interests, both domestically and internationally. As late as the 1980s, for example, Prime Minister González reversed his own (and his party's) position on taking Spain out of the North Atlantic Treaty Organization (NATO). He did so in part to mollify the Spanish military, which favored NATO membership, and in part to satisfy business interests, which viewed NATO membership and Spain's desired membership in the EU as conjoined. José María Aznar's decision, despite overwhelming popular opposition, to support the U.S.-led invasion of Iraq (breaking with France and Germany, Spain's traditional European allies) contributed to the conservatives' upset loss in the 2004 general elections.

The Legislature

Spain's Constitution specifies that the parliament, the **Cortes Generales** or Cortes, is the repository of national sovereignty (Article 1.3). However, although Spain is formally a parliamentary system, its legislature has not been the most powerful political institution. The framers of the Constitution took great pains to create a strong executive and in the process weakened the legislature.

The negotiated transition to democracy also initially weakened the Cortes. In order to avoid potentially dangerous political confrontation, most key policies during the first years of democracy resulted from an informal consensus among party elites. This consensus ended in 1979, and from 1979 to 1982, there was a precarious minority government. However, by 1982, when the Spanish Socialist Workers Party (PSOE) won the first absolute majority in the young democracy, the party easily controlled the Cortes because of its voting strength and extraordinary party discipline. From 1982 to 1989 and again from 2000 to 2004, there were majority governments that had no effective political opposition, so they could ignore the opposition and further weaken the parliament. After 1989, when the Socialists lost their majority, and under the 1996–2000 conservative minority government, the Cortes became more assertive and adversarial.

Spain's legislature consists of two houses: the **Congress of Deputies** (lower house) and the **Senate** (upper house) (see again Figure 8.2). Each house elects a president, and the President of the Congress of Deputies is the equivalent of the Speaker of the British House of Commons. The chamber presidents have the power to enforce the rules of their respective houses. The King formally proposes prime ministerial candidates to the lower house's president.

Both houses are organized around "party groups" comprised of a minimum of deputies (fifteen in the lower house or five or more deputies who won at least 15 percent of the vote in a given region). Most parliamentary groups are made up of deputies from the same party. Members who do not have a party group to join (members of small, mostly regional parties) are forced to join the "mixed group." Party groups, in turn, dominate the running of each chamber. They determine who is allowed to participate in debate and who sits on committees. Party group leaders become the big hitters within the legislature, and in each house they sit on the Council of Party Spokesmen, chaired by the chamber president. This group sets the agenda for the legislature and assigns tasks to committees.

Congress of Deputies The lower and more powerful house of the legislature contains 350 members elected to four-year terms. The Congress of Deputies must pass all national laws and budgets. Yet, compared with their European counterparts, Spain's parliamentarians are fairly weak. The vast majority of laws passed by the Cortes originate with the government.[7] The Cortes strictly limits the activities of individual members to influence legislation, and officially designated parliamentary groups introduce almost all legislation that originates within the Congress.

The legislature has yet to play much of a "watchdog" role and has generally been ineffective in controlling the executive. The Constitution's framers saw to it that the Cortes could not assert itself too boldly vis-à-vis the executive branch. The **constructive vote of no confidence**, similar to that used in Germany, requires the members of the Congress of Deputies to agree on a replacement for the prime minister before they can vote out the incumbent. To date no prime minister has been removed from office by such a vote. In its first twenty years, the Congress of Deputies produced few investigative commissions of real importance. However, more recently, the Cortes has asserted itself more. As in the United Kingdom, Spanish members of parliament question Cabinet members during a weekly question time. Parliamentary groups may force a public debate on key policy issues in order to embarrass or challenge the government. Either house of parliament can require Cabinet members to testify at hearings.

Parliamentary committees do play a crucial role in the legislative process. Every proposed law must be scrutinized and approved and can be amended by standing committees. Since the majority party in the Cortes has always dominated the committees, governments get their way with most legislation, but committees can and sometimes do substantially alter legislative bills.

The role of the Cortes as a recruiting mechanism for executive positions is limited because Cabinet members do not need to be members of the parliament, though in fact about 60 percent are. There is higher turnover in the Spanish legislature than in most Western European legislatures. This is partly due to the low prestige and few incentives attached to being a deputy. The Cortes is not well connected to the organized interests or decisionmaking centers, and a 1983 law prohibits a member of parliament from holding certain jobs. In addition, salaries are very low, and resources available to deputies are strictly controlled by leaders of the parliamentary groups. Individual deputies thus have relatively little power.

The day-to-day weakness of the Cortes should not obscure the crucial legitimating function it performed in the consolidation of democracy in June 1977, when it was the only elected body in the country. The relative balance among parliamentary forces encouraged cooperation among them. Initially, the Cortes played a key role in ratifying agreements. Parliamentary representatives from different regions pushed through regional autonomy accords. A small number of parliamentarians representing most political groups in fact wrote the Constitution.

The Senate Spain's upper house is composed of 259 members, 208 elected under a plurality system that has made it far less representative than the lower house and 51 indirectly elected through Spain's 17 **Autonomous Communities**, identified in the map at the beginning of this chapter. The Senate was originally intended to be representative of Spain's regions, but the parliaments of the Autonomous Communities, rather than the Senate, have performed this function. The Senate suffers because it is widely regarded as a superfluous body. Its main power is that it has two months to review bills passed by the Congress of Deputies. Several Spanish governments and senators themselves have called for an overhaul of the chamber to make it truly representative of the Autonomous Communities, but such reform will require a constitutional amendment, and to date the political will has been lacking.[8]

Spain's lower house, the Congress of Deputies, is charged with the most important duties—formally electing the prime minister, approving or rejecting votes of confidence submitted by the prime minister, passing censure motions against the government, ratifying decrees or laws, passing the government budget, and authorizing states of emergency. The Senate can initiate legislation, but this rarely happens, and it can amend lower-house laws, but the amendments must always be hammered out in a joint Congress of Deputies–Senate committee. A simple majority in the Congress can override Senate amendments and vetoes of Congress legislation. The Senate can delay legislation for a maximum of two months for ordinary bills and twenty days for urgent ones. The Spanish Senate thus has far more power than the British House of Lords, but considerably less than the U.S. Senate.

The Legislative Process

Most laws originate as Council of Ministers–sponsored *proyectos de ley* (government bills), although *proposiciones de ley* (private-member bills) occasionally pass. Figure 8.3 illustrates how such proposals become law. Once sent to the Congress of Deputies leadership and published in the official bulletin of the Congress, a bill is sent to a legislative committee for amendments. A legislative proposal that survives this scrutiny must then be approved by a majority of the Congress. Once it has obtained a majority in the Senate, the bill is submitted to the monarch (who must ratify it within fifteen days) and published in the official State Bulletin.

The Judicial System

Reforming Spain's judicial system was one of the greatest challenges facing the democratic regime.[9] Under the Franco regime, the courts had little independence, and the government directly appointed most judges. The courts were identified with harsh repression against those who opposed the dictatorship. As late as September 1975, and despite an international outcry, Francoist courts sanctioned the execution without trial of Basque terrorists arrested under martial law.

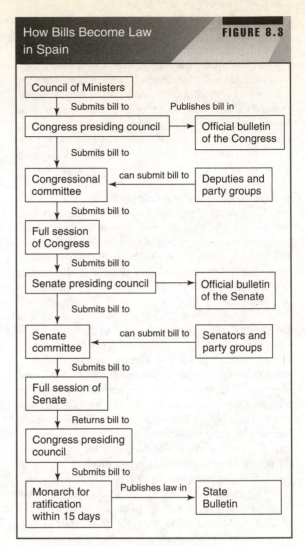

How Bills Become Law in Spain

FIGURE 8.3

Source: Peter J. Donaghy and Michael T. Newton, *Spain: A Guide to Political and Economic Institutions* (Cambridge, England: Cambridge University Press, 1987), p. 59.

In an attempt to depart from this authoritarian legal tradition, the 1978 Constitution established a **Constitutional Court** as the supreme arbiter in political disputes and attempted to give it independence from the state. The Court consists of 12 members, all professional lawyers or judges. The Cortes selects eight of the judges (four per house, approved by three-fifths of its members); the government proposes two names, subject to the legislature's approval; and the General Council of the Judiciary (discussed later) names the final two. Its members must be independent of any party and cannot actively participate in them. Members are appointed to nine-year terms, with a third of the Court renewed every three years. The government or legislature cannot dismiss Constitutional Court judges, and the Court controls its own budget and organization.

The Constitutional Court can declare any law or government decree unconstitutional; it has the power to rule on a direct appeal by the prime minister, fifty members of either house, assemblies of Spain's Autonomous Communities, or lower court judges. In some cases individual citizens may appeal to the Court if they feel that their constitutional rights have been violated. The legislature or the government may also ask the Court to rule on the constitutionality of pending legislation.

To date, the Constitutional Court has played a significant role in limiting Spain's government. For example, in 1983 it ruled unconstitutional a major law intended to rationalize (and in some cases slow down) the devolution of power to Spain's Autonomous Communities. In 1993 it struck down key provisions of a government antiterrorism bill that would have facilitated police searches of private homes. The conservative opposition has unsuccessfully appealed to the Constitutional Court in an attempt to overturn a whole host of social reform legislation passed by the Zapatero government since its election in 2004, including the controversial legalization of same-sex marriages.

For matters that are not of a constitutional nature, the highest court is the **Supreme Court (Tribunal Supremo)**. The powers of the Supreme Court have been eroded by the creation of the Constitutional Court (generally seen as the most powerful court in Spain) and by the devolution of many of its powers to the Autonomous Communities. Still, the Supreme Court has the final word in the enforcement of the penal code. In July 1988 the Supreme Court demonstrated its power and independence when it sentenced a former Socialist Cabinet member to prison for his role in a government-sponsored antiterrorist death squad.

Each of the seventeen Autonomous Communities has its own High Court of Justice *(Tribunales Superiores de Justicia),* which oversees the administration of justice in each region. These are the highest courts at the regional level and are charged with, among other things, resolving electoral disputes. Each high court has three chambers dealing with civil/penal, administrative, and social matters.

One of the most interesting offices created by the 1978 Spanish Constitution is the **Defensor del Pueblo**, or Ombudsperson, appointed by the Cortes for a period of five years. Because the appointment requires the approval of a three-fifths majority in each house, the Defensor is intended to be a nonpartisan individual. The position was designed to be a watchdog over the administration and to investigate citizen complaints in their dealings with officialdom. The Defensor reports yearly to the Cortes with a summary of complaints against state agencies.

The Spanish judiciary is supervised by the General Council of the Judiciary, created in an attempt to insulate judges from political pressure. The Council has twenty members, ten approved by each house of the legislature, for five-year terms.

The Spanish judiciary has clearly made a lot of progress since the Franco regime. Spanish judges cannot be easily removed by the government, are forbidden from holding any other public office, and cannot be members of any political party or trade union. Since the 1980s the judiciary has played an increasingly aggressive role in combating corruption and overturning governing policies. In a number of highly publicized corruption scandals beginning in 1990, Spanish judges were put in the spotlight, investigating and prosecuting cases against a variety of top Spanish officials. These investigations greatly enhanced the prestige of Spain's judiciary, converting some judges into national heroes with name recognition and popularity ratings rivaling those of the top political leaders (see Box 8.1).

While some Spanish conservatives suspected that the Socialist governments of the 1980s and 1990s manipulated the judiciary, those governments tended to view the judiciary and its increasingly assertive behavior as conservative and anti-Socialist. During the long Socialist tenure in office, the judiciary attempted to prevent government incursions against civil liberties. In the context of rapidly rising crime and the continued war against terrorism, and as an attempt to mollify the police and military, the Socialists passed the Public Security Law and gave permanent status to a controversial 1977 antiterrorism law. These measures, among other things, gave police broad powers to enter private homes without a court order if they suspected criminal activity and to hold suspects incommunicado for long periods of time. In 1995 Prime Minister González admitted that police units had top political leaders under surveillance, increasing

Some Spanish judges have become celebrities in the international arena, as well as at home. Baltazar Garzón, a young, independent, and aggressive investigative judge of Spain's National Court, has become an international phenomenon due to his attempt to bring former Latin American military rulers to justice for human rights abuses committed against Spanish citizens during the 1970s and 1980s. Garzón formally requested the extradition of former Chilean dictator Pinochet (who was receiving medical treatment in the United Kingdom) to Spain in 1998, provoking strong opposition from the Chilean government. Despite obvious opposition to Garzón's action (the Aznar government did not want to endanger Spain's close relations with Latin America), the government made no attempt to stop the extradition. The British ultimately refused to extradite Pinochet, but the incident was another sign of the growing independence and prestige of Spain's judiciary. In April 2005 Garzón sentenced a former Argentine naval officer to 640 years in prison for human rights abuses under the Argentine military junta in the 1970s and 1980s.

Garzón has also waged a long-standing campaign against Basque terrorism, seizing assets from the radical Batasuna party and ordering organizations associated with terrorism to pay damages for terrorist attacks. In late 2003 Garzón brought charges against international terrorist Osama Bin Laden.

In October 2008 Garzón ordered the first judicial investigation into executions of political prisoners during the Franco era. Garzón called for the opening of nineteen mass graves thought to contain the bodies of opponents of Franco who were summarily executed during the Franco dictatorship. Garzón's order drew protests from some Spanish conservatives who accused the judge of reopening old wounds.

demands on the courts for protection of civil liberties against a powerful government. Spanish civil libertarians sought protection from the courts and were partly successful in weakening the law. In 1999 Spain's Constitutional Court dealt a blow to the Aznar government when it overturned the convictions of twenty-three Basque politicians who had been jailed for airing an election broadcast that allegedly supported Basque terrorists. In short, a healthy tension between the government and the judiciary has been an important feature of Spain's political culture.

Spain's Autonomous Communities

Despite the long history of regional nationalism, Spanish history offers no precedent for a successful decentralization of power. Past attempts to give autonomy to Spain's regions (usually Catalonia and the Basque Country) alienated the Spanish right, and attempts at decentralization during the Second Republic helped provoke the Spanish Civil War and precipitated the destruction of democracy. Under Franco all power was centralized in Madrid. Provincial governors,

appointed by the dictator and under direct orders of the Ministry of the Interior, ran local government and appointed local officials. Thus, the founders of Spain's democracy after Franco's death addressed this issue with caution. After protracted debate and much compromise, the 1978 Constitution attempted to establish a middle ground between federalism (favored by the left and by regional nationalists) and a unitary state (favored by the right). The result, agree almost all observers, is a confusing and often contradictory arrangement.

Spain's 1978 Constitution recognizes the right to regional autonomy through the Autonomous Communities (ACs), carefully avoiding the terms *state* and *nation* and not defining what an AC is or specifying the exact powers it enjoys. The Constitution left the nuts and bolts of the autonomy-granting process to future legislatures. Moreover, as a result of the interparty bargaining process (in which the Catalans, but not the Basques, were directly represented), the Constitution provided for a faster route to autonomy for "historic" regions like Catalonia, the Basque Country, and Galicia, which had a history of separate languages and national identity. While all regions aspiring to AC status had to apply for it and complete a tedious set of procedures, the historic regions faced far fewer obstacles.

By 1979 autonomy statutes had been approved for Catalonia and the Basque Country, setting off a frenzy in which every region of Spain demanded autonomy. This resulted in the formation of seventeen ACs through **devolution**, a chaotic process that frustrated regional nationalists and centralizing rightists alike and that may have encouraged the attempted coup of February 1981 (the coup leaders had plans to rein in the devolution process). As a result of the attempted coup, the governing center-right Union of the Democratic Center (UCD), together with the opposition Socialists, passed a controversial measure designed to slow down the devolution process. The measure gave Spanish law priority over AC law, even in the historic regions. Infuriated Basques and Catalans got the Constitutional Court to throw out about one-third of the law in 1983, effectively killing the measure. By then the governing Socialists were not as jittery about a military coup, and they began to expedite devolution. By February 1983 all seventeen Autonomous Communities were in place, and by the end of that year, all had held a regional election.

Currently, all ACs have their own statutes of autonomy, and each has its own unicameral legislature, a president, an AC public administration, and an AC High Court of Justice. However, unlike in purely federal systems, each AC has slightly different powers, depending on the negotiations between Madrid and the AC and on the timing and route to autonomy taken by the AC. The AC government of the Basque Country, for example, had the greatest amount of power. By the early 1990s, the Socialist government made efforts to transfer identical powers to all ACs, raising fears among Catalans and Basques that they were being stripped of their special privileges as "historic" ACs. Under current rules regional and central governments share powers in many areas (education, health, law and order, and civil service, among others), but not in those areas specifically reserved for the central government (defense, foreign policy, and economic policy, among others). In practice the exact powers enjoyed by the central government and the ACs remain vague. However, even under the conservative Aznar governments, the process of devolution, though uneven, continued, and AC governments today have more power than ever.

Since the 2004 election of Socialist Prime Minister Zapatero, three ACs (Catalonia, Valencia, and Andalucia) have had revised autonomy statutes approved by the legislature and via regional referendums. The most controversial revision was the new Catalan Autonomy Statute (approved in 2006), which defines Catalonia as a nation, grants it greater control over its tax revenue, and requires public-sector employees to know Catalan. The Popular Party and even some within the Socialist Party opposed that statute. The head of the Spanish Army was arrested and removed after he stated that the statute endangered the unity of the Spanish state, and thus might justify military intervention. Zapatero hopes to revise all 17 Autonomy Statutes by the end of his second term. However, Zapatero's support for greater regional autonomy was not unlimited. When in 2004 the Basque regional government proposed a referendum that would define the Basque Country's relationship to Spain as one of "free association," in what many saw as a prelude to independence, Zapatero opposed the measure, and the legislature rejected it.

SPANISH POLITICAL CULTURE

During Franco's traditional authoritarian regime, Spaniards were encouraged to stay out of politics and to focus their attentions on their families, their work, and other diversions such as sports and the state-controlled television. Spain became a political desert, and fear of police repression kept it that way for the vast majority of Spaniards. Public opinion research conducted during Franco's rule documented the consequences of authoritarian rule for Spain's political culture. When Spaniards were asked in 1966 whether "it is better for one person to have all the authority and make all the decisions for us, or for a group of people elected by all citizens to make the political decisions," only 35 percent opted for the more democratic answer.[10] At the time of the democratic transition, about one-half of Spanish respondents gave authoritarian responses on this and other questions.

By the 1960s, however, Spain's isolation from the democratic world had ended due to emigration, tourism, increasing exposure to European ideas, and the concomitants of economic growth. Studies conducted in the 1960s and 1970s began to document the modernization of Spain's political culture. Still, on the eve of the transition, many scholars pondered whether a democracy could be constructed with Spain's authoritarian culture.

Such fears have proved to be unfounded. With a few exceptions, after three decades of democracy the political culture of Spaniards is no longer very different from that of other European countries. By 1980, 50 percent of Spanish survey respondents agreed that "democracy is preferable to any other form of government," and by 2000 that figure had risen to 88 percent, similar to other European democracies.[11] A 2008 survey showed that 66 percent of Spanish respondents were very or fairly satisfied with democracy, among the highest levels within the EU (the EU average was 58 percent). Fifteen percent claimed to be dissatisfied with democracy in Spain, far less than the EU average of 22 percent.[12] The fear that the economic crisis of the mid-1970s and the persistence of extraordinarily high levels of unemployment might erode the legitimacy of democratic rule proved unwarranted. Indeed, Spanish survey results demonstrate that "support for democracy rose despite poor state performance" and confirm that the behavior of Spanish political elites and the centrist orientation of Spain's party system prevented political polarization that might otherwise have overwhelmed Spain's young democracy.[13]

Spain may have a democratic political culture, but legacies of authoritarian rule remain, and in some ways Spain's political culture deviates from the European norm. Spaniards continue to express less interest in politics and participate less in politics than do most of their Western European counterparts. Spanish political parties and trade unions have the lowest per capita membership in Western Europe, and confidence in those institutions is especially weak (see Figure 8.4). According to the 1996 World Values Survey, only 36 percent of Spaniards

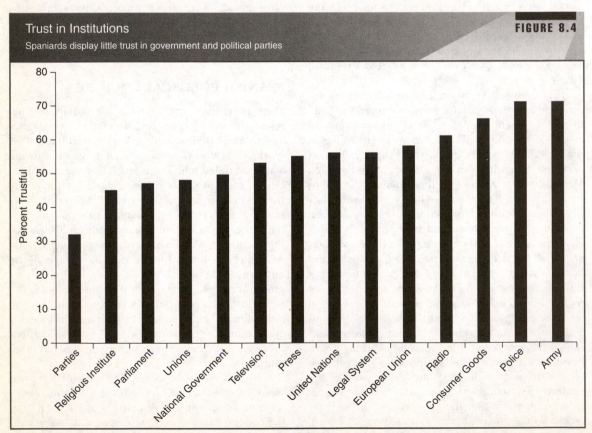

Trust in Institutions   **FIGURE 8.4**

Spaniards display little trust in government and political parties

Source: *Eurobarometer 68* (Fall 2007). Downloaded from http://ec.europa.eu/public_opinion/archives/eb/eb68/eb68_en.htm. Figure presents the percentage of respondents expressing trust in each institution.

reported membership in any organized group.[14] Fewer Spaniards identified with a political party than did the citizens of most other industrial democracies. Spaniards interviewed for opinion research continue to express very low levels of trust in their politicians and very low political efficacy.[15]

Yet, there is little evidence to support the idea that Spain is experiencing a crisis of political participation.[16] Recent opinion studies suggest that most types of political participation have either remained stable or increased slightly. Spaniards are increasingly likely to associate with political groups that are independent from political parties or trade unions. Spain ranked third among West European countries in a measure of the amount of popular protest activity, and Spaniards have consistently taken to the streets in large numbers to contest a whole host of issues across the political spectrum.[17] Younger Spaniards, who were not subjected to Franco's depoliticization, score roughly the same as do their European counterparts, suggesting that they have a different, more democratic political culture than their elders. Moreover, despite Spaniards' lack of political participation, voter turnout has remained relatively robust (though somewhat lower than elsewhere in Europe).

Spain's global sociopolitical orientations are broadly similar to those of other European societies. Spaniards are moderately inclined toward social reformism, and very few take extreme positions on any issue. Spaniards generally rank the values of liberty and equality about equal.

A number of researchers have studied the major political cleavages in society. One study concluded that region, religion, and class, together with generational conflict, are the "master cleavages of Spanish politics."[18] However, in contrast to the Second Republic, Spain is now overwhelmingly urban, literate, and industrialized. Reduced church attendance, greater geographical mobility, emigration, and exposure to mass media have made Spain a less parochial society. The intensity of these "master cleavages" therefore has diminished considerably, and they no longer threaten democratic rule. Moreover, none of the cleavages is closely linked with partisan identification, a factor that has facilitated the consolidation of democracy.

The regional cleavage, initially feared to be the intractable schism most likely to undermine Spanish democracy, is less important than expected. This has partly been the result of the massive internal demographic shift within Spain that brought many immigrants to the Basque Country and Catalonia. These immigrants are less parochial and more attached to a Spanish national identity. Only in the Basque Country and, to a lesser extent, in Catalonia are there significant feelings of alienation toward the Spanish state. Because the regional cleavage is not strongly related to left and right (there is a weak relationship between regionalism and leftism), the danger posed by the regional cleavage has been lessened.

Moreover, the intensity of regional nationalism is not even easily related to the attachment to a regional language.[19] Indeed, in the Basque Country, where radical and violent nationalism has been strongest, 57 percent of those polled claim that they cannot understand Euskera, the regional language. In Catalonia 97 percent of respondents claim to understand Catalan, but nationalism there has been far more moderate than in the Basque Country. In Galicia 99 percent of respondents claim to understand the regional language, but radical nationalism has been virtually nonexistent.

POLITICAL SOCIALIZATION

Education

Contemporary Spain is a highly educated and literate nation. Only 2 percent of Spaniards (mostly older citizens) are illiterate. Franco invested significant resources in education during the economic boom of the 1960s, and since democratization Spain's educational system has received a considerable boost. Unlike in the United Kingdom, education in Spain has been remarkably accessible to people of all social classes and to women (there are more women students than men students in Spanish universities), and there is little of the elitism surrounding education that exists in the United Kingdom. The desire to obtain a college education, for example, does not vary considerably among classes. There is no Spanish equivalent of Britain's Oxford or Cambridge and no well-established hierarchy among Spain's universities.

About one-third of schoolchildren are educated at private schools, half of which are owned by religious orders and the rest secular. Because of the shortage of schools, early democratic governments, like their predecessors from the Franco regime, allowed some Catholic private schools to provide state-subsidized places for students. In return the Socialists required private schools to set standardized admissions procedures and form representative governing bodies. In addition, teachers in these private schools were paid directly by the state, giving the state greater control. Students in these schools had the option of not taking religion classes. These and other measures were deeply resented by many middle-class parents, and by the Catholic Church, as state encroachment on their educational freedom. Protests over Socialist educational policy produced some of the largest mass demonstrations of the democratic period, but the protests and an appeal to the Constitutional Court failed to stop the reforms. Currently about 90 percent of secular private schools and 98 percent of religious schools are run with taxpayers' money.

The Socialists made educational reform one of their chief priorities, and in the early 1990s, they overhauled the entire structure of Spanish education. The government attempted to alleviate a significant source of educational inequality by providing free preschool for children ages 4 to 6. Spanish children now start primary education at age 6 and then progress to secondary education (ages 13 to 16). Students can then leave school or pursue a *Bachillerato* (high school diploma) from ages 16 to 18. After completing this degree, students can either enter university or attend state-funded vocational schools. A higher percentage of Spaniards attend university than in the United Kingdom, France, or Germany. However, given the high rate of course repetition (due to the high failure rate in Spanish university courses), the real figure is probably quite a bit lower.[20] The relatively open access to higher education produces serious overcrowding at the relatively small number of Spanish universities.

The Role of the Media

Visitors to Spain often note the plethora of periodicals on news kiosks and are impressed with their variety and sophistication. However, a 2004 survey showed that only 27 percent of Spaniards read a newspaper daily, well below the EU average of 41 percent.[21] Yet, newspaper readership has grown quickly since the birth of democracy. Moreover, the relative absence of tabloids, which are so popular in other European countries, partly explains the low readership statistics. Even the most sensationalistic

Spanish dailies contain serious news coverage. Despite small readership, the Spanish press has often played an important role in politics. During the PSOE tenure in office, during the 1980s and early 1990s, when there was little parliamentary opposition and scrutiny, the press brought a number of important scandals to the public's attention.

Television, however, is the most important medium in Spain, and it has been argued that "Spain is a nation of TV addicts."[22] After the British, Spaniards spend more time than any other Europeans watching TV. One study showed that about 70 percent of Spaniards formed their political views based on what they had seen on television.[23]

Given the importance of television, control of that medium has been a political tempest since 1977. Prime Minister Suárez, a former director of the Francoist television monopoly, RTVE (Spanish Radio and Television), dragged his feet when it came to relinquishing state control of the electronic media. Once in office, the PSOE continued to manipulate the electronic media, and state television was unabashedly pro-government in the 1986 NATO referendum.

Slowly, however, the state monopoly of the electronic media has decreased, in part because of the creation of regional television channels. Spain's state television monopoly ended in 1990 with the birth of private television channels. According to one expert on the media, the Socialists begrudgingly granted privatization of television, but this "is likely to be seen with hindsight as one of their most valuable contributions to the consolidation of democracy, comparable with their taming of the army."[24] Despite the proliferation of private television and radio outlets since that time, the state is still the biggest owner of mass media. Private television has eroded the state monopoly, but by 2002 TVE-1 (the main state network) still topped the ratings (with about a 32 percent market share).[25]

INTEREST GROUPS

Under Franco the state controlled virtually all interest groups and incorporated both employees and employers in a state-dominated organization. Even the Catholic Church was subject to state control. During the transition organized interests played a secondary role and were not a crucial force pressuring for democratization.

Trade Unions

Franco's regime depended on labor repression and exclusion, despite some liberalization in the 1960s. Opposition trade unions differed in their approach to the Francoist trade union structure. The Communist **Workers' Commissions (CC.OO)** sought to infiltrate the official trade unions, while the PSOE-affiliated **General Confederation of Workers (UGT)** boycotted them. In the democratic period, these two trade union organizations became the chief rivals for the allegiance of Spanish workers.

Spain has the lowest unionization rate in Europe, and unions are divided ideologically, tactically, and regionally. Today only about fifteen percent of salaried workers are unionized, down from a high of 57.8 percent in 1978; much higher figures are found in Italy, Greece, and Turkey.[26] The weakness of trade unions would lead one to expect a high level of labor conflict, and, indeed, over the last decade, Spain has had the second highest strike rate in Europe (see Figure 8.5).

Although organizationally weak, Spanish trade unions have considerable influence. The 1980 Workers Statute codified worker representation in the workplace and gave trade unions a role in the process. In firms with ten to fifty employees, workers are represented by up to three elected delegates. In larger firms workers' councils are elected. Unions that elect at least 10 percent of council delegates are entitled to participate in collective bargaining negotiations. Workers can vote for representatives even if they do not belong to a union, an unusual feature that contributes to low levels of union membership. Thus, even though union membership is low, 80 percent of Spanish workers vote in workers' council elections.

The role of trade unions changed during the first two decades of democracy. The UGT and the CC.OO entered the democratic period as "transmission belts" for the leftist parties with which they were affiliated. Ties between the UGT and the PSOE were especially strong. PSOE members were required to join the UGT

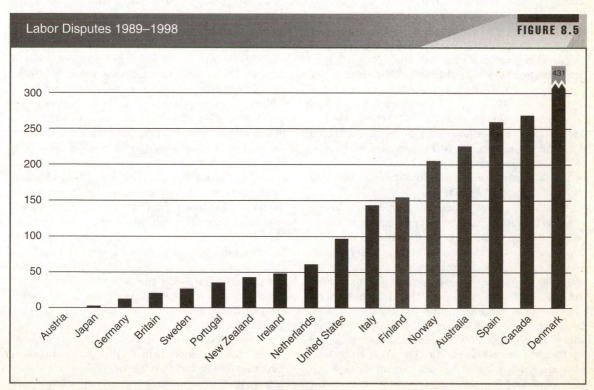

Labor Disputes 1989–1998   FIGURE 8.5

Source: Office for National Statistics. *The Economist*, April 22, 2000, p. 96.

and to work with the union. A similar, but somewhat looser relationship existed between the CC.OO and the PCE, the Spanish Communist Party. In the early democratic period, the desire to consolidate democracy took precedence over worker demands. The *Moncloa Pacts* of October 1977, a landmark economic accord between the center-right UCD government and the leftist political parties, required trade unions to toe the party line and accept major sacrifices. Trade unions were bitterly disappointed by the policies of the Socialists between 1982 and 1996. The Socialists' restructuring of the economy and the resulting rise in unemployment infuriated the union movement. By 1986 the UGT and the PSOE were in open conflict. The UGT leader quit his PSOE seat in the Cortes and formally broke ties with the Socialists. In the 1989 elections, the UGT refused to endorse the Socialists. Since the late 1980s, the UGT and CC.OO have often coordinated activities.

Business Organizations

Business associations are stronger and more unified than is organized labor. Near the end of the Francoist regime, a number of entrepreneurial organizations were tolerated, and the **Spanish Confederation of Entrepreneurial Organizations (CEOE)** emerged as the most important of these. The CEOE claims to incorporate 75 percent of firms and an even larger percentage of Spain's total production. It is probably the most successful peak business organization in Southern Europe. Founded in 1977, the CEOE has 133 affiliated associations and 1.3 million affiliated firms. It includes a very broad spectrum of businesses. In 1983 it incorporated the main small and medium business organization, and most regional business groups belong to the CEOE.

The CEOE took a hands-off approach to the democratic transition. Only after the attempted coup of 1981 did the CEOE make clear commitments to the democratic system. However, the organization played an important role as spokesperson for business interests in the tripartite wage agreements reached during the late 1970s and early 1980s. The CEOE has tended to maintain its distance from political parties. It supports parties of the right and center, but its relationship with the PSOE has been far better than the PSOE–trade union relationship. The CEOE has been a pro–free market force, complaining about high energy costs and foreign competition. It opposes tax policies that it believes hurt business and limit investment, and it steadily assails "unproductive" public spending. A constant goal of the CEOE is to revise what it views as overly restrictive laws regarding the hiring and firing of workers, many of which date from the Francoist era. Employers claim that they need more flexibility in hiring workers in order to compete with foreign enterprise.

Agricultural lobbies are very weak in Spain, a reflection of the fact that the importance of agriculture in Spain has steadily declined. By 2003 agriculture employed only 7 percent of the population and accounted for 3.6 percent of the gross domestic product (GDP). Agricultural lobbies are divided between high-tech interests that want further EU integration and smaller farmers who fear European competition.

The Armed Forces

Spain's military has a long history of political involvement. Since the early nineteenth century, military officers regularly tried to depose governments in support of both conservative monarchist and liberal agendas: From 1820 to 1936, there were 44 pronunciamientos (military uprisings), culminating with the antidemocratic rebellion led by General Franco. The humiliating defeats suffered by the military as Spain lost the last pieces of its empire, from Cuba to Morocco, made the armed forces defensive and sensitive to criticism by civilians. For most of the twentieth century, civilians accused of offending the military's honor were subject to military courts, a measure repealed only in 1978.

The Spanish Civil War was a turning point in the history of the armed forces. A significant minority of the military remained loyal to the democratic Republic, and this faction was purged when Franco won control of the government. The armed forces became a far more conservative institution. Under Franco the military had a prominent political role, although the regime was never a pure military dictatorship: Members of the armed forces held 32 of the 114 Francoist Cabinet posts. Military men sat on the boards of state-owned companies. Most importantly, the military gained control over all police forces, intelligence organizations, and customs. As a result of this beneficial treatment, the military was the group most consistently loyal to Franco.

During the transition the military begrudgingly accepted the authority of Franco's designated successor, King Juan Carlos, and his prime minister, Adolfo Suárez. Military leaders, however, vigorously opposed aspects of the democratization process, especially the legalization of the Communist Party. Military hard-liners felt increasingly uneasy during the first UCD governments because of increased terrorism (usually directed against military members), the rapid devolution of powers to Spain's regions, and squabbling and chaotic governments. Weak UCD governments failed to act decisively in the face of repeated acts of military insubordination, which culminated in a 1981 failed coup by disaffected sectors of the military. The coup failed when the King, as commander in chief, rallied loyalist sectors in defense of democracy.

Ironically, it was the Socialist government after 1982 that finally tamed the military. The strength and determination of the PSOE allowed it to act decisively vis-à-vis the military, and most observers would rank the Socialists' reform of the military as their single most important achievement in office. The Socialists streamlined and modernized the army. The PSOE decision to join NATO gave the Spanish military an international role and reduced its focus on domestic security. Most importantly, the PSOE consistently imposed severe punishment on members of the military for insubordination. Spanish law now prohibits political or union activity by active military personnel, who must permanently leave the armed forces if they run for office. The Spanish police forces have been thoroughly civilianized. The military presence in Spanish politics is now negligible. Statements in 2006 by the head of Spain's army, protesting the new Autonomy Statute for Catalonia, resulted in his arrest and firing.

During the first decades of democracy, a constant point of contention was the requirement that all Spanish males complete military service. In the 1980s several political parties (though not the PSOE) advocated abolition of the draft. The PSOE liberalized provisions for conscientious objections and cut the length of military service. The conservative Aznar government eliminated conscription in 1999, and since that time Spain has struggled to attract volunteers. Defense spending rose steadily as a percentage of GDP from 1975 to 1985, a reflection of attempts to modernize the armed forces. Since 1985, however, the military budget has fallen steadily as a percentage of GDP. Spain currently spends only 1.2 percent of its GDP on the military, the second lowest in NATO.

The Catholic Church

Religion is still the strongest cleavage dividing Spaniards. The intensity of the religious question reflects the prominent role of the Catholic Church in Spanish history and the resentment that this role has often created. During the transition to democracy, the Catholic Church did not play an active political role. This neutrality reflected the fact that the Church had long ceased to be a unified supporter of authoritarian rule. By the mid-1950s Catholic progressives began using the Church's autonomy to engage in social activism. By 1975 much of the Church, though not most of the top leadership, actively opposed the continuation of authoritarian rule. The bystander role taken by the Church during the transition was one reason that a successful Catholic political party never emerged.

During the democratic regime, the Catholic Church has gradually become a more vocal participant in the political process. Church representatives weighed in during the writing of the Constitution, expressing their concerns on issues such as abortion and divorce. In the 1979 elections, the Church fought hard to prevent a Socialist victory, publishing a number of documents warning of the dangers of a PSOE government. The Church's pugnacious stance against divorce helped spark the breakup of the UCD in the early 1980s. In the 1980s and early 1990s, the Church reacted strongly to the Socialists' proposed changes in education. On the eve of the March 2000 general elections, the Church angered many Spaniards when it openly endorsed the PP.

Much of the defensive posture adopted by the Church results from its weakening presence in Spanish society.[27] In a 1990 survey, 87 percent of respondents said they were members of a religious community (and 99 percent of these were Catholic). However, the data reveal a dramatic decline in religious practice. In 2002 only 19 percent of Spaniards said they were practicing Catholics and regular churchgoers.[28] Moreover, church attendance is dropping quickly in most urban and wealthy areas and among younger Spaniards. About one-half of Spaniards report going to church only once a year or less.[29] The number of Spaniards dedicating themselves to becoming priests or nuns is falling precipitously.

Democracy has meant a considerable loss of influence and wealth for the Church. Since 1976 Spanish heads of state no longer appoint Spanish bishops, and the revision of the Spanish-Vatican Concordat in 1979 prepared the groundwork for the separation of the Church and the state. State support for the Church will eventually be phased out, but no Spanish government has yet been willing to pull the plug entirely. Currently, Spanish taxpayers may opt to dedicate part of their taxes to the Church, but only about one-third do so.

The ability of the Church to influence voter choice appears to be very weak. Spanish society has rapidly become more secularized. Few Spaniards believe that religious issues should be considered when voting.[30] Research has also shown that large percentages of Spaniards oppose the official Church policy on a variety of issues. Religion continues to be a very strong cleavage in Spanish politics, but the relationship between religiosity and voting is strongest at the political extremes: The PP does best among the most religious, and the United Left does best among atheists. The relationship is weaker in the political center. Indeed, about one-third of the most religious Catholics vote for the PSOE.

The Church, however, continues to be an important actor in Spanish politics. Pronouncements by the Bishops Conference, a top Church leadership body, carry considerable weight and are followed closely by the press. The Church continues to administer about one-third of Spanish schools, though it now has less control over curriculum in many of them. The Church publishes a daily newspaper and owns a radio network. For decades Spaniards have also speculated about the power of Opus Dei (God's Work), a secretive Catholic lay organization founded in 1928. During the Francoist regime, this organization rose to prominence in Spanish business and education. Opus Dei members supposedly occupied about a quarter of university professorships during the Franco period. The Opus Dei still runs an important private university, the University of Navarre, and a prestigious business school in Barcelona. Several members of Prime Minister José María Aznar's Cabinet had close ties to Opus Dei. In 2001 the Aznar government passed a controversial law requiring that all students in Spanish schools take a graded course on either Catholicism or "world religions." The Church is backed by its most important affiliated interest group, the National Confederation of Parents of School Children (CONCAPA), which claims a membership of over three million.

The election of Zapatero in 2004 mobilized the Church against a whole host of PSOE reforms. Zapatero moved quickly to pass legislation legalizing gay marriage, making divorce and abortion easier to obtain, removing religious symbols from all state institutions, and removing the compulsory religious education that the previous government had mandated. Zapatero refused to meet the Pope during the Pontiff's trip to Spain in 2006. Spain's bishops convened a massive protest in Madrid during the 2008 electoral campaign, dubbing it "Christian Family Day," hoping to prevent the reelection of Zapatero. However, public opinion polls have consistently shown that a majority of Spaniards support Zapatero's social policies, and the Church has been unable to stop their implementation. Zapatero pushed forward with his secularizing agenda, and in 2009 pushed legislation that would liberalize Spain's restrictive abortion laws.

Other Groups

Since the return of democracy, many interest groups have formed, and some have acquired significant political and economic power. One of the most fascinating and unusual examples is the Spanish Organization of the Blind (ONCE). Created by Franco's government in 1939 to employ the many who lost their vision while fighting in the Civil War, ONCE was allowed to run tax-exempt lotteries throughout Spain. By 1950 ONCE had used the profits to set up a welfare system for its own members. The organization was forced to reorganize and democratize after 1977, but it has still managed to control Spanish lotteries. The wealth of ONCE has become immense, and the organization now invests in a plethora of Spanish businesses, including one of Spain's top private television stations.

As in much of Europe, Spaniards have been attracted to a whole host of "single-issue" interest groups. However, environmental, peace, and feminist groups, to mention a few, are less developed in Spain than in most of Western Europe. The Franco regime's restrictions on participation are partly responsible for the relative weakness of these organizations in Spain. Many political activists in the 1960s and 1970s focused their energy on the struggle against Franco, which weakened single-issue groups. In the 1980s a strong peace movement arose in opposition to Spain's participation in NATO, but the decision of the governing Socialists to remain in NATO dealt the movement a major blow.

Polls show that awareness of environmental issues is growing rapidly in Spain. Nevertheless, Spain had no major environmental party until the 1993 creation of Los Verdes (The Greens), and in large part because of a lack of strategic and organizational unity, the Spanish environmental movement has yet to have the kind of impact that has occurred in other parts of Europe.[31] As noted later in this chapter, Spanish women's groups had significant success in the 1980s and 1990s, but the results came more through the efforts of women in the established political parties (especially the Socialist Party) than in independent feminist groups. Citizens have increasingly organized to protest Basque terrorism and have been led by a number of groups including Association of Victims of Terrorism (AVT).

One highly visible group has been the Association for the Recovery of Historical Memory (ARMH), founded in 2000 by a group of archeologists and forensic experts. The organization coordinated attempts to exhume mass graves of those killed during the Franco dictatorship. Over two decades after the end of the dictatorship, the ARMH began the first real national dialogue about Franco's treatment of his opponents. The ARMH's efforts contributed to the wide-ranging 2007 Historical Memory Law, which recognizes the rights of those who suffered persecution under Franco. Among other provisions, the law requires local governments to assist with the exhumation and proper burial of Spaniards who were executed during the dictatorship.

ELECTORAL COMPETITION IN SPAIN

The Political Party System

Political parties were banned during the almost four decades of authoritarian rule in Franco's Spain. The official Francoist National Movement never functioned as a mobilizing party; rather, it operated bureaucratically. Franco vilified modern political parties as parasitic organizations unable to act in the common interest. To a considerable extent, the nature of political parties in contemporary Spain—weak organizations with scant membership—can be explained by this long hiatus in party politics.

Spanish parties have the lowest percentage of the electorate as members in Western Europe. Spain's two largest parties, the PP and the PSOE, each have only about half a million members.[32] They make relatively little effort to recruit new members. With the exception of the Spanish Communist Party (PCE), no party emerged from Francoism with a strong membership base. Given the clandestine conditions under which parties had to operate during the dictatorship, mass membership was not a goal they pursued. During the transition hundreds of parties emerged on the left, right, and center of the political system. In the first elections in

1977, what distinguished these parties most was the popularity and name recognition of key leaders, not the size of their membership. It is also important to remember that the Spanish party system was created in the 1970s, well into the age of modern mass media. Unlike other European party systems, where mass membership parties predated the electronic media, Spain's party system emerged in an era when image mattered far more than organizational strength. Finally, given the negotiated nature of Spain's transition, political mobilization was discouraged. Party leaders entered into a series of "bargains" with each other, and mass membership parties were not seen as facilitating such elite-level bargaining. Spain's political leaders remembered that in the Second Republic radicalized party masses had made political compromise impossible.

The personalism of Spanish politics and the weak ideological content share much in common with the trend in Europe as a whole. However, the same factors that limit party membership in Spain exaggerate personalism. Memories of the Spanish Second Republic and the Civil War, still reasonably fresh among older Spaniards, emphasize the dangers of ideology. Four decades of authoritarianism stripped most Spaniards of ideological passion: The regime inculcated them with an apolitical orientation more than any ideology. During the transition the emergence of hundreds of "new" political parties all competing for electoral survival meant that name recognition and simple slogans, rather than complex ideological messages, were at a premium. Personalism was better suited for political campaigns that depended largely on television advertising. Finally, until very recently Spanish political leaders purposely restrained themselves from presenting an ideologically charged image, fearing that polarization would threaten the transition to democracy.

The hierarchical and rather authoritarian internal workings of the political parties of today are partially related to the characteristics noted earlier. Low membership facilitates strong internal control by party leaders. The importance of personalism, itself facilitated by ideological weakness, gives party leaders (especially charismatic ones) excessive influence over their parties. Lack of ideology often facilitates internal factions that seek to impose a stronger ideological vision on the party. Such internal ideological struggles have destroyed a number of political parties, including the Union of the Democratic Center (UCD), the governing party from 1977 to 1981, and have severely weakened others, such as the Spanish Communist Party (PCE). The electorate has consistently punished parties that display internal turmoil. Spain's most successful parties, consequently, have limited internal dissent and imposed strict party discipline. Hierarchical control within parties is facilitated by Spain's closed-list electoral system, which gives party leaders (not the voters) control over the order in which party candidates for office appear on electoral lists. The electoral system also discriminates against small nationwide parties, making it more costly for dissatisfied party factions to bolt and form separate organizations. Finally, the Cortes has procedural rules that severely penalize small parties and that give almost no voice to party backbenchers.

The Major Parties

The political parties have undergone widespread and pervasive changes since the first elections in 1975. In order to simplify the discussion here, the parties are organized into several broad categories: the Communist left, the Socialists, parties of the center and right, and regional parties.

The Communist Left During the Second Republic, the **Spanish Communist Party (PCE)** was a marginal electoral force, but it came to play an important role during the Civil War. Under Franco the PCE, though illegal, was the only opposition force with any real presence inside Spain, conducting some guerrilla operations against the regime in the 1940s and 1950s. As a result, it was harshly repressed. By the mid-1950s the party had almost been eliminated within Spain, and many of its leaders were in exile.

In the 1950s the PCE became one of the pioneers of *Eurocommunism,* distancing itself from the Soviet Union and from Marxist-Leninist ideology and accepting democratic electoral politics. During the transition the PCE supported the monarchy, acted moderately and responsibly, and participated in the elite compromises that were required to write the Constitution. The PCE had hoped to dominate the left after the 1977 elections. Instead, it polled just under 10 percent, well behind the Socialists. Voters were not entirely convinced of the democratic credentials of the Communists. At the same time, the moderation of the PCE program made it appear similar to that of the Socialists, robbing the Communists of their distinctiveness. The definitive blow to the PCE occurred in the 1982 general elections. The Communists were

drubbed and won only 4 percent of the vote, down from almost 11 percent in the previous election. As a result of internal schisms, PCE membership plummeted from a high of 240,000 in 1978 to only 55,000 in 1991.[33]

The remains of the Eurocommunist wing of the party, together with other leftist parties, formed a coalition called **United Left (IU)**. This coalition was initially formed as an anti-NATO protest movement, uniting Communists, environmentalists, and feminists. After 1986 the IU became the only real leftist opposition to the Socialists, operating as a relentless and sometimes very effective critic of their economic policies. It argued that Socialist neoliberal economic policies disproportionately hurt the poor. The coalition's "green" and feminist emphases also made it a strong critic of the Socialists in these areas. After the IU mounted an energetic attack on the Socialist government over corruption charges, the IU in 1996 polled over 10 percent of the vote and won 21 seats. Since then the IU has experienced a rapid decline, winning only two seats and under 4 percent of the vote in the 2008 elections, rendering it unable to form its own parliamentary group. The Socialists under Zapatero have successfully adopted many of the issues (like women's issues, gay rights, regional autonomy, and the environment) that had made the IU distinctive. Given close competition between the PSOE and PP, many on the left have preferred to back the Socialists in order to prevent a conservative victory.

The Socialists The **Spanish Socialist Workers Party (PSOE)** was a dominant force during the first two and a half decades of Spanish democracy.[34] Its long tenure in government—from 1982 to 1996 and from 2004 to the present—and its internal unity and discipline have made it highly successful.

During the Second Republic, the PSOE became the largest single party in Spain. However, it was badly divided between reformist social democrats (who were strongly anti-Communist and deeply committed to democratic procedures) and revolutionary socialists (whose main commitment was to the working class and whose loyalty to the democratic Republic was "conditional").[35] During the Republic many Socialist leaders supported democracy only if it delivered the specific policy outcomes (workers' rights and the building of socialism) that they desired.[35] When the right won the elections of 1934, many of these leaders turned against the Republic and called for revolution. The PSOE spearheaded a protracted armed uprising by workers in northern Spain. In the eyes of many contemporary Spanish socialist intellectuals, the divisions within the PSOE and the weak commitment to parliamentary rule contributed to the downfall of democracy. As a result, the PSOE suffered four decades of repression and exile during Franco's rule.

Throughout most of the Franco regime, the bulk of the Socialist leaders were in exile, and those who remained in Spain were eclipsed by the better organized PCE. Beginning in the 1950s, however, a new generation of PSOE leaders based inside Spain began to revive the party. In 1974 a group of young militants, led by Felipe González, gained control of the PSOE. Under its new leaders, the party made spectacular gains in organizational strength from 1974 to the first elections in 1977. During that period its membership grew from 3,500 to 51,000 and then doubled again by 1979.[36]

The young leadership moved the PSOE toward the center. After four decades of Francoist rule, the PSOE leadership came to realize that a highly ideological campaign would not win votes. The PSOE leaders, unlike their predecessors in the Second Republic, believed that the consolidation of democracy was more important than ideological purity.

The PSOE's success in the first general elections exceeded all expectations: The Socialists took second place, with over 29 percent of the vote and 33.7 percent of the seats in the Congress of Deputies (see Table 8.2). It trounced the PCE, clearly established itself as the hegemonic force on the left, and earned the right to play a large role in the writing of the new constitution. The party's leadership eliminated the Marxist, class-based definition of the party and affirmed the ideological pluralism of the PSOE. They purged some of the more radical proposals from its electoral platform and pledged to become more of an interclass "catchall" party.

These moves resulted in an unprecedented victory in the 1982 elections. The PSOE won 48.1 percent of the valid votes and 57.7 percent of the seats in the Congress of Deputies. The election resulted in the first instance of party alternation in the new democracy and produced the first government that contained no former Francoist leader. It also produced the first single-party majority government in Spain's history.

The new Socialist government gained an unprecedented degree of control in a system that gives majoritarian governments extraordinary power. From the start of its term, the Socialists moved quickly to pursue a controversial neoliberal macroeconomic policy that clearly favored integration of Spain into the world economy, economic growth, and the building of infrastructure over full employment. The Socialists spent lavishly for the 1992 World's Fair in Seville and the Barcelona Olympics, including a controversial high-speed train from Seville to Madrid.

The hegemony enjoyed by the PSOE resulted in an aloofness and arrogance on the part of the government. Scandals involving the abuse of public offices continued to surface. Perhaps the most damaging scandal involved a secret government-run death squad aimed at Basque terrorists, for which a number of top Socialist officials were jailed. By the 1993 elections, the PSOE's majority was in jeopardy. The Socialists kept their status as the largest party, but fell seventeen seats short of a majority. The PSOE had to depend on centrist regional parties to prop up a minority government, and a third of the members of the new Cabinet did not even belong to the PSOE.

The PSOE is structured much like other Social Democratic parties in Europe, but it is unusually centralized. It is formally federal, with the local *agrupación* (party branch) as its primary structure, electing provincial and regional bodies. In 1979 the party leadership embraced a shift to a much more disciplined party structure. The party enacted rule changes to inhibit factionalism and to reinforce party stability. After the PSOE defeat in the 1996 elections, many members felt that the Socialist leadership had gotten out of touch with the rank and file. Consequently, the 1997 PSOE Congress adopted a primary election system for candidates for local and regional posts, and this was later extended to the selection of Socialist candidates for head of government. The use of party primaries to select candidates was a first for Spanish political parties, and it augured well for an internal democratization of the PSOE. After the Socialists lost power in 1996, the party continued to struggle at the polls.

The PSOE was drubbed in the 2000 elections—it lost sixteen seats in the lower house and over 1 million votes—leading to an internal struggle for power. In July 2000 the Socialists elected **José Luis Rodríguez Zapatero** as their new leader (Box 8.2). Zapatero represented a new generation of Socialist "whiz kids" who sought to further democratize party institutions and to resuscitate the PSOE's image. His party's upset victory in the March 2004 elections propelled him to the forefront of Spanish politics rather quickly. After nine years of conservative rule, the new prime minister moved quickly to implement a series

TABLE 8.2

Percentage of the Vote and Number of Seats in the Congress of Deputies, 1977–2008

	1977 %	1977 #	1979 %	1979 #	1982 %	1982 #	1986 %	1986 #	1989 %	1989 #	1993 %	1993 #	1996 %	1996 #	2000 %	2000 #	2004 %	2004 #	2008 %	2008 #
Popular Party (and Predecessors), nationwide conservatives (AP/CP/PP)	8.40	16	6.05	9	26.36	106	25.97	105	25.79	106	34.76	141	38.79	156	44.52	183	37.71	148	39.94	154
Union of the Democratic Center, nationwide centrists (UCD/CDS)	34.44	166	34.84	168	6.77	12	9.22	19	7.89	14	—	0	—	—	—	—	—	—	—	—
Spanish Socialist Workers Party (PSOE)	29.44	118	30.40	121	48.11	202	44.06	184	39.60	176	38.76	159	37.63	141	34.16	125	42.59	164	43.87	169
Spanish Communist Party/United Left	9.33	20	10.77	23	4.02	4	4.63	7	9.07	17	9.55	18	10.54	21	5.45	8	4.96	5	3.77	2
Convergence and Union, Catalan centrists (CIU)	0.94	2	2.69	8	3.67	12	5.02	18	5.04	18	4.94	17	4.60	16	4.19	15	3.23	10	3.03	10
Basque National Party, Basque centrists (PNV)	1.62	2	1.88	7	1.88	8	1.53	6	1.24	5	1.24	5	1.27	5	1.53	7	1.63	7	1.19	6
Others	16.40	26	13.60	14	9.19	6	9.57	11	11.37	14	10.75	10	7.17	11	10.15	15	9.88	13	8.20	8
Total	100	350	100	350	100	350	100	350	100	350	100	350	100	350	100	350	100	350	100	350

Source: Ministerio del Interior http://www.elecciones.mir.es/MIR/jsp/resultados/index.htm), accessed March 25, 2009.

BOX 8.2

José Luis Rodríguez Zapatero

Spain's current prime minister, José Luis Rodríguez Zapatero, was only 15 years old when dictator Francisco Franco died. He comes from an affluent family in the Castilian province of León, with a long history of involvement in politics. Like his father, Zapatero became a lawyer before entering politics. In 1986 Zapatero became the youngest-ever member of parliament, and he rose rapidly through the ranks of the PSOE. Backed by the "New Wave" faction of young Socialists, Zapatero narrowly won the party leadership election in 2000 at the age of 39, without ever having served in the government. After his equally surprising election as prime minister in 2004, the opposition dubbed him "Bambi" in order to highlight his lack of experience.

Zapatero has been a controversial prime minister, moving quickly to pass a wide range of controversial social legislation, including the legalization of gay marriage, measures to reduce domestic violence against women, amnesty for illegal immigrants, and liberalization of abortion.

Zapatero's grandfather was a liberal army officer executed by Franco's regime after the Spanish Civil War. Zapatero's government passed a Law of Historical Memory that seeks to help exhume the bodies and remove the stigma associated with Spaniards executed by Franco. Zapatero's government was the first to officially denounce the Franco regime as illegitimate.

---

of controversial social reforms, including the legalization of gay marriage and the easing of abortion restrictions. His first foreign policy move was to withdraw Spanish troops from Iraq. Despite being derided by the conservative opposition for his inexperience, Zapatero accomplished a remarkable amount in his first term and was reelected in 2008.[37]

Parties of the Center On the eve of Spain's first elections in 1977, countless groups claimed to be "centrist." These included timid Francoist reformers who emerged in the twilight of the Franco regime, anti-Franco opposition figures, Christian Democrats, liberals, monarchists, and Social Democrats. In early 1977 those groups coalesced in the **Union of the Democratic Center (UCD),** led by Adolfo Suárez, the Francoist bureaucrat responsible for stewarding the transition to democracy.

The UCD experiment was initially very successful. Backed by the still powerful state media and bureaucracy and fronted by Spain's most popular and charismatic leader, the UCD easily won the first two democratic elections. Running campaigns based solely on the image of its popular leader, the UCD advocated a cautious support for devolution of power to the regions, a separation of church and state, military reform, and economic restructuring. It polled well among rural voters, women, and Catholics. In retrospect these victories were extremely important for the viability of

Spanish democracy. The UCD brought to power a coalition of Francoist reformers and moderate democratic opposition members, thus bridging the gap between authoritarianism and democracy. It proved that those who had played a role in the Francoist regime could have a place in the new democracy. Indeed, in the first democratic legislature forty-four UCD members of the Congress of Deputies were former members of the Francoist legislature, and almost half of the party's members were officeholders (mostly middle-level bureaucrats) under Franco.[38] Suárez and the UCD were thus in an ideal position to negotiate a democratic constitution that could appeal to a wide range of voters.

Once in power, however, the UCD proved to be unwieldy. The ideological diversity of "centrists" was a fatal flaw, especially for a party that had to oversee constitutional compromise. The tension between its Christian Democratic right and its Social Democratic left eventually tore the UCD apart. Suárez had alienated sectors of the military because of his role in the transition, and his government was unable to discipline the increasingly restive armed forces. Suárez resigned in January 1981 after he failed to acquire greater control over squabbling party leaders. The attempted military coup of February 23, 1981, accelerated the intramural chaos in the UCD. Soon the UCD's Social Democrats bolted the party, some joining the PSOE, while some of its Christian Democrats joined the rightist Popular Alliance. The 1982 elections marked one of the largest electoral defeats of a governing party in Spain's electoral history and dealt the UCD, which dropped from 168 seats to only 12 a deathblow.

Since the demise of the UCD, no centrist party has been able to achieve national electoral success. The main reason has been that after the Socialist victory in 1982, the centrist political space grew smaller. The PSOE's move toward the center deprived other parties of that space, and the right's moderation and drift toward the political mainstream had a similar effect.

Parties of the Right   Spanish parties of the right have a long history of weakness and disunity. Some have argued that the Spanish right has never had to organize, given that its historical interests have usually been well protected. When its interests were threatened, the Spanish right supported authoritarian rule. During the Second Republic, the main party of the right eventually supported Francoist authoritarianism.

After 1977 the Spanish right was confronted with a difficult problem. It was initially unable and unwilling to distance itself from the Franco regime, and that identification hurt it at the polls. Attempts by rightist leaders to draw on the legacy of Spanish conservatism in the late nineteenth and early twentieth centuries had little resonance.

Spain's main conservative party, the Partido Popular (PP), or Popular Party, began as the Popular Alliance (AP) in October 1976, drawing recruits largely from the former top-level apparatus of the Francoist state. Manuel Fraga, a well-known minister under Franco, led the party. The well-organized and well-funded AP had high hopes for electoral success until Adolfo Suárez and the UCD entered the 1977 electoral campaign. Compared with the UCD and the youthful Suárez, Fraga and his party appeared more authoritarian and less committed to democracy. The AP campaign stressed the need for order and continuity. It accepted regional autonomy, but rejected federalism or regional independence. It opposed divorce and abortion and advocated support for the police and the armed forces. The AP performed poorly in the first democratic elections, winning only 16 of the 350 seats in the Congress of Deputies, with only 8.4 percent of the vote. In the Basque Country and Catalonia, the AP won almost no support.

In retrospect it is clear that the post-Francoist right faced some serious obstacles. The right might have expected active support from the Catholic Church, but the Church (itself divided) refused to endorse any one political party. A more serious obstacle was the regional question. The Spanish right has a long history of opposing political decentralization, and, therefore, conservatives in Spain's most important regions have backed regional instead of Madrid-based conservative parties. The absence of a single party capable of representing national and regional conservatives has weakened the right.

The dismal electoral results of 1977 encouraged the AP to ally with two small centrist parties (one Liberal and one Christian Democratic) under the name Popular Coalition (CP). Despite the reorganization, the CP won only nine seats in the Congress of Deputies and 6 percent of the vote in 1979, leading many observers to predict the disappearance of the right altogether. This might have been the outcome had the governing UCD not suddenly imploded in the 1982 elections. The Popular Coalition, in alliance with regional conservative parties, reaped the benefits, winning 26.4 percent of the vote and 106 seats in the Congress of Deputies. About half of former UCD voters switched to the AP in 1982.[39] Despite the raised expectations, the CP failed to improve on its 1982 performance in the 1986 general elections, and the rightist coalition disbanded.

In 1988 the AP once again attempted to polish its image. It took a new name, the **Popular Party (PP)**, and sought to integrate former UCD leaders, but it failed to make gains in the 1989 elections. In 1990 the PP selected a new leader, **José María Aznar**, the young president of the Castilla-León Autonomous Community.[40] Aznar promoted a modern Christian Democratic image and tried to purge the party of its extreme right. He also waged a relentless campaign against PSOE corruption. His steady, if not flamboyant, leadership of the PP paid dividends in the 1993 elections, when the party made significant gains, and in the 1996 elections, when the PP finally took power. In the 1980s the right had moved from being a vehicle for the former Francoist elite to being a more mainstream party. The PP's membership rose from 5,000 members in 1979 to 220,000 by October 1986, and younger Spaniards made up much of the new membership. The PP victory in the 1996 general elections finally enabled the Spanish right to demonstrate its credentials as a modern, democratic party.

Aznar's first term in office allayed any fears that Spanish conservatives could not be trusted to uphold democratic rule. Under the PP Spain prospered, with annual growth rates averaging 3 percent, and unemployment fell by 8 percent. Aznar's willingness to enter into negotiation with Basque nationalists, coupled with his hard line during the bargaining process, won him much support. Voters in the March 2000 elections rewarded the PP. It became the first conservative party in Spanish history to win an absolute majority of legislative seats (see Table 8.2).

During his eight years in office, Aznar provided a stark contrast to his flamboyant predecessor. However, like González, Aznar kept an iron grip on his party, even handpicking his successor (Mariano Rajoy) to head the PP ticket in the 2004 elections after Aznar decided not to pursue a third term. Aznar can take credit for almost a decade of rapid economic growth and real progress in the war against Basque terrorism. Yet his aloof style, his conservative social policies, and especially his support for the invasion to remove Saddam Hussein's regime in Iraq all contributed to a decline in his popularity and the PP's loss in the 2004 elections.

Since losing power in 2004, the party has been led by Mariano Rajoy, who has attempted to move the PP toward the center. After his party's second consecutive loss in 2008, Rajoy faced an internal rebellion from the party right, which advocates a harder line on issues like regional devolution and immigration, and opposition from moderates who reject Rajoy's strategy of political polarization. The PP has vehemently opposed the social reforms proposed by the Socialists after 2004; its deputies voted against the law legalizing same-sex marriage and the Historical Memory Law, and the party abstained on the Law of Equality Between Men and Women.

Catalonian Parties Spain's regional parties have played an important role in its democratic system, both in the Autonomous Communities and, to a lesser extent, in the national party system. It is impossible here to cover all the regional groups, but it is important to touch on the major parties in the two most important regions, Catalonia and the Basque Country.

The Catalonian party system has been fairly stable from the start, dominated by the Democratic Convergence of Catalonia (CDC), which has run in elections together with a smaller group, the Democratic Union of Catalonia (UDC), in a coalition called **Convergence and Union** (*CiU*).[41] (See Table 8.3.) The CDC was founded near the end of the Francoist regime. CiU remains the leading electoral force in Catalonia, and it is currently the third largest electoral force in the national legislature. Despite winning a plurality of seats in the 2003 regional elections, the CiU lost power to a coalition of socialists and Catalonian leftists.

The CiU has operated very much as a Catalonian "catchall" party of the center. Its founder, Jordi Pujol, dominated it from the start. Pujol spent two years in jail under Franco, and he later became a leading force behind the Banca Catalana, a regional bank. Pujol won the first election to the restored *Generalitat* (Catalonian government) in 1980—and five subsequent elections. Pujol's political longevity gave him immense prestige within Catalonia and considerable respect nationwide. However, his active promotion of Catalonian interests abroad often angered Madrid. After the March 1996 elections, he lent his party's support to the PP government of Aznar despite the Spanish right's historical opposition to regional devolution. (See Box 8.3.) He was able to exact promises

Percentage of the Vote and Number of Seats in the Catalonian Legislature, 1999–2006						**TABLE 8.3**
	1999		**2003**		**2006**	
	%	#	%	#	%	#
CiU (centrist nationalists)	38	56	31	46	32	48
PP (national right)	10	12	12	15	11	14
ERC (republican left of Catalonia)	9	12	16	23	14	21
PSC-PSOE (Catalonian Socialists)	38	52	31	42	27	37
PSUC/IC/ICV (Catalonian Communists, United Left, and Greens)	3	3	7	9	10	12
Others	2	0	3	0	6	3
Total	100	135	100	135	100	135

Source: *Anuario El País* (various years) and www.elmundo.es.

The success of Spain's devolution can be seen on many levels. In Catalonia street signs appear in Catalan, and a majority of children learn both Catalan and Castilian. The large majority of citizens in Catalonia now speak Catalan. In Catalonia and the Basque Country, there are regional police forces and television and radio stations that broadcast in regional languages. All seventeen ACs have their own elected governments and court systems, and each has control over territorial planning, social services, and cultural policy.

from the PP regarding regional devolution. However, Pujol always kept his distance from the national government, steadfastly refusing to accept cabinet positions.

The CiU is best viewed as a centrist political party with a blend of Christian Democratic and nationalist ideology. It advocates a more formally federal system, but has come to accept the system of Autonomous Communities. It is a party that has also represented the small- and medium-sized Catalonian bourgeoisie. Despite its early flirtation with Social Democratic ideas, it has generally promoted market economics and free enterprise. A main emphasis of the CiU, and an area where it has had a significant impact, is its policy to restore the Catalan language to a position of dominance in Catalonia. By the mid-1980s over 85 percent of the schools in the region offered some classes in Catalan, compared with about 3 percent at the start of the democratic period. The CiU controlled the regional government from the transition to democracy until 2003.

Basque Parties Unlike the Catalonian party system, the situation in the Basque Country has been very volatile and extremely polarized.[42] As in Catalonia, the dominant party in the region, the **Basque Nationalist Party (PNV)**, has been a centrist force. The PNV was an important regional force during the Second Republic, and it had a long history of opposition to and fierce repression by Franco during the authoritarian regime. Partially due to this painful past and partially due to a strong and violent pro-independence movement, the PNV has been less accepting of the Autonomous Community status than has the CiU in Catalonia. Unlike the CiU, the PNV formally opposed the Constitution of 1978.

Juan José Ibarretxe, the PNV president of the Basque Country from 1999 to 2009, proposed a referendum on the right to self-determination (though not necessarily independence) for the Basque Country and has called for the unilateral creation of a "free associated state" with ties to Spain. That plan was strongly opposed by both the PP and the PSOE. The PNV governed the Basque Country since the approval of the Basque Autonomy Statute in 1979, but from 1986 to 2009 it did so in coalition with other parties. In national elections the PNV has consistently made a strong showing, and like the CiU in Catalonia, it has done best when national centrist parties are weakest (see Table 8.4). In the 2001 regional elections, it experienced a breakthrough, winning 42.7 percent of the vote. However, the PNV and the planned referendum on independence were dealt a severe blow in the April 2005 regional elections. The PNV lost its majority in the regional legislature, and the anti-referendum opposition made important gains. Despite retaining a plurality of votes and seats in the 2009 regional elections, the PNV was pushed out of power for the first time by a coalition of non-nationalist parties led by the Socialists.

In contrast to Catalonia, there has been a consistently strong nationalist left presence in the Basque Country. The Euskadiko Euskerra (EE), or Basque Left, represented the regional left until it split during the transition to democracy. It lost much of its support to the radical Basque left party, **Herri Batasuna (HB)**, the political arm of the terrorist organization ETA. Unlike the other Basque parties, the HB (renamed Euskal Herritarrok, or EH, in 1998) is an antisystem party (i.e., it rejects the Spanish Constitution), and like ETA it promotes the independence of the region from Spain. It has done surprisingly well in

Percentage of the Vote and Number of Seats in the Basque Legislature, 1998–2005						TABLE 8.4	
	2001		2005		2009		
	%	#	%	#	%	#	
PNV (Basque Nationalist Party)	43	33	39	29	39	30	
HB (radical Basque left)	10	7	13	9	—	—	
EA (moderate breakaway from PNV)	—	—	—	—	4	1	
PSE-PSOE (Basque Socialists)	18	13	23	18	31	24	
PCE/IU (Basque Communists)	6	3	5	3	3	1	
PP (national right)	23	19	17	15	14	13	
Others	0	0	3	1	9	7	
Total	100	75	100	75	100	75	

Source: *Anuario El País* (various years), www.elmundo.es, and www.elpais.es.

regional and national elections and has won seats in every national election between 1979 and 1996, peaking with five deputies in 1986. Initially, its members elected to the national parliament refused to occupy their seats as a sign of protest against the Spanish state. When HB deputies finally agreed to take their seats in 1989, they were expelled from the legislature for refusing to take the required oath to the Constitution. After 1986 the HB strength in national elections waned, and it won only two seats in the 1993 and 1996 elections. HB's successor, EH, boycotted the 2000 general elections and encouraged voters to abstain. Shortly before the 2001 Basque elections, Spain's highest court upheld a government ban of EH. In the 2005 regional elections, the radical Basque left, running under yet another moniker, continued to garner about a tenth of the vote. In the 2009 elections the courts banned two new parties that were deemed to have links to ETA.

The Electoral System

Spain's electoral system was one of the many compromises that resulted from the negotiated transition to democracy. The left insisted on proportional representation, while the right advocated a single-member district/plurality system. The compromise called for proportional representation for the Congress of Deputies, but with strong "corrective" measures to favor the major parties and to prevent excessive fragmentation of the legislature. Conservatives won some additional victories such as the use of a plurality system for the Senate.

Spain's Congress of Deputies employs a modified system of proportional representation, using Spain's 50 unevenly sized provinces (generally smaller than the ACs) as constituencies. All provinces, regardless of size, receive a minimum of two deputies in the lower house and then additional seats for each 144,500 citizens. Conservatives initially supported this electoral system, since urban areas that were thought to favor the left were underrepresented. In the first democratic elections, the small size of electoral districts and the overrepresentation of conservative rural districts made it easier for the UCD to win elections. Spain's electoral system favors large parties over small ones, especially in smaller electoral districts. It also favors small parties whose vote is concentrated geographically, as is the case with Spain's many regional parties. Spanish parties must receive over 3 percent of the vote to win seats in the legislature, a measure that also limits the success of small parties. Spain's electoral system is, in the words of one scholar, "strikingly unproportional."[43]

Elections for the Congress of Deputies employ the closed-list system of presenting candidates: The content and order of party lists are set by party leaders, not by voters. Moreover, candidates on party lists are not required to be members of that party. Both these provisions have weakened party rank and file vis-à-vis party leaders. For elections to the Senate, voters select up to three names from a single list of all candidates who run in a given province, and the recipients with the most votes are elected. In addition, some senators are appointed directly by the Autonomous Communities.

The electoral system for the Cortes has had its intended outcome. It has often produced governments with a majority or plurality large enough to govern alone. Spain's party system is still highly fragmented, but it would undoubtedly be more so were it not for the electoral laws. In the 2008 elections, when the PSOE and PP gained seats, both major parties would have lost seats to smaller parties had Spain employed larger electoral districts and a more proportional allocation of seats. The PSOE and PP won 92% of the seats in the lower house with only 84% of the vote. Small parties find it difficult to survive on the national level as a result of both the electoral system and Spain's system of party finance. On the national level at least, two large parties have increasingly dominated the party system.

Strict laws govern the financing of political parties, but these laws have not been followed very closely during the first three decades of Spanish democracy. Spain's political parties can raise their funds through public financing (which makes up the bulk of their budgets), membership dues, and private donations.[44] The state reimburses parties for electoral expenses based on the number of seats they win in an election. The system clearly favors large incumbent parties, since campaign funds must be raised up front, often by bank loans. Since 1987 a parliamentary Audit Commission inspects party finances, but critics have argued that financing rules have been only sporadically enforced. A series of party financing scandals made headlines in the 1980s and early 1990s as Spanish parties ran up gigantic debts. The incessant schedule of elections (national, regional, municipal, and European) began to take its toll on party coffers. With few dues-paying members and almost no unpaid volunteers, both major parties were tempted to trade political favors for campaign contributions.

Sources of Party Support

Most scholars have argued that social class is not an important basis of party support in Spain, despite the fact that its indicators of inequality rank among the highest in Europe. The growth of a large middle class, the increased social mobility since the 1960s, and the long tenure in power of the Socialist Party (which enjoyed strong support from all social classes) have all helped to weaken this once divisive cleavage. As noted in Table 8.5, the income levels of party supporters are not dramatically different across parties, although slightly more PP supporters than PSOE supporters are in the highest income level.

Several studies point to the surprising continued strength of the religious cleavage in Spanish politics. McDonough and his colleagues found that religion is a much stronger cleavage than is class or region, even though the latter two are still important, and the religious cleavage appears to have been somewhat resistant to economic and social modernization. Table 8.5 reveals that PP supporters are over twice as likely as PSOE supporters (and seven times as likely as supporters of the leftist IU) to say that they regularly attend church. Moreover, religion no longer polarizes Spanish political culture as it once did. McDonough and his colleagues concluded that by the mid-1990s "religious attachments have little to do with popular attitudes toward democracy or toward government in Spain. . . . The day of mobilization against the political system on the basis of religion seems to be over."[45]

Campaigns and Elections

Unlike in the United States, Spanish citizens of voting age are automatically registered to vote. The Central Electoral Junta is responsible for drawing up a list of eligible voters. An Electoral College, made up by citizens chosen randomly, counts the votes and oversees elections. Ultimately, the Constitutional Court is responsible for ensuring that elections are free and fair. As can be seen in Figure 8.6, Spaniards turn out to vote in large numbers, despite the fact that elections (national, AC, municipal, and European Parliament) have been held frequently. In 2008 voter turnout was a respectable 75 percent.

Spanish electoral campaigns are short affairs. Until 1994 campaigns lasted three weeks, but since then they have been reduced to only two weeks, in order to save time and money. The day before elections is designated a "day of reflection," and all advertisements and campaign activities are banned. In the early years of Spanish democracy, parties used mass rallies to build enthusiasm. In recent years such mass electoral events have become rarities, and parties rely heavily on the mass media to get out the word. Spanish parties are allocated free time on television according to their performance in the last election, thus favoring incumbents. Both the UCD and the

Social Bases of Party Support in Spain, 2007 Church attendance and age affect support for the PP and PSOE		**TABLE 8.5**				
		PP	**PSOE**	**IU**	**CiU**	**PNV**
Gender	Male	45.6%	50.8%	50.7%	45.3%	23.1%
	Female	54.4	49.2	49.3	54.7	76.9
	Total	100.0	100.0	100.0	100.0	100.0
Age	18–34	20.5%	26.9%	33.3%	18.7%	15.4%
	35–54	34.1	39.7	50.7	30.6	23.1
	Over 54	45.5	33.3	16.0	50.7	61.5
	Total	100.0	100.0	100.0	100.0	100.0
Income Level	Lower	33.2%	48.1%	36.9%	34.7%	7.7%
	Middle	50.9	36.4	29.2	48.0	23.1
	Higher	15.9	15.5	33.9	17.3	69.2
	Total	100.0	100.0	100.0	100.0	100.0
Education Level	Lower	57.1%	55.3%	32.8%	56.0%	61.5%
	Middle	22.0	24.5	33.7	28.0	30.8
	Higher	19.9	19.8	33.1	16.0	7.7
	Don't know, don't respond	1.0	0.4	0.4	0.0	0.0
	Total	100.0	100.0	100.0	100.0	100.0
Church Attendance	Seldom/never	33.4%	56.9%	88.2%	50.0%	45.5%
	Occasionally	34.0	29.2	7.5	19.4	9.1
	Regularly	31.7	13.6	4.3	29.4	45.4
	Don't know, don't respond	0.4	0.3	0.00	1.2	0.0
	Total	100.0	100.0	100.0	100.0	100.0

Source: Centro de Investigaciones Sociológicas, May 2007. Retrieved March 25, 2009 from www.cis.es/cis/opencms/-Archivos/Marginales/2700_2719/2701/Cru270100RECUERDO.htm.

PSOE were criticized when in office for using the state media to enhance their political fortunes. The growing importance of private television and radio channels has limited somewhat the ability of governments to manipulate the media in their favor. A relatively new approach that reflects the importance of television in electoral campaigns is the televised debate between party leaders. In the 1993 electoral campaign, Felipe González and José María Aznar engaged in a series of debates that drew a huge national audience and that did much to enhance the image of the little-known Aznar. In 2008 Zapatero and PP leader Rajoy faced off in two fierce televised electoral debates, which, according to major polls, were won by the Socialist leader.

Spanish electoral campaigns in the decade after the transition to democracy were mild affairs. Given the fragility of the transition to democracy, political elites from the major parties went out of their way not to polarize the political environment. In recent years campaigns have become more hard-nosed. The 2004 and 2008 electoral campaigns were especially hard fought. In 2004 new leaders headed both major parties. Counting on his comfortable lead in the polls, PP candidate Mariano Rajoy refused to debate his Socialist opponent, a move that some believe damaged Rajoy's candidacy. Meanwhile, Socialist leader José Luis Rodríguez Zapatero hammered the governing conservatives on a whole host of issues ranging from the U.S.-led invasion of Iraq to the PP's controversial National Water Plan. The Madrid terrorist bombings, only three days before the elections, cast a pall over what had been a hard-fought campaign.

The 2008 electoral campaign was the most bitterly contested since the return of democracy, taking place in the midst of a growing economic crisis, rising concerns over immigration, and a resurgence of Basque terrorist violence. The PP, still stinging from its unexpected loss in the 2004 elections, attacked the PSOE for being too soft on Basque

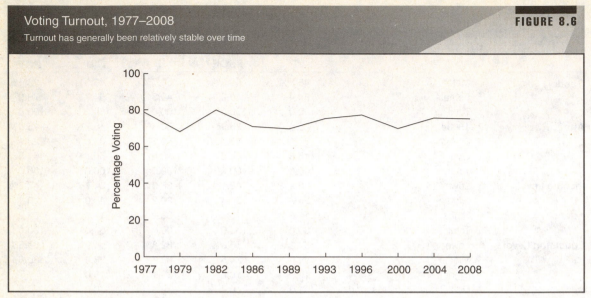

Voting Turnout, 1977–2008
Turnout has generally been relatively stable over time

FIGURE 8.6

Note: The figure presents the actual voters as a percentage of potential voters.

Sources: International Institute for Democracy and Electoral Assistance, http://www.idea.int/vt/country_view.cfm?CountryCode=ES (accessed March 25, 2009); Ministry of the Interior, http://www.elecciones.mir.es/MIR/jsp/resultados/index.htm (accessed on March 25, 2009).

terrorism and illegal immigration, and for not paying enough attention to the growing economic crisis. Some observers viewed the campaign as a sign that Spain was becoming dangerously polarized, while others viewed it as proof that Spain's democracy was mature and consolidated.

The Party System

During the first two decades of democracy, there was constant change in Spain's party system, with parties rising and falling almost overnight. The presence of separate regional party systems in some of Spain's most important Autonomous Communities makes any simple characterization of the Spanish party system very elusive. In several recent elections, these regional parties have played a crucial role in supporting minority governments of one of the two major parties.

However, it is possible to point to some constant features of Spain's party system. First, since 1979 two major parties (though not always the same two) have increasingly dominated the electoral landscape (see again Table 8.2). In every general election between 1977 and 2008, the two largest parties have won over

80 percent of the seats (the figure in 2008 was 92 percent). Between 1977 and 1981, the UCD and the PSOE were dominant; since then the PP and the PSOE have dominated.

Second, there has been a small, but consistent and important presence of regional parties throughout Spain. The success of such parties, which are largely middle-of-the-road, goes hand in hand with the inability of a national centrist party to achieve electoral success since the demise of the UCD. In the 2008 elections, regional parties won 24 seats (about 7 percent of the total) in the lower house of the Cortes. Given that the PSOE lacks a parliamentary majority, regional parties have often had considerable influence despite their small number of seats.

Third, despite the fluctuation in the party system, the Spanish electorate has remained remarkably stable. Opinion research consistently shows that Spanish voters are clustered just to the right or left of center.[46] With the exception of the Basque Country (where antisystem parties have consistently drawn significant support), Spain's party system is less polarized than those of many other European countries.

Consequently, a fourth feature of the party system is the failure of national parties that are perceived to be at the political extremes. The PCE (and later the IU) has been unable to convince voters that it has moved toward the center and as a result has been condemned to no more than one-tenth of the vote (in the 2008 elections, it received under 4 percent). The PP, in contrast, has left behind an older generation of leaders identified with Franco and moderated its image. Even in the Basque Country, only a relatively small minority (about 10 percent) has backed radical nationalist parties.

Fifth, as noted earlier, Spaniards are not very attached to political parties, and they have comparatively weak party identification, partly a result of the changing party landscape.[47] Spanish political parties have very few members and are organizationally very weak. Consequently, Spaniards place great weight on the popularity of party leaders, and image means a great deal.

Studies of electoral volatility (shifts in individual voting behavior from one election to the next) show that the change in Spanish parties has not mirrored a change in voter orientation. Except for the watershed election of 1982, the volatility of the Spanish voters has not been much higher than the average in other European elections.[48] A more specific measure of voting change is "interbloc" volatility, which is a shift from right-center to left voting or vice versa. Spain has had high total volatility, but very low levels of interbloc volatility. Even in the party system realignment of 1982, relatively few voters crossed the divide between left and right.

POLICY PERFORMANCE AND OUTCOMES

Does politics matter? Does public policy change when there is a change in political regime? The transition from Francoist authoritarianism to democracy in Spain provides an opportunity to examine these questions. There has been a dramatic shift in public policy outputs between the two regimes. Under Franco Spain was far below other Western industrialized states in its levels of taxation and state public spending. As a result, the provision of many public services approached third world levels. By the mid-1980s, after only a decade of democracy, Spain's public policy outputs were very close to the European norm. Figure 8.8 compares some measures of public policy outputs during two regimes.

The Size and Scope of Spanish Government

Spain is often identified with strong leaders like Ferdinand and Isabel and Francisco Franco. Historically, however, the Spanish state was weak compared to other European nations. It often was unable to collect taxes or enforce laws. Even dictatorships were far from all-encompassing in their power. Franco shelved the totalitarian project proposed by some of his supporters early in his regime. Part and parcel of this legacy is Spain's long history of bureaucratic inefficiency and stagnation, and the inability to enact

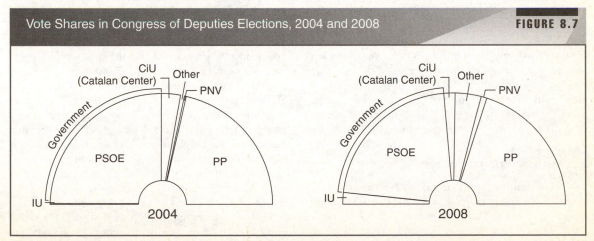

Vote Shares in Congress of Deputies Elections, 2004 and 2008

FIGURE 8.7

CiU (Catalan Center)   Other   PNV   Government   PSOE   PP   IU   2004

CiU (Catalan Center)   Other   PNV   Government   PSOE   PP   IU   2008

Source: Ministerio del Interior, http://www.elecciones.mir.es/MIR/jsp/resultados/index.htm), accessed March 25, 2009.

civil service reform has plagued authoritarian and democratic regimes alike.

From 1982 to 1996, Spain's Socialist government tried hard to tame the bureaucracy. Under the Socialists the *reforma de los relojes* (reform of the clocks) required civil servants to work strict schedules, mandated that government offices remain open between 9 A.M. and 2 P.M., and attempted to streamline the bureaucratic maze facing Spaniards who sought government services. In 1984 the Socialists formally banned the practice of *pluriempleo* (state employees holding multiple jobs). These reforms have been only partially successful. Moreover, with regional devolution state bureaucracies have often been replaced with Autonomous Community offices that may operate no more efficiently.

In 1990 there were about 2 million people dependent in some way on the public purse. About one-third were employed in the state's central administration (including the military, police, legal corps, and social security staff); about one-quarter were employed by Autonomous Communities. By 1993 public-sector employees represented just over 20 percent of the country's salaried workers—a figure that may seem large, but that is actually in line with the percentages in other European nations.

Due in part to the Francoist legacy, the Spanish state owns and operates many business enterprises and plays an important role in many traditional (and declining) industries such as mining, iron, steel, and shipbuilding. In 1986 there were 180 companies in which the state held a direct majority share through three large state holding companies, along with 300 subsidiaries and more than 500 minority holdings. Together they accounted for about 5 percent of the total labor force and about 9 percent of the industrial sector's labor force, which in comparative perspective is rather insignificant. Spanish governments of the left and right have undertaken a gradual and carefully controlled privatization of state holdings, beginning in 1986 with the privatization of the automobile maker SEAT (later sold to Germany's Volkswagen), and including, more recently, the state airline IBERIA.

Economic Performance

The economy in Spain stagnated for the first two decades of Franco's regime, and only in 1963 did real wages recover to the pre–Civil War level of 1936. After World War II, Spain was ostracized by the international community. Franco initially pursued a policy of autarky (self-sufficiency through high levels of protectionism), which led to widespread suffering. By the early 1950s, this policy had failed, and Spain was going bankrupt. Franco switched course and began to liberalize the economy in order to attract foreign capital. The result was the economic "miracle" of the 1960s. Spain's cheap labor (due to repression of unions) and low taxes, combined with state protection of key industries, produced extraordinarily rapid industrial development.

By 1975 Spain was suffering from the side effects of this rapid growth. The OPEC oil crisis of the 1970s hit oil-dependent Spain particularly hard. Inflation, historically very low under Franco, was beginning to increase. Wages that had been kept artificially low during decades of authoritarian rule were now under pressure to rise. Spain's traditionally low budget deficit began to grow as governments during the transition to democracy sought to satiate pent-up demand for public services. Most ominous, however, was the widespread economic crisis symbolized by many of Spain's overprotected and increasingly obsolete industrial plants.

The first democratic governments were unable to address the impending economic crisis. The UCD governments were too weak, and major economic policies were implemented through pacts negotiated between the UCD and parties of the left. The desire to consolidate democracy took precedence over economic reform. As a result, the economy stagnated from 1975 to 1982 as growth slowed to only 1.5 percent. Inflation soared, unemployment climbed, and industrial production and investment declined. The budget deficit skyrocketed. Spain's economic crisis at the time was the most severe in all of Western Europe.

High levels of unemployment have plagued Spain since its democratic transition. Unemployment rose from under 5 percent in 1975 to over 22 percent in 1996, but then steadily declined until the recent global economic crisis. Yet, for many reasons Spain continues to have a very serious unemployment problem (the rate in 2009 was about 17 percent). Franco avoided high unemployment because of the massive migration of Spaniards to other European nations and the low number of women in the workforce. Europe's economic crisis in the 1970s and the return of democracy reversed this outflow of the labor force. Democratization also brought a rapid entry of women into the workforce. The delayed effects of the 1960s baby boom that accompanied the economic "miracle" also swelled the labor market. Franco's use of state protectionism prolonged the life of many industries, but Spain's entry into the Common Market made continued state support for inefficient enterprises untenable. In the 1980s and 1990s, the Socialists' policy of closing down and streamlining such industries threw many Spaniards out of work. The rapid rise in wages after democracy was not accompanied by a rise in productivity, and, as a result, many firms became less competitive.

Between 1982 and 1996, the Socialists attempted to restructure the economy and prepare it for full integration into the international economy.[49] In order to carry out this policy, the government implemented tough austerity measures, many of which hurt poor Spaniards the most. On its first day in office, the PSOE announced a devaluation of the currency and a dramatic rise in energy prices. The 1983 Law of Reconversion and Reindustrialization started the process of closing down the most inefficient of Spain's industries. As noted earlier, the Socialists liberalized labor laws, giving employers more freedom to hire and fire workers and thus infuriating Spain's trade unions. Spain's deficit was cut in half between 1982 and 1990, and the rate of public expenditure growth fell dramatically. Tax reform increased the state's revenue, and inflation fell considerably. In the second half of the 1980s, the economic growth rate was about 5 percent annually—on average, twice that of the European Community. In short, the Socialists were remarkably effective in reforming the Spanish economy. Ironically, some of these neoliberal measures were similar to those adopted by Thatcher's Conservative Party in Britain. The Socialists defended their record in office by noting the dramatic growth between 1982 and 1989 in expenditures on public pensions, public health, unemployment benefits, and education. Indeed, the Socialists unquestionably made vast improvements in Spain's welfare state, even though their main concerns were economic growth and European integration. The real wages of workers improved more than 6 percent during the Socialist period in office.[50] It is also true that once Spain joined the EU in 1986 and endorsed the European Monetary System in 1989, it had little leeway in its macroeconomic policy.

However, critics have attacked the Socialist policies of the 1980s and 1990s as hurting the poor and failing to reduce inequality. The percentage of Spaniards living in poverty stayed constant during their period in office at about 20 percent of the population—far above the EU average of 14 percent. Income inequality declined sharply at the start of the democratic period, but held constant (with a very slight decline) during the fourteen years of Socialist government.

After 1996 the conservative government continued most of the Socialist economic policies, and it accelerated the privatization of state industries, including some of the most profitable pieces of the public sector. Parts of the state telephone and energy-generating monopolies were sold. The PP announced a drastic budget cut of $1.6 billion and called for the elimination of over 6,000 public-sector jobs. The conservatives also reduced taxes on small and medium-sized enterprises and cut capital gains taxes to 20 percent. In 2003 Spain's overall rate of taxation (35.4 percent of GDP) was the lowest in the EU, where the average was 41 percent.[51] Aznar reduced Spain's budget deficit, limited the public debt, and tamed inflation so as to comply with the EU standards required for participation in the proposed single European currency. By May 1997 Spain had met EU goals and by 1998 it qualified for participation in the new European currency (see Chapter 12).

In recent years the trend of continued growth, declining inflation, and a dropping deficit has been maintained (see Table 8.6). For much of Aznar's eight years in power, Spain had the fastest-growing economy among the four largest nations in the

Spain's Recent Economic Success					TABLE 8.6
	1993	**1996**	**1999**	**2004**	**2007**
Real GDP growth (%)	−1.2	2.4	3.7	2.8	3.8
Inflation (% change in consumer prices)	4.6	3.6	2.9	2.8	2.8
Unemployment (% of labor force)	23.7	22.2	15.4	11.1	8.3

Sources: *Anuario El País* (various years).

Eurozone. Aznar imposed substantial cuts in spending on social programs, and Spain's level of spending on social programs dropped to one of the lowest in Europe.[52]

Since the Socialists returned to power in 2004, the Zapatero governments have largely continued the market-friendly policies of the Aznar administrations by cutting personal and business tax rates and continuing to reduce Spain's public debt.[53] The economy continued to flourish until 2007, when Spain's housing boom ended and when inflation and unemployment rates began to increase.

The Spanish Welfare State

By the 1980s Spain was spending a greater proportion of national income on social security (which includes health care, old age pensions, family support, and support to persons with disabilities) than was the United States, Britain, Canada, Switzerland, or Australia, and it is currently in the middle of the pack among OECD nations.[54] This largesse is a relatively recent phenomenon and is mostly the result of the democratic regime. In 1960 Spain spent about 2 percent of its GDP on social security, by 1990 that figure had risen to about 15 percent, and in 1995 it peaked at about 19 percent. Likewise, education spending, which lagged during the Francoist regime, doubled between 1975 and 2001, as noted in Figure 8.8.

Democratic governments have overhauled and enhanced the welfare system. All citizens are now entitled to receive welfare benefits. A basic pension is guaranteed to all Spanish citizens regardless of the amount they have paid into the system. Spain's social security agency has seen its share of the national budget grow steadily, while the amount of its budget contributed by employers and employees has gradually declined (the state currently contributes about one-third of the total cost of social security, similar to other European countries).

The National Health System created in 1986 replaced a variety of insurance schemes with an integrated public system that provides universal medical coverage. Universal coverage for all but the wealthiest 1 percent of the population was achieved by 1991. About one-quarter of Spanish health care is private, and private providers are often contracted by the state to perform health services. A drawback to the extended coverage is the increase in waiting lists, and investment in health care that has not kept up

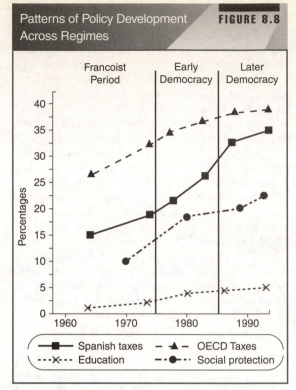

FIGURE 8.8

Patterns of Policy Development Across Regimes

Source: Richard Gunther, "The Impact of Regime Change on Public Policy: The Case of Spain," *Journal of Public Policy* 16, no. 2 (1996): 177, 179.

with increased demand. Still, Spain is one of the healthiest societies in the world and has the highest life expectancy in the EU. Infant mortality has plummeted and is lower than in the United States and most EU countries. In addition, the PSOE established a fairly extensive rural subsidy and jobs program, targeting Andalucia and Extremadura, the poor southern provinces. Though criticized for their inefficiency, these programs have significantly improved living standards in the south.

Spain's benefits for the elderly are among the most generous in the world. As a percentage of former earnings, only Sweden's are higher. With the economic crisis of the 1970s and 1980s, the pension system teetered on the verge of bankruptcy. The Socialists overhauled the system, restricting access to pensions based on disability and imposing stricter limits on the value of retirement benefits.

Spain's high unemployment rate has focused attention on unemployment benefits. At the end of the

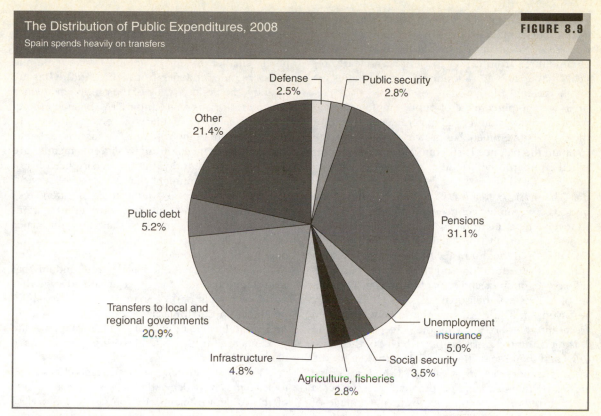

The Distribution of Public Expenditures, 2008
Spain spends heavily on transfers

FIGURE 8.9

- Defense 2.5%
- Public security 2.8%
- Other 21.4%
- Pensions 31.1%
- Public debt 5.2%
- Transfers to local and regional governments 20.9%
- Unemployment insurance 5.0%
- Social security 3.5%
- Infrastructure 4.8%
- Agriculture, fisheries 2.8%

Source: Ministerio de Hacienda y Economía. Retrieved from www.meh.es/Portal/Estadistica+e+Informes/Presupuesto+y+cuentas+publicas, March 25, 2009.

Franco regime, only 62 percent of Spaniards were eligible for such benefits.[55] The Socialists attempted to tighten up the criteria for receiving benefits, but in one of the few areas where they responded to trade union pressure, they raised that figure to about 70 percent by 1993. Under the Socialists the number of Spaniards receiving unemployment benefits rose dramatically. In 2002 the Aznar government restricted those benefits. The government did not give in to union pressure, even after a nationwide general strike. Unlike many European countries, there is no safety net for those who do not qualify for benefits. These individuals are forced to depend on their families for support. Spain's unemployment rate has been especially high among young people, and first-time job seekers do not qualify for unemployment benefits. Workers who qualify for benefits receive an amount that varies according to how much a worker has contributed to unemployment insurance over his or her career, but that is

limited to six years. After six years, a very small unemployment "subsidy" is available.

Figure 8.9 shows that a large part of public expenditures in Spain goes into transfers to individual citizens or to local and regional governments. The transfers to subnational governments support many educational and health policies that are administered at those levels. Pensions account for the largest part of transfers to individuals. In contrast, Spain spends less than many other European countries on national defense and public security, and it does not have to make particularly large public debt payments.

Regional Devolution

Spain's democracy has gone a long way toward solving the historical conflict between center and periphery. But the constitutional solution has involved compromise, and a small minority of

Spaniards remain dissatisfied. There can be no doubt that democratization has created a genuine devolution of power. A look at the shift in public expenditures from center to periphery clearly reveals that Spain's 17 Autonomous Communities get an increasingly large share of the pie (see Figure 8.9). The percentage of public employees who work for regional and local governments instead of the central government has grown steadily, although in Spain the balance is still tilted toward the center when compared with federal systems in Germany and the United States.[56]

The most contentious issue between the central and AC governments concerns funding. The ability to receive revenue from Madrid or to raise it locally varies considerably from region to region. Under the Socialists a gradual transfer of funds, especially in the areas of education and health care, began to take place, often raising cries of favoritism. The ability of ACs to levy their own taxes has not been fully resolved, and little AC revenue is now generated from internal taxes. With the exception of the Basque Country and Navarre, which tax their citizens and then repay the central government for the cost of its services, most of the AC budgets come from a portion of central government taxes collected in each region. Currently, the exact percentage of such taxes going to AC governments is determined by a complex and controversial formula that considers population, area, industrialization, migration patterns, and poverty levels. The bottom line, however, is that ACs remain heavily dependent on the central state financially.

One problem faced by the central government is income disparities among regions. Since the transition to democracy, many leaders in Madrid have sought to finance ACs in a way that would equalize the wealth among Spanish regions. Article 2 of the Spanish Constitution calls for a leveling of income between regions, and the Inter-Territorial Compensation Fund was established to achieve this. Since 1975 Spanish regions have become more equal, though this has in part resulted from the equalization efforts of the EU. However, Spain's two wealthiest regions and the regions with the greatest autonomy (the Basque Country and Catalonia) view such leveling as a drain on their economies. In addition, such solidaristic policies exacerbate the deep-seated view in both regions that Madrid has historically taken from these regions more than it has given back.

A more localized but still serious tension between center and periphery concerns the minority of individuals in the Basque Country (and to a much smaller extent, Catalonia) who continue to desire independence from Spain. In the Basque Country, the political wing of the pro-independence Basque terrorist organization ETA (Basque Homeland and Liberty) regularly receives between 10 and 15 percent of the vote in elections. Those favoring independence through violent means are clearly a small minority, but the persistence of pro-independence sentiment alarms many observers. The most prominent Basque leadership often lacks the political will and unity to confront and marginalize terrorism. In contrast to Catalonia, the major Basque political forces are ambiguous in their support for Spain's constitution. The centrist Basque National Party has called for a referendum that would give Basques the power to decide whether or not to remain part of Spain. Demands for independence in Catalonia have always been weaker. And in the Basque Country as well as Catalonia, the percentage of those polled favoring independence has steadily dropped.

The conservative Aznar governments (1996–2004) took a dim view of demands to increase the autonomy of the AC governments. In contrast, the Socialists under Zapatero have supported revised autonomy statutes that give ACs greater autonomy and have overseen the approval of new statutes in Catalonia, Andalusia, and Valencia.

In only two regions, Catalonia and the Basque Country, is there a large population with a truly dominant ethnic identity.[57] In other regions citizens clearly accept both national and regional identifications.[58] Even in the Basque Country and Catalonia, however, a sizeable group, though not a majority, feels equally attached to Spain and the region. And in those two regions, a majority (56% in the Basque Country and 69% in Catalonia) expresses some type of dual regional and Spanish identity.[59] In Catalonia a significant percentage (12%) view themselves as only Spanish.

The trend toward devolution now appears to be unstoppable. By 2006 the central government controlled only 46 percent of all public spending, compared with 87 percent in 1981—one clear sign that the ACs are increasingly important.[60] There is now a growing realization that Spain is moving toward a federal model of government. As a result, there are renewed calls for revamping the Senate into a genuinely regional body. Concerns that the electoral victory of José María Aznar in 1996 would stem the devolution process were unfounded. Lacking a parliamentary majority, Aznar cut political deals with centrist regional groups that assured a continuation of the devolution process. However, once in opposition the conservatives did oppose the revised Catalan Autonomy Statute approved in 2006, arguing that it threatened the unity of the Spanish state.

Terrorism

Terrorism—one of the most intractable problems of democracy in Spain—had its origins in the Francoist regime. The terrorist group **Basque Homeland and Liberty** (*ETA*—Euskadi ta Askatassuna) emerged in opposition to Francoist repression and has carried out the vast majority of terrorist attacks since the transition to democracy.

Democracy has not solved the problem of domestic terrorism, but there has been a decline in the incidence of terrorism over the past decade. As a result of democratization and devolution of powers to the regions, a major faction of ETA quit the armed struggle in 1977, backing a leftist Basque political party. Curiously, however, ETA continued to grow, and terrorist acts did not cease. Most targets of ETA terrorism have been members of the state security forces, but innocent bystanders are regularly murdered in ETA attacks. ETA's constant attacks on military personnel were a source of frustration for the armed forces and may have precipitated the attempted coup of 1981.

There is much speculation about why democratization did not eliminate Basque terrorism. Although it is thought to have no more than 500 members, ETA's continued existence has been aided by its secretive structure (it is organized into small cells) and its constant campaign of robbery and extortion that give the organization substantial resources. Popular support for ETA and the behavior of Basque political elites are also important factors. The constitution's failure to recognize the Basque Country's right to self-determination alienated many Basques. Until fairly recently political leaders at both the central and the regional levels lacked the unity and resolve to combat terrorism. Many leftists, and Basques of all political stripes,

sympathized with ETA during the dictatorship and found it hard to denounce the organization after 1977. The Basque Nationalist Party (PNV), for example, refused to refer to ETA as "terrorist." The Basque clergy condemn ETA, but often equate it with police repression. In addition, ETA receives support from foreign terrorist groups, and the French government tolerated the presence of Basque terrorists within its borders until the mid-1980s. ETA's political front, Herri Batasuna (HB), and its various successors have fared well in regional elections.

Nevertheless, democratic leaders, while unable to stop Basque terrorism, may be slowly winning the political battle. An accord between Spain and France in 1984 tightened the screws on ETA. Spain's entry into the EU and NATO and the September 11, 2001, attacks in the United States gave Spain important allies in the fight against terrorism. Most importantly, the tide of popular opinion within the Basque Country appears to have turned decidedly against ETA. The new Basque police force has improved the image of government. In January 1988 all Basque political forces, except the pro-ETA HB, signed an antiterrorism pact. The leading Basque political party, the PNV, has been more openly critical of ETA, even though it often disagrees with the government in Madrid over how to best stop terrorism. Polls now regularly show that an overwhelming majority of Basques favor the disarming of ETA. In recent years massive demonstrations against terrorism have become commonplace.

Unfortunately, just as the threat of domestic terrorism appeared to subside, a new terrorist threat surfaced with the March 2004 Madrid bombings, carried out by Islamic radicals (see Box 8.4).

Immigration

The last decade has seen an unprecedented explosion of immigration to Spain, and, as a result, immigration is now a major political issue for the first time in Spanish history. The dimensions of the crisis are dramatic: From 2003 to 2007, the number of foreign-born residents in Spain doubled to about 4 million (the actual numbers may be as high as 5 million), or about 10 percent of the Spanish population. It is estimated that over 600,000 immigrants arrived in Spain in 2005 alone. Immigrants have arrived from three main regions: Africa, Latin America, and Eastern

BOX 8.4

Terrorism and Democratic Elections

Early in the morning on March 11, 2004, a series of explosions destroyed several commuter trains in Madrid. The acts of terror killed 191 people and injured over 1,500. In a country all too accustomed to terrorist acts perpetrated by Basque nationalists, the March 2004 attacks stood out as the worst single act of terrorism in Spanish history. The Aznar government, backed by the state-owned media, initially blamed ETA for the massacre, and it stubbornly stuck to this interpretation even as evidence mounted that Islamic radicals were responsible. On the eve of general elections, many Spaniards suspected that Aznar's government was trying to capitalize on his party's tough anti-ETA policies, while diverting attention away from his very unpopular support for the U.S.-led invasion and occupation of Iraq. Only three days after the attacks, Spanish voters handed Aznar's conservatives a stunning defeat. Some foreign observers called the vote a victory for terrorism, arguing that the violence had provided a last-minute boost for Spain's Socialist Workers Party, which had openly opposed Spain's role in the occupation of Iraq. Others countered that the conservatives were punished for having falsely blamed ETA for the bombings and for having long pursued a foreign policy that was opposed by a vast majority of Spaniards. Still others questioned whether democracies should conduct national elections in the immediate aftermath of such traumatic attacks.*

*An excellent overview of the 2004 elections is Raj Chari, "The Spanish 2004 General Election: Terrorism as a Catalyst for Change?" *West European Politics* 27 (November 2004): 954–963.

Europe. Africans have tended to arrive illegally, gaining entry through the Canary Islands (only 70 miles off the coast of Morocco), through Spain's Moroccan enclaves of Ceuta and Melilla, or via the narrow Strait of Gibraltar. Latin Americans have integrated more easily into Spanish society, given their language skills. The bulk of immigrants from Eastern Europe have come from new members states of the EU, especially Romania.

The Socialist administrations of Zapatero have tended to take a tolerant view of immigration. Socialists noted that immigrants contributed a great deal to Spain's recent economic boom, helping to offset Spain's low birth rate (the lowest in Western Europe). Moreover, during most of the last decade, Spain's unemployment rate declined even as millions of immigrants entered Spain. In 2005 Zapatero passed an amnesty law that gave resident status to over half a million illegal immigrants, arguing that the law would deliver a blow to the underground economy, while increasing Spain's tax revenue.

Opinion polls show that concern about immigration has risen substantially in recent years. Immigrants are often blamed for crime and other social problems. After the March 2004 terrorist attacks in Madrid, immigrants from Africa were viewed with increasing suspicion. Riots by immigrant communities in France were a model for many Spaniards of what could go wrong. As the Spanish economy slowed in 2007, immigrants more easily became scapegoats. Immigration suddenly became politicized during the 2008 electoral campaign. During the televised election debates, Popular Party leader Mariano Rajoy blasted the Zapatero government for encouraging a flood of immigrants. He called for all immigrants to sign a legally binding immigrant contract requiring them to learn Spanish and to respect Spanish customs. Polls taken after the debates showed that a majority of Spaniards supported the plan.

The issue of immigration did not prove decisive in the 2008 legislative elections, but the Zapatero government is aware that there is popular support for a policy to stop illegal immigration. In June 2008 Spain increased the period during which it can detain illegal immigrants from 40 to 60 days. Spain has supported EU legislation that will create a common European immigration policy. Nevertheless, to date it has resisted (and has been a harsh critic of) the kind of harsh crackdown on immigrants adopted by some other countries, such as Italy.

Women in Spain

During the Franco regime, males had statutory power over women within Spanish families, and women needed permission from their husbands for a wide variety of activities. Women had no control over family assets. Penalties for adultery were far harsher for women than for men. Contraception, divorce, and abortion, to which many women sought access, were all strictly illegal. The government banned women's organizations, except for the patronizing "Women's Section" of the official party (which sponsored courses on how to be a good wife and mother).

How successful has democracy been in promoting equality for Spain's women? The answer to this question is generally encouraging, but not without some important qualifications.[61] Much of the struggle for women's rights after 1975 was subordinated to the struggle to consolidate democracy. The first UCD governments abolished some of the most egregious legislation from the Francoist period, and the Constitution of 1978 gave women and men legal equality, but many aspects of the document disappointed the women's movement and particularly those on the left. For example, on the issue of abortion the framers of the Constitution rejected the wording proposed by the left and instead stated, "All have the right to life," possibly implying constitutional protection of the fetus. The Constitution gives male heirs to the throne precedence over females.

The consolidation of democracy did, however, facilitate the passing of laws that gave basic rights to women. By 1978 parliament had abolished some sexist laws, like criminalization of adultery for women, and had legalized contraceptives. Divorce was legalized in 1981, and then only after a bitter struggle that helped destroy the governing UCD. After 1982 the PSOE government actively sought to promote women's causes, and feminists were able to obtain important political positions. The most important innovation was the creation of the Spanish Women's Institute, a powerful governmental institution. With Cabinet backing it pursued myriad actions to improve the lot of women. It attempted to eliminate all legislation that discriminated against women, improve women's health (a landmark 1985 health bill included provisions for state-funded family planning), promote women's participation in society, and encourage equal sharing of domestic responsibilities.

As a result, the lives of Spanish women improved considerably in the first two decades of democracy. As women have had increased opportunities to enter the labor market and as contraception has become widely available, there has been a rapid decline in birthrates. By 1990 Spain's birthrate was one of the lowest in Europe. Publicly funded preschool for 3- to 6-year-olds, a crucial issue for women, has been extensively implemented. Spanish women have made enormous strides in higher education. By the end of the Francoist regime, only about one-third of university students were women, compared to over one-half today. Unemployment has been a matter of particular concern for women, who work disproportionately in lower-paying and less secure jobs. In 1992 women on average earned only 72.5 percent of what men were paid, reflecting the lower skill levels and often part-time nature of their jobs. These jobs are also less secure, as the unemployment rate for women (about 30 percent) is almost double that of men and the highest in Europe.[62]

Spain's Socialists can take credit for increasing the role of women in politics, a profession reserved for men until very recently. The PSOE introduced a quota system requiring that a quarter of all party-controlled public posts be given to women. At the start of the Socialists' tenure in office, only 5 percent of political appointments went to women; by 1991 this figure had increased to 13 percent. About 25 percent of the members of the Spanish legislature elected in 2004 were women, well above the European average of 16 percent.[63] Despite the continued strength of Spanish *machismo* and the persistence of discrimination against women, signs of change are everywhere. Women judges, Cabinet ministers, and (since 1993) bullfighters have changed the traditional image of Spanish women. José Luis Rodríguez Zapatero, a self-defined "radical feminist," took office in 2004, pledging to make women's issues a priority. His government passed tough new laws against domestic violence, liberalized Spain's divorce laws, and relaxed restrictions on abortion. Women make up over one-half of Zapatero's Cabinet, including the deputy prime minister, a first for Europe. In 2007 the Socialists passed a Law for Equality Between Men and Women that addresses the paucity of women on the boards of directors of major Spanish corporations, requires political parties to allocate 40 percent of electoral lists to women, creates paternity leaves for fathers, and extends maternity leave for women.

Foreign Policy

Spain was not an important international actor during the Franco regime. The international community ostracized authoritarian Spain during the first part of Franco's rule. The isolation was partly broken in the 1950s, when the United States began to value Spain's role as an anti-Communist bulwark. A 1953 agreement between Spain and the United States gave the United States valuable military facilities on Spanish soil in exchange for American economic aid and political support. Membership in the United Nations came soon after, in 1955, and relations with Spain's European neighbors began to thaw (a trade agreement with the European Economic Community was signed in 1970), although they remained cool until after the death of the dictator in 1975.

Under the first UCD governments, Spain's relations with the world rapidly normalized. Spain applied for membership in the European Community and NATO, improved relations with its neighbors, and formally renounced its last colonial claims in North Africa. After Spain's four decades of isolation, the decision to join the EU was supported by almost every Spanish political force and took on almost mythical significance. Spain, along with Portugal, joined the EU in 1986 after intense and protracted negotiations. Spain quickly became one of the strongest proponents of monetary integration. Despite the enormous sacrifices required over the last two decades in order to integrate into the EU, Spaniards continue to be among the strongest supporters of European integration and a common foreign policy. A 2008 poll showed that 65 percent of Spaniards believed that EU membership has been good for Spain, far above the average European level.[64] Spaniards were also among the most enthusiastic backers of the new European currency, the euro.

Integration into NATO proved far more controversial. Much of the left and a sector of the governing UCD were opposed to NATO membership when the government first proposed it in 1977, but they were unable to stop the process, and Spain was formally admitted in May 1982. Spanish voters narrowly supported continued NATO membership in a March 1986 referendum convened by the Socialists. In 1988 the Socialists carried through on the pledge to reduce the U.S. military presence by

renegotiating Spain's military agreement with the United States. The 1995 appointment of Javier Solana, a former Socialist cabinet minister, as the first Spanish NATO Secretary General, ended doubts about Spain's commitment to the organization. In 1996 the conservative government of Prime Minister Aznar fully integrated Spain into NATO's military command. Despite strong domestic opposition, Spain sent 1,000 troops to participate in NATO's Kosovo operation in 1999 and later sent small contingents to both Afghanistan and Iraq. Aznar's uncompromising support for the U.S.-led invasion of Iraq proved extremely unpopular from the start. Polls showed that about 90 percent of the public opposed the invasion at the start, and a similar percentage continued to oppose the war by early 2004. After his 2004 electoral victory, Socialist Prime Minister Zapatero immediately fulfilled a campaign pledge to withdraw Spain's 1,300 troops from Iraq, while offering to beef up Spain's contingent in Afghanistan.

Spain's relationship with its southern neighbor Morocco remains a source of tension. Morocco, a former Spanish colony, resents Spain's continued occupation of two enclaves on Morocco's Mediterranean coast. Spain is concerned about the growing flood of illegal immigrants who cross the Strait of Gibraltar to seek employment in Europe. Racial tensions between African migrant workers and Spanish citizens exploded in southern Spain in February 2000, leading to considerable violence. In 2002 Moroccan forces briefly occupied a Spanish islet off Morocco's coast. The 2004 Madrid railway bombings, carried out largely by Moroccan-born terrorists, convinced the newly elected Socialist prime minister of the need to improve Spanish-Moroccan relations, and his first foreign visit was to Morocco.

One unresolved foreign policy issue concerns the status of **Gibraltar**, a tiny (just over two square miles) British dependency on the southwest portion of the Iberian Peninsula that juts out into the Mediterranean Sea. Great Britain won the "rock" from Spain in 1704, but Spain claims sovereignty over Gibraltar. In protest over Britain's refusal to "return" Gibraltar, Franco closed the border between Gibraltar and Spain in an attempt to cut off and strangle the enclave. Instead, the policy only strengthened the resolve of Gibraltar's residents to remain British citizens. Only after the election of a Socialist government in 1982 was the border between Spain and Gibraltar normalized, but Spain continues its claim over the rock. Fortunately, this issue no longer endangers Spain's relations with Britain—indeed, Spain and the United Kingdom both backed the invasion of Iraq to depose Saddam Hussein—and the dispute is no longer imbued with the emotion that was present during the Franco years. An April 1999 accord between Spain and the United Kingdom has opened the way for future negotiations over the territory and promises to further ease tensions.

Spain enjoys special ties to its former colonies in Latin America, having assumed the role of cultural leader of the 300 million Spanish speakers worldwide. It attempts to represent the interests of Latin America within the EU. In addition, Spanish governments have been harsh critics of human rights violations in Latin America. Socialist support for Sandinista Nicaragua and Castro's Cuba created friction with the Reagan and Bush administrations during the 1980s. One of the first foreign policy acts of the conservative Aznar government was to cut off official Spanish aid to Cuba, an act that drew praise from the United States. However, in 1997 the new conservative government locked horns with the Clinton administration over U.S.-Cuban policy. PP Foreign Minister Abel Matutes blasted U.S. attempts to penalize Europeans who invested in Cuba, threatening the United States with retaliation. Spain has played an active role in the negotiation and enforcement of peace proposals in Nicaragua and El Salvador and has played a key role in United Nations missions in both countries.

Beginning with the 2004 electoral campaign, foreign policy issues that were long kept off the domestic political agenda have become particularly divisive.[65] Aznar's cozy relationship with the Bush administration, his decision to send Spanish troops to Iraq, and his confrontational policies toward Morocco ended decades of broad consensus between the PP and the PSOE on major foreign policy issues. Zapatero's foreign policy has departed substantially from that of his conservative predecessor. In addition to withdrawing Spanish troops from Iraq, the Socialists have deemphasized relations with the United States and United Kingdom and have sought to exercise political influence via the EU. Spanish relations with the United States have become more tense, and Zapatero has not been invited to the White House.

Zapatero has sought a less confrontatic with Morocco and Cuba.

THE PEACEFUL DISAPPEARANCE OF THE TWO SPAINS

For students of comparative politics, Spain's remarkable transition to democracy and its ability to overcome dangerous historical cleavages offer numerous lessons. Most importantly, the transition to democracy demonstrates that the art of politics—especially creative leadership and political compromise—can solve seemingly intractable political problems. The transition was successful in large part because of the ability of Juan Carlos and Adolfo Suárez to use Francoist political structures to promote democratic reform and to the willingness of democratic opposition leaders to tolerate such a strategy. Skilled political leadership was not the only explanation for Spain's successful democratization. As noted in Chapter 1, the relationship between economic development and democracy is complex, and this is certainly illustrated in the Spanish case. Rapid economic development under Franco after 1960 began to change Spanish society in ways that the dictator could not have foreseen. The urbanization, secularization, greater education, and increasing wealth of Spaniards all eroded historical cleavages. The opening of Spain to foreign investment ignited the economic boom, and the opening of Spanish society to foreign influence began to foster a democratic political culture.

Not all political cleavages have been mitigated by skilled leadership and economic modernization. As we have seen, the center-periphery issue continues to challenge Spanish democracy, but by 2008 only Basque terrorism remained as a reminder of this persistent problem. Small sectors of Spain's armed forces still admire Spain's authoritarian past, but the vast majority have accepted democratic rule. After 2004 the Catholic Church led a bitter opposition against a whole host of social reforms passed by the Socialists, and Spanish conservatives fiercely opposed plans for greater regional autonomy. On the whole, however, the historic divide between the "two Spains" has been replaced by a united, vibrant, and modern democracy that has fully integrated with its European neighbors. The political issues that divide Spaniards are being peacefully contested within the confines of a successful constitutional democracy.

REVIEW QUESTIONS

- Describe Spain's historical cleavages. Are any of those cleavages still important?

- Describe Spain's transition to democracy. How did that transition facilitate the consolidation of democracy?

- Has Spain's system of regional devolution been successful? What are some outstanding issues regarding Spain's system of Autonomous Communities?

- What are some of the main characteristics of Spain's political party system?

- What are the main aspects of Spain's immigration challenge?

- What are some major concerns of Spanish foreign policy?

KEY TERMS

Autonomous
Communities (ACs)
Aznar, José María
Basque Homeland and
Liberty (ETA)
Basque Nationalist
Party (PNV)
Basques
Castilians
Catalans
Congress of Deputies
Constitutional Court
constructive vote of
no confidence

Convergence and
Union (CiU)
Cortes Generales
Defensor del Pueblo
devolution
Franco, Francisco
Galicians
General Confederation
of Workers (UGT)
Gibraltar
González, Felipe
Herri Batasuna (HB)
King Juan Carlos
Popular Party (PP)

President of the
Government
Reconquista
Rodríguez Zapatero,
José Luis
Senate
Spanish Civil War
(1936–1939)
Spanish Communist
Party (PCE)
Spanish Confederation
of Entrepreneurial
Organizations
(CEOE)
Spanish Inquisition

Spanish Second
Republic
(1931–1936)
Spanish Socialist
Workers Party
(PSOE)
Suárez, Adolfo
Supreme Court
two Spains
Union of the
Democratic
Center (UCD)
United Left (IU)
Workers' Commissions
(CC.OO)

SUGGESTED READINGS

Balfour, Sebastian. *The Politics of Contemporary Spain.* London: Routledge, 2005.

Encarnacíon, Omar. *Spanish Politics.* Malden, MA: Polity Press, 2008.

Field, Bonnie N., and Kerstin Hamann (eds.), *Democracy and Institutional Development: Spain in comparative Theoretical Perspective.* London: Palgrave Macmillan, 2008.

Gibbons, John. *Spanish Politics Today.* Manchester, England: Manchester University Press, 1999.

Gunther, Richard, and J. Montero. *The Politics of Spain.* England: Cambridge University Press, 2009.

Gunther, Richard, J. Montero, and J. Botella. *Democracy in Modern Spain.* New Haven, CT: Yale University Press, 2004.

Gunther, Richard, G. Sani, and G. Shabad. *Spain After Franco.* Berkeley: University of California Press, 1986.

Hanley, David, and John Loughlin, eds. *Spanish Political Parties.* Cardiff: University of Wales Press, 2006.

Heywood, Paul. *The Government and Politics of Spain.* New York: St. Martin's Press, 1995.

Hooper, John. *The New Spaniards.* London: Penguin, 1995.

Lieberman, Sima. *Growth and Crisis in the Spanish Economy, 1940–1993*. London: Routledge, 1995.

Magone, José. *Contemporary Spanish Politics*. Second Edition London: Routledge, 2009.

McDonough, Peter, Samuel H. Barnes, and Antonio López Pina. *The Cultural Dynamics of Democratization in Spain*. Ithaca, NY: Cornell University Press, 1998.

Pérez-Díaz, Víctor M. *Spain at the Crossroads: Civil Society, Politics, and the Rule of Law*. Cambridge: Harvard University Press, 1999.

Share, Donald. *Dilemmas of Social Democracy: The Spanish Socialist Workers Party in the 1980s*. Westport, CT: Greenwood Publishers, 1989.

_____. *The Making of Spanish Democracy*. New York: Center for the Study of Democratic Institutions/Praeger Publishers, 1986.

Threlfall, Monica, Christine Cousins, and Celia Valente. *Gendering Spanish Democracy*. London: Routledge, 2006.

INTERNET RESOURCES

Office of the President: **www.la-moncloa.es**

Spain's lower house: **www.congreso.es**

Spanish Socialist Workers Party: **www.psoe.es**

Partido Popular: **www.pp.es**

Izquierda Unida: **www.izquierda-unida.es**

CiU, the leading Catalan Party: **www.convergencia.org**

PNV, the leading Basque Party: **www.eaj-pnv.com**

Directory of Spanish political resources on the Web: **www.sispain.org/SiSpain/english/index.html**

El País, Spain's leading daily newspaper: **www.elpais.es**

El Mundo, Spain's second major Spanish daily newspaper: **www.elmundo.es**

La Vanguardia, a leading daily from Barcelona: **www.lavanguardia.es**

ENDNOTES

1. A January 2009 Centro de Investigaciones Sociológicas (CIS) Public Opinion Barometer survey reported that the top four problems identified by Spaniards were the economy, unemployment, immigration, and terrorism. www.cie.es/opencm/es1_encuestas/estudios/ver.jsp?estudios=9040 Study #2782, accessed March 25, 2009.

2. Cristina Fernández and Carolina Ortega, "Labor Market Assimilation of Immigrants in Spain," *Spanish Economic Review* 10 (2008): 83–107.

3. According to a CIS poll in May 2004, 53 percent of Spaniards felt there are too many immigrants in Spain. http://www.cis.es/cis/opencm/ES/1_encuestas/estudios/ver.jsp?estudio=3954, study #2565, accessed March 25, 2009.

4. Paul Preston, *The Spanish Civil War: Reaction, Revolution and Revenge* (London: Harper Perennial, 2006).

5. Donald Share, *The Making of Spanish Democracy* (New York: Praeger Publishers and the Center for the Study of Democratic Institutions, 1986), 86–118.

6. Donald Share, *Dilemmas of Social Democracy: The Spanish Socialist Workers Party in the 1980s* (Westport, CT: Greenwood, 1989).

7. José Magone, *Contemporary Spanish Politics* (London: Routledge, 2009), 113.

8. See Elisa Roller, "Reforming the Senate: Mission Impossible?" *West European Politics* 25, no. 4 (October 2002): 69–72.

9. An outstanding overview is Thomas Lancaster and Michael Gates, "Spain," in *Legal Traditions and Systems,* ed. Alan Katz (New York: Greenwood Press, 1986), 360–380.

10. Frederick Weil, "The Sources and Structure of Legitimation in Western Democracies," *American Sociological Review* 54 (October 1989): 691.

11. From Richard Gunther, J. Montero, and J. Botella, *Democracy in Modern Spain* (New Haven, CT: Yale University Press, 2004), 163.

12. *Eurobarometer,* 69, July 2008, p. 5. http://ec.europa.eu/public_opinion/archives/eb/eb69/eb_69_first_en.pdf, accessed March 25, 2009.

13. Weil, "The Sources and Structure of Legitimation," p. 696; Mariano Torcal Loriente, "El orígen y desarrollo del apoyo a la democracia en España," *Revista Española de Ciencia Política* 18 (2008): 29–65.

14. Gunther, Montero, and Botella, *Democracy in Modern Spain,* 147.

15. The discussion below draws heavily on Gunther, Montero, and Botella, *Democracy in Modern Spain,* 146–197.

16. Laura Morales, "¿Existe una crisis participativa? La evolución de la participación política y el asociacionismo en España," *Revista Española de Ciencia Política* 13 (October 2005): 51–87.

17. Taehyun Nam, "Rough Days in Democracies: Comparing Protests in Democracies" *European Journal of Political Research* 46, no. 1 (January 2007): 97–120.

18. Peter McDonough, Samuel H. Barnes, and Antonio Lopez Pina, "Social Identity and Mass Politics in Spain," *Comparative Political Studies* 21, no. 2 (July 1988): 200–230.

19. Gunther, Montero, and Botella, *Democracy in Modern Spain,* 180.

20. Hooper, *The New Spaniards* (London: Penguin: 1995, First Edition), 269.

21. Centro de Investigaciones Sociológicas, "Opinion publica ante la Union Europea" (Spring 2004). http://www.cis.es/cis/opencm/ES/1_encuestas/estudios/ver.jsp? estudio=3974, study #2566, accessed March 25, 2009.

22. *Eurobarometer,* 52, April 2000, p. 15 http://ec.europa.eu/public_opinion/archives/eb/eb52/eb52_en.htm, accessed March 25, 2009.

23. Hooper, *The New Spaniards,* 307.

24. Hooper, *The New Spaniards,* 306.

25. Karen Sanders with María José Canel, "Spanish Politicians and the Media: Controlled Visibility and Soap Opera Politics," *Parliamentary Affairs* 57, no. 1 (January 2004): 200.

26. Heywood, *Government and Politics of Spain,* (New York: Saint Martin's Press, 1995), p. 250; Kerstin Hamann, "Unions and Industrial Relations in Spain" in Bonnie Field and Kerstin Hamann (eds.), *Democracy and Institutional Development: Spain in Comparative Theoretical Perspective* (London: Palgrave Macmillan,2009), 162.

27. Hooper, *The New Spaniards,* 133.

28. Dale Fuchs, "New Law Requires Roman Catholicism Classes in Spain's Schools," *New York Times,* December 21, 2003, 15.

29. Gunther, Montero, and Botella, *Democracy in Modern Spain,* 143.

30. José Ramón Montero, "Religiosidad, ideología y voto en españa," *Revista de Estudios Políticos* 83 (January–March 1994): 85.

31. John Karamichas, "Developments in Spanish Greens: Change of Course or Repetition?" *Environmental Politics* 11, no. 1 (Spring 2002): 178–183.

32. Gunther, Montero, and Botella, *Democracy in Modern Spain,* 147 and 263.

33. Paul Heywood, "The Spanish Left: Towards a Common Home?" in *West European Communist Parties After the Revolutions of 1989,* ed. Martin Bull and Paul Heywood (London: St. Martin's Press, 1994).

34. On the PSOE, see Share, *Dilemmas of Social Democracy.*

35. Juan J. Linz, "From Great Hopes to Civil War: The Breakdown of Democracy in Spain," in *The Breakdown of Democratic Regimes: Europe,* ed. Juan J. Linz and Alfred Stepan (Baltimore, MD: Johns Hopkins University Press, 1978), 166.

36. See Share, *Dilemmas of Social Democracy,* 28.

37. Paul Kennedy, "Phoenix from the Ashes: The PSOE Government Under Rodríguez Zapatero, 2004–2007: A New Model for Social Democracy?" *International Journal of Iberian Studies* 20, no. 3 (2007), 187-206.

38. Kenneth Medhurst, "Spanish Conservative Politics," in *Conservative Parties in Western Europe,* ed. Zig Layton-Henry (London: Macmillan, 1982), 313.

39. Heywood, *Government and Politics of Spain,* 204.

40. On the PP, see John Gilmour, "The Partido Popular," in *Spanish Political Parties,* ed. David Hanley and John Loughlin (Cardiff: University of Wales Press, 2006), 21–45.

41. John Etherington and Ana-Mar Fernández, "Political Parties in Catalonia," in *Spanish Political Parties,* ed. David Hanley and John Loughlin (Cardiff: University of Wales Press, 2006), 74–107.

42. Francisco Letamendia, "Basque Political Parties," in *Spanish Political Parties,* ed. David Hanley and John Loughlin(Cardiff: University of Wales Press, 2006), 108–141.

43. Richard Gunther, "Electoral Laws, Party Systems, and Elites: The Case of Spain," *American Political Science Review* 83, no. 3 (September 1989): 840.

44. Magone, *Contemporary Spanish Politics,* 141-148

45. McDonough, Barnes, and Lopez Pina, "The Nature of Political Support," in *Comparative Political Studies* 27, No. 3 (October 1994): 335–336.

46. Gunther, Montero, and Botella, *Democracy in Modern Spain,* 170–171.

47. Leonardo Morlino, "Political Parties and Democratic Consolidation in Southern Europe," in *The Politics of Democratic Consolidation,* ed. Richard Gunther, P. Nikiforous Diamandorous, and Hans-Jurgen Puhle (Baltimore, MD: Johns Hopkins University Press, 1995), 331–332.

48. Morlino, "Political Parties," 319.

49. Sebastián Etchemendy, "Revamping the Weak, Protecting the Strong, and Managing Privatization," *Comparative Political Studies* 37, no. 4 (August 2004): 623–651.

50. Maravall, "Politics and Policy: Economic Reforms in Southern Europe," in Luiz Carlos Bresser Pereira et al., eds., *Economic Reforms in New Democracies* (Cambridge: Cambridge University Press, 1993), 108, argues that despite huge crisis and unemployment, earnings per worker actually rose 6.2 percent in terms of real earning power between 1983 and 1991.

51. OECD, *Economic Survey, Spain* (2003) OECD is the publisher, New York is place of publication, full citation: vol. 2003, no. 7, 39–99.

52. Gunther, Montero, and Botella, *Democracy in Modern Spain,* 370.

53. On the economic record of the PSOE under Rodríguez Zapatero, see Paul Kennedy, "Phoenix from the Ashes: The PSOE Government Under Rodríguez Zapatero, 2004–2007," *International Journal of Iberian Studies* 20, no. 3 (2007): 187–206.

54. Francis G. Castles, "Welfare State Development in Southern Europe," *West European Politics* 2 (April 1995): 292. This is an excellent overview of the Spanish welfare state, from which this section draws heavily.

55. Hooper, *The New Spaniards,* 245.

56. Gunther, Montero, and Botella, *Democracy in Modern Spain,* 298.

57. Eduardo López-Aranguren and Manuel García Ferrando, "Nacionalismo y regionalism en la España de los autonomías," in *España a debate,* ed. José Beneyto Vidal (Madrid: Teenos, 1991), 177–190.

58. Luis Moreno, *The Federalizaton of Spain* (London: Frank Cass, 2001).

59. Montserrat Guiberneau, "National Identity, Devolution, and Succession in Canada, Britain, and Spain," *Nations and Nationalism* 12, no. 1 (2006): 66.

60. Magone, *Contemporary Spanish Politics,* 212.

61. The best overview of the women's movement in Spain, from which this section borrows heavily, is Monica Threlfall, Christine Cousins, and Celia Valente, *Gendering Spanish Democracy* (London: Routledge, 2006).

62. Monica Threlfall, "Feminist Politics and Social Change in Spain," in Monica Threlfall, ed., *Mapping the Women's Movement* (London: Verso, 1996), 141.

63. Based on information from The Inter-parliamentary Union. Retrieved _March 25, 2009 from www.ipu.org

64. *Eurobarometer* #69, (Spring 2008). http://ec.europa.eu/public_opinion/archives/eb/eb69/eb_69_first_en.pdf, accessed March 25, 2009.

65. Richard Gillespie, "Spanish Foreign Policy: Party Alternatives or the Pursuit of Consensus?" *Journal of Southern Europe and the Balkans* 9, no. 1 (April 2007): 29–45.

POLITICS IN RUSSIA

Thomas F. Remington

Country Bio

RUSSIA

Population
142.2 million

Territory
6,593,000 square miles

Year of Independence
1991

Year of Current Constitution
1993

Head of State
President Dmitrii Anatol'evich Medvedev

Head of Government
Premier Vladimir Vladimirovich Putin

Language(s)
Russian, other languages of ethnic nationalities

Religion
Russian Orthodox 70–80%, other Christian 1–2%, Muslim 14–15%, Buddhist 0.6%, Jewish 0.3%; other or non-religious 5–15%

ENSURING CONTINUITY OF POWER

On May 7, 2008, **Dmitrii Anatol'evich Medvedev** took the oath of office as president of the Russian Federation. The solemn ceremony—attended by his predecessor, Vladimir Putin, and the Russian Orthodox Patriarch of Russia, Alexii II—signaled that the leadership was united around the choice of the new president. Elsewhere in the former Soviet Union, the succession from one president to another has sometimes triggered a struggle for power among contending political forces, leading to popular uprisings with unpredictable outcomes.[1] The Russian authorities were determined not to allow a similar disruption in the transfer of power from one president to the next.

The succession was smooth, but hardly democratic. Although a presidential election had been held on March 2, every detail was closely controlled so that no serious challenge to Medvedev could arise. Once Putin had decided that Medvedev would succeed him—a choice he announced the previous December—the Kremlin took no chances on the outcome. The state-controlled mass media, regional governors, big business, and the election commission all fell in line. The manipulated election process demonstrated to the world and to any would-be opponents that Medvedev was backed by a united front of all the authorities.

Adding to the display of continuity was the fact that Vladimir Putin himself stayed on in power as prime minister. Medvedev's first act as newly inaugurated president was to name Putin as head of government. This neat exchange—Putin made Medvedev his successor, Medvedev kept Putin in power—solved several problems. Putin's exceptional popularity among the public and the authorities' fear of a destabilizing split among the ruling elite made it desirable to find a postpresidency role for Putin that would ensure continuity and legitimate the new president. At the same time, the authorities deemed it important to observe the niceties of constitutional law, which require that a president serve no more than two consecutive terms. Putin's move therefore allowed the leadership to comply with the constitution, while retaining power.

Yet, this improvised arrangement of shared power opened up huge uncertainty. No one in the political elite could be certain whether Putin was really still in charge and Medvedev was just a figurehead, whether Putin really intended to give up near-autocratic power and turn his attention instead to the details of managing the government, or whether this was a fragile temporary truce that would result in one or the other of the two men ultimately triumphing over the other. Observers noted that the constitution makes the prime minister first in line to succeed the president. So if Medvedev decided to step down prematurely or met with an unfortunate accident, Putin would automatically succeed him and become acting president (much as Putin had become acting president eight years before when Yeltsin resigned the presidency six months ahead of time). Then Putin could presumably be elected to a new term as president in his own right—the constitution only bars a president from serving more than two *successive* terms. No one could be sure what would happen next, but few thought that the duo of Putin as prime minister and Medvedev as president could last long: Most expected that sooner or later one or the other of them would be forced out.

The peculiarity of the situation arose from the fact that Russia's constitution, like that of France and many other countries, provides both for a directly elected president and a prime minister who must enjoy the confidence of parliament. France under the constitution of the Fifth Republic has demonstrated that a president of one party can coexist tolerably well with a prime minister of an opposing party so long as they agree on how to divide responsibilities and do not fight too openly. But Russia has never had successful experience with the sharing of power between two leaders, one with overall responsibility for guiding the state and the other in charge of the government. As Boris Yeltsin once put it, "in Russia, only one person can be number one." Under Communist rule (which lasted from the Bolshevik Revolution in 1917 until the collapse of the Soviet Union in 1991), the regime worked out a division of power between the Communist Party and the government. The party's leader was always the supreme leader in the country, and the head of government was always subordinate. If a similar logic prevails now, Putin, as prime minister, will have to content himself with managing the economy, and Medvedev, as president,

will have final say in all policy matters at home and abroad. Whatever happens, by ensuring a seamless succession from Putin to Medvedev, Russia has launched yet another constitutional experiment, the outcome of which is highly uncertain.

CURRENT POLICY CHALLENGES

Dmitrii Medvedev took over as president at a particularly auspicious point. After a decade of calamitous economic decline in the 1990s following the breakdown of the Soviet regime, Russia's economy has entered a sustained period of recovery. Russia's role as a leading world exporter of fuels and metals (Russia is second only to Saudi Arabia as a world exporter of oil) means that the high world prices for oil, gas, and other commodities have brought prosperity. Until the financial crisis of 2008, the gross national product grew annually in the range of 7–8 percent since 1999, and the government initiated major programs to rebuild schools, hospitals, housing, and agricultural infrastructure. Wages and pensions have risen significantly, while poverty and unemployment have plummeted. Public opinion surveys suggest that the population is pleased with the current trends: 60 percent of the population believes the country is headed in the right direction. Compare that with the nadir of the troubles of the 1990s: For example, in early 1999, only 6 percent thought the country was going the right way. In 2008, 73 percent of the country expressed approval of Medvedev's performance as president.[2] However, the rapidity and severity of the economic crisis that unfolded in 2008–2009 pose a grave challenge to the Putin-Medvedev leadership.

A question debated actively in Russia and abroad is how much credit Vladimir Putin and his authoritarian style of rule deserve for Russia's turnaround (Box 9.1). Behind this question lie two widespread beliefs: First, after a turbulent political transition, a spell of authoritarian rule is often the only way that a country can make a decisive turn toward economic growth and prosperity, with democracy possible only once the institutions of market capitalism are firmly installed (many point to China as a case in point). Second is the idea that whatever the experience of other countries, Russia can only be governed autocratically.

An alternative view is that Putin's actions as leader had relatively little to do with Russia's success. Skeptics argue that any country where oil and gas

Vladimir Putin

Vladimir Vladimirovich Putin was born on October 7, 1952, in Leningrad (called St. Petersburg since 1991). In 1970 he entered Leningrad State University and specialized in civil law. Upon graduation in 1975, Putin worked for the KGB and was first assigned to counterintelligence and then to the foreign intelligence division. Proficient in the German language, he was sent to East Germany in 1985. In 1990, after the Berlin Wall fell, Putin went back to Leningrad, working at the university, but in the employ of the KGB. When a former professor of his, Anatolii Sobchak, became mayor of Leningrad in 1991, he went to work for Sobchak.

In 1996 Putin took a position in Yeltsin's presidential administration. He rose rapidly. In 1998 Yeltsin named Putin head of the FSB (the Federal Security Service—successor to the KGB) and in March 1999 secretary of the Security Council. In August 1999 Yeltsin appointed him prime minister. Thanks to his decisive handling of the military operation in Chechnia, Putin's popularity ratings soared. On December 31, 1999, Yeltsin resigned, making Putin acting president. Putin ran for the presidency and, on March 26, 2000, won with an outright majority of the votes.

Over time, Putin's political persona grew clearer. Uncomfortable with the give and take of public politics, he prefers the hierarchical style of organization used in the military and police. He is a pragmatist with no particular affection for either the Soviet or the tsarist order. Capable of projecting an affable, relaxed demeanor on some occasions, on others he can be brusque, even crude. Like many previous Russian rulers, he has made the consolidation of his own political power his first priority.

---

make up over 60 percent of exports would have realized a huge windfall from the sharp increase in world oil prices. (From 1999 to 2008, the average price of a barrel of crude oil on world markets rose tenfold—from $10 to $100.) From that standpoint, Putin was not so much clever as lucky.

But whichever perspective is right, the fact remains that Medvedev faces serious challenges over the longer run. He and Putin have both repeatedly warned that Russia must not allow itself to become economically dependent on its petroleum resources for economic growth, but must instead generate technological innovation and continuing productivity improvements. "The main problem of the Russian economy today is its extreme inefficiency," Putin declared shortly before stepping down as president. "Labor productivity in Russia remains unacceptably low. We have the same expenditures of labor as in the most developed countries but in Russia they bring several times less return. And that is doubly dangerous in conditions of growing global competition and rising costs for skilled labor and energy."[3] The plunge in world energy prices at a time of sharp worldwide recession in 2008–2009 has confirmed Putin's warning.

Both Putin and Medvedev are well aware of the dangers of the "resource curse": that is, the idea that in countries with windfall revenues from natural resources, the leaders avoid investing in the skills and knowledge of the population, and the societies wind up with lower levels of development than in resource-poor countries.[4] Russia's leaders have worked to invest the oil revenues in projects intended to improve the country's living standard and educational level, stimulate the development of small business, and invest in new and promising technologies.

At the same time, they have frankly acknowledged the grim demographic realities: Russia's population is declining each year as a result of the excess of deaths over births, and the economy is becoming increasingly dependent on migrant labor from China, Central Asia, and elsewhere. Inequality across regions and social groups is rising. A recent National Human Development Report written by a team of Russian experts noted that some regions of Russia live at a level of human development comparable to that of Central Europe, while others are closer to an African level.[5]

But while Russian leaders have admitted the gravity of the problems the country faces, they have been unable to break through the obstacles standing in the way of solving them. Three in particular have proven to be stumbling blocks: the long experience of Russian bureaucrats in defeating any reforms that weaken their power; the vast physical span of the country, which impedes efforts to unite groups in society around broad common interests; and the legacy of the Soviet development model, which concentrated resources in giant state-owned enterprises—often located in remote, harsh regions—that are difficult, if not impossible, to convert into competitive, viable capitalist firms operating in a global market. Therefore, while Russia has enjoyed a substantial economic recovery in the 2000s, thanks to its reserves of natural resources, the sustainability of its progress over the longer term remains in doubt.

HISTORICAL LEGACIES

The Tsarist Regime

The Russian state traces its origins to the princely state that arose around Kiev (today the capital of independent Ukraine) in the ninth century. For nearly a thousand years, the Russian state was autocratic. That is, it was ruled by a hereditary monarch whose power was unlimited by any constitutional constraints. Only in the first decade of the twentieth century did the Russian tsar agree to grant a constitution calling for an elected legislature—and even then, the tsar soon dissolved the legislature and arbitrarily revised the constitution.

In addition to autocracy, the historical legacy of Russian statehood includes *absolutism, patrimonialism,* and *Orthodox Christianity. Absolutism* means that the tsar aspired to wield absolute power over the subjects of the realm. *Patrimonialism* refers to the idea that the ruler treated his realm as property that he owned, rather than as a society with its own legitimate rights and interests.[6] This concept of power continues to influence state rulers today. Finally, the tsarist state identified itself with the *Russian Orthodox Church.* In Russia, as in other countries where it is a dominant religious tradition, the Orthodox Church ties itself closely to the state, considering itself a national church. Traditionally, it has exhorted its adherents to show loyalty and obedience to the state in worldly matters, in return for which the state treated it as the state church. This legacy is still manifested in the present-day rulers' efforts to associate themselves with the heritage of the church and in many Russians' impulse to identify their state with a higher spiritual mission.

Absolutism, patrimonialism, and orthodoxy have been recurring elements of Russian political culture. But alternative motifs have been influential as well. At some points in Russian history, the country's rulers have sought to modernize its economy and society.

Russia imported Western practices in technology, law, state organization, and education in order to make the state competitive with other great powers. Modernizing rulers—such as Peter the Great (who ruled from 1682 to 1725) and Catherine the Great (from 1762 to 1796)—had a powerful impact on Russian society, bringing it closer to West European models. The imperative of building Russia's military and economic potential was all the more pressing because of Russia's constant expansion through conquest and annexation of neighboring territories and its ever-present need to defend its borders. The state's role in controlling and mobilizing society rose with the need to govern a vast territory. By the end of the seventeenth century, Russia was territorially the largest state in the world. But for most of its history, Russia's imperial reach exceeded its actual grasp.

Compared with other major powers of Europe, Russia's economic institutions remained backward well into the twentieth century. However, the trajectory of its development, especially in the nineteenth century, was toward that of a modern industrial society. By the time the tsarist order fell in 1917, Russia had a large industrial sector, although it was concentrated in a few cities. The country had a sizeable middle class, although it was greatly outnumbered by the vast and impoverished peasantry and the radicalized industrial working class. As a result, the social basis for a peaceful democratic transition was too weak to prevent the Communists from seizing power in 1917.

The thousand-year tsarist era left a contradictory legacy. The tsars attempted to legitimate their absolute power by appealing to tradition, empire, and divine right. They treated law as an instrument of rule, rather than a source of authority. The doctrines that rulers should be accountable to the ruled and that sovereignty resides in the will of the people were alien to Russian state tradition. Throughout Russian history, state and society have been more distant from each other than in Western societies. Rulers and populace regarded one another with mistrust and suspicion. This gap has been overcome at times of great national trials, such as the war against Napoleon and later World War II. Russia celebrated victory in those wars as a triumphant demonstration of the unity of state and people. But Russia's political traditions also include a yearning for equality, solidarity, and community, as well as for moral purity and sympathy for the downtrodden. And throughout the Russian heritage runs a deep strain of pride in the greatness of the country and the endurance of its people.

The Communist Revolution and the Soviet Order

The tsarist regime proved unable to meet the overwhelming demands of national mobilization in World War I. Tsar Nicholas II abdicated in February 1917 (March 1917, by the Western calendar). He was replaced by a short-lived provisional government, which, in turn, fell when the Russian Communists—Bolsheviks, as they called themselves—took power in October 1917 (November, by the Western calendar). Their aim was to create a socialist society in Russia and, eventually, to spread revolutionary socialism throughout the world. Socialism, the Russian Communist Party believed, meant a society without private ownership of the means of production, one where the state owned and controlled all important economic assets and where political power was exercised in the name of the working people. **Vladimir Ilyich Lenin** was the leader of the Russian Communist Party and the first head of the Soviet Russian government. (Figure 9.1 lists the Soviet and post-Soviet leaders since 1917.)

Under Lenin's system of rule, the Communist Party controlled all levels of government. At each level of the territorial hierarchy of the country, full-time Communist Party officials supervised government. At the top, final power to decide policy rested in the Communist Party of the Soviet Union (CPSU) Politburo. Under **Joseph Stalin**, who took power after Lenin's death in 1924, power was even further centralized. Stalin instituted a totalitarian regime intent on building up Russia's industrial and military might. The state survived the terrible test of World War II, ultimately pushing back the invading German army all the way to Berlin. But the combined cost of war and terror under Stalin was staggering. The institutions of rule that Stalin left behind when he died in 1953 eventually crippled the Soviet state. They included personalistic rule, insecurity for rulers and ruled alike, heavy reliance on the secret police, and a militarized economy. None of Stalin's successors could reform the system without undermining Communist rule itself.

As vast as the Soviet state's powers were, their use was frustrated by bureaucratic immobilism. As in any organization, overcentralization undermined the leaders' actual power to enact significant policy change—or even to recognize when serious policy change was needed. The center's ability to coordinate bureaucratic agencies in order to execute its initiatives was frequently undermined by tacit resistance to the

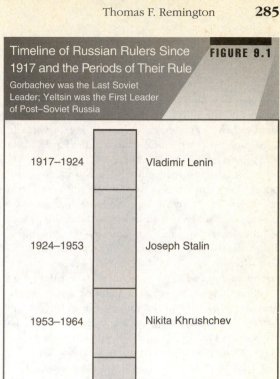

Timeline of Russian Rulers Since 1917 and the Periods of Their Rule **FIGURE 9.1**

Gorbachev was the Last Soviet Leader; Yeltsin was the First Leader of Post–Soviet Russia

1917–1924	Vladimir Lenin
1924–1953	Joseph Stalin
1953–1964	Nikita Khrushchev
1964–1982	Leonid Brezhnev
1982–1984	Yuri Andropov
1984–1985	Konstantin Chernenko
1985–1991	Mikhail Gorbachev
1991–1999	Boris Yeltsin
2000–2008	Vladimir Putin
2008–	Dmitrii Medvedev

center's orders by officials at lower levels, distortions in the flow of information up and down the hierarchy, and the force of inertia. Bureaucratic officials were generally more devoted to protecting and advancing their own personal and career interests than to serving the public interest. By the time **Mikhail Gorbachev** was elected General Secretary of the CPSU in 1985, the political system of the Soviet Union had grown top-heavy, unresponsive, and corrupt. The regime had more than enough power to crush any political opposition. However, it was unable to modernize the economy or improve living standards for the population. By the early 1980s, the economy had stopped growing, and the country was unable to compete militarily or economically with the West.

After the deaths of three elderly leaders in quick succession in 1982, 1984, and 1985, the ruling party Politburo turned to a vigorous young (54-year-old) reformer named Mikhail Gorbachev to lead the country. Gorbachev quickly grasped the levers of power that the system granted the general secretary. He moved both to strengthen his own political base and to carry out a program of reform.[7] Emphasizing the need for greater openness—**glasnost'**—in society, Gorbachev stressed that the ultimate test of the party's effectiveness lay in improving the economic well-being of the country and its people. Gorbachev not only called for political democratization, but also legalized private enterprise for individual and cooperative businesses and encouraged them to fill the many gaps in the economy left by the inefficiency of the state sector. He welcomed the explosion of new informal social and political associations. He made major concessions to the United States in the sphere of arms control, which resulted in a treaty that, for the first time in history, called for the destruction of entire classes of nuclear missiles.

Gorbachev railroaded his proposals for democratization through the legislature. In 1989 and 1990, Gorbachev's plan for free elections and a working parliament was realized as elections were held and new deputies were elected at the center and in every region and locality. When nearly half a million coal miners went on strike in the summer of 1989, Gorbachev declared himself sympathetic to their demands.

Gorbachev's radicalism received its most dramatic confirmation through the astonishing developments of 1989 in Eastern Europe. All the regimes making up the Communist bloc collapsed and gave way to multiparty parliamentary regimes in virtually bloodless popular revolutions. The Soviet Union stood by and supported the revolutions. The overnight dismantling of communism in Eastern Europe meant that the elaborate structure of party ties, police cooperation, economic trade, and military alliance that had developed with Eastern Europe after World War II vanished. Divided Germany was allowed to reunite.

In the Soviet Union itself, the Communist Party faced a critical loss of authority. The newly elected governments of the national republics making up the Soviet state one by one declared that they were sovereign. The three Baltic republics declared their intention to secede from the union. Between 1989 and 1990, throughout the Soviet Union and Eastern Europe, Communist Party rule crumbled.

Political Institutions of the Transition Period: Demise of the Soviet Union

Gorbachev's reforms had consequences he did not intend. The 1990 elections of deputies to the supreme soviets in all fifteen republics and to local soviets stimulated popular nationalist and democratic movements in most republics. In the core republic of Russia itself, Gorbachev's rival Boris Yeltsin was elected chairman of the Russian Supreme Soviet in June 1990. As chief of state in the Russian Republic, Yeltsin was well positioned to challenge Gorbachev for preeminence.

Yeltsin's rise forced Gorbachev to alter his strategy. Beginning in March 1991, Gorbachev sought terms for a new federal or confederal union that would be acceptable to Yeltsin and the Russian leadership, as well as to the leaders of the other republics. In April 1991 he reached an agreement on the outlines of a new treaty of union with nine of the fifteen republics, including Russia. A weak central government would manage basic coordinating functions. But the republics would gain the power to control the economies of their territories.

Gorbachev had underestimated the strength of his opposition. On August 19, 1991, a conspiracy of senior officials placed Gorbachev under house arrest and seized power. In response, thousands of citizens in Moscow and St. Petersburg rallied to protest the coup attempt. The coup collapsed on the third day, but Gorbachev's power had been fatally weakened. Neither the union nor the Russian power structures heeded his commands. Through the fall of 1991, the Russian government took over the union government, ministry by ministry. In November 1991 President Yeltsin issued a decree formally outlawing the Communist Party of the Soviet Union. In December Yeltsin and the leaders of Ukraine and Belarus formally declared the Union of Soviet Socialist Republics dissolved. On December 25, 1991, Gorbachev resigned as president and turned the powers of his office over to Boris Yeltsin.[8]

Political Institutions of the Transition Period: Russia 1990–1993

Boris Yeltsin was elected president of the Russian Federation in June 1991. Unlike Gorbachev, Yeltsin was elected in a direct, popular, competitive election, which gave him a considerable advantage in mobilizing public support against Gorbachev and the central Soviet Union government (see Box 9.2).

Like Gorbachev before him, Yeltsin demanded extraordinary powers from parliament to cope with the country's economic problems. Following the August 1991 coup attempt, parliament delegated to him emergency decree powers to cope with the economic

crisis. Yeltsin formed a government led by a group of young, Western-oriented reformers determined to carry out a decisive economic transformation. The new government's economic program took effect on January 2, 1992. Their first results were felt immediately as prices skyrocketed. Quickly, many politicians began to distance themselves from the program: Even Yeltsin's vice president denounced the program as "economic genocide." Through 1992 opposition to the reforms grew stronger and more intransigent. Increasingly, the political confrontation between Yeltsin and the reformers on the one side and the opposition to radical economic reform on the other became centered in the two branches of government. President Yeltsin demanded broad powers to carry out the reforms, but parliament refused to go along. In March 1993 an opposition motion to remove the president through impeachment nearly passed in the parliament.

On September 21, 1993, Yeltsin decreed the parliament dissolved and called for elections for a

---

Boris Yeltsin: Russia's First President

BOX 9.2

Boris Yeltsin, born in 1931, graduated from the Urals Polytechnical Institute in 1955 with a diploma in civil engineering and worked for a long time in construction. From 1976 to 1985, he served as first secretary of the Sverdlovsk *oblast* (provincial) Communist Party organization.

Early in 1986 Yeltsin became first secretary of the Moscow city party organization, but he was removed in November 1987 for speaking out against Mikhail Gorbachev. Positioning himself as a victim of the party establishment, Yeltsin made a remarkable political comeback. In the 1989 elections to the Congress of People's Deputies, he won a Moscow at-large seat with almost 90 percent of the vote. The following year he was elected to the Russian republic's parliament with over 80 percent of the vote. He was then elected its chairman in June 1990. In 1991 he was elected president of Russia, receiving 57 percent of the vote. Thus, he had won three major races in three successive years. He was reelected as president in 1996 in a dramatic, come-from-behind race against the leader of the Communist Party.

Yeltsin's last years in office were notable for his lengthy spells of illness and for the carousel of prime ministerial

appointments. The entourage of family members and advisors around him, dubbed colloquially "the Family," seemed to exercise undue influence over him. Yet, infirm as he was, he judged that Russia's interests and his own would be safe in Vladimir Putin's hands. Yeltsin's resignation speech was full of contrition for his failure to bring a better life to Russians. After retiring, Yeltsin stayed out of the public eye. He died of heart failure on April 23, 2007, and was buried in Moscow with full honors.

Yeltsin's legacy is mixed. He was most effective when engaged in political battle, whether he was fighting for supremacy against Gorbachev or fighting against the Communists. Impulsive and undisciplined, he was gifted with exceptionally keen political intuition. He regarded economic reform as an instrument in his political war with the Communist opposition and used privatization to make it impossible for any future rulers to return to state socialism. Imperious and willful, he also regarded the adoption of the 1993 constitution as a major achievement and willingly accepted the limits on his presidential power that it imposed.

new parliament. Yeltsin's enemies barricaded themselves inside the parliament building. After a ten-day standoff, the dissidents joined with some loosely organized paramilitary units outside the building and attacked the Moscow mayor's offices adjacent to the Russian White House. They even called on their followers to "seize the Kremlin." Finally, the army agreed to back Yeltsin and suppress the uprising by force, shelling the parliament building in the process.

The violence of October 1993 cast a long shadow over subsequent events. Yeltsin's decree meant that national elections were to be held for a legislature that did not constitutionally exist, since the new constitution establishing these institutions was to be voted on in a referendum held in parallel with the parliamentary elections. Yet for all the turmoil, the constitution approved in the December referendum has remained in force since then.

THE CONTEMPORARY CONSTITUTIONAL ORDER

The Presidency

Yeltsin's constitution combined elements of presidentialism and parliamentarism. (See Figure 9.2 for a schematic overview of the Russian constitutional structure.) Although it provided for the separation of the executive, legislative, and judicial branches and for a federal division of power between the central and regional levels of government, it gave the president wide power. The president is directly elected for a six-year term and may not serve more than two consecutive terms. The president names the prime minister to head the government. Yet, the government must have the confidence of parliament to remain in power. Although the constitution does not call the president the head of the executive branch, he is so in fact by virtue of his

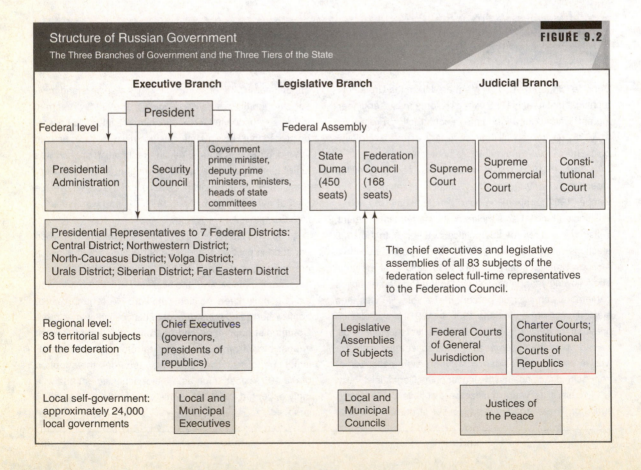

Structure of Russian Government   **FIGURE 9.2**
The Three Branches of Government and the Three Tiers of the State

Executive Branch   **Legislative Branch**   **Judicial Branch**

President

Federal level   Federal Assembly

| Presidential Administration | Security Council | Government prime minister, deputy prime ministers, ministers, heads of state committees | State Duma (450 seats) | Federation Council (168 seats) | Supreme Court | Supreme Commercial Court | Constitutional Court |

Presidential Representatives to 7 Federal Districts:
Central District; Northwestern District;
North-Caucasus District; Volga District;
Urals District; Siberian District; Far Eastern District

The chief executives and legislative assemblies of all 83 subjects of the federation select full-time representatives to the Federation Council.

Regional level: 83 territorial subjects of the federation — Chief Executives (governors, presidents of republics) — Legislative Assemblies of Subjects — Federal Courts of General Jurisdiction — Charter Courts; Constitutional Courts of Republics

Local self-government: approximately 24,000 local governments — Local and Municipal Executives — Local and Municipal Councils — Justices of the Peace power to appoint the prime minister and the rest of the government and his right to issue **presidential decrees** with the force of law. (The decree power is somewhat limited in that decrees may not violate existing law and can be superseded by legislation.)

Over the years since the constitution was approved, some informal practices have come to govern the exercise of central power. For example, the president and government divide executive responsibility. The government, headed by the prime minister, is primarily responsible for economic and social policy. The president directly oversees the ministries and other bodies directly concerned with coercion, law enforcement, and state security—the "power ministries." These include the Foreign Ministry, Defense Ministry, Ministry of Internal Affairs (which controls the regular police and security troops), Federal Security Service (FSB—formerly the KGB), and several other security and intelligence agencies. The president and his staff set overall policy in the foreign and domestic domains, and the government develops the specific proposals and rules carrying out this policy. In practice, the government answers to the president, not parliament. The government's base of support is the president, rather than a particular coalition of political forces in parliament. This arrangement appears to be continuing under the duo of President Medvedev and Prime Minister Putin, although it may not last.

Despite the pronounced presidential tilt to the system, the parliament does have some potential for independent action. Its ability to exercise its rights, however, depends on the composition of political forces represented in parliament and the cohesiveness of the majority. Parliament's approval is required for any bill to become law. The State Duma (the lower house of parliament) must confirm the president's nominee for prime minister. If, upon three successive votes, the Duma refuses to confirm the nomination, the president must dissolve the Duma and call new elections. Likewise, the Duma may vote to deny confidence in the government. If a motion of no confidence carries twice, the president must either dissolve parliament or dismiss the government. During Yeltsin's tenure as president, the Duma was able to block some of Yeltsin's legislative initiatives. Since 2003, however, it has largely been a rubber stamp. The constitution allows for a variety of types of relationships among the president, government, and parliament, depending on the degree to which the president dominates the political system.

In addition to these powers, the president has a number of other formal and informal powers in his constitutional capacity as "head of state," "guarantor of the constitution," and commander in chief of the armed forces. He oversees a large presidential administration, which supervises the federal government and keeps tabs on regional governments. Informally, the administration also manages relations with the parliament, the courts, big business, the media, political parties, and major interest groups.

The president also oversees many official and quasi-official supervisory and advisory commissions, which he creates and directs using his decree power. One is the **Security Council**, chaired by the president. Besides the president, the Security Council consists of a permanent secretary, the heads of the power ministries and other security-related agencies, the prime minister, and the chairs of the two chambers of parliament. Its powers are broad, but shadowy. Putin used it to formulate policy proposals not only in matters of foreign and defense policy, but also on selected issues having to do with the organization of the executive branch.

Another prominent advisory body is the **State Council**, which comprises the heads of the regional governments and thus parallels the Federation Council. Still another is the **Public Chamber**, which is made up of 126 members from selected civic, sports, artistic, and other nongovernmental organizations (NGOs). Its purpose is to deliberate on matters of public policy, make recommendations to parliament and the government on pending policy issues, and link civil society with the state. Like the State Council, it is a quasi-parliamentary deliberative body that the president can consult at will. All three bodies duplicate some of the deliberative and representative functions of parliament—and therefore weaken parliament's role. They illustrate the tendency, under both Yeltsin and Putin, for the president to create and dissolve new structures answering directly to the president. These improvised structures can be politically useful for the president as counterweights to constitutionally mandated bodies (such as parliament), as well as providing policy advice and feedback. They help ensure that the president is always the dominant institution in the political system, but they undermine the authority of other formal institutions.

The Government

The *government* refers to the senior echelon of leadership in the executive branch. It is charged with formulating the main lines of national policy (especially in the economic and social realms) and overseeing their implementation. (The president oversees the formulation and execution of foreign and national security policy.) In this respect the government corresponds to the Cabinet in Western parliamentary systems. But in contrast to most parliamentary systems, the makeup of the Russian government is not directly determined by the party composition of the parliament. Indeed, there is scarcely any relationship between the distribution of party forces in the Duma and the political balance of the government. Nearly all members of the government are career managers and administrators, rather than party politicians. Overall, the government is not a party government, but reflects the president's calculations about how to weigh considerations such as personal loyalty, professional competence, and the relative strength of major bureaucratic factions in selecting Cabinet ministers. Although there is recurrent discussion of the idea that the party that forms the majority in the Duma should have the right to name the head of the government, no president has been willing to move toward instituting this model—no doubt out of fear that it would reduce his freedom of action in governing.

The Parliament

The parliament—called the Federal Assembly—is bicameral. The lower house is called the **State Duma**, and the upper house, the **Federation Council**. Legislation originates in the Duma. As Figure 9.3 shows, upon passage in the State Duma, a bill goes to the Federation Council for consideration. The Federation

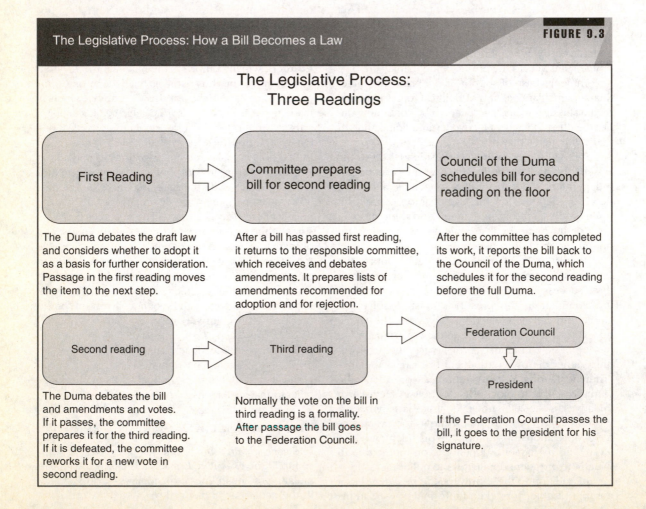

The Legislative Process: How a Bill Becomes a Law

FIGURE 9.3

The Legislative Process: Three Readings

First Reading

The Duma debates the draft law and considers whether to adopt it as a basis for further consideration. Passage in the first reading moves the item to the next step.

Committee prepares bill for second reading

After a bill has passed first reading, it returns to the responsible committee, which receives and debates amendments. It prepares lists of amendments recommended for adoption and for rejection.

Council of the Duma schedules bill for second reading on the floor

After the committee has completed its work, it reports the bill back to the Council of the Duma, which schedules it for the second reading before the full Duma.

Second reading

The Duma debates the bill and amendments and votes. If it passes, the committee prepares it for the third reading. If it is defeated, the committee reworks it for a new vote in second reading.

Third reading

Normally the vote on the bill in third reading is a formality. After passage the bill goes to the Federation Council.

Federation Council

President

If the Federation Council passes the bill, it goes to the president for his signature.

Council can only pass it, reject it, or reject it and call for the formation of an agreement commission (consisting of members of both houses) to iron out differences. If the Duma rejects the upper house's proposed changes, it can override the Federation Council by a two-thirds vote and send the bill directly to the president for his signature.

When the bill has cleared parliament, it goes to the president. If the president refuses to sign the bill, it returns to the Duma. The Duma may pass an amended version by a simple absolute majority, or it may override the president's veto, for which a two-thirds vote is required. The Federation Council must then also approve the bill by a simple majority if the president's amendments are accepted or by a two-thirds vote if it chooses to override the president. On rare occasions the Duma has overridden the president's veto; it has overridden the Federation Council more frequently. In other cases the Duma has passed bills rejected by the president after accepting the president's proposed amendments. Under President Yeltsin political forces opposed to Yeltsin, particularly Communists and nationalists, held the majority in the Duma. But parliament and the president generally worked to head off major confrontations.

Until recently the Duma's 450 members were equally divided between deputies elected by a plurality rule in 225 single-member districts and 225 deputies elected through proportional representation (PR) in a single national electoral district. A party receiving at least 5 percent of the vote on the party-list ballot was entitled to as many of the party-list seats in the Duma as its share of the party-list vote. As in other PR systems, votes cast for parties that fail to clear the barrier are redistributed to winning parties. Since the 2007 Duma election, all 450 deputies are elected proportionally from party lists in a single nationwide district, and the threshold for winning seats rose to 7 percent.[9]

The parties clearing the 7 percent threshold form their own factions in the Duma. According to newly amended Duma rules, deputies may not switch faction membership (those who leave or are expelled lose their seats). Faction leaders are represented on the governing body of the Duma, the Council of the Duma. Factions are the main site of political discussion in the Duma and give members a channel for proposing bills to the chamber.

Since the December 2003 elections, the Kremlin has enjoyed the support of a commanding majority in the Duma, where the **United Russia** party holds two-thirds of the seats. United Russia holds twenty-six of the thirty-two committee chairmanships and eight of the eleven seats of the Council of the Duma, which is the steering body for the chamber. Since United Russia deputies vote with a high degree of discipline, the Duma consistently delivers the president solid legislative majorities. Other factions have very little opportunity to influence the agenda, let alone the outcomes of legislative deliberations. Therefore, United Russia's control over the agenda and voting has turned the Duma into a rubber stamp for the executive branch.

Each deputy is a member of one of thirty-two standing committees. Bills submitted to the Duma are assigned to committees according to their subject matter. The committees collect and review proposed amendments before reporting out the bills for votes by the full chamber with the committee's recommendations.

The Federation Council is designed as an instrument of federalism in that (as in the U.S. Senate) every constituent unit of the federation is represented by two representatives. Thus, the populations of small ethnic-national territories are greatly overrepresented, compared with more populous regions. The Federation Council has important powers. Besides acting on bills passed by the lower house, it approves presidential nominees for high courts, such as the Supreme Court and the Constitutional Court. It must approve presidential decrees declaring martial law or a state of emergency and any acts altering the boundaries of territorial units. It must consider any legislation dealing with taxes, budget, financial policy, treaties, customs, and declarations of war.

Until a major reform was pushed through by President Putin in the spring of 2000, the Federation Council's members were the heads of the executive and legislative branches of each constituent territory of the federation. Now, however, each governor and each regional legislature names a representative to the Federation Council to serve on a full-time basis. The governors name their representatives, who are then confirmed by the legislatures. The regional legislatures elect their delegates and can recall them.

There is considerable dissatisfaction over the current role of the Federation Council. Many believe that the chamber's members should be popularly elected. This must be reconciled, however, with the constitutional rule that the two members of the chamber from each of Russia's territorial subjects must represent its executive and legislative branches.

Executive-Legislative Relations

Relations between president and parliament during the 1990s were often stormy. The first two Dumas, elected in 1993 and in 1995, were dominated by the Communist and other leftist factions hostile to President Yeltsin and the policies of his government. This was particularly true in areas of economic policy and privatization. On other issues, such as matters concerning federal relations, the Duma and president often reached agreement—sometimes against the resistance of the Federation Council, whose members fought to protect regional prerogatives.

The 1999 election produced a Duma with a pro-government majority. President Putin and his government built a reliable base of support in the Duma for their legislative initiatives made up of a coalition of four centrist political factions. The 2003 election produced a still wider margin of support for the president in the Duma and an overwhelming majority for the United Russia party—which means that the president does not need to expend much effort in bargaining with the Duma to win its support for his policies. The Fifth Duma, elected in December 2007, is also dominated by the United Russia party and has continued to give its loyal support to the Medvedev-Putin team.

Although the level of voting discipline within the majority party is similar to that in a Westminster-style parliament, as is the practice of reliably supporting the government's initiatives, the relationship between the Duma and the government is somewhat different. In a Westminster-type setting, the government needs to maintain a majority in parliament. If it loses its majority, it must face the voters in a new election. Majority Members of Parliament would prefer to hold onto their seats as long as possible and vote for the government's proposals so as to avoid a parliamentary dissolution and new election. By the same token, the government is normally unwilling to face a revolt on the floor of Parliament and the possible loss of its majority. Thus, the government and the majority party need each other. In Russia the parliamentary deputies have almost no political resources outside the party, so the government has a much stronger hand in instructing them how to vote. A deputy who defies party discipline can be expelled and has very few alternatives. A major shift in the alignment of political forces in society, however, could lead to a different relationship between executive and legislative power.

The Constitutional Court

The 1993 constitution provides for judicial review by the **Constitutional Court**. Its nineteen members are nominated by the president, but are subject to confirmation by the Federation Council. The court is empowered to consider the constitutionality of actions of the president, the parliament, and lower-level governments. The court has carefully avoided issuing any decisions restricting presidential powers in any significant way. However, it has decided a number of thorny constitutional issues, including the relations between the two chambers of parliament and the delineation of powers between the central and regional governments. It has consistently defended the rights of individual defendants in the criminal justice system against actions of federal and regional authorities. The court has also tended to uphold the sovereignty of federal law over the rights of the constituent territories of the federation.

Since Putin took office in 2000, the court has taken care to avoid crossing the president. Nevertheless, even the possibility that it might exert a measure of independent political influence led Putin to move the seat of the court to St. Petersburg in 2008. This may have been intended as a means to distance the court from the tight web of governing bodies located in Moscow and thus to marginalize it politically. Conceivably, however, it might wind up increasing the court's independence.

Central Government and the Regions

Following the breakup of the Soviet Union, many Russians feared that Russia would also dissolve into a patchwork of independent fiefdoms. Certainly, Russia's territorial integrity was subjected to serious strains. Under President Yeltsin the central government granted wide autonomy to regional governments in return for political support. Yeltsin went so far as to sign a series of bilateral treaties with over forty regions to codify the respective rights and responsibilities of the federal government and the individual regional governments. Under Putin, however, the pendulum of federal policy swung back sharply toward centralization.

The demographic factor is one reason that Russia did not break up. Eighty percent of Russia's population is ethnically Russian. None of its ethnic minorities accounts for more than 4 percent of the total (the Tatars form the largest of the ethnic minorities, constituting about 5.5 million of Russia's total population of 142 million). Rebuilding national community in post–Soviet Russia has been helped by Russia's thousand-year history of statehood. Yet, until 1991 Russia was never constituted as a nation-state: Under the tsars it was a multinational empire, and under Soviet rule it was nominally a federal union of socialist republics. State policy toward nationality has also varied over the centuries. In some periods Russia recognized a variety of distinct ethnic-national communities and tolerated cultural differences among them. In other periods the state pressured non-Russian groups to assimilate to Russian culture.

Russia was formally established as a federal republic under the Soviet regime. In contrast to the Soviet Union, of which it was the largest component, only some of Russia's constituent members were ethnic-national territories.[10] The rest were pure administrative subdivisions, populated mainly by Russians. The non-Russian ethnic-national territories were classified by size and status into autonomous republics, autonomous provinces, and national districts. In many of them, the indigenous ethnic group constituted a minority of the population. As of 2008 Russia comprises 83 constituent territorial units, officially termed "subjects of the federation." They represent six different types of units. Republics, autonomous districts (all but one of them located within other units), and the one autonomous *oblast* give formal political representation to ethnic minorities; *oblasts* (provinces), *krais* (territories), and two cities of federal status (Moscow and St. Petersburg) are treated as ordinary administrative subdivisions with no special constitutional status.

One of the centralizing measures President Putin pursued is the absorption of smaller ethnic districts into larger surrounding units. In most of these cases, the smaller ethnic district was impoverished and hoped for better living standards as part of a consolidated territory.[11] The mergers also reduced the patronage rights and political voice that came with an ethnic district's status as a constituent unit of the federation.[12]

The ethnic republics jealously guard their special status. From 1990 to 1992, all the republics adopted declarations of sovereignty, and two made attempts to declare full or partial independence from Russia. Only one, however, the Chechen Republic (**Chechnia**), resorted to arms to back up its claim. Chechnia is one of a belt of predominantly Muslim ethnic republics in the mountainous region of the North Caucasus, between the Black and Caspian seas. Chechnia's president declared independence from Russia in 1991, an act Russia refused to recognize, but did not initially attempt to overturn by force. When negotiations failed, however, in December 1994 Russian forces attacked the republic directly, subjecting its capital city, Groznyi, to devastating bombardment. This forced tens of thousands of Chechen and Russian residents to flee and led to a protracted, destructive war. Fighting ceased in the summer of 1996, but resumed in 1999. Federal forces had established control over most parts of Chechnia by early 2000, but Chechen guerrillas continue to carry out ambushes and suicide attacks against federal units.

In the mid-1990s, a radical fundamentalist form of Islam replaced national independence as the guiding ideology of the Chechen rebel movement. The guerrillas have resorted to terrorist attacks against civilian targets both in the North Caucasus region and in Moscow. One of the most shocking of these incidents was the seizure of a school in the town of Beslan, near Chechnia, in September 2004 (see Box 9.3). The brutal methods used by federal forces to suppress the uprising have fueled continuing hatred on the part of many Chechens against the federal government, which, in turn, facilitates recruitment by the terrorists. With time, order has been restored under the sometimes brutal rule of Ramzan Kadyrov, and much of Groznyi has been rebuilt. Attacks and reprisals continue to occur occasionally, however, especially in ethnic republics neighboring Chechnia, where unemployment and poverty are severe.

Chechnia, fortunately, was an exceptional case. In the other twenty ethnic republics, Moscow reached an accommodation granting the republics a certain amount of autonomy in return for acceptance of Russia's sovereign power. All twenty-one ethnic republics have the constitutional right to determine their own form of state power so long as their decisions do not contradict federal law. All twenty-one have established presidencies. In many cases the republic presidents have constructed personal power bases around appeals to ethnic solidarity and the cultural autonomy of the indigenous nationality. Often they have used this power to establish personalistic dictatorships in their regions.

President Putin made clear his intention to reassert the federal government's authority over the regions. The reform of the Federation Council in 2000 was one step in this direction. Another was Putin's decree of May 13, 2000, which created seven new "federal districts." He appointed a special presidential representative to each district who monitors the actions of the regional governments within that district. This reform sought to strengthen central control over

BOX 9.3

Beslan

September 1 is the first day of school each year throughout Russia. Children, accompanied by their parents, often come to school bringing flowers to their teachers. A group organized by the Chechen warlord Shamil Basaev chose September 1, 2004, to carry out a horrific attack. A group of heavily armed militants stormed a school in the town of Beslan, located in the republic of North Ossetia, next door to Chechnia. They took over 1,000 schoolchildren, parents, and teachers hostage. The terrorists crowded the captives into the school gymnasium, which they filled with explosives to prevent any rescue attempt. The terrorists refused to allow water and food to be brought into the school. Negotiations over the release of the hostages failed.

On the third day of the siege, something triggered the detonation of one of the bombs inside the school. In the chaos that followed, many of the children and adults rushed to escape. The terrorists fired at them. Federal forces stormed the school, trying to rescue the escaping hostages and to kill the terrorists. Many of the bombs planted by the terrorists exploded. Ultimately, about 350 of the hostages died, along with most of the terrorists.

The media covered the events extensively. The Beslan tragedy had an impact on Russian national consciousness comparable to that of September 11 in the United States. While there had been a number of previous attacks tied to Chechen terrorists, none had cost so many innocent lives.

Putin claimed that the terrorists were part of an international terrorist movement aimed ultimately at the dismemberment of Russia itself and avoided linking the incident to Russian policy in Chechnia. In response to the crisis, Putin called for measures to reinforce national security. He also demanded increased centralization of executive power, including an end to the direct election of governors. Most observers assumed that Putin had wanted to make these changes anyway and that the Beslan tragedy simply gave him a political opening to enact them. Beslan was a tragic indication that the insurgency that began in Chechnia is spreading throughout the North Caucasus region.

---

the activity of federal bodies in the regions. Often, in the past, local branches of federal agencies had fallen under the influence of powerful governors.

Still another very important measure was the abolition of direct popular election of governors, including the presidents of the ethnic republics. Before 2005 regional chief executives were chosen by direct popular election. Since 2005, however, the president nominates a candidate to the regional legislature, which then approves the nomination (no legislature has dared to oppose one of Putin's appointments). Many citizens supported this change, believing that the institution of local elections had been discredited by corruption and fraud and that elections were more often determined by the influence of wealthy insiders than by public opinion. Critics of the reform accused Putin of creating a hypercentralized, authoritarian system of rule. Putin clearly hoped that appointed governors would be more accountable and effective, but past experience suggests that centralizing power by itself is unlikely to improve governance in the regions in the absence of other mechanisms for monitoring government performance and for enforcing the law.

Below the tier of regional governments are units that are supposed to enjoy the right of self-government—municipalities and other local government units. Under new legislation the right of local self-government has been expanded to a much larger set of units—such as urban and rural districts and small settlements—raising the total number of local self-governing units to 24,000. In principle, local self-government is supposed to permit substantial policy-making autonomy in the spheres of housing, utilities, and social services (and to reduce the federal government's burden in providing such services). However, the new legislation—which is being phased in gradually—provides no fixed, independent sources of revenue for these local entities. They thus depend for the great majority of their budgets on the regional governments. For their part the regional governments resist allowing local governments to exercise any significant powers of their own. In many cases, the mayors of the capital cities of regions are political rivals of the governors of the regions. Moscow and St. Petersburg are exceptional cases because they have the status of federal territorial subjects like republics and regions. Other cities lack the power and autonomy of Moscow and St. Petersburg, and they must bargain with their superior regional governments for shares of power.

Russia's postcommunist constitutional arrangements are still evolving. The political system allows considerable room for the arbitrary exercise of power and even, as under President Putin, the evisceration of democracy. Both Yeltsin and Putin interpreted their presidential mandates broadly, and although President Medvedev has called for adherence to the rule of law, it is likely that he will also find it expedient on occasion to push the limits of presidential power.

The constitutional arrangements established under President Yeltsin have the potential to evolve toward democracy or to be used for authoritarian rule, depending on the inclinations of the leaders and the balance of forces in the country. Russia's future political evolution depends on more than its formal institutional arrangements. The informal traditions and understandings surrounding formal rules strongly shape the way officeholders wield power and determine how effectively institutions hold leaders accountable for their actions. Informal rules can be far more important than formal rules. If rulers can circumvent formal limits on their power, constitutional structures may become irrelevant to the actual exercise of power.

Under Vladimir Putin Russia's system of rule became a hybrid regime that includes elements of democracy within a largely authoritarian framework. In this system elections are held regularly, and opposition forces are allowed a small, marginal role. The ruling authorities decide how much freedom to allow opposition groups to organize and campaign, and they exercise substantial control over television and radio, although allowing much greater freedom to the print and Internet media. Business is given wide sway to pursue its economic interests, but may not finance a political challenge to the authorities. Above all, elections are not allowed to result in a loss of power for the ruling authorities. There is still considerable room for the articulation of interests and the discussion of policy alternatives. At the same time, corruption is rampant, and occasional murders of outspoken journalists and politicians go unpunished. The suppression of democratic freedoms is far more effective at pushing political opposition to the sidelines than at giving the authorities an independent means of controlling the bureaucracy.

Over the eight years of his presidency, Putin reversed the disarray of the early postcommunist period by constructing a hybrid democratic/authoritarian regime.

Without explicitly violating any constitutional limits on his power and without abolishing elections or other formal democratic rights, Putin effectively negated the constitutional constraints on executive power. Putin stands in sharp contrast to Yeltsin in terms of the use of presidential power. Yeltsin used his presidential powers erratically and impulsively. But Yeltsin respected certain limits on his power: He did not suppress media criticism, and he tolerated political opposition. Faced with an opposition-led parliament, Yeltsin was willing to compromise with his opponents to enact legislation. However, Yeltsin grew dependent on a small group of favored **oligarchs** (business magnates with strong connections to government) for support and allowed them to accumulate massive fortunes and corrupt influence. Likewise, Yeltsin allowed regional bosses to flout federal authority with impunity because he found it less costly to accommodate them than to fight them.

The loss of state capacity under Yeltsin illustrates one danger of an overcentralized political system. When the president does not effectively command the powers of the office, power drifts to other centers of power. Putin's presidency illustrates the opposite danger. When Putin took over, he was faced with the task of reversing the breakdown of political control and responsibility that had accelerated under Yeltsin. Although he publicly called for a system based on respect for the rule of law, he steadily restored authoritarian methods of rule. Although Dmitrii Medvedev often refers to freedom and democracy as necessary for Russia, it is likely that any moves he makes toward liberalizing the system will be modest and gradual.

RUSSIAN POLITICAL CULTURE IN THE POST-SOVIET PERIOD

Russian political culture is the product of centuries of autocratic rule, rapid but uneven improvement of educational and living standards in the twentieth century, and rising exposure to Western standards of political life. The resulting contemporary political culture is a contradictory bundle of values: A sturdy core of belief in democratic values is accompanied by a firm belief in the importance of a strong state and sharp disillusionment with the results of the reforms of the late 1980s and early 1990s. In a 2005 survey, 66 percent of Russians agreed that "Russia needs democracy," but 45 percent said that the kind of democracy Russia needs is "a completely special kind corresponding to Russian specifics."[13] A survey shortly before the December 2007 election found that almost two-thirds of the public did not believe the elections would be free or fair; yet, a majority believed that their lives would improve thanks to the elections.[14] Asked whether they believed they could have any influence on policy decisions in the country, 83 percent said no.[15] But two-thirds of voters thought that democratic elections are at least somewhat important to the country, and a majority said that as president, Dmitrii Medvedev would pursue policies that would strengthen democracy.[16] Can such contradictory beliefs about democracy be reconciled?

In interpreting such results, we must remember that Russians judge political principles such as democracy according to their effect on preserving the integrity of the state. Many Russians cannot forgive Gorbachev and Yeltsin for pursuing policies that resulted in the breakup of the Soviet state, widespread poverty, the amassing of great wealth by a few individuals using unscrupulous methods, and the loss of status as a great world power. Many associate concepts such as "democracy" and the "market economy" with misguided or malevolent efforts to remold Russia along Western lines. The restoration of the state's power and prestige, therefore, is a criterion for judging the worth of principles such as freedom and democracy. That helps explain why many Russians praise Putin for strengthening democracy and hope Medvedev will continue his policies. Far from seeing "freedom" and "order" as necessary enemies, many recognize that freedom is only possible in an ordered society. But if forced to choose between freedom and order, Russians divide rather evenly. For example, in an international survey conducted under the auspices of the British Broadcasting Company, 47 percent of Russians (compared with 40 percent internationally) said that stability and peace are more important concerns than freedom of the press, whereas 39 percent (versus 56 percent globally) gave priority to press freedom.[17]

We can understand these competing influences on Russian political culture when we consider the long-term forces (such as the rapid rise in educational levels of the population in the Soviet period) shaping it, as well as the impact of recent history.

The reforms of the late 1980s and early 1990s raised expectations that Russia would enjoy a significant rise in living standards once it got rid of communism. The sharp fall in living standards that followed the collapse of the old regime dispelled any notion that changing that political and economic system could turn the country around overnight.

Still, the years of economic recovery and political stability after 1999 have tempered some of the sharp disappointment that Russians felt with the change in regime and have erased much of the nostalgia for the old Soviet order. Both optimism and personal happiness have risen significantly in recent years. In December 2007, 40 percent of Russians reported that they were looking ahead to 2008 with optimism; a year before only 30 percent expressed optimism about the coming year.[18] Over the past ten years, the number of people considering themselves happy rose from 60 percent to 77 percent, while the number reporting that they are unhappy fell from 25 percent to 15 percent.[19] More people are willing to look back and say that the radical reforms of the economy beginning in 1992 brought greater good than harm (43 percent said more good than harm, while 35 percent said more harm than good in a December 2007 poll).[20] Russians even have more faith in the ruble as a currency after long preferring the dollar or the euro to the ruble: In April 2008, 61 percent (compared with 37 percent in July 2002) said they had more confidence in the ruble than in the dollar or the euro.[21] A similar number—61 percent—now believe that it was a good thing that Russia became independent of the Soviet Union. Ten years before, only 27 percent thought so.[22]

One reason Russians are willing to sacrifice democratic rights for political security is the widespread view that political order is fragile, a view that the authorities have worked hard to keep alive. Russians have long been taught that a weakening of the internal cohesion of the state invites predation from outside powers, and many episodes of Russian history bear out this belief. The Putin leadership pointed to the popular uprisings in Ukraine, Georgia, and elsewhere not as signs of a democratic spirit in the face of attempted election fraud by local strongmen, but as proof that outside powers (such as the U.S. Central Intelligence Agency and other Western intelligence services) were fomenting unrest in order to overthrow the legitimate state authorities. Asked what they consider the main internal threat facing Russia today, Russians expressed fear about political instability connected with political succession (16%), struggle among competing factions in power (12%), loss of control by the central government over the regions (9%), separatism in the North Caucasus (4%), and loss of control over the regions in the Far East located near China (4%).[23]

Surveys also show that citizens have little faith in most present-day political institutions, although, as Figure 9.4 shows, they have a good deal of confidence

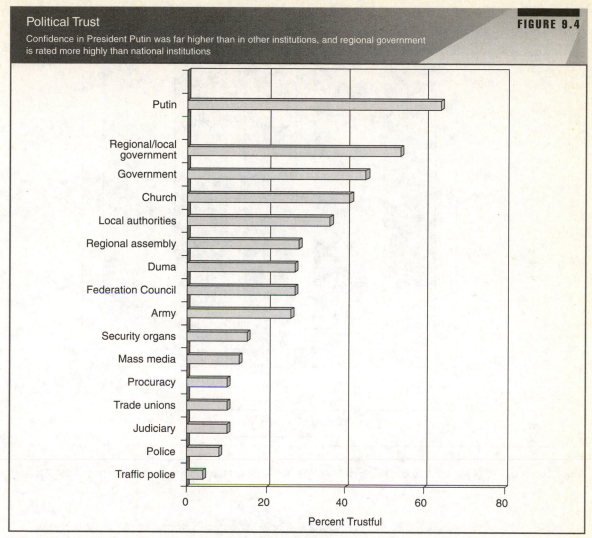

Political Trust

FIGURE 9.4

Confidence in President Putin was far higher than in other institutions, and regional government is rated more highly than national institutions

Percent Trustful

Sources: Putin trust: Fond obshchestvennogo mneniia, July 2008. Retrieved from bd.fom.ru/report/map/projects/dominant/dom0826/d082621#Abs3. All other items: Fund for Public Opinion, May 2007. Retrieved July 11, 2008 bd.fom.ru/report/cat/power/pow_rei/d071901

in the president and government. Confidence in elective bodies such as the parliament is low, and in the law enforcement and security organs, it is even lower, while it is higher in local and regional government and higher still in the Orthodox Church.

Some of Putin's popularity rubbed off on the state's political institutions. Still, Russians distinguish between the constitutional framework of the state and the personalities of the leaders. Few Russians thought that power should transfer with Putin from the presidency to the prime ministership; two-thirds preferred

maintaining a system of "strong presidential power."[24] Neither did most Russians want to see presidential power increased.[25] As Figure 9.5 shows, by a wide margin Russians believe that there should be a political opposition to the authorities. Russians exhibit a strong sense of skepticism about and mistrust of most institutions of the state; yet, by a two-to-one margin, most Russians believe they cannot solve their problems without it.[26] Most accept that the state requires firm guidance by a capable president and give Putin credit for having restored order and purpose to the state.

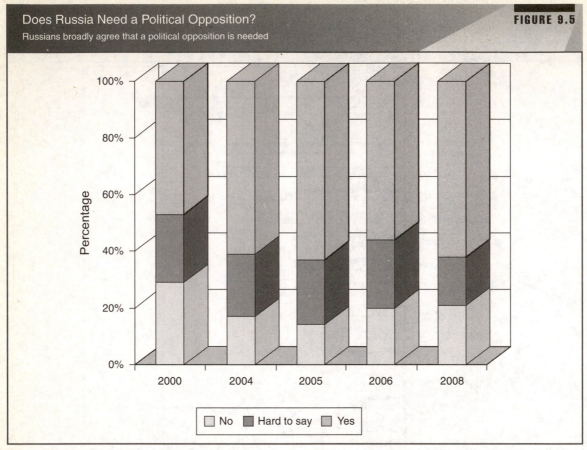

Does Russia Need a Political Opposition?   FIGURE 9.5

Russians broadly agree that a political opposition is needed

Note: Percentages are percentages of those responding.

Source: Levada Center, "Politicheskaia oppozitsiia v Rossii," July 2008. Retrieved July 11, 2008, from www.levada.ru/ press/2008073102.html

Therefore, although there continues to be a strong foundation of support for democratic values, that support is contingent on whether these values will help hold the country together or pull it apart.

The political culture thus combines contradictory elements. Russians do value democratic rights, but experience has taught them that under the banner of democracy, politicians can abuse their power to the detriment of the integrity of the state and the well-being of society. They also feel powerless to affect state policy. Little wonder that a leader such as Putin can command such widespread support despite the general mistrust Russians have for the post-Soviet political institutions. Russians see him as restoring order following a protracted period of social and political breakdown. As Richard Rose and his colleagues argued, the reason

Russians generally approved of the Putin regime was not because they considered it to be ideal, but because it improved economic well-being and in any case they saw little prospect for changing it.[27]

Surveys also reveal considerable continuity with the past in support for the idea that the state should ensure society's prosperity and the citizens' material security. More so than residents of Western Europe or the United States, Russians believe that the state is responsible for providing a just moral and social order, with justice being understood more as social equality than as equality before the law. This pattern reflects the lasting influence of traditional conceptions of state and society on Russian political culture. Still, few would support the reestablishment of Soviet rule or a reversion to a military dictatorship.

Political culture is also shaped by slower acting, but more lasting influences, including the succession of generations, rising educational levels, and urbanization.[28] These are mutually reinforcing changes as new generations of young people are exposed to fundamentally different influences than those to which their parents were exposed, while the older generations tend to have lower levels of education and less exposure to the more cosmopolitan way of life of cities.

Political Socialization

The Soviet regime devoted enormous effort to political indoctrination and propaganda. The regime controlled the content of school curriculums, mass media, popular culture, political education, and nearly every other channel by which values and attitudes were formed. The heart of Soviet doctrine was the Marxist belief that the way in which a society organizes economic production—feudalism, capitalism, socialism, and so forth—determines the structure of values and beliefs prevalent in the society. The idea was that the ruling class in each society determines the basic ideology of the society. Therefore, Soviet propaganda and indoctrination emphasized that Soviet citizens were part of a worldwide working-class movement to overthrow capitalism and replace it with socialism, in which there would be no private property. Needing to knit together a highly diverse multinational state, the Soviet regime downplayed national feeling and replaced it with a sense of patriotic loyalty to the Soviet state and to the working class's interests in the worldwide class struggle.

Today the ideological content of Russian education has changed significantly, and there is much less overt political control over the formation of attitudes and values. In place of the idea of the class struggle and the international solidarity of the working class, textbooks stress love for the Russian national heritage. Historical figures who in the Communist era were honored as heroes of the struggle of ordinary people against feudal or capitalist masters are now held up as great representatives of Russia's national culture.[29] Schoolbooks and mass media place heavy emphasis on loyalty to Russia as a state. This theme underlies Russia's effort to create a new sense of national community within the country's post-Soviet state boundaries.

The authorities have also turned to the Orthodox Church as an aid in political socialization. They regard the Church as a valuable ally in building patriotic loyalty, national pride, and a framework of ethical values.

The Church, in turn, seeks to protect its traditional status as Russia's state church, enabling it to block other Christian denominations from proselytizing in Russia. As of the fall of 2006, a course on the fundamentals of Orthodox culture had been introduced into the school curriculum in nearly twenty regions, and about 20,000 Orthodox priests were serving as chaplains in the armed forces.[30] The Church's rising influence in the schools has prompted a backlash among many intellectuals, who protest that teaching religion in the schools violates the constitutional provision that Russia is a secular state.[31] But many people, whether religious or not, deplore the decay of morals in society and the relentless rise of consumerism and materialism as Russia opens itself to the global capitalist system. They see the Church, with its long history of partnership with the state, as a way of restoring traditional moral values in society.

In the 1990s the regime generally respected media freedom. Under Putin, the authorities moved to set limits on the media (particularly television), but did not institute an elaborate political socialization system such as the Soviet state employed. Nevertheless, the authorities have used the media to build support for their foreign and domestic policies. The overall political line under Putin and Medvedev has been that Russia is rejecting totalitarian communism on the one hand and unbridled oligarchic capitalism on the other and is restoring continuity with the best traditions of Russia's political history. Both, however, have repeatedly insisted that Russia must make use of democracy and capitalism, although in its own way.

The media system is stratified. Television reaches almost everyone and is by far the most important source of news for the population. Accordingly, it is subjected to the tightest political control by the authorities, who give the editors of the main broadcast programs regular guidance on what to cover and what not to cover. Print and Internet media are allowed much more freedom, but they reach a far smaller audience, so they are of less immediate concern to the authorities.[32] Aware of the stultifying effects of the old Soviet system of ideological control over communications, the authorities' strategy is defensive, in that they want to prevent organized groups from challenging their claim to power, rather than being overtly ideological.

Russian political socialization is therefore much less subject to direct state control than it was in the Soviet era, and even then, awareness of the political and economic standards of the outside world filtered into the consciousness of the Soviet population.

Today's authorities want to use schools and communications media to build loyalty to the state and its leaders, confidence in the future, and acceptance of a centralized regime, while at the same time spurring Russians to modernize the economy.

POLITICAL PARTICIPATION

In a democracy citizens take part in public life both through direct forms of political participation (such as voting, engaging in party work, organizing for a cause, demonstrating, and lobbying) and through indirect forms of participation (such as holding membership in civic groups and in voluntary associations). Both kinds of participation influence the quality of government. By means of collective action, citizens signal to policymakers what they want government to do. Through these channels of participation, activists rise to positions of leadership. But, despite the legal equality of citizens in democracies, levels of participation in the population vary with differences across groups in resources, opportunities, and motivations. The better off and the better educated are disproportionately involved in political life everywhere, but in some societies, the disproportion is much greater than in others. And where deep inequalities in the distribution of wealth and income reinforce differentials in political voice between rich and poor, democracy itself is at risk.[33]

The Importance of Social Capital

A healthy fabric of voluntary associations has long been recognized as an important component of democracy. Participation in civic life builds social capital—reciprocal bonds of trust and obligation among citizens that facilitate collective action. Where social capital is significant, people treat one another as equals, rather than as members of social hierarchies. They are more willing to cooperate in ways that benefit the society and improve the quality of government by sharing the burden of making government accountable and effective.[34] For example, where people feel less distance from and mistrust toward government, governments are better able to float bonds to provide improvements to community infrastructure. People are more willing to pay their taxes, so that government has more revenue to spend on public goods—and less ability and less incentive to divert it into politicians' pockets. Both capitalism and democratic government rest on people's ability to cooperate for mutual benefit.

In Russia, however, social capital has historically been scarce, compared with West European societies, and participation in civic activity has been extremely limited. Moreover, state and society have generally been separated by mutual mistrust and suspicion. State authorities have usually stood outside and above society, extracting what resources they needed from society, but not cultivating ties of obligation to it. The Communist regime further depleted the stock of social capital by coopting associations useful for the state and repressing those that threatened its interests. Therefore, social capital not only in Russia, but also throughout the former Communist bloc, is significantly lower than in other parts of the world.[35]

The weakness of intermediate associations linking political elites to ordinary citizens widens the felt distance between state and society. Thus, although Russians turn out to vote in elections in relatively high numbers, participation in organized forms of political activity is low. Opinion polls show that most people believe that their involvement in political activity is futile, and they have little confidence that they can influence government policy through their participation. Although there was an intense surge in political involvement in the late 1980s and early 1990s when controls over political expression and association were lifted, it ebbed substantially over the 1990s.

Membership in voluntary associations in contemporary Russia is extremely low. According to survey data, 91 percent of the population does not belong to any sports or recreational club, literary or other cultural group, political party, local housing association, or charitable organization. Four percent belong to sports or recreation groups, and 2 percent each say that they belong to a housing bloc, neighborhood association, or cultural group. Only half a percent reports being a member of a political party. About 9 percent report attending church at least once a month, and about 20 percent say that they are members of trade unions. Attending religious services and being a member of a trade union are very passive forms of participation in public life. Yet, even when these and other types of participation are taken into account, almost 60 percent of the population still is outside any voluntary public associations.[36] For example, today some 87 percent of Russian Orthodox believers are not members of a congregation, going to church only occasionally.[37]

This is not to say that Russian citizens are *psychologically* disengaged from public life or that they are socially isolated. Half of the Russian adult population reports reading national newspapers "regularly" or "sometimes," and almost everyone watches national television "regularly" (81%). Sixty-nine percent read local newspapers "regularly" or "sometimes." Sixty-six percent discuss the problems of the country with friends "regularly" or "sometimes," and 48 percent say that people ask them their opinions about what is happening in the country. A similar percentage of people discuss the problems of their city with friends.[38] Russians do vote in high proportions in national elections—higher in fact than those of their American counterparts.[39]

Moreover, Russians prize their right *not* to participate in politics. Today's low levels of political participation are a reflection of the low level of confidence in political institutions and the widespread view that ordinary individuals have little influence over government. In the 2003 Duma elections, 4.7 percent of the voters expressed their dissatisfaction with the array of choices offered by checking the box marked "against all" on the party-list ballot.[40] But the authorities worried that this was too attractive a means of expressing disaffection and eliminated the option from later elections.

Elite Recruitment

Elite recruitment refers to the institutional processes in a society by which people gain access to positions of influence and responsibility. Elite recruitment is closely tied to political participation because it is through participation in community activity that people take on leadership roles, learn civic skills (such as organization and persuasion), develop networks of friends and supporters, and become interested in pursuing political careers.

In the Soviet regime, the link between participation and elite recruitment was highly formalized. The Communist Party recruited the population into a variety of officially sponsored organizations—such as the Communist Party, youth leagues, trade unions, and women's associations. Through such organizations the regime identified potential leaders and gave them experience in organizing group activity. The party reserved the right to approve appointments to any positions that carried high administrative responsibility or that were likely to affect the formation of public attitudes. The system for recruiting, training, and appointing individuals for positions of leadership and responsibility in the regime was called the **nomenklatura** system. Those individuals who were approved for the positions on nomenklatura lists were informally called "the nomenklatura." Many citizens regarded them as the ruling class in Soviet society.

The democratizing reforms of the late 1980s and early 1990s made two important changes to the process of elite recruitment. First, the old nomenklatura system crumbled along with other Communist Party controls over society. Second, although most members of the old ruling elites adapted themselves to the new circumstances and stayed on in various official capacities, the wave of new informal organizations and popular elections brought many new people into elite positions. Today the contemporary Russian political elite consists of a mixture of career types: those who worked their way up through the state bureaucracy and those who entered politics through other channels, such as elective politics or business.

Today some of the old Soviet institutional mechanisms for recruitment are being restored. In the Communist regime, the party maintained schools to train political leaders, where rising officials received a combination of management education and political indoctrination. Today most of those schools serve a similar function as academies for training civil servants and are overseen by the presidential administration. The authorities are working to systematize the selection and training of officials in order to ensure that a competent and politically reliable cadre is available for recruitment not only to state bureaucratic positions, but even for management positions in major firms.[41]

There are two major differences between elite recruitment in the Communist regime and that in the present. The nomenklatura system of the Soviet regime ensured that in every walk of life, those who held positions of power and responsibility were approved by the party. They thus formed different sections of a single political elite and owed their positions to their political loyalty and usefulness. Today, however, there are multiple elites (political, business, professional, cultural, etc.), reflecting the greater degree of pluralism in post-Soviet society.

Second, there are multiple channels for recruitment to today's *political* elite. Many of its members come from positions in the federal and regional executive agencies. Putin relied heavily on the police (the regular police and the security services) and the military as sources of personnel for his senior-level appointments.[42] He also turned to colleagues he had worked with closely in St. Petersburg in the 1990s; an example is President Dmitrii Medvedev. Medvedev has worked closely with Putin since 1990 when he became an advisor to Putin, who was serving as a deputy to the mayor. Medvedev then moved with Putin to Moscow in 1999 when Putin was made deputy head of the presidential administration under Yeltsin. Putin gave him ever broader responsibilities, first as head of the presidential administration and then as first deputy chairman of the government. This pattern of close patron-client relations, where a rising politician brings members of his "team" with him each time he moves up the career ladder, is a common feature of elite recruitment in Russia. One effect is to generate competition between rival groups of clients, sometimes called "clans." In Russia's case there has been persistent behind-the-scenes rivalry between two such clans, both composed of associates of Putin. One is close to the security services, while the other, with a slightly more liberal cast, is made up of trained lawyers. When Putin chose Medvedev as his anointed successor, it was seen as a serious blow against the first group.[43]

The Soviet elite recruitment system produced many of today's successful businesspeople as old guard bureaucrats discovered ways to cash in on their political contacts and get rich quickly. Money from the Communist Party found its way into the establishment of many new business ventures, including several of the first commercial banks. Insiders took advantage of their contacts to obtain business licenses, office space, and exclusive contracts with little difficulty. Some bought (at bargain basement prices) controlling interests in state firms that were undergoing privatization and a few years later became millionaires.

Today's business elite is closely tied to the state both because state officials keep business on a short leash and because business provides material and political benefits to officials. In some cases bureaucratic factions form around particular enterprises and industries such as the oil or gas industry. Businesses need licenses, permits, contracts, exemptions, and other benefits from government. Political officials, in turn, need financial contributions to their campaigns, political support, favorable media coverage, and other benefits that business can provide. In the 1990s the close and collusive relations between many businesses and government officials nurtured widespread corruption and the meteoric rise of a small group of business tycoons, or oligarchs. They took advantage of their links to Yeltsin's administration to acquire control of some of Russia's most valuable companies. The prominence of the newly rich fed a public backlash that made it politically viable for Putin to suppress some of them and destroy their business empires by police methods. And in many cases the state takeover of private firms ended up concentrating wealth and power in the hands of well-connected state officials (often from the security services) who have treated the firms as private fiefdoms, rather than increasing their productivity or accountability.[44]

INTEREST ARTICULATION: BETWEEN STATISM AND PLURALISM

The political and economic changes of the last two decades in Russia have had a powerful impact on the way social interests are organized. A diverse spectrum of interest associations has developed. The pattern of interest articulation, however, reflects the powerful impact of state control over society, as well as the sharp disparities in wealth and power that formed during the transition period. A few organizations have considerable influence in policymaking, while other groups have little.

The Communist regime did not tolerate the open pursuit of any interests except those authorized by the state. Interest organizations—such as trade unions, youth groups, professional societies, and the like—were closely supervised by the Communist Party. Glasnost' upset this statist model of interest articulation by setting off an explosion of political expression. This, in turn, prompted new groups to form and to make political demands. It is hard today to imagine how profound the impact of glasnost' was on Soviet society. Almost overnight, it opened the floodgates to a growing stream of startling facts, ideas, disclosures, reappraisals, scandals, and sensations. In loosening the party's controls over communication sufficiently to encourage people to speak and write freely and openly, the regime also relinquished the controls that would have enabled it to rein in political expression when it went too far.

As people voiced their deep-felt demands and grievances, others recognized that they shared the same beliefs and values and made common cause with them, sometimes forming new, unofficial organizations. Therefore, one result of glasnost' was a wave of participation in "informal"—that is, unlicensed and uncontrolled—public associations. When the authorities tried to limit or prohibit such groups, they generated still more frustration and protest. Associations of all sorts formed, including groups dedicated to remembering the victims of Stalin's terror, ultranationalists who wanted to restore tsarism, and nationalist movements in many republics. The explosion of the nuclear reactor at Chernobyl in 1986 had a tremendous impact in stimulating the formation of environmental protest, linked closely to nationalist sentiment in Belarus and Ukraine.[45]

The elimination of the state's monopoly on productive property resulted in the formation of new interests, among them those with a stake in the market economy. Now groups can form to represent a diversity of interests, compete for access to influence and resources, and define their own agendas. The Justice Ministry estimates that there are nearly half a million NGOs, although probably no more than a quarter of them are active at any given time.[46]

In some cases NGOs are the successors of recognized associations of the old regime, such as official trade unions. Often these groups cling to their inherited organizational assets and continue to seek "insider" access to the state. Other groups sprang up during the glasnost' period or later, but must cooperate with local authorities in order to gain access to meeting places and media attention.

There were elements of corporatism in the state's relations with interest groups under Putin because of the regime's preference for dealing directly with controllable umbrella organizations representing particular segments of society. An example is the formation of the Public Chamber to create a state-approved platform for the activity of selected NGOs. Operating within the limits set by the regime, the Public Chamber has been able to serve to some extent as a channel of communication between the public and the authorities.[47] Similar chambers have been created in many regions. Overall, however, the pattern of interest group activity is more pluralist than corporatist because in most cases interest associations are too numerous, too weak internally, and too competitive for corporatism to succeed. But under Putin, interest articulation did become more statist as the regime gradually increased political controls on nongovernmental associations.

A law enacted at the beginning of 2006 imposed new restrictions on NGOs, making it easier for the authorities to deny them registration and to shut them down. At the same time, the authorities warned that foreign intelligence services were sponsoring Russian NGOs for the purposes of intelligence gathering and subversion. The political atmosphere for NGOs became considerably chillier.

Let us consider three examples of associational groups: the **Russian Union of Industrialists and Entrepreneurs (RUIE)**, the **League of Committees**

of Soldiers' Mothers**, and the **Federation of Independent Trade Unions of Russia (FITUR)**. They illustrate different strategies for organization and influence and different relationships to the state.

The Russian Union of Industrialists and Entrepreneurs

Most formerly state-owned industrial firms are now wholly or partly privately owned. More and more industrial managers respond to the incentives of a market economy, rather than to those of a state socialist economy. Under the old regime, managers were told to fulfill the plan regardless of cost or quality. Profit was not a relevant consideration.[48] Now most managers seek to maximize profits and increase the value of their firms. Although many still demand subsidies and protection from the state, more and more want an environment where laws and contracts are enforced by the state, regulation is reasonable and honest, taxes are fair (and low), and barriers to foreign trade are minimized. These changes are visible in the political interests of the association that represents the interests of big business in Russia, the Russian Union of Industrialists and Entrepreneurs (RUIE). The RUIE is the single most powerful organized interest group in Russia. Its membership comprises both the old state industrial firms (now mostly private or quasi-private) and new private firms and conglomerates.

In the early 1990s, the RUIE's lobbying efforts were aimed at winning continued state support of industrial firms and planning for a slow transition to a market economy. The RUIE also helped broker agreements between business and labor, and it was a source of policy advice for government and parliament. In 2000 the Putin administration let it be known that it wanted the oligarchs to join the RUIE and the RUIE to become the unified voice of big business. The Putin leadership also sponsored two other business associations to articulate the interests of small and medium-size business.

Over time the RUIE's role has changed according to the opportunities and limits set by the state authorities. In the 2000s it has been a loyal source of policy advice and political support for the government. It has expanded its in-house capacity for working with the government in drafting legislation. On a number of issues, such as tax law, pension policy, bankruptcy legislation, regulation of the securities market, and the terms of Russia's entry to the World Trade Organization, the RUIE has been active and

One of the most widely publicized episodes of the Putin era was the state takeover of the powerful private oil company, Yukos, and the criminal prosecution of its head, Mikhail Khodorkovsky. At the time of his arrest in October 2003, Khodorkovsky was the wealthiest of Russia's new postcommunist magnates. His career began in the late 1980s when he started a bank. Later he acquired—at a bargain basement price—80 percent of the shares of the Yukos oil company when the government privatized it. At first, like some other newly wealthy tycoons, Khodorkovsky sought to squeeze maximum profit from the firm by stripping its assets. Soon his business strategy changed, and he began to invest in the firm's productive capacity. He made Yukos the most dynamic of Russia's oil companies. As he improved the efficiency and transparency of the firm, the share prices rose and, with them, Khodorkovsky's own net worth. At its peak in 2002, the company's assets were estimated at about $20 billion, of which Khodorkovsky owned nearly $8 billion.

Seeking to improve his public image, Khodorkovsky created a foundation and launched several charitable initiatives. He recruited some distinguished international figures to his foundation's board. He became active in Russian politics, helping to fund political parties and sponsoring the election campaigns of several Duma deputies. Critics accused him of wanting to control parliament and even of wanting to change the constitution to turn it into a parliamentary system. There was talk that he intended to seek the presidency.

By spring 2003, the Putin administration decided that Khodorkovsky and Yukos had grown too independent. In a series of actions, several top figures in Yukos and associated companies were arrested and charged with fraud, embezzlement, tax evasion, and even murder. In December 2003, the government began issuing claims against the company for billions of dollars in back taxes and froze the company's bank accounts as collateral against the claims. When Yukos failed to pay the full tax bill, the government seized its main production subsidiary and auctioned it off to a firm that, three days later, sold it to Russia's only state-owned oil company, Rosneft'. In October 2003 Khodorkovsky was arrested and charged with fraud and tax evasion. In May 2004 he was sentenced to nine years' imprisonment and sent to a prison camp in Siberia. In 2006 the last remnants of the company were forced into bankruptcy.

Whatever the regime's motives—political, economic, or both—the Yukos affair shows that the authorities are willing to manipulate the legal system for political purposes when it suits them and that the fight to redistribute control of Russia's natural resource assets remains a driving force in politics.

influential in shaping policy. For the most part, it works behind the scenes to lobby for its interests, but occasionally, if it feels its voice has been ignored, it applies pressure more publicly.[49]

Yet the limits of RUIE's power as the collective voice of big business are clear. When the Putin regime began its campaign to destroy the Yukos oil firm starting in July 2003 (see Box 9.4), the RUIE confined itself to mild expressions of concern. Its members, evidently fearful of crossing Putin, chose not to defend Yukos's head, Mikhail Khodorkovsky, or to protest the use of police methods to destroy one of Russia's largest oil companies. Instead, they promised to meet their tax obligations and to do more to help the country fight poverty. Perhaps if big business had taken a strong and united stand, they could have influenced state policy. But the desire by each individual firm to maintain friendly relations with the government and the fear of government reprisals undercut big business's capacity for collective action.

The League of Committees of Soldiers' Mothers

The Soviet regime sponsored several official women's organizations, but these mainly served propaganda purposes. During the glasnost' period, a number of unofficial women's organizations sprang up. One such group was the Committee of Soldiers' Mothers. It formed in the spring of 1989 when some 300 women in Moscow rallied to protest the end of student deferments from military conscription. Their protest came hard on the heels of Gorbachev's withdrawal of Soviet forces from the decade-long war in Afghanistan, where over 13,000 Soviet troops were killed in bitter and demoralizing fighting. In response to the Soldiers' Mothers' actions, Gorbachev agreed to restore student deferments. Since then the Soldiers' Mothers' movement has grown, with local branches forming in hundreds of cities and joining together in the League of Committees of Soldiers' Mothers. Their focus has expanded somewhat, but remains centered on the problems of military service. The league presses the military to end the brutal hazing of recruits, which results in the deaths (in many cases by suicide) of hundreds of soldiers each year. The league also advises young men on how to avoid being conscripted.[50]

The onset of large-scale hostilities in Chechnia in 1994–1996 and 1999–2000 stimulated a new burst of activity by the league. It helped families locate soldiers who were missing in action or captured by the Chechen rebel forces. It sent missions to Chechnia to negotiate for the release of prisoners and to provide proper burial for the dead. It collected information about the actual scale of the war and of its casualties. It also continued to lobby for decent treatment of recruits. Through the 1990s it became one of the most sizeable and respected civic groups in Russia. It can call on a network of thousands of active volunteers for its work. These volunteers visit wounded soldiers in hospitals and help military authorities identify casualties. One of the movement's greatest assets is its members' moral authority as mothers defending the interests of their children. This stance makes it hard for their opponents to paint them as unpatriotic.

The league plays both a public political role (for instance, it lobbied to liberalize the law on alternative civil service for conscientious objectors, and it fights for an end to the brutality in the treatment of servicemen[51]) and a role as service provider. Much of its effort is spent on helping soldiers and their families deal with their problems.

Like many NGOs, the League of Committees of Soldiers' Mothers cultivates ties with counterpart organizations abroad, and it has won international recognition for its work. For some groups such ties are a source of dependence, as organizations compensate for the lack of mass membership with aid and know-how from counterpart organizations abroad. However, the league enjoys a stable base of public support in Russia. Its international ties have also probably helped protect the group in the face of the sometimes hostile attitude of the authorities.[52]

The Federation of Independent Trade Unions of Russia

The Federation of Independent Trade Unions of Russia (FITUR) is the successor of the official trade union federation under the Soviet regime. Unlike the RUIE, however, it has poorly adapted itself to the postcommunist environment, even though it inherited substantial organizational resources from the old Soviet trade union organization. In the Soviet era, virtually every employed person belonged to a trade union. All branch and regional trade union organizations were part of a single labor federation, called the All-Union Central Council of Trade Unions. With the breakdown of the old regime, some of the member unions became independent, while other unions sprang up as independent bodies representing the interests of particular groups of workers. Nonetheless, the nucleus of the old official trade union organization survived in the form of the FITUR. It remains by far the largest trade union federation in Russia. Around 95 percent of all organized workers belong to unions that are, at least formally, members of the FITUR. The independent unions are much smaller. By comparison with big business, however, the labor movement is fragmented, weak, and unable to mobilize workers effectively for collective action.

The FITUR inherited valuable real estate assets from its Soviet-era predecessor organization, including thousands of office buildings, hotels, rest homes, hospitals, and children's camps. It also inherited the right to collect workers' contributions for the state social insurance fund. Control of this fund enabled the official trade unions to acquire enormous amounts of income-generating property over the years. These assets and income streams give leaders of the official unions considerable advantages in competing for members. But the FITUR no longer has centralized control over its regional and branch members. In the 1993 and 1995 parliamentary elections, for instance, member unions formed their own political alliances with parties. Thus, internal disunity is another major reason for the relative weakness of the FITUR as an organization. Much of its effort is expended in fighting independent unions to win a monopoly on representing workers in collective bargaining with employers, rather than in joining with other unions to defend the interests of workers generally.[53]

The ineffectiveness of the FITUR is also illustrated by the tepid response of organized labor to the severe deterioration in labor and social conditions in the 1990s, when there was much less labor protest than might have been expected. There were some strikes and protests, mainly over wage arrears. Surveys found that in any given year in the 1990s three-quarters of all workers received their wages late at least once.[54] Teachers were particularly hard hit by the problem of unpaid wages. Waves of strikes by teachers shut down thousands of schools in the late 1990s. After 1999 strikes subsided as the economy began to recover. Recent research shows that much of the labor protest was actually organized not by the unions, but by governors seeking to pressure the central government for more money.[55]

Why are unions so weak? One reason is that workers depend on the enterprises where they work for a variety of social benefits that are administered through the enterprise, such as housing, recreation facilities, and medical and day care services.[56] Another, however, is the close relationship between the leadership of the FITUR and government authorities. As a result, it is very difficult for labor to mount collective actions. Workers generally feel unrepresented by their unions.[57]

New Sectors of Interest

In a time when people's interests are changing rapidly, interest groups search for new roles. Some old groups decline, while new organizations form. In Russia many new associations have formed around the interests of new categories of actors. Bankers, political consultants, realtors, mayors of small cities, mayors of large cities, judges, attorneys, auditors, television broadcasters, political consultants, and numerous other professional and occupational groups have formed associations to seek favorable policies or set professional standards. Environmental groups, women's organizations, human rights activists, and many other cause-oriented groups have organized. Most of these operate in a particular locality, but a few have national scope.

The rules of the game for interest articulation changed sharply after the Soviet regime fell and are continuing to change as the postcommunist regime redefines the framework for relations between state and society. In the Yeltsin period, lobbying frequently took corrupt forms, including bribery of parliamentary deputies and government officials. By the end of the 1990s, more collective action by business and other sectors of interest was evident, and there was more open bargaining over the details of policy.

In the 2000s, however, policymaking is more centralized again, and interest groups are more dependent on the goodwill of the authorities for their ability to operate. The authorities have created corporatist structures such as the Public Chamber for consultation between the state and civil society and have tightened controls over NGOs. Still, interest articulation is mainly pluralistic, with tens of thousands of nonstate associations competing to voice their interests through the mass media, the parliament, and the government. Despite the political controls, public pressure expressed through interest groups does have some impact on policymaking.

PARTIES AND THE AGGREGATION OF INTERESTS

Interest aggregation refers to the process by which the demands of various groups of a society are pooled to form programmatic options for government. Although other institutions also aggregate interests, in most countries political parties are the quintessential structure performing this vital task. How well parties aggregate interests, define choices for voters, and hold politicians accountable is of critical importance to democracy.

Although Russia's party system in the 1990s was fluid and fragmented, a clear structure has emerged in the 2000s in which the United Russia party dominates, while other parties are marginal. In the 1990s there was considerable turnover in the parties from one election to the next. Voters had little sense of attachment to parties and more often associated them with particular politicians' personalities than with specific ideological stances. Most parties had very weak roots in society, although parties guided the work of the State Duma through their parliamentary factions.[58]

Russia's party system has undergone a major transformation in the 2000s. The authorities have succeeded in creating a single party that dominates elections. Russians term such a party a **party of power**, indicating that the party serves the collective interests of those holding office: For them it is a vehicle for career advancement, while for the voters it is the electoral face of the state. In the 1990s there were several short-lived attempts to form parties of power, but in the 2000s the United Russia party has become *the* unquestioned party of power. United Russia presently casts such a long and commanding shadow over the political system that some observers believe that the Kremlin seeks to turn it into a replica of the ruling Communist Party of the Soviet era.

Political parties tend to be prominent in national and regional legislative elections, but much less so in presidential elections. Because Russia's presidential system encourages the president to avoid making commitments to parties, presidential races usually concentrate attention on the candidates' personalities, rather than on their policy programs. Moreover, the fact that the winning party in parliament does not form the government tends to undercut politicians'

loyalty to parties. Instead, the Kremlin uses parties to control politicians' careers and to build legitimacy for its power by winning elections.

Elections and Party Development

Table 9.1 indicates the official results of the party-list voting in the 1993, 1995, 1999, 2003, and 2007 elections. The table groups parties into five categories that have characterized party identities since the early 1990s: *democratic* (those espousing liberal democratic

| Party-List Vote in Duma Elections Since 1993 | | | | | TABLE 9.1 |
| Support for United Russia has grown at the expense of support for democratic, Communist, and nationalist parties | | | | | |
Party	**1993**	**1995**	**1999**	**2003**	**2007**
Democratic Parties					
Russia's Choice	15.5	3.9	—	—	—
Union of Rightist Forces (SPS)	—	—	8.5	4.0	0.9
Yabloko	7.8	6.8	5.9	4.3	1.5
Party of Russian Unity and Concord (PRES)	6.7	—	—	—	—
Democratic Party of Russia (DPR)	5.5	—	—	0.2	0.1
Centrist Parties					
Women of Russia	8.1	4.6	2.0	—	—
Civic Union[a]	1.9	1.6	—	—	—
Parties of Power					
Our Home Is Russia	—	10.1	1.2	—	—
Fatherland—All Russia (OVR)	—	—	13.3	—	—
Unity/United Russia[b]	—	—	23.3	38.2	64.3
A Just Russia	—	—	—	—	7.7
Nationalist Parties					
Liberal Democratic Party of Russia (LDPR)[c]	22.9	11.2	5.9	11.6	8.1
Congress of Russian Communities (KRO)[d]	—	4.3	0.6	—	—
Motherland (Rodina)	—	—	—	9.2	—
Leftist Parties					
Communist Party of the Russian Federation (CPRF)	12.4	22.3	24.2	12.8	11.5
Agrarian Party	7.9	3.8	—	3.6	2.3
Other parties failing to meet 5% threshold	10.9	26.8	12.5	11.1	2.1
Against all[e]	4.3	2.8	3.3	4.7	—

[a]In 1995 the same alliance renamed itself the Bloc of Trade Unionists and Industrialists.
[b]In 2003 Unity ran under the name United Russia, following a merger with the Fatherland party.
[c]In 1999 the LDPR party list was called the Zhirinovsky bloc.
[d]In 1999 this party was called the Congress of Russian Communities and Yuri Boldyrev Movement.
[e]In 2007 the "Against all" option was not available.

Source: Compiled by author from reports of Central Electoral Commission. See http://cikrf.ru.

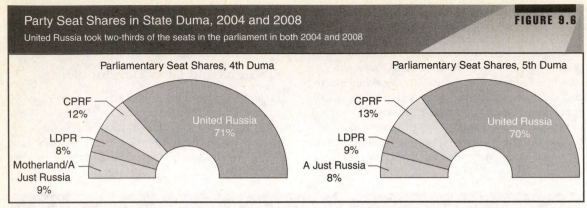

FIGURE 9.6

Party Seat Shares in State Duma, 2004 and 2008

United Russia took two-thirds of the seats in the parliament in both 2004 and 2008

Parliamentary Seat Shares, 4th Duma

CPRF 12%
LDPR 8%
Motherland/A Just Russia 9%
United Russia 71%

Parliamentary Seat Shares, 5th Duma

CPRF 13%
LDPR 9%
A Just Russia 8%
United Russia 70%

Notes: Figures taken as of May 2004 and January 2008. Percentages shift with time as members change factional affiliations. Note that United Russia was the result of a merger of the Fatherland Pary and United and that A Just Russia formed in 2006 from the merger of Motherland, the Pensioners' Party, and the Party of Life.

Source: Compiled by author from reports of State Duma.

principles), *leftist* (those advocating socialist and statist values), *centrist* (those mixing leftist and liberal democratic appeals), *nationalist* (those highlighting ethnic nationalism, patriotism, and imperialism), and *parties of power*.

Figure 9.6 shows how the election results translated into the distribution of seats in the Duma to various party factions following the 1999, 2003, and 2007 elections. Note how the spectrum of parliamentary parties has dwindled as United Russia has come to occupy a dominant position. It has been aided by some strategic engineering of the electoral system that has included tightening the rules for party registration, raising the threshold for representation from 5 percent to 7 percent, switching to an all-PR Duma, and prohibiting deputies from leaving their factions without losing their seats. Above all, the increasing use of electoral fraud to ensure overwhelming victories for United Russia has padded its margin. In the nearly twenty years since contested elections first were held, the party system has evolved from being one with many weakly supported parties to an authoritarian dominant party system.[59]

From the Multiparty System to the Dominant Party Regime

The multiparty system arose with the elections under Gorbachev to the reformed Soviet and Russian Republic parliaments. Democratically oriented politicians

coalesced to defeat Communist Party officials in the 1989 and 1990 elections and, once elected, formed legislative caucuses in parliament. There they fought with Communist, nationalist, and agrarian groups. These parliamentary factions became the nuclei of political parties in the parliamentary election of December 1993.

Polarization and the Party System Elections in the late 1980s and early 1990s were aligned around two poles, one associated with Yeltsin and the forces pushing for democracy and a market economy, the other fighting to preserve the old system based on state ownership and control of the economy. Other parties positioned themselves in relation to these poles. For instance, Vladimir Zhirinovsky's nationalistic **Liberal Democratic Party of Russia (LDPR)** claimed to offer an alternative to both the democrats and the Communists, appealing to xenophobia, authoritarianism, and the nostalgia for empire. The party's unexpectedly strong showing in the 1993 election was a signal of widespread popular discontent with the Yeltsin economic reforms.

The main anchor of the left (statist and socialist) pole of the spectrum has been the Communists (**Communist Party of the Russian Federation**, or *CPRF*), who are the heirs of the old ruling Communist Party of the Soviet Union and who espouse a mixture of communist and nationalist principles.

On the right, or pro-market and pro-democracy, side of the spectrum have been several parties whose fortunes have fallen dramatically since the 1990s. One of these is *Yabloko*. Yabloko has consistently defended democratic principles and a social democratic policy in the economy and has opposed some of the policies pursued by Yeltsin and Putin that have sought to dismantle most of the old state supports and controls in the economy. It is no longer represented in the Duma because it has failed to attract enough votes to clear the 7 percent threshold.

Elections in the early to mid-1990s reflected the polarization between democrats and Communists, but also tended to produce a fragmented field of parties. In the 1993 and 1995 Duma elections, neither pro-democracy parties nor Communists won a clear majority, although democrats were in the minority, while Communists, nationalists, and their allies had a majority of seats. Except for a few parties (the CPRF, the LDPR, and Yabloko), most parties had shallow roots and tended to spring up shortly before elections. Many sought to avoid taking a clear programmatic stance, instead claiming to be "centrists" and pragmatists who would steer between the opposing poles of the democrats and Communists.

Presidential elections have not tended to stimulate party development as much as parliamentary elections have because they have revolved more around the personalities of the candidates. When Boris Yeltsin ran for reelection in 1996, he started out with an approval rating in the single digits (and even considered canceling the election at one point), but ultimately rallied his strength and succeeded in persuading voters that the election was about a choice between him and a return to communism. Yeltsin's displays of vigor during the campaign, his lavish promises to voters, and his domination of the media all contributed to a surge in popularity and a victory over Gennadii Ziuganov, his Communist rival (see Table 9.2).[60] The campaign took its toll on Yeltsin, however. Soon afterward he had major heart surgery, and for much of his second term, he was in poor health.

Building the Party of Power The 1999 election was dominated by the question of who would succeed Yeltsin as president. Many federal and regional officeholders wanted to rally around a new "party of power" in order to protect their jobs. A group of backroom Kremlin strategists formed a movement called Unity in the late summer of 1999. They wanted to create an electoral bloc that state officials throughout the country could rally around in the race for the Duma. They also intended it to serve as a political vehicle for Vladimir Putin, whom Yeltsin had just named prime minister and anointed as his successor. Conveniently for Putin, within days of Unity's formation and Putin's appointment, Chechen rebels launched raids into the neighboring region of Dagestan. Bombings of apartment buildings—officially blamed on Chechen terrorists—also occurred in Moscow and other cities. Putin's decisive handling of the military operations against the Chechen guerrillas gave him and the Unity movement a major boost in popularity. Unity, which had not even existed until late August, won 23 percent of the party-list vote in December.

The presidential election of 2000 occurred ahead of schedule due to President Yeltsin's early resignation. Under the constitution the prime minister automatically succeeds the president if the president leaves office early, but new elections must be held within three months. Accordingly, the

Presidential Election, 1996 **TABLE 9.2**
Yeltsin edged out the Communist candidate in the first round and then won decisively in the second round

	First Round (June 16, 1996)	Second Round (July 3, 1996)
Boris Yeltsin	35.2%	53.8%
Gennadii Ziuganov	32.0	40.3
Alexander Lebed	14.5	—
Grigorii Yavlinskii	7.3	—
Vladimir Zhirinovsky	5.7	—
Svyatoslav Fedorov	0.9	—
Mikhail Gorbachev	0.5	—
Martin Shakkum	0.3	—
Yurii Vlasov	0.2	—
Vladimir Bryntsalov	0.1	—
Aman Tuleev	0.0	—
Against all candidates	1.5	4.8

presidential election was scheduled for March 26, 2000. The early election gave the front-runner and incumbent, Putin, an advantage because he could capitalize on his popularity and the country's desire for continuity. Putin ran the Russian equivalent of a "rose garden" campaign, preferring to be seen handling the normal daily business of a president, rather than going out on the hustings and asking for people's votes. He counted on the support of officeholders at all levels, a media campaign that presented a "presidential" image to the voters, and the voters' fear that change would only make life worse. His rivals, moreover, were weak. Several prominent politicians prudently chose not to run against him. Putin's strategy worked brilliantly: He won an outright majority in the first round (see Table 9.3).

The 2003 and 2004 Elections Under Putin the ideological divide between Communists and democrats that had marked the transition era disappeared. The political arena was dominated by the president and his supporters. The loyal pro-Putin party Unity was renamed United Russia after it absorbed a rival party, Fatherland (headed by Moscow mayor Yuri Luzhkov). United Russia held a near monopoly in the party spectrum, squeezing other parties to the margins. A series of changes in the electoral law made it

increasingly difficult for all but a few parties to compete in elections, while the Kremlin mounted a major effort to pressure regional governors and big business to back United Russia.

The Kremlin's success in making United Russia the dominant party was demonstrated vividly in the 2003 parliamentary election. United Russia won 38 percent of the party-list vote and wound up with two-thirds of the seats in the Duma. The Communists suffered a severe blow, losing almost half their vote share, and the democrats did even worse. For the first time, none of the democratic parties won seats on the party-list vote. The result underscored Putin's drive to eliminate any meaningful political opposition. Such an impressive showing for United Russia assured Putin's reelection as president. The March 2004 race was a landslide. Putin won easily with 71.3 percent of the vote, while his Communist rival received less than 14 percent of the vote (see Table 9.3). European observers commented that the elections were "well administered," but hardly constituted "a genuine democratic contest" in view of the president's overwhelming control of media coverage of the race and the absence of genuine competition.[61]

United Russia's dominance was confirmed in the 2007 Duma election. Shortly before the election, Putin declared that he would head the party's list (though he said he would not join the party and he did not intend to take his Duma seat).[62] This indicated that Putin intended to use the party as a basis for his power even after he left the presidency. Even though the Kremlin created a second party of power (called A Just Russia) as a mechanism to siphon off some votes on the left side of the spectrum and to offer an alternative outlet for some politicians who could not be accommodated in United Russia, United Russia's overwhelming success was never in doubt, and it went on to win 64.3 percent of the vote. The authorities used a variety of methods to manipulate the election, ranging from grossly unequal access to the media for the parties to outright falsification of results in many regions (in some districts, the reported vote for United Russia was greater than 100 percent of the registered voters).[63]

Similarly, the authorities took no chances in the 2008 presidential election. Again, they violated numerous provisions of the law in order to guarantee the desired outcome—for example, by disqualifying potentially serious opposition candidates, pouring large resources from the state budget into Medvedev's campaign, giving Medvedev disproportionate media coverage, and ignoring challenges brought by opposition groups and election rights NGOs over violations of the

Russian Presidential Elections in the 2000s **TABLE 9.3** Putin and Medvedev won in the first round by wide margins in each race	2000	2004	2008
Vladimir Putin	52.9	71.3	—
Gennadii Ziuganov (CPRF)	29.2	—	17.7
Vladimir Zhirinovsky (LDPR)	2.7	—	9.3
Grigorii Yavlinskii (Yabloko)	5.8	—	—
Nikolai Kharitonov (CPRF)	—	13.7	—
Dmitrii Medvedev	—	—	70.2
Andrei Bogdanov (DPR)	—	—	1.3
Other	6.5	10.7	—
Against all candidates	1.8	3.4	—

Legend: CPRF: Communist Party of the Russian Federation; LDPR: Liberal Democratic Party of Russia; DPR: Democratic Party of Russia.

Note: The "Against all candidates" option was not available on the 2008 ballot.

election law. Medvedev would probably have won in any case, but the large-scale manipulation of the election signaled to voters and opponents alike that the authorities were in complete control of the succession. The authorities managed the outcome so successfully that Medvedev officially won over 70 percent of the vote—about 1 percentage point below Putin's reported margin in 2004 (see Table 9.3).

The establishment of the dominant party regime has changed the way parties represent different social groups. In the 1990s there were some systematic links between particular social groups and particular parties. For instance, younger and better educated voters tended to support the democratic parties, while older and less educated voters supported Communist and nationalist parties. But as the United Russia party has gained dominance, it has appealed to all parts of the society. As a result, social structure has become less and less significant as an influence on voting, while voters' attitudes toward the authorities in general and toward Putin in particular have become the most important predictor of voting preferences.

Table 9.4 indicates that voters of all camps tend to see United Russia as the embodiment of President Putin's political legacy. The challenge for United Russia in the future will be to establish a basis of support that goes beyond simply its identification with Putin. The party will need to cultivate more lasting attachments based on its ability to deliver policy benefits to the voters. Putin and other Kremlin officials have warned the party that it cannot hope to feed off the Kremlin's life-support system forever—though they are unwilling to cut it loose.

For other parties the 2007–2008 elections confirmed the new reality that United Russia is likely to enjoy a dominant position for years to come. Other parties have been relegated to playing a small, marginal role in national politics and concentrating their efforts on winning seats in regional parliaments.

THE POLITICS OF ECONOMIC REFORM

The Dual Transition

Russia's postcommunist transition was wrenching because the country had to remake both its *political* and its *economic* institutions following the end of communism. The move to a market economy created opportunities for some—and hardships for many more. Democratization opened the political system to the

Grounds for Support of United Russia — Support for United Russia strongly reflects attitudes toward Vladimir Putin	**TABLE 9.4**
Wanted to support Putin	46%
I like this party, I trust it	32
I don't especially like this party, but the others are even worse	3
I wanted to vote the same way as everyone else	2
I was forced to vote for it but I didn't especially want to	<1
Other	<1
Hard to answer	15

Source: All-Russian Center for the Study of Public Opinion (VTsIOM), "Political Attitudes and the Vote for United Russia," Press Release No. 840, December 19, 2007. Retrieved July 11, 2008, from wciom.ru/arkhiv/tematicheskii-arkhiv/item/single/9406.html (survey conducted December 8–9, 2007; N = 1,600).

influence of groups that could organize to press for exclusive economic benefits for themselves. Many people who had modest, but secure livelihoods under the Soviet regime were ruined by inflation and unemployment when the planned economy broke down. A smaller number took advantage of opportunities for entrepreneurship or exploited their connections with government to amass sizeable fortunes. One reason Vladimir Putin was so popular was that people gave him credit for restoring growth and prosperity to the economy and cracking down on some of the tycoons who had amassed great fortunes by dubious means.

Stabilization Russia pursued two major sets of economic reforms in the early 1990s, macroeconomic stabilization and privatization. Stabilization, which in Russia came to be called **shock therapy**, is a program intended to stop a country's financial meltdown. This required a painful dose of fiscal and monetary discipline by slashing government spending and squeezing the money supply. Structural reform of this kind always lowers the standard of living for some groups of the population in the short run.

Initially, many expected that the greatest enemies of stabilization would be those whose living standards suffered as a result of the higher prices and lower incomes, such as workers in state enterprises and pensioners. In practice, however, those who benefited from the early steps to open the economy and privatize state assets proved to be the greatest obstacles to further reform because they exploited their privileged access to the authorities to lock in their own gains and to oppose any subsequent measures to expand competition. Among these were officials who acquired ownership rights to monopoly enterprises and then worked to shut out potential competitors from their markets, state officials who benefited from collecting "fees" to issue licenses to importers and exporters or permits for doing business, and entrepreneurs whose firms dominated the market in their industry.[64] A fully competitive market system, with a level playing field for all players, would have posed a threat to their ability to profit from their privileged positions.

From Communism to Capitalism
Communist systems differed from other authoritarian regimes in ways that made their economic transitions more difficult. This was particularly true for the Soviet Union and its successor states. For one, the economic growth model followed by Stalin and his successors concentrated much production in large enterprises. This meant that many local governments were entirely dependent on the economic health of a single employer. The heavy commitment of resources to military production in the Soviet Union further complicated the task of reform in Russia, as does the country's vast size. Rebuilding the decaying infrastructure of a country as large as Russia is staggeringly expensive.

The economic stabilization program began on January 2, 1992, when the government abolished most controls on prices, raised taxes, and cut government spending sharply. Almost immediately, opposition to the new program began to form. Economists and politicians took sides. The shock therapy program was an easy target for criticism, even though there was no consensus among critics about what the alternative should be. It became commonplace to say that the program was all shock and no therapy.

By cutting government spending, letting prices rise, and raising taxes, the stabilization program sought to create incentives for producers to increase output and find new niches in the marketplaces. But Russian producers did not initially respond by raising productivity. As a result, society suffered from a sharp, sudden loss in purchasing power. People went hungry, bank savings vanished, and the economy fell into a protracted slump. Firms that were politically connected were able to survive by winning cheap credits and production orders from the government,

which dampened any incentive for improving productivity. Desperate to raise operating revenues, the government borrowed heavily from the International Monetary Fund (IMF) and issued treasury bonds at ruinously high interest rates. IMF loans came with strings attached—the government pledged to cut spending further and step up tax collections as a condition of accepting IMF assistance, which fueled the depression further. Communists and nationalists got a rise out of audiences by depicting the government as the puppet of a malevolent, imperialist West.

Privatization
Stabilization was followed shortly afterward by the mass **privatization** of state firms. In contrast to the shock therapy program, privatization enjoyed considerable public support, at least at first. Privatization transfers legal title of state firms to private owners. Under the right conditions, private ownership of productive assets is usually more efficient for society as a whole than is state ownership because in a competitive environment owners are motivated by an incentive to maximize their property's ability to produce a return. Under the privatization program, every Russian citizen received a voucher with a face value of 10,000 rubles (around $30 at the time). People were free to buy and sell vouchers, but they could be used only to acquire shares of stock in privatized enterprises or shares of mutual funds investing in privatized enterprises. The program sought to ensure that everyone became a property owner instantly. Politically, the program aimed to build support for the economic reforms by giving citizens a stake in the outcome of the market transition. Economically, the government hoped that privatization would eventually spur increases in productivity by creating meaningful property rights. Beginning in October 1992, the program distributed 148 million privatization vouchers to citizens. By June 30, 1994, when the program ended, 140 million vouchers had been exchanged for stock out of the 148 million originally distributed. Some 40 million citizens were, in theory, share owners. But these shares were often of no value because they paid no dividends and shareholders exercised no voting rights in the companies.

The next phase of privatization auctioned off most remaining shares of state enterprises for cash. This phase was marked by a series of scandalous sweetheart deals in which banks owned by a small number of Russia's wealthiest tycoons wound up with title to some of Russia's most lucrative oil, gas, and metallurgy firms for bargain basement prices. The most notorious of these arrangements became known as the **loans for**

Russian Annual GDP Growth and Price Inflation Rates, 1991–2007	TABLE 9.5

Russia has enjoyed sustained growth in the 2000s, after a dismal decade in the 1990s

	1991	1992	1993	1994	1995	1996	1997	1998	1999	2000	2001	2002	2003	2004	2005	2006	2007
GDP	−5	−14.5	−8.7	−12.6	−4.3	−6	0.4	−11.6	3.2	7.6	5	4	7.3	7.1	6.4	7.4	8.1
Inflation	138	2323	844	202	131	21.8	11	84.4	36.5	20.2	18.6	15.1	12	11.7	10.9	9	11.9

Note: GDP is measured in constant market prices. Inflation is measured as the percentage change in the consumer price index from December of one year to December of the next.

Source: Press reports of Russian State Statistical Service (www.gks.ru).

shares scheme. It was devised in 1995 by a small group of business magnates with strong connections to government who persuaded Yeltsin to auction off management rights to controlling packages of shares in several major state-owned companies in return for loans to the government. If the government failed to repay the loans in a year's time, the shares would revert to the banks that made the loans. The government, as expected, defaulted on the loans, letting a small number of oligarchs acquire ownership of some of Russia's most valuable companies.[65]

Consequences of Privatization On paper, privatization was a huge success. By 1996 privatized firms produced about 90 percent of industrial output, and about two-thirds of all large and medium-sized enterprises had been privatized.[66] In fact, however, the actual transfer of ownership rights was far less impressive than it appeared. For one thing, the dominant pattern was for managers to acquire large shareholdings of the firms they ran. As a result, management of many firms did not change. Moreover, many nominally private firms continued to be closely tied to state support, such as cheap state-subsidized loans and credits.[67]

The program allowed a great many unscrupulous wheeler-dealers to prey on the public through a variety of financial schemes. Some investment funds promised truly incredible rates of return. Many people lost their savings by investing in funds that went bankrupt or turned out to be simple pyramid schemes. The Russian government lacked the capacity to protect the investors. Privatization was carried out before the institutional framework of a market economy was in place. Markets for stocks, bonds, and commodities were small in scale and weakly regulated. The legal foundation for a market economy has gradually emerged, but only after much of the economy was already privatized. For much of the 1990s, the lack of liquidity in the economy meant that enterprises failed to pay their wages and taxes on time, trading with one another using barter.

The government fell into an unsustainable debt trap. Unable to meet its obligations, it grew increasingly dependent on loans. As lenders became increasingly certain that the government could not make good on its obligations, they demanded ever higher interest rates, deepening the trap. Ultimately, the bubble burst. In August 1998, the government declared a moratorium on its debts and let the ruble's value collapse against the dollar. Overnight the ruble lost two-thirds of its value, and credit dried up.[68] The government bonds held by investors were almost worthless. The effects of the crash rippled through the economy. The sharp devaluation of the ruble made exports more competitive and gave an impetus to domestic producers, but also significantly lowered people's living standards.

As Table 9.5 shows, economic output in Russia fell for a decade before beginning to recover in 1999. The recovery was not due to a structural reform of the economy. There has not been a substantial overhaul of the banking system or of the way industry is managed. The economy is still vulnerable to a downturn in the international economic situation because Russia remains highly dependent on exports of natural resources: Oil and gas make up over half of Russian exports and a fifth of Russian gross domestic product (GDP).[69] Still, a number of branches besides energy are showing real vigor—among them, construction and retail trade. Following the 1998 crash, several sectors (such as agriculture) got a boost from the drop in the ruble's exchange value as their prices became competitive and imported products became more expensive. As the economy revived, enterprises were able to pay off arrears in back wages and taxes. In turn, these taxes allowed government to meet its own obligations, in turn allowing consumer demand for industry's products to rise, and so on. These trends have raised living standards noticeably.

Unemployment has fallen since the August 1998 crisis, and the number of people living in poverty has declined by over one-third, from over 30 percent to under 20 percent. The leaders have expressed satisfaction with the favorable trends in the economy, but warn that they are not sufficient to achieve sustained and balanced development. Both Putin and Medvedev have called for reducing the economy's reliance on natural resource exports and increasing its capacity for innovation. However, some of Putin's actions—such as the renationalization of a number of firms and the creation of large state-owned holding companies—tended to undermine incentives for raising productivity. The narrowness of the foundation on which Russia's recovery was based became acutely evident when the world economic crisis struck in 2008–2009. Russia's stock market lost three-quarters of its value in half a year. Credit markets froze up and industrial production plummeted. Unemployment rose. Revenues from energy exports fell sharply. Fears of social unrest spread. The crisis demonstrated how vulnerable Russia was to changes in world financial and energy markets.

Social Conditions Living standards fell sharply during the 1990s. A small minority became wealthy, and some households improved their lot modestly. Most people, however, suffered a net decline in living standards as a result of unemployment, lagging income, and nonpayment of wages and pensions.

Income inequality grew sharply both during the period of economic decline in the 1990s and again during the period of economic recovery in the 2000s. This has been caused by many factors. In the 1990s it was the result of the lag of wage increases behind price inflation, the sharp rise in unemployment, the deterioration of the pension and other social assistance systems, and the concentration of vast wealth in the hands of a small number of people. In the 2000s poverty has decreased significantly, along with unemployment, and pension levels have risen. Yet, inequality continues to rise as a result of large disparities in wage levels (two workers in the same occupation and in the same region might have widely different wages depending on where they work),[70] the extremely high earnings of managers in industries such as energy and finance, and the Putin regime's shift to a flat (13%) income tax and abolition of estate taxes. As a result of both government policy and current economic trends, therefore, economic prosperity is benefiting those at the upper end of the income distribution much more than it is those at the lower end. This helps explain the sharp rise in the number of Russian billionaires. According to *Forbes Magazine*'s list, the number of billionaires in Russia shot up from 60 to 110 between 2007 and 2008.[71] Something like twelve of them have seats in the Federation Council.[72]

One commonly used measure of inequality is the Gini index, which is an aggregate measure of the total deviation from perfect equality in the distribution of wealth or income. In Russia the Gini index nearly doubled during the early 1990s, rising from 26 in 1987–1990 to 48 in 1993–1994. Inequality in Russia was higher than in any other postcommunist country except for Kyrgyzstan.[73] As the economy began to recover and poverty fell, the Gini index declined slightly, to just under 40, before creeping back up in the mid-2000s to over 40 (approximately equal to the level of income inequality in the United States). In 2006 the richest tenth of the population in Russia received 15.3 times as much income as did the poorest tenth, up from 14 times in 2002. The actual level of income inequality is probably considerably greater than the official figure because of the large scale of unreported, "off-book" income due to tax evasion.

The continuing rise in inequality and the absence of a growing middle class constitute a matter of some concern to Russian leaders. In his address to the State Council on February 8, 2008, President Putin declared that the current level of income inequality was "absolutely unacceptable" and should be reduced to more moderate levels; he called for measures that would bring about an expansion of the middle class. Its share of the population, he declared, should reach 60 or even 70 percent by 2020.[74]

An especially disturbing dimension of the social effects of transition has been the erosion of public health. Although public health had deteriorated in the late Communist period, the decline worsened after the regime changed. Mortality rates have risen sharply, especially among males. Life expectancy for males in Russia is at a level comparable to that in poor and developing countries. At present, life expectancy at birth for males is just under fifty-nine years and for females seventy-two years. The disparity between male and female mortality—enormous by world standards—is generally attributed to the higher rates of abuse of alcohol and tobacco among men. Other demographic indicators are equally grim. Prime Minister Fradkov told a Cabinet meeting in July 2006 that only 30 percent of newborn children "can be described as healthy" and that "there are more than 500,000 disabled children in need of various forms of treatment, and also some 730,000 orphans or abandoned children."[75] Rates of incidence of HIV and other infectious diseases, murders, suicides, drug addiction, and alcoholism are rising.

Russia's leaders consider the demographic crisis to pose a grave threat to the country's national security both because of the growing shortage of labor in some regions (experts believe that there are 12 or 14 million illegal immigrants in Russia, about the same number as in the United States) and because of the army's inability to recruit enough healthy young men.[76] Every year Russia's population declines by about three-quarters of a million people due to the excess of deaths over births. Demographers estimate that Russia's population could fall by over one-third by 2050. In his 2006 message to parliament, President Putin called for a series of measures to raise birthrates, reduce mortality, and stimulate immigration.

Setting the country on a path of self-sustaining economic growth, where workers and investors are confident in their legal rights, requires a complete overhaul of the relationship of the state to the economy. The Soviet state used central planning to direct enterprises on what to produce and how to use resources. Much of the economy was geared to heavy industry and defense production, and government ministries directly administered each branch of the economy. The postcommunist state must have an entirely different relationship to the economy in order to stimulate growth. It must set clear rules for economic activity, regulate markets, enforce the law, supply public goods and services, and promote competition. Shifting the structure of the state bureaucracy and the attitudes of state officials has been a Herculean task.

We can get some idea of the legacy of the communist system in the way the state was intertwined with the economy by looking at the structure of the state budget. Figure 9.7 shows the breakdown of spending for the 2007 federal budget. Total spending was set at 5.4 trillion rubles, or about US$220 billion. The share spent on national defense (at 15%) probably understates the actual amount. The shares of

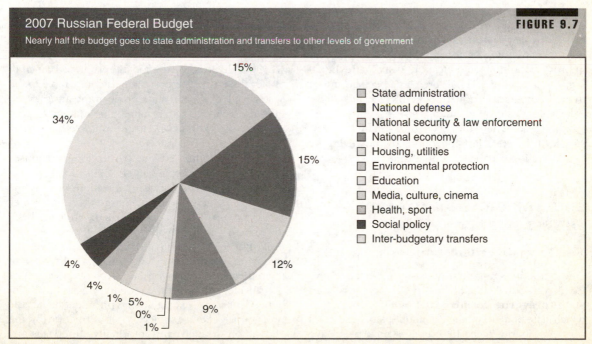

2007 Russian Federal Budget

FIGURE 9.7

Nearly half the budget goes to state administration and transfers to other levels of government

- State administration
- National defense
- National security & law enforcement
- National economy
- Housing, utilities
- Environmental protection
- Education
- Media, culture, cinema
- Health, sport
- Social policy
- Inter-budgetary transfers

Source: Russian Ministry of Finance (www.minfin.ru).

spending on general administration (15%), law enforcement (12%), and subsidies to various regional development funds (34%) are high, compared with other countries, and indicate how substantial the central government's role is in state and society. Over half the government's revenues come from oil and gas revenues, a degree of dependence on resource rents that Russia's government knows to be unhealthy over the long term.[77]

The government also recognizes that the oil- and gas-fueled budget surpluses pose a serious danger of creating inflationary pressures in the economy. For this reason, like some other oil-rich states, Russia has created a "stabilization fund" that removes some of the revenues generated by high world energy prices from circulation and uses them to pay off external debt. In 2007 the government divided the stabilization fund into two portions, one called the reserve fund, to be used in the event of a serious fall in government revenues, and the other called a national welfare fund, to be used mainly to shore up the pension system. By the beginning of 2008, the reserve fund held about $120 billion in assets and the national welfare fund about $30 billion. The Putin and Medvedev governments have held firm in the face of mounting political pressure to spend down these funds, conscious of the serious risk of wrecking the country's finances through inflation if they do so. The country's fiscal surplus has made it possible, however, for the government to launch ambitious programs of spending on four high-priority projects to improve conditions in education, health care, housing, and agriculture. The reserve fund became crucial in enabling Russia's government to cover its deficits as its revenues dropped and its social spending obligations rose when the 2008-2009 financial crisis struck. If the crisis lasts beyond 2009, however, the fiscal situation may become untenable.

RULE ADJUDICATION: TOWARD THE RULE OF LAW

The Law-Governed State

One of the most important goals of Gorbachev's reforms was to make the Soviet Union a **law-governed state (pravovoe gosudarstvo),** rather than one in which state bodies and the Communist Party exercised power arbitrarily. Since 1991 the Russian leaders have asserted that the state must respect the primacy of law over politics—even when they took actions grossly violating the constitution. The difficulty in placing law above politics testifies to the lingering legacy of the old regime's abuse of the legal system. Presidents Putin and Medvedev have repeatedly declared their commitment to the principle of the rule of law (in a strange, but memorable phrase, Putin once called for the "dictatorship of law"), even when their actions have flagrantly infringed on the independence of the judiciary.

The struggle for the rule of law began well before Gorbachev. After Stalin died, his successors ended mass terror and took significant steps to reduce the use of law for political repression. Still, throughout the late Soviet era, the Communist Party and the KGB often used legal procedures to give the mantle of legal legitimacy to acts of political repression. Although the prosecution of political dissidents has ended, the use of the legal system for political purposes by state authorities continues. Reforms in the 1990s took some steps toward making the judiciary independent of the authorities, but in the 2000s, political control over the legal system has increased.

The major institutional actors in the legal system are the **procuracy**, the courts (judiciary), and the bar. Each has undergone substantial change in the postcommunist period.

The Procuracy Russia's legal system traditionally vested a great deal of power in the procuracy, which was considered to be the most prestigious branch of the legal system. The procuracy is comparable to the system of federal and state prosecuting attorneys in the United States, but has more wide-ranging responsibilities and is organized as a centralized hierarchy headed by the procurator-general. The procuracy is charged with fighting crime, corruption, and abuses of power in the bureaucracy. It seeks to ensure that all state officials and public organizations observe the law. It investigates criminal charges and prosecutes cases in court. The procuracy has traditionally been the principal check on abuses of power by state officials. But it is inadequately equipped to meet the sweeping responsibilities assigned to it because of the difficulty of effectively supervising the vast state bureaucracy. Although the procuracy is nominally independent of the executive, the president names the procurator-general (subject to confirmation by the Federation Council) and informally supervises any politically significant cases.

The Judiciary In contrast to the influence that the procuracy has traditionally wielded in Russia, the bench has been relatively weak. Trial judges are usually the least experienced and lowest paid members of the legal profession—and the most vulnerable to external political and administrative pressure. In a few instances, judges have been murdered when they attempted to take on organized crime. Many judges have left their positions to take higher-paying jobs in other branches of the legal profession, and caseloads have risen substantially.

State officials pay lip service to the principle of judicial independence, but often violate it in practice by pressuring judges to render particular judgments in politically sensitive matters. At the same time, many reforms since the end of communism are intended to make the administration of justice more effective, and some increase the rights of defendants in criminal cases. For example, in the 1990s, trial by jury in major criminal cases was introduced in several regions on an experimental basis and since then has spread throughout the country in serious criminal cases. The goal of adopting the jury system was to make the judicial system more adversarial, so that the prosecution and the defense have equal status in the courtroom and the judge becomes a neutral arbiter between them.[78] In a number of high-profile cases, juries have acquitted defendants when they found the procuracy's case unconvincing.

The Russian judiciary is a unitary hierarchy. All courts of general jurisdiction are federal courts. There are also other specialized types of courts in addition to federal courts of general jurisdiction—among them, the commercial courts, the constitutional courts of ethnic republics, the local municipal courts (equivalent to justices of the peace), and the military courts. Most criminal trials are held in district and city courts of general jurisdiction, which have original jurisdiction in most criminal proceedings. Higher-level courts, including regional and republic-level courts, hear appeals from lower courts and have original jurisdiction in certain cases. At the pinnacle of the hierarchy of courts of general jurisdiction is the Russian Supreme Court, which hears cases referred from lower courts and also issues instructions to lower courts on judicial matters. The Supreme Court does not have the power to challenge the constitutionality of laws and other official actions of legislative and executive bodies. The constitution assigns that power to the Constitutional Court. Under the constitution, the judges of the Supreme Court are nominated by the president and confirmed by the Federation Council.

There is a similar hierarchy of courts hearing cases arising from civil disputes between firms or between firms and the government called **commercial courts (arbitrazhnye sudy)**. Like the Supreme Court, the Supreme Commercial Court is both the highest appellate court for its system of courts and the source of instruction and direction to lower commercial courts. As with the Supreme Court, the judges of the Supreme Commercial Court are nominated by the president and confirmed by the Federation Council. In recent years the Supreme Commercial Court has handed down a number of major decisions that clarify the rules of the economic marketplace.

The Ministry of Justice oversees the court system and provides for its material and administrative needs. Its influence over the legal system is limited, however, because it lacks any direct authority over the procuracy.

The Bar Change of another sort has been occurring among those members of the legal profession who represent individual citizens and organizations in both criminal and civil matters: advocates (*advokaty*). They are comparable to barristers in Great Britain and litigating attorneys in the United States. Their role has expanded considerably with the spread of the market economy. They have long enjoyed some autonomy through their self-governing associations, through which they elect officers and govern admission of new practitioners. In the past their ability to use their rights was limited, but in recent years their opportunities have risen markedly. Private law firms are proliferating. The profession is attractive for the opportunities it provides to earn high incomes. A number of lawyers have become celebrities by taking on high-profile cases.

Constitutional Adjudication One of the most important reforms in postcommunist Russia's legal system is the establishment of a court for constitutional review of the official acts of government. The Constitutional Court has authority to interpret the constitution in a variety of areas. It has ruled on several ambiguous questions relating to parliamentary procedure. It has overturned some laws passed by national republics within Russia and has struck down several provisions of the Russian Criminal Code that limited individual rights. Generally, in disputes between individuals and state authorities, the court finds in favor of individuals, thus reaffirming the sphere of individual legal rights. It has consistently upheld the sovereignty of the federal constitution over regional governments.

The most important challenge for the court, however, is the huge domain of presidential authority. The court has been reluctant to challenge the president. One of its first and most important decisions concerned a challenge brought by a group of Communist parliamentarians to President Yeltsin's decrees launching the war in Chechnia. The court ruled that the president had the authority to wage the war through the use of his constitutional power to issue decrees with the force of law. In other, less highly charged issues, the court established legal limits to the president's authority. For instance, the court ruled that Yeltsin could not refuse to sign a law after parliament had overridden his veto. However, in the more authoritarian climate of the 2000s, the court has not issued any rulings restricting the president's powers. Generally, the court is sensitive to the political climate surrounding it and takes care not to issue a ruling that would be ignored or opposed by the president.

Obstacles to the Rule of Law

Movement toward the rule of law continues to be hampered by the abuse of legal institutions by the political authorities and by endemic corruption in state and society.

In the post-Soviet state, the security police continue to operate autonomously. In the Soviet period, the agency with principal responsibility for maintaining domestic security was called the KGB (State Security Committee). The KGB exercised wide powers, including responsibility for both domestic and foreign intelligence. Since 1991 its functions have been split up among several agencies. The main domestic security agency is called the Federal Security Service (FSB). Although the structure and mission of the security agencies have changed, they have never undergone a thorough purge of personnel. No member of or collaborator with the Soviet-era security services has been prosecuted for violating citizens' rights. In contrast to Eastern Europe, there has been no review of officials' records for past collaboration with the secret police. This is one of several ways in which post-Soviet Russia has still not put its Communist past behind it.

The security police are regarded as one of the more professionally competent and uncorrupted state agencies. However, despite being assigned new tasks, such as fighting international narcotics trafficking and terrorism, they still demonstrate a Soviet-style preoccupation with controlling the flow of information about the country. For example, in 2001 the security police sent a directive to the Academy of Sciences demanding that scholars report all contacts with foreigners. Many similar Soviet-era police practices have been revived under Putin.

President Putin also resumed the Soviet-era practice of using the legal system to suppress potential political opposition. An example is the series of legal maneuvers taken against the owners of independent media in the early 2000s. These included police harassment and criminal prosecution, as well as civil actions such as bankruptcy proceedings. For example, the owners of two television companies were forced to divest themselves of their media holdings and transfer ownership to companies loyal to the administration. As a result, Russia's two relatively autonomous national television companies lost their political independence, one respected liberal newspaper was shut down, and the entire media establishment was sent a strong signal that it would be wise to avoid crossing the current administration. Today only a small number of print media have retained a measure of political independence.

In the 1990s the bankruptcy laws were often used by businesses to drive rivals into bankruptcy in order to take them over; today state companies use civil and criminal laws for the same purpose—to force a private company to sell out at a bargain price so that it can then be taken over and its assets stripped. For example, the state used charges of tax evasion and theft to force the Yukos oil firm into bankruptcy so that its most profitable elements could be sold at a low price to the state oil company, Rosneft'. These forced hostile takeovers are called *reiderstvo* (raiding).[79]

Corruption Another obstacle to the rule of law is endemic corruption. Corruption increased substantially after the Soviet period. It is widespread both in everyday life and in dealings with the state. A large-scale survey by a Moscow research firm gives some indication of the nature and scale of corruption. At least half the population of Russia is involved in corruption in daily life. For instance, the probability that an individual will pay a bribe to get an automobile inspection permit is about 60 percent. The likelihood of paying a bribe to get one's child into a good school or college or to get good grades is about 50 percent. There is a 26 percent chance of paying a bribe to get a favorable ruling in a court case. The areas where the largest sums are spent are health care, education, courts, and automobile inspections; these alone account for over 60 percent of the money paid in bribes.[80]

President Medvedev has declared fighting corruption to be a top priority of his administration. As a result, the topic has been given increasing public attention. Experts believe that the scale of corruption grew considerably in the 2000s, no doubt because of the flood of oil revenues into the country. One estimate is that the total volume of corrupt transactions doubled between 2006 and 2008, from $240 billion (approximately equal to the total national budget) to $480 billion (approximately one and one-half times the size of the national budget).[81]

Corruption is hardly unique to Russia or to the former Communist world. However, it is especially widespread in Russia and the other former Soviet states. Corruption on this scale imposes a severe drag on economic development, both because it diverts resources away from public needs and because it undermines people's willingness to invest in productive activity.[82] Moreover, much corruption is tied to organized crime, which bribes government officials for protection and drives out legal businesses. The corruption of the police and courts ensures that many crimes go unpunished and forces legal businesses to compete in the corruption market with illegal ones.

Corruption in Russia has deep roots, and many Russians assume that it is ineradicable. Comparative studies of corruption demonstrate, however, that a culture of corruption can be changed by changing the expectations of the public and the government.[83] The key is for the political leadership to make a serious effort to combat corruption and to back up this commitment with institutional reform and sustained attention to the problem.

Since the early 1990s, there have been a number of reforms, such as the adoption of trial by jury and the creation of the Constitutional Court, that have the potential to strengthen the judiciary's independence from both political pressure and corruption. However, the authorities' habitual use of the procuracy and the courts for political purposes and the powerfully corrosive effect of corruption continue to subvert the integrity of the legal system. In the long run, movement toward the rule of law will require that power be sufficiently dispersed among groups and organizations in the state and society so that neither private nor state interests are powerful enough to subordinate the law to their own purposes.

RUSSIA AND THE INTERNATIONAL COMMUNITY

Russia's thousand-year history of expansion, war, and state domination of society has left behind a legacy of autocratic rule and a preoccupation with defending national borders. The collapse of the Soviet regime required Russia to rebuild its political institutions, economic system, national identity, and relations with the outside world. During the Soviet period, state propaganda used the image of an international struggle between capitalism and socialism to justify its repressive control over society and its enormous military establishment. Now the country's leaders recognize that only through international integration can Russia hope to prosper. Today's leaders aim to capture the benefits of economic integration with the developed capitalist world, while at the same time building an authoritarian political order at home featuring direct state control of the strategically important sectors of the economy.

Gorbachev, Yeltsin, Putin, and Medvedev all asserted that the integration of Russia into the community of developed democracies is strategically important for Russia. Gorbachev was willing to allow Communist regimes to fall throughout Eastern Europe for the sake of improved relations with the West. Yeltsin accepted the admission of East European states into the North Atlantic Treaty Organization as a necessary condition for close relations with the United States and Europe. Putin repeatedly emphasized that he regarded Russia's admission to the World Trade Organization as critical for Russia's long-term economic success. Following the September 11, 2001, terrorist attacks on the United States, Putin immediately telephoned U.S. President George W. Bush to offer his support. Putin clearly saw an advantage for Russia in aligning itself with the United States against Islamic terrorism, which it identified as an immediate threat to its own security. Putin cited Russia's own war in Chechnia as part of the global struggle against Islamic terrorists.

At the same time, Russia has not accepted the constraints of international law. It has expanded its military presence in several former Soviet republics, pressuring them to become satellites of Russia. In August 2008 it launched a well-prepared military invasion of independent, pro-Western Georgia after Georgia attempted to use force to take back control over a Russia-backed breakaway region, South Ossetia. The overwhelming Russian response was clearly intended to subjugate Georgia to Russia's interest in preserving a buffer of subordinate states in the territory of the former Soviet Union.

Likewise, in its brutal military campaigns in Chechnia from 1994 to 1996 and then again from 1999 to 2006, Russia refused to allow international human rights organizations to monitor Russian practices, which included mass bombardment of civilian areas. In 2007 Russia resumed the Cold War–era practice of sending its strategic bombers on long-distance missions over the Atlantic, Pacific, and Arctic oceans to demonstrate the global reach of its military power. As its economic and military power has revived, Russia has attempted to establish itself as a counterweight to American power and to rebuild Russian influence in the former Soviet region.

Russia's quasi-imperial behavior in parts of the former Soviet Union and its refusal to be bound by democratic principles have kept it from becoming fully integrated into the international community. Yet, it is far more open than it was under Soviet rule, and its leaders recognize that they cannot retreat into isolation and autarky. They are also aware of the grave vulnerabilities Russia faces—its declining population, aging infrastructure, dependence on immigrant labor, and overreliance on natural resources for state revenues. Thus, while they seek to be a hegemonic power in the territory of the former Soviet Union, they also do not want to resurrect Russia's role as the United States's enemy in the bipolar world; they would prefer that Russia be one of several major powers in a multipolar world.

Russia's vast territory, weak government capacity, and tradition of state domination over society make it likely that the primary objective of its leaders for the foreseeable future will be to strengthen the state, in both its internal and its international dimensions. The end of the Communist regime and the dissolution of the Soviet Union damaged the state's capacity to enforce the laws, protect its citizens, and provide basic social services. Favorable economic conditions in the 2000s enabled the state to rebuild its power at home and abroad, but the crisis of 2008–2009 revealed Russia's susceptibility to trends in international financial and energy markets. In the long run, self-sustaining economic development will require the rule of law and effective institutions for articulating and aggregating social interests. The viability of Russia's postcommunist state will ultimately depend on how responsive and adaptive its institutions are to the demands of Russia's citizens in a globalized and interdependent world.

REVIEW QUESTIONS

- How did Yeltsin's "shock therapy" program contribute to the constitutional crisis of 1993?
- What effects did the constitutional struggles of 1992–1993 have on the features of the 1993 constitution?
- How did President Putin go about strengthening the power of the central government vis-à-vis regional governments? What were his reasons for shifting the balance of power in this way?
- What are the main similarities and differences between the channels of elite recruitment under the Soviet system and today?
- Most Russians evaluate the pre-Gorbachev Soviet system favorably, yet would prefer not to bring it back. How would you explain this apparent contradiction?
- Why has United Russia been so successful as a "party of power"?
- What are the main obstacles to the rule of law in Russia? What changes in the political system would be required to overcome them?

KEY TERMS

Chechnia
commercial courts (*arbitrazhnye sudy*)

Communist Party of the Russian Federation (CPRF)

Constitutional Court
Federation Council

Federation of Independent Trade Unions of Russia (FITUR)

glasnost'
Gorbachev, Mikhail
law-governed state
(*pravovoe
gosudarstvo*)
League of Committees
of Soldiers' Mothers
Lenin, Vladimir Ilyich

loans for shares
Medvedev, Dmitrii
Anatol'evich
Nomenklatura
oligarchs
party of power
presidential decrees

privatization
procuracy
Public Chamber
Russian Union of
Industrialists and
Entrepreneurs
(RUIE)

Security Council
shock therapy
Stalin, Joseph
State Council
State Duma
United Russia

SUGGESTED READINGS

Aslund, Anders. *Russia's Capitalist Revolution: Why Market Reform Succeeded and Democracy Failed*. Washington, DC: Peterson Institute for International Economics, 2007.

Baker, Peter, and Susan Glasser. *Kremlin Rising: Vladimir Putin's Russia and the End of Revolution*. New York: Scribner, 2005.

Breslauer, George W. *Gorbachev and Yeltsin as Leaders*. Cambridge, England: Cambridge University Press, 2002.

Colton, Timothy J. *Yeltsin: A Life*. New York: Basic Books, 2008.

Fish, M. Stephen. *Democracy Derailed in Russia: The Failure of Open Politics*. Cambridge, England: Cambridge University Press, 2005.

Hale, Henry. *Why Not Parties in Russia? Democracy, Federalism, and the State*. Cambridge, England: Cambridge University Press, 2006.

Hellman, Joel S. "Winners Take All: The Politics of Partial Reform in Postcommunist Transitions." *World Politics* 50, no. 1 (1998): 203–234.

Hill, Fiona, and Clifford Gaddy. *The Siberian Curse: How Communist Planners Left Russia Out in the Cold*. Washington, DC: Brookings Institution, 2003.

McFaul, Michael. *Russia's Unfinished Revolution: Political Change from Gorbachev to Putin*. Ithaca, NY: Cornell University Press, 2001.

Rose, Richard, William Mishler, and Neil Munro. *Russia Transformed: Developing Popular Support for a New Regime*. Cambridge, England: Cambridge University Press, 2006.

Sakwa, Richard. *Putin: Russia's Choice*. London: Routledge, 2004.

Shleifer, Andrei, and Daniel Treisman. *Without a Map: Political Tactics and Economic Reform in Russia*. Cambridge, MA: MIT Press, 2000.

White, Stephen, Richard Rose, and Ian McAllister. *How Russia Votes*. Chatham, NJ: Chatham House, 1997.

INTERNET RESOURCES

The main institutions of the federal government—the president, the parliament, and the government: **www.gov.ru/index.html** (Most of the content accessible through this site is in Russian, but some resources are in English.)

An e-mail newsletter containing news stories and commentary: **www.cdi.org/russia/johnson**

A wide range of political resources: **www.politicalresources.net/russia.htm**

The University of Pittsburgh links to resources on Russia: **www.ucis.pitt.edu/rccsweb**

A joint Internet project by a team of Russians and Americans: **www.friends-partners.org**

The *Moscow Times* is an English-language daily newspaper primarily for expatriates: **www.moscowtimes.ru/**

The University of Strathclyde's Center for the Study of Public Policy provides public opinion and electoral information from Russia: **www.RussiaVotes.org**

ENDNOTES

1. Henry E. Hale, "Regime Cycles: Democracy, Autocracy and Revolution in Post-Soviet Eurasia." *World Politics* 58 (2005): 133–165.

2. From surveys conducted by Russia's premier polling organization, the Levada Center. The "right/wrong direction" survey was posted on April 2, 2008, to their website: www.levada.ru/press/2008040201.html. Results of the survey on approval of the president available at www.levada.ru/press/2008061102.html.

3. Putin's address to the State Council, February 8, 2008. Retrieved from the presidential website: president. kremlin. ru/text/appears/2008/02/159528.shtml.

4. The resource curse has also been linked to the perpetuation of autocracy, since rulers in resource-rich countries prefer to receive revenues from extractive industries, rather than building up a broad base of tax revenues in exchange for political representation by the citizens. On the "resource curse," see Jeffrey D. Sachs and Andrew M. Warner, "Natural Resource Abundance and Economic Growth," NBER Working Paper no. 5398, December 1995; and Michael L. Ross, "The Political Economy of the Resource Curse," *World Politics* 51, no. 2 (1999): 297–322.

5. United Nations Development Programme Russia. *National Human Development Report, Russian Federation 2006/2007: Russia's Regions: Goals, Challenges, Achievements* (Moscow: United Nations Development Programme, 2007), 8.

6. Richard Pipes, *Russia Under the Old Regime,* 2nd ed. (New York: Penguin Books, 1995).

7. Archie Brown, *The Gorbachev Factor* (New York: Oxford University Press, 1996).

8. For a comparison of the leadership styles of Gorbachev and Yeltsin, see George W. Breslauer, *Gorbachev and Yeltsin as Leaders* (Cambridge, England: Cambridge University Press, 2002); see also Archie Brown and Lilia Shevtsova, eds., *Gorbachev, Yeltsin, and Putin: Political Leadership in Russia's Transition* (Washington, DC: Carnegie Endowment for International Peace, 2001); Lilia Shevtsova, *Putin's Russia* (Washington, DC: Carnegie Endowment for International Peace, 2003); and Richard Sakwa, *Putin: Russia's Choice* (London: Routledge, 2004).

9. Many observers agreed that the point of the reform was to weaken the influence of local interests on Duma deputies, further centralizing power in the executive.

10. On nationality policy in the Soviet Union, see Terry Martin, *The Affirmative Action Empire: Nations and Nationalism in the Soviet Union, 1923–1939* (Ithaca, NY: Cornell University Press, 2001).

11. Julia Kusznir, "Russian Territorial Reform: A Centralist Project That Could End Up Fostering Decentralization?"

Russian Analytical Digest no. 43 (June 17, 2008). Retrieved from www.res.ethz.ch/analysis/rad.

12. J. Paul Goode, "The Push for Regional Enlargement in Putin's Russia," *Post-Soviet Affairs* 20, no. 3 (July–September 2004): 219–257.

13. From a survey conducted by the widely respected Levada Center in June 2005.

14. Brian Whitmore, "RFE/RL Poll Finds Russians Skeptical About Elections, Hopeful for Future," *RFE/RL Newsline,* November 16, 2007.

15. L. D. Gudkov, B. V. Dubin, and Yu. A. Levada, *Problema <elity> v segodniashnei Rossii: Razmyshleniia nad rezul'tatami sotsiologicheskogo issledovaniia* (Moscow: Fond Liberal'naia missiia, 2007), 136.

16. Whitmore, "RFE/RL Poll"; *RFE/RL Newsline,* March 14, 2008.

17. Reported in Polit.ru, December 10, 2007; full report in BBC World Service Poll, "World Divided on Press Freedom." Retrieved December 10, 2007, from www. globescan.com/news_archives/bbc75. Thirteen other countries from the developed and developing worlds were surveyed.

18. *RFE/RL Newsline,* December 28, 2007.

19. Retrieved May 22, 2008, from Kommersant.ru.

20. Retrieved January 11, 2008, from Polit.ru.

21. *RFE/RL Newsline,* April 14, 2008.

22. *Nezavisimaia gazeta,* June 11, 2008.

23. Levada Center. Retrieved February 14, 2008, from www.levada.ru/press/2008020800.html

24. *RFE/RL Newsline,* March 31, 2008.

25. *RFE/RL Newsline,* September 18, 2007.

26. *RFE/RL Newsline,* October 3, 2007.

27. Richard Rose, Neil Munro, and William Mishler, "Resigned Acceptance of an Incomplete Democracy: Russia's Political Equilibrium," *Post-Soviet Affairs* 20, no. 3 (2004): 195–218.

28. Donna Bahry, "Society Transformed? Rethinking the Social Roots of Perestroika," *Slavic Review* 52, no. 3 (1993): 512–554.

29. Elena Lisovskaya and Vyacheslav Karpov, "New Ideologies in Postcommunist Russian Textbooks," *Comparative Education Review* 43, no. 4 (1999): 522–532.

30. *RFE/RL Newsline,* February 15, 2006; August 31, 2006.

31. Some 1700 scientists and other professionals sent an open letter to President Putin calling for an end to religion courses in state schools. See Polit.ru, April 16, 2008.

32. On television, see Ellen Mickiewicz, *Television, Power, and the Public in Russia* (Cambridge, England: Cambridge University Press, 2008); on the

regime's media policies more generally, see Sarah Oates, "The Neo-Soviet Model of the Media," *Europe-Asia Studies* 59, no. 8 (2007): 1279–1297; on the Internet, see Marcus Alexander, "The Internet and Democratization: The Development of Russian Internet Policy." *Demokratizatsiiya* 12 (2004): 607–627, and Anton Troianovski, "Playing by New Rules: Soft Power and the Fight for Russian Cyberspace" (senior thesis, Harvard University, 2008).

33. Daron Acemoglu and James A. Robinson, *Economic Origins of Dictatorship and Democracy* (Cambridge, England: Cambridge University Press, 2006); for studies of the effects of inequality on democracy in the United States, see Theda Skocpol and Lawrence R. Jacobs, *Inequality and American Democracy: What We Know and What We Need to Learn* (New York: Russell Sage, 2005).

34. Robert D. Putnam, *Making Democracy Work: Civic Traditions in Modern Italy* (Princeton, NJ: Princeton University Press, 1993).

35. Marc Morje Howard, *The Weakness of Civil Society in Post-Communist Europe* (Cambridge, England: Cambridge University Press, 2003).

36. Richard Rose and Neil Munro, *Elections Without Order: Russia's Challenge to Vladimir Putin* (Cambridge, England: Cambridge University Press, 2002), 224–225; Richard Rose, *Getting Things Done with Social Capital: New Russia Barometer VII* (Glasgow: Center for the Study of Public Policy, University of Strathclyde, 1998), 32–33.

37. Emil' Pain, "Ot vlasti avtoriteta k vlasti normy," *Nezavisimaia gazeta,* May 20, 2008.

38. Rose, *Getting Things Done.*

39. Turnout for the December 2003 parliamentary elections was reported to be 55.45 percent and for the presidential election in March 2004, 64.4 percent. In the United States, turnout of the voting-age population for the closely contested presidential election in 2000 was 51.3 percent.

40. A reform sponsored by President Putin and the United Russia Party has moved to eliminate the "against all" option from future elections. Although the goal is to force voters to support one of the given parties, many observers—including the chairman of the Central Election Commission—warn that this change will reduce electoral turnout.

41. Eugene Huskey, *Nomenklatura Lite? The Cadres Reserve (Kadrovyi reserv) in Russian Public Administration* (NCEEER Working Paper) (Washington, DC: National Council for Eurasian and East European Research, 2003).

42. Olga Kryshtanovskaya and Stephen White, "Putin's Militocracy," *Post-Soviet Affairs* 19, no. 4 (2003): 289–306.

43. Another feature of this rivalry is that the *siloviki*—the group of security types, headed by Igor' Sechin, a former military intelligence (GRU) official—is tied to the state oil company, Rosneft'. Sechin is chairman of the Rosneft' board. The rival clan of "liberals" has ties to Gazprom (until he became president of Russia, Medvedev was chairman of the board of Gazprom). Gazprom and Rosneft' have fought openly over control of oil and gas assets.

44. William Tompson, "Back to the Future? Thoughts on the Political Economy of Expanding State Ownership in Russia," *Les Cahiers Russie–The Russia Papers* (6) (2008).

45. Jane I. Dawson, *Eco-nationalism: Anti-nuclear Activism and National Identity in Russia, Lithuania, and Ukraine* (Durham, NC: Duke University Press, 1996).

46. *RFE/RL Newsline,* April 18, 2006.

47. For example, in July 2008, the Public Chamber issued a report on the state of freedom of speech in two Russian regions, as well as a handbook on the rules for military conscription. Kommersant.ru, July 2, 2008; Leonid Fedorov, "Svobodu slova postavili na uchet," *Nezavisimaia gazeta,* July 1, 2008.

48. In a system where all prices were set by the state, there was no meaningful measure of profit in any case. Indeed, relative prices were profoundly distorted by the cumulative effect of decades of central planning. The absence of accurate measures of economic costs is one of the major reasons that Russia's economy continues to be so slow to restructure.

49. A sore point has been fire safety inspections. Businesses regularly complain that these are usually shakedown efforts by state officials whose inspections invariably discover numerous violations of fire safety rules—which can be resolved by a bribe. The RUIE has pushed openly to reduce the powers of the fire safety inspectors.

50. Article 59 of the constitution provides that young men of conscription age who are conscientious objectors to war may do alternative service, rather than being called up to army service. Legislation specifying how this right may be exercised finally passed in 2002.

51. The chairwoman of Soldiers' Mothers recently estimated that some 3,500 servicemen lose their lives each year as a result of "various accidents and suicides." *RFE/RL Newsline,* February 14, 2008.

52. Several authors have examined the effect of Western aid on NGOs in Russia and other post-Communist countries. See Sarah L. Henderson, *Building Democracy in Contemporary Russia: Western Support for Grassroots Organizations* (Ithaca, NY: Cornell University Press, 2003); Thomas Carothers and Marina Ottaway, eds., *Funding Virtue: Civil Society Aid and Democracy* (Washington, DC: Carnegie Endowment for International Peace, 2000); and Sarah E. Mendelson and John K. Glenn, eds., *The Power and Limits of NGOs: A Critical Look at Building Democracy in Eastern Europe and Eurasia* (New York: Columbia University Press, 2002).

53. The FITUR reached a Faustian bargain with the government over the terms of a new labor relations code, which was adopted in 2001. Under the new legislation, employers no longer have to obtain the consent of the unions to lay off workers. But collective bargaining will be between the largest union at each enterprise and the management unless the workers have agreed on which union will represent them. Thus, the new labor code favors the FITUR at the expense of the smaller independent unions.

54. Richard Rose, *New Russia Barometer VI: After the Presidential Election* (Studies in Public Policy no. 272) (Glasgow: Center for the Study of Public Policy, University of Strathclyde, 1996), 6; and Rose, *Getting Things Done,* 15.

55. Graeme B. Robertson, "Strikes and Labor Organizations in Hybrid Regimes," *American Political Science Review* 101, no. 4 (2007): 781–798.

56. Linda J. Cook, *Labor and Liberalization: Trade Unions in the New Russia* (New York: Twentieth Century Fund Press, 1997), 76–77.

57. A recent survey in Nizhnii Novgorod found that 81 percent of workers said their interests were either not protected at all or protected insufficiently; 85 percent did not consider themselves members of a trade union, but 58 percent said they desired to belong to a union that would actually defend their interests. Ol'ga Morozova, "Profsoiuzy ne pomogaiut," Vedomosti.ru, July 8, 2008.

58. Two recent books detail the obstacles to the formation of a stable competitive party system: Henry Hale, *Why Not Parties in Russia?* (Cambridge, England: Cambridge University Press, 2006); and Regina Smyth, *Candidate Strategies and Electoral Competition in the Russian Federation: Democracy Without Foundation* (Cambridge, England: Cambridge University Press, 2006).

59. Ora John Reuter and Thomas F. Remington, "Dominant Party Regimes and the Commitment Problem: The Case of United Russia." *Comparative Political Studies* 42:4 (2009), pp. 501-526; Smyth. *Candidate Strategies and Electoral Competition*; Hale, *Why Not Parties in Russia?*

60. Stephen White, Richard Rose, and Ian McAllister, *How Russia Votes* (Chatham, NJ: Chatham House, 1997), 241–270.

61. Quoted from a press release of the election observer mission of the Organization for Security and Cooperation in Europe, posted to its website immediately following the election, as reported by *RFE/RL Newsline,* March 15, 2004.

62. In all, 108 candidates on the United Party list declined to take their seats in parliament. Such candidates were used as "locomotives"—they were used to attract votes, but had no intention of serving in the Duma once the party won.

63. On the scale of fraud in recent Russian elections, see Mikhail Myagkov, Peter C. Ordeshook, and Dmitri Shakin, *The Forensics of Election Fraud: Russia and Ukraine* (Cambridge: Cambridge University Press, 2009).

64. Joel S. Hellman, "Winners Take All: The Politics of Partial Reform in Postcommunist Transitions," *World Politics* 50, no. 1 (1998): 203–234.

65. An excellent account of the "loans for shares" program, based on interviews with many of the participants, is Chrystia Freeland, *Sale of the Century: Russia's Wild Ride from Communism to Capitalism* (New York: Crown, 2000), 169–189.

66. Joseph R. Blasi, Maya Kroumova, and Douglas Kruse, *Kremlin Capitalism: Privatizing the Russian Economy* (Ithaca, NY: Cornell University Press, 1997), 50.

67. Blasi, Kroumova, and Kruse, *Kremlin Capitalism;* Michael McFaul, "State Power, Institutional Change, and the Politics of Privatization in Russia," *World Politics* 47 (1995): 210–243.

68. Thane Gustafson, *Capitalism Russian-Style* (Cambridge, England: Cambridge University Press, 1999), 2–3, 94–95.

69. Organization for Economic Co-operation and Development, *OECD Economic Survey of the Russian Federation, 2004: The Challenge of Sustaining Growth* (Paris: OECD, 2004). Retrieved from www.oecd.org/document/62/0,2340,en_2649_201185_32474302_1_1_1,00.html.

70. Simon Clarke, "Market and Institutional Determinants of Wage Differentiation in Russia," *Industrial and Labor Relations* 55, no. 4 (2002): 628–648.

71. Nikolaus von Twickel, "Rich Get Richer as Poor Get Poorer," *Moscow Times,* August 8, 2008.

72. Heidi Brown, "Russia: The World's Richest Government." Retrieved April 2, 2008, from www.forbes.com/2008/03/28/russia-billionaires-duma-biz-cz_hb_0401russiapols_print.html.

73. World Bank, *Transition: The First Ten Years—Analysis and Lessons for Eastern Europe and the Former Soviet Union* (Washington, DC: World Bank, 2002), 9.

74. Quoted from Vladimir Putin's address to an expanded session of the State Council, February 8, 2008, "On the Strategy of Development of Russia to 2020." Retrieved from president. kremlin.ru/text/appears/2008/02/ 159528.shtml.

75. *RFE/RL Newsline,* July 20, 2006.

76. Russian military commanders reported that one-third of the men they had called up in the fall of 2004 were unfit to serve as a result of health problems. Polit.ru, December 9, 2004.

77. *RFE/RL Newsline,* August 18, 2006.

78. A vivid portrait of a recent jury trial in Moscow is presented by Peter Baker and Susan Glasser, *Kremlin Rising: Vladimir Putin's Russia and the End of Revolution* (New York: Scribner, 2005), 231–250.

79. The use of police intimidation to force private owners to sell to state companies was described in a revealing newspaper interview in late 2007. Maksim Kvashe,

"Partiiu dlia nas olitsetvoriaet silovoi blok, kotoryi vozglavliaet Igor' Ivanovich Sechin." *Kommersant,* November 30, 2007, p. 20.

80. G. A. Satarov, *Diagnostika rossiiskoi korruptsii: Sotsiologicheskii analiz* (Moscow: Fond INDEM, 2002), 16–17.

81. Nikita Krichevskii, "Aktual'nye predlozheniia na vechnuiu temu: kak dolzhna stroit'sia strategiia bor'by s korruptsiei," *Nezavisimaia gazeta,* June 11, 2008.

82. Joel S. Hellman, Geraint Jones, and Daniel Kaufmann, *"Seize the State, Seize the Day": State Capture, Corruption, and Influence in Transition* (Policy Research Working Paper no. 2444) (Washington, DC: World Bank Institute, September 2000).

83. Susan Rose-Ackerman, *Corruption and Government: Causes, Consequences and Reform* (Cambridge, England: Cambridge University Press, 1999), pp. 159–174.

POLITICS IN POLAND

Ray Taras

Country Bio

POLAND

Population
38.5 million

Territory
120,700 square miles

Year of Independence
1918

Year of Current Constitution
1997

Head of State
President Lech Kaczyński

Head of Government
Prime Minister Donald Tusk

Language
Polish

Religion
Roman Catholic 95%; Eastern Orthodox,
Protestant, and other 5%

If 1989 remains a remarkable year, an *annus mirabilis,* in Central and Eastern European history, arguably 2004 represents a less dramatic, but symbolically more significant *caesura,* the year that yielded the fruits of the victory over communism—full membership in the European Union (EU). The fifteen-year interlude was marked by political debate and constitutional wrangling over what type of democratic system Poland should adopt, high expectations about the prosperity that the free market would bring, and subsequent disenchantment among some sections of society when the political and economic dividends of regime change benefited only a few groups and were underwhelming anyway. Being formally admitted into the EU after successfully meeting a plethora of stringent legal, political, and economic conditions represented a historic breakthrough for Poland and other postcommunist accession states.

When 1989 began, Communist parties ruled in eight East European countries: Poland, Czechoslovakia, East Germany, Hungary, Bulgaria, Romania, Yugoslavia, and Albania. By Christmas day, when Romanian dictator Nicolae Ceausescu and his wife Elena were executed, Communist leaders remained firmly in control of only Albania. With the opening of the Berlin Wall in November, Communist East Germany was about to disappear, and the breakup of socialist Yugoslavia into separate nation-states had become irreversible. The year 1989 marked not only a historic regime change in the region therefore, but a reconfiguration of countries and borders as well.

EU enlargement in May 2004 institutionalized the geopolitical shift in Central and Eastern Europe. By far the largest of the ten countries acceding to the EU was Poland, but it was the inclusion of the three small Baltic republics that illustrated how differently Europe was now configured. The year 2004 was a "minor miracle" for some countries, then, and 2007 marked a historic year for Bulgaria and Romania, which brought the total of EU member states to twenty-seven.

A saying that captures the character of political change in Central Europe is that if it took Poland ten years to overthrow communism, it took Hungary ten months and Czechoslovakia ten days (the so-called velvet revolution). Poland had indeed struggled longer to end Communist rule, and it was precisely by virtue of this fact that the other overthrows were swifter. Similarly, Poland negotiated hard with the EU in obtaining as favorable terms of entry as possible, thereby allowing other applicants to gain concessions as well.

The breakthroughs of 1989 and 2004 originated in an earlier development that had taken place in Poland—the birth of **Solidarność (Solidarity)** in August 1980. Starting off as a trade union and led by a fiery shipyard electrician, **Lech Wałęsa**, Solidarity grew into a 10-million-member national movement that expressed public discontent with the Polish Communist regime. Its dramatic rise—and fall, as martial law imposed in December 1981 made the organization illegal—got the attention of the Kremlin, which feared that its control over the Communist parties of Eastern Europe could unravel. Without Solidarity, therefore, there may never have been Mikhail Gorbachev, a man who was selected to revitalize the Soviet Union, but who inadvertently brought about its demise.

If Poland was pivotal to the chain of events that produced the 1989 and 2004 breakthroughs in the region, can we say that Poland serves as the model democracy and market economy in today's Central Europe? What problems does Poland face in raising its political and economic development to the level found in the long-standing EU member states? Is Poland's exceptionalism—as a trigger of change in the region—a thing of the past? Or has Polish exceptionalism, as manifested in the country's nationalistic, religious turn in recent years, now become an obstacle to deeper European integration?

CURRENT POLICY CHALLENGES

Poland may have spearheaded democratization in Central Europe and blazed the path to EU membership, but it confronts a series of challenges that will determine whether liberalism is going to emerge as the dominant ideology of its political system. The rise to power of conservative Catholic groups in the mid-2000s has led to a renewed and expanded campaign to "decommunize" Poland, which some analysts claim was only haphazardly carried out in the years after the Communist system fell. The campaign led to the enactment of the 2007 lustration (or purification) law that

was to subsume some 700,000 citizens in public and professional life. It aimed at purging from politics and the professions anyone from schoolteachers who had at one time belonged to socialist organizations to Solidarity founder, Nobel Peace Prize laureate, and first democratically elected president of the Third Republic Wałęsa, who was implicated in alleged collaboration with the Communist secret police. Significantly, the clergy was exempted from undergoing lustration even though some Catholic priests—and even a few members of the ecclesiastical hierarchy—had had dubious working relationships with Communist officials. The institution put in charge of investigating political crimes committed in the Communist era was the portentously titled Institute of National Remembrance, a government body set up in 1998. Not surprisingly, this antiCommunist crusade was accompanied by broader political attacks on such liberal principles as individual rights, freedom of speech and thought, equal political rights, the rule of law, tolerance, and separation of church and state.

Constructing a state that prizes liberal values, then, remains a fundamental policy challenge in a Poland twenty years removed from the Communist era. In contrast, the task of finding the right institutional tools to consolidate democracy is largely complete. A noteworthy exception is the political party system, which until recently has remained fluid. Policy is difficult to formulate when the key political actors are in constant flux. Where most European states have fairly stable two- or multiparty systems that rarely change, Poland's has displayed little continuity from one election to the next. True, until 2005 we can conceptualize electoral battles as regular showdowns between a left-of-center secular political bloc and a more conservative, nationalist camp. The makeup of the left-of-center, social democratic bloc was unproblematic: It was anchored by the offshoot of the former Communist Party that had transformed itself in the 1990s into a credible democratic party. The lynchpin of the conservative camp, by contrast, was different from one election to the next as right-wing parties scrambled to form viable electoral alliances. By 2005 the social democrats had fragmented, too, triggering a new stage of party alignment. Effective policies are the product of an effective party system, and Poland has been hobbled by this systemic flaw.

Apart from the crisis of liberalism and the unstable party system, a third policy challenge is adopting economic policy that addresses growing inequalities while simultaneously dealing with the global financial crisis.

Poland's evolution into a flourishing capitalist system has been impressive (as we describe later in the section on policy outcomes). But this progress has produced a social stratum of winners—primarily well-educated urbanites employed in such areas as finance, management, and highly specialized professions—and a much wider one of losers—the poorly educated blue-collar workers, inhabitants of less prosperous regions, and inhabitants of rural areas. Economic transformation has reduced social mobility, while widening income differentials—the top 10 percent accounts for over 25 percent of total income, while the bottom 10 percent has only a 3 percent share. The problems of Polish agriculture—which is labor intensive and inefficient—have been chronic and, for a time, resulted in occasionally violent social protests. The troubled agrarian sector received some relief with the country's participation in the EU's Common Agricultural Policy, which offers direct subsidy payments for crops, while implementing price support mechanisms. On the other hand, many citizens, including farmers, remain leery of foreign ownership of Polish land—an unavoidable, if deferred, consequence of EU membership.

A fourth policy challenge, crafting new security arrangements in a changing geopolitical environment, has been an overriding concern for Polish policymakers since the dismantling of the Soviet bloc. Joining NATO in 1998 constituted a major step toward enhancing national security, but an unexpected series of developments has eroded the luster of NATO membership. First, the responsibilities of alliance membership have triggered new challenges. NATO's interventionism in conflicts in the Balkans, its peacekeeping commitments there and combat role in Afghanistan, the resurgence of Russia and Europe's energy dependence on it, and the ambiguous security status of Ukraine, Poland's large eastern neighbor, add up to new security dilemmas. Secondly, Poland remains torn by conflicting imperatives—paying heed to EU foreign policy orientations within the overall framework of the evolving Common Foreign and Security Policy (CFSP) and prioritizing its bilateral security arrangements with the United States. Instead of fudging the choice or playing both sides against each other, in 2003 Polish leaders came out squarely in favor of President George W. Bush's decision to wage war in Iraq. Indeed, after Britain, Poland initially represented the most important ally the United States had in "stabilizing" Iraq after the invasion. The fallout from that decision has been serious, and core EU member states like France and Germany ridiculed Poland's decision. To make matters worse, Poland gained fewer lucrative business contracts from its engagement in Iraq than had been anticipated. Bandwagoning with the world's only superpower seemed the unassailably rational thing to do in 2003, but the fiasco in Iraq led to a gradual drawdown of Polish forces. Poland thus went from being a founding member of the "Coalition of the Willing" in Iraq to, by the end of 2008, one of the last to join the "Coalition of the Leaving." Can Poland improve its reputation in Europe, tarnished by the intervention in Iraq?

The fifth and final policy challenge for Poland is to satisfy the criteria of Europeanness, that is, to negotiate a twenty-first-century European identity. While such an identity may only be notional, it is clear what it should entail: cooperating with other EU states in implementing the 2007 Lisbon treaty (a European quasi-constitution that would be a step on the road to European federalism), fulfilling the budgetary criteria required to participate in the euro monetary zone, and adopting a value system more traditionally associated with Western than Eastern Europe. This signifies a secular rather than a religiously informed world outlook, an emphasis on multiculturalism rather than homogeneity, and a more tolerant, inclusive attitude toward minority groups, immigrants, and the nations of the region in place of an apprehensive, even xenophobic one. As we shall see next, Poles claim that their history proves that they have always been European. From the perspective of Brussels or Strasburg, however, where Western European politicians may still be skeptical about a long-sovietized Slavic bloc of nations attempting to embrace Europe with difficulty, the case is not self-evident. How seamlessly Polish policymakers work with their counterparts from the longer-standing EU member states is an intriguing question to consider.

THE MAKING OF MODERN POLAND

Every nation takes a selective approach to its own history: It focuses on a handful of recorded events, great leaders, and rival nations and transforms them into a core history. Often this core history establishes the political traditions of a nation and weaves credible myths that help shape contemporary political attitudes and behavior.[1] Especially if a country has undergone regime change, as Poland did after 1989, there will be efforts to legitimate the new system by invoking old traditions. What are the most salient aspects of Polish history that have popular currency today and help give legitimacy to (or bring into question) the country's present path of political development?

Defining Features and Historical Development

Today's Poland occupies a location centered in the lowlands of the Northern European Plain that is remarkably similar to the site of the first Polish state established a millennium ago. Geographically, it is the "heart of Europe,"[2] and, therefore, it is correct to view Poland as a Central European nation. Because Russia ruled the eastern part of the country throughout the nineteenth century and the Polish Communist state formed part of the Soviet bloc from 1945 to 1989, Poland is identified as Eastern European up to the 1990s. In terms of surface area, Poland is large by European standards, just slightly smaller than unified Germany.

The vast majority of Poland's population is Roman Catholic. About one-third still lives in the countryside, even though the country was industrialized under Communist rule and, after 1989, the service sector grew exponentially. The capital, Warsaw, has become a major European financial center, as well as the seat of the national government. Other major cities are Łódź, Kraków, Wrocław, Poznań, and Gdańsk. Greater trade with the West has transformed much of Poland, especially the cities, and it is visibly more cosmopolitan than a few decades ago.

Poles form part of the Slavic world. Their language belongs to the western Slavic group that includes Czech and Slovak. Some historical evidence indicates that the original home of all Slavs was the territory ruled by Polish kings in the fourteenth century. Even today Poles frequently give the impression that Poland—rather than the larger Russian nation—represents the heart of the Slavic world. Most Poles would certainly argue that they, not the Russians, form an integral part of the European tradition.

Poland's first king, **Mieszko I**, converted to Christianity in 966 in order to bolster the country's alliances in the face of a Germanic threat. But a Rus invasion in 981 stripped the country of much of its lands. The dilemmas Mieszko faced presaged those of a thousand years later—an observation not lost on Poles who have cursed their disastrous geopolitical position. That is why EU membership in 2004 is considered so historic.

An important historical debate touches on whether Poland has constituted an ethnically homogeneous or a multinational state. History provides ambiguous evidence on this matter. For the first four centuries, Poland consisted largely of related tribes, but in 1370 a Polish-Lithuanian union was created that transformed the country into a multinational state. The union's expansive borders stretched from the Baltic Sea in the north to the Black Sea in the south. The adage that to be Polish means to be Catholic is therefore inaccurate, given the ethno-religious diversity of Poland in medieval times. Thus, about 80 percent of the world's Jews lived in Poland in the Middle Ages, causing one writer to note that "in no other country than ancient Israel, have Jews lived continuously for as many centuries, in as large numbers, and with as much autonomy as in Poland."[3] During his 1997 pilgrimage to his home country, Pope John Paul II highlighted the culture that Catholic and Jewish Poles had helped forge over the centuries. He drew attention to the idea that Polishness was not the making solely of Catholic Poles.

The ecumenical approach of Pope John Paul II departs from a more proprietary attitude traditionally taken by the Catholic Church toward Poland. The role of Catholicism in the making of the Polish nation is evident from the time of Mieszko, but in the mid–fifteenth century, the ruling gentry began to define Poland's role in Europe in terms of an **antemurale christianitatis**—that is, the easternmost bulwark of Roman Catholicism. Poland was regarded as a nation lying on the fault line of Western and Eastern civilizations. In the following centuries, a Polish version of manifest destiny was elucidated that highlighted the country's role as defender of Western Christian civilization. No better example of Poland's success in playing this role can be found than the defeat inflicted by King Jan Sobieski in 1683 on the Turkish armies outside of Vienna, thereby saving Europe from Islam.

Internally, Poland's political system came to be increasingly decentralized, offering a spectacular exception to the rule of absolute monarchies found in most European states of the late Middle Ages. The nobility, or *szlachta,* embraced a radical new formula: "one nobleman, one vote." Power became vested in this class, not in the monarchy, leading to a crude kind of proto-democracy—what was to be known as **szlachta democracy**. The state enacted constitutional laws that incorporated the ideas of liberty, equality, and government based on the consent of a significant part of the nation. The system of elective kings became the political cornerstone of this so-called Republican Commonwealth, which lasted until the **partitions** of Poland in the late eighteenth century.

Fear of absolutist government, rather than a precocious commitment to democratic ideas, led to constitutional arrangements fostering "unrule" in the country. It was behind the adoption of the best known principle of the Commonwealth, the **liberum veto**, which allowed a single member of the **Sejm** (or parliament) to veto any act presented to this body. The szlachta's rationale was that "[t]he liberum veto would defend the sovereignty of the individual. God and Europe would defend that of the Republic."[4] The flaw in the logic was that God and Europe did not rescue Poland from the partitions. Although the Polish state had devised an ingenious system of checks and balances to preserve the democracy of the gentry, when skillfully exploited by Poland's foes, it led to the destruction of the Commonwealth.

Three times between 1772 and 1795 lands that formed part of the Polish-Lithuanian Commonwealth were partitioned among its powerful neighbors—Russia, Prussia, and Habsburg Austria. An independent Polish state was all but doomed when Stanisław Kościuszko led a failed national insurrection in 1794 that led to bloody reprisals by Russian troops. By the terms of the third partition, signed in October 1795, all remaining Polish lands were divided up, the king was forced to abdicate, and the name *Poland* was supposed to disappear from world maps forever.

How did Poles respond to the loss of statehood? Adam Mickiewicz, a nineteenth-century romantic writer acclaimed as national poet, compared Poland to Christ, destined to suffer on the cross to redeem the sins of other nations so that they, too, might become worthy of liberty. Mickiewicz broached an important theme running through modern Polish history, that of **romantic insurrectionism**. During the nineteenth century, Poles staged a series of uprisings, the fiercest taking place in 1830 and 1863. All were crushed by the partitioning powers.

An alternative, more pragmatic approach to rebuilding the Polish nation was charted.[5] Positivism entailed the belief that reason, intelligence, and "organic work"—a spirit of industriousness raising the social, economic, and cultural level of the nation—would promote Poland's economic and therefore political development. Positivism was influential in the struggle of Poles to forge a civil society—fusing an individual's private and public spheres—while remaining outside the reach of alien state structures. "Poland never had an autonomous State in modern times," wrote one scholar. "The idea of civil society thus provided the only ideological alternative to foreign domination."[6]

The task of constructing an independent civil society was resumed almost a century later when Poles organized resistance to the Communist regime.

Interwar and Communist Poland

When Poland regained independence in November 1918, it had less to do with romantic insurrectionism, positivism, or the building of a civil society. It owed more to the collapse of empires and to the role played by the Western Allies. The tsarist empire in Russia disintegrated in November 1917 when the Bolsheviks seized power, and Austria and Germany were defeated a year later to end World War I. For a time at least, Poland's nemeses were gone. To be sure, in 1920 Polish leader **Józef Piłsudski**, considered the father of the reborn Polish state, faced off against Russian armies intent on bringing Bolshevism to the country. His forces stymied the Soviet advance and then moved eastward, conquering large parts of Ukraine and Belorussia for the new Polish state.

This expanded state turned out to be ethnically more heterogeneous than Woodrow Wilson had anticipated in his Fourteen Points, announced in January 1918. The thirteenth point referred to a "united, independent and autonomous Poland with free unrestricted access to the sea" and situated on "territories inhabited by an indubitably Polish population." Nevertheless, in 1921 about 30 percent of the population was made up of minority groups. These included up to 6 million Ukrainians, 3 million Jews, 1.5 million Belorussians, and more than 1 million Germans.

Deprived of statehood for over a century, Poland's new leaders gave priority to nation-building over safeguarding the rights of minorities. If anti-Semitism never became official government policy, it was not energetically resisted by successive interwar governments. They took a heavy-handed approach to dealing with Eastern Orthodox communities of Ukrainians and Belorussians now living inside Polish borders, and Lithuanian Catholics were victims of discriminatory practices as well.

Piłsudski's regime was a personal dictatorship concealed in a parliamentary guise. After the **May 1926 coup**, which he orchestrated, even that role for parliament was eliminated as rigged elections, internment of opposition officials, and widespread censorship brought his misnamed *sanacja* (purification) regime into disrepute. Following his death in 1935, the "colonels' regime" abandoned all pretense of democracy, and fascist tendencies surfaced. Fear of

Communism increased, strikes were violently suppressed, and the living conditions of the peasantry worsened. What is more, Poland's foreign policymakers were at a loss to forge alliances that would counter the dual threats emanating from Nazi Germany and Stalinist Russia.

Poles' historical anxiety about partition was reawakened by two insidious international agreements signed just prior to and toward the end of World War II. In August 1939 a secret protocol of the **Ribbentrop-Molotov pact**, officially announced as a nonaggression treaty between Hitler's Germany and Stalin's Soviet Union, partitioned Poland again. When the Germans invaded on September 1, 1939, and the Russians took their turn on September 17, they each claimed their prearranged spoils.

The very survival of the Polish nation was in question during the German occupation, which lasted until 1945. One-fifth of Poland's prewar population, more than 6 million people, was killed, the highest casualty rate of any nation in the war. Some 3 million Polish Jews (90 percent) were exterminated, together with 3 million other Poles. Resistance to German occupation was relentless, but two insurrections stand out. It took one month of savage repression for German forces to liquidate the Jewish ghetto of Warsaw in April–May of 1943. In all, 60,000 Jews were killed. In the sixty-three-day-long Warsaw uprising that began on August 1, 1944, nearly 200,000 Poles lost their lives. Russian forces remained on the other side of the river, offering no help, as the capital was destroyed.

The brutal Russian occupation of eastern Poland during the war added to the nation's suffering. From the experience of World War II, Poles learned that insurrections did not lead to national independence; agreements concluded among the great powers, as happened at Yalta, did.

The **Yalta agreement** was the second destructive international event for Poland in the twentieth century. The February 1945 meeting of Churchill, Roosevelt, and Stalin at the Crimean resort of Yalta de facto incorporated Poland into the Soviet bloc and deprived it of political independence. Churchill was persuaded that "free and unfettered elections" called for by the Yalta accord would indeed take place. By summer 1945 Poland's provisional government was stacked with Communists and the prospect of free elections became an illusion. The United States and Britain extended diplomatic recognition to the Communists anyway.

The sovietization of Poland began when the Red Army entered Warsaw in January 1944 to liberate it from German occupation. The process accelerated during Stalin's last years, when all political freedoms and political opposition had been erased, and Poland's system—its institutions, processes, ideology, economy—resembled that of the Soviet Union. A Communist Party—called the **Polish United Workers' Party (PUWP)**—headed by an all-powerful Politburo and its leader, the first secretary, had a monopoly over decisionmaking.

The brief thaw in the Soviet Union that followed Stalin's death in 1953 provided a chance for Polish Communist leaders to ease the Kremlin's hold on the country and effect some political liberalization. In 1956 workers in Poznań staged protests demanding bread and freedom. While swiftly quashed, the unrest ushered in the celebrated **Polish October**, with a new Communist leadership promising a Polish road to socialism, political reform, and expanded cultural freedoms. By 1960, however, the bleakness, austerity, and repressiveness of life under Communism had returned.

In an uncanny repeat of 1956, strikes in shipyards on the Baltic coast in December 1970—again brutally repressed by the Communist authorities—triggered another change in Communist leadership and another promise of liberalization. Even if the promise was again not kept, strike organizers like Wałęsa mastered the art of organizing resistance. The Catholic Church was no longer alone in standing up to the Communist rulers, even though the much-loved Primate of the Catholic Church, **Cardinal Stefan ń Wyszyński**, continued to personify opposition to Marxist ideology. He died in 1981, shortly after Solidarity was organized, and Wałęsa became the natural candidate to succeed him as de facto leader of a nationwide anti-Communist movement. Another famous opposition organization, established in 1976 to defend workers who had gone on strike that year and faced reprisals, was the **Committee for Workers' Self-Defense (KOR)**. It brought together a score of dissidents—like **Adam Michnik** and **Jacek Kuroń**—who figured prominently in the Solidarity organization in 1980, at the 1989 roundtable talks that paved the way for democracy, and in the politics of the **Third Republic**—the name of Poland's political system after 1989.

For Poles, before the historic years of 1989 and 2004 there had been 1980. That summer an unprecedented wave of strikes spread across the country. Initially, the demands were only economic (higher wages, lower prices for food products), but by August the strikers, led by Wałęsa, demanded recognition of an independent trade union. The union chose

Solidarity for its name and presented twenty-one demands, economic and political, to the Communist authorities. After a tense standoff when the threat of a Soviet invasion seemed imminent, Wałęsa prevailed, and a political revolution followed. The Communist monopoly on power had been broken, and Solidarity quickly transformed itself into a social movement.

Under pressure from the Kremlin, the Communist leadership drew up contingency plans to crush Solidarity. **General Wojciech Jaruzelski** was put in charge of preparing **martial law**. When it was imposed on December 13, 1981, Solidarity leaders were taken by surprise. Most were rounded up and interned, and the trade union was declared illegal. Scores of people lost their lives during the first months of martial law, but a Soviet invasion that might have produced a catastrophe was averted. For the next seven years, Jaruzelski did not allow Solidarity and its leaders back into political life.

To be sure, the Communist system could boast of some successes between 1945 and 1989. The proportion of the labor force employed in the agricultural sector was halved, from 54 percent in 1950 to 27 percent in 1990.[7] Data presented in Table 10.1 on such factors as per capita gross domestic product (GDP), urbanization, educational attainment (number of students enrolled in primary schools, number of graduates from high school and college), and media diffusion (numbers of radios, televisions, telephones, and passenger cars) also reveal some modest achievements in the Communist period. Overall, the population was increasingly better educated and more informed (the falloff in the number of high school and college graduates in the 1980s was largely the result of demographic factors such as lower reproduction rate and out-migration).

Among the other successes claimed by the Communist regime was the fact that per capita GDP had increased tenfold, and real income had nearly tripled between 1955 and 1981—the peak year. Undoubtedly, people's living standards improved in this period, evidenced by an estimated threefold increase in the consumption of meat—historically a reliable indicator of living standards—and about a halving of the consumption of potatoes—a staple food for those who are less well off. The best evidence that the Polish economy was in crisis in the 1980s and early 1990s was the observation that average Poles were

Indices of Economic and Social Change

TABLE 10.1

Over the last decade Poles have approached the living standards found in Western Europe and the number of college graduates has skyrocketed

	1946	1950	1960	1970	1980	1990	2000	2007
Economy								
Per capita gross domestic product	—	$271	$564	$955	$4,276	$4,099	$9,844	$16,300
Urban population (%)	33.9	36.8	48.3	52.3	58.8	61.8	61.8	61.2
Workforce outside of agriculture (%)	—	46.4	56.7	65.7	70.3	73.2	72.0	84.0
Education								
Students in primary schools (000s)	3,322	3,360	4,963	5,389	4,260	5,276	3,221	2,375
High school graduates (000s)	26	111	105	365	552	440	554	399
College graduates (000s)	4	15	21	47	84	52	304	410
Communications and Transport								
Registered radios (000s)	—	1,464	5,268	5,658	8,666	10,944	9,313	—
Registered televisions (000s)	—	—	426	4,215	7,954	9,919	9,069	—
Telephone (000s; includes cell after 2000)	—	194	535	1,070	1,943	3,293	17,695	51,753
Registered passenger automobiles (000s)	—	40	117	479	2,383	5,261	9,991	14,589

Note: Net material product rather than GDP is used before 1980; GDP based on purchasing power parity (PPP) is used after 1990.

— signifies no data available.

Sources: Główny Urząd Statystyczny, *Mały Rocznik Statystyczny Polski 2008* (Warsaw: GUS, 2008). Retrieved December 2, 2008, from www.stat.gov.pl/gus/45_737_PLK_HTML.htm. Also Central Intelligence Agency, *The World Factbook*. Retrieved December 2, 2008, from www.cia.gov/library/publications/the-world-factbook/geos/pl.html#Comm.

again substituting potatoes for meat in their diet. Indeed, during the late Communist period poverty affected all social groups. Between 1981 and 1990 (a period that corresponds to the Jaruzelski era), real income fell by one-third—a bottom line that more than anything explains the Communists' desperate effort to persuade Solidarity to share political responsibility.[8]

Resistance to Communism, of course, was driven by noneconomic factors, too, not the least of which was the moral bankruptcy of Marxism.[9] Organized resistance reflected the contrasting political traditions of the country: revolutionary romanticism versus political pragmatism; a multinational, civic understanding of the state versus an ethnic, religious one; an orientation toward Western Europe versus self-consciousness about lying on the eastern edge of Western civilization. In her poem "Possibilities," 1996 Nobel Prize–winning poet Wisława Szymborska captured the eternal moral choices that have pervaded Polish history:

> I prefer when I like humans,
> Than when I love humanity.
> I prefer not to believe,
> That reason is responsible for everything.
> I prefer moralists, who promise me nothing.
> I prefer conquered to conquering countries.
> I prefer the hell of chaos than the hell of order.[10]

The Democratic Transition

A paradoxical aspect of the democratic breakthrough in Poland is that it was not the direct result of popular unrest. We have noted the social upheavals of 1956, 1970, and 1980, but in 1989 little or no mass political mobilization took place. Strikes had recurred in the summer of 1988, but they were not on the scale of the summer of 1980. If the year 1989 is associated in Eastern Europe with images of large-scale popular rallies in Prague, Bucharest, Vilnius, and, of course, Berlin, Warsaw is conspicuous by its absence.

Regime change was the product, instead, of a pacted transition between Communist and opposition elites. The first indication of a shift in the Communist leadership's approach to resolving crises came in August 1988 when the interior minister (responsible for state security) publicly called for **roundtable talks** with representatives of various social groups. "I stipulate no preconditions regarding the subject of the talks nor regarding the composition of participants," he announced.[11] "Talks about talks" commenced in August 1988, and soon afterward a debate took place on state

television between Wałęsa (for nearly a decade a "non-person" not allowed to appear in public after Solidarity was banned) and the head of the Communist trade union. Wałęsa scored a resounding debating victory, and Solidarity was set to return to center stage.

The roundtable of February–April 1989 consisted of representatives of the Communist leadership, called the "coalition-government" side, and those of the democratic movement, the "opposition-Solidarity" side. The leadership of the Catholic Church was officially not involved in the roundtable talks and declared its neutrality, though its representatives invariably backed positions advocated by Solidarity. Six hundred individuals participated in the roundtable negotiations, but the most important discussions, centering on establishing conditions for a **pacted transition**, involved private meetings between top party and Solidarity leaders held at a villa in Magdalenka. The secretive nature of discussions at Magdalenka led some observers to claim that a covert deal was worked out between the elites. This conspiracy theory formed the basis for allegations, repeated by conservative leaders for the next two decades, that in exchange for withdrawing from politics, the ruling Communist class (the **nomenklatura**) had been promised a free hand in privatizing state assets. The 2007 lustration law was intended once and for all to eliminate the presence of former Communists in high political and economic posts.

At the center of roundtable negotiations was the return of Solidarity to national politics. A compromise worked out at the roundtable designated 35 percent of Sejm seats as open contests, while the remaining 65 percent was set aside for the Communists and their allies. The elections for the 35 percent of seats were to be "nonconfrontational," which meant that the Communists should not be the target of a negative campaign. Finally, this **contract Sejm** was to be a one-time arrangement, and the following legislative elections were to be fully free.

An important political institution reestablished by the roundtable agreement was the presidency (abolished in 1952). Both sides agreed that a president could serve as a stabilizing force and a symbol of continuity during the transition. The obvious Communist candidate was Jaruzelski, and even much of Solidarity recognized the advantage of having the long-serving leader preside over the transition. When Solidarity won all the contested Sejm seats in the June 1989 election, the arrangement it proposed—"your President, our Prime Minister"—seemed both sensible and generous.

The roundtable agreement also restored an upper house of parliament, the Senate, abolished in 1948. Since it was not invested with much power, elections to it were to be free. The Senate contest thus offered Solidarity the chance to demonstrate its strength throughout the country. The roundtable pact contained multiple mutual checks and balances and, it appeared, could not possibly produce a lopsided public defeat for the Communists. It was crafted to ensure that the transition would be gradual and would pose no risk to either the old or the new elite. All those premises changed once the election results were known and once events in other Communist countries began to outpace the speed of the Polish transition.

In terms of the popular vote in the June election, the government (Communist) side obtained just over one-quarter of all valid votes cast (26.8%), while Solidarity tallied 69.9 percent (the remainder went to independents). Solidarity swept all contested Sejm seats and 99 out of 100 Senate seats. Worse for the Communist side, of the 65 percent of seats set aside for it, the majority of its candidates did not win 50 percent of the votes, thereby necessitating a second round of elections.

Turnout for the first round of this historic election was an unimpressive 63 percent of eligible voters. One explanation for this was that the public might have viewed the election as a deal cut by two establishment parties—the Communists and Solidarity. The same suspicions aroused by the talks in Magdalenka—"elites talking to elites"[12]—may have spread to sections of the population as they contemplated whether voting really was meaningful.

The election results produced a domino effect on other provisions of the roundtable agreement. Jaruzelski announced he would not be a candidate for the presidency, but after Wałęsa stated that he did not wish to stand at this time (partly to allay Kremlin fears that too much change was happening too quickly), the General reversed his decision and in July was elected by a slim majority of the two houses.

This left one other issue to be resolved in the summer of 1989—the formation of a government. Since the Communist bloc held a working majority in the contract Sejm, Jaruzelski nominated his interior minister to the post of prime minister. This, however, would have left both major offices in the hands of the electorally repudiated Communist party. The surprise defection of two small Communist satellite parties from the government camp sealed the fate of the Communists. In August Tadeusz Mazowiecki—

Catholic intellectual, editor of an important Solidarity newspaper, and long-time Wałęsa advisor—was appointed prime minister—the first non-Communist one in East Europe since Stalin's time. Few participants at the roundtable talks a few months earlier could have foreseen this dramatic turn of events that was quickly to result in regime change.

STRUCTURE OF THE POLITICAL SYSTEM

What distinguishes a democracy from an authoritarian system of government? According to a U.S. think tank, Freedom House, political rights and civil liberties are basic to democracy. "Political rights enable people to participate freely in the political process, including through the right to vote, compete for public office, and elect representatives who have a decisive impact on public policies and are accountable to the electorate." In turn, "civil liberties allow for the freedoms of expression and belief, associational and organizational rights, rule of law, and personal autonomy without interference from the state." Since 1995 a panel of Freedom House experts has given Poland its top ranking on its political rights. In recent years Poland has also moved to the top score on civil liberties.[13]

Another important feature of democracy is that political outcomes should be determined by rules of the game designed and accepted by the main political actors. These rules are outlined in a country's constitution, they can be found in laws passed by an elected assembly or approved in a general referendum, and they can be based on conventions and traditions that have developed over time. Rules identify the jurisdiction and powers of various government institutions—president, prime minister, cabinet, parliament. Rules also determine how officeholders of such institutions are to be picked.

The interwar experience influenced the design of the post-1989 democratic system. Indeed, continuity was highlighted by naming the new system the Third Republic. Interwar Poland had been the **Second Republic**, while the Communist regime was not numbered, since it was not regarded as an independent Polish state (though some facetiously called it the Second-and-a-Half Republic).

The structure of the new government, illustrated in Figure 10.1, did incorporate vestiges of its Communist predecessor. Democratizing the political system meant designing new institutions and formulating legal

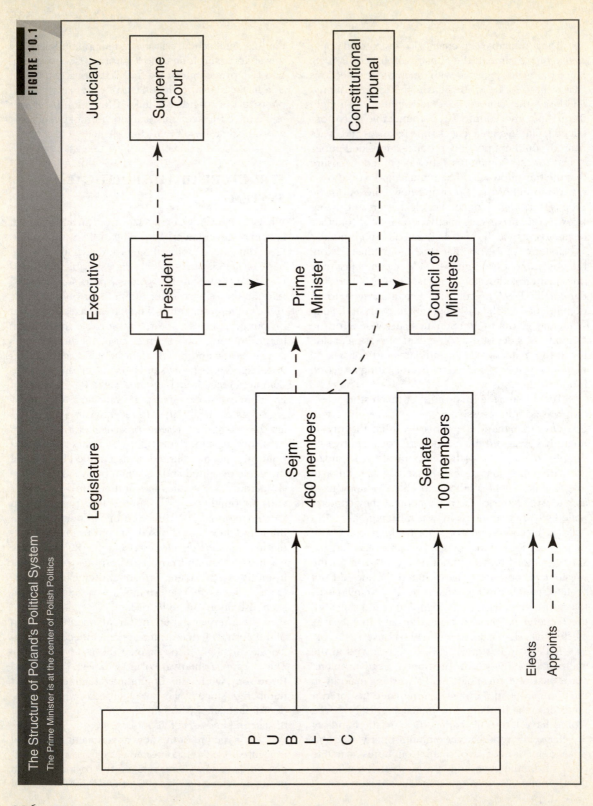

FIGURE 10.1

The Structure of Poland's Political System

The Prime Minister is at the center of Polish Politics

provisions in place of Communist ones. Among the institutional changes were the following:

1. replacing the constitution of July 22, 1952;
2. introducing an electoral law allowing for a multiparty system;
3. changing the official symbols and terms of the Communist system (the country's official name, coat of arms, flag, and anthem);
4. reintroducing such political institutions as the presidency, the Senate, and a reformed local government system;
5. providing the legal framework for private ownership;
6. safeguarding the independence of the judiciary; and
7. enshrining principles incorporating political rights and civil liberties.

Adopting a new constitution was the most urgent issue, since other changes would follow from it. Because the stakes were high, it took seven years of wrangling before a draft was passed by parliament and then approved in a national referendum. There was widespread disagreement about what the new constitution should include. Even the preamble proved contentious because opinions differed as to whether it was the Polish nation (an ethnic category) or the citizens of Poland (a civic understanding) that were the subject of the document. There was disagreement, too, about whether the special role of Catholicism in the country should be explicitly mentioned (as was the case in the Irish constitution). The constitution adopted in 1997 avoided making choices on these matters and instead contained references to both the Polish nation and its citizens and to Catholicism and other religious faiths. The noncontroversial approach taken contributed to a low turnout for the referendum: Only 43 percent of the electorate turned out at the polls, and just 53 percent of them voted in favor of its adoption. Those opposing it were primarily motivated by the desire to deprive the left-of-center government that had cobbled the document together of a success; their substantive disagreement was minor.

Before this constitution was passed, the distribution of power between the branches of government resembled that of the interwar republic up to 1926. The power of the executive branch—defined as including both president and prime minister—was circumscribed. A form of "Sejmocracy" emerged in which little could get done without the legislature's approval.

Even the pivotal **Balcerowicz plan** of January 1990, which created a free market, would not have passed had not its author, finance minister Leszek Balcerowicz, surprised the Sejm with a bill he demanded it approve immediately.

Wałęsa, who became president in December 1990 after winning direct elections, fought hard against this Sejmocracy and often invoked the interwar experience. The chaos and paralysis that a powerful legislature had produced back then had convinced Piłsudski that a strong executive was essential to political efficacy and stability; that was why he undertook the 1926 coup. While no evidence exists that Wałęsa was plotting a coup, he clearly favored a strong presidential system. Accordingly, during his five-year term as president, he undermined the authority of a succession of prime ministers, in the process heightening the political instability he condemned. He did his best to prevent a parliamentary system from being institutionalized, but the Sejm just as effectively rebuffed his attempts to expand presidential powers. When in 1995 the Sejm began to consider various drafts of a new constitution, Wałęsa's was the only version of seven that proposed a presidential system. His failure to get reelected was in good measure a popular vote against establishing a strong executive branch. The new president, **Aleksander Kwaśniewski**, was quick to emphasize that he was a "parliamentarian" and was content to preside over rather than dominate Polish politics. Wałęsa's defeat signified not only a shift in power from Solidarity to ex-Communist forces, but also a change from an activist to a deliberative presidency.

The President

The constitutional role of the president in the current political system is circumscribed. An interim constitution adopted in 1992 termed Poland "a Presidential-parliamentary system of government," but the **constitution of 1997** dropped this phrasing. Article 10.1 of Chapter 1 declares that "the system of the Polish Republic is based on the separation and balance of legislative authority, executive authority, and judicial authority." The presidency is considered a part of the executive branch, which also includes the **Council of Ministers** (Article 10.2).

The president is elected directly by majority vote. If no candidate obtains a majority, a second round of elections is held two weeks later between the top two vote-getters from the first round. The term of office is five years, with a two-term limitation. There is no vice president, and in the event of the president's incapacity or death, the marshal of the Sejm (similar to the U.S. Speaker of the House) temporarily holds the office until new elections are held.

The constitution designates the president as head of state and commander in chief of the armed forces. A political convention has emerged that the president should not officially belong to a political party, but this has been purely symbolic, and all three Third Republic presidents have unabashedly backed their "party of origin" once in office. Chapter 5 of the 1997 constitution enumerates the specific powers of the president. Article 126.1 declares that the president is "the supreme representative of the Polish Republic and guarantees the continuity of state authority." Enumerated powers include the right to designate the prime minister (though not cabinet ministers), initiate legislation, veto bills (which the Sejm can override by a three-fifths majority), refer bills to the Constitutional Court for a ruling as to their constitutionality, under certain conditions dissolve parliament and call early elections, call a referendum, oversee defense (indirectly through the Defense Ministry and through appointing the chief of the General Staff of the armed forces) and national security matters (together with the National Security Council), declare martial law if the Sejm is unable to meet quickly, and represent the state in foreign relations. The president can issue decrees and administrative acts, the latter requiring the prime minister's countersignature. The officeholder also has a constitutionally recognized Presidential Chancellory (Article 142.2b) to help him or her carry out duties.

Despite these diverse formal powers, the Polish president does not have the political clout that his counterpart in France, who heads a semi-presidential system, has. This may be due in part to the diffidence and discretion exercised by Kwaśniewski during his two terms as president. It may be that even with a divided parliament for much of this period, it and the president shared similar political values and goals. Indeed, only in the last two years of Kwaśniewski's presidency did serious rifts arise over such fundamental questions as the direction of Polish foreign policy and the country's role in the EU. Finally, parties in the Sejm were reluctant to stake their political capital by challenging a very popular president. They were content to let Kwaśniewski act as "the supreme representative of the Polish Republic" who "guarantees the continuity of state authority."

His successor, elected in 2005, harbored greater ambitions for the presidency. From the outset Lech Kaczyński, a former advisor to Wałęsa, did not see the office as requiring nonpartisanship. Especially after his identical twin brother, Jarosław, became prime minister the following year, his stated objective was to make a clean institutional break from the Third Republic. He believed the government had come under the control of a "network" of big business interests, corrupt politicians, Communist-era secret service agents, and secular leftist intellectuals. The formal structure of power had to be changed, and nothing less than a new constitution that would establish a Fourth Republic could achieve this. President Lech Kaczyński became a polarizing figure, perhaps more clearly reflecting what the office was really intended to be like.

The Legislature

The legislative branch is made up of two chambers: the lower house (Sejm) consists of 460 deputies, and the upper house (Senate) is made up of 100 members. On some occasions the two meet together as the National Assembly. Direct elections to both houses must be held no more than four years apart. Early elections can be held if (1) a government cannot be formed; (2) a vote of no confidence in an existing government is passed (however, the notion of a "constructive" no-confidence vote, which is not mentioned in the constitution, but has been used in Poland and resembles that found in Germany, would mean that the current government would be replaced or reconstitute itself—not that elections should follow); or (3) the president decides, under certain conditions, to dissolve the legislature. As in most parliamentary systems, the prime minister, or head of the government, seeks to influence the timing of elections to coincide with an upswing in his or her party's fortunes.

The Sejm enacts legislation through three readings of a bill, after which it is sent to the Senate for approval. The Senate can make changes to the bill or even vote it down, but the Sejm can have its way by enacting the bill again with a simple majority vote. The bill becomes law when the president signs it. The power of the Senate is limited, and there have been calls for its abolition. We should recall that it was little more than a bargaining chip, rather than an issue of substance, at the roundtable talks.

The Sejm is at the center of Polish politics, then. It is where the competitive party system functions for most of the year (the Sejm recesses briefly in summer). The extended, often-heated debates on legislative bills give the lower house the constant visibility that the presidency does not possess. The most controversial issues of Polish politics after 1989 have been extensively debated in the Sejm: enacting a new constitution, defining the official place of the Catholic Church in society, determining women's access to abortion, drafting legislation on the privatization of state-owned industry, clarifying the public role that former Communist officials could play in a democratic Poland, reorganizing local government (from forty-seven to sixteen regions) and the health care system, ratifying membership in NATO, approving the EU accession treaty and the 2007 Lisbon treaty and, not least, passing government budgets.

Prime Minister and Cabinet

According to Article 146.1 of the constitution, "The Council of Ministers carries out the domestic and foreign policies of the Polish Republic." Article 146.2 also gives it residual powers—that is, those not explicitly assigned to other bodies. Another key function of the Council of Ministers (synonymous with the government, or cabinet) is determining the annual budget. The constitution sets out the principle of the collective responsibility of this body to the Sejm, as well as the individual responsibility of each minister for the work of his or her department to the Sejm. Like the president, the government can issue decrees within its own area of jurisdiction.

Twenty years into the life of the Third Republic, the office with the most influence in shaping national politics has become that of prime minister. The prime minister is officially nominated by the president, but is usually the leader (or a high-ranking member) of the largest party in parliament. A party's hold on the prime ministership privileges it in the political system. Thus, from 1993 to 1995 President Wałęsa's power was neutralized by a prime minister coming from the ranks of the opposing SLD camp. Similarly, for several years after 1997 President Kwaśniewski's power was weakened by the presence of a prime minister from the opposing Solidarity Electoral Action (AWS) bloc. A further example: Conflict soon developed between President Kaczyński and his brother's successor as prime minister, Donald Tusk, whose party won the 2007 parliamentary elections.

It has been rare for a single party to obtain an absolute majority of parliamentary seats, so prime ministerial turnover and cabinet reshuffles have been commonplace (see Figure 10.2). Between 1989 and the end of 1997, nine persons were nominated as

FIGURE 10.2 Presidents and Prime Ministers of Poland, 1989–2009. Presidents offer continuity to the political system

Prime Minister	Year	President
Donald Tusk	2007	
Jarosław Kaczyński	2006	
Kazimierz Marcinkiewicz	2005	Lech Kaczyński
Marek Belka	2004	
Leszek Miller	2001	
Jerzy Buzek	1997	
Wlodzimierz Cimoszewicz	1996	
Józef Oleksy	1995	Aleksander Kwaśniewski
Waldemar Pawlak	1993	
Hanna Suchocka	1992	
Waldemar Pawlak	1992	
Jan Olszewski	1991	
Jan Krzysztof Bielecki	1990	Lech Wałęsa
Tadeusz Mazowiecki	1989	Wojciech Jaruzelski

prime minister. Over the next decade, there were five more, with the longest serving having been Jerzy Buzek, of AWS, who held the office from 1997 to 2001.

Has this turnover of governments produced political instability? The democratic system has widespread support, whether measured by public opinion polls or by party leaders' commitment to play by the rules of the game. The complex six- and seven-party coalition governments of the early 1990s, with their "carousels" of incoming and outgoing ministers, gave way in the later 1990s to two-party coalitions where ministerial shuffles were rarer. The reason for greater government stability lay in the electoral law of 1993, which rewarded parties winning the most votes with a disproportionate number of parliamentary seats. The Sejm became more powerful and autonomous and could now insist on the accountability of governments to it. It could force changes in the prime minister and other cabinet ministers, in this way ensuring that a government was more responsive to elected representatives.

The grounds on which a government falls and another one is constituted is the best barometer of the health of a democratic system. Poland has moved away from government crises triggered by destabilizing struggles for power between president and prime minister (as in the case of Wałęsa versus Prime Minister Jan Olszewski in 1992), to crises grounded in policy differences between coalition partners (as that on taxation between the AWS and UW in 2000), to seamless replacement of a tarnished prime minister by a new appointee from the same party (as with Marek Belka's takeover from Leszek Miller in 2004) or by a more senior official in that party (as when Jarosław Kaczyński replaced Kazimierz Marcinkiewicz in 2006), to begrudging cohabitation between opposing political camps (as with President Lech Kaczyński and Prime Minister Donald Tusk after 2007). These cases illustrate that the rules of the game have taken root and political crises are resolved by using them.

The Judicial Branch

The 1997 constitution designates the court system and tribunals as a separate branch of authority. The judicial system is made up of the Supreme Court, general courts, administrative courts (including the Supreme Administrative Court), and military courts.

The **Supreme Court** is the forum of last resort for appeals against judgments in lower courts. The chief justice and other justices on it are appointed by the president on the advice of the National Judicial Council. They have life terms, cannot be removed, are independent, and cannot belong to a political party or trade union.

Another judicial body is the **Constitutional Tribunal,** which, as in France and Germany, rules on the constitutionality and offers binding interpretations of laws, delimits the jurisdiction of different branches of government, and undertakes other kinds of judicial review. The Constitutional Tribunal consists of fifteen justices elected by the Sejm for one term lasting nine years. In its early years, justices on the Constitutional Tribunal saw its mission as laying the foundation for a democratic, law-based state and were very proactive (some would say overly so) in shaping Polish legislation to reflect the principles and values found in Western countries.

A further important judicial body is the **Tribunal of State**. The leaders of all important national institutions—the president, the prime minister, individual ministers, the head of the National Bank, members of the National Radio and Television Council, the head of the Chief Inspectorate (which controls the work of the state administration and other state institutions), and the head of the armed forces—must answer to the Tribunal of State for the constitutionality of their acts.

The Polish Third Republic also has a civil rights ombudsperson. This official is chosen by the Sejm for a five-year term and is responsible for determining whether citizens' rights and freedoms are infringed upon by state bodies. The officeholder is authorized to act in court on behalf of citizens whose charges have been substantiated. Since the office was created in the last years of the Communist regime, all five ombudspersons have been legal scholars, underscoring the professionalization of this post. On average the office receives about 50,000 letters from citizens per year, and the majority deal with such routine issues as housing, pensions, taxes, and workers' rights. The 1997 constitution also established an ombudsperson for children's rights.

The Advantages of Institutional Experimentation

There is much to be said for Poland's trial-and-error approach to institution-building since 1989. Organizational theorist Douglass North has explained why some societies develop efficient, adaptive, growth-promoting institutions and others do not. The key lies in a society's openness to institutional innovation, as well as its commitment to institutional elimination: "It is essential to have rules that eliminate not only failed economic organization but failed political organization as well. The effective structure of rules, therefore, not only rewards successes, but also vetoes the survival of maladapted parts of the organizational structure."[14] Poland has deftly carried out creative and flexible institutional adaptation, and it should be no surprise that it has recorded both political stability and economic success.

Many political structures have been overhauled since the democratic breakthrough. Some were completely discarded and replaced by new ones. Functional ministries such as defense, foreign affairs, and internal affairs were remodeled and restaffed. The Supreme Court and the Constitutional Tribunal were invested with added responsibilities. A new State Security Agency (UOP) replaced the feared Communist security apparatus, though it still figured at the center of a controversy in 1995–1996 when several of its officials backed the internal affairs minister's claim that the then prime minister had worked for Soviet intelligence. The charges were not proved, and the security apparatus again came under attack, as in the Communist period, for playing dirty politics.

Other institutions inherited from the antecedent regime have sometimes surprisingly survived, even if in an overhauled form. These include the Central Office of Planning, the Main Statistical Office, the National Bank, the Chief Inspectorate, the ombudsperson, and the Office of the Council of Ministers. New institution-building was aimed at speeding up economic transformation and has included both the Economic and the Social Committees of the Council of Ministers, for a time the Ministry of Property Transformation (or Privatization), the Ministry of Foreign Economic Cooperation, and the Anti-monopolies Office. Institutional elimination has occurred when the changing context required it. Thus, the government eliminated the Privatization Ministry in 1996 to reflect the fact that the state should not be in the business of creating a market economy.

Special mention must be made of the **Institute of National Remembrance (INR),** whose mission is to serve as a Commission for the Prosecution of Crimes Against the Polish Nation, whether committed by the Nazis in World War II (there are few of these left) or the Communists in the People's Republic (a much wider pool of people). Established by a special legislative bill approved in 1998 shortly after a right-wing party alliance took control of parliament, it is headed by an independent president aided by a large support staff. The scope and notoriety of the INR increased after the Kaczyńskis initiated their decommunization program. The 2006 law on lustration transferred prosecutory powers, held until then by the public interest prosecutor and special lustration court, to the INR. Files were compiled on fifty-three categories of people, born before August 1972, who had held positions of public responsibility (for example, lawyers, journalists, and academics, in addition to state officials). These 700,000 people were required to make declarations about whether they had worked for the Communist secret services, which would be checked against their files. Those not making such a declaration could lose their jobs. Just before the deadline in May 2007 for submission of all declarations, the Constitutional Court ruled that several articles of the lustration law were unconstitutional. While the decision put an end to the lustration process, there was no guarantee that INR files damaging to certain individuals would not be made public.

On balance, institutional experimentation and innovation have allowed Poland to consolidate its democracy. However, we should recognize that certain types of institutions can also weaken a democratic system.

POLITICAL CULTURE

We need to be circumspect about advances in Poland's democratic politics. As one academic cautioned, "[I]f the state institutions and political elites were quite successful in adapting themselves to the procedural requirements of liberal democracy, they were less successful in forging links with society."[15] The charge that political elites are out of touch with public opinion can be heard in many contemporary democracies, and Poland is no exception. Can it be that the same Polish society that toppled Communism finds itself estranged today from its elected representatives and embraces a value system different from that of its leaders? Examining a country's political culture can provide an answer to this important question.

Political culture is the notion that political values, attitudes, and behavior are deeply embedded in—not transient to—a particular nation. Political culture is rooted in the more enduring political orientations of a country. We have noted the rebellious streak cutting through Polish history and the strong distrust of authoritarian government. If we focus on more recent trends—for example, electoral behavior after 1989—we may be able to identify emerging features of political culture.

Based on voting preferences, we find that Poles' political preferences have been fickle since the democratic breakthrough. At the same time, surveys of citizen attitudes indicate that a value system is emerging that is significantly different from the one that supposedly existed under the Communist regime. On the basis of short-term trends, can we speak of a culture shift toward democratic values in Poland? Or is an irreversible cultural break with the past yet to occur?

Values and Identity

Norms about the community a citizen lives in are important in defining his or her place in a postmodern world characterized by fragmentation and transience. Have Poles been able to maintain a strong sense of national identity and continue to take pride in their nation and state? Or, with so much global culture shift generally and the rapid transition from a political identity imposed by Russia to one shaped by the values of the West in Central Europe specifically, are Poles unclear and anxious about the community they live in?

In the World Values Survey of forty-three nations conducted at a time when Poland was in its early transition years (1991–1993), the country placed third in identifying "the country as a whole" as "the geographical group you would say you belong to first of all."[16] In answer to the question "How proud are you to be Polish?" 69 percent answered "very proud"—putting it in fourth place.[17] Paradoxically, though, Poles ranked next to last when asked if they trusted people of their own nationality.[18] Both a sense of national identity and of patriotism seemed ingrained in Poles at the time of democratic transition in the early 1990s (also see Chapter 2).

Also noteworthy is the inclusive rather than exclusionary understanding of citizenship that Polish respondents have provided. Whereas sharply drawn ethnic boundaries would reflect a less open attitude to minorities, inclusiveness would suggest tolerance and liberalism. A 1994 survey asked respondents who they think is Polish. The most common answers were someone who speaks Polish (cited by 96% of respondents), someone whose citizenship is Polish (92%), someone whose parents are Polish (82%), or someone who lives in Poland (80%). Surprisingly, little more than one-half (57%) said that a Pole is someone who is Catholic.[19] These answers on national identity

underline a more liberal orientation than that displayed a decade later by the Kaczyński brothers.

Indeed, in 2007, even as the twins pressed for a more Catholic Poland that would incorporate conservative social values, twice as many Poles had a positive view of liberalism—understood as entailing freedom of speech and thought, tolerance, and openness to change—as those viewing it negatively. Conversely, conservatism—defined as an adherence to traditional values, faithfulness to long-standing principles, and the questioning of change and innovation—was supported by only 15 percent of respondents; 20 percent opposed it.[20] These results suggest that Poles may have voted in the Kaczyńskis for reasons other than their conservative political program—in particular, for their anticorruption platform. The quandary for a parliamentary democracy was that, once in office, these leaders would go ahead and implement some of their conservative, even illiberal, ideas.

Democratic Norms

A key aspect of political culture is citizen attitudes toward the system of government. For a democratic culture to take root in Poland, authoritarian attitudes have to be replaced with those supporting political pluralism. A more participant culture where citizens are informed about politics and make political demands is a further indication of a modern democratic system. Some scholars have highlighted the deferential, subject culture of many Slavic societies where citizens passively obey government officials, a tendency that may have been reinforced by Soviet-style authoritarianism.[21] Others have stressed the distinctiveness of national cultures—in the case of Poland, the experience of insurrectionism and antiauthoritarianism—and their general incompatibility with the Communist normative system.[22] Others still point to the more recent experience of building a civil society—a private sphere of life for citizens free of government interference—that was undertaken in Poland in the mid-1970s, earlier than in other states in the region. Learning how to organize outside of the structures of power facilitated the transition to democratic processes, it is argued, and laid the groundwork for the spread of liberal values.

Early in the transition, Poles expressed relatively little confidence in the emergent system. For example, in 1993, 52 percent of Poles surveyed claimed they were dissatisfied with the way Polish democracy functioned; 36 percent said they were satisfied. Dissatisfaction with Polish democracy peaked in 2003, after four years of a left-of-center government that had been implicated in a number of high-profile financial scandals: 71 percent of respondents were unhappy with the democratic system and only 20 percent happy. But a sharp turnaround followed, and by late 2007, shortly after the election of a centrist government led by Donald Tusk, for the first time a plurality of Poles expressed satisfaction rather than dissatisfaction with the working of democracy (by a 46% to 42% margin).[23] The close association in the minds of Poles of the health of the democratic system with the popularity of the government at its head is an obvious conclusion of these survey results. Ideally, of course, democracy is most secure when citizens value it in its own right.

An important reason undergirding dissatisfaction was the sense that political institutions were not really representing citizen interests. In 1992, just after the democratic breakthrough, a poll found that only 26 percent of respondents agreed "there are now organizations, associations, or unions in Poland that serve the interest of people like you"; 53 percent disagreed. This view has not changed much since then. Associated with this assessment is the public's sense of political inefficacy and powerlessness. Thus, if in 1992 only 7 percent of respondents believed they had influence on the country in general, the high water mark of 19 percent was reached in 1997, and it has not risen for a decade. Indeed, a remarkable (for a democracy) 83 percent in 2004 claimed that they had no influence on national affairs.[24] A positive development is that since 2007 a majority of Poles have asserted that it *is* significant to them whether Poland has a democratic or an undemocratic government.[25]

Twenty years after the democratic breakthrough, Poles have fewer and fewer doubts that the democratic system is superior to the former authoritarian regime. They are more pleased than other postcommunist nations that Communism has been laid to rest. When asked in 1999 to reflect on whether the collapse of Communism was a good thing, 80 percent of Poles (a figure similar to that of West Europeans) said yes, and only 6 percent said no; the approval rate in other Central European countries was about 70 percent.[26] In 2004, in answer to the question whether the change of regime made fifteen years earlier was worth it, 65 percent of Poles said yes, and only 21 percent said no.[27]

To be sure, Poles' trust or distrust in particular political institutions in the Third Republic system indicates how skeptical they remain of aspects of democratic governance. In a 2008 survey, the work of legislative

institutions (both the Sejm and the Senate)—the core of representative government—received more negative than positive ratings (Figure 10.3). In a survey of public trust in institutions, political parties, which populate these representative bodies with members, were held in the least esteem among all the country's institutions. The only other organization that evoked more distrust than trust was churches of all denominations apart from Catholic, which was highly trusted.[28] This differentiated evaluation of churches is a significant finding and calls into question Poles' tolerance of other religious and ethnic groups (for instance, Orthodoxy is the main religion of the country's Ukrainian and Belarussian minorities).

Levels of trust in a series of institutions pivotal to the functioning of democracy—the government, state administration, court system, ombudsperson, press—were high in 2008, indicating that Poles are selective in their valuating of Third Republic organizations. We can suggest therefore that in insisting on a more representative, effective democratic system that offers citizens real opportunities to influence politics—and in rejecting the temptation to be sentimental about the Communist *ancien régime*—Poles today have by and large embraced democratic norms. If anything, they favor more democracy than the political institutions are delivering.

This is a departure from the prevailing culture of the early 1990s. Back then the World Values Survey had spotlighted an aspect of Polish exceptionalism: "[A]lmost all of the socialist or ex-socialist societies . . . are characterized by (1) survival values, and (2) a strong emphasis on state authority, rather than traditional authority. Poland is a striking exception, distinguished from the other socialist societies by her strong traditional-religious values."[29] It is a "hyper-Catholic society . . . manifesting relatively traditional cultural values across a wide range of areas. Not only in religion, but also in politics, gender roles, sexual norms, and family values, their values are far more traditional than those generally found in industrial societies."[30]

Religion continues to be at the center of national politics. The Kaczyńskis skillfully used Catholic identity and values (discussed below) to win the presidential as well as legislative elections in 2005. There has been no emphatic break from Poland's traditional religious value system; in fact, it has been consolidated. If religion continues to represent a political cleavage cutting across Polish society—an unusual phenomenon for an EU state—the positive side of this is that it has

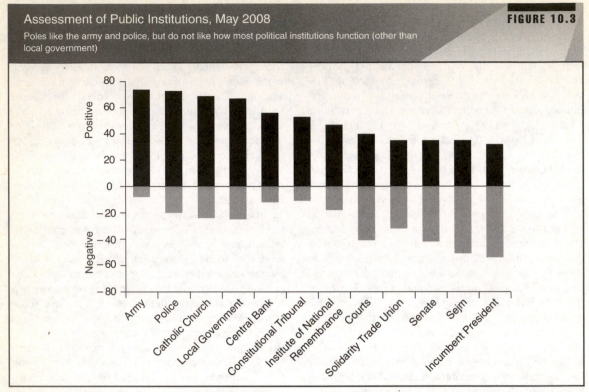

Assessment of Public Institutions, May 2008   **FIGURE 10.3**

Poles like the army and police, but do not like how most political institutions function (other than local government)

Note: The answer "difficult to say" is excluded from the results.

Source: Centrum Badania Opinii Spolecznej (CBOS), "Opinie o dzialalności instytucji publicznych," May 2008. Retrieved October 19, 2008, from www.cbos.pl/.

reduced the salience of the democratic-Communist divide that marked the country's politics in the early transition years.

Social and Economic Values

To what extent did a Communist value system take hold in Poland? If we assume that the core values of this system were social justice and egalitarianism, then large sections of Polish society internalized such ideals during the Communist period.[31] But Communist values also prescribed deference to authority, the centrality of the common good, and, officially at least, a nonconsumerist way of life. In these areas Polish political culture proved resilient to the Communist regime's indoctrination efforts.

At the outset of the 1990s, Poland ranked twenty-eighth out of forty-three societies in terms of espousing postmaterialist values. What are these? "Materialist priorities are tapped by emphasis on such goals as economic growth, fighting rising prices, maintaining order and fighting crime; while post-materialist values are reflected when top priority is given to such goals as giving people more say on the job or in government decisions, or protecting freedom of speech or moving toward a less impersonal, more humane society."[32] The economic **shock therapy** that Polish society experienced in the early 1990s forced citizens to shift to materialist (survival) priorities. This contrasted with the more idealistic project of building a civil society espoused by dissidents in the 1970s and 1980s.

Early in the 1990s, the uncertain consequences of the transition to a market economy and democracy were reflected in public opinion that revealed considerable anxiety. Egalitarianism, the core value of the socialist normative order, carried over to the democratic system, though with weaker societal commitment to it. One study carried out in the first years of the transition discovered that the issues considered important by the public—unemployment, inflation, agriculture, poverty, crime, and housing—were egalitarian in nature.[33] Another study found that the policy of decommunizing public life was ranked last of eleven priorities identified by respondents (only 9% mentioned it). When asked what type of society was preferable—one in which individual interests dominated or one in which the state provided citizens with guarantees—Polish respondents displayed a slight preference for the latter.[34] Statist attitudes holding that it is the duty of the state to safeguard minimum living standards for everybody survived regime change. In the second half of the decade, the egalitarian mindset weakened as large numbers of Poles found employment in the more remunerative private sector. A 2000 report concluded that Poles now put freedom before equality in social life if faced with the choice.[35]

Today's political culture reflects the effects of twenty years of democratic experience. Some statist values remain, but among young people in particular, they have given way to individualist ones. Political behavior, a central aspect of political culture, is now channeled through the ballot box, though for a time public demonstrations (against abortion and EU agricultural products; for health care reform and farm subsidies) also reflected the more participatory culture. Some skeptics have detected a lag between the precocious growth of democratic institutions and a more gradual transformation of societal values. However, if there is a democratic deficit in the country, it is located not in its political culture, but in the poorly functioning institutions of representative government.

POLITICAL SOCIALIZATION

The transition to democracy led to a dramatic change in the form and content of political socialization in the country—that is, the values that political authorities, using a variety of means, want their citizens to internalize. The very roles in politics that were to be played by the school, the family, the newspaper, and the church service were redefined. The meanings of patriotism, citizenship, and personal success were revised. Political socialization tells us as much about the nature of a political system as the institutions it establishes.

Communist Indoctrination

The Communist regime had made political indoctrination one of its priorities. An elaborate network of interlocking organizations was set up to carry out Communist political teaching. The state based the education system on a curriculum and incentive system that rewarded those who internalized—or at least paid lip service to—socialist values. Socialization into the Marxist system of values extended from universal state-run child-care facilities that allowed both parents to work (and drew their attention to the "magnanimity" of the Communist welfare system) to universities and vocational colleges where students were trained to move smoothly into the labor market.

Parallel to the school system were youth organizations that prepared members for leadership roles. Once in the workforce, individuals were recruited into various types of trade unions and professional associations. These organizations served as the schools of socialism. When not at school or work, citizens were encouraged to take part in the self-management of housing blocks where they lived. All these agents of socialization were supposed to ensure that social justice, order, and equality of condition were maintained.

The media, too, were in the hands of the party-state. For many decades Poles' sources of political information were radio, television, and newspapers—all subject to the scrutiny of censors. The Communist "propaganda of success" permeated news content, reaching its peak in the 1970s by glorifying a mini-economic boom (the fact that it was produced by enormous Western loans was not mentioned). Political socialization then praised the consumer culture, proclaiming that Communist economic planning had laid the foundation for a society of plenty. The virtue of austerity inculcated in the 1950s and 1960s was replaced by the call for people to enrich themselves and join the ranks of the "red bourgeoisie."

Patriotism was a central feature of Communist propaganda, even if its meaning was distorted by the principle of proletarian internationalism, which prescribed a special relationship with the Soviet Union. Throughout the existence of the People's Republic, there was an underlying tension discernible in propaganda between Polish patriotism and political russophilism. It even divided the Communist elite and in some measure contributed to the collapse of Communism—a system identified by many as an alien, Russian-imposed ideological aberration.

Retooling Political Socialization

The new democracy overhauled the content and methods of political socialization. The agents of socialization located in the public sphere—schools, mass organizations, workplaces, and neighborhood groups—were relegated to a secondary role behind more traditional sources of values—peer group, family, and church. The privatization of public life occurred in tandem with the privatization of the economy. There was now not one overarching value system propagated to all groups in society, but several different ones. Children of working-class families were taught the value of solidarity, while those of the middle class learned about individualism. More than ever, peasant children were brought up to be good Catholics.

As just about anywhere, young people rebelled against the values of their elders. In the early 1990s, some of the most serious instances of political violence involved young anarchists. Initial enthusiasm about politics triggered by regime change was displaced by a waning interest among the young in the political concerns of their parents' generation. The number of drug users grew, and young victims of AIDS were often forced onto the streets to beg, since there were no treatment centers for them. The pervasiveness of Western youth culture was seen in styles of dress (from preppy khakis to cargo pants), ways of speaking (creeping anglicisms), and tastes in music (rap). Indigenous popular musical forms emerged (for example, discopolo, popular among rural youth), but in the cities it was American-style hip-hop that had the greatest appeal.

Socialization within the family produced an ethnic revival as people discovered long-suppressed identities—Jewish, German, Silesian, Ukrainian, Lemko, Kashub. The religious and cultural institutions of minority peoples were revived and began to function as agents of socialization. For minority groups the family, especially when it transmitted a maternal language and distinct cultural heritage, reemerged as a chief instrument of value dissemination.

Catholicism and Political Values

In the communist era, the Catholic Church served as the alternative to socialist indoctrination. After the democratic breakthrough, it attempted to inculcate Christian values even more aggressively. This created an unexpected backlash against the Church. Many Poles came to regard the Church as too influential in political life in the 1990s. Outward signs of religiosity—attending mass, receiving first communion, making pilgrimages to the monastery at Częstochowa, turning out in enormous numbers for the Pope's visits—

remained pervasive. But, simultaneously, certain sections of Polish society were moving toward a more secular outlook. Both Pope John Paul II and **Cardinal Józef Glemp**, Primate of the Polish Catholic Church since 1981, had to caution Poles against submitting to the appeal of materialism. If Poles remained largely a devout, believing people, they began to differentiate faith in God from faith in the Church's role in politics.

Since the 1990s there has even been a rise in anticlericalism. Arguably, it was sparked by the Church's attempt to replace the state as the dominant agent of political socialization. One Polish scholar described the negative impact that the Church was having in a capitalist society: "Catholicism has once again shown itself as a historical factor making pro-capitalist changes harder. Its communalism, pressure to subordinate the interests of the individual to those of the community, its dislike of the creation and use of wealth by the individual . . . were an important binding agent of dislike of the 'new.'"[36]

The Church's role in cultural transmission can be exaggerated. Until 2005 it sided with losing conservative parties in a series of elections. Its intervention on the issue of abortion triggered a backlash. Many Polish Catholics were disappointed in the leadership offered by Cardinal Glemp, who they viewed as too conservative and nationalistic. A large number were upset at his ineptness in dealing with controversies involving the Nazi death camp at Auschwitz. First, a plan was announced to put up a Carmelite convent close by, then ultranationalist Poles erected crosses on a nearby hillside to highlight the deaths of Catholics in Auschwitz, and, finally, a developer proposed to build a shopping plaza in the area. Many Poles found Glemp's unwillingness to support protests organized by Jewish groups unseemly.

The Church's blunders did not hobble it for long. Its influence on politics strengthened as Poland became poised to join the EU. Its biggest coup was finally backing a winning party, the Kaczyńskis' Law and Justice (PiS), in 2005. The party's double (presidential and parliamentary) election victory put its leaders in the presidential and prime ministerial offices. Fears of a loss of Poles' Catholic identity in a secular or Protestant-dominated EU were being effectively exploited. Important to these developments was a conservative Catholic radio station, **Radio Maryja**, part of a larger media group, which attracted several million listeners with its nationalist, anti-European, antigay, antifeminist, and occasionally anti-Semitic (see below) programming. Prime Minister Jarosław Kaczyński, as well as other leading politicians of the radical right, took part in its radio shows; he even described Radio Maryja as a bastion of freedom and source of "comfort and hope."[37]

An explicitly Catholic (if somewhat smaller) party, the League of Polish Families (LPR), was a political extension of the radio station. Its leader was a featured speaker at the 2007 World Congress of Families, a conservative umbrella group of pro-family organizations of different denominations that met in Warsaw. The Congress explained its rationale for selecting the Polish capital as its site: "Europe is almost lost; to a demographic winter and to the secularists. . . . Almost alone, Poland has maintained strong faith and strong families, though even Poland comes under severe pressure to change. Poland has saved Europe before. It is likely she will save Europe again. On family and population questions, Europe is the battleground in the early years of the twenty-first century, and Poland is the pivot point."[38] Although President Kaczyński served as honorary patron, few Poles paid much attention to the event.

Catholicism's transmission of family values has focused on a micro-organizational level. In the difficult transition years, the Catholic family performed the role of support group for its members. Many Poles who had endured economic hardships became receptive to Catholicism's appeal. The notions of a common good and a spiritual mission for Poles were attractive at a time of upheaval.

The Church is sometimes accused of playing an insidious role in the socialization of women. Whereas officially the Communist system treated the liberation of women as a high priority, Catholicism has stressed the unique role that women have to play as mothers and as the nucleus of the family. If the Communist system effectively imposed a double burden on women—as indispensable participants in the labor market and as homemakers—the Church has taken a more one-sided view, seeing women as being the givers of life, raising children to be practicing Catholics, and forming the hearth of the family. The Communist regime, officially at least, sought to radicalize women and invited their participation in politics. In contrast, the Church has encouraged women to perform traditional roles such as raising children, cooking, and going to church—and if they are to vote it, should be for Catholic candidates.[39] Clearly, the Church has failed in the first task: The fertility rate has fallen from 2.2 children per woman in 1987 (enough to keep the population size constant) to 1.3 in 2008, putting it in 208th position of 220 countries ranked. This may be represented as Polish women's "revenge of the non-cradle." Higher living costs and child expenses combine with some women's deliberate choice to work, rather than rearing children, to explain the falling demographics (seen elsewhere in Central Europe as well).

In the 1990s women were the main victims of the transition to a market economy, accounting for nearly two-thirds of the nonmanual unemployed. Finding new employment was much more difficult, not helped by the dismantling of the state-run childcare system. None of this has been the direct result of the Church resocializing females to take up their traditional roles, but many clerics have not concealed their satisfaction that economic imperatives have succeeded in changing women's roles in line with Catholic teachings.

Compulsory religious education in schools and an ultraconservative abortion law were the Church's doings, however. Because women account for a greater proportion of believers, they face greater moral agonizing than men when deciding whether to conform to Catholic teaching. By internalizing Catholic values, Polish women may thus be tempted to reject some of the emancipatory ideas commonplace in Western countries. We should stress nevertheless that even when Catholic values lead to the emergence of conservative attitudes among Polish women, it does not follow that they are less emancipated than their Western cohorts, only that their strategies for advancement are different.

The Media Battles

Television, radio, and the press are major agents of socialization in any society. Since 1989 the political knowledge of Polish citizens has expanded as government-controlled media have democratized and other private media outlets have been established. If there is a problem with media content today, it is that Polish firms own few newspapers and newsmagazines; bias in journalism is often a by-product of foreign ownership. Although French and Italian media conglomerates operate in Poland, the country's western neighbor has the largest presence; some have even spoken of Poland as a German media colony.

To be sure, the most widely read newspaper, *Gazeta Wyborcza* (*Electoral Gazette*), is largely Polish owned and secular oriented. It was established in 1989 by former dissident Michnik to break the state monopoly on the media and has since become a very successful commercial venture. A Polish edition of *Newsweek,* started up after 2000, has also become a success story and has edged out long-standing Polish newsmagazines (like *Polityka*) as the most widely read weekly.

Citizens have many news sources (including from Western Europe) to tap. The state still controls two television channels, a number of national radio stations, and a nationwide newspaper (*Rzeczpospolita*). But these now face stiff competition from privately owned media. For example, in 2001 an ownership group controlled by the Franciscan order established a Catholic television station (TV Puls). It featured family and religious television programming to counter the supposed excess of violence and sex on the commercial networks. But in a sign of the times, in 2007 a Rupert Murdoch–owned consortium took over TV Puls, and it now shows programs like *The Simpsons*.

Sporadic attempts have been made to control the mass media in democratic Poland. One, inspired by the Church, was the antipornography law passed by the Sejm, which provided for jail sentences for newsagents who sold even soft porn like *Playboy*. The bill was vetoed in 2000 by President Kwaśniewski. Control over television has sparked the fiercest political battles. Governments of both the left and right have operated under the same assumption as in the Communist period—control over television and radio broadcasting helps win public support for incumbent leaders. Thus the SLD government of 1993–97 stacked the committee overseeing the media, the National Broadcasting Council (NBC), with its own supporters and filled the post of director of state television with a person from its own ranks. In turn the AWS-led Buzek government of 1997–2001 tried to do the same. On its return to power, the SLD went one step further and became enmeshed in the so-called **Rywingate** scandal in 2002. Its fallout crippled the left-of-center government, paving the way for the conservative electoral sweep of 2005.

Rywingate centered on apolitical leaders' efforts to manipulate the media. In 2002 entrepreneur Lew Rywin (who produced Roman Polanski's Oscar-winning movie *The Pianist*) visited *Gazeta Wyborcza* editor Michnik and offered to make changes to the media bill pending in the legislature that would allow the newspaper's parent company to enter the television business. Rywin claimed to be acting on behalf of top people in the ruling Social Democratic party, including the prime minister. In exchange he requested a $17.5 million bribe from Michnik. Although he is a controversial figure, former anti-Communist underground leader Michnik is generally viewed as highly ethical, even incorruptible. The *Gazeta Wyborcza* editor taped his conversation with Rywin and eventually made it public.

The bribery scandal involving the media bill—together with charges of other SLD financial wrongdoings—reduced voter support for the ex-Communists to single digits. Rywingate forced the prime minister to resign the day after presiding over Poland's entry into the EU. In short order the scandal was to undermine the SLD's pivotal role in national politics, and it has never recovered.

Under the conservative government that followed, the politically overhauled NBC was caught in a different controversy—it was accused of bias in investigating media wrongdoing. In 2006 the NBC fined a commercial television station for allowing a well-known literary critic to satirize a woman who recited prayers on Radio Maryja (unknown to the critic, it turned out that the woman was disabled, making the satire more distasteful). But the NBC did not fine or condemn Radio Maryja for allowing a series of anti-Semitic remarks to be broadcast—for example, statements that "the Holocaust industry" of international Jewry wanted to squeeze billions of dollars from Poland through property restitution laws and that "the men from Judea" running secular newspapers (a coded reference to Michnik and *Gazeta Wyborcza*) act as a fifth column. Prime Minister Kaczyński lashed out at the media "oligarchs" and even compared *Gazeta Wyborcza* to the former Communist Party newspaper.

In sum, the political battles waged over the control of television and radio have been ruthless. The stakes involve control over both a primary agent of political socialization and the financial windfalls that can come from media ownership. The politicized control over the media was bad enough to earn Poland last place among all EU countries in the 2007 and 2008 annual reports on world press freedom.[40]

POLITICAL PARTICIPATION

The transition from Communism to democracy involved a fundamental change in the nature of political participation. The Communist system exhorted citizens to take part in politics through voting in elections, attending mass rallies and meetings, and joining many different types of organizations that supposedly made inputs into the political system. Of course, voting was purely a ceremonial function, attending rallies was of no more than symbolic importance, and joining various organizations was primarily a form of manipulated participation.

The introduction of electoral democracy meant that voting now had real significance. In the space of twelve years, Poland had eight national elections: five parliamentary elections (1989, 1991, 1993, 1997, and 2001) and three presidential elections (1990, 1995, and 2000). Add to this three national referendums (1996, 1997, and 2003), and we can see the participatory demands made on Poles. It should not be surprising therefore that as meaningful participatory opportunities have expanded under democracy, the rate of participation has dropped off (Figure 10.4). The turnout for presidential contests has ranged from a high of 68 percent in the 1995 runoff to a low of just under 50 percent in the 2005 first round. Parliamentary elections were drawing about one-half of the electorate until 2005, when just 41 percent showed up to oust the SLD government and replace it with Law and Justice. The highest turnout for a referendum was 59 percent in 2003 (on EU accession), while in local

elections a respectable 46 percent went to the polls in 2006. In the case of the European Parliamentary elections in 2004, an embarrassing one-fifth voted, less than half the average turnout in Western Europe.

There are many explanations for citizen nonvoting apart from the frequency of elections in Poland. Political parties have not always offered clear and consistent programs, making partisan identification difficult. Until recently, there was near consensus among parties that market reform, less government, and NATO and EU membership were indispensable, blunting voters' interest. By and large, political leaders have lacked charisma. Exhaustion with politics after the struggles with the Communist regime in the 1980s led to greater citizen apathy. The opportunity to live a private life and ignore political involvement altogether is welcome after the constant mobilization and countermobilization of the 1980s. An optimistic view is that the political system simply is not overloaded with pressing citizen demands expressed through the ballot box. Finally, as we have seen, it is possible that the mild skepticism with electoral democracy that we have noted is turning off a section of voters.

In what ways does the public take part in politics? The demise of the Communist Party in 1990 left

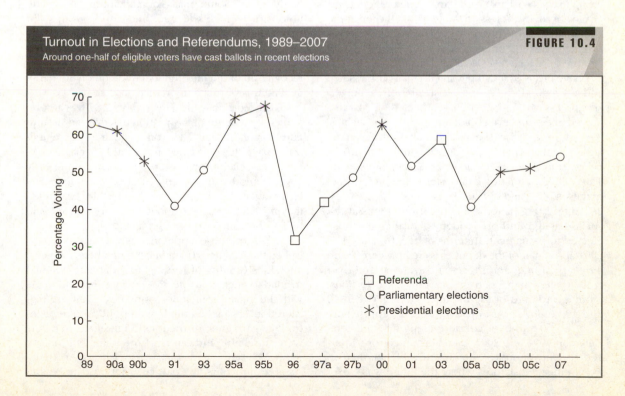

Turnout in Elections and Referendums, 1989–2007
Around one-half of eligible voters have cast ballots in recent elections

FIGURE 10.4

□ Referenda
○ Parliamentary elections
✳ Presidential elections

Percentage Voting

no mass-membership political parties in existence. Parties today are primarily electoral machines seeking to win over voters. Once they secure representation in the Sejm, they become parliamentary parties seeking to influence policymaking. Combined with a falloff in membership in mass organizations (trade unions, farmers' groups, student organizations) and a widespread reticence (or even apathy) about participating in civil society after concluding the struggle against Communism, citizens have become less effective in aggregating their interests. Intermediary organizations between state and society are lacking (some that do exist are discussed later). Direct political action, as through demonstrations, has also fallen off in the last ten years. A general disaffection with partisan politics is discernible in many established democracies and may be catching up with Poland.

LEADERSHIP RECRUITMENT

Who are Poland's new political elites, and from where are they recruited? If we focus on those individuals who have held executive power as either president or prime minister, we arrive at a very heterogeneous group in socio-occupational terms. One president was an electrician by profession (Wałęsa); another an apparatchik in the former Communist bureaucracy, specializing in youth and physical education (Kwaśniewski); and the third a lawyer (Lech Kaczyński). Prime ministers have included a Catholic intellectual, businessmen and lawyers, a farmer, a physicist, a historian, university professors and economists (including Marxist-trained ones), and even Communist Party apparatchiks. Most of these very well educated individuals (even the farmer held an engineering degree) finished their university studies when Poland was a Communist system. Their different training demonstrates the professional pluralism of Poland's political elite.

Interesting patterns emerge if one looks at the social background of a wider political elite—those elected to parliament. In terms of age, from 1991 to 2001 about half of the deputies were between 40 and 49 years of age, and those who were 60 and over made up less than 5 percent. After the 2007 elections, around one-third of the deputies were between 40 and 49, and older groups were better represented, with the 60-and-over cohort making up 9 percent. Between 1991 and 2001, men accounted for 87 percent of the deputies, significantly higher than in Communist legislatures where the figure was closer

to 75 percent. Women made some inroads in the 2007 elections, taking 20 percent of the seats. In that year a remarkable 91 deputies had received a higher education. The best-represented occupations in 2007 were those in administration (16 percent), followed by educators (15 percent), legal professionals (13 percent), engineers and computer scientists (11 percent), and economists (10 percent). About two-thirds of the deputies were serving just their first or second term, testifying to the high rate of turnover and the low rate of incumbency in the legislature.

Perhaps the most important question Poland must now ask about its political elite is one that has been debated for years in the United States and other older democracies: Do economic and political elites overlap, or have pluralism and circulation of elites become regularities? While it appears that wealthy Poles have generally steered clear of high politics, this is not to say that they do not influence the economic decisions that may affect them.

INTEREST GROUPS

Under the Communist system, interest groups did not really exist. Some mass organizations like trade unions, a women's league, and youth groups did nominally participate in the policy process, but they had no influence on issues outside of their respective jurisdictions. That was why the regime's begrudging recognition of the independent trade union Solidarity in 1980 was of such importance.

The democratic breakthrough in 1989 was accompanied by a surge of associational activity in Eastern Europe, conceptualized by one scholar as a "repluralization of politics."[41] One study found over 2,000 voluntary associations in existence in Poland in the early 1990s,[42] another estimated that there were up to 500 environmentalist groups alone,[43] and a third concluded that in 1995 "there were about 40 groups which could be sensibly called women's groups."[44]

Most of these spontaneously created groups lacked the resources (membership numbers, finances) and skills (quality of leadership, negotiation skills) needed to engage in effective policy concertation. As with the initial proliferation of parties (370 were registered in 1993 when the law on political parties introduced tougher restrictions), aggregate numbers were unreliable indicators of the place held in the political system by voluntary associations. An analysis of groups pursuing particular interests in Poland

BOX 10.1

The 1979 Pilgrimage of Pope John Paul II to Poland

In 1978 a Polish cardinal, Karol Wojtyła, was elected Pope of the Roman Catholic Church. In 1979 he returned to Communist-ruled Poland on a Papal visit organized by the Polish Catholic Church. In 1980 the independent trade union Solidarity was formed, stripping the Communist Party of its monopoly on power. Nine years later Solidarity defeated the Communist Party in free elections. Does the end of communism, then, originate with the election of a Polish Pope?

Certain American journalists have fostered a myth about John Paul II's role in the fall of communism. They depict him as a lonely hero in a Cold War thriller, a priest who from the start was slipping in and out of darkened doorways in the war against the Evil Empire. At the moment of perfect ripeness, Karol Wojtyła has himself elected Pope, flies home, and ignites the fuse he spent years fashioning. If the myth were pitched as a feature film, it would be John Wayne meets John Le Carre.

The revolution launched by John Paul's return to Poland is one that conjures roads lined with weeping pilgrims, meadows of peaceful souls singing hymns, and most of all, of people swaying forward as one—reaching for the extraordinary man in white as he is borne through their midst. . . .

John Paul II's 1979 trip was the fulcrum of revolution which led to the collapse of communism. Timothy Garton Ash put it this way, "Without the Pope, no Solidarity. Without Solidarity, no Gorbachev. Without Gorbachev, no fall of communism." (In fact, Gorbachev himself gave the Kremlin's long-term enemy this due, "It would have been impossible without the Pope.")

It took time; it took the Pope's support from Rome—some of it financial; it took several more trips in 1983 and 1987. But the flame was lit. It would smolder and flicker before it burned from one end of Poland to the other. Millions of people spread the revolution, but it began with the Pope's trip home in 1979. As General Jaruzelski said, "That was the detonator."*

*Jane Barnes and Helen Whitney, "John Paul II and the Fall of Communism" *Frontline* (1999). Retrieved September 24, 2008, from http://www.pbs.org/wgbh/pages/frontline/shows/pope/communism/.

---

must begin with two long-powerful institutions, the Catholic Church and the military.

The Catholic Church

The Church has played a historical role in Polish politics. Its significance in engaging the Communist regime in a battle for the minds of citizens from the 1940s to the 1980s—a battle that the Church won handily—can hardly be overstated. (See Box 10.1.) Not surprisingly, the Church adopted a triumphalist attitude when the Communist regime collapsed. Indeed, some Church leaders unabashedly admitted that they had violated the terms of the roundtable agreement that required its neutrality. The Church used every means at its disposal—the pulpit, its printing facilities, its meeting rooms, its many voluntary workers, and, above all, its good name—to persuade citizens to vote against Communist candidates. Communist rulers who had so often tricked others into making deals that the rulers had no intention of keeping (as when they registered Solidarity as a legal trade union in late 1980

and then banned it in late 1981) were now themselves taken in by the Church's pledge to act as an impartial mediator of the 1989 election.

We have described how the role of the Church in the Third Republic, especially in facilitating cultural transmission, came under fire, only to rebound under the Kaczyńskis. The highly unpopular, restrictive abortion bill that had to be vetoed by the president, the requirement that public schools provide religious education (though pupils can opt out of it), the principle that Catholic values should permeate public broadcasting, and the tough law on pornography that again required a presidential veto alienated many of the faithful, not to mention non-Catholics. Occasional anti-Semitic sentiments expressed by a few members of the Episcopate, lay Catholic groups, individual priests, and Radio Maryja broadcasters have been a further blemish on the Church.

Anticlerical politicians were able to capitalize on the Church's growing unpopularity. Kwasniewski made known his indignation: "We are not going to have a theocratic state in the middle of Europe at the end of the twentieth century."[45] A 1994 survey found that 71 percent of respondents believed that the Church had too much influence in public life. The Church had been the most trusted of all institutions in Poland throughout most of the 1970s and 1980s; however, public confidence in the Church plummeted from 90 percent before communism's fall to only 50 percent in 1994. Nevertheless, the resilience of this millennium-old Polish institution was shown in a ringing public endorsement in 2008: Nearly 80 percent of respondents expressed trust in it, with a trifling 8 percent expressing distrust.[46]

The Church's reduced political influence in the 1990s was displayed in its inability to have many of the principles it embraces made into law. When the Sejm debated writing a new constitution, the Church made the case for a preamble identifying Christian values as the set of principles underlying Polish society, for recognition of the Church's special role in the country, for rejection of the notion of a secular state, and for a constitutional ban on abortion. The Church did not give up when these efforts failed at home, and the EU agreement in 2004 on a European constitution was delayed by the insistence of Poland (and Spain) that its preamble refer to Europe's Christian heritage; this effort was also unsuccessful.

The Church's international reach was demonstrated by the **Concordat**, signed by Polish and Vatican representatives in 1993, but approved by the government only in 1998 when the Sejm was controlled by a Catholic-oriented party alliance. The 1993 draft began with this assertion: "The Catholic religion is practiced by the majority of the Polish population." A similar clause in the interwar constitution had become a source of controversy, since, at the time, Poland had large ethnic and religious minorities. The 1993 Concordat institutionalized Catholic education in schools, and Church marriages were now to have the same legal status as civil ones (though the Church was prudent enough not to press for changes to existing divorce laws). One writer summarized Church ambitions this way: "Anyone who naively believes today that church-state conflict was invented by the communists and, with their demise, this chapter is closed for all time is making a major and possibly costly mistake."[47]

The Military

A central issue in the politics of new democracies is civil-military relations. A democracy requires civilian oversight of the military because civilian leaders are accountable to the electorate, while military ones are not. In Poland's case fulfilling eligibility requirements for NATO entailed raising standards for civilian political control over the military establishment.

Complicating the problem were the influence and visibility that the Polish military gained in politics in the last years of Communist rule. With the imposition of martial law to crush the Solidarity movement, the distinction between the military and the Communist Party became blurred: General Jaruzelski went from being defense minister to prime minister, Communist Party leader, and head of the Military Council for National Salvation—the body that ruled Poland for a year when martial law was imposed. As we have seen, in 1989 the Sejm elected Jaruzelski as the first president of democratic Poland, and he held the office until direct elections in 1990. An earlier military figure, Piłsudski, became the role model for the new president, Wałęsa.

The first test of civilian control of the military in democratic Poland came with the so-called Parys affair in 1992. An upstart politician, Jan Parys, was named defense minister in a virulently anti-Communist government. He quickly announced a purge of former Communist Party members from the military. Since the interim constitution gave the president powers in defense and security matters, however, Wałęsa believed that he was the guarantor of civilian oversight of the military. He selected a general congenial to the military to be the new chief of the General Staff. Defense Minister Parys objected and suggested that Wałęsa was planning a coup with the help of military leaders. The military felt that it was caught in a power struggle between the executive and legislative branches of government. This struggle was resolved in dramatic fashion when the president got enough support in the Sejm to force the government's resignation in 1992.

For its part, the General Staff has had reason to question the wisdom of strict civilian supervision of the military. A 50 percent cut in the size of the armed forces, budgetary cutbacks (until 1995), and clumsy civilian meddling in personnel matters led to "a siege mentality among the Polish senior officer corps."[48] This was exacerbated by the decision in 2003 by the SLD government to send Polish troops to Iraq to head the only non-American or -British "stabilization sector." In addition to deploying 2,500 soldiers of its own, the Polish military was put in command of troops from some twenty other countries.

The cross-party support for the Bush administration's war in Iraq turned into a fiasco.[49] When Spain withdrew its troops after the 2004 Madrid bombings, Poland became the largest non-Anglo-American force left. The majority of Poles—usually pro-American—began to express opposition to the military engagement and in the fall of 2004 the defense minister announced a major drawdown of Polish troops in Iraq. While the army has continued to be the most trusted institution in the country (Figure 10.3), it is significant that party leaders across the political spectrum who had made the Iraq decision have become more and more unpopular.

It is difficult to criticize the Polish General Staff for its belief that civilian control has produced greater political wrangling and bad decisions. A recent example lends weight to this proposition. In 2008 the Tusk government concluded a treaty with a lame duck Bush administration to allow a missile shield to be based in Poland (see below). It angered the Russians and hardened their resolve to defend their sphere of influence, illustrated by their military intervention in Georgia. It seems safe to say that the General Staff's respect for the political establishment has diminished as a result of a series of questionable processes and decisions.

Trade Unions

If the Catholic Church and the military are integral aspects of Polish political life, the same can no longer be said of trade unions, even though one, Solidarity, brought down the Communist regime. As with their counterparts in many other countries, the overall membership and political influence of Polish labor unions have declined dramatically over the past two decades. Between 1982 and 2005, the degree of unionization fell from 80 to 14 percent, turning Poland into an EU country with one of the lowest levels of unionization. In 2002 only about 6 percent of the adult population (or 18 percent of the workforce) belonged to a trade union. Fifty-two percent of all members are women, giving the lie to the stereotype of union members as predominantly male; the highly feminized educational and health care sectors account for this pattern. Particularly worrying to union organizers is the fact that only 2 percent of employees under 25 belong to a union.

Today the two largest organizations, Solidarity and the All-Poland Alliance of Trade Unions (OPZZ), have a combined membership of about 2 million. Solidarity's decline is especially striking. (See Box 10.2.) From a peak of nearly 10 million in 1981, member-

ship fell off throughout the 1980s when it was banned by the Communist authorities, but also after the democratic breakthrough. An economic recession, a persistently high unemployment rate (approaching 20 percent), an expanding private sector, major cuts in the size of state industry, unpopularity among young people entering the workforce, and a global decline in unionized labor slashed membership.

The much-disparaged former pro-Communist trade union OPZZ is today the equal of Solidarity, even though its membership has fallen to one-third of what it was in 1994. Until recently the union enjoyed a privileged representational status as a distinct group within the parliamentary caucus of the SLD—for example, in 1993 it accounted for 61 of the SLD's 171 deputies. Under a system of corporatism (discussed next), it is the state that usually determines how interest groups are to be represented. In Poland corporatism was stood on its head: The interest structure (the OPZZ) helped determine state representation (in SLD governments). After 2001 the SLD moved toward the model of the British Labour Party's decreasing dependence on trade unions. The OPZZ was deprived of its special status within the party and no longer had its own bloc of deputies.

A Polish sociologist argued that "[systemic transformation disintegrates older interest structures and forms new ones."[50] Following a capitalist transformation, workers' interests have been "decomposed" into specific occupations—textile worker, coal miner, lathe operator—and, further, into particular firms.[51] Interest structures of the future are likely to reflect such differentiated socio-occupational categories of workers, so the future of centralized trade unions is not promising. Indeed, wage bargaining sometimes takes place at the level of the plant: Other bargaining is conducted industrywide—for example, among coal miners or among schoolteachers.

Organized labor in Poland, once of legendary stature, has become fragmented. Successive Polish governments have succeeded in reducing union influence in politics—a strategy that paid off for leaders like Britain's Margaret Thatcher and U.S. President Ronald Reagan. To be sure, unions institutionally participate in policy discussions on economic questions that concern them—in particular, through the Tripartite Commission discussed later. But even here, on such a fundamental issue as wages, unions have not had much success. In 2007 the OPZZ and Solidarity joined forces in a campaign to increase wages, which had fallen by 36 percent in real terms between 2000

The rise and fall of Solidarity is a story about timeliness and obsolescence, about a romantic idea and political infighting, about historical agency and fate. In 2001, just before parliamentary elections were held, *The Economist* reflected:

Solidarity has had its ups and downs since the heroic days of 1980–81, when, at the Gdańsk shipyard and in the coal mines, trade-unionists like the young Lech Wałęsa, later President Wałęsa, raised the banner that in time swept away Soviet-imposed communism and helped to bring down that tyranny in Russia itself. But today's down may prove the end. That is a sad thought for all who remember the heroic past. But Poland's voters have to live in the world as it is.

In 2000, President Aleksander Kwaśniewski, a Politburo member in the former Communist Party and a founder of the post-Communist Alliance of the Democratic Left, was reelected in a landslide. Solidarity-backed presidential candidates could not muster enough votes to force a runoff election. Another landslide victory for the post-Communists—and a further resounding defeat for Solidarity—was about to be

recorded in the 2001 elections to the Sejm. Solidarity was not even going to reach the threshold needed to win seats in parliament. It would be relegated to the legislative sidelines, just like before the democratic breakthrough in 1989.

Solidarity is already a husk of its former self. Its free-marketeers and pragmatists have defected in droves to new parties, or simply dropped out. Only trade-union diehards, old-guard Catholic nationalists and loyalists who see nowhere else to go remain within the movement, as it flounders to find a plausible electoral platform.

Goodbye to Solidarity, then? Probably. And those heroic days, and the Gdańsk shipyard? Well, the shipyard, privatized in 1998, employs 3,800 people against 18,000 in 1980, and its workers were protesting this week against further layoffs. And Mr. Wałęsa? Voted out of the presidency in 1995, and his image fallen much lower since, in last year's presidential election he won just 1 percent of the vote.*

*From "The End of Solidarity: Poland's Coming Election," *The Economist,* August 16, 2001, 27.

---

and 2005. After many years of declining use of the strike tactic—the low point was 2005, when only 8 strikes encompassing just 2,000 workers took place—unions resorted to it again in 2007, when nearly 2,000 strikes were staged involving some 60,000 employees and costing 186,000 lost working days. The strike action of nurses and doctors was particularly well supported by the Polish public, but their monetary gains were limited. It is hard to see how organized labor can regain its clout, especially during a financial crisis.

Business Groups

Many new institutions represent the interests of Poland's emergent entrepreneurial class. Owners and executives of private businesses have organized into a number of national bodies. The most prestigious business lobby group is the Business Center Club, affiliating 1,200 companies and controlling over $30 billion in capital. Medium and small entrepreneurs are organized into the Polish Confederation of Private Employers, the Association of Polish Crafts, and

the Polish Federation of Independent Entrepreneurs. For managers of state-owned enterprises, the Polish Confederation of Employers is the principal lobby group. An umbrella organization, the Polish Chamber of Commerce, has over 500,000 affiliated companies. There are also sixty regional Chambers of Commerce.

The question facing Polish employers, as with their counterparts elsewhere, is whether they are better off in a unified, centralized organization that lobbies the government (as in France or Germany) or in an individualistic, highly decentralized business lobby (as in Britain or the United States). Whether business interests do become more confederated or remain decentralized may not be that important anyway in determining how much clout the lobby has. As in most democracies, the more important test is whether a pro-business or pro-labor party is in power.

Minority Groups

Limited ethnic politics occurs in Poland. Of all registered minority associations, nearly half are German, most of them based in provinces bordering on the German Federal Republic, where this minority is concentrated. The German minority has consistently been represented in the legislature. The 1993 electoral law exempted parties of national minorities from having to reach a 5 percent threshold to obtain Sejm seats, allowing the German coalition to win four seats that year. In the 2007 elections, however, only one member of the German minority bloc was voted into the Sejm. The most influential German organization in the country is the Social-Cultural Association of the German Minority in Silesia. Supported by the German government, it has managed to carve out a measure of autonomy for itself.

Also functioning in democratic Poland are Ukrainian, Lithuanian, and Belarussian minority associations based in the eastern provinces. None currently has parliamentary representation. Numerous religious and secular Jewish associations exist, subsumed under the Coordinating Committee of Jewish Organizations. The Jewish Historical Institute is particularly active in trying to keep alive the centuries-old Jewish presence in Poland. Thanks to the efforts of Jewish organizations, in 1997 the Sejm enacted a law providing for restitution of Jewish communal property to remaining Jewish communities (fewer than 10,000 Jews live in Poland today). Both Polish and Jewish leaders have undertaken efforts to overcome negative stereotypes of each other. Stereotypes die hard, however. In the mid-1990s Poles rated Jews near the top of their list of groups having too much influence in the political system. This perception has continued to shape the politics of the conservative right.

THE PARTY SYSTEM

Democracy is inextricably linked to political pluralism, a multiparty system, and free elections. In Poland the development of a competitive party system, where two or more parties seek electoral support to gain political influence, has taken many twists and turns since the 1990s. Parties have come and gone; they have splintered, and they have entered into a variety of electoral pacts with changing names. A typical case of this is the conservative Catholic movement. Having started its political life as the Christian National Union, it ran in the 1991 Sejm election as Catholic Electoral Action and in the 1993 election as Fatherland. In 1995 it formed part of the Alliance for Poland supporting Wałęsa's presidential bid. For the

1997 legislative election, it joined with Solidarity under the banner *Solidarity Electoral Action (AWS),* for the 2001 election, it was part of Solidarity Electoral Action of the Right; and for the 2005 and 2007 Sejm elections, its main embodiment was the Law and Justice. Such party malleability largely reflects political and personal battles for leadership over a movement.

The **electoral law of 1993** was designed to reduce party fragmentation and increase the stability of the party system. Parties that receive less than 5 percent of the popular vote now do not gain representation in the Sejm. Conversely, the larger vote-getting parties get a disproportionately larger number of seats than their share of the vote entitles them to. The ex-Communists best adapted to the new law by presenting a united coalition of the left in each election. Nevertheless, the 1993 electoral law has not consolidated the party system, and under the Kaczyńskis there was even talk of moving to a single-constituency first-past-the-post system.

Current Parties

Until recently all major parties in Poland have shared some common characteristics. They have accepted the rules of the game of the Third Republic and have abided by the outcomes generated by these rules. There has been no threat, by former Communists or the right, to employ extraparliamentary means to obtain power. No major party has voiced a principled objection to a cornerstone of domestic policy—transition to a market economy— and by and large, all major parties accept a Western-oriented foreign policy, though whether the EU or the United States should be Poland's primary security guarantor has been in dispute.

The need to form broad-based coalitions that appeal to cross-sections of the electorate to win a large bloc of seats has explained the consensual politics of Polish parties. The AWS, for example, was a **catch-all party**—that is, an umbrella organization for numerous political groups—and it advanced a broad political program. Political expediency—to drive the ex-Communists from power in the 1997 parliamentary elections—united the disparate forces on the right. Once in power, however, the alliance proved so diverse that over the next four years it was plagued by internal disputes. From governing party it went after the 2001 election to an organization without any elected deputies in the Sejm.

Another catch-all party that eventually became a victim of its diverse policy orientations was the *Freedom Union (UW)*. In 1991 it posted the strongest electoral showing of any party, owing in large measure to its leaders' claim that it had no ideology or program. The UW had at various times included a left-of-center, welfare-state faction represented by former dissident Kuroń; a centrist Catholic section comprised of Mazowiecki supporters; and a neoliberal economic group headed by Balcerowicz. A series of poor electoral showings beginning in 1993 left the party out of the Sejm after 2001. Even with leaders having name recognition and a core following among the better-educated, secular, urban public, it disappeared from the political scene. It was overhauled, and in 2007, under the name *Civic Platform,* it won a plurality of seats in elections and formed the government. The troubling vacuum found in the political center was filled. The party's image as a responsible political actor also attracted the new business class, this at a time when government financial scandals and radical antiestablishment movements plagued national politics.

The head-to-head contest between the Catholic conservative Law and Justice and the centrist Civic Platform is a relatively recent phenomenon. Law and Justice triumphed in the 2005 presidential and parliamentary elections, while Civic Platform took the 2007 Sejm elections. Before them, beginning with the 1993 elections, the dominant party in terms of vote-getting and membership numbers was the SLD, the social democratic successor to the former Communist Party. The SLD resembled a catch-all umbrella organization that included various unions and parties. Much of the electorate came to regard the SLD as a European social democratic party, and only a minority still clung to the view that it was a successor party of the Communists. But the party's image of modernity was tarnished by old-fashioned financial scandals (above all, Rywingate). Rebranded as the **Alliance of the Democratic Left (SLD),** it won only about 10 percent of the vote in the 2005 presidential and Sejm elections and got up to 13 percent in the 2007 Sejm elections under the label *Left and Democrats.*

A regular coalition partner for SLD-led governments and, in 2007, for Civic Platform is the Polish Peasant Party (PSL). Also a descendant of a Communist-era party, the PSL defends private farmers whose economic interests have been undermined by the transition to a market economy and membership in the EU. Because the rural population accounts for over one-third of the electorate, the PSL has a large potential constituency. It is one of only four parties with seats in the Sejm after the 2007 elections.

For a time the most breathtaking—and many would contend dangerous—phenomenon in the party system was the rise of Self-Defense. It was unrepresented in the Sejm until 2001, but at one point in the spring of 2004—just before Poland's formal accession into the EU—it had obtained the declared support of one out of four Poles, making it the second most popular party in the country. Much of its success—and notoriety—is attributable to its populist leader, Andrzej Lepper, a frequent organizer of illegal and often violent agrarian protests since the 1990s. Radically agrarian, anticapitalist, anti-EU, antiestablishment, and, to some extent, pro-Russian, Self-Defense quickly became the consummate aggregator of the protest vote. It served as a coalition partner of Law and Justice after the 2005 elections, but overplayed its hand. Lepper was outmaneuvered by Jarosław Kaczyński and quickly lost political credibility. The combination of financial scandals in Self-Defense and the deradicalization of agrarian politics as EU farm subsidies kicked in led to the movement's disappearance from the Sejm after 2007.

A second nationalist, anti-EU, and antiestablishment party that has risen to prominence in recent years is the League of Polish Families (LPR). A conservative Catholic party, it made common cause with the secular Self-Defense movement to vehemently attack Polish policy on Iraq, demand the resignation of the corrupt SLD government, and insist on German war reparations even after Polish and German leaders had agreed in 2004 to waive reciprocal war claims. Its primary constituency remains conservative Catholics.

Table 10.2 depicts the nature of the left/right division within Polish politics. No one a decade ago could have predicted how the party system in existence today would reflect this left/right division, since the actors have changed so much. It remains to be seen whether the parties dominant today will survive any longer than their predecessors after an electoral setback.

Election Results

One criterion by which democratic consolidation is measured is holding a minimum of two free elections. Already in 1993 this criterion had been satisfied. Some political scientists believe that a smooth turnover of government from incumbents to opposition has to occur before we can speak of a consolidated democracy. This has happened regularly in Poland—in fact, five

Main Political Orientations of the Polish Electorate	TABLE 10.2
The most important cleavage today is between a liberal and a Catholic conception of Poland	

Left of Center	Right of Center
Secular	Catholic
Western	Nationalistic
Urban	Rural
Interdependent	Protectionist
Civic rights	Law and order
Socially liberal	Family values
Political pluralism	Autocratic style
Postcommunist	Anticommunist
Pro-EU	Euroskeptic
Future oriented	Tradition bound

times. Since 1991 no government has been able to get reelected, with Solidarity-based and conservative blocs losing power in 1993, 2001, and 2007 and SLD-led coalitions being voted out in 1997 and 2005. As for the presidency, in his 1995 reelection attempt Wałęsa suffered a narrow defeat at the hands of Kwaśniewski, who subsequently was reelected in 2000.

Electoral outcomes have forced parties to form coalition governments around the party that has won the plurality of Sejm seats. In this way Poland resembles Germany, rather than Britain or the United States, where winning parties capture the majority of seats. A political party must therefore do well both in elections and in coalition-building to gain a share of power. Let us briefly review the Third Republic's electoral history.

Presidential Elections In order to win the first direct presidential election, held in 1990 (Table 10.3), a strong organizational basis was crucial, and former Solidarity union head Wałęsa had a distinct advantage over other candidates. He had secured the support of Solidarity groups and Catholic parties, while his most serious rival, Prime Minister Mazowiecki, lacked any prior organization on which to base his campaign. The SLD and PSL, which were well organized, were both tainted by their Communist pedigrees.

In the first round, Wałęsa led the field, but was well short of the 50 percent needed to avoid a runoff. The greatest shock was the elimination of Mazowiecki

Presidential Election Results, 1990–2005		TABLE 10.3
Poles have elected three presidents in four elections since the democratic breakthrough		

	First Round (%)	Second Round (%)
1990 Candidate (Party)		
Lech Wałęsa (Solidarity KO)	40.0	74.3
Stanisław Tymiński ("X")	23.1	25.7
Tadeusz Mazowiecki (ROAD)	18.1	
1995 Candidate (Party)		
Aleksander Kwaśniewski (SLD)	35.1	51.7
Lech Wałęsa (nonparty)	33.1	48.3
Jacek Kuroń (UW)	9.2	
2000 Candidate (Party)		
Aleksander Kwaśniewski (SLD)	53.9	
Andrzej Olechowski (nonparty)	17.3	
Marian Krzaklewski (AWS)	15.6	
2005 Candidate (Party)		
Lech Kaczyński (PiS)	33.1	54.0
Donald Tusk (PO)	36.3	46.0
Andrzej Lepper (SO)	15.1	

Sources: Główny Urząd Statystyczny, *Maly Rocznik Statystyczny Polski 2008* (Warsaw: GUS, 2008).

and the second-place showing of political outsider Stan Tymiński, a Polish emigrant to Canada who claimed to have established successful businesses there and in Peru. The embarrassment produced by his performance, which was the result of a protest vote by citizens unhappy with the many problems caused by the transition, led nearly all political actors to rally around Wałęsa in the runoff. Three of four voters supported the Solidarity head in the second round.

In 1995, 13 candidates contested the first round of the presidential elections. Wałęsa sought to establish himself as the only "electable" candidate of the center-right, and his campaign posters accurately depicted the choice in the election: "There are many other candidates. There is only one Wałęsa" The first round was indecisive, with Kwaśniewski edging out Wałęsa by 35 percent to 33 percent.

Two television debates prior to the runoff were crucial in determining the result. Kwaśniewski's youthfulness (he was 41), eloquence, and good manners stood in sharp contrast to a particularly ill-tempered and agitated Wałęsa. With a high turnout in the second round, Kwaśniewski won by a very slim margin: 51.7 percent to 48.3 percent. The election verdict was neither a repudiation of capitalism nor nostalgia for communism, but a "retrospective" verdict—rejection of "five more years of this."

The 2000 election held none of the suspense of the previous one. The feeling was that the only person who was more popular than Kwaśniewski and who could defeat him in an election was his wife. Twelve candidates entered the contest, and Kwaśniewski won a handy majority in the first round, 37 percent ahead of the second-place finisher. Wałęsa got just 1 percent of the vote.

The reelection of Kwaśniewski was a milestone in contemporary Polish history. It showed that a party system based on the distinction drawn at the 1989 roundtable between a left-wing bloc and a Solidarity camp had become anachronistic. The top two vote-getters—Kwaśniewski and Andrzej Olechowski—were Communist-era officials. The right was in disarray, but so were centrists, as well as those leftists with no associations to the former Communist Party.

Since Kwaśniewski could not run for a third term, the 2005 presidential election was an open contest. Twelve candidates were on the final ballot, including the fringe candidate Tymiński who had gotten as far as a runoff in 1990. This time he received 0.2 percent of the vote, testimony to the far more professional nature of Polish politics today. The two leading vote-getters, Tusk and Kaczyński, were both politicians of the right of center and had been parliamentary allies when conservative groups were weak in the Sejm. At the time of the election, Kaczyński had been serving as mayor of Warsaw and had adopted more nationalistic, anti-Communist, and economically statist positions than had the socially more liberal Tusk, who had once headed the country's most noliberal party. Kaczyński campaigned on an anticorruption program, encapsulated in his slogan "strong president, honest *Poland*." Winning in the first round and leading in opinion polls for a while, Tusk argued for an "honest president, strong *Poland*." In the runoff between the two, Kaczyński, a master political infighter and strategist, attacked the entire legacy of the Third Republic—its self-interested elites, corruption, and accommodation of ex-Communists. He won surprisingly comfortably.

Parliamentary Elections The first parliament to be elected freely was the product of a complicated electoral law. In 1991 anywhere from 7 to 17 members in each of 37 constituencies were elected, for a total of 391 seats. Sixty-nine other deputies were elected indirectly, from the "national lists" the parties presented; seats were apportioned according to the share of the vote parties obtained in the constituencies (Table 10.4).

The effect of the electoral law was to provide just about any party gaining votes with Sejm representation. The institutional designers of the new system wanted to make sure that no political force went unrepresented and that each could expect greater gains from participating in the electoral process than from carrying on political activity outside of it. At this time groups had more to lose from opting out of the electoral process than from staying in. If they faired poorly in one election, they could always hope to do better the next time.

The 1991 elections were contested by parties having many different programs (the most frivolous was the Beer Lovers' Party). When President Wałęsa dissolved this unmanageable legislature in 1993, 29 parties were represented in the Sejm. Not surprisingly, the electoral law passed in 1993 sought to limit party fragmentation: 391 seats were contested in multimember constituencies, and 69 others were distributed to individual parties receiving at least 5 percent of the national vote. Parties that formed electoral alliances had to clear an 8 percent threshold. The law produced the desired effect. Only one electoral alliance, the SLD, surpassed the 8 percent threshold, and just five individual parties crossed the 5 percent threshold.

Parliamentary Election Results

TABLE 10.4

Most leaders have been in politics since the democratic breakthrough, but the parties they head are relatively new

Party	1991	1993	1997	2001	2005	2007
Alliance of the Democratic Left (SLD)[a]	12.0%	20.6%	27.1%	41.0%	11.3%	13.2%
Polish Peasant Party (PSL)	8.7	15.3	7.3	9.0	7.0	8.9
Freedom Union (UW)[b]	12.3	10.7	13.4	3.1	—	—
Civic Platform (PO)	—	—	—	12.7	24.1	41.5
Self-Defense (SO)	—	2.8	—	10.2	11.4	1.5
Law and Justice (PiS)	—	—	—	9.5	27.0	32.1
League of Polish Families (LPR)	—	—	—	7.9	8.0	1.3
Union of Labor (UP)[a]	—	7.2	4.7	—	3.9	—
Confederation for an Independent Poland (KPN)	7.5	5.6	—	—	—	—
Solidarity Electoral Action (AWS)[c]	5.1	4.6	33.8	5.6	—	—
Center Accord (PC)	8.7	4.5	—	—	—	—
Liberal Democratic Congress (KLD)	7.5	3.8	—	—	—	—
Catholic Election Action (WAK)	8.7	—	—	—	—	—
Other parties and Independents	29.5	24.9	13.7	0.4	7.0	1.3

[a]In 2001 and 2007, the SLD and UP ran as one party under a different name.
[b]In 1991 and 1993, the UW ran as the Democratic Union (UD).
[c]In 1991 and 1993, the AWS electoral alliance ran as the Solidarity Party.
— signifies the party did not exist or did not run

Sources: Główny Urząd Statystyczny, *Mały Rocznik Statystyczny Polski 2008* (Warsaw: GUS, 2008).

Were it not for personal rivalries and internal disputes within the Solidarity camp, which led to a split in the popular vote, the election result would not have proved to be a stunning victory for the ex-Communists. Moreover, economic shock therapy had created a political backlash, and the SLD got much mileage from its slogan: "It doesn't have to be like this."

Four years later the SLD became victim of an anti-incumbent backlash. Its slogan of "A good today, a better tomorrow," rebounded against it. Although the breakdown in voting between left and right was not much different than in 1993, the center-right ran as a relatively united electoral coalition under the AWS banner. Within AWS the largest bloc of seats (52) went to representatives of the Solidarity trade union, followed closely by Catholic groups (45). Paradoxically, AWS chose an Evangelical Lutheran, Buzek, as prime minister. Its coalition partner was the underachieving, but ambitious Freedom Union, which had won 60 seats. Since the UW held the balance of power in parliament, had both a prestigious past and leaders with name recognition, and was popular with Western politicians, it was able to obtain influential ministerial posts in the AWS-led government. For example, Balcerowicz returned to his posts of deputy prime minister and finance minister, his party colleague Geremek became foreign minister, and Poland's first female prime minister, Hanna Suchocka, was appointed justice minister.

The center-right fragmented again before the 2001 parliamentary election. By contrast, the SLD teamed up with a small leftist party to earn 41 percent of the vote and close to a majority of Sejm seats. Indeed, the SLD's share of the vote increased for the third election in a row. An unsettling development in 2001 was the rise of radical nationalist parties like Self-Defense and the League of Polish Families, which together gained close to 100 seats. A more reassuring development was that two new conservative parties, which offered moderate programs at that time, Civic Platform and Law and Justice, won slightly over 100 seats.

By 2005 the SLD government had shot itself in the foot. A turnover of party leaders; financial scandals; high unemployment; cuts in health, education, and welfare programs; and an antisecularist backlash led to its defeat. Together, Law and Justice and Civic

Platform received over half of all votes cast and were separated from each other by only a few percentage points. This election was distinctive for the main parties' use of American-style campaigns, including professional campaign managers, television ads, televised candidate debates, and billboard advertising.

The 2007 rematch between Law and Justice and Civic Platform generated the highest voter turnout since 1989. The Kaczyńskis had polarized society and had damaged Poland's international reputation by some of their faux pas, whether involving clumsiness in dealings with German Chancellor Angela Merkel or the dramatic increase in the visibility of Catholicism in domestic politics. Despite ideological affinities, Law and Justice launched relentless attacks on Civic Platform. It called for a clean break with the Third Republic, which it alleged had fallen under the control of ex-Communists, corrupt officials, and extortionists. For its part Civic Platform emphasized that Poles should once again feel good about their country. Tusk's party beat out Law and Justice by 43 seats and went on to form a government coalition with the PSL. It was in large measure a victory of the young urban electorate over the older rural Catholic electorate (Table 10.5).

Party Support in 2007 Sejm Elections

TABLE 10.5

Better-educated urbanites with higher-paid jobs helped usher the centrist Civic Platform into power

	Civic Platform (%)	Law and Justice (%)	Alliance of the Democratic Left (%)	Polish Peasant Party (%)
Age				
18–24	56	22	11	6
25–39	52	24	12	8
40–59	40	33	13	10
60 and older	30	40	17	8
Sex				
Women	46	30	13	8
Men	42	31	14	9
Residence				
Large cities (over 500,000)	56	25	14	3
Smaller cities (200,001–500,000)	52	26	15	4
Towns (51,000–200,000)	49	27	16	5
Rural areas	30	38	10	16
Education				
Primary	27	43	10	12
Vocational	31	39	12	11
Secondary	45	29	14	8
Higher	56	21	14	6
Occupation				
Manager	57	21	13	6
Entrepreneur	54	26	11	6
Farmer	12	41	7	30
Blue-collar worker	35	38	12	10
Clerical worker	48	26	15	9
Retired	32	38	18	8
Student	59	21	11	6
Unemployed	41	31	13	7

Source: Osrodek Badania Opinii Publicznej (TNS OBOP), Exit Poll, October 21, 2007. Data provided to the author by Jacek Raciborski.

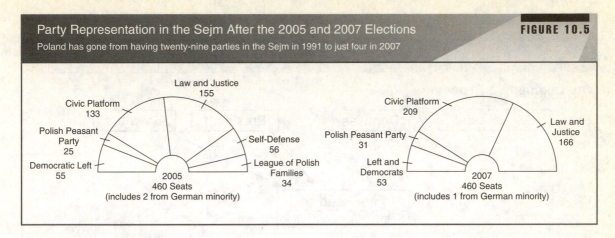

FIGURE 10.5

Party Representation in the Sejm After the 2005 and 2007 Elections

Poland has gone from having twenty-nine parties in the Sejm in 1991 to just four in 2007

2005
460 Seats
(includes 2 from German minority)

Civic Platform 133
Law and Justice 155
Polish Peasant Party 25
Self-Defense 56
Democratic Left 55
League of Polish Families 34

2007
460 Seats
(includes 1 from German minority)

Civic Platform 209
Law and Justice 166
Polish Peasant Party 31
Left and Democrats 53

Above all, for most of the two-thirds of Poles who voted for a party other than Law and Justice, the 2007 election put an end to an embarrassing two-year period when Poland had seemed to be the laughingstock of Europe.

European Parliament Elections In June 2004 Poland held elections for fifty-four seats in the European Parliament. All the major political parties contested this first European election since Poland joined the EU, but the turnout was a disappointing 21 percent. The result confirmed Civic Platform as the most important political force in the country: It garnered 24 percent of the vote and won fifteen seats. The nationalist Euroskeptic League of Polish Families came next with 15 percent and ten seats, and the other anti-EU party, Self-Defense, did worse than expected with an 11 percent voting share and six seats. Law and Justice placed just ahead of Self-Defense with 13 percent and seven seats. The election proved a disaster for the ruling SLD: It obtained 9 percent of the vote and only five seats. Three other parties (the Freedom Union and Polish Peasant Party with four seats each and Social Democracy with three seats) combined for 18 percent of the vote.

The results of elections to the European Parliament occasionally reflect a voter backlash against an incumbent government. That was the case in 2004. But the June 2009 European Parliament elections seemed to consolidate the gains that Civic Platform had registered over the Law and Justice in national elections two years earlier, hinting at greater party alignment and electoral stability.

THE POLICYMAKING PROCESS

In a democratic system, we can identify four distinct phases in the policymaking process: policy initiation, the legislative process, policy implementation, and judicial review. In the first phase, civic organizations and specialized interest groups generally play a central role. Political parties also serve as aggregators of interests that help shape policy formulation. The second phase, the legislative process, is where ideas about policy are turned into specific parliamentary bills, to be debated and voted upon (Figure 10.6). One study broke down the initiators of bills submitted to the Sejm between 1997 and 1999: 46 percent were sponsored by individual deputies, 43 percent were presented by the government, and the rest were initiated by senators, the president, and civic initiative.[52]

Bills with the highest probability of being enacted are those proposed by the government. Thus, approximately two-thirds of government-sponsored bills between 1997 and 2001 became law, compared to about 40 percent for both deputy- and president- sponsored bills. This is because all members of the ruling coalition that commands a majority of seats in the Sejm (the exception is a minority government, which, by definition, does not command a majority) are expected to vote for coalition-initiated bills. Successful bills go through three readings in the legislature, though the first reading can be held in a Sejm committee if the bill is not concerned with the constitution, budget, state institutions, and civil rights. The fullest and most partisan debates take place during the second plenary reading when party discipline is crucial in determining a bill's

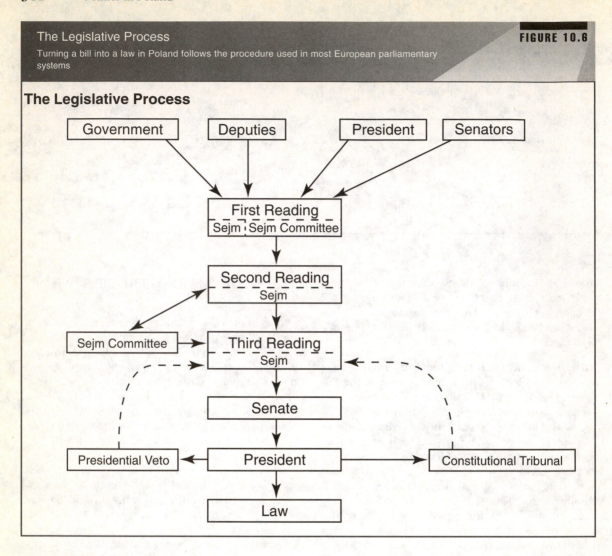

FIGURE 10.6

The Legislative Process

Turning a bill into a law in Poland follows the procedure used in most European parliamentary systems

The Legislative Process

fate. In general, Polish parties are not as disciplined as those in Britain (with its system of three-line whips requiring Members of Parliament to vote as party leaders require) or as lax as those in the United States (where crossover voting is a regular feature).

After a bill has received a second reading, the third reading is usually a formality, though technical considerations may require that a committee carry out revisions. In general, only about half of all bills introduced in the Sejm successfully make it through the third reading.[53]

After leaving the Sejm, a bill must be considered by the Senate within fourteen days. Any Senate objections can be overruled by an absolute majority in the Sejm, so cases of Senate blockage are now rare. The president's signature is the final stage in a bill becoming law. The president has the right to veto a whole bill (not just one part of it), but a 60 percent Sejm majority may override the veto. Kwaśniewski vetoed six laws passed by the AWS government, and only one veto was overridden (significantly, this was his veto of the law establishing an Institute of National Remembrance). Instead of vetoing a bill, the president can refer it to the Constitutional Tribunal to test its constitutionality. Kwaśniewski did this to four AWS government bills, two of which were deemed constitutional and two of which were ruled unconstitutional.

The legislative process offers interest groups three key occasions to influence policy: (1) when the government is drafting a bill for introduction in the Sejm; (2) between the first and second readings, when a Sejm committee is reviewing the bill; and (3) before the president signs it into law. In the first case, lobbying is directed at the party of government, as well as at the various advisory bodies connected to the cabinet (especially the Economic Committee of the Council of Ministers). In the second case, interest groups lobby Sejm committee chairs, parliamentary caucus leaders, and backbench deputies. In the third case, the president's Chancellory is likely to be the target of intense lobbying. This is not to suggest that Polish interest groups have professionalized their lobbying techniques on the scale of their U.S. counterparts. As the policy cases we consider next indicate, ad hoc groups have often been involved in the policymaking process.

A third phase is carrying out policy. This is the role of the state and local bureaucracies, with the Council of Ministers and individual ministers overseeing the process. Civil servants have generally had to be accountable to political leaders for administering policy, but some of them have been political appointees of the government in power. Both the SLD and Law and Justice were particularly guilty of appointing their people to high positions in the civil service.

The fourth phase occurs when policy comes under judicial review—for example, for infringing upon an individual's constitutional rights. This is the function of Poland's judicial system and in some cases, where the appellant wants to go further, the European Court of Human Rights (ECHR). In 2007 Polish citizens brought over 5,000 cases to the ECHR.

The state occasionally serves as a mediating actor and facilitator in the policy process. One example in Poland involves the process that resulted in the 1992 Pact on State Enterprises. Initiated by Labor Minister Kuron and hammered out by trade unions, business groups, and ministry officials, it was designed to bring labor peace to the country. The pact gave rise to the Polish Tripartite Commission for Social and Economic Issues, whose task was to draft legislation following consultations and negotiations among representatives from business and labor organizations, as well as from the state. The process of **tripartism**, as it became known, faced the problem of how to distribute influence among the participants. By the mid-1990s the trade union movement was so decentralized that labor's representatives to tripartite negotiations came from several different organizations—Solidarity, the OPZZ, and smaller unions. The business side was also not fully represented on the Tripartite Commission: the Confederation of Polish Employers (KPP) was the main business group included, but it did not represent the rapidly expanding private sector that employed nonunionized workers. Despite such initial shortcomings, the Tripartite Commission played an influential role in shaping policies on the restructuring of the mining industry, health care and pension reforms, employment, and indexation of salaries to inflation rates. In 2001 a new act on the Tripartite Commission was passed. For a trade union or business group to gain representation, the act specified that it had to have 300,000 employees. The body's representative nature was enhanced, and the partners involved in social dialogue were formalized.

There are a dozen or so unions representing various groups in the agricultural sector. The most important are those affiliated with Rural Solidarity and Self-Defense. Agricultural unions do not have the equivalent of a tripartite commission in which to negotiate, and this has led to much direct action. The Ministry of Agriculture in Warsaw was a regular target of farmer protests; those organized by Self-Defense sometimes resulted in violent skirmishes. "Bargaining" in the agrarian sector is not unlike that in France, then. In 2002 the Polish government negotiated a favorable deal for farmers in its accession terms with the EU (see subsequent discussion), and protests have become less common.

POLICY OUTCOMES

Three major policy issues dominated Polish politics after 1989: (1) establishing a free market economy, (2) framing a national security policy, and (3) integrating into EU structures. Only the second, determining a security framework, still has loose ends; the other two, a market economy with a shrinking public sector and harmonization of Poland's institutions and laws with those of the EU, have all but been completed. We also need to consider a fourth policy outcome that has blemished the country's transition record—corruption.

Free Market Reform

Economic reform began in Poland while the Communist Party was still in power. In 1987 Poland joined the World Bank and took the first steps toward economic decentralization and price liberalization. In a referendum that year, two-thirds of voters expressed support for rapid economic change. In 1988 parliament adopted a law promoting private enterprise, and in the first half of 1989, as roundtable talks were being held, 1,300 private ventures were registered, many set up by members of the Communist Party establishment.

The Solidarity-based governments from 1989 to 1993 accelerated this economic transformation. Policies implemented included restricting the money supply; controlling hyperinflation, while freeing the prices of nearly all products from state controls; limiting the budget deficit (5% of GDP was the target); promoting currency convertibility (helped by the creation by Western institutions of a złoty stabilization fund); and developing incentives for private enterprise.

Poland's economic policy was shaped by the International Monetary Fund (IMF) and overseen by Balcerowicz, appointed minister of finance and head of economic reform in 1989. At the beginning of 1990, he introduced a crash stabilization package—popularly termed shock therapy or the big bang approach. Its main features were a balanced government budget; strict fiscal, monetary, and income policies; and convertibility of the złoty. IMF aid was contingent on keeping close to the 5 percent target.

The Balcerowicz plan also entailed structural adjustment of the economy that was highlighted by far-reaching privatization. Privatization laws in 1990 converted 40 percent of state-owned firms into public corporations and created additional opportunities for setting up brand new private firms. One Polish economist concluded that privatization of state-owned juggernauts was poorly conceived, but fortunately was not critical to successful economic transformation. The country's remarkable economic growth was spurred mostly by "creating conditions for virtually unrestricted entry of private firms into all sectors of the economy and fields of activity."[54]

Jeffrey Sachs, a Harvard-based advisor to the Polish government, had recommended the big bang approach to economic reform. He recognized the quandary of such an approach: "Why should something 'so good' feel 'so bad.'"[55] Sachs was one of the first to draw the comparison between Poland's and Spain's economic development after 1950. Both countries had similar economic conditions then: comparable population sizes, large agricultural sectors, peripheral European locations lagging behind in modernization, and Catholicism. "Spain shot ahead of Poland in the next thirty-five years. Spain started to catch up with the rest of Western Europe, while Poland fell farther behind."[56] Economic integration with Europe was the major factor ensuring Spain's success.

On the other hand, a critic of the Balcerowicz plan questioned the assumptions and process of shock therapy. "The architects of reform were persuaded that their blueprint was sound—no, more: the only one possible."[57] Reform was unresponsive to public preferences: "Radical reform was a project initiated from above and launched by surprise, independently of public opinion and without the participation of organized political forces," and accordingly "had the effect of weakening democratic institutions."[58] A case in point was the passage of the Balcerowicz plan. The Sejm was "given sixteen pieces of legislation and told that it must approve the nine most important before the end of the month to meet the IMF conditions."[59]

The process of reform might have been contentious, but the success of the reforms—at least until the onset of the global financial crisis in 2008—was undeniable. According to the World Bank, annual GDP growth from 1993 to 2007 averaged over 5 percent. Poland was the first country in Central Europe to have its GDP surpass its 1989 level. Even though privatization of state-owned industrial enterprises proved laborious, the country quickly became the most privatized economy in the region. By 2007 three-quarters of employed people were working in the private sector. A buoyant stock market and robust consumer demand were other immediate products of the successful transition to a market economy. By the end of the 1990s, Poland had attracted more foreign direct investment than any country in the region. The structure of the economy was increasingly modern and postindustrial: By the end of 2007, the service sector accounted for two-thirds of GDP and employed about 60 percent of the workforce. Compared to the sluggish modernization of the average Polish household under communism (see indicators in Table 10.1), more and more Poles are living a materialist Western lifestyle. At the end of 2007, 99 percent of them had televisions and refrigerators at home, nearly 80 percent had cell phones, 53 percent had cars, 50 percent had personal computers, and 37 percent had personal computers with Internet access.

We know that capitalism produces losers, as well as winners. Unemployment remained stubbornly high, hovering near 20 percent of the labor force, when Poland joined the EU in 2004. Double-digit inflation was at first not contained, thereby adversely affecting the millions in Poland (pensioners, persons with disabilities, students) on fixed incomes. But over time EU membership produced economic improvements that no Polish government had been able to effect. By 2007 unemployment had been reduced to 10 percent, while consumer price increases were limited to about 4 percent. The exchange rate had seen the zloty strengthen in relation to U.S. currency, going from around 4.5 to about 3 to the dollar in 2009. While 17 percent of Poles continued to live below the poverty line, an average annual growth rate in Polish GDP of around 5 percent—even in 2008—spread wealth around, if not evenly.

The world financial crisis that began in 2008 seemed to affect Poland less drastically than other EU countries. In March 2009 the World Bank forecast a positive GDP growth rate of 0.5% for Poland in 2009 while other countries' GDPs were contracting.[60] To be sure, unemployment was rising, the government breached the Maastricht Treaty's 3 percent threshold for a budget deficit as it tried to stimulate growth through spending, and the złoty declined against the euro, putting off to 2013 or later Poland's entry into the eurozone.[61] Polish financial markets were hit hard, and vulnerable Western banks that dominated the country's banking sector added to the sense of crisis. Having survived the shock therapy of the early 1990s may, paradoxically, have prepared Poles to ride out the current economic turmoil in a sanguine way.

Security Policy

The idea of *antemurale christianitatis* has strong contemporary resonance in security matters. Since the democratic breakthrough, Polish politicians have debated the most effective way to achieve long-term national security. Throughout the 1990s the consensus was that Poland should press for swift integration into European security structures. The continued fear of a Russian return to imperial behavior—seemingly confirmed with Vladimir Putin becoming its president in 2000—convinced many leaders that Poland's role should, once again, be that of a rampart defending Western civilization against the East. Many foreign policy planners believed that this role could be effectively played within NATO, which Poland joined in 1998, as well as by a close bilateral security arrangement with the United States.

Significant changes having an impact on Poland's security occurred immediately after the collapse of the Soviet Union. The number of neighbors increased from three (the Soviet Union, Czechoslovakia, and

East Germany) to seven (Russia, Lithuania, Belarus, Ukraine, Slovakia, Czech Republic, and Germany). On the east, Poland's borders are with states (Belarus and Ukraine) suffering from varying degrees of political and economic instability. On the north, Poland's frontier with Russia—the Kaliningrad region—is a source of concern because it is separated from the rest of the Russian Federation and Moscow demands unimpeded land access to it. The issue has become more complex since Poland joined the EU because Brussels requires external borders with non-EU-member-states be made very secure.

In many ways NATO membership was of little help in dealing with the type of security threats that arose after September 11, 2001 The calculus of those who developed Poland's foreign policy was to lend support to the world superpower, rather than backing the major EU states that opposed the U.S. invasion of Iraq. For this policy decision, Poland was given the cold shoulder by French and German leaders. One German newspaper dubbed the country the "Trojan ass" of Europe. Poland's Iraq gamble did not pay off, whether measured in terms of achieving its military objectives, receiving profitable contracts for Polish companies to rebuild Iraq, showing Europe that Poland was now an important international player, or bolstering Poles' pro-Americanism (Box 10.3).

Despite these failures, in 2008 Poland strengthened security ties with the United States by signing a controversial missile shield treaty. Under the treaty the United States would base ten missile interceptors in Poland—officially aimed at preventing an air attack of a rogue Middle East state, but viewed by Russia as a threat to itself—in return for a battery of American air-defense Patriot missiles staffed by a U.S. army battalion stationed in Poland. The Kremlin forcefully condemned the treaty; as significantly, a number of EU states became convinced that Poland's security dependence on the United States was a mistake that weakened European unity and raised tensions with Russia.

Regardless of which party is in power, Poland has preferred to obtain security guarantees from the United States, rather than from Europe. It is highly skeptical of the effectiveness of the EU's nascent Common Foreign and Security Policy. Poland's enthusiastic support for NATO membership for Ukraine and Georgia puts it at odds with three of the EU's most powerful members—France, Germany, and Italy. Russia responded to what it viewed as Poland's initiatives to encircle it with unfriendly regimes and destabilizing

BOX 10.3

Are Poles Becoming Anti-American?

Polls of Poles have repeatedly shown how pro-American this Central European nation is. Even as anti-American sentiments spread across the world following the 2003 U.S. invasion of Iraq, Poland seemed to be immune to the malaise.

Western visitors here have often been surprised by Poland's avid pro-Americanism. For some it's a pleasant surprise: They find none of the anti-American stereotypes common elsewhere in Europe. For others it's an unpleasant one: What about the victims of America's imperial power?

Poles managed to find something deeply admirable in all American presidents: They appreciated Carter for his human rights agenda, Reagan for his gut anti-communism, Bush Senior for overseeing the end of the Cold War and Clinton for his commitment to an inclusive globalization.

Until now. George W. Bush has managed to do what 45 years of Communist rule could not: puncture the image of essential American goodness that has always been the United States' key selling point. Poles are now asking whether it pays to be America's friend.

The Iraq war has been the turning point. Poland was one of America's most zealous supporters, the leader of what Defense Secretary Rumsfeld dubbed the "new Europe." Unlike the situation in other supportive European countries, all major political parties supported the war. People elsewhere argued over whether Iraq really had weapons of mass destruction, but in Poland the calculus was more simple: America requested our help, so we gave it.

Then came the torture at Abu Ghraib, showing irrefutable images of an America not to their liking. Bit by bit, the evidence grew that this was not the war the liberals had signed up for. Moreover, America seemed incapable of listening even to its allies.

This has led to an unprecedented anti-American backlash in Poland. In September 2004 President Kwasniewski, one of Bush's strongest supporters, urged the U.S. president to abandon his "neoconservative divide-and-rule policy."

Adam Michnik once quipped that "Poland is more pro-American than America is." Bush has changed that.*

*David Ost, "Letter from Poland," *The Nation,* October 4, 2004, 3.

---

missile systems by declaring it would target Poland with nuclear weapons. The salience of the security dilemma—efforts made to enhance one's own national security can lead to countermeasures by the opposing side that actually undermine that security—is clear. It appears, then, that the outcome of the country's foreign policy behavior—risky given Poland's proximity to Russia and the skepticism of much of the Polish public itself —has been to make Poland more under threat than most of its neighbors.

Europeanness

Poland joined the EU six years after the start of accession negotiations in 1998. Polish leaders had been talking of EU membership from 1989 on, but the process proved slower and more complex than the euphoria after the democratic breakthrough had suggested. It was only in 2000 that Poland submitted a detailed timetable to the EU Enlargement Commissioner for enacting 150 laws needed before accession could occur.

Poland's first years in the EU were shaped by a series of transitional arrangements. It had a five-year period to reach a financial balance between contributions it paid into the EU general budget and funds it drew out of that budget. A twelve-year moratorium (five years longer than any other candidate country negotiated) has been placed on the purchase of Polish land by EU nationals—a highly emotional subject, especially with regard to Germans whose ancestors came from territories that Poland acquired after World War II. A five-year transition period, ending in 2009, was agreed upon for the purchase of vacation homes.

With regard to labor migration, a formula was adopted involving a maximum seven-year transitional period. Polish citizens' right to work in EU countries could be restricted by those countries through 2009. To be sure, Britain, Ireland, and Sweden opened their labor markets immediately after EU enlargement. By 2009 about 300,000 Poles had migrated to Britain. Remaining EU states could keep their labor markets closed to Poles and other eastern

Europeans through 2011, after which the EU becomes a fully free labor market.

The impact of the EU's Common Agricultural Policy on Poland's farmers was at the center of accession negotiations. Under the agreement reached, the EU is phasing in direct aid for Polish farmers over ten years, starting with 25 percent of the full EU rate in 2004, 30 percent in 2005, and so on. The Polish government is required by the EU to contribute financial assistance to farmers for this period through agreed upon topping up rates.

Poland therefore has been easing itself into EU structures. In 2008 it joined the Schengen zone, which suspends all border controls between its members (it includes most EU states plus a few others like Norway and Liechtenstein). One of the biggest disagreements between Poland and the more powerful EU states was over the Lisbon treaty, which is to implement federalizing reforms, including a more visible and stable EU presidency. Poland prefers a loose association over a deeper form of integration. President Kaczyński traveled to the EU summit in Lisbon

in 2007 to sign the agreement, and the treaty was approved by the Sejm. But conservative politicians in the country were hoping that the Irish would vote a second time, in 2009, to reject the treaty in a referendum, thereby scuttling the project for good.

EU membership is accelerating Poland's acquisition of a European identity. (See Box 10.4.) A crucial aspect in this process is the adoption of what we can term the *acquis communantaire culturel,* the modal European culture that shapes political and economic practices in the EU. The question arises, then, of how Poles think they differ today from the typical European. Generally, Poles consider themselves more religious, patriotic, altruistic, and family oriented than typical Europeans (Table 10.6). They also see themselves as poorer, more dishonest, and lacking in self-confidence, education, and culture. While these images have endured, in 2008 Poles saw themselves as embodying more of the traits of "Europeans."

A Polish sociologist highlighted the problems caused by the uneven development between

---

Are Poles Warming Up to the European Union?

BOX 10.4

One of the fiercest opponents of Poland's membership in the European Union has been a radical peasant leader, Andrzej Lepper, who claimed that Polish farmers would be devastated by EU competition. In October 2004 fate played a joke on Lepper. He became one of the first 5,000 Polish farmers to receive money from the European Union, which Poland joined on May 1, 2004.

Lepper, the leader of the anti-European Samoobrona Party, received nearly $2,400 as the start of multiyear payments from the EU's generous farm subsidy plan. The joke is that this tidy sum could be Lepper's political undoing. His support has come from the countryside, where he set up Samoobrona, or Self-Defense, in 1992 to campaign against Polish entry into the EU.

As EU farm subsidies started arriving for Poland's 1.4 million farmers, Lepper's support began crumbling. His sometimes violent campaigning among farmers to stop Poland from joining the EU rapidly lost appeal. His doomsday predictions that farmers would be forgotten and left to starve were proved wrong.

The EU had never been popular in the depths of the Polish countryside, where populist politicians like Lepper often joined ranks with the local and still powerful Roman Catholic Church to oppose joining the Union. The Church, which played a big role in opposing the Communist regime, fears a democratic Poland will follow other European countries by becoming more secular. But the Church is losing influence in rural areas as young people leave for the more "secular" towns and cities in the hopes of finding jobs.

Even mainstream Polish politicians tried to use Euroskepticism to extract concessions from Brussels during difficult accession talks. As the largest of the 10 new members, Poland had made so many demands that it exasperated its negotiating partners. Yet months after joining, the mood in Poland toward the EU is improving, with opinion polls showing 75 percent supporting Europe.*

*Judy Dempsey, "Euroskepticism Fades in Polish Countryside," *International Herald Tribune,* November 2, 2004, 3.

	TABLE 10.6

Image of the "Typical Pole" and the "Typical European"

Poles' perceptions of themselves are positive, but the stereotypical European still looks better

	Typical Pole		Typical European	
	2004	**2008**	**2004**	**2008**
Lives well	15%	—	84%	—
Lives poorly	72	—	4	—
Is religious	90	—	34	—
Is not religious	5	—	43	—
Is patriotic	72	—	51	—
Is not patriotic	20	—	28	—
Work is most important	25	—	52	—
Family is most important	61	—	25	—
Helps others	51	—	35	—
Only looks after his own interests	39	—	48	—
Is sure of himself	32	44%	81	93%
Is confused	57	56	7	7
Is educated	63	59	83	81
Is uneducated	25	41	5	19
Is cultured	57	64	69	81
Lacks culture	32	36	16	19
Works hard	76	83	78	71
Works poorly	15	17	8	29
In a difficult situation works with others	64		55	
Works on his own	26	—	21	—
Is honest	47	57	56	82
Is dishonest	34	43	18	18

Note: The answer "difficult to say" is excluded from the 2004 results. Respondents who took the 2008 survey could not answer "difficult to say."
— signifies question not asked.

Sources: Centrum Badania Opinii Spolecznej (CBOS), "Typowy Polak i Europejczyk—Podobieństwa i różnice," April 2004. Retrieved October 5, 2004, from www.cbos.pl. For 2008, "Wizerunek Polaka i Europejczyka." Online survey retrieved September 20, 2008, from www.ankietka.pl/survey/results/id/4870/wizerunek-polaka-i-europejczyka.html.

institutional and cultural growth: "To be already in Europe, in a political and even an economic sense, is not yet the same as becoming a fully fledged European citizen. Joining the realm of European states and markets is not the same as entering European civil societies. Only the latter will signify a true and ultimate return to Europe."[62] The cultural divide between Western and Central Europe has been reduced, but Poland must do more to make what remains of the divide not politically salient.

Corruption

A dividing line that persists between Western and formerly Communist Europe is transparent versus corrupt practices. Just before the enlargement decision, the European Commission gave Poland a top grade for meeting its political criteria, but singled it out for persisting corruption. A 2000 World Bank report had identified corruption "at the highest levels" as Poland's most serious problem. In its 2008 report, Transparency International, the international nongovernmental organization monitoring corruption, listed Poland fifty-eighth—the lowest rank given to a Central European or Baltic state.[63] Finally, the World Economic Forum's 2008–2009 report on global competitiveness pointed to tax regulations and inefficient government bureaucracy—as well as corruption—as "the most problematic factors for doing business" in Poland.[64]

Having both a history of democracy and wealth inhibits corrupt practices. Until recently Poland had neither. Credible political institutions also help prevent corruption, and as robust as Poland's institutions may be, they are still only twenty years old. Still, how do we explain Poland's notoriety as one of the EU's most corrupt polities (to be sure, the 2007 admission of Bulgaria and Romania did draw attention away from Poland)?

A partisan explanation would place the blame on the former Communists who governed Poland for eight of twelve years, ending in 2005. Rywingate provided evidence of this, but a second major scandal, the Orlen affair in 2003, pointed to corruption at the very top. President Kwaśniewski himself was indirectly implicated—though never charged–in a bribery attempt that involved Poland's largest oil company (and seventh largest company of any kind in Eastern Europe), PKN Orlen. Kwaśniewski was to help privatize a major Polish oil refinery, which would then be sold to a Russian energy company. To make matters worse for the former Communist, the Russian company representative had purportedly worked in the KGB. The deal fell through when the scandal broke, and the electoral backlash against the SLD was dramatic. The Kaczyńskis derived extensive political dividends from their anticorruption drive, especially since the public was unwilling to tolerate such "un-European" practices. However, corruption has hardly been a monopoly of the former Communists, and some politicians in other parties have felt that it is their turn to profit from being in power.[65] Still, the argument of incumbents about corrupt practices that "they did it first" has few takers today in Polish society.

CONCLUSION

Studying the democratic process is important in a country that was a precocious exponent of the idea, but that also was a victim of authoritarian rule. Zbigniew Brzezinski cautioned that "[t]hough the notions of 'democracy' are fashionable, in much of the world the practice of democracy is still quite superficial and democratic institutions remain vulnerable."[66] To a great degree, new democratic regimes are judged by their current performance, thereby making them more vulnerable to the effects of economic or social crisis.

This chapter has described the great strides that Poland has made to consolidate its democracy. The policy process is squarely based on political institutions that provide for generally fair outcomes. As in many established democracies, problems remain with institutional arrangements. An important one in Poland concerns what Bingham Powell has suggested is the need for a majoritarian vision. For it to exist, "a single cohesive party or at least an identifiable preelection coalition must gain unblocked control of the policymaking process to offer voters the forward-looking mandate conditions and retrospective accountability conditions necessary for the majoritarian vision."[67] Governments led by the SLD, a party whose origins lie in the Communist period, came close to approximating majoritarian processes, but governments of the center and right have not. Today it is Civic Platform, a center-right party, that is best placed to meet the majoritarian test. The Polish public seems to recognize this majoritarian imperative: Support is growing for replacement of the proportional representation electoral system with a simple majority one.[68]

In economic terms history as it has been played out in Poland has vindicated Adam Smith in his emphasis on the intimate relationship between commerce and liberty. Or, as Barrington Moore put it, there can be no democracy without a bourgeoisie.[69] The steady expansion of a Polish middle class should reassure us about the prospects for democratic stability in the country. But its possible contraction as a result of a worldwide economic downturn would be a reason for concern.

REVIEW QUESTIONS

- Is decommunization of public life as urgent a policy challenge as addressing growing social and economic inequalities?

- What unique features of Polish history appear to shape its contemporary politics? What are the lasting legacies of the Communist era?

- What was unusual about the processes that led to a democratic breakthrough in Poland? Was the roundtable agreement a success precisely because its conditions were not honored?

- Identify examples of institutional experimentation after 1989. Which of these was most consequential for consolidating the political system?

- Describe the political successes and failures of the Catholic Church since 1989. What are its most important resources? Have political authorities stood up to it?

- What explains the proliferation and constant overhauling of political parties? Can we view the changing party system as a sign of strength or weakness in the Third Republic?

- What explains the inability of successive Polish governments to be reelected? To what extent are policy differences between government and opposition the reason?

- Identify the policy area that has marked Poland's great success since 1989. Why?

KEY TERMS

Alliance of the Democratic Left (SLD)

antemurale christianitatis

Balcerowicz plan

catch-all party

Committee for Workers' Self-Defense (KOR)

Concordat

constitution of 1997

Constitutional Tribunal

contract Sejm

Council of Ministers

electoral law of 1993

Glemp, Cardinal Józef

Institute of National Remembrance

Jaruzelski, General Wojciech

Kwaśniewski, Aleksander

liberum veto

martial law

May 1926 coup

Michnik, Adam

Mieszko I

nomenklatura

pacted transition

partitions

Piłsudski, Józef

Polish October

Polish United Workers' Party (PUWP)

Radio Maryja

Ribbentrop-Molotov pact

romantic insurrectionism

roundtable talks

Rywingate

Second Republic

Sejm

shock therapy

Solidarity (Solidarność)

Supreme Court

szlachta democracy

Third Republic

Tribunal of State

tripartism

Wałęsa, Lech

Wyszyński, Cardinal Stefan

Yalta agreement

LIST OF PARTY ABBREVIATIONS

AWS   Solidarity Electoral Action (Akcja Wyborcza Solidarność)

LPR   League of Polish Families (Liga Polskich Rodzin)

OPZZ   All-Poland Alliance of Trade Unions (Ogólnopolskie Porozumienie Związków Zawodowych)

PiS   Law and Justice (Prawo i Sprawiedliwość)

PO   Civic Platform (Platforma Obywatelska)

PSL   Polish Peasant Party (Polskie Stronnictwo Ludowe)

SLD   Alliance of the Democratic Left (Sojusz Lewicy Demokratycznej)

UW   Freedom Union (Unia Wolności)

SUGGESTED READINGS

Castle, Marjorie. *Triggering Communism's Collapse: Perceptions and Power in Poland's Transition*. Lanham, MD: Rowman and Littlefield, 2003.

Castle, Marjorie, and Ray Taras. *Democracy in Poland*. Boulder, CO: Westview Press, 2002.

Davies, Norman. *God's Playground: A History of Poland*, vols. 1–2. New York: Columbia University Press, 2004.

Dunn, Elizabeth C., Bruce Grant, and Nancy Ries, eds. *Privatizing Poland: Baby Food, Big Business, and the Remaking of Labor*. Ithaca, NY: Cornell University Press, 2004.

Ekiert, Grzegorz, and Jan Kubik. *Rebellious Civil Society: Popular Protest and Democratic Control in Poland, 1989–1993*. Ann Arbor: University of Michigan Press, 1999.

Kemp-Welch, Anthony. *Poland Under Communism: A Cold War History*. Cambridge, England: Cambridge University Press, 2008.

Longhurst, Derry. *The New Atlanticist: Poland's Foreign and Security Priorities*. Oxford, England: Blackwell, 2005.

Michnik, Adam. *Letters from Freedom: Post–Cold War Realities and Perspectives*. Berkeley: University of California Press, 1998.

Millard, Frances. *Polish Politics and Society*. London: Routledge, 1999.

Prazmowska, Anita J. *A History of Poland*. Harmondsworth, Middlesex, England: Palgrave Macmillan, 2004.

Sachs, Jeffrey. *Poland's Jump to the Market Economy*. Cambridge, MA: MIT Press, 1994.

Sanford, George. *Democratic Government in Poland*. Harmondsworth, Middlesex, England: Palgrave Macmillan, 2004.

Simon, Jeffrey. *Poland and NATO: A Study in Civil-Military Relations*. Lanham, MD: Rowman and Littlefield, 2003.

INTERNET RESOURCES

Introductory guide to Poland: poland.gov.pl

General information for visitors, businesspeople, and people of Polish origin: polandonline.com

Online Polish-language free encyclopedia: **pl.wikipedia.org/wiki**

Current political and economic news: poland.pl

Current statistical data: **www.stat.gov.pl/english/index.htm**

The Polish edition of the weekly *Newsweek:* **www.newsweek.pl**

An English-language daily news site: **www.warsawvoice.pl**

ENDNOTES

1. On the role of history in creating unique social characteristics in Poland, see Adam Podgorecki, *Polish Society* (New York: Praeger, 1994), ch. 4.

2. This is the title of a history of Poland: Norman Davies, *Heart of Europe: A Short History of Poland* (New York: Oxford University Press, 1984).

3. Earl Vinecour, *Polish Jews: The Final Chapter* (New York: New York University Press, 1977), 1.

4. Jerzy Lukowski, *Liberty's Folly: The Polish-Lithuanian Commonwealth in the Eighteenth Century, 1697–1795* (London: Routledge, 1991), 25.

5. The romanticism versus pragmatism dichotomy is described by Adam Bromke, *Poland's Politics: Idealism vs. Realism* (Cambridge: Harvard University Press, 1967).

6. Adam B. Seligman, *The Idea of Civil Society* (New York: Free Press, 1992), 8.

7. Data reported in Irving Kaplan, "The Society and Its Environment," in *Poland: A Country Study,* ed. Harold D. Nelson (Washington, DC: U.S. Government Printing Office, 1984), 107.

8. Glówny Urzqd Statystyczny, *Rocznik Statystyczny 1991* (Warsaw: GUS, 1991), 24–26, 26–38.

9. See John Clark and Aaron Wildavsky, *The Moral Collapse of Communism: Poland as a Cautionary Tale* (San Francisco: Institute for Contemporary Studies Press, 1990).

10. This is my translation.

11. *Zycie Warszawy,* August 27–28, 1988.

12. Jadwiga Staniszkis, *The Dynamics of the Breakthrough in Eastern Europe: The Polish Experience* (Berkeley: University of California Press, 1991), 199.

13. Freedom House, *Freedom in the World 2007: The Annual Survey of Political Rights and Civil Liberties* (Washington, DC: Freedom House, 2007).

14. Douglass C. North, *Institutions, Institutional Change, and Economic Performance* (Cambridge, England: Cambridge University Press, 1992), 81.

15. Frances Millard, *Polish Politics and Society* (London: Routledge, 1999), 177.

16. Ronald Inglehart, Miguel Basanez, and Alejandro Moreno, *Human Values and Beliefs: A Cross Cultural Sourcebook* (Ann Arbor: University of Michigan Press, 1997), tab. V320. See also Ronald Inglehart, *Modernization and Postmodernization: Cultural, Economic, and Political Change in 43 Societies* (Princeton, NJ: Princeton University Press, 1997).

17. Inglehart, Basanez, and Moreno, *Human Values and Beliefs,* tab. V322. Ahead of Poland were Ireland, the United States, and India.

18. Inglehart, Basanez, and Moreno, *Human Values and Beliefs,* tab. V340. With an 82 percent rate of trust in their own nationality, Poles were approximately 15 percent below the mean, but still 27 percent ahead of the most trustless nationality, the Russians, at 55 percent.

19. Centrum Badania Opinii Spolecznej (CBOS), Fall 1994.

20. Centrum Badania Opinii Spolecznej (CBOS), "Spoleczna percepcja konserwatyzmu i liberalizmu," August 2007. Retrieved January 22, 2008, from www.cbos.pl. About 40 percent of respondents said they had an indifferent opinion of both conservatism and liberalism.

21. For a discussion of the congruence between a country's history of authoritarianism and communist totalitarianism, see Stephen White, John Gardner, and George Schopflin, *Communist Political Systems: An Introduction* (New York: St. Martin's, 1987), ch. 2.

22. See Janina Frentzel-Zagorska, "Civil Society in Poland and Hungary," *Soviet Studies* 42, no. 4 (October 1990): 759–777.

23. Centrum Badania Opinii Spolecznej (CBOS), "Demokracja—oceny, postawy, perspektywy," July 2008. Retrieved November 6, 2008, from www.cbos.pl.

24. Centrum Badania Opinii Spolecznej (CBOS), "Poczucie wplywu na sprawy publiczne," June 2004. Retrieved October 30, 2004, from www.cbos.pl.

25. Centrum Badania Opinii Spolecznej (CBOS), "Demokracja—oceny, postawy, perspektywy," July 2008. Retrieved October 11, 2008, from www.cbos.pl.

26. Reported in *Business Central Europe,* December 1999/January 2000, 59.

27. Centrum Badania Opinii Spolecznej (CBOS), "Polacy o zmianach po 1989 roku," June 2004. Retrieved October 11, 2004, from www.cbos.pl.

28. Centrum Badania Opinii Spolecznej (CBOS), "Zaufanie społeczne w latach 2002–2008," February 2008. Retrieved April 11, 2008, from www.cbos.pl.

29. Inglehart, Basanez, and Moreno, *Human Values and Beliefs,* 27.

30. Inglehart, Basanez, and Moreno, *Human Values and Beliefs,* 30–31.

31. George Kolankiewicz and Ray Taras, "Poland: Socialism for Everyman?" in *Political Culture and Political Change in Communist States,* ed. Archie Brown and Jack Gray (New York: Holmes and Meier, 1979), 101–130.

32. Inglehart, Basanez, and Moreno, *Human Values and Beliefs,* 19. See Table V405 for country rankings.

33. Ireneusz Bialecki and Bogdan W. Mach, "Orientacje społeczno-ekonomiczne posłów na tle pogladów społeczeństwa," in *Poczatek parlamentarnej elity: poslowie kontraktowego Sejmu,* ed. Jacek Wasilewski and Wlodzimierz Wesolowski (Warsaw: IFIS PAN, 1992), 129–131.

34. Mary E. McIntosh and Martha Abele MacIver, "Coping with Freedom and Uncertainty: Public Opinion in Hungary, Poland, and Czechoslovakia 1989–1992," *International Journal of Public Opinion Research* 4, no. 4 (Winter 1992): 381–385.

35. Centrum Badania Opinii Spolecznej (CBOS), "Freedom and Equality in Social Life," February 2000. Retrieved June 25, 2000, from www.cbos.pl.

36. Jan Winiecki, "The Reasons for Electoral Defeat Lie in Non-Economic Factors," in *Five Years After June: The Polish Transformation, 1989–1994,* ed. Jan Winiecki (London: Centre for Research into Communist Economies, 1996), 87.

37. Richard Bernstein, "Culture War Seen in Polish Broadcasting Case," *International Herald Tribune,* May 4, 2006.

38. World Congress of Families IV, Planning Meeting, October 23–25, 2005, Rockford, IL. Cited in "Poland Digs In Against Tide Toward Secularism," *Chicago Tribune,* June 5, 2006.

39. For a detailed study, see Marilyn Rueschmeyer, ed., *Women in the Politics of Post-Communist Eastern Europe* (Armonk, NY: M. E. Sharpe, 1994).

40. Reporters Without Borders, "Press Freedom Index" 2008–2009. Retrieved April 23, 2009, from http://www.rsf.org/article.php3?id_article=29031.

41. Sharon Wolchik, "The Repluralization of Politics in Czechoslovakia," *Communist and Post-Communist Studies* 26, no. 4 (December 1993): 412–431.

42. Grzegorz Ekiert and Jan Kubik, *Rebellious Civil Society: Popular Protests and Democratic Consolidation in Poland, 1989–1993* (Ann Arbor: University of Michigan Press, 1999).

43. Piotr Glinski, "Environmentalism Among Polish Youth: A Maturing Social Movement," *Communist and Post-Communist Studies* 27, no. 2 (June 1994): 156–158. See also Barbara Hicks, *Environmental Politics: A Social Movement Between Regime and Politics* (New York: Columbia University Press, 1996).

44. Millard, *Polish Politics and Society,* p. 121.

45. Survey data and Kwaśniewski's statement are from Tom Hundley, "Catholic Church Losing Clout in Poland," *Chicago Tribune,* November 13, 1994.

46. Centrum Badania Opinii Spolecznej (CBOS), "Zaufanie społeczne w latach 2002–2008," February 2008. Retrieved April 11, 2008, from www.cbos.pl.

47. Stanislaw Podemski, "Zadowoleni i niespokojni," *Polityka* 32 (August 7, 1993): 1.

48. Andrew A. Michta, "Civil-Military Relations in Poland After 1989: The Outer Limits of Change," *Problems of Post-Communism* 44, no. 2 (March–April 1997): 64.

49. For example, see Ray Taras, "Poland's Diplomatic Misadventure in Iraq," *Problems of Post-Communism* 51, no. 1 (January–February 2004), 3–17.

50. Włodzimierz Wesołowski, "Transformacja charakteru i struktury interesów: aktualne procesy, szanse i zagrożenia," in *Spoleczenstwo w transformacji: ekspertyzy i studia,* ed. Andrzej Rychard and Michal Federowicz (Warsaw: IFIS PAN, 1993), 138.

51. Wesołowski, "Transformacja charakteru i struktury interesu," 133.

52. Dariusz Chrzanowski, Piotr Radziewicz, and Wojciech Odraważ-Sypniewski, *Analiza projektów ustaw wniesionych do Sejmu III kadencji* (Warsaw: Sejm Chancellery, 2000), 3.

53. Sejm RP, *Informacja o dzialalnosci Sejmu II i III kadencji.* Retrieved February 4, 2004, from www.sejm.gov.pl.

54. Jan Winiecki, "The Sources of Economic Success: Eliminating Barriers to Human Entrepreneurship—A Hayekian Lesson in Spontaneous Development," in Winiecki, *Five Years After June,* 41.

55. Jeffrey Sachs, "Western Financial Assistance and Russia's Reforms," in *Making Markets: Economic Transformation in Eastern Europe and the Post-Soviet States,* ed. Shafiqul Islam and Michael Mandelbaum (New York: Council on Foreign Relations Press, 1993), 146.

56. Jeffrey Sachs, *Poland's Jump to the Market Economy* (Cambridge, MA: MIT Press, 1994), 25.

57. Adam Przeworski, "Economic Reforms, Public Opinion, and Political Institutions: Poland in the Eastern European Perspective," in *Economic Reforms in New Democracies: A Social-Democratic Approach,* ed. Luis Carlos Bresser Pereira, Jose Maria Maravall, and Adam Przeworski (Cambridge, England: Cambridge University Press, 1993), 183.

58. Przeworski, "Economic Reforms, Public Opinion, and Political Institutions," 180.

59. Przeworski, "Economic Reforms, Public Opinion, and Political Institutions," 176.

60. World Bank, "Global Economic Prospects 2009," March 31', 2009. Retrieved April 23, 2009, from http://www.worldbank.org/.

61. "Economic Data: Poland," *Economist Intelligence Unit*, March 14, 2009. Retrieved April 22, 2009, from http://www.economist.com/countries/poland/index.cfm.

62. Piotr Sztompka, "The Intangibles and Imponderables of the Transition to Democracy," *Studies in Comparative Communism* 24, no. 3 (September 1991): 311.

63. Transparency International, "2008 Corruption Percerptions Index." Retrieved April 16, 2009, from http:// www.transparency.org/policy_research/surveys_indices/ cpi/2008.

64. World Economic Forum, "The Global Competitiveness Report 2008-2009" (Retrieved April 23, 2009, from http://www.weforum.org/documents/gcr0809/index.html.

65. The slogan attributed to the 1997–2001 Solidarity government was "TKM" (*teraz kurwa my*)—an acronym for the loosely translated "F—, it's our turn now!"

When Solidarity left government in 2001, 70 percent of Poles claimed it had received kickbacks, compared to 55 percent who said that about SLD when it left government in 1997.

66. Zbigniew Brzezinski, *Out of Control: Global Turmoil on the Eve of the 21st Century* (New York: Collier Books, 1993), 216.

67. G. Bingham Powell, Jr., *Elections as Instruments of Democracy: Majoritarian and Proportional Visions* (New Haven, CT: Yale University Press, 2000), 234.

68. A September 2004 public opinion survey report found 43 percent of respondents in favor of a simple majority single-constituency system, 16 percent in favor of proportional representation, and 28 percent indifferent (13 percent answered don't know). Centrum Badania Opinii Społecznej (CBOS), "Wybory wiekszościowe czy proporcjonalne?" September 2004. Retrieved January 10, 2005, from www.cbos.pl.

69. Barrington Moore, *Social Origins of Dictatorship and Democracy* (Boston: Beacon Press, 1966), ch. 7.

POLITICS IN BULGARIA

Tatiana P. Kostadinova

Country Bio

BULGARIA

Population
7.3 million

Territory
42,683 square miles

Year of Independence
1908

Year of Current Constitution
1991

Head of State
President Georgi Parvanov

Head of Government
Prime Minister Sergei Stanishev

Language
Bulgarian, Turkish 9.6%, Roma 4.1%

Religion
Bulgarian Orthodox 82.6%, Muslim 12.2%, unaffiliated or other 5.2%

When fireworks lit the night sky on the eve of 2007, Bulgaria was celebrating not just another new year, but also what many perceived as a return to Europe. On January 1, a long-lasting dream came true—the country became a full member of the European Union (EU). After a forty-five-year experience with communism, Bulgaria underwent a difficult transition to a democratic political system and a market economy starting in 1989. One important element of this transformation was the pursuit of EU membership, which Bulgarians desired as a magical solution to the difficult challenges facing the nation. Despite the achievement of this goal, Bulgaria remains a country whose income is among the lowest in Europe, its political system is contaminated by rampant corruption, and the people are becoming increasingly disengaged from politics.

Bulgaria's effort to democratize has been crippled by the legacies from the previous Communist regime. After the installation of the Communist regime in the mid-1940s, the country developed a political and economic system closely following the model promoted by Stalin in the Soviet Union. Political scientists, historians, and journalists counted Bulgaria as one of the most loyal allies of the Soviet Union in the years of the Cold War. Bulgaria was a reliable partner in the Moscow-dominated integration structures in Eastern Europe. The Bulgarian Communist leaders coordinated policymaking and personnel changes with the Kremlin, often going too far in their desire to please the Soviet leaders.

Unlike Poland, Hungary, and Czechoslovakia, Bulgaria did not experience a popular upsurge against the Communist dictatorship, nor was there a genuine effort by the Communist Party to reform itself into a more tolerant, humane, and inclusive organization. The wind of change that swept through Eastern Europe in the late 1980s reached Bulgaria at a time when its economy was still entirely dependent on

Soviet markets and energy supply, its political opposition was too young and not ready to lead, and its civil society was underdeveloped and weak.

The totalitarian system had a tight grasp on society. But once the East European communist regimes started to fall in 1989, Bulgaria followed the lead. Competitive politics took root amidst sharp political confrontation when the former Communist Party and the opposition exchanged victories. A democratic process of free and fair elections got under way, but so did public suspicions about secret agreements between elites to spare those who were guilty of Communist crimes. To many Bulgarians this was the price of a "gentle revolution" paid by a nascent opposition seeking legitimization and power.

Politics in Bulgaria has become less ideological and more pragmatic in the twenty-first century. Tired of the prolonged reforms and political confrontations in the 1990s, large groups of voters are now attracted to populist promises for nonpartisan governance and a new morality in politics. While Bulgaria successfully concluded its accession to the European Union, serious economic and social policy challenges raise questions about the country's potential to develop more accountable and citizen-oriented politics.

CURRENT POLICY CHALLENGES

The first cluster of contemporary policy challenges involves economics. In 2002 Bulgaria had a functioning market economy. This came late in the transition due to the lack of consensus about the speed of reform and the desired extent of government intervention in the economy. People preferred a gradual path to economic transformation to the shock therapy model used in Poland. Large-scale **privatization** did not start until the mid-1990s.

These policy choices have had a pronounced impact on Bulgaria's macro- and microeconomic performance. The country has one of the lowest income levels in Europe; it is the poorest member of the European Union today. There has been steady economic growth in the last several years, but this growth does not translate into individual benefits. When Simeon Saxkoburggotski came to power in 2001, he promised to improve things in 800 days, but failed to deliver. And so did the Socialists, who won the election in 2005 on a platform promising a 20 percent increase in salaries and pensions. One of the most urgent tasks for the current and future governments is

to facilitate economic development and raise people's living standards.

There is an urgent need for tax and business reform. In the 2000s more than 30 percent of the state revenues come from income taxes.[1] The value-added tax (VAT) on business profits is 20 percent since the country joined the EU. While these numbers are comparable to the averages for the other new East European members of the EU, they are still too high for a nation that needs economic growth. Bulgarian and foreign experts also agree that the existing regulatory climate is not favorable to developing nascent businesses. The government requires too many license procedures and permits for the registration and operation of private enterprises. Partially due to high taxes and excessive regulation in the private sector, a parallel "shadow" economy accounts for up to a third of the gross domestic product (GDP). Relaxing the regulatory burden on business would bring relief to the private sector and reduce the mass practice of bribing public officials. Facing serious problems with corruption and criticism from international financial institutions, the Bulgarian ruling elite have to find the political will to reduce the role of the state in business regulation.

A second important policy challenge is promoting population growth. The population shrank from 9 million in 1988 to 7.3 million in 2006. This demographic trend results from declining birth rates and migration to Western countries to find better opportunities. Moreover, those who leave are the younger, better educated, and more entrepreneurial. The segment of the population that is age 65 and above increased from 11 percent in 1985 to 17 percent in 2006, while children decreased from 21 percent of the population to 14 percent. The slowdown of the economy and the high unemployment rates of the 1990s made it difficult for the government to provide even small monthly pensions for the aging population. According to some estimates, three-fourths of the population (retired workers, children, and the unemployed receiving social benefits) is supported by the work of the remaining one-fourth.[2]

These problems have led to limitations in social services. In order to complete structural reform and to handle inflation, the government drastically cut public spending on education and health care in 1998–1999. More often than before, couples live together without marrying and families choose to raise just one child because of their limited economic means. The current and future governments need to formulate a comprehensive social policy program that supports motherhood, provides for the daily needs of families, and cares for the elderly. However, such a policy program requires a strong economy and responsible political elites.

A third policy challenge is the demand for strong measures against corruption. No country is immune to corruption, but the problem is very serious in Bulgaria. According to Transparency International, Bulgaria ranks among the most corrupt European nations. Many EU officials fear that Bulgaria is incapable of detecting, preventing, and punishing those who participate in corruption in the public sector. Much of the necessary anticorruption legislation and structures have already been put in place, but the nation needs a genuine commitment by political elites to implement these policies.

Finally, the most significant foreign policy challenge is solving the issue of energy dependence. Bulgaria is integrated into the EU and NATO, but recent contracts with Russia to supply gas to and build pipelines through Bulgaria raise new security concerns. The issue is sensitive because Bulgaria, as a loyal satellite of the Soviet Union, was heavily dependent on the Kremlin both politically and economically during the Cold War period. Moreover, as an exporter of electricity for other Balkan countries, Bulgaria agreed to close the older nuclear reactors as part of its accession to the EU. This produced higher electricity costs for consumers. Dependence on Russian gas becomes even more troubling, given Russia's efforts to conclude separate deals with the European nations and the lack of a unified EU energy strategy. Diversifying the composition of Bulgaria's energy portfolio is one solution promoted by economists, but this is problematic in the context of gas supply agreements with Russia.

HISTORICAL LEGACY

In many ways Bulgarian politics cannot be fully comprehended without reference to the national historical experience. The Bulgarian state is one of the oldest in Europe, and its people think of themselves as citizens of a country with an ancient history. Once a mighty medieval kingdom with lands bordering three seas, Bulgaria then went through turbulent events in which it lost and restored its statehood. Tolerance, endurance, and adaptation helped the people survive painful defeats and destructive ideologies. Interruptions in the

history of their state, however, left an imprint on the way social conflicts are resolved and political choices are made.

The Balkan invasion of the Ottoman Turks in the late fourteenth century disrupted the natural social, political, and cultural development of Bulgaria. The conquerors differed a great deal in their language, religion, and state traditions. As a result, the nation experienced Renaissance, industrialization, and modernization much later than did most other European countries. A national bourgeoisie emerged, secular schools opened, and a liberation movement gained strength in the nineteenth century.

Liberation from Ottoman domination in 1878 led to the restoration of the state and to new challenges, although the formal announcement of independence from the Ottoman Empire was not made until 1908. Bulgaria became a constitutional monarchy, but the political institutions and processes were not truly democratic. Election results were often manipulated, and political opponents were persecuted. Liberation also did not fully solve the national problem because significant territories populated by ethnic Bulgarians were left out. Consequently, revision of borders remained the main goal of Bulgarian foreign policy during the interwar period. By the time Europe and the world celebrated the end of World War II, Bulgaria had fought and lost three wars for liberation.

The Communist Regime

Along with other East European nations such as Poland and Czechoslovakia, Bulgaria became part of the Soviet bloc after World War II. The resulting political and economic changes were fundamental. In 1946 a referendum rejected the monarchy in favor of a republican form of government. All non-Communist political parties were banned; many opposition leaders were either sent to prison or executed. A 1947 Constitution changed the name of the country to People's Republic of Bulgaria. The new political system, however, was less about governance by the people than about governance in the name of one group, the working class.

A totalitarian state suppressed the development of autonomous organizations, imposed censorship, persecuted dissent, and promoted the collective interest over that of the individual. The state encouraged political participation, but only the **Bulgarian Communist Party (BCP)** and its satellite organizations were available for membership. The Marxist-Leninist

Postwar Bulgarian Political Developments	**FIGURE 11.1**

1944	Red Army invasion
1946	Referendum rejects monarchy
1947	Opposition banned BCP prevails Communist Constitution
1950s	Agricultural collectivization completed
1954	Zhivkov becomes First Secretary of BCP
1960s	Industrial growth
1970s	Political and ideological stagnation
1980s	Acceleration of foreign debt
1985	Campaign against ethnic Turks
1989	Zhivkov resigns UDF is formed
1990	First free elections
1991	New Constitution
1997	UDF accelerates economic reform
2001	
2004	Joins NATO
2007	Joins EU

ideology of class struggle became a dominant philosophy, taught in schools and studied at the workplace. The BCP was portrayed as the leading political factor in the country, taking care of the working people and guarding the socialist fatherland from the evil capitalism. Nobody was supposed to criticize or question the Communist Party; disagreement with and failure to accept the norms of the communist ideology were punished as crimes.

The economic transformation of socialist Bulgaria followed the principles of modernization, urbanization, industrialization, and social equality. At the end of the war, Bulgaria was poor, predominantly rural, and industrially underdeveloped. The BCP followed closely the Soviet economic model: Under slogans of equality and no exploitation, the new regime nationalized private enterprises and consolidated agrarian land in collective farms. Since the BCP held total control over the economy, most of the decisions on the economy were made by the Political Bureau (**Politbureau**) and then "sent down" to the state administration for implementation.

In a relatively short period of time, economically backward Bulgaria made significant progress toward modernization and urbanization. By the 1960s the structure of the economy was altered irreversibly and deep demographic and social changes were evident in the population. To many citizens those were positive developments that made their country a modern industrialized nation, with opportunities for everyone to study, receive health care, and have a job. The nature of economic relationships, however, discouraged individual incentive and promoted inefficiency. By the late 1970s, the model had already been exhausted, and the economic output did not provide the social benefits that the BCP promised. The Communist government took loans from international financial institutions and accumulated a huge foreign debt.

Power was concentrated in the hands of the BCP Politbureau, led by the first secretary. For thirty-five years (1954–1989), one man, **Todor Zhivkov**, occupied this highest post. He also headed the state administration by becoming chairman of the Council of Ministers (prime minister) in 1962 and president of the State Council in 1971. The political system was stable and rigid, with limited potential for reform.

Thus, the party elite were extremely confused when the new Soviet leader, Mikhail Gorbachev, implemented policies providing for more transparency in public life in the late 1980s (see Chapter 9). The lack of a genuine commitment to reform on the part of

Zhivkov prevailed. Only after the communist regimes in Poland, Hungary, and East Germany conceded in the spring and summer of 1989 did part of the Communist elite in Bulgaria overthrow Zhivkov. As elsewhere in Eastern Europe, the fall of the totalitarian regime was affected by a weakened capacity of the state to provide for its citizens; inflexibility of the system, which needed to reform itself in the face of challenges; and loss of political support from Moscow.

The Democratic Transition

Most Bulgarians believe that the birthday of the nation's democratic transition is November 10, 1989. On that day, at a meeting of the BCP Central Committee, a group of soft-liners led by Foreign Minister Petar Mladenov forced Todor Zhivkov to resign. Observers argue that the event of November 10 was nothing but a "palace coup d'etat." Zhivkov was removed from the top of the BCP's leadership, but his ideological comrades kept the power in their hands. Yet, following that date and in the context of the unfolding revolutions all over Eastern Europe, the Bulgarian society erupted: Parties and independent unions formed within days, and citizens went out in the streets to demand more freedom and to denounce the BCP. Similar to Poland and Hungary, Bulgaria held **national round table** talks to lay the foundations of a peaceful transition to a more democratic system.

The round table negotiations between the BCP and the opposition Union of Democratic Forces (UDF) took place in January–March 1990. The two parties agreed on dismantling BCP organizations at workplaces, implementing a new electoral system for election of a Grand National Assembly, and recognizing the right to private property. Those agreements had a binding character and were approved by the still acting National Assembly. Negotiations in the spring of 1990 legitimized the UDF as the main anti-Communist force in Bulgaria.

The most important achievements of Bulgaria's democratic transition in the 1990s were in the areas of institution-building and competitive electoral politics. A new Constitution was inaugurated in the summer of 1991. In the course of several years, a tremendous amount of work was done to adopt new legislation. During the 1990s the electoral arena was dominated by two political platforms, those of the former BCP (now the Bulgarian Socialist Party or BSP) and the anti-Communist UDF. Peaceful transitions of power took place three times in ten years, indicating that

elites had accepted the rules set at the beginning of transition.

Economic transformation was not as successful as institutional reform. Unlike other post-Communist countries, the former Communist Party won the first multiparty election in 1990 and postponed reforms. The UDF prevailed in the second election in 1991, but did not have a majority in the National Assembly to complete privatization. A leftist government headed by Zhan Videnov led the country to the deepest economic crisis of the transition. In 1996 several banks declared bankruptcy, inflation went up by 120 percent, and the state grain reserve was sold abroad by businessmen close to the government. After a decisive electoral victory in 1997, the UDF formed a cabinet that carried out the long overdue market reforms.

In 2001 voters supported a new political force, a movement led by former king Simeon Saxkoburggotski (Box 11.1). He ran a populist campaign on the platform of "clean" politics and rapid improvement in the living standard of common people. Those promises were not kept, but the UDF never recovered to win another election. The pattern of BSP–UDF alternation in power of the 1990s is long gone. A center-left coalition government was formed in 2005, which finalized the process of Bulgaria's EU accession.

SOCIAL FORCES

Bulgaria experienced major social and demographic changes after World War II and the introduction of a Soviet economic model of development. Agricultural collectivization led many peasants to migrate to the cities, where they found jobs in the new factories and plants. More workers specialized in the engineering and mid-level technical careers required by an industrial economy. Women gained significant political and economic rights in the 1947 Constitution that proclaimed gender equality as a policy goal of the Communist government. Some of those social trends continued after 1989: Women are still in the labor force in large numbers, literacy rates are among the highest in the world, and birth rates are in decline.

More-substantial social changes occurred in the economic area. The transition from centrally planned economy to a market economy, the restoration of rights over property nationalized in the late 1940s, and the opening of the country for foreign trade generated opportunities for enrichment, but also produced

BOX 11.1

Ex-King, Party Leader, and Prime Minister

One unique event in Bulgaria's political life after 1989 was the inauguration of former king Simeon Saxkoburggotski (Saxe-Coburg Gotha) as prime minister. He held this office from 2001 through 2005. The story of his life is perhaps more unusual than the saga of any other monarch in the modern world.

Simeon II, the first son of King Boris III and Queen Johanna, was born in 1937. He was baptized in the Eastern Orthodox tradition and kept this religious affiliation throughout the years. King Boris died unexpectedly after returning from a visit with Hitler in August 1943. At the age of 6, Simeon II inherited the crown; a regency council was appointed to govern the country until he reached adulthood. After the formation of a Communist-controlled government in September 1944, the three regents, including Simeon's uncle Kiril, were tried by a People's Court as enemies of the nation. In 1946 a referendum determined that the country would become a republic, and Simeon, his mother, and his sister were deported.

The royal family in exile received political asylum from the Spanish government. In Spain Simeon II graduated from the Lycée Français with majors in law and political science. In 1962 he married Doña Margarita Gomez-Acebo y Cejuela, a cousin of Juan Carlos, King of Spain. They had five children, all of whom carry Bulgarian names.

When the democratic transition in Bulgaria started, Simeon II restored his Bulgarian citizenship and received a Bulgarian passport. In the spring of 2001, the former king of Bulgaria moved back; he organized a political movement (National Movement Simeon II), won half of the seats in the National Assembly, and became prime minister.

Simeon II likes to distance himself from the "usual" politicians. He is not a party member, but "the party leader." As prime minister he avoided answering questions before the parliament and preferred to communicate with the nation via the media. Public trust in him was ruined by scandals around improper restoration of ownership over estates that Simeon II claimed as property of the royal family. The image of the former king as a nonpartisan and uncorrupt leader who came to save his nation was vastly compromised.

---

inequalities. The economic divide often overlaps partially with other traditional divisions in Bulgaria, such as residence, ethnicity, and gender. This section focuses on each of these cleavages separately.

Income Inequalities

If the main division during the time of communism was along the line of party membership, today it is along that between the haves and the have-nots. Before 1989 the modest, yet guaranteed standards of living included equal provision of social services and only small disparities in household incomes. Since full employment was one of the tenets of the socialist economic model and both men and women were in the labor force, the average household had two wage earners. The extent to which salaries varied in Communist Bulgaria depended on the degree of education and the years of working experience. Overall, employees with the same level of education were entitled to a certain salary that would increase with the passage of certain periods of time. Most people

owned their homes, but a family was not allowed to possess a second house or apartment.

Yet, one group with a higher social and economic status emerged. Those in the BCP leadership and the state administration had privileges assuring a life that the common people could not enjoy. They were able to buy a car without waiting for years, obtain a telephone line connection, travel to nonsocialist countries, and get a bigger home in a better neighborhood. Members of the BCP had better chances for being promoted, and so did their children.

The transformation to a market economy, with postponements and complications, created new and deeper economic divisions. This immediately produced a small group of rich capitalists and a large population of people with shrinking resources. Individuals close to the previous regime enriched themselves by expropriating public property and funds, which they quickly invested and turned into millions. At the same time, a huge majority of the people became poorer as the previous system of social welfare deteriorated. When privatization and restructuring accelerated in the mid-1990s, unemployment levels grew rapidly.[3] The income gap between the new capitalists and the rest of the population widened further, as fewer could work and support their families and the pensions for retired workers were depreciated. Since then, Bulgaria has implemented various structural reforms, and living standards have rebounded.

Income inequality has increased since the start of the transition. Despite the clear indications of macroeconomic stabilization after the completion of market reform, many Bulgarians believe that their well-being has not improved very much. Public opinion polls show that about two-thirds of the population feel that they are poor.[4] The economic distance between rich and poor is comparable to that in other Central and East European countries. The level of poverty, however, is slightly higher than the poverty levels in Romania and Latvia and significantly exceeds the levels measured in Hungary and Poland.

Rural/Urban Disparities

Rural areas are quite distinct from big cities in terms of economic and cultural characteristics. There are also significant regional differences, especially between Sofia and the rest of the country. These contrasts are not new and should not be attributed solely to the transition. Before 1989 living standards in the villages were considerably lower than those in the cities. Backwardness, underdeveloped infrastructure and communication networks, and limited access to health care were distinctive features of life in rural Bulgaria.

Things did not improve dramatically after 1989. Restoration of private land ownership in the early 1990s did not bring the expected revival of agricultural production, for many of the new landowners chose not to return, but to stay in the cities. To many Bulgarians, especially to the youth, village life is not attractive—there are no jobs, no opportunities, and no entertainment of their liking. As a result, schools were closed for lack of students, and houses were abandoned. Public expenditures for social programs and infrastructure in the 1990s were lower for the rural areas, while the lion's share went to the big cities.

Poverty has struck the rural areas more than the cities. Unemployment, a main source of hardship, has declined to around 7 percent (2007), but it affects certain groups disproportionately. Poverty in the villages and small towns is worse because of its magnitude. In 2001 about one-third of the population lived in the countryside, but households there made up two-thirds of the poor. Poverty rates are four times higher in rural areas than in cities. Between 1995 and 2001, agricultural income decreased significantly. This is not surprising, given that in 2001 only a quarter of all rural residents 15 years of age and older had a job.[5]

Life in the largest cities continues to be very different from the everyday experiences of people in the small towns. In the past the Communist authorities inhibited migration to the capital city of Sofia. After 1989 the restrictions were lifted, and the inhabitants of the largest city increased to 1.4 million, or 17.4 percent of the total population. Better economic opportunities and a favorable investment climate are the reasons that Sofia maintains the lowest unemployment rates in the country. Other regions that prospered during the transition are those around Varna and Bourgas, Bulgaria's biggest ports on the Black Sea. Since the accession of the country to the EU, the Danube River town of Ruse and its surroundings have benefited from the opening of the border with Romania and the increased commercial and tourist flows. Better infrastructure, access to modern communications, and Western-like stores in the cities stand in sharp contrast to the backwardness of rural areas. Surveys show that urban citizens have not only a different lifestyle, but also distinct political views and party affiliation.

Ethnic Divisions

Another source of social division is ethnicity. Because of its geographic location, the country has become the homeland for groups with different cultures, traditions, and religions: Bulgarians, Turks, Roma, Jews, Armenians, and other smaller minority groups. Historically, Bulgarians have shown tolerance toward ethnic minorities. This tolerance is based more on accepting differences between groups than on being proud to belong to a multiethnic society.[6] While relations with ethnic Jews and Armenians have been friendly over the years, interactions with the Turkish and Roma minorities have been more difficult.

Relations between ethnic Bulgarians and Turks are largely a product of history. Years after the liberation in 1878, memories of "the Turkish yoke" fueled hostility and mistrust toward ethnic Turks. The BCP preached equality of races, but in practice did not respect minority rights. In the mid-1980s, Zhivkov started a campaign for "revival" of the national consciousness of the ethnic Turks. Under the theory that their ancestors were Bulgarian and Christian, converted to Islam during the Ottoman invasion, the regime forced the

Turks to adopt Slavic names and forbid the use of their mother language and traditional attire, as well as the practice of Islamic rites. In the spring of 1989, Zhivkov pushed for the deportation of thousands of Turks to neighboring Turkey.

Post-Communist Bulgaria has made significant progress in improving relations between ethnic Bulgarians and Turks. At present schools offer education in the Turkish language in schools in regions with mixed population, the daily news is broadcast in Turkish on national television channels, and new mosques are being built where they did not exist before. Against the background of violent ethnic wars in former Yugoslavia, analysts often cite Bulgaria as an example of a successful "ethnic model." But achievements have not come without opposition from nationalistic circles. To the extent to which conflict exists, it is based on misperceptions and prejudice about the "real" intentions of the minority group, blaming the Turks for disloyalty to the Bulgarian state and for separatist aspirations.

While the conflict with the Turkish minority is more political in nature, the problematic relationship between the majority group and the Roma has social roots. Most of the problems of the Roma community are economic and social. Workable policy solutions for education, housing, work, health, and public safety needs have not yet been found. Marginalized from the rest of society, most Roma people live in distinct communities, are rarely employed, and have substandard living conditions. Sadly, they are more likely to commit crimes and to end up in jail. The Roma think of themselves as a group victim, increasingly helpless and isolated.[7]

Bulgarian discrimination against the Roma is widespread. Many Bulgarians believe that the Roma living on social security are lazy and do not look for jobs and that Roma families do not send their children to school and encourage them to steal. While providing some temporary relief, government policies of compensation for Roma electricity and heating expenses in some places have not facilitated inclusion. On the contrary, these have sparked more hostility among Bulgarians who feel unhappy about the way public money is being used.

Gender Differences

Bulgaria's gender divide shares common features with those in other post-Communist states, although it went through a unique development in recent years. During the communist era, gender equality was preached as a major social achievement in the modernizing society. The 1947 Constitution declared women equal to men and provided legal guarantees for their active involvement in public life. Women were engaged in the labor force, although in lower-level positions compared to men with the same education and skills. Due to these gender equality provisions and liberal abortion policies, the traditional role of women, limited to housekeeping and motherhood, changed. To make sure women were engaged in social and political life, the Communist Party used quotas for female representation in its own structures, in parliament, and in local government. The socialist policies of inclusion resulted in a well-educated female labor force and facilitated the entry of women into the social and political elite.

The gender divide did not disappear after 1989. Actually, the status of women was somewhat degraded as transition unfolded. Facing the challenges of economic and political competition, many women withdrew from the public to the private sector. The socialist model had become part of the past, and the loss of social security made some women prefer to commit themselves entirely to the family. They continue to be well educated, as shown by the almost equal literacy rates across genders. However, women are much more likely to be unemployed and to receive lower salaries than men. Old stereotypes that certain professions are more suitable for men still exist; men are twice as likely to be hired as "operators of equipment, machines and vehicles," while women outnumber men in the service sector.

Women's political involvement after 1989 has been very different from that of men. Similar to other East European countries, Bulgaria had female legislative representation in the 20–30 percent range. Although a significant number of women became skillful and knowledgeable in the public arena, they did not really compete to win those positions. Once the Communist regime collapsed, Bulgarian women lost the momentum to become more actively involved in politics. The few women's associations that formed after 1989 have been organizationally weak and underdeveloped.[8] The first competitive multiparty elections resulted in a significant drop in the share of female deputies in the National Assembly.

Female representation in the parliament and the government has substantially improved in the last two elections. A major change occurred in 2001 when Simeon Saxkoburggotski's movement formed a coalition with the Bulgarian Women's Party in order to participate in the parliamentary election.[9] Simeon himself encouraged the inclusion of more women, arguing that their participation would "make politics more humane and therefore, more successful."[10] The extraordinary circumstances of 2001 resulted in the election of a larger number of female candidates, a phenomenon that had diffusion effects on other parties. In 2005 women again won a significant share of legislative representation by obtaining 22 percent of the seats in the National Assembly.

THE NEW DEMOCRATIC STRUCTURES OF GOVERNMENT

As with other post-Communist states, an urgent task after the fall of the totalitarian regime was to create new democratic institutions. The government structure that had served the BCP and the socialist state had to be replaced by a new system of democratic governance. The national round table in 1990 recognized that a new basic law was needed to further legislation reforms. They therefore called for the election of a Grand National Assembly. The spring 1990 election was the first competitive multiparty contest in post-Communist Bulgaria. The Communists won an absolute majority of seats, which gave them an advantage in influencing the constitution-making process. In a climate of severe political confrontation between the BSP's "socialist democracy" and the UDF's Western-type liberal democracy, sixteen drafts were submitted and debated. Despite the opposition of some UDF representatives, the Grand National Assembly passed a new basic law in July 1991.

Bulgaria's 1991 Constitution was a "quick fix" law, but it played an important role by defining the main rules of the political game and preventing institutional chaos.[11] The key political players, including those who opposed its adoption, have respected the constitutional provisions. The new political system is based on the principle of clear division of power, and the rules for interaction are broadly recognized as "the only game in town." Despite some talk about possible amendments, the Constitution has not been seriously contested.

Article 1 of the Constitution establishes Bulgaria as "a republic with a parliamentary form of government" whose power is derived from the people. Most importantly, a provision that no political party or group may "usurp the expression of the popular sovereignty" sharply contrasts the previous constitutional role of the Communist Party. Separate articles establish that Bulgaria is a "law-governed state" and assure equality of all citizens before the law. The Constitution guarantees the rights to free association, religious practice, and political participation, as well as the protection of families and the right to free choice of residence, property, and employment. It specifically cites the rights of citizen access to information and mass media free of censorship. Despite the vagueness and inconsistencies in some parts of the Constitution, it provides the foundations of a democratic political system based on pluralism and respect for human rights. The Constitution contributed to political stability in the volatile environment of transition.[12]

The Legislature

Bulgaria's national legislature is the **National Assembly**. In the communist era, the National Assembly met only briefly to rubber-stamp decisions already made by the BCP. Since the collapse of the Communist regime, the National Assembly has functioned on a full-time basis.

The National Assembly consists of 240 members, called "people's representatives" or deputies, who are equivalent to members of parliament in other countries (see Figure 11.2). The deputies are directly elected by the people for four-year terms. Members of the National Assembly come from different parties and form parliamentary groups that are proportionately represented in the governance of the National Assembly. Deputies cannot hold another public office. If approved as prime minister or minister, the deputy resigns from his/her parliamentary seat. In its first session, the National Assembly elects a chairman, usually from among the largest parliamentary group, and vice chairmen, nominated by the larger elected parties. The structure of the National Assembly includes permanent committees that facilitate the legislative work and ad hoc committees that investigate particular issues of public concern.

The Constitution empowers the National Assembly with more authority than is given to any other government body. The National Assembly has law-making powers and exercises parliamentary control over the cabinet and the prime minister. Any deputy or member of the cabinet can introduce a bill, which then becomes a law if approved on two readings by a majority of those present, except when a qualified majority is constitutionally required. The parliament establishes taxes, schedules elections for president,

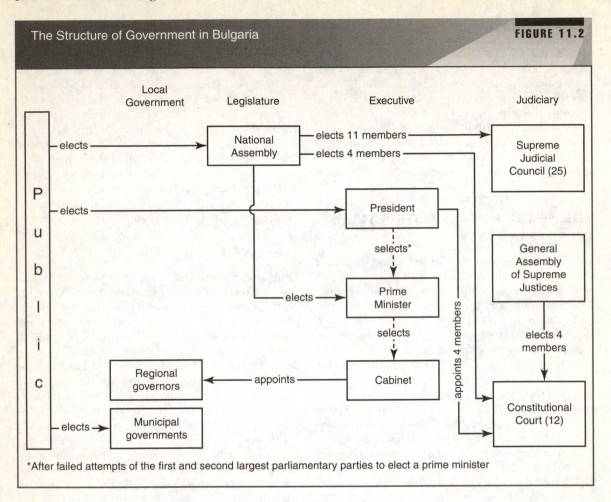

The Structure of Government in Bulgaria

FIGURE 11.2

*After failed attempts of the first and second largest parliamentary parties to elect a prime minister

approves the use of the armed forces, and ratifies international agreements.

The National Assembly also has important powers with regard to the executive branch. It elects, on a motion from the president, a prime minister by simple majority. It can also dismiss the prime minister by passing a motion of no confidence with a majority vote. Individual representatives can question the prime minister and members of his cabinet about government and about policies or their implementation, much like British Members of Parliament can question their prime minister in the House of Commons. Opposition deputies have effectively used these questions to challenge ministers on national radio and television.

The National Assembly has managed an unprecedented amount of legislative work. All spheres of government and public life needed new laws. In fulfilling these tasks, the National Assembly achieved some success, but also showed deficiencies that delayed some important legislation. Initially, the deputies' lack of professional skills and knowledge was one source of delay. This problem was especially serious for the UDF, which relied on just a few experts in constitutional law, while many of its deputies were writers, artists, singers, and journalists. With the passage of time, the National Assembly became more informed and accomplished.

Intense political confrontation between the main parties was another source of stalemate. Because the plenary sessions of the first National Assemblies were broadcast live on the national radio, many deputies gave partisan speeches to introduce themselves and their party's policy positions. The UDF used this forum to expose the crimes of the Communist regime in long and passionate revelations from the floor. Through the 1990s conflict prevailed within the National Assembly, and approval of key pieces of legislation often proved difficult. Yet, there was always consensus in one particular area: the well-being of the deputies. Increases in salaries, long vacation times (for "meetings with constituents"), luxurious automobiles purchased for parliamentary use, and other perks were easily passed by impressive multiparty majorities. Deputies were well paid, providing them a high standard of living and opportunities for enrichment. It is not surprising that many opinion polls reveal deep public disappointment with their representatives in the National Assembly.

Prime Minister and Cabinet

The executive branch is dual—that is, it consists of the **prime minister**, who heads the cabinet (**Council of Ministers**), and the president. Experts usually classify Bulgaria as semi-presidential because executive power is shared.[13] Authority is distributed very unevenly between the prime minister (and the cabinet) and the president. The former is much more powerful than the latter.

Since the adoption of the new Constitution in 1991, Bulgaria has had six prime ministers (see Table 11.1). Although not required by the Constitution, the practice is that the leader of the party with the largest parliamentary delegation becomes prime minister. The first UDF government, led by Filip Dimitrov, was short-lived; it lost a vote of confidence after a year. A cabinet of experts headed by Lyuben Berov governed between 1992 and 1994. The 1994 election did produce a clear winner, and Zhan Videnov became prime minister, but his government resigned within two years under the pressure of mass anger and frustration over failed policies. The president then appointed a caretaker cabinet that ruled until new elections in 1997. Since then, politics has stabilized: Two parliaments and two prime ministers, **Ivan Kostov** (UDF) and **Simeon Saxkoburggotski** (National Movement Simeon II or NMSS), have served full terms of four years each. Currently, Prime Minister Sergei Stanishev (BSP) is completing a full term as well, which ends in the summer of 2009.

The prime minister directs and coordinates the work of the entire cabinet, assisted by deputy prime ministers. The Constitution assigns the Council of Ministers the responsibility of implementing domestic and foreign policies, as well as preserving public order and national security. The concentration of so much executive power in the hands of the prime minister does not make this office too independent. Unlike the president, who is directly elected, the prime minister is selected by the majority in the National Assembly. He or she can be dismissed by a no-confidence vote, which in order to be passed, needs the support of half of all representatives in the National Assembly.[14]

The prime minister also has important influence over the composition of the cabinet because he or she proposes the structure and the members of the

---

Bulgaria's Executives   TABLE 11.1

The BSP and the UDF have controlled the executive branch most of the time after 1989

Prime Minister, Party, Term (Cabinet coalition)	President, Party, Term
Sergei Stanishev, BSP, 2005– (BSP, NMSS, MRF)	Georgi Parvanov, BSP, 2006–
Simeon Saxkoburggotski, NMSS, 2001–2005 (NMSS, MRF)	Georgi Parvanov, BSP, 2001–2006
Ivan Kostov, UDF, 1997–2001 (UDF)	Petar Stoyanov, UDF, 1996–2001
Zhan Videnov, BSP, 1995–1997 (BSP)	Zhelyu Zhelev, UDF, 1992–1996
Lyuben Berov, Independent, 1992–1994 (expert, backed by MRF and BSP)	Zhelyu Zhelev, UDF, 1990–1992
Filip Dimitrov, UDF, 1991–1992 (UDF)	Petar Mladenov, BSP, 1990
Dimitar Popov, Independent, 1990–1991 (BSP, UDF, Independents)	
Andrei Loukanov, BSP, 1990	

Council of Ministers to the National Assembly for approval. Moreover, the Constitution states that the National Assembly may elect or dismiss the entire cabinet, not individual ministers. These provisions give the prime minister tools to rectify apparently failing performance by replacing a few ministers and to accommodate political conflicts through appointments. For instance, Prime Minister Berov recast his cabinet several times to meet the criticisms of the public and ensure a new supporting parliamentary majority.

In the case of coalition governments, the prime minister's job of keeping the cabinet coherent is even more complicated because of multiple participants' conflicting interests. To resolve the crisis generated by scandals about improper allocation of government contracts, Stanishev made both personnel and structural changes in the Council of Ministers. He strengthened his position by eliminating rivals within his party and by establishing a new balance among the coalition partners in the cabinet.

President

Under the 1971 Constitution, the National Assembly elected the **president** with a two-thirds majority. This arrangement initially served the former Communists well. In 1990 they won the parliamentary election. Incumbent President Petar Mladenov, one of the architects of the November 10 removal of Zhivkov, stayed in office. However, he was forced to resign in the summer after the public learned that he intended to use the army against participants in an anti-Communist demonstration.[15] Then the National Assembly elected UDF leader **Zhelyu Zhelev** as president.[16] The 1991 Constitution changed the process. The president and the vice president are now directly elected by voters for a five-year term, renewable only once. The current president, Georgi Parvanov, was reelected in 2006 to serve a second term.

The decision to have a directly elected head of state was a sharp departure from the past. This weakened the parliament to a degree and gave the president moral grounds to speak and act in the name of the people. This arrangement reflected the political situation as the 1991 Constitution was being drafted. In the summer of 1991, the BSP did not expect to win the upcoming parliamentary election and, therefore, preferred to reduce the importance of the National Assembly. They also thought that holding a separate presidential election would give them another opportunity to compete for power. The UDF also supported a directly elected president, hoping that Zhelev would use his incumbency advantage and keep the post (which happened). The 1991 Constitution kept the office of the vice president from the previous Constitution, ensuring succession and opportunities for mitigation of intraparty conflicts. Among all new East European democracies, Bulgaria is the only country that has a vice president.

By law, the Bulgarian president has limited powers. The Constitution designates the president as the head of state and supreme commander in chief of the armed forces. The president has the power to appoint a prime minister–designate, nominated by the party with the largest share of parliamentary seats. The president can dissolve the National Assembly and call a new election, but only after three failed attempts to elect a prime minister and a cabinet. Compared to Poland's president, the Bulgarian president is much weaker: He cannot initiate legislation, and the National Assembly can easily override his veto with an absolute majority (consider the three-fifths requirement for the Polish Sejm). Yet, if overridden by the National Assembly, the president can still turn to the Constitutional Court for a ruling on the constitutionality of a bill. The president has used this opportunity on several occasions in which the Court ruled against the National Assembly.

The controversy between the president's legitimacy from direct election and the limited presidential powers has been a continuing issue. All three Bulgarian presidents have clearly favored a stronger presidency. Zhelev talked about establishment of a "presidential republic." Stoyanov referred to the limited role attributed to his office by the Constitution. Parvanov has proposed the idea that presidential powers be expanded and reinforced.

Despite complaints about too many constitutional constraints, the presidents have been more influential than expected. They have criticized their party when in control of the National Assembly (Zhelev), played a crucial role during deep political crises (Stoyanov), and helped the formation of a ruling coalition (Parvanov). The presidents have tried to build an image of nonpartisan politicians who unite the nation and serve the interest of the broader public. Some of them promised things during their election campaigns that they could not deliver, given the limited presidential authority allowed by law. Parvanov, in particular, used the term *social president* to imply commitment to fairer incomes and benefits. Until now, attempts to expand the scope of presidential powers have remained suggestive because a two-thirds majority in the National Assembly is required to make constitutional changes.

The Judicial System

The 1991 Constitution established judicial structures to promote the principle of the rule of law. Politicians faced two challenging issues in creating a post-Communist judiciary: deciding the fate of judges and prosecutors associated with the crimes of the previous regime and defining the power of the new judicial institutions relative to other branches of government. Decisions over judicial appointments and dismissals, tenure, and executive supervision were largely determined by who had decisionmaking power and whether they expected to win the next election.[17] The leaders of the BSP realized that their public support was steadily declining at the time the 1991 Constitution was crafted. They therefore favored a judiciary insulated from political pressure and supervision. Sensitive questions, such as personnel changes through lustration of judges in high-level positions, came to the agenda only after the former Communist Party was removed from power as a result of the 1991 election.

Three groups of authorities comprise the judicial system: the courts, the public prosecution, and the preliminary investigation offices. The Supreme Judicial Council runs the operation of the judicial system. The 1991 Constitution empowers the Council to appoint, promote, and remove from office judges, prosecutors, and public investigators. The Council also proposes a budget bill for the operation of the entire judicial system to the National Assembly for adoption.

The Supreme Judicial Council has twenty-five members who have five-year terms and cannot serve two consecutive terms. The National Assembly elects eleven members, and other judiciary bodies elect eleven. The three remaining members are selected by the heads of other courts and the prosecutor general. The Council gathers at least once every three months, summoned either by the minister of justice or by one-fifth of its members.

The Supreme Cassation Court is the highest judicial institution dealing with criminal, merchant, and civil cases. Another institution, the Supreme Administrative Court, deliberates on appeals and complaints

against acts of the prime minister and the cabinet, heads of state departments, the Supreme Judicial Council, the Bulgarian National Bank, and district governors. The Supreme Administrative Court provides an opportunity for society to challenge in court the acts of the administration.

The **Constitutional Court** is a new legal institution, established only in 1991. It consists of twelve members: One-third are elected by the National Assembly, another third are appointed by the president, and the rest are elected by the members of the other courts. Their terms are nine years, with no opportunity for reelection or reappointment.

Along with evaluation of the consistency between presidential decrees/legislation and the Constitution, this Constitutional Court interprets the basic law. Its decisions are final and binding. The court's reputation has remained relatively high over the years in the eyes of the public, the media, and the elite. The court has made major contributions to the democratic process. These include interpretations of the constitutional rights of citizens to free speech, instructions on the constitutional frames for negotiating NATO membership, and affirmation of the constitutionality of the MRF, which helped enormously the process of accommodation of ethnic conflict.[18]

In the last several years, the government adopted constitutional amendments aimed at reforming the judicial system in order to comply with the process of EU accession. In 2003 the National Assembly limited the immunity of magistrates from prosecution and bounded their irremovability. Another amendment created an institution new to Bulgaria—the **ombudsman**, elected by the National Assembly for a five-year term. The ombudsman intervenes in cases when citizen rights and freedoms have been violated by state or municipal officials. Just in the first year after the establishment of the ombudsman, 1,100 complaints were filed with this office. The significance of this institutional reform is substantial, given the limited access of individual citizens to the courts in the upper layer of the judicial system.

Local Governments

Bulgaria has a unitary system of government. Geographically, power is more concentrated in the central government, while local administrative units possess limited autonomy. The Ministry for Regional

Development is responsible for the smooth perform-ance of regional and municipal administrations. Re-cruitment, operation, and funding of local government structures depend heavily on funding from the national budget.[19]

The country has a two-tier system of local gover-nance that combines regional and municipal structures. At the regional level, the national territory is divided into twenty-eight units, called regions, that are en-trusted with harmonizing national and local interests.[20] The municipality level is where local self-governance is exercised in practice. Currently, there are 262 muni-cipalities with their own executive bodies.

The role of regional governments is to represent the central state in local matters. They are headed by governors appointed by the Council of Ministers and deputy governors appointed by the prime minister. Consequently, appointments to these posts have been driven more often by partisan interests than by the need for regional representation. For example, as a coalition partner in the 2001–2005 NMSS govern-ment, the MRF received the post of governor of the Sofia region even though voter support for the MRF there was just 1.3 percent. The regional governors' main task is to coordinate the activities of state agen-cies and local authorities in the region. In doing that the regional governors make sure that state policies are implemented as required by law, state property is protected, and administrative control over municipal bodies is properly exercised.

In contrast, the municipalities are smaller admin-istrative and territorial units where voters are repre-sented more directly. The citizens of a municipality elect both a municipal council and a mayor for four-year terms. The former is an assembly that has the right to adopt normative acts on issues important for the municipality and not in violation of state laws and orders. The 1991 Local Self-Government and Lo-cal Administration Act gives the mayor executive powers to implement decisions made by the council; if unlawful, his or her acts may be repealed by the regional governor.[21]

Local governments in Bulgaria face serious chal-lenges. In a country with a traditionally centralized system of government, it is difficult for municipalities to achieve the autonomy they need to solve local problems. Post-1989 legislation in this area has helped define more clearly the role of the central gov-ernment and the responsibility of municipalities in empowering people to self-govern the town or village where they live. In 1996 the National Association of Municipalities was created to strengthen relations be-tween municipalities and facilitate their interactions with the state.

Another challenge is how to finance local gov-ernment operations in the difficult times of transition. Municipal fees and state subsidies are the most sig-nificant sources of revenues. In most places the mu-nicipal councils decide to spend the bigger portion of the budget on education, health care, and social ser-vices. Yet, they do not have the necessary resources to accommodate many who were left without a job and to maintain the local infrastructure. Municipal public officials and administrators often beg the cen-tral government for help and understanding about the complex problems they try to solve with very limited funds.

Bulgaria's EU accession contributed to the process of decentralization of regional and local gov-ernment. In distributing assistance funds, the EU requires well-functioning regions and sufficient ad-ministrative capacity. In 2002 the Bulgarian govern-ment adopted a program for financial decentralization to support the application of the European Charter of Local Government. European funding enables local authorities to become more involved in investment in infrastructure projects. The structural funds from Brussels increase the autonomy of municipalities and their ability to provide citizens with services. Still, the disparity between responsibilities and means at the local government level is significant.

In summary, the new political system reflects two main trends. First, it follows the example of the European parliamentary tradition in that more power is concentrated in the hands of the National Assem-bly. The National Assembly affects the origin and the work of the executive: It selects the prime minister and questions members of the cabinet on a weekly basis. Second, the specific design of the institutions of government and their functions are marked by the high uncertainty in which they were created. The de-sire to avoid concentration of authority in one insti-tution and the fear of losing elections led to the Constitution including multiple centers of power.

POLITICAL CULTURE

Bulgarians often argue that the choices made by their political elites and their country's fate carry the marks of the past. Therefore, any effort to establish whether culture is congruent with democratic governance would be incomplete without considering history. The legacy of Ottoman domination, the failure of the interwar national unification project, and the communist experience all shaped the way people think of politics. Moreover, a five-century foreign occupation remains relevant to the national psychology. Contemporary policy failures are often blamed on the Turks, on the backwardness of the sultans' empire, on the "hostile" Muslim religion of the conquerors, and on Turks' continued presence after the war of liberation. The long isolation from the rest of Europe further damaged national self-esteem. And the extermination of Bulgarian medieval elites is believed to have left the people without native political leadership. Some go as far as claiming that the long Ottoman domination developed a "slavery culture" of obedient behavior, conformity, and passive acceptance of life conditions despite low-voice murmuring and hidden anger. A common explanation of why Bulgaria did not have an anti-Communist uprising as in Hungary in 1956 or in Czechoslovakia in 1968 is that long foreign domination discouraged opposition behavior and the will for change.

The Communists' coming to power after World War II was welcomed by many as a promise for modernization of Bulgarian society. But falling under the Kremlin's control soon became yet another source of frustration and disappointment. Even today comments that Bulgaria has always made the wrong choices—joining Germany in two World Wars and the Soviet Union later—can be heard in the bars and coffeehouses. Nihilism and disbelief in the nation's potential to solve its own problems have generated strong self-criticism, which underestimates obvious achievements. Many people justify unsuccessful outcomes by blaming "certain external" forces and international conspiracies directed against the country. These legacies from the past still affect the way some Bulgarians, mostly the older generation and rural residents, perceive reform, democratization, and prosperity. A belief that change is possible penetrated the society after 1989, but pessimists still challenge this belief as too naïve.

The Bulgarian transition exhibits some of the unique characteristics of the transformation of popular views about politics in Eastern Europe post-1989. People's attitudes toward the two central goals of post-Communist reform, democracy and market economy, followed different paths of change. Unlike right-wing totalitarian dictators, the ruling Communists spoke highly of the value of democracy. The Communist propaganda, however, emphasized that they were not praising the Western type of liberal democracy. Instead, the Communists claimed they were developing a new, superior type of democracy, "socialist democracy." This may explain why, since the very first days of the transition, the goal of achieving democracy has remained uncontested among all major groups in society. What had to be realized anew was the meaning of "representative, competitive" democracy, which the people did not recognize fully.

In contrast, the Communist state had condemned the market economy as a bourgeois economic model that created capitalists and bred inequality. Consequently, changing individuals' perceptions about wealth and profit after 1989 has been much more difficult than establishing the value of democracy. This involved a shift from economic values focused exclusively on socialist ideals (e.g., from equality to accepting unequal individual benefits from work and private incentive).[22] Traditionally egalitarian in their perception of society, Bulgarians still question inequality in paychecks and pensions. Most social groups, excluding students and intellectuals, think that the highest income should not exceed the lowest by more than three times.

The public's enthusiasm about being engaged in the governance of their country played a positive role in the early days of the transition. Negative memories of the recent communist past and its policies of coercion initially prompted approval of democratic and market reforms. Similar to other East European states, Bulgaria chose the path of simultaneous political and economic changes. Over time, however, a transformation of such magnitude proved complicated and painful, requiring political will and determination from elites and sacrifice from ordinary citizens. Has the public remained committed to democratic reforms after experiencing the hardships of economic restructuring and the loss of previous security networks? Or is nostalgia for the relative material security of the recent past suffocating the desire for political freedoms? Stable public support for democratic performance becomes a key determinant of the legitimacy of Bulgaria's new political system. The rest of this section discusses different aspects of the political culture and how they agree with the goals set by the democracy project.

National Identity and Pride

Scholars maintain that positive attitudes toward the country and its achievements are core elements of political culture, especially in times of serious challenges (see Chapter 2). The intensity of national identification contributes to strong emotional ties. They bring people together and strengthen their will to overcome difficulties in turbulent times.

The Communist regime muted "patriotic" feeling and underscored the importance of internationalism and solidarity with working people all over the world. Before 1989, the Communist Party portrayed national pride as a bourgeois affection, inferior to love for the Soviet Union and its socialist achievements. Ironically, in the 1980s and right after transition started, the Communists spurred nationalist sentiments in some parts of the country against the Turkish Muslim minority. Patriotism and national pride had been suppressed for so long that national flags were hard to find in stores in the early 1990s. Celebrating the victories of the Bulgarian soccer team at the 1994 World Cup in the United States, Bulgarians were short of flags and jerseys with their national colors.

Public opinion polls reveal that a majority of the people are proud to call themselves Bulgarian. Yet, the feeling of national pride is not as widespread as it is in most other EU member states (see Figure 2.1 in Chapter 2). More revealing, about one-fourth of the population is not proud of their country at all. The reasons for the weaker national sentiment in Bulgaria are complex. Bulgarians are very proud of the beauty of their land and of its national achievements in the areas of culture and sports. At the same time, the shadow of the past, as described in the previous section, and the disturbances of the 1990s have suppressed feelings of self-esteem.

Another indicator of how people feel about their country is their perception of the new political system. In general, when citizens believe that the political order is right for their nation, they might overlook some deficiencies in policymaking. This is especially important when the government is carrying out difficult reforms with high costs for large segments of society.

More than half of the public agrees that democracy is better than any other form of government, although it may still have some problems.[23] However, at least two-thirds of all Bulgarians remain dissatisfied with the functioning of democracy in their country.[24] The big question is whether a majority will continue to support the political system, given the economic challenges of the transition. There are troubling signs that the low living standards may undermine democratic values. A growing number of people believe that their society needs more equality and justice, even if this requires certain limitations on individual freedoms.[25]

Political Process and Institutions

Social optimism in Bulgaria is among the weakest in Europe: Just four out of ten Bulgarians, compared to nine out of ten Europeans, are happy with their lives.[26] Deep disappointment with the process of government and the behavior of elites is characteristic of how Bulgarians feel today. As Figure 11.3 shows, the most trusted national institutions are the electronic media, television and radio, followed by the army. Strikingly low are the levels of confidence in the cabinet (lowest in the EU), the national parliament (second lowest after Poland), and the political parties. These numbers are not surprising, given the widespread belief that Bulgarian politicians are very corrupt and political parties raise money by making illegal deals with suspicious donors. According to some public opinion polls, over 80 percent of Bulgarians believe corruption is widespread and malignant.[27]

For Bulgarians discouraged and frustrated with national politicians, the EU has emerged as a symbol of hope. They enthusiastically express much more confidence in the EU than in their national institutions. In 2007 the EU Parliament was thought to be a trustworthy democratic body by 58 percent of the public and the EU Commission by 46 percent.[28]

Policy Expectations

Bulgaria's institutional shift toward a new system based on pluralism and competition happened relatively quickly. It was very difficult for many people to organize their own lives in the new setting. Until 1989 the path to professional success required Communist Party membership; the transition to a market economy brought confusion about how to succeed under the new conditions. Another source of disorientation was the changing role of the state. In the communist period, people were told that the BCP would take care of all their needs. After 1989 the BCP lost its political monopoly, but the inertia remained to rely on the state for one's well-being.

Even today many people wait for support from the state before they themselves try to solve the problem. This phenomenon is much more characteristic of members of the older generation, who do not have the youth, skills, and knowledge needed to compete and survive. With GDP levels significantly lower than in other EU member countries, Bulgaria lacks the economic potential to satisfy such expectations of assistance. Consequently, voters feel betrayed and shift

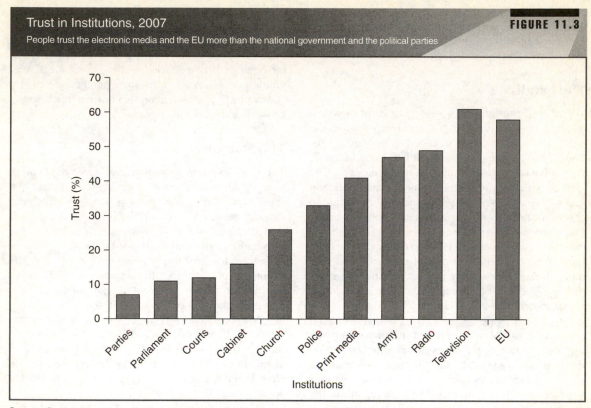

Trust in Institutions, 2007

People trust the electronic media and the EU more than the national government and the political parties

FIGURE 11.3

Source: Commission of the European Union, Eurobarometer 68: Public Opinion in the European Union, National Report on Bulgaria, Fall 2007. Retrieved 10 May 2008 from ec.europa.eu/public_opinion/archives/eb/eb68/eb68_bg_nat.pdf.

their support in favor of the next new politician or party with an attractive populist appeal.

For most citizens capitalism is the model of affluent modern societies. If a market economy helped West European nations develop strong economies after World War II, Bulgaria would benefit from adopting it. At the same time, expectations for active involvement of the state in managing the economy and in solving social problems are also high. Inflation and unemployment are the most important problems that Bulgarians expect their government to solve.[29] They insist that politicians in power increase pensions, provide quality health care services, and ensure public safety by reducing crime. Fewer expectations exist for active environmental and housing policies, given the reduced industrial production and the fact that a large proportion of Bulgarians own their homes.

Overall, the public expects more socially oriented and transparent policies from their government. They are very disappointed with their low living standards and consider the economic transition

a failure. Moreover, they continue to lose confidence in the ability of the Bulgarian institutions to address corruption. Trusting European institutions more, many people expect that Brussels (i.e., the EU) will impose serious measures, including sanctions, to alleviate the problem. More than ever before support for representative government is dependent on economic progress and transparent policies. Democracy is still fragile in Bulgaria.

POLITICAL SOCIALIZATION

The process of formation of beliefs and attitudes about politics has changed dramatically with the democratic transition. The Communist regime had a powerful propaganda system to shape the minds of people through various channels such as the schools and the media. This also muted more traditional factors, including the family and the church. The role of each of these socialization agents changed after the transition. This section discusses from whom the common Bulgarian learns about liberal democracy and its institutions and about the responsibilities of elected officials and those who elect them.

The Family

The role of the family as an environment in which children first learn about politics changed when the Communist regime was installed in the late 1940s. The traditional multigenerational family model broke down as young people moved to the cities to find jobs in factories and their elders remained in the villages. The average family became smaller, with two children and two working parents. Both husbands and wives worked and had equal rights to vote and become a party member. However, they did not have much time to spend in political conversations with their children. In addition, the totalitarian regime suppressed freedom of speech and expression through brutal means and intimidation, which limited political discourse. State Security, the Communist secret service, had a broad network of informers. In many instances family members were recruited to spy on their spouses. Even at home honest conversations about politics and politicians were not safe. Parents worried that if they talked about the regime in the presence of children, then friends, classmates, or teachers would learn what they said. Therefore, they normally preferred to keep silent. They could praise the Communist Party before the children, but would not dare talk about the courage of a grandfather who opposed joining the collective farm.

The post-Communist transition generated changes in the family and in its socializing role. Families are now even smaller and rarer than before. By 1998 more than half of the women with children had only one child, and the proportion of those who decided not to give birth had increased.[30] Out-of-wedlock births are not the exception anymore, given the increase in young couples who live together without being married. The once conservative society is now tolerant of this situation, blaming the economy for the lack of commitment to the traditional family format.

The transition to a pluralistic representative democracy, free of ideological pressures, also changed the climate within the family. People are no longer afraid to speak up in public and at home. Now parents can teach their children what to value in politics and can openly express their preferences and affiliations. Unlike in other nations, Bulgarian families spend a lot of time discussing politics, after work and at the dinner table. Interestingly, however, generational gaps are growing wider, with younger cohorts accusing their parents of not opposing the Communist regime earlier. More pragmatic and better equipped to meet the challenges of the future, young people do not share their parents' ideological (Communist or anti-Communist) burden or interest in conversations about the past.

The Schools

The school system, once a central agent of Communist propaganda among students, also went through significant changes. The pre-1989 universal free education system was skillfully used for the dissemination of Marxist-Leninist ideas, glorification of the Communist Party and its leadership, and inculcation of faithful love for the Soviet Union. Organs of the Communist Party and the Ministry of Education tightly controlled the content of textbooks used from first grade through college. Elective courses were not an option, and curiosity about Western societies was muted. All students studied history and literature through the prism of Marxist theory and socialist realism. Because the Communist leadership was so close to the Kremlin, all Bulgarians were supposed to speak some Russian, which was included in the school curriculum. The school, as a place where children spent a lot of time together, turned into a fruitful opportunity for the transmission of ideas and beliefs to young people who had no access to alternative sources of information.

Schools have also been effective in socializing the young because education is traditionally valued in Bulgaria and families sacrifice scarce resources to send their children to study. This is shown by the high rates of enrollment and graduation at all levels of education, both before and after 1989. Aside from the ideological character of much of the material taught in communist times, high school graduates had excellent preparation in natural sciences, mathematics, and foreign languages, including Western languages. The start of market reform affected the quality of education, for the state could now spend less for the maintenance of buildings, school supplies, and teacher salaries. At the same time, the first private schools were created, which challenged the public education system. By the mid-1990s the legalization of new private and state-subsidized educational facilities led to a substantial increase in the number of college students. Some may argue that people tend to stay in school during difficult economic times. Still, in 1994 Bulgarians ranked "social prestige" and "greater independence" higher than "income" and "finding a job abroad" as advantages that a higher education diploma might give them.[31] Important structural changes also occurred. Between 1960 and 1985, more students were enrolled in technical and engineering disciplines, and the reforms after 1990 generated high interest in the study of economics and law. Consequently, the number of students in economics doubled, and the number of those studying law increased by ten times within five years.[32]

The school system is undergoing a difficult transformation from centralization to modernity and autonomy. The rejection of censorship facilitated this process. Today students are exposed to a variety of teachings and viewpoints. They have a better and more sophisticated understanding of the market economy than do their parents, and they are more pragmatic in deciding on what jobs to search for and where.

A difficult challenge for the state is determining how to keep schools open in places with declining population, to secure heating for classrooms in the cold winters, and to increase the pay for good teachers in public institutions. Despite some successful efforts to repair school buildings and to provide students with hot milk and breakfast, more is needed to improve learning conditions and help the development of civic values. Another difficult problem is the notoriously low rate of school graduation for minority children, especially the Roma. Solving the problem of their educational attainment is part of the bigger challenge of integrating the Roma into society.

The Media

The press and broadcast media, once under the total control of the state and the Communist Party, underwent major changes after 1989. This included changes in ownership, program content, and relations with society. During Communist rule, restrictive ideological canons and censorship suffocated any effort at independent journalism. A few national newspapers, organs of the Communist Party and its satellite organizations, had large circulations and cost almost nothing. They presented the usual propaganda, speeches of party leaders and materials written by journalists loyal to the regime. The state-run television and radio programs were also heavily censored; until the mid-1970s the Friday television programming was received directly from Moscow.

Gorbachev's liberalization policies in the Soviet Union caused confusion in Bulgaria because of their appeals for more transparency and openness in politics. Ironically, once forced to subscribe to Soviet periodicals at work and at school, in the late 1980s Bulgarians sought out magazines and newspapers coming from the Soviet Union. Zhivkov's regime was reluctant to implement Gorbachev's reforms, yet stopping Soviet newspapers seemed equally undesirable. In the last several years of Communist rule, tentative attempts to advance independent opinions on current events or forbidden topics were made by anchors of news programs on national radio and television broadcasts.

After the abolition of censorship and the state monopoly, the media sector expanded rapidly. Hundreds of privately owned newspapers publish nationally or regionally. The major dailies include *24 Chasa (24 Hours), Trud, Dnevnik, Sega,* and the BSP's *Duma.* Challenged by the new competitive economic environment, many of the print media became commercial and less professional. Political news and analyses, even in the large newspapers, are swamped in commercials, horoscopes, and even pornography. To attract more potential buyers, most papers rely on color and scandalous news and sacrifice quality of reporting.

The Constitution guarantees freedoms of expression and citizen access to information, but the public is concerned that the press is not as independent as one would wish. The public sees the owners of some dailies as connected to corporate interests and serving certain circles of the political elite. Newspapers have failed to become reasonably reliable sources of information because data and news reporting are manipulated through deliberate selection or misrepresentation. It is difficult to determine whether the papers are presenting hard facts or mere interpretations. The public is suspicious about both the integrity of the press and the professional ethics of journalists.[33]

Marketization of electronic media led to the entry of foreign and domestic private broadcast stations, which soon became quite popular. After an initial surge of foreign entertainment, the national channel Horizont has regained its previous status as the most listened to programming. It balances Bulgarian with foreign elements in its broadcasting schedule.[34] The privately owned Darik Radio has high-quality daily coverage of news in a distinct format. Thanks to the reporting of Darik journalists, the public received timely information on the protests before the National Assembly that led

Along with the political and social transformation, Bulgarian culture went through fundamental changes after 1989. The abolition of centralized management and control opened the doors to the establishment of private publishing enterprises and film and music producers. Censorship over content and ideology was lifted, which gave rise to new styles and genres. The propaganda machine of the Communist regime is long gone, but so also are generous state subsidies for culture. The new market-driven pop culture combines free expression and controversial artistic values.

A vicious cycle of empty studios and high ticket prices hurt domestic performance arts. Almost all movies shown in theaters are foreign imports of low artistic quality. The average person will not pay to see a mediocre movie, but will watch television, which offers entertainment of the same quality, but for much less. A disproportionate amount of television viewing time is devoted to Western-type soap operas and reality shows. American soap operas such as *Guiding Light* and *The Bold and the Beautiful* and serials

from Mexico and other Latin American countries are broadcast in prime time. Bulgarian versions of *Jeopardy, Big Brother,* and *Survivor* are among the most watched game programs.

In the music sector, a new *popfolk* genre dominates after the disappearance of state-sponsored popular music and as an alternative to Anglo-American rock and jazz. Known also as *chalga*, this form of music brings together modern instruments, Oriental rhythms, Roma roots, and traditional Bulgarian and Balkan folk elements. *Chalga* has been criticized for the simple and often vulgar lyrics, the sexuality of female performers, and the materialistic values imposed as a substitute for social engagement. Fans argue that this is music for the common people, who are sick of politicians and the intelligentsia and who want to be happy, have beautiful women, and drive Mercedes and BMWs, too. The magnitude of the *chalga* effect cannot be ignored, given that it constitutes more than 80 percent of the entire music production in Bulgaria.

to the resignation of the Socialist government in the spring of 1997. Today the national television networks face serious competition from Nova Television and 7-Dni, which are widely viewed by those who subscribe to cable service. In addition, the cable companies broadcast international news programs, including those from CNN and EuroNews.

Public opinion of television and radio broadcasts is generally highly positive. This is quite interesting, given the marketization and commercialization of the media and the quest for sensationalism among journalists. Still, as in the past, the morning talk shows and the evening news blocs have large audiences. It is still very expensive for the common person to buy newspapers every day, while it is much cheaper to get information on political matters from national television. In addition, the electronic media offer news coverage of relatively good quality that competes for more viewers by adding entertaining elements in their daily programs.

The current information environment is thus much different than before 1989. On the one hand, the broadcast media offer many cheap and low-quality products reflecting foreign mass culture; these programs

are being watched with huge interest. On the other hand, viewers receive extensive information on domestic and foreign affairs presented by more objective and critical reporters. As much as the broadcast media are commercialized, they remain the best and most affordable sources of information for the general public.

CITIZEN PARTICIPATION

Citizen political participation is a defining characteristic of a democratic system. There are many ways in which people can engage, from writing letters to public officials, to voting, to marching in protests and demonstrations. While people in a totalitarian country are forced to take part in symbolic activities that are supposed to legitimize the system, citizens of democratic states act to express their views voluntarily. Democratic transitions are often accompanied by great enthusiasm and popular drive for political action.

In Bulgaria political mobilization reached its peak in 1990. Hundreds of thousands demonstrated in the streets of the large cities, demanding "Democracy! Markets! Europe!" Eighteen years later disappointment and disengagement characterize mass political activism. Indifference and apathy are reinforced by fatigue from a prolonged transition with no promise for immediate prosperity. People are somewhat tired of politics, but they realize that, unlike under the Communist regime, now they do have the right to choose not to vote or not to demonstrate.

The post-1989 period of democratic transition is a history of behavioral extremes. Remarkable levels of enthusiasm and political mobilization alternated with deep disappointment over unfulfilled expectations and with passive waiting. In 1990 citizens were for the first time free to protest the BCP's past and present policies, support the UDF's demands at the round table talks, and volunteer in the first multiparty elections. By 1996 enthusiasm waned, together with the hope for real reform and economic revival. In 1997 the emergence of a united opposition to the disastrous Videnov government awoke millions, who put pressure on the cabinet to resign through street protests and demonstrations. However, new fatigue and suspicions of corruption caused another wave of popular disengagement in the early 2000s.

Bulgarians now rarely participate in demonstrations; despite anger toward the political elite, only 4 percent said they protested in 2001.[35] Other forms of participation, such as contacting a public official with demands or opinions, are also seen only occasionally. Even election campaigns do not excite and involve ordinary citizens as much as they did before. An overwhelming 93 percent of Bulgarians admit that they do not talk to others to convince them to vote for a particular party, nor do they attend political meetings or put up posters.

The most direct form of participation, the act of voting, does not excite people at present. In the communist past, Bulgarians were forced to go to the polls and cast a ballot with the name of a single candidate for the post, the only one nominated by the Communist Party. To ensure the legitimacy of the system domestically and internationally, the Communist authorities reported turnout rates as high as 99 percent. Although artificially inflated, the numbers of citizens who turned out to vote were still quite high due to the pressure put on them to show up and vote.

The nature of the entire electoral process changed dramatically after the start of transition. In the election of 1990, the first multiparty competitive race in Bulgaria, over 90 percent of the electorate participated without being forced by the law or by a party. As Figure 11.4 shows, however, turnout rates have been declining. In only five cycles of parliamentary

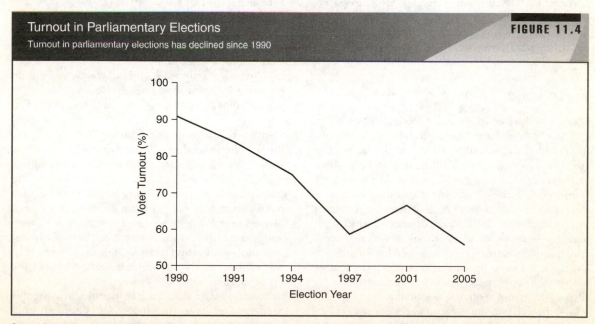

Turnout in Parliamentary Elections
Turnout in parliamentary elections has declined since 1990

FIGURE 11.4

Source: International Institute for Democracy and Electoral Assistance, *Voter Turnout Online*. Retrieved 26 January 2008 from www.idea.int/vt.

elections, participation dropped to 56 percent. Local government elections do not excite people either, with voting rates under 50 percent. Bulgaria is not an exception in this regard; similar trends occurred in the other post-Communist transitional democracies.

The declining voter turnout at all levels of government is a troubling sign of voter alienation from politics. Interestingly, clear majorities among the electorate believe that it is important who is in power (59 percent) and that whom people vote for definitely makes a difference (52 percent).[36] However, they are increasingly losing interest in voting. Some feel tired of the long transition, which took so much effort and hardship, but did not produce the higher living standards people expected. Others believe that the low participation rates indicate a crisis of representation.

Disappointment with party politics has resulted in the election of populist figures who claim they will "clean up" politics and bring a "new" morality.[37] Skeptical voters are ready to support any new names on the ballot just to get rid of the old ones. Many voters eventually feel deceived and misused and decide not to go to the polling stations at all. Even more concerning is a growing trend of vote-buying in the last few years. In the minds of some voters who are disillusioned with politics, the opportunity to earn some money for casting a ballot is attractive, given how much those who get elected benefit later. If strict regulations on election campaigning and transparent government policies are not enforced, political participation may continue to decline. This is evidence that the democratic transition is still incomplete.

ELITE RECRUITMENT

Changes in the procedures for recruitment of public officials have reshaped the national elite. In the past loyalty to the Communist Party was the main criterion for selecting ministers, deputies, and high-level bureaucrats. A small circle around Zhivkov nominated people for office, and those decisions were not open to objection. The party elite—members of Politbureau and the Central Committee and party secretaries of regional organizations—were people recognized as active in the "struggle" for socialism in Bulgaria. Younger recruits to state and party leadership positions were identified among functionaries of the youth organization, the Komsomol.

With the 1989 introduction of a political model based on competition and accountability, elite recruitment became more transparent and democratic. The president and members of National Assembly are elected in direct free elections where parties compete for the support of voters. Parties use procedures for election of national and regional executive bodies by delegates representing rank-and-file members.

A closer look at the individual characteristics of deputies reveals distinct patterns. The previous Communist quota system of representation for all social groups does not exist anymore. After the transition, the group of deputies with liberal professions—that is, scientists, educators, and physicians—has been dominant in the National Assembly. Engineers and economists are another significant group. The most striking difference from the communist era is the near absence of workers in the National Assembly. Party leadership bodies reflect a similar social profile where the well educated, most often economists and lawyers, emerge as chairmen and council members.

The political and the economic elites differ from each other in terms of continuity. The familiar faces of Communist Party functionaries could be recognized among the BSP deputies in the first transitional National Assembly. However, many of them never ran again. Successive elections returned a new group of legislators to office. Only half of the current deputies have served in at least one of the previous assemblies. The incumbency factor has contributed to increased professionalism in the work of the legislators, but concerns also grow that the same politicians get access to the distribution and redistribution of national wealth. Party leaders tend to approve the candidacies of potentially disciplined legislators, and this trend will likely continue in the future.

The economic elite, in contrast, have gone through a less profound change. Because transition was peaceful and its terms were negotiated, the former economic elite managed to survive and accumulate wealth under the new market conditions. The weakness of state institutions in the last years before 1989 and the first years of democratic transition allowed for the economic consolidation of the **nomenklatura**, those holding high-level positions in the Communist Party and the state administration. Ownership of state assets and enterprises was secretly transferred, and money was then safely deposited in international banks. Former members of the Politbureau and the Central Committee occupy top positions in financial institutions, in banks, and on company executive boards. People describe this phenomenon as a transformation of the former communists into the new capitalists—the economic elite largely stayed the same.

The presence of the old *nomenklatura* spurs waves of frustration and calls for justice. However, proposals to ban former Communist functionaries from public office (**lustration**) and to open the confidential files of State Security met serious opposition. Some people believe that those who were part of the totalitarian structures should not be elected or appointed to high positions. Others, mainly BSP supporters, think that imposing restrictions on participation in public life for a significant group of the population is undemocratic and would not help heal the wounds of the past. As a result, Bulgaria did not get a lustration law. In 1992 the government attempted to adopt provisions preventing former members of the BCP leadership from holding high-level positions. The Constitutional Court outlawed most of these as unconstitutional.

Equally painful have been the efforts to open the archives of State Security and publicize the files of government officials. A 1997 law almost succeeded, but the Constitutional Court ruled that its implementation would jeopardize the work of important institutions.[38] A new law, strongly supported by nongovernmental organizations and the media, finally opened the archives in December 2006. Since then, a parliamentary committee responsible for reviewing the files has announced the names of dozens of secret agents who occupied public office after 1989.

Bulgaria has been among the last post-Communist states to deal with the past by exposing current politicians linked to State Security. Politicians from almost all parties, especially the Socialists, resisted the disclosure of such embarrassing information to the general public. Interestingly, however, revealing the secret past of prominent politicians did not always have the expected effect. The leader of the MRF, Ahmed Dogan, was revealed as a former secret agent of State Security, but was not punished at the ballot box, and neither was his party. President Parvanov, also disclosed as a collaborator, does not seem threatened by public outrage. The lustration laws came so late in the transition that the political elite feel safe from the shadows of the communist past.

INTEREST GROUPS

The broad network of associations, societies, and unions functioning in Bulgaria before World War II died after the Communist takeover. In the totalitarian state, trade unions, women's and youth organizations, and professional groups functioned under the close control of the Communist Party. At present, interest groups are numerous and independent from the state, but they show some weaknesses when representing particular policy demands. A major obstacle to the effective operation of these groups is the absence of regulation setting parameters for their activities. At present Bulgaria still has not adopted a law on interest groups and lobbying. This section focuses on several organizations that claim to speak on behalf of groups with distinct interests.

Trade Unions

Trade unions are powerful voices expressing working people's interests. While membership has declined to about 20 percent of the workforce since 1989, now working people organize voluntarily in unions free of government control.

The two major trade union organizations today are the **Confederation of Independent Trade Unions in Bulgaria (CITUB)** and the **Confederation of Labor** Podkrepa (Support). The former is a successor of the state-controlled organization of all employees in Communist Bulgaria. Because it is ideologically more to the left and has connections to the past regime, CITUB enters into preelection coalitions with leftist parties led by the BSP. The latter, Podkrepa, is one of the first anti-Communist groups that formed in February 1989, following the example of Poland's Solidarity. Initially, **Podkrepa** was much more engaged in politics than was CITUB. The union was a cofounder of the UDF; its president, Konstantin Trentchev, was an active negotiator for the opposition at the round table talks; and other of its leaders were elected to the National Assembly. Once the UDF formed its first cabinet, it was difficult for *Podkrepa* to stay with the party in power and defend workers' interests in enterprises still owned by the state. The two trade unions have consistently fought to protect workers' rights to employment, stable salaries, and social security.

Given the difficulties the nation experienced on the road to market reform, CITUB and *Podkrepa* faced an almost impossible combination of tasks. They promoted reforms, but also had to stand for the interests of workers when privatization increased unemployment and high inflation rates eroded wages. Early in the transition, the government recognized the unions as important partners. Along with business, they were included in the Tripartite Commission that sought consensus decisions on reforms. The understanding that social peace was impossible without the active involvement of all three players—state, business, and labor—facilitated an active social dialogue based on partnership.[39]

The two confederations led numerous protests, demonstrations, and strikes to force the government to act to relieve the economic and social pressures of transition. In the fall of 2001, CITUB and Podkrepa organized their first joint demonstration under the slogan "No to Poverty, Misery, and Unemployment." Twelve thousand protesters sent a declaration to the National Assembly with demands for new employment policies, the liberalization of the price of labor, an increase in people's incomes, and transparent privatization. Several months later trade union and employer representatives signed with the government a document called Charter for Social Cooperation, creating a partnership that would reach broad consensus on the completion of the economic reforms.

A new wave of protests demanding "Solidarity for Rights and Justice" spread across the country in 2003, with the enthusiastic participation of unionized and nonunionized workers, the unemployed, retired workers, and students. Especially tense and massive was the 2007 general strike of teachers who were protesting their poor working conditions and demanding a salary increase. The unions directed the strike, which went on for weeks. At the end, the government agreed to a 22.5 percent increase in teachers' monthly wages. The outcome showed that the influence of CITUB and Podkrepa was increasing and that any party in government had to consult them when drafting social policies in the future.

Businesses

The most influential organizations of employers include the **Bulgarian Industrial Association (BIA)**, the Bulgarian Chamber of Commerce and Industry (BCCI), the Union of Economic Enterprising (UEE), and the *Vuzrazhdane* Union of Private Producers (VUPP). Among them, BIA is the oldest nongovernmental business organization; its origin can be traced back to 1980. It has a matrix structure of representation, with industrial branches horizontally and national and regional organizations vertically. This allows BIA to be very effective in multilevel bargaining on economic and social issues with the government and the unions. BIA has emerged as a trustworthy negotiation partner, expressing the interest of the business community in creating conditions for fair competition. Its commitment to modernization and innovation is

best indicated by the fact that scientific organizations, such as the Bulgarian Academy of Sciences, have become members and partners.

The business organizations protect their members by influencing legislation and negotiating labor-state-industry relations. BIA and BCCI have sat on parliamentary committees since 1997 to convey and protect the interests of business. Representatives of these organizations turn to the Council of Ministers to discuss their demands because it is the most active initiator of legislation.

There are two main areas in which businesses still expect to see better results: taxation of profit and license regulation. High taxes have hurt small and medium-size enterprises enormously. According to global rankings on economic freedom, Bulgaria is one of the countries that most heavily regulates business. In addition to these problems, businesses and their organizations complain that political parties and public officials approach them with bribe requests. Therefore, BIA and BCCI support legislation on lobbying and anticorruption measures.

Environmental Groups

The environmental movement was at the forefront of the social effort for democratization in Bulgaria in the late 1980s. The first "green" groups that formed in opposition to the Communist regime called for both a clean environment and human rights. These organizations functioned under the conditions of a totalitarian system. Their activists were intellectuals, dissidents, and both members and nonmembers of the BCP. They claimed that the right of people to clean air and clean water was not political, but human, and that the authorities should respect it. The regime contested the autonomy of those groups and the political issues they addressed.

In 1987 the first open public demonstrations targeted the pollution of the city of Ruse by a Romanian plant across the Danube River. Learning about the outburst of social protest and the ignorance of Communist officials, intellectuals in Sofia founded the National Committee for the Ecological Salvation of Ruse. The committee did not last long because State Security threatened its members and forced them to dissolve the organization. The environmental cause, however, was not dead. New groups pushed for more government attention to the problems of the environment.

In the spring of 1989, BCP dissidents and nonparty members formed **Ecoglasnost**, the most active environmental organization of the early transition years. Its members circulated petitions for the conservation of rivers and mountain areas and submitted them to the National Assembly. In interviews on Radio Free Europe, they also openly denounced the Communist government's discrimination against the Turkish minority. Ecoglasnost leaders were founders of the UDF. As active members of the Grand National Assembly, they participated in the preparation of environmental laws and achieved the closing down of polluting enterprises. Soon conflicts over the future of the organization and its relations with the government and the BSP led to internal splits. A more leftist Political Club "Ecoglasnost" remained active in politics, and its members ran for office with the UDF and later in BSP-led coalitions. The more rightist National Movement Ecoglasnost stayed in the UDF.

The environmental movement in Bulgaria has lost most of the momentum it had in the first years of transition. The fact that politics became very polarized in the 1990s may have had an impact, but the main reason was the weakened public interest in the environment. Previous demands for green policies were displaced by social tensions over economic issues. New environmental groups emerged, but they have not come close to the influence Ecoglasnost once had in the National Assembly.

The Church

As the representative of the nation's largest religious group, the **Bulgarian Orthodox Church (BOC)** has not been as strong as one might expect in the new climate of freedom of worship. Christianity, like other religions, was rejected and its members persecuted during the communist era. The BCP tightly controlled the Holy Synod; the head of the church, the patriarch, was selected with the approval of the Politbureau.

Unlike the Catholic church, which played an active role in Central and Eastern Europe, the BOC was not an agent mobilizing people for dissent and opposition to the totalitarian regime. Surprisingly, the churches filled with people in the months after Zhivkov's removal. Attendance at sermons, baptisms, and religious weddings all became part of the big transformation, although more a symbolic than a real change in a predominantly atheist society.

One of the reasons for the failure of the BOC to emerge as a spiritual leader of Christians is the accommodative behavior of the high-level clergy in the past. As became known after 1989, many priests, including bishops, worked for State Security and provided information on political views inside the ministry. In violation of the secrecy of confession, listening equipment was installed in some of the largest cathedrals. Another reason for the subsequent withdrawal of many potential parishioners was the split within BOC after 1989, which brought much confusion and disappointment. Accusing the patriarch of loyal service to Zhivkov, opposition to the Holy Synod emerged within the UDF, led by Hieromonakh Christophor Subev. Subev organized prayers for the emerging democracy, offered alternative Christmas and Easter liturgies, and called for Patriarch Maxim's resignation. The conflict deepened during the 1990s. This divided the clergy, and politicians supported different factions: The BSP supported the old patriarchy and the UDF the alternative synod. After 2001 Patriarch Maxim prevailed, and the struggle within the BOC ended.

For most Bulgarians the split in the BOC was shameful; hopes died that it could unite people, despite their partisan divisions, around a core set of Christian values. The BOC lost an excellent opportunity to establish itself as spiritual leader. Instead, its most important role today is to maintain a long tradition of celebrating Christian holidays in a country where almost half of the population does not identify with any religion.

Overall, representation of group interests is still deficient. Various organizations mushroomed since 1989, but many of them lack resources or represent causes that few people consider urgent. The problems of economic transition made unions and employer associations dominant in the nongovernmental sector and weakened the green agenda. Youth and women's organizations face challenges when connecting to parties to promote family- and gender-related legislation. In a context of completed market reform, interest groups are now searching for more effective ways to transmit initiatives generated by civil society.

POLITICAL PARTIES

Political parties are important participants in the democratic process of governance; they aggregate the interests of citizens into packages of policies and instruments for their implementation (see Chapter 3). Having clear party platforms that people can relate to is crucial for the performance of any democracy. In the last eighteen years, Bulgaria went through a complex process of transition from a one-party to a multiparty system. Since the fall of the Zhivkov regime, more than three hundred parties have been registered. However, many of them have not functioned effectively for years. The story of post-1989 party-building is full of splits, mergers, reoccurrences, and alignment. Historically, some organizations date back to the times before the Communist takeover in the mid-1940s, while others are brand new. Ideologically, the spectrum of parties today offers voters a variety of policy programs from which to choose. This section focuses on the major parties in Bulgaria, starting from the left and moving to the right.

Bulgarian Socialist Party

The **Bulgarian Socialist Party (BSP)** is broadly considered the primary successor of the Bulgarian Communist Party. It inherited the assets of the BCP and claims to represent those who continue to believe in social equality and government intervention in the economy. The BSP was one of the major parties involved in the transition. It was organizer of and active participant in the national round table talks, and its candidates won several elections. The BSP elite drafted important legislation and governed the country in one-party and coalition cabinets.

Similar to other Communist parties in Central and Eastern Europe, the BCP changed its name early in the transition to show that it was becoming a modern leftist party. The term *Socialist* was supposed to convey a social democratic image of a Scandinavian type and to distance it from its haunting past. In practice, the BSP was not very successful in reforming itself. It remains quite rigid, organizationally and ideologically. Compared to other parties, the BSP has a very bureaucratic apparatus that is centralized and consolidated around mutual interests. The party's access to state resources was a tremendous electoral advantage, especially at the beginning of the transition. The BSP transferred to its ownership many BCP buildings and conveyed state-owned companies and funds into the hands of loyal supporters. Party membership declined after 1989, but the party remains the largest one in Bulgaria, and its supporters are the most loyal and disciplined. At present, the BSP holds the two highest positions in the executive branch; President Parvanov is a former and Prime Minister Stanishev is the current secretary of the party.

To show a commitment to democratic pluralism, BSP allows internal factions, such as the conservative Marxist Platform, the pro-Western The Road to Europe, and the reform-oriented Alliance for Social Democracy. Still, with the exception of the Euroleft, which split in 1997, the BSP and its factions remain unified. Through skillfully selected rhetoric and symbols, the party managed not only to survive the first difficult electoral contests, but also to retain positions leading to power (see Figure 11.5). The BSP presents itself as defender of the socially weak, while at the same time having top businessmen in its ranks. Observers have illustrated this strange situation by the stunning contrast between images of "red voters" and "red millionaires."

Discrepancies between the BSP's socialist appeal and its actual policies make people doubt whether the party will be able to keep its social base. For example, in 2005 the Socialists promised their voters an income increase of 20 percent. So far, they have not delivered, and support for them is decreasing. As people increasingly see disagreement between the BSP's ideology and its policies, the problem of how well the party represents the interests of leftist voters becomes more troubling (Box 11.3).

Movement for Rights and Freedoms

In the political center, the **Movement for Rights and Freedoms (MRF)** has established itself as an influential political player. The MRF was formed in the spring of 1990 by a group of politicians led by Ahmed Dogan, a participant in the ethnic Turks' clandestine resistance against the Communist regime. The MRF is broadly known as the "Turkish party" in Bulgaria, although the Constitution forbids the formation of parties on ethnic and religious grounds. On the premise that the Constitution had to be enforced, a group of BSP deputies appealed to the Constitutional Court for a ruling on the right of the MRF to run in the 1991 election. The judges nominated by the UDF prevailed, arguing that there was nothing inspiring ethnic hatred in the MRF's registration documents. Since then, the MRF has come to play the role of a "balancer" in Bulgarian politics by supporting, at different times, UDF- and BSP-led cabinets.

Organizationally, the MRF is very centralized, with all structures directly controlled by its leader, Dogan. In all parliamentary elections, the MRF has consistently won the votes of ethnic Turks and Muslims, who are disciplined voters and turn out to vote at rates higher than those of the supporters of other groups. With its stable electoral support, the MRF has been an attractive partner for politicians running in

Party Vote Shares

The fragmentation of the party vote shares is increasing

FIGURE 11.5

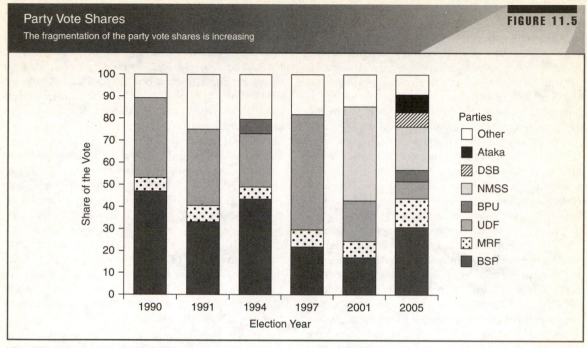

Note: BPU (Bulgarian People's Union) is a coalition including the Bulgarian Agrarian People's Union, the Internal Macedonian Revolutionary Organization, and the Union of Free Democrats.

presidential elections. Both Zhelev and Parvanov gained the vote of the MRF, which does not field candidates of its own. Since 2001 the MRF has been a coalition partner in the NMSS and the BSP cabinets, holding one deputy ministerial post and the agriculture and the environment ministries.

The ideological profile of the MRF is more difficult to define. The party elite are composed of affluent, well-established politicians. They claim that their organization stands in protection of democratic values, but internal party democracy is not a characteristic feature of the MRF. The gap between the party's

---

Between the "Red Grandmas" and the "Red Cell-Phones"

BOX 11.3

After the democratic transition the BSP described itself as "left" and concerned for the "socially weak." In fact, despite its leftist rhetoric the BSP follows rightist policies. Its electorate comprises big business and a multitude of pauperized citizens counting on its "social policies." The press has long noted this disparity and described it as a contrast between the "red grandmas" and the "red cell-phones." The party provided leftist rhetoric to the former, while shaping its policies to the interests of the latter. The BSP used its administrative leverage to reward older cadres with key economic

positions. In the resulting environment of large-scale plunder and tax evasion, even such minimal "social" measures as holding down the prices of vital commodities . . . or subsidizing unprofitable enterprises to avoid raising the level of unemployment became self-defeating because they could only be carried out at the expense of profitable enterprises.

Source: Roumen Daskalov, "A Democracy Born in Pain," in *Bulgaria in Transition: Politics, Economics, and Culture After Communism*, ed. John D. Bell (Boulder, CO: Westview Press, 1998), p. 19.

high-level political leaders and its voters is bridged for the most part by ethnicity. MRF supporters are predominantly Muslim, socially weak, and geographically concentrated in areas severely hit by economic reform. For years the MRF supported government interventionist policies and effectively stopped privatization of state enterprises in the tobacco sector. The continued access to state resources provided by the MRF assured stable voter support and consolidated the position of Dogan as leader.

There are two main challenges facing the MRF as a party. The first is whether it can expand its base of support to include ethnic Bulgarian voters. The MRF leadership has made a genuine effort to break the ethnic capsule and transform the MRF into a national party by including other nationalities among its candidates. Dogan has nominated non-Turkish politicians and experts for appointments allocated to the MRF. These tactics work at the elite level, but the result at the voter level is still uncertain. The second challenge is partially related to the MRF's long presence in power. In a 2005 interview, given two days before the election, Dogan openly admitted the existence of linkages between the MRF and a "loop of firms." The national media accuse the MRF of a surfeit of power and its leader of extreme enrichment, themes that make the public very unhappy with an organization still considered as ethnic.

National Movement Simeon II

One of the youngest and electorally most successful parties in Bulgaria is the **National Movement Simeon II (NMSS)**. This organization emerged as a nonparty nationwide movement in 2001, upon the return of the former king of Bulgaria, Simeon II Saxkoburggotski. It was later transformed into a party. The NMSS is a leader-oriented party in which all important decisions, including deputy nominations and suspensions of deputy mandates, are made unilaterally by the leader, Simeon (see Box 11.1). In 2001 the NMSS won a sweeping victory over the older parties due to its leader's charisma and the public's dissatisfaction with the harsh economic policies of the UDF government (see Figure 11.5). The party has been in power in coalition with the MRF between 2001 and 2005 and with the BSP and the MRF after 2005.

Ideologically, the NMSS defines itself as a liberal party defending such values as individual freedom and responsibility, morality and decency, justice and tolerance, equal opportunities, and solidarity. Its goals include increasing the living standards of all Bulgarians,

facilitating the market economy, and introducing institutions to combat corruption and limit crime. The NMSS is very diverse, with factions representing the interests of various clusters within Bulgaria's emerging middle class. Simeon was initially surrounded by young experts in international financing and banking, the "Bulgarian yuppies," who became ministers in his first cabinet. Other groups within the NMSS represent lawyers, economists, and people in the arts. Internal discipline is maintained exclusively through loyalty to Simeon Saxkoburggotski, yet a few splits have occasionally undermined party cohesion.

The NMSS has recently lost much of its glamour as a "king's" party. NMSS ministers were accused of corrupt behavior and irregular contacts with suspicious businessmen. Bulgarians do not believe anymore in the tale of the "king-savior." Gradually, voters have withdrawn much of their previous support, and Simeon's party won just one seat in the European Parliament election in 2007. According to new surveys, the party might have problems electing representatives to the next National Assembly.

Citizens for European Development of Bulgaria

Significant for the future fortunes of the NMSS was the separation of one of its most popular activists, Boyko Borisov. Borisov was a favorite of Simeon II's and held the prestigious post of secretary of the Ministry of Interior in the NMSS government. After the 2005 election, Borisov felt he was not being treated fairly and left to form a political movement of his own, **Citizens for European Development of Bulgaria (CEDB)**.

The new party is the latest "star" in the sky of Bulgaria's political life. The CEDB has not yet participated in parliamentary and presidential elections, but it has won two other significant contests. Borisov was elected mayor of Sofia, the first non-UDF politician to win this post after 1989. In May 2007 CEDB won the largest share of the vote in Bulgaria's first election of representatives to the European Parliament, which translated into five seats. The young party's success can be attributed mainly to the personality of its leader. Borisov became popular when he worked for the police; his image of an energetic person fighting those who violate the public order won him fame and the mayoral seat. Ideologically, the party identifies itself as a center-rightist organization, and its program and appeals are broadly populist. However, some Bulgarian voters feel uneasy with the presence of too many former State Security officers in the CEDB and with Borisov's close friendship with prominent Socialist functionaries.

Union of Democratic Forces

Just to the right of the political center stands the **Union of Democratic Forces (UDF),** the oldest and most prominent anti-Communist party in Bulgaria. It was created in December 1989 as an umbrella organization uniting eleven groups and parties. These included human rights and environmental groups; the first independent trade union, Podkrepa; and several old parties banned by the Communists. At that time the UDF resembled other catch-all anti-Communist organizations in Central and Eastern Europe, such as Solidarity in Poland and Civic Forum in the Czech Republic. Its first chairman, Zhelyu Zhelev, was a dissident before 1989; later he became the first elected president of Bulgaria.

The UDF has undergone significant organizational changes since its first appearance on the political scene. Initially, it was to remain a loose confederation with mainly coordination functions. Its founders realized that the constituent groups were too diverse for a centralized and coherent organization and that they needed space to develop their own structures. As a result of splits within the UDF in 1991, several member groups (the Social-Democratic Party, the Liberals, and the Agrarian Union–Nikola Petkov) left to run on their own in the parliamentary election that fall. Despite disagreements, the UDF won and formed its first government with Prime Minister Filip Dimitrov. The next big change in the organizational life of the UDF happened in 1997 when, under Chairman Kostov's leadership, it was transformed into a single party.

Since the days of its creation, the UDF has represented the interests of Bulgarians with anti-Communist, pro-democracy, pro–market reform, and pro-Western orientations. The anti-Communist "rightist project" for Bulgaria was most fully realized during the party's second time in power, between 1997 and 2001. The UDF cabinet led by Ivan Kostov relied on its majority support in the National Assembly; it also had President Stoyanov on its side. Serving a full term in office, the UDF government carried out long-delayed, important, but unpopular reforms: privatization and structural reform, reform of the health care system, financial stabilization, and administrative reform. After siding with the West during the Kosovo crisis, Bulgaria was formally invited to negotiate membership in the EU and NATO.

Unlike the BSP, the UDF has weaker control over its parliamentary group and the voting behavior of its members. Internal personal conflicts and destructive fights have hurt the image of the organization in the eyes of its supporters. The defeat in the 2001 election placed the UDF in opposition. Blamed for the loss, Kostov announced his decision to resign as party leader, but the crisis deepened. Once the largest political force, the UDF is now struggling to keep its position as fourth in terms of the size of its parliamentary delegation. Unable to find an effective way to articulate the new demands of its constituents and mobilize them to vote, the UDF keeps losing election after election.

Democrats for Strong Bulgaria

In a search for "new" political representation in the early 2000s, some supporters of the UDF explored the formation of another party through small citizen groups. They discussed policy matters online and formed a citizen association, Dialog. Its members appealed to former Prime Minister Kostov and other parliamentarians to draft an agenda for development of the country after the transition. A nationwide campaign created **Democrats for Strong Bulgaria (DSB)** in 2004. The party is committed to the revision of concession contracts signed by Simeon's cabinet, which placed a heavy burden on taxpayers; abolition of immunity status for deputies and magistrates; and completion of administrative reforms. Its foreign policy priorities include two important security issues: the energy dependence on Russia and the future enlargement of the EU in the Balkans.

The DSB is the single Bulgarian party formed as a result of a grassroots movement. Its organizational life is based on solid democratic principles, but its electoral success remains modest. Some of the former anti-BSP voters had shifted their preferences toward the NMSS; many simply do not vote anymore. Another obstacle to the growth of the party is the personality of DSB leader Kostov, whom critics accuse of a "commander" style of leadership. A charismatic politician, with a clear vision for the future, Kostov is now equally strongly respected by DSB followers and despised by political opponents. It has become clear that without recruitment of new, younger people as leaders and formation of partnerships with other rightist parties, the DSB would not be able to expand its influence on policies it championed from the beginning. An important step in this direction was made with the formation of a DSB/UDF pre-electoral coalition for participation in the upcoming 2009 parliamentary election.

Ataka

The **Ataka** (National Union Attack) was registered just two months before the 2005 parliamentary elections as a coalition among the National Movement for the Salvation of the Fatherland, the Bulgarian National Patriotic Party, and the Union of Patriotic Forces and Military of the Reserve-Defense. Its members call themselves patriots, but analysts describe the party as xenophobic, anti-Semitic, and racially biased. Volen Siderov, Ataka's leader, and other party functionaries have used harsh words to criticize the Bulgarian political elite, the "privileged" treatment of minorities, and Bulgaria's engagement in NATO and in the current Iraq war. Their rhetoric is softer on Bulgaria's EU membership, but very disapproving of full compliance with Brussels, including the shutting down of two reactors at the Kozloduy nuclear plant.

Ataka did surprisingly well in elections, winning twenty-two seats in the National Assembly in 2005 and three seats in the European Parliament in 2007 (see Figure 11.5). Its candidate for the presidency was a top second in the first round of the 2006 presidential election and lost to the incumbent in the runoff. Ataka's electoral success is considered troubling both at home and abroad. In Bulgaria people think that the gains of the MRF, and especially its continuous presence in the executive, triggered the need for the formation of a nationalistic party. They argue that the MRF and Ataka reinforce each other, each giving the other a reason to exist. As a result of the discriminatory platform of and inflammatory speeches made by Ataka's deputies, politicians from all other parliamentary parties have distanced themselves from the nationalistic organization.

The Party System

One of the first important tasks of a transition from totalitarianism to democracy is the development of a system that represents the interests of various social groups. It is well known that some systems are more permissive because they have lower thresholds for representation, introduce less-rigid conditions for party registration, and enhance the financing of organizational activities. The **proportional representation** (PR) system of election of deputies and easy

preregistration requirements facilitate multipartyism in Bulgaria. Given the important institutional reforms and the changing patterns of voter identification, what kind of a party system exists in Bulgaria today?

In the course of twenty years, Bulgaria's one-party system has been transformed into a fragmented multiparty system. Today there are more than three hundred organizations registered as parties, and just about two dozen run in elections. The shape of the party system has not been the same since the start of democratic transition. Three parties—the BSP, UDF, and MRF—have obtained permanent parliamentary representation. While they dominated the National Assembly in the 1990s, new entrants such as the NMSS, Ataka, and the DSB challenged the "bipolar model" in 2001 and 2005. The success of the newcomers can be partially explained by the fact that only 4 percent of the vote is needed for an organization to win seats. Limitations on access to state subsidies have not effectively reduced the number of parties. So many small nonparliamentary parties still exist because of the incentive to run in local elections and win seats on city and municipal executive councils.

One of the major disadvantages of excessive multipartyism is the failure to build stable governing majorities. Bulgaria applies proportional representation, an electoral formula associated with party fragmentation, but four out of six post-1989 parliamentary elections produced majoritarian winners. The dominance of the Communist/anti-Communist cleavage in the 1990s resulted in a configuration dominated by two large parties, the BSP and the UDF. This is changing, though, as shown by the fragmented party vote shares in the last elections (see Figure 11.5).

ELECTORAL COMPETITION

Electoral reform was recognized early in the transition as important for holding free and competitive elections. Reform brought two major changes in the system of parliamentary elections. The first change was introduced after heated debates at the national round table in early 1990. The ex-Communists and the opposition had different visions about how the seats in the constituent assembly should be allocated. The BSP representatives preferred a majoritarian system because theirs was the only party that had the resources to run individual candidates in district races.[40] The UDF leaders insisted on proportional rules and multimember districts. They hoped that such an arrangement would allow them run an ideological, anti-Communist, party-labeled campaign. In addition, the opposition did not have the organizational network, personnel, and media access for local campaigning. The round table decided in favor of a mixed system. According to the new rules, 200 assembly seats were to be competed in majoritarian single-member districts and 200 seats in twenty-eight multimember districts through closed-list PR. A 4 percent threshold in the proportional distribution was set to reduce parliamentary fragmentation and facilitate the consolidation of the party system. By combining two methods of election, the mixed system of 1990 allowed both individual candidates and party-ranked candidates to run.

Bulgaria used the mixed system for just one election. In July 1991, before its dissolution, the Grand National Assembly adopted a new electoral law. The switch was caused by changes in the party system. By the summer of 1991, the BSP had suffered a significant withdrawal of party members and a further decline in public support. The Socialists were not certain how many votes they would receive in the fall election, so competing in majoritarian districts seemed too risky. For its part the opposition was shaken by splits over the new Constitution. Under conditions of growing uncertainty for both the BSP and the UDF, the electoral system was changed once again. The new election law of 1991 created a closed-list PR system with 240 parliamentary seats allocated in thirty-one electoral districts, retaining the 4 percent nationwide threshold.

The basic formula for election of deputies was kept virtually intact after 1991. It made parties central players in the electoral game. Party leaders are extremely powerful, for they play the role of gatekeepers who control nominations and parliamentary mandates. For this reason attempts to alter the system of elections have failed until recently. The issue became salient again, however. Now, common Bulgarians know much more about proportional and majoritarian representation and strongly favor the latter as a remedy for corrupt party politics. A new electoral law was passed by the National Assembly in April 2009, which made thirty-one of the deputy seats majoritarian and raises an eight percent threshold for coalitions of parties. Many see these changes as an attempt by the ruling coalition to reduce the chances of the rightist DSB/UDF alliance of winning any representation.

Parliamentary and Presidential Elections

In the nineteen years after the end of the Communist regime, Bulgaria held six parliamentary and four presidential elections, all of them recognized by international organizations as free and fair. The electoral campaign starts two months before ballots are cast. The first elections were marked by fierce competition between parties, big outdoor demonstrations, audacious speeches, and voter mobilization. With each subsequent election cycle, the initial enthusiasm cooled down and people became more indifferent to the outcome. A common campaigning strategy in recent years is to accuse the other side of corruption and to "reveal" yet another State Security agent running for office. Elections have lost some of their fervor as contests of ideas.

Election returns show that Bulgarians understand and use their power to vote incumbents out of office when things are bad. Since the beginning of transition, no party has won two elections in a row. The BSP and the UDF dominated the party system in the 1990s; they alternated in power with or without the support of the MRF. Between 1991 and 1997, the turbulent time of aborted reforms, Bulgarian governments could not carry out their full term, and preliminary parliamentary elections had to be called. Conditions were extremely volatile in the early spring of 1997 when, in the midst of a severe crisis, the incumbent government resigned and the BSP returned the mandate for formation of a new cabinet back to the president. This opened the door for a new election. Starting with the victories of the UDF in 1997 and the NMSS in 2001, the governments have served full four-year terms. The current tripartite cabinet of the BSP, MRF, and NMSS is also completing its term. The governing coalitions after 2000 have been durable, albeit fragmented (see Figure 11.6).

Presidential elections are less dramatic, for both the elite and the public understand that the Constitution assigns the president fewer powers. Still, presidential contests are also competitive; a second round has always been necessary to determine a final winner. The UDF and BSP candidates won those contests after rallying the support of broad coalitions. Zhelev's and Parvanov's victories came following parliamentary elections won by their own parties; Stoyanov prevailed when the ruling BSP had already lost control over the economy.

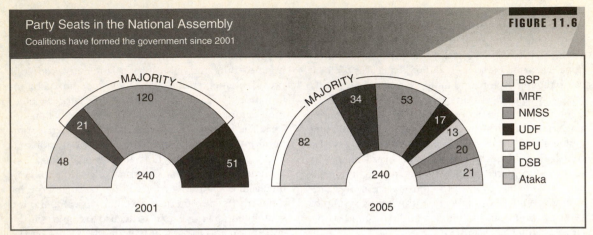

FIGURE 11.6

Party Seats in the National Assembly
Coalitions have formed the government since 2001

Legend: BSP, MRF, NMSS, UDF, BPU, DSB, Ataka

2001: 240, MAJORITY, 48, 21, 120, 51

2005: 240, MAJORITY, 82, 34, 53, 17, 13, 20, 21

Note: BPU (Bulgarian People's Union) is a coalition including the Bulgarian Agrarian People's Union, the Internal Macedonian Revolutionary Organization, and the Union of Free Democrats.

Social Bases of Party Support

Voters are now presented with numerous choices at elections, but how do they select a party? In developed democracies people learn about parties and attach to them in an environment of established democratic structures and processes. Citizens there have a more complete idea of what their interests are and who can better represent them. In a post-Communist setting, social restratification and party-building take place simultaneously, making it difficult for voters to attach to a party. Two decades after the fall of the totalitarian regime, about 40 percent of Bulgarians say they feel close to a party, and their social characteristics show particular patterns of political support.

As in the early years of the transition, the Socialists draw more electoral support from the rural areas. As Table 11.2 shows, in 2007 the BSP's voters tended to be over 60 years of age and were more likely women. In contrast, the base of the two rightist parties, the UDF and the DSB (the anti-Communist opposition of the 1990s), is in Sofia and the large cities. Bulgarians with primary or lower education levels are almost absent in the UDF/DSB base. The two parties' strength comes from middle-aged voters, the generation of those who filled the streets of Sofia in the cold winters of 1990 and 1997.

The ethnic MRF and the nationalistic Ataka have demographically distinct voter bases. The MRF is extremely strong in rural Bulgaria, much more so than any other Bulgarian party, while Ataka persists in the towns. Their bases are almost reversed with regard to

the age of the main voter groups: Most of the MRF supporters are younger and less educated people, while Ataka attracts more voters among older Bulgarians and high school graduates. The larger share of both parties' support comes from male voters.

The voters of the two centrist parties, the NMSS and the CEDB, have similar socio-demographic profiles. This is not very surprising, given their similar origin and message. Simeon's and Borisov's parties draw more voters from among the urban, better educated, and younger population of Bulgaria. After the NMSS's failure to win a second mandate and the scandals surrounding Simeon's restored estates, the king's party has been losing support across all social sectors. The CEDB quickly filled this vacuum and is now the new centrist party that draws support from groups previously represented by the NMSS and the UDF. By joining the European People's Party, Borisov tried to present the CEDB as a rightist party. A failure of the tripartite Stanishev government might help the CEDB expand its base with young urban voters who are abandoning the NMSS.

THE POLICYMAKING PROCESS

Policymaking is a very different process now than during communism. The transformation of an idea for government action into a policy may start as a measure discussed by the cabinet, a demand raised by workers during a strike, or a recommendation by a nongovernmental organization. Legislating policies

| Characteristics of Party Supporters, 2007 | | | | | | | **TABLE 11.2** |
| The BSP draws its support from older voters, while the CEDB is strong in the cities | | | | | | | |

	BSP	MRF	NMSS	CEDB	UDF	DSB	Ataka
Residence							
Sofia	24.5	1.0	7.4	26.7	8.6	14.6	9.4
Large town	19.6	2.1	14.8	32.1	7.2	4.8	14.8
Small town	24.3	13.4	5.5	22.4	3.7	4.0	16.6
Village	22.3	43.5	3.6	10.3	2.5	1.0	9.5
Education							
College	24.3	4.8	8.5	26.6	6.9	7.0	10.7
High school	18.9	18.5	6.2	23.9	4.6	3.3	14.8
Primary & lower	24.1	46.6	2.4	6.3	1.5	1.4	10.5
Age							
18–30	9.5	27.1	9.6	27.9	4.7	3.5	10.5
31–40	10.0	25.6	7.2	28.9	5.3	4.1	10.9
41–50	14.6	22.8	6.7	25.9	5.2	4.4	9.8
51–60	21.7	15.7	5.6	21.9	4.8	4.4	15.1
61+	39.9	12.1	3.9	10.8	4.2	4.2	14.2
Gender							
Male	19.7	22.0	5.4	20.1	5.5	3.7	15.3
Female	23.8	17.1	7.1	22.5	4.1	4.5	10.0

Source: Alpha Research, Exit Poll for European Parliament Election, May 21, 2007. Retrieved 28 April 2008 from www.aresearch.org.

is a complex process in which the three main branches of government are involved. Policy implementation is entirely in the hands of the cabinet and the local administration. The policies and their success are shaped by the governing majorities, as well as by the process of Europeanization, which mitigates sharp ideological differences.

The Constitution establishes a three-stage process by which a policy proposal becomes a law (see Figure 11.7). In the initiation stage, members of the National Assembly and the Council of Ministers introduce the bill; the president does not have this power. The ministers assign experts within their administration to prepare the draft legislation, which is then discussed and approved at meetings of the cabinet. The procedure requires that the sponsors of the bill provide motives that focus on the expected consequences of implementation. Within three days after submission, the National Assembly chair distributes the draft legislation for review to the relevant committees and determines which one among them will play a leading role during the deliberations.

The National Assembly considers the legislative draft in committee meetings and at plenary sessions. Members of standing committees study the policy proposal to assess its importance and discuss findings at joint sessions. They prepare a statement with opinions and justifications and present it to the chair of the leading committee and the chair of the National Assembly. This statement is based on additional research and may also incorporate data and advice provided by experts and representatives of nongovernmental organizations. Within a two-month period after initial introduction, the legislative draft, together with the motives and a report from the leading committee, is distributed to all deputies. They debate and vote on the bill in two readings, first on the entire text as a whole and then paragraph by paragraph and article by article.

At the stage of enactment, the president either signs the bill and sends it to the *Official Gazette* for

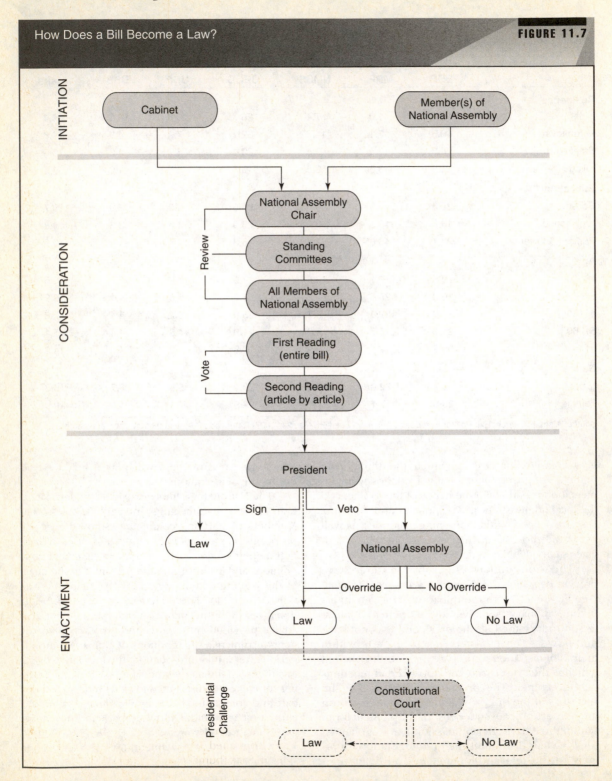

How Does a Bill Become a Law?   FIGURE 11.7

promulgation or returns it for further consideration. If the National Assembly decides to stick to the initially adopted version, the president may decide to turn to the Constitutional Court for a ruling on the constitutionality of the bill.

POLICY OUTPUTS

While the choice of policy measures is important, their outcomes are not determined solely by what is adopted as laws and procedures. The results of public policies are often affected by other factors, including government capacity for enforcement, demographic burden, and international markets. In the case of Bulgaria, the public expects and politicians promise benefits to buffer pressures from the transition, but budgetary constraints hinder generous support to all who need it. The introduction of competitive politics increased the role of some social groups, among them pensioners, who are the largest and most active voting segment of the electorate. At the same time, smaller and less vocal groups in need, such as orphans and persons with disabilities, receive less assistance and attention. Policy outcomes are also shaped by international institutions and Bulgaria's engagement in global initiatives. Governments, regardless of their ideology, are bound by commitments to fiscal discipline made before the International Monetary Fund and other financial institutions abroad. Promises to minimize the budget deficit shaped distinct outcomes: Compliance hindered the generous distribution of social benefits, but helped fulfill the requirements for EU accession earlier than expected.

The rest of this section focuses on the results of policy implementation in three key areas (market reforms, welfare, and foreign policy) and the obstacles to transparent governance. All of them are important for the future of democracy in Bulgaria. The transition to a market economy has been one of the main goals of the post-Communist transformation. In the eyes of a majority of the people, how well the nascent democratic system performs is demonstrated by whether the government takes good care of those in need. Integration into European structures has been desired as a guarantee for democratic governance, economic prosperity, and national security. Achievements in each of these areas have been overshadowed by the spread of corrupt practices that have hurt fair and accountable policy implementation.

Market Reform Policies

The development of **market reform** policies has been extremely difficult. There was no previous world experience with the transformation of a totally centralized system into a market economy. As elsewhere in the post-Communist world, Bulgarian elites chose to carry out simultaneous political and economic reforms, a decision that further complicated the transition to free markets. Issues such as the speed and mode of privatization confused Bulgaria's policymakers, who were concerned about the electoral cost of radical solutions. The lack of commitment to quick reforms in the early 1990s and losses suffered from the international embargo over neighboring Yugoslavia made things worse. The country fell into a deep economic crisis; bank after bank declared bankruptcy in the summer of 1996. The series of failures confirmed the difficulty of creating a market economy through policies favoring government intervention.[41]

A package of policies adopted by the 1997–2001 UDF cabinet of Ivan Kostov effectively carried out market reforms. The government closed down many losing state enterprises and cut subsidies allowed by the previous Socialist cabinet. Privatization was accelerated; the number of companies privatized in 1998 alone equaled the total for the entire 1989–1997 period.[42] The UDF cabinet made the critical decision to introduce a **currency board** as an instrument to keep inflation down and stabilize the economy. The new regime pegged the exchange rate of the local currency, the lev, to the German mark and later to the euro. Critics at the time opposed this policy, arguing that it would expose the domestic economy to disturbances in the foreign currency to which the lev was tied. Soon the results of Kostov's policies proved such concerns were wrong.

The triple-digit inflation of 1996–1997 was replaced by 5.7 percent inflation after 1998. Strict financial discipline and stabilization helped to substantially cut down the budget deficit; the amount of foreign direct investment in 1998–2002 surged to ten times the 1990–1996 levels. Years of negative growth of the economy ended and were followed by a period of stable annual increases in the GDP (see Figure 11.8). In three consecutive years, 2004–2006, Bulgaria maintained a 7 percent GDP per capita growth rate, one of the highest rates in Europe. These positive trends were continued under the centrist government of Simeon Saxkoburggotski.

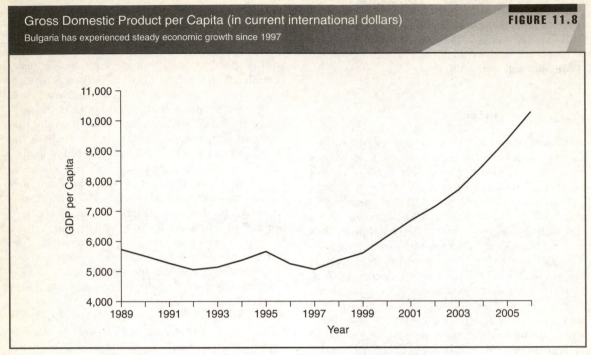

Gross Domestic Product per Capita (in current international dollars)
Bulgaria has experienced steady economic growth since 1997

FIGURE 11.8

Source: World Bank, *World Development Indicators Online*. Retrieved 3 May 2008 from www.worldbank.org.

Welfare Policies

Macroeconomic stability is important, but individual citizens want to feel economic improvement in the everyday life of their families. The implementation of policies aimed at the introduction of a market economy incurred awful hardships for the ordinary household. Governments had to remain committed to financial discipline and at the same time find ways to alleviate problems related to unemployment and deteriorating living standards. As Figure 11.9 reveals, spending on social protection is the largest category of central government expenditures. Two social assistance instruments that proved successful were the guaranteed minimum income and the energy benefit programs. Designed to provide relief for households hit by the reforms, they partially filled the gap of the lost social services. Through these programs, cash and in-kind assistance is provided to the poorest 20 percent among the Bulgarian population.

After 1997 living standards started to improve. To deal with unemployment, the Ministry of Labor and Social Policy developed programs to provide more

job opportunities for young people and facilitated vocational education and training. The outcomes are encouraging, with unemployment rates dropping from a high of 18 percent in 2000 to 6–7 percent in 2007. Yet, government policies have not been very effective in improving the lives of particular groups. Most of the older, retired people still live below the poverty line. The indexing of pensions lags behind the rising costs of heating, basic food, and other consumer goods. Often the government decides to increase pensions on the eve of elections or before Christmas (the so-called thirteenth payment), but the extra money is too little to bring substantial improvement.

The provision of quality health care to those in need is hindered by incomplete reform of the health care system. A centrally managed health insurance fund and private providers have replaced the free medical service of the communist era. The Health Insurance Act of 1998 introduced this reform. However, the system has not worked well and urgently needs repair. The Ministry of Healthcare, the manager of the health insurance structure, occasionally declares a

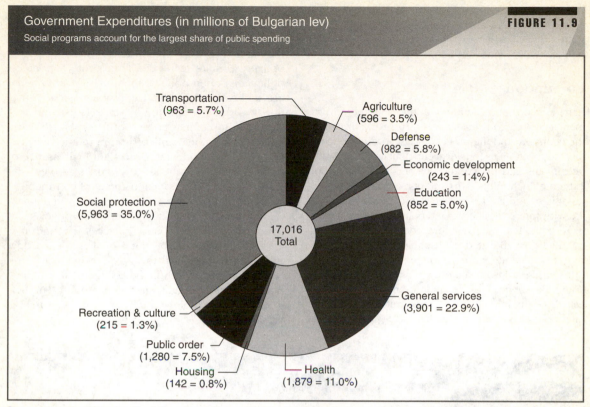

Government Expenditures (in millions of Bulgarian lev)
Social programs account for the largest share of public spending

FIGURE 11.9

Transportation
(963 = 5.7%)

Agriculture
(596 = 3.5%)

Defense
(982 = 5.8%)

Economic development
(243 = 1.4%)

Education
(852 = 5.0%)

Social protection
(5,963 = 35.0%)

17,016
Total

General services
(3,901 = 22.9%)

Recreation & culture
(215 = 1.3%)

Public order
(1,280 = 7.5%)

Housing
(142 = 0.8%)

Health
(1,879 = 11.0%)

Source: International Monetary Fund, *Government Finance Statistics Yearbook,* Washington, D.C.: International Monetary Fund, 2007, 92–94.

deficiency of funds. Further, reimbursement of physicians for services provided is difficult to monitor, and employers who misreport wages to reduce payments remain unpunished.

Foreign Policies

Bulgaria has achieved its two main foreign policy goals: NATO and **EU accession**. In 1994 Bulgaria joined NATO's Partnership for Peace program and three years later applied for full membership. At the 2002 summit of the Atlantic Pact in Prague, seven post-Communist states including Bulgaria received invitations to join. Initially, the BSP opposed membership in the Western military alliance, arguing in favor of neutrality and against the 1999 intervention of NATO in Serbia. By 2000, however, a consensus emerged among all political forces and a majority of the public in support of membership. As a NATO

member, Bulgaria transformed its troops into a professional army and built compatible arms and communications. The country participates in NATO's peace missions in Kosovo and Afghanistan and sent troops in support of the American effort in Iraq.

The road to EU membership was longer and more complicated. Bulgaria signed an association agreement in 1993, submitted its application for membership in 1995, and started negotiations for accession in 2000. Despite progress made in many policy areas, Bulgaria, along with Romania, was left out of the group of ten countries that joined the EU in 2004. At the time of accession in January 2007, justice system reform and anticorruption policies remained areas of concern. As a result, the EU imposed restrictions on the free movement of Bulgarian workers to other EU member states. The European Commission kept the right to enforce other safeguard measures if needed. Bulgaria has been closely monitored by

Brussels, and the findings so far are not satisfactory. As the European Commission concluded in 2007, the right policies have been adopted, but there is lack of political will to enforce them.

Corruption

Rampant corruption seriously undermines the government's policy efforts in key areas. The marketization of the economy and the process of privatization opened many opportunities for illegal enrichment. Bribing public officials and police and customs officers, paying extra money to physicians and nurses, and buying admission to and grades in high schools and universities are widespread. Politicians and political parties also engage in malfeasance at unprecedented levels. Public contracts are allocated to "friendly" firms, loyal supporters and donors are appointed to attractive positions, and parties raise money in violation of the law and make themselves dependent on corporate interests. Vote-buying decides election outcomes in many races for positions in local government (see Box 11.4).

Anticorruption policies have not been effective so far. Links among politicians, parties, big businesses, and organized crime weaken the ability of the nascent political system to develop transparent policies. To hide secret deals and protect sponsors, politicians "open political umbrellas" over criminal acts and crooked groups. The problem is not institutional, some people argue, since legislation and structures to combat corruption do exist. Bulgaria joined international anticorruption treaties and developed a national strategy to fight malfeasance of different types. Yet, the legal system has shown a remarkable inability to sanction crimes of corruption.

Membership in the EU was not an immediate remedy for the failure of anticorruption policies. On the contrary, the distribution of accession funds created yet another opportunity for illegal exchange. Brussels's response was to stop financing many projects. Under pressure from the EU, more effort is now being put into the fight against corruption. The Bulgarian public wholeheartedly welcomes Brussels's harsh warnings.

Sneakers for Votes

BOX 11.4

The so-called sneaker trick, invented by businessman Alexander Tassev, will remain notorious the modern history of Bulgarian elections. He used to distribute one running shoe to Roma voters in the region of Kyustendil before voting. Upon exiting the polling station, the voter received the second shoe.

This episode is just one element in a scheme of corrupt exchange between some businesses and political parties. In this cycle a businessman makes investments (buys votes) in a party candidate and thus manipulates the election outcome. In return he is awarded an advantage in the bidding for a government contract, which he receives with no outside competition. If a participant in the exchange does not stick to his promises, organized crime elements are the enforcers. This scheme is often used in Bulgaria to win elections and buy political influence.

Tassev did not win an election himself. In 1995 he ran for a seat on the municipal council of Kyustendil and lost. In 1997 he paid for a safe seat in the parliamentary group of the Bulgarian Business Bloc, but the same seat had been sold to two people, and Tassev remained out of the National Assembly.

"There was hardly anybody who did not know him," commented Lyudmil Stoyanov, the mayor of Kyustendil and a favorite of Tassev. Tassev made a bid on him, instead of his former protégé Kiril Aleksov from BSP. The NMSS candidate won with 14,644 votes over the 14,100 of his opponent. The rumor had it that "the difference was bought out." Tassev had the protection of the municipal council in Kyustendil. Before his death he had seven or eight council members who paid him back with either a concession or something else. Emil Koshlukov, a former member of the parliament, affirmed that Tassev obtained concessions for ballots. For example, one of Tassev's firms won an uncontested bidding process for the delivery of fuels to the municipality. The mayor did not think that was wrong.

In May 2007 Tassev was shot dead with two bullets while in his Mercedes.

Source: Christi Petrova, *The Kings of Smuggling* (Sofia: Sluntze, 2007), 57–64.

PROSPECTS FOR DEMOCRACY IN BULGARIA

Bulgaria's transition from communism to democracy has been an ambitious journey full of challenges, uncertainties, hardships, and achievements. From the very beginning, the goals were to develop a system of representative government, a state governed by the rule of law, a prosperous economy driven by private entrepreneurship, and close cooperation and partnership with the West. By the mid-1990s citizens felt deeply disappointed and discouraged by the protracted reforms. In his farewell address to the nation, President Zhelev declared the transition failed, pointing at the inability of the country to carry out the necessary economic and social changes.

The 1997 electoral victory of the UDF marked the start of real reforms and became a watershed in the development of the Bulgarian transition. The subsequent results confirm that a successful transformation required a resolute political elite to take responsibility and call on the public for sacrifice. The policies of gradual reform aimed at softening the pain of the shift did not work; they just prolonged the agony of economic uncertainty for hundreds of Bulgarian families.

For observers from outside, the course of the democratic transition in Bulgaria may look messy and uncertain. In the mixed record of success, achievements are often obscured by current problems that do not seem to receive immediate attention. Commentators have either bypassed Bulgaria when acclaiming the East European revolutions or referred to its bumpy progress to emphasize the success of front-runners Poland, Hungary, and the Czech Republic. One cannot fully assess the Bulgarian transition, however, without comparing political life now to the situation twenty years ago. During this time Bulgaria has managed to build new democratic institutions for representative government, to hold free and fair elections of public officials, to develop a multiparty system, and to maintain a vibrant political life based on pluralism and civil liberties. At the time when ethnic war broke out in neighboring Yugoslavia, Bulgarian elites managed to avoid conflict by engaging representatives of the ethnic Turkish community in the national and local governments. Although delayed, integration into NATO and the EU was accomplished, and membership is broadly expected to contribute to national security and to a more prosperous future.

Still, much more could have been achieved in the years of transition. It seems that the reason for this is not a failure to establish democratic institutions and structures. Bulgaria has quite successfully done that with the adoption of a new Constitution, legislative reform, and competitive party politics. Instead, the democratic process is deficient, impaired, and incomplete. Policy decisionmaking is often not transparent, politicians are not held accountable, and the public interest is vulnerable to malfeasance. Many people blame the way the transition started, through negotiations between elites who bargained behind the scenes and struck secret deals for protection for the old guard and access to power for the opposition. The files of State Security were either deliberately destroyed or selectively used to compromise UDF leaders. Major laws on economic restructuring were passed as early as 1991, but reforms were delayed while circles close to the BSP were allowed to strip assets from the state and carry out a "quiet privatization." Extensive anticorruption and party finance legislation was introduced, but not enforced. The justice system, with its new structures, was granted independence, but it failed to act on dozens of "mafia-style" killings, and the guilty remain at large.

Perhaps the most serious threat to democratic consolidation in Bulgaria now is the mass disappointment with politics that alienates citizens from the political process. Disgusted with politicians who misuse power for personal enrichment, ordinary citizens have lost much of the trust they once had in the new elites. The PR system for the election of deputies facilitated the transition from a one-party to a multiparty system, but its closed-list version deprived voters of the opportunity to elect those for whom voter needs come first. The number of Bulgarians who demand electoral reform is now on the rise. Hope is also strong that membership in the EU, similar to the currency board ten years ago, will help strengthen financial discipline and overcome the difficulties in governance. Although real problems exist, the process of democratization in Bulgaria is irreversible, as demonstrated by the sound public rejection of corrupt practices and the thrust for European norms of honest and accountable government.

KEY TERMS

Ataka

Bulgarian Communist
Party (BCP)

Bulgarian Industrial
Association (BIA)

Bulgarian Orthodox
Church (BOC)

Bulgarian Socialist
Party (BSP)

Citizens for European
Development
of Bulgaria
(CEDB)

Confederation of
Independent Trade
Unions in Bulgaria
(CITUB)

Confederation of Labor
Podkrepa

Constitutional Court

Council of Ministers

Currency board

Democrats for Strong
Bulgaria (DSB)

Ecoglasnost

EU accession

Kostov, Ivan

Lustration

Market reform

Movement for Rights
and Freedoms (MRF)

National Assembly

National Movement
Simeon II (NMSS)

National Round Table

Nomenklatura

Ombudsman

Politbureau

President

Prime Minister

Privatization

Proportional
representation

Saxkoburggotski,
Simeon

Union of Democratic
Forces (UDF)

Zhelev, Zhelyu

Zhivkov, Todor

SUGGESTED READINGS

Bell, John D., ed. *Bulgaria in Transition: Politics, Economics, Society, and Culture After Communism*. Boulder, CO: Westview Press, 1998.

Crampton, Richard I. *Bulgaria*. Oxford History of Modern Europe. New York: Oxford University Press, 2007.

Ganev, Venelin I. *Preying on the State: The Transformation of Bulgaria After 1989*. Ithaca, NY: Cornell University Press, 2007.

Genov, Nikolai, and Anna Krasteva, eds. *Recent Social Trends in Bulgaria 1960–1995*. Montreal: McGill-Queen's University Press, 2001.

Giatzidis, Emil. *An Introduction to Post-Communist Bulgaria: Political, Economic, and Social Transformations*. Manchester, England: Manchester University Press, 2002.

Melone, Albert P. *Creating Parliamentary Government: The Transition to Democracy in Bulgaria*. Columbus: Ohio State University, 1998.

INTERNET RESOURCES

National Assembly: **www.parliament.bg**

Council of Ministers of Republic of Bulgaria: **www.government.bg**

Bulgarian News Agency: **www.bta.bg**

Bulgarian National Radio: **www.bnr.bg**

St. St. Cyril and Methodius National Library: **www.nationallibrary.bg**

ENDNOTES

1. Georgi Angelov, "Bulgaria—State and Perspectives in Late 2004," in *Anatomy of the Transition: The Economic Policy of Bulgaria from 1989 to 2000,* ed. Asenka Hristova, Vladislav Slantchev, Georgi Angelov, Georgi Stoev, Dimitar Tchobanov, Krasen Stantchev, Lachezar Bogdanov, and Martin Dimitrov (Sofia: CIELA, 2004), 17.

2. Angelov, "Bulgaria," 19.

3. Agency of Employment, Statistics and Analyses: Summary Data on the Labour Market. Retrieved 31 March 2008, from www.az.government.bg.

4. World Bank, Human Development Section Unit, Europe and Central Asia Region, *Bulgaria: Poverty Assessment,* Report No. 24516-BUL World Bank: Washington, D.C., October 29, 2002.

5. World Bank, *Bulgaria: Poverty Assessment.*

6. Evgenii Dainov, *Their Voices: Minorities in Bulgaria, Government Policies and the Media* (Sofia: Centre for Social Practices, 2005). Retrieved 10 April 2008 from www.csp-sofia.org/PDF/Bg/policy.Paper.pdf.

7. Nikola Lalov, "The Negativism Towards the Turks Is Declining," *Mediapool,* April 4, 2008. Retrieved 10 April 2008 from www.mediapool.bg.

8. Dobrinka Kostova, "Bulgaria: Economic Elite Change During the 1990s," in *Elites After State Socialism: Theories and Analysis,* ed. John Hingley and Gyorgy Lengyel (Lanham, MD: Rowman & Littlefield, 2000), 199–207; "Alternative Women's Organization Established," AU1803141190 Sofia Domestic Service in Bulgarian, 17 March 1990. *FBIS–EEU* (Foreign Broadcast Information Service, Daily Report: Eastern Europe). New Cannon, March 19, 1990, 16.

9. The court refused to register Simeon II's organization soon enough to participate in the 2001 election. The announced decision referred to irregularities in the registration documents.

10. Speech of Simeon Saxkoburggotski, "The Political System and Its Morals Need Immediate Change," 6 April 2001. Retrieved 19 March 2008 from www.ndsv.bg/content/315.html.

11. Venelin I. Ganev, "Bulgaria: The (Ir)Relevance of Post-Communist Constitutionalism," in *Democratic Consolidation in Eastern Europe,* ed. Jan Zielonka (Oxford, England: Oxford University Press, 2001).

12. Ganev, "Bulgaria," 192.

13. Instead of being concentrated into a single institution, as is the case in presidential systems in, for example, the United States. See Chapter 4 in this book.

14. Jon Elster, Claus Offe, and Ulrich K. Preuss, *Institutional Design in Post-Communist Societies: Rebuilding the Ship at Sea* (Cambridge, England: Cambridge University Press, 1998), 98.

15. In the late evening hours of December 14, 1989, the National Assembly was holding a session expected to revoke Article 1 of the current constitution, establishing the leading role of the Communist Party. After it became clear that the Assembly had no genuine intention to do that, at least so soon, angry people gathered in front of the Assembly to express their frustration. Facing pressure from the demonstrators who were threatening to storm the building, President Mladenov uttered the phrase "Let the tanks come!" This moment was caught on tape by a cameraman standing nearby and later broadcast again and again on the national TV channel. After all, no tanks were brought and no guns were fired, but Mladenov's words cost him the post.

16. This vote was quite surprising because the National Assembly was dominated by the BSP. However, Zhelev chose General Atanas Semerdjiev from the former Secret Service as vice president. To many, this compromise was the result of a secret deal struck between the reformers within the former Communist Party and within some circles within the UDF. Whatever the truth, the opposition got an important office in the administration that it kept through elections for the next ten years.

17. Pedro C. Magalhaes, "The Politics of Judicial Reform in Eastern Europe," *Comparative Politics* 32, no. 1 (October 1999): 43–62.

18. Venelin I. Ganev, "The Bulgarian Constitutional Court, 1991–1997: A Success Story in Context," *Europe-Asia Studies* 55, no. 4 (June 2003): 597–611.

19. Yuliyana Chavdarova Galabinova, "The Process of Decentralization in Bulgaria and the Necessity to Introduce Regional Self-Government," *Amfiteatru Economic* 19 (February 2006): 1–9.

20. Emilia Kandeva, *Introduction to Comparative Local Government in Central and Eastern Europe: A Balkan Perspective* (Budapest: Open Society Institute, 2001).

21. Emilia Drumeva, "Local Government in Bulgaria," in *Local Government in Central and Eastern Europe,* ed. Emilia Kandeva (Budapest: Open Society Institute, 2001).

22. Emil Giatzidis, *An Introduction to Post-Communist Bulgaria: Political, Economic and Social Transformation* (Manchester. England: Manchester University Press, 2002), 111; Roumiana Deltcheva, "New Tendencies in Post-totalitarian Bulgaria: Mass Culture and the Media," *Europe-Asia Studies* 48, no. 2 (1996): 305–315.

23. These data come from *The Comparative Study of Electoral Systems,* CSES Module 2 Full Release [dataset]. June 27, 2007, version. Retrieved 11 May 2008 from www.cses.org.

24. Commission of the European Union, Eurobarometer 68: Public Opinion in the European Union, National Report on Bulgaria, Fall 2007. Retrieved 12 April 2008 from ec.europa.eu/public_opinion/archives/eb/eb68/eb68_bg_nat.pdf.

25. Commission of the European Union, Eurobarometer 66: Public Opinion in the European Union, National Report on Bulgaria, Fall 2006. Retrieved 12 April 2008 from ec.europa.eu/public_opinion/archives/eb/eb66/eb66_bg_nat.pdf.

26. Commission of the European Union, Eurobarometer 66: Public Opinion in the European Union, National Report for Bulgaria.

27. *The Comparative Study of Electoral Systems* (Module 2). The widespread perception of corruption within the

Bulgarian political elite is also confirmed by yearly data from the *Transparency International Corruption Perceptions Index.* Retrieved 11 May 2008 from www.transparency.org.

28. Commission on the European Union, Eurobarometer 68: Public Opinion in the European Union, National Report on Bulgaria.

29. Commission on the European Union, Eurobarometer 66: Public Opinion in the European Union, National Report for Bulgaria; Commission on the European Union, Eurobarometer 68: Public Opinion in the European Union, National Report on Bulgaria.

30. Maria Nikolova, "Women's Employment in the Private Sector and Their Demographic Behavior," in *Labor, Employment and Unemployment,* ed. Katya Vladimirova (Sofia: University of National and World Economy Press, 2000), 94.

31. Anna Krasteva, "Values," in *Recent Social Trends in Bulgaria 1960–1995,* ed. Nikolai Genov and Anna Krasteva (Montreal: McGill-Queen's University Press, 2001), 483–487.

32. Mariana Zakharieva, "Vocational and Professional Education," in *Recent Social Trends in Bulgaria 1960–1995,* ed. Nikolai Genov and Anna Krasteva (Montreal: McGill-Queen's University Press, 2001), p. 434.

33. Dean Kruckeberg and Katerina Tsetsura, *A Composite Index by Country of Variables Related to the Likelihood of the Existence of 'Cash for News Coverage'* (Gainesville, Florida: Institute of Public Relations and the International Public Relations Association, 2003).

Retrieved 20 May 2008 from www.instituteforpr.org/research_single/ index_of_bribery.

34. Roumiana Deltcheva, "New Tendencies in Post-totalitarian Bulgaria: Mass Culture and the Media," *Europe-Asia Studies* 48, no. 2 (1996): 305–315.

35. *The Comparative Study of Electoral Systems* (Module 2).

36. *The Comparative Study of Electoral Systems* (Module 2).

37. Tatiana Kostadinova, "The Impact of Finance Regulations on Political Parties: The Case of Bulgaria." *Europe-Asia Studies* 59, no. 5 (2007): 807–827.

38. Mark S. Ellis "Purging the Past: The Current State of Lustration Laws in the Former Communist Bloc," *Law and Contemporary Problems* 59, no. 4 (Autumn 1996): 181–196.

39. Elena A. Iankova, "Multi-level Bargaining During Bulgaria's Return to Capitalism," *Industrial and Labor Relations Review* 54, no. 1 (October 2000): 115–137.

40. *Kruglata Masa* (The Round Table), Stenographic notes (Sofia: Zhelyu Zhelev Foundation, 2000), 402–404.

41. Asenka Hhristova and Krassen Stanchev "Start of Economic Reforms in Bulgaria," in *Anatomy of the Transition: The Economic Policy of Bulgaria from 1989 to 2000,* ed. Asenka Hristova, Vladislav Slantchev, Georgi Angelov, Georgi Stoev, Dimitar Tchobanov, Krasen Stantchev, Lachezar Bogdanov, and Martin Dimitrov (Sofia: CIELA, 2004), 58.

42. Neven T. Valev, "From a Currency Board to the Euro: Public Attitudes Toward Unilateral Euroisation in Bulgaria," *Comparative Economic Studies* 48 (2006): 480–496.

POLITICS IN THE EUROPEAN UNION

Alberta Sbragia and Francesco Stolfi

Country Bio

EUROPEAN UNION

Population
493 million

Territory
2,610 million square miles

Year of Legal Creation
1958

President
Rotates among member states

Language
German 16.6%, English 12.0%, Italian 12.0%, French 11.0%, Spanish 8.0%, Polish 7.8%, other 32.6%

Religion
Roman Catholic 55%, Protestant 18%, Orthodox 8%, Muslim 2%, Jewish 0.2%, other and unaffiliated 16.8%

On September 8, 2008, three men traveled to Moscow to meet Dmitry Medvedev and Vladimir Putin, respectively president and prime minister of Russia. The three men were Nicolas Sarkozy, president of France; José Barroso, president of the European Commission; and Javier Solana, the high representative for the Common Foreign and Security Policy of the European Union (EU). They were in Moscow to broker an agreement to end the tense standoff between Russia and Georgia after the tiny Caucasus republic had invaded the Russian-backed separatist region of South Ossetia a month before. They reached a deal; Russia withdrew its troops from Georgia and accepted 200 EU observers at the border between Georgia and South Ossetia. NATO, however, was furious, as the deal allowed Russia to keep a large number of troops in South Ossetia, while the United States complained that some European countries were too dependent on Russian gas and thus too subject to Russia's will. This episode underscores some key features of the EU. It acts through its own supranational institutions, as well as through its member states; its political power potentially puts it in conflict with other international organizations and with the United States; and for all its activism, it remains weak when it is confronted with countries using traditional state power.

The **European Union (EU)** represents a remarkable attempt by the nation-states of Europe to construct a framework of governance to make collective decisions about a broad range of issues. As an organization the EU is far more legally authoritative and institutionally sophisticated than any other international body. The twenty-seven member nations have not renounced the vigorous pursuit of their "national interest" in any policy area. Yet, by agreeing to pursue that interest within an organization such as the EU, the member states recognize the ultimate superiority of multilateral decisionmaking and action in a variety of policy areas.

The term *European Union* is often used interchangeably with the term *European Community*. The original European Economic Community (EEC), established with the Treaty of Rome in 1958, gradually came to be known as the European Community (EC). The Treaty of Maastricht in 1992 changed the name of the European Community to the European Union. In certain legal contexts, however, the term *European Community* is still used. In this chapter we determine usage by what is most appropriate, given the historical period being discussed.

Although the EU resembles an international organization in certain ways, it is in fact very different. To begin with, it includes institutions that are not directly controlled by the member states and that exercise real policymaking power. The EU is similar to a national political system, but it is clearly distinct from the other political systems discussed in this book. For example, it does not have its own military or its own police force, and it does not belong to the United Nations. It is not a sovereign entity in the way that traditional nation-states are sovereign in international affairs. Furthermore, it is governed without a prime minister and a cabinet, which are found in traditional parliamentary democracies. Rather than being governed by an elected government, a group of institutions collectively makes EU policy. Although the EU produces binding laws, the fact that it does so without having a traditional "government" is perhaps the EU's most confusing feature.

The EU is an experiment in "pooling sovereignty." National governments have agreed to restrict their own ability to make decisions unilaterally. They have agreed to make decisions in concert with other member governments and with institutions that are not under their control. In many policy areas, a national government, when outvoted by other governments, must comply with the decision it opposed. This process does not cover all policy areas, but it does cover many. Unilateral decisionmaking by national governments has become less frequent as the EU's policy agenda has gradually expanded.

Belonging to the EU has serious consequences for member states. A significant share—between 30 and 50 percent—of all domestic legislation originates from the EU. Membership in the EU is not to be taken lightly, for it changes the policy processes and the policy outcomes of national political systems. Membership carries with it serious and binding economic and political commitments. Individual nations belonging to the EU can be increasingly thought of as member states of a larger collectivity that shapes their policy options. However, membership does not change the culture of a country—the same language is spoken before and after accession, for example. A nation's "way of life" goes on after accession as it did before. A country makes a serious political and economic commitment when it joins the European Union, but it does not commit to changing its culture and history.

POLICY CHALLENGES

The very success of the EU underpins its biggest challenges. As it has become a byword for economic prosperity and democracy, this increases the pressure to include more and more members. From the original six members, the EU now counts twenty-seven member states. This huge increase in size creates problems that have not been solved yet. Some analysts believe that with the Eastern enlargements of 2004 and 2007 (in which the EU increased almost twofold, from fifteen to twenty-seven members), the EU has in fact bitten off more than it can chew.

Three related challenges have come to the fore. First, the newer member states are much poorer and much more agricultural than the older members. In 2008, for example, Poland, the largest of the twelve new member states, had a per capita gross domestic product (GDP) that was only 55 percent of the EU average; Bulgaria's was only 39 percent of the EU average.[1]

The second challenge is institutional: restructuring the policymaking institutions of the larger EU to avoid gridlock. The Lisbon Treaty (see below) tried to answer this question. After its rejection by Irish voters in June 2008, the EU is left—not for the first time—to ponder how to combine decisionmaking efficiency and democratic legitimacy.

Finally, the EU now includes most of Scandinavia, key Mediterranean countries, and former Soviet satellites. As the economies of the twenty-seven become more intertwined and as more policy areas are included in an integrated Europe's policy portfolio, questions of national identity are more salient. European cultures reflect many centuries of disparate historical experiences, and the current economic convergence is proceeding far more quickly than cultural (or linguistic) convergence. Although the EU is firmly committed to protecting cultural diversity, the tension among culture, economics, policy, and identity are more pronounced now that the EU includes such a wide range of nations. Even in Ireland, a country that has benefited enormously from its membership in the EU, one of the most important reasons for voting "no" to the Lisbon Treaty was defending Irish national identity.[2] To what extent will the average person accept being made into a "European" in political and economic terms before feeling that his or her identity is being fundamentally threatened? That question has not yet been answered.

The question of a "European" identity is further complicated by the issue of whether Turkey actually belongs in the EU. The question of whether accession negotiations should begin with Turkey (which was officially accepted as a candidate country in 1999) divides mass electorates (which generally oppose Turkish membership) from their elected leaders (many of whom support it). The very difficult historical relationship between Christian Europe and Muslim Turkey (and its predecessor, the Ottoman Empire) has brought issues of identity to the fore as the debate over Turkish accession has developed. The consequence of such a debate over "European" identity is unpredictable. Ironically, the debate over Turkey may make "the 27" feel more European than they did before Turkish membership came onto the political agenda. Yet, the question of Turkish accession also presents an opportunity for the EU. Given the capabilities of the Turkish military, an EU with Turkey as a member could play a major role in geopolitics. The Turkish question may well force the EU to choose between cultural affinity and a major geopolitical role.

WHY "EUROPE"?

At its core, the EU is rooted in the desire to transcend European history, a history filled with "rivers of blood," to use Winston Churchill's famous phrase. European integration is an attempt to change the geopolitics of Europe. By entangling the domestic institutions of individual nation-states within the institutions of the EU, integration has changed (hopefully forever) the relations among European states. Such a change in international relations, however, has "fed back" into national political systems. Domestic policies, institutions, and modes of governance have been changed by virtue of belonging to the EU.

The integration effort was initially anchored in the belief that it represented the best answer to "the

German Question" after World War II. That is, integration (rather than confrontation) was the best way to keep Germany firmly in the company of peaceful democratic nations and to keep it from playing a destructive role in postwar European geopolitics. The attempt to ensure that Germany was a cooperative rather than a threatening neighbor led to a historic restructuring of relations among European states. This also significantly influenced domestic politics and policy.

Although the fear of potential German aggression was an initial motive for European integration, there are other important spurs to integration. European business firms' fear of losing competitiveness relative to American and Japanese firms is one such spur. People accept that international problems such as environmental pollution, illegal immigration, and organized crime require transnational solutions. The European difficulties in dealing with the various Balkan crises, including Kosovo, have pushed governments to increase their coordination in the defense area.

National governments have sometimes led this effort at integration. At other times they have acquiesced in accepting it, or they have resisted it. Whatever their stance toward European integration, national governments play a key role in shaping and directing it. The institutions of the EU not controlled by the member states, including the European Court of Justice, also can keep the process of integration moving, especially when the member states do not exercise leadership.

The EU is now so important that much of what happens in national capitals cannot be understood without considering Brussels. However, neither can one understand what happens in Brussels without taking national capitals into account.[3] Brussels is not nearly as divorced from national politics as Washington is from the politics of state capitals in the United States.

The EU's political system is entangled with the politics of its constituent member states, while simultaneously having its own separate institutional identity and political dynamics. That balance between entanglement and autonomy makes it both complex and fascinating.

Schuman, Monnet, and the European Coal and Steel Community

European integration is linked to the creation of institutions that have some autonomy apart from the member governments. While member governments remain pivotal, they are not the only important actors.

The existence of such independent institutions—cohabiting with institutions that are more tightly controlled by member governments—is known as **supranationality. Intergovernmentalism,** by contrast, refers to institutional arrangements in which only national governments matter in the making of policy.

The effort toward European integration—understood as having a supranational component—dates from May 9, 1950, and the **Schuman Plan** (see Figure 12.1). On that day French Foreign Minister Robert Schuman proposed the creation of an international organization to coordinate activity in the coal and steel industries. Designed to ensure Franco-German reconciliation, Schuman's proposal represented a reversal of French foreign policy toward Germany. France changed from a policy of unremitting hostility to one of reconciliation. Schuman envisioned a Germany embedded in an integrated framework as the way to constrain German might. Schuman's own life experience encouraged him to shape "French foreign policy to his vision of a Europe in which France and Germany were reconciled and the suffering of the border provinces ended."[4] (See Box 12.1.)

The Plan had been designed by Jean Monnet, then general commissary for the French Plan of Modernization and Equipment. Monnet underscored the strategic importance of having a "supranational" component in any initiative designed to achieve integration. In his view, supranationality was necessary to prevent the old interstate balance of power dynamics from becoming preeminent. Monnet was to play a critical role in the process of European integration throughout the following decade and beyond, so much so that he is sometimes referred to as "Mr. Europe."

The Franco-German relationship lay at the core of the Schuman Plan. That relationship remains the central one within the process of European integration. France is Germany's key interlocutor in Europe, and Germany is France's key referent. When they agree on the need for further integration, France and Germany provide the political energy, the driving force, and the momentum for achieving further integration.

In addition to reversing French foreign policy toward Germany, the Schuman Plan invited democratic nations in Europe to join in forming an international organization outlined in the plan. Germany, Italy, Belgium, Luxembourg, and the Netherlands (the latter three known as the Benelux countries) responded. The United Kingdom (UK) rejected the invitation to participate in the European Coal and Steel

	The Timetable for European Integration	FIGURE 12.1

1950	Schuman Plan
1952	Treaty of Paris—European Coal and Steel Community (ECSC)
1958	Treaty of Rome—European Economic Community (EEC)
1973	Britain, Denmark, and Ireland join the EC
1979	Direct election of the European Parliament
1981	Greece joins the EC
1986	Spain and Portugal join the EC
1987	Single European Act (SEA)
1993	Maastricht Treaty
1995	Austria, Sweden, and Finland join the EU
1999	Introduction of the euro as a "virtual" currency; Treaty of Amsterdam
2002	The euro is introduced into daily use
2003	Treaty of Nice
2004	Cyprus, Czech Republic, Estonia, Hungary, Latvia, Lithuania, Malta, Poland, Slovakia, and Slovenia join the EU
2007	Bulgaria and Romania join the EU; Treaty of Lisbon

Community (ECSC) negotiations, which was a defining moment for the future relationship between the UK and an integrated Europe. The six nations signed the Treaty of Paris, which established the ECSC, on April 18, 1951. The ECSC focused on economics as the most appropriate arena for integration. Integration would foster interstate trade and the prosperity that flows from such trade, and integration would expand by the results of such trade. This view has

BOX 12.1

Robert Schuman: A True "European"

Robert Schuman's life story reflects the history of Europe in the twentieth century. He was born in Luxembourg in 1886 and was raised in the German-speaking part of Lorraine. He attended German universities and then was drafted into the German Army in World War I. Schuman became a French citizen in 1919 when Alsace-Lorraine was restored to France under the Treaty of Versailles. He was elected to the French Parliament in 1919, but refused to serve under the Vichy Regime. The Gestapo imprisoned him for condemning the expulsion of the French population of Lorraine. He escaped in 1942 and became active in the French Resistance. As the war was ending, he helped to found the Christian Democratic Party (MRP) in 1944. Between November 1947 and December 1952, Schuman served as either prime minister or foreign minister of France. In November 1950 he proposed the Schuman Plan, which was the catalyst for European integration. Between 1958 and 1963, Schuman served as a member of the European Assembly, the forerunner of the European Parliament.

---

shaped the evolution of European integration and its substantive policy core: economics, economic policy, and trade in the pursuit of economic prosperity.

This concern with prosperity also presumed that prosperity facilitates peace. Because the interwar years (1918–1939) had seen economic tumult in Europe and the simultaneous rise of fascism and Nazism, economic prosperity was considered necessary for both democracy and peace. Although the ECSC was overshadowed by future developments in integration, it represented the first key step in overcoming the ancient divisions of continental Europe.

The Cold War, the United States, and European Integration

The United States influenced European integration in the 1950s in a number of ways. The postwar period (especially 1947–1950) was crucial in institutionally linking the United States to Europe. On June 5, 1947, the United States announced the **Marshall Plan** (1948–1951). By insisting that Europe coordinate requests for Marshall Plan aid, rather than each country dealing bilaterally with the United States, the plan helped set the stage for European integration, "not least in the fostering of new modes of thinking."[5] Later, the United States provided strong support for both the Schuman Plan and the European Economic Community.

While the Marshall Plan linked the United States and Europe economically, Americans also became involved militarily. In April 1949 the Atlantic Pact was signed, and the **North Atlantic Treaty Organization (NATO)** was born. Through NATO the United States and Canada committed themselves militarily to European defense.

The incorporation of both American troops and Germany in NATO within the context of the Cold War created the framework for European security and defense policy even after the end of the Cold War. This took these issues off the agenda of European integration. The Bretton Woods system took international monetary policy off the agenda. The path of integration was profoundly shaped by the fact that European integration occurred within the "NATO–Bretton Woods system," in which the United States exercised hegemony in the West.

The European Economic Community

In May 1955 the Assembly of the ECSC asked the foreign ministers of the six members to draft new treaties to further European integration. The **Treaty of Rome** established the **European Economic Community (EEC)** and came into force on January 1, 1958.

The Treaty of Rome included a much wider range of economic arenas and modified the institutional structure of the ECSC in important ways. Unlike the ECSC, the EEC has remained at the core of the integration process. The close working relationship that gradually developed among the six countries operating within the ECSC transferred over into the EEC. The Treaty of Rome called for the creation of a common market—the free movement of people, goods, services, and labor—among the six signatories.

It called for a common agricultural policy (included in order to convince the French parliament to ratify the treaty). It also called for measures to move the EEC beyond a mere common market. It embodied both economic and political objectives: "Whilst the Treaty of Rome is virtually exclusively concerned with economic cooperation, there was (and remains) an underlying political agenda. There is no doubt that its architects saw it . . . as another step on the road to political union."[6]

The Expansion of Europe

- Since the formation of the Common Market, the membership has grown from six to twenty-seven. In the 1960s the UK finally applied for membership in the EEC. After two vetoes by France's President De Gaulle, the UK, Ireland, and Denmark (for whom the UK was a key trading partner) finally joined in 1973. This happened after Georges Pompidou replaced De Gaulle as president of France. Norway had also applied and been accepted, but its electorate rejected membership in a referendum in 1972. In 1981 Greece joined, and in 1986 Spain and Portugal did the same. The accession of all three was viewed as consolidating their transition to democracy and as widening European integration to the Mediterranean.
- In 1995 Austria, Sweden, and Finland joined; Norway's electorate again refused accession in a referendum.
- On May 1, 2004, ten new countries—Cyprus, Czech Republic, Estonia, Hungary, Latvia, Lithuania, Malta, Poland, Slovakia, and Slovenia—joined the EU in what is referred to as the "big bang enlargement."
- Bulgaria and Romania joined in 2007.

In addition, the EU made it clear that the EU map would not be completed without all the Balkan countries. Croatia is supposed to join in the next few years, as are Macedonia and Serbia. More controversially, Turkey was also recognized as a candidate country in 1999, and accession negotiations began in 2005. However, the problems raised by the ratification process of the Lisbon Treaty have put further enlargement in jeopardy. Key countries such as France and Germany have argued that enlargement should be placed in abeyance until a way is found to streamline the overall decisionmaking process.

The Single European Act

In 1985 the member states decided to amend the Treaty of Rome, and the **Single European Act (SEA)** came into force in 1987. The SEA changed the decision rules for legislation creating the internal market from unanimity to qualified majority voting. (A qualified majority is a supermajority, requiring more votes for approval than does a simple majority.) A single national government could no longer veto legislation for the creation of the market. Furthermore, the SEA increased the powers of the European Parliament and increased the EC's powers on environmental protection issues.

The adoption of a single market was a milestone in the history of European integration. It was as important as the interstate commerce clause in the U.S. Constitution. Just as that clause undergirded the growth of federal power in nineteenth-century America, the single market represented a major step in European integration and the power of the EC institutions.

A single market minimizes nontariff barriers. Such barriers are often tied to cultural traditions, which means that overriding them can be politically sensitive. By examining barriers from the perspective of whether they inhibit exports to a certain country, the single market opens to scrutiny institutional arrangements in both the public and the private sectors. Germany could not exclude beer made in an "un-German" way, Italy could not exclude pasta made with "foreign" wheat, and so forth.

The creation of a truly European market was above all a project of regulatory reform—national deregulation combined with re-regulation at the EC level. The EC strengthened market forces to improve the ability of European firms to compete globally. Regulation was implemented by Brussels, rather than at the national level. The EC set up regulatory agencies—such as the European Agency for the Evaluation of Medicinal Products to regulate pharmaceuticals—that complement national regulatory frameworks. Furthermore, environmental regulation is increasingly concentrated at the EC level. Finally, the European Commission exercised its powers in the area of competition policy (which covers antitrust and state aids) much more aggressively.[7] Protected markets, such as those in the telecommunications and air transport sectors, were gradually liberalized (so that phone calls and intra-European air travel became far cheaper than they had been). Economic integration gradually eroded or eliminated such protectionist policies. By the late 1990s, the EC's regulatory reach was so important that some analysts considered it a "regulatory state."[8]

The Maastricht Treaty

Analysts generally viewed the single market of the late 1980s as a success. Business investment climbed, and Europe enjoyed a new sense of economic optimism. Under these circumstances an initiative to move to a European central bank and a common currency as an extension of the single market attracted support.

While that effort was under way, the Berlin Wall fell in November 1989. German unification, once barely considered, now became a reality (see Chapter 7). A new Germany was on the scene. Would it continue to face westward—toward Brussels—or would it face toward the East? What role would the new Germany play in a Europe fundamentally changed by the end of the Cold War? How could Europe "contain" this economic powerhouse, which had just added more than 16 million inhabitants? These questions were especially pressing, as the problems—and especially the huge costs—associated with German unification were still unacknowledged by most observers.

One response was a new version of the old "German question." Europe moved toward a new treaty that would bind Germany even more firmly to the West by further tying German institutions to those of the EC. The result was the **Treaty of European Union (TEU)**, usually referred to as the **Maastricht Treaty,** after the small Dutch town in which the final negotiations took place in December 1991.

The Maastricht Treaty came into effect in November 1993. It was another milestone in the history of European integration. It moved the process of European integration into two critical new policy areas, as well as entrenching the EC's pivotal role in monetary policy. The treaty is complex. It changed the name of the European Community to the European Union. Most importantly, it changed the structure of the EC by establishing three "pillars," or policy areas, in which the EC institutions played different roles. The Treaty of Amsterdam and the Treaty of Nice (see below) retained this structure.

In the Maastricht, Amsterdam, and Nice treaties, the European Council and the Council of Ministers were important in all three pillars. The other EC institutions were central only in pillar one. The more federally inclined members of the EU saw the pillar structure as a transition phase, one that would ultimately lead to all three areas of policy being brought under the EC's institutions. The more intergovernmentalist members viewed the pillar structure as a safeguard against precisely that kind of evolutionary development.

Pillar One: The Extension of the Treaty of Rome

Pillar one, as defined by Maastricht, encompasses **Economic and Monetary Union (EMU)**—including a new **European Central Bank** and a common currency (the euro), as well as incorporating all the monetary policy areas previously under the EC's jurisdiction. The *acquis communautaire*—all the accumulated laws and judicial decisions adopted since the signing of Treaty of Rome—belong to the first pillar. For example, the single market, agriculture, environmental policy, regional policy, research and technological development, consumer protection, trade policy, fisheries policy, competition policy, and transportation policy all fall under pillar one.

Decisionmaking procedures within pillar one are firmly rooted within the traditional EC institutions, while expanding the Parliament's decisionmaking power. Pillar one policy areas fall under the jurisdiction of the institutional machinery of the European Commission, the European Parliament, the Council of Ministers, the presidency, the European Court of Justice, the European Council, and the new European Central Bank. Under Maastricht, however, the UK and Denmark could opt out of the common currency as well as several other provisions if they so wished. In September 2000 the Danish public voted against adopting the euro, and in 2003 Swedish voters also rejected the euro in a referendum. In general, pillar one includes everything that the "old" EC included, plus the new European Central Bank and the euro for those countries that joined the Eurozone.

Pillars Two and Three: An Intergovernmental Compromise

Pillars two and three expanded the scope of the EU by encompassing policy areas that had been outside the scope of European integration. Pillar two refers to *Common Foreign and Security Policy (CFSP),* and pillar three refers to **Justice, Freedom and Security** (internal security). The institutional structures governing pillars two and three differ from those of pillar one. In both pillars the Council of Ministers, rather than the Commission, was primarily responsible for action, unanimous voting was required, the Parliament was largely excluded, and the European Court of Justice did not exercise jurisdiction.

The fact that the Council of Ministers, rather than the European Commission, was the key institution represented a compromise. On one side were those countries that favored a more "federal" model of integration and therefore supported giving the Commission powers in these areas. On the other side were those governments (the UK and France) that were worried about sovereignty. Pillars two and three therefore were brought within the process of integration, but were governed by the European Council and the Council of Ministers, the most intergovernmental institutions within the EU's institutional framework.

Treaty of Amsterdam

The **Treaty of Amsterdam** came into effect in 1999 and significantly changed the policy and institutional landscape established by the Maastricht Treaty. First, most issues of pillar three were placed within pillar one. This significantly strengthened the policy reach of the Commission and the influence of the European Court of Justice. The treaty also enhanced the power of the Commission president vis-à-vis the other commissioners. Second, the treaty increased the power of the European Parliament by both simplifying and expanding the use of co-decision in a wide range of issue areas. Third, the powers of the EU in several policy areas—including public health (which is critical to the European welfare state) and foreign and security policy (both of which are very sensitive for national sovereignty)—were enhanced. Public health is firmly under the EU's institutions in pillar one, while the CFSP is firmly in intergovernmental pillar two.

The transfer of most policy areas within the "old" pillar three to pillar one was a very significant step in the process of European integration. Experts traditionally viewed internal security as absolutely central to national sovereignty. In the post-Amsterdam period, issues such as asylum, immigration, and judicial cooperation in civil matters came within the Commission's policy remit and the jurisdiction of the European Court of Justice, with some restrictions. In Maastricht, the member states had given up their sovereignty in monetary policy by accepting the euro, but they had been very reluctant to "Europeanize"

internal security. Spurred by the dismantling of internal border controls in the expanding Schengen area[9] and by the common need to deal with immigration into the EU, the member states agreed to "pool" their sovereignty in the area of Justice, Freedom and Security (in the United States, the Department of Justice is concerned with most of the same issue areas). Intergovernmental pillar three of the Maastricht Treaty was widely viewed as a failure. Thus, the Treaty of Amsterdam signaled the new willingness of the member states to be more effective by bringing it under the Commission's umbrella.

In a similar vein, in October 1999 the member states agreed to numerous initiatives to further integration in this extremely sensitive area. Only two policy areas—police cooperation and judicial cooperation in criminal matters—remain within the "new" pillar three after Amsterdam, and, even here, the member states were willing to be less intergovernmental. The European Court of Justice was completely excluded in the old pillar three, but has a limited role in the post-Amsterdam pillar three. Furthermore, the Commission, as well as the member states, has the right of initiative in all matters falling under pillar three. This is an expansion of the role of the Commission. Some convergence of criminal legislation is now possible, so some analysts viewed Amsterdam as contributing "towards creating a common European criminal law."[10] The European Police Office (EUROPOL), originally set up by the Maastricht Treaty, has stronger powers and a more operational role. Eurojust was created in 2002; this body brings together judges and prosecutors from the member states with the purpose of increasing the coordination of investigations.

Finally, in reaction to the September 11, 2001, terrorist attack on the United States and the March 11, 2004, terrorist attack on a Madrid train station, the EU further strengthened its role in the area of Justice, Freedom and Security. The member states created a European Arrest Warrant to make the arrest and extradition of fugitives within the EU more efficient and appointed an EU antiterrrorism "czar." In 2005 the EU also set up its own European Police College (CEPOL), located in England, to provide seminars and courses for senior police officers. However, the EU has not created a European version of the U.S. Central Intelligence Agency (CIA). Intelligence gathering remains a strictly national function, but now national intelligence agencies cooperate a great deal more than in the pre-2001 period.

The Amsterdam Treaty enhanced the powers of the EU in the area of the CFSP. Institutionally, the secretary-general of the Council of Ministers was also appointed as the high representative for the EU Common Foreign and Security Policy ("Mr. CFSP"). Javier Solana, widely respected in his previous posts as secretary-general of NATO foreign affairs minister of Spain, was appointed to that position when the Treaty of Amsterdam came into effect.

The Treaty of Nice

The **Treaty of Nice**, the fourth revision of the Rome treaties, entered into force on February 1, 2003. The treaty prepared the EU for its enlargement to Central and Eastern Europe. In particular, the treaty streamlined decisionmaking in the EU's institutions. Making decisions with twenty-five (and then twenty-seven) countries would be much more difficult than with fifteen countries. Streamlining decisionmaking, however, necessarily changes the distribution of power within the institutions. In particular, the small states, which had historically been overrepresented in the EU's institutions, fought to keep their privileged position. The large states argued that, since enlargement would add so many small states to the Union, maintaining the privileges of small states would lead to an unbalanced EU, in which the populous member states would lose their appropriate role. The members reached a final deal in the early morning hours of the last day of the Nice European Council in December 2000.

In addition to finding a compromise between the demands of the small and large member states (in which the small states did relatively well), the Treaty of Nice introduced some important changes. Institutionally, it allowed each member state to appoint only one commissioner (previously, the larger member states had appointed two commissioners). Second, it introduced qualified majority voting in choosing the president of the Commission and increased the office's power vis-à-vis other commissioners. Third, there was a new weighting of votes in the Council of Ministers (that weighting represented the concrete results of the compromise between the large and small states). Fourth, qualified majority voting (as opposed to unanimity) was extended to roughly thirty new policy areas. It strengthened the EU's role in the area of security and defense and created a new **Political and Security Committee (PSC)**.[11] Irish voters rejected the Nice Treaty in a referendum in 2001, but they subsequently accepted it in a 2002 referendum.

Failure to Launch and the Treaty of Lisbon

Between February 2002 and July 2003, a Convention for the Future of Europe drafted a constitutional treaty to make the working of the EU institutions more efficient in light of the upcoming Eastern enlargement and also to make the EU more democratic by increasing the role of its directly elected Parliament. The twenty-five governments of the member states agreed to the final version of the treaty in 2004. However, the apparent constitutional nature of the treaty made it necessary to submit it to popular referendums in some of the member states. The French and Dutch voters rejected it in 2005. The rejection partly reflected the internal political dynamics of France and the Netherlands, but it was also the product of the national governments' habit of blaming the EU for many unpopular—albeit often necessary—measures.

The rejection of the constitutional treaty sent shock waves throughout the EU. After a "pause of reflection," the member states again attempted to reform the EU. The negotiations were sometimes acrimonious. For instance, the Polish government claimed that its demands for adjustments to the voting system in the Council of Ministers were "worth dying for"[12] and even demanded voting rights for its war dead.[13]

The result was the **Treaty of Lisbon,** signed in Portugal's capital in December 2007. This treaty essentially incorporated the constitutional treaty rejected by the voters, discarding the most obvious symbols of sovereignty for the EU (such as a national anthem, a motto, and a flag). The main thrust of the treaty was to simplify the operation of the EU institutions and at the same time to make them more democratically accountable. With the exclusion of the CFSP, all policy areas would be brought into pillar one, and the co-decision legislative procedure—in which the Parliament was essentially the equal of the Council of Ministers—would be extended to most policy areas. Even in an area as sensitive as Justice, Freedom and Security, the policies that the Amsterdam Treaty left out of pillar one would be brought into it, thus completing the trajectory that had started with the Maastricht Treaty.

European citizens would acquire the power of initiative: At least a million voters could ask the Commission to take a specific initiative. Importantly, Parliament would also become the coequal of the Council of Ministers in budgetary decisionmaking. The treaty would simplify decisionmaking within the European Commission by limiting the number of commissioners to two-thirds of the number of member states. It would also extend qualified majority voting in the Council of Ministers to a number of new policy areas and would introduce (to be implemented from 2014 on) a new voting system whereby decisions in the Council of Ministers would be approved if supported by 55 percent of the member states representing at least 65 percent of the EU population. Alongside the rotating presidency of the European Council and the Council of Ministers, the treaty would create the position of president of the European Union, elected by the European Council by qualified majority vote. Moreover, the treaty would establish a position that essentially would amount to that of a foreign affairs minister of the EU. The new high representative of the EU for foreign affairs and security policy would merge the preexisting positions of high representative for CFSP and of European commissioner for external relations.

The Lisbon Treaty would also make the Charter of Fundamental Rights legally binding for the member states. However, the UK and Poland would be given an exception so they would not be legally bound by it, the former because it feared it might weaken the operation of the free market and the latter because it feared it might force Poland to accept gay marriage. The UK and Ireland would also have "opt-outs" with regard to policies for immigration, visas, and external borders.

However, in June 2008 Ireland, the only country where it was subject to a popular vote, rejected the Lisbon Treaty. The treaty must be ratified by every one of the twenty-seven member states before it can enter into effect. The Irish vote put the entire ratification process in disarray. In the months following the rejection, the Irish government secured from the other governments a set of guarantees that Irish sovereignty would not be reduced in key areas valued by Irish voters, such as neutrality or abortion. A new referendum will probably take place in late 2009.

THE INSTITUTIONS

The institutional structure of the EU is based on the complex divisions represented by different institutions in different policy areas (see Figure 12.2). The sophisticated policymaking process normally associated with the EU resides in pillar one. This includes key policymaking institutions such as the European Commission, the Council of Ministers, the European

Parliament, the European Council, the European Court of Justice, and the European Central Bank. The European Council and the Council of Ministers also have jurisdiction over pillars two and three.

Whereas the other institutions all interact with one another, the European Central Bank (located in Frankfurt, Germany) is very independent from all the other institutions. However, Justice, Freedom and Security within pillar one still excludes the Parliament. The European Commission, Council, and Parliament are the central policymaking actors in areas such as immigration, visa policy, and asylum policy. In pillars two and three, the European Council and the Council of Ministers are the key institutional actors.

The European Commission

The **European Commission**, located in Brussels, is the EU's most visible institution in day-to-day policymaking. Its institutional mission within the EU is to promote integration. Toward that end the Commission is made up of the College of Commissioners, the decisionmaking body within the Commission, and civil servants that do the important technocratic work typical of all bureaucracies. The College of Commissioners is the political (although not in a partisan sense) component of the Commission, while the civil servants are the administrative sector. The term *Commission* is used in the press to refer to the civil servants, the College, or both.

The Commission is composed of twenty-seven commissioners who collectively make up the College of Commissioners. Each commissioner is appointed by the head of a member state, but once appointed, the commissioner is able to act independently of his country's national government. A commissioner does not take instructions from the national government and can operate quite autonomously. That independence gives the Commission as a whole its supranational authority and power.

Each commissioner serves for a five-year term and can be reappointed if the national government so wishes. Each has one vote. Each is in charge of certain policy areas (environment, trade, external relations, agriculture, research and technology, transport, or telecommunications, for example). When they meet collectively every Wednesday, they are known as the College of Commissioners.

The president of the Commission is the most important commissioner; the Treaty of Amsterdam and the Treaty of Nice enhanced his influence within the

The Structure of the European Union

FIGURE 12.2

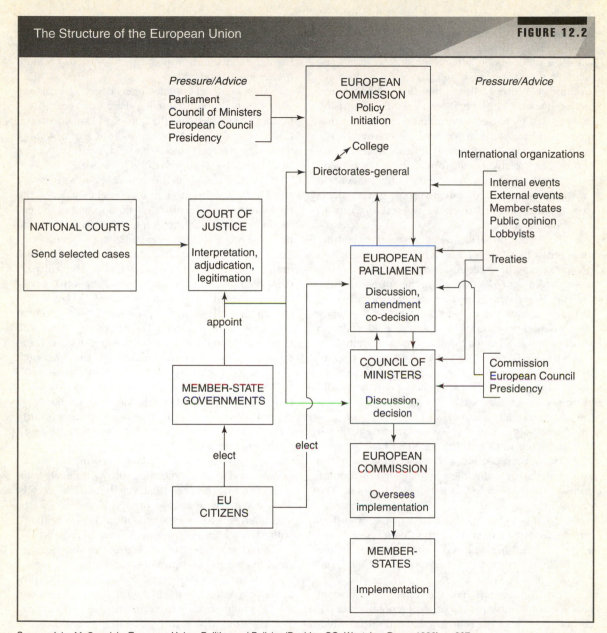

Pressure/Advice

Parliament
Council of Ministers
European Council
Presidency

EUROPEAN COMMISSION
Policy Initiation

College

Directorates-general

Pressure/Advice

International organizations

Internal events
External events
Member-states
Public opinion
Lobbyists

Treaties

NATIONAL COURTS

Send selected cases

COURT OF JUSTICE

Interpretation, adjudication, legitimation

EUROPEAN PARLIAMENT

Discussion, amendment co-decision

appoint

MEMBER-STATE GOVERNMENTS

COUNCIL OF MINISTERS

Discussion, decision

Commission
European Council
Presidency

elect

elect

EU CITIZENS

EUROPEAN COMMISSION

Oversees implementation

MEMBER-STATES

Implementation

Source: John McCormick, *European Union: Politics and Policies* (Boulder, CO: Westview Press, 1996), p. 207.

Commission. In the post-Nice era, the European Council nominally chooses the president by qualified majority voting. However, in June 2004 the European Council selected by consensus the current Commission president, Jose Manuel Barroso of Portugal. The reliance on consensus, rather than qualified majority voting, acknowledged the political reality that a Commission president would be ineffective if one of the large member states opposed his appointment. (In fact, Barroso was selected after one or more of the large member states in effect vetoed other candidates.) The European Parliament then must approve the European Council's nomination. Typically, a president from a small country succeeds one from a large country (Barroso is from Portugal, a small country, while his predecessor, Romano Prodi, was from Italy, a large country). Strong Commission presidents leave an imprint: Walter Hallstein, the first president, and Jacques Delors (1985–1995) both led the Commission in ways that increased its profile and prestige. Commission presidents, however, are constrained by the fact that they do not appoint their fellow commissioners and have relatively little formal control over them. Even Jacques Delors at the height of his power and prestige was unable to convince some governments to reappoint commissioners he wanted to return to the Commission.

The Treaty of Nice, however, strengthened the president's hand to some extent. For example, the president may now request a member of the Commission to resign after obtaining the approval of the College. Jose Barroso, the first Commission president in the post-Nice era, took advantage of his newly strengthened position to give desirable portfolios to small countries. The fact that France, traditionally a very influential country in the EU, was given responsibility for transport, rather than a more prestigious assignment, was a sign that President Barroso would not be shy about using the new powers of the Commission president.

Nonetheless, the role of the president of the Commission is not similar to that of a prime minister. The Commission president is not accountable to the European Parliament in the way that a national prime minister is responsible to a national parliament. The president is appointed by the national governments, rather than being elected, whereas prime ministers are elected. In a similar vein, the Commission is not a "government" in that it is not selected by either the voters (as is the president of France) or the legislature (as are prime ministers).

The Commission has a number of important powers, but its most pivotal power is contained in pillar one: It is the only institution that can propose legislation in pillar one. Neither the Council of Ministers nor the European Parliament can initiate legislation. The Commission's monopoly over policy initiation is one of its most important formal powers. Although the initiation power is limited by the Parliament's power to ask for a legislative proposal, the fact that the Commission drafts the proposal gives it important leverage in the legislative process. This power enables the Commission to shape the policy agenda.

The Commission also manages the EU's budget, is involved in external relations, monitors the application of EU law in the member states, and generally makes the arguments and proposals necessary to promote further integration.

The College of Commissioners decides by majority vote which proposals for legislation to send to the Council of Ministers and the European Parliament. The College can also decide to take antitrust action (without the approval of the Council of Ministers) and can argue cases before the European Court of Justice.

The Commission's bureaucracy, although very small in comparison to national bureaucracies, is the most important administrative component of the entire EU and is key to the Commission's ability to promote the process of integration. Sometimes known as Eurocrats, officials who work for the Commission are multilingual and highly educated. They typically receive their position after passing a competitive examination. They do the initial drafting of the legislation (which the College then approves) and are present at the negotiations within the Council of Ministers on all proposals from the College of Commissioners. Commission officials are emphatically not the functional equivalents of international civil servants, such as officials who work for global international organizations such as the United Nations. Commission officials are viewed as having much more authority when dealing with national officials than are traditional international civil servants.

The operations of its civil servants allow the Commission to play a complex role. Commission officials often operate very effectively behind the scenes. They consult with a wide variety of interest groups and often receive complaints about noncompliance with EU laws from citizens in the member states.

Fundamentally, the Commission promotes European integration and provides the administrative resources absolutely essential for policymaking in a system as complex as the EU. Without the Commission the EU would not have an administrative apparatus.

The Commission is at the heart of the EU because of its centrality in defining problems and formulating policy, its access to significant administrative resources, and its links to a variety of groups throughout the EU. However, in recent years its centrality in EU policymaking has suffered significantly. This is due to the lackluster performance of the Commission presidents, the rise of new actors in the European policymaking process (notably the European Parliament; see below), and the assertiveness of the member states.

Thus, for instance, the response to the economic and financial crisis that began in 2008 was managed by the individual member states, while the Commission was largely sidelined.

The EU has a policymaking body not directly controlled by the member states and able to wield important influence. This clearly distinguishes the organization from all other international bodies. The Commission as an institution symbolizes that supranational dimension within European integration that Jean Monnet so vigorously promoted.

The Council of the European Union (Council of Ministers)

The Council of the EU is usually referred to as the **Council of Ministers**. It adopts EU legislation and develops the budget along with the Commission and the Parliament. It is the top decisionmaking body. Its decisions, often made in conjunction with the European Parliament in pillar one, become EU law. Its members are ministers from national governments. If a national government loses an election, the ministers from the new government immediately participate in the Council's decisionmaking process.

The Council of Ministers, as the EU's main legislature, is a more powerful decisionmaker than either the Commission or the Parliament. It, rather than the Parliament, formulates the EU's trade policy and is the dominant actor in the area of Justice, Freedom and Security. Above all, it adopts EU legislation that is then incorporated into national legal codes. It does not, however, participate in the formation of the Commission and cannot dismiss it.

Technically speaking, there are nine Councils of Ministers, and the term *Council of Ministers* is applied to each sectoral council. Each council is composed of the relevant ministers from each of the member-state governments (or someone delegated to represent them). Hierarchically, the most important is the General Affairs and External Relations Council (GAERC), which brings together the foreign affairs ministers. The GAERC deals with external relations and with horizontal matters, such as the coordination of decisions and the preparation of and follow-up with the European Council, as well as institutional and administrative questions. The GAERC meets at least once a month. Other councils also meet frequently, reflecting the fact that the EU is more active in certain policy areas than others. For example, the Council of Agriculture and Fisheries meets at least

once a month, whereas the Council of Environment Ministers meets once formally and once informally within every three-month period.

All ministers operating within a council do not carry the same weight, as they have unequal voting power. In a similar vein, not all councils are equal in significance. Although the most important is the GAERC, finance ministers are constantly competing with foreign ministers for influence. In pillar one the Council of Economic and Finance Ministers (especially the Euro-Group) comes next in the hierarchy of influence. The Justice, Freedom and Security Council became important after the Maastricht Treaty came into effect and is now a key council in both pillar one and pillar three.

The Council of Ministers is the EU institution in which national interests are represented, defended, and ultimately compromised in the interest of reaching agreement. It is a "club" in the sense that the participants understand that ultimately compromises will have to be made by everyone and acknowledge that the Council of Ministers is not a traditional international organization. Although each council zealously guards its prerogatives and keeps a close eye on activities to ensure that the Commission does not encroach on its territory, it must be emphasized that the Council of Ministers is very much an EU institution. While it represents national interests, it does so within the framework of European integration. Member states, by operating within the framework of the Council of Ministers, accept an institutional framework that leads to a collective—rather than a unilateral—decision. By participating in the Council of Ministers, national governments give up the maneuverability and autonomy that are implicit in national (unilateral) decisionmaking. It is for that reason that "Euroskeptics" argue that participation in the EU means giving up sovereignty—defined as the ability to make unilateral decisions.

In contrast, the power of the Council of Ministers ensures that the EU always adopts legislation that meets with the approval of most or all of the member states' governments. The EU does not impose legislation on national governments—they adopt the legislation themselves in the Council of Ministers (and in many areas in partnership with the European Parliament). Opposition parties in national parliaments, however, do not have access to Council of Ministers meetings, so the EU enhances the power of those political parties that are in government at the national level.

The Council of Ministers plays a stronger role in pillars two and three than it does in pillar one. In pillar one the policymaking process gives important roles to both the Commission and the Parliament (the latter, however, is excluded from Justice, Freedom and Security even in pillar one), and the European Court of Justice can be central. The Commission plays a smaller role and the Parliament has no role in the policymaking process within pillars two and three.

The culture of the Council of Ministers is based on negotiation and is predisposed toward finding agreement: The whole system depends on a crucial assumption that there is give and take between the positions of the member states and that, whatever the starting positions of the members, there is *both* scope for those positions to evolve and a predisposition to find agreement. Thus, atmospherics, mutual confidence, and trust are important ingredients.

The member governments, acting within the Council of Ministers, are engaged in an institutional process that is unlike that of any other legislative body in the world. Multinational, bound by EU rather than international law, and (in pillar one) engaged in important relationships with the European Commission and the European Parliament, the Council of Ministers "locks" national ministers into an ongoing cooperative venture that includes a shared and enlarging policy agenda. It is that "locking" effect that helps ensure that national officials do not decide to act unilaterally, rather than multilaterally.

Although some analysts view the Council of Ministers as blocking further integration, other attempts at regional integration throughout the world highlight the importance of having national ministers involved in the nitty-gritty of policymaking at the European level. The Council of Ministers, in essence, is the guarantor of European integration in that national governments must participate in it and cannot ignore it. Without the Council of Ministers, the actions of the Commission and the Parliament could conceivably be ignored by national governments, but their membership in the Council of Ministers helps ensure that these national governments address the issues proposed by the Commission.

The European Council

The key strategic institution within the EU is clearly the **European Council**. Strictly speaking, it does not form part of the Council of Ministers hierarchy, but it is closely linked to it. The European Council does not adopt legislation, leaving that to the Council of Ministers. Instead, it sets out the key guidelines for action and future development. Prime ministers (the president in the case of Cyprus, France, and Finland), foreign ministers, the Commission president, and another designated commissioner attend the European Council. The foreign ministers provide the institutional continuity between the Council of Ministers and the European Council.

The European Council meets formally four times a year in "summits" held in Brussels since the 2004 enlargement. (If a presidency decides to organize an informal summit, it can organize it wherever it wants.) These meetings receive far more publicity than do meetings of the various sectoral councils and may well symbolize the European Union for the average citizen.

The European Council usually operates through unanimity even when it is not required to do so. The European Council now "occupies a position at the apex of the EU's institutional system, overseeing the work of each of the three pillars, and the specialized sectoral Councils which operate therein. It monitors their work, sets framework principles to guide their future deliberations, takes or clears major political decisions, and frequently engages in trouble-shooting."[14] It is the European Council, for example, that decided key issues such as whether enlargement to Eastern Europe would occur, when it would occur, and whether Turkey could begin accession negotiations.

Representatives of the member state government holding the **presidency of the European Council and the Council of Ministers** chair the European Council and the Council of Ministers. Every six months the presidency of the EU rotates so that each member government has the powers of the presidency in both the European Council and the Council of Ministers. The head of state or government of the country holding the presidency, along with the Commission president and the high representative for foreign and security policy of the Council of Ministers, represents the EU at summit meetings with non-EU leaders. For example, in the second half of 2008 France held the presidency, and in summer 2008 French President Nicolas Sarkozy met with Russian Prime Minister Vladimir Putin to broker an agreement to stop hostilities between Russia and Georgia. Most burdensome perhaps is the fact that officials representing the member state government holding the presidency chair all of the hundreds of meetings that go on in the Council of Ministers.

Finally, the European Council controls the agenda and negotiations of the **Intergovernmental Conference (IGC),** which is called to revise treaties.

The most difficult compromises are made at the IGC—the Single European Act, the Maastricht Treaty, the Treaty of Amsterdam, the Treaty of Nice, and the Lisbon Treaty were all agreed to at the end of negotiations by the European Council. Only prime ministers (accompanied by their foreign ministers) or heads of state have the political power necessary to make concessions that are very difficult for national governments to accept, but that are critical for the success of negotiations.

The European Parliament

The **European Parliament** is the only supranational assembly in the world whose members are chosen by voters, rather than by governments. The European Parliament is also the only parliament in the world with two homes (see Box 12.2). Its 785 members serve five-year terms congruent with the commissioners' five-year terms. **Members of the European Parliament (MEPs)** are elected at the same time across the EU, but each country uses its own electoral system (a uniform EU electoral system does not yet exist). Because of the disproportionate influence of small countries in the EU (discussed later), members represent constituencies vastly different in size.

When the ECSC was formed, the Parliament was originally located at Strasbourg. The city is still the official seat of the Parliament, even though the building that houses it now stands empty for 300 days a year. Most of the Parliament's work has gradually moved to Brussels, where the other EU institutions are. France, however, insists that some of the work be done in Strasbourg, even adding a protocol to the 1997 Amsterdam Treaty to that effect. The Parliament and the member states (and in particular, France)

have repeatedly locked horns on the issue. MEPs have often tried to end this cumbersome arrangement, even launching a petition of European voters to stop the circus. However, the final decision rests with the member states, and it is therefore likely that the circus will not end anytime soon.

Turnover is very high after each parliamentary election.[15] In the last elections (2004), 43 percent of the elected MEPs from the 15 pre-enlargement countries were newcomers.[16] This compares to less than 15 percent who were newcomers after recent elections to the U.S. Congress. Some MEPs continue on to distinguished careers in national politics, especially in France (where ten of the sixteen prime ministers and four of the six presidents in the Fifth Republic were MEPs). Roughly 30 percent of the MEPs in the 2004–2009 Parliament are women, with the highest proportion in the Swedish delegation (58 percent) and the lowest in the delegations from Malta and Cyprus (none).[17]

The Parliament argues that as the only directly elected European institution (it became directly elected in 1979), it is closer to the citizens of Europe than either the European Commission or the European Council. Thus, the Parliament has pressured, coaxed, threatened, and in general become an important presence on the political scene. Since the Treaty of Amsterdam went into effect in 1999, it has strongly influenced most legislation falling under pillar one. The Treaty of Nice further reinforced the Parliament's role of co-legislator with the Council of Ministers. The Parliament can only ask the Commission to draft proposals, rather than initiating its own draft proposals. However, in those areas in which it has jurisdiction, the Parliament can offer amendments that can substantially change the proposal

---

A Traveling Circus?

BOX 12.2

The European Parliament's members "migrate" between Brussels in Belgium (which is effectively the capital of the EU, as most of the key EU institutions are located there), where it meets most of the time, and Strasbourg in France, where it meets for twelve sessions per year. This "transhumance" or "traveling circus" as the many critics of this

arrangement call it costs 200 million euros per year (15 percent of the operating costs of the EP) and involves the use of fifteen trucks to shuttle files between the two locations, with a significant impact in terms of CO_2 emissions. The problem is further increased by the fact that the European Parliament's Secretariat is in yet another location (Luxembourg).

offered by both the Commission and the Council of Ministers. In recent years the Parliament had about 80 percent of its amendments accepted by the Council of Ministers. This indicates that it is effective in shaping legislation.[18]

The Parliament controls (within limits) so-called noncompulsory spending. This includes spending not directed toward agricultural support or based on international agreements with third countries. The proportion of noncompulsory spending as a percentage of the total budget has increased over time. Currently, it is over 50 percent. In fact, the granting of budgetary authority to the Parliament in 1975 was a key step that has undergirded the subsequent increases in parliamentary power.

The Maastricht Treaty strengthened the Parliament's formal powers, and the Amsterdam, the Nice, and (if it is ratified) the Lisbon treaties further extended the co-decision procedure for legislation. The Parliament's co-decision power allows it to stop legislation that it does not want, even if the Council of Ministers unanimously supports it. In cases in which the Parliament and the Council of Ministers approve different versions of a piece of legislation, conciliation talks are held to try to agree on a compromise. If such talks fail, the legislation dies.

Parliament also has the right to approve the president of the Commission, as well as giving a formal vote of approval of the College of Commissioners as a whole. Finally, it approves the president of the European Central Bank. The Parliament must assent to certain international agreements, including accession treaties and association agreements.

Most of the Parliament's work is done in committee. Each committee can decide whether its work will be done in public view or in closed session. Committees in most national parliaments work in closed session, but most European parliamentary committees now work in public. Each MEP is a full member of at least one committee. Final parliamentary approval has to be granted in plenary sessions, and at times committee recommendations are overridden in the plenary sessions.

The European Court of Justice

The **European Court of Justice** (ECJ; renamed the **Court of Justice of the European Union** by the Lisbon Treaty) is located in Luxembourg. It is a powerful supranational institution that makes law through judicial review. The ECJ is composed of one judge from each member state (chosen by the national government). Judges serve renewable six-year terms of office. They elect one of the sitting judges as president. The ECJ established the Court of First Instance in November 1989. That court has a more limited jurisdiction and cannot hear what might be termed constitutionally important cases.

The ECJ is often the arbiter in disputes between an individual member state and the Commission. It also handles interinstitutional disputes—for example, between the Commission and the Council of Ministers. Individual citizens can bring cases before these courts only if an EU action directly harms them. It is typically easier for a firm to claim such harm than for a noneconomic actor. Nongovernmental groups such as environmental organizations do not have easy access to the ECJ. Since the Treaty of Nice, the European Parliament can also bring a case to court. The ECJ has jurisdiction over issue areas falling within pillar one, as well as very limited jurisdiction in pillar three.

Most of the ECJ's cases come from national courts asking for a preliminary ruling. The national court then takes the ECJ's preliminary ruling and delivers it as its own opinion. Therefore, national judges are an important factor in developing the effectiveness of the EU's legal order.

Initially established as an international court operating under the constraints of international law, the ECJ rather quickly began to represent the "European interest" in its own right. After the Treaty of Rome went into effect, the ECJ "constitutionalized" the international law under which it was operating. Rather than simply becoming an international court with limited impact, it gradually evolved into a powerful body. In some striking, albeit limited, ways, it resembles the U.S. Supreme Court. Its influence in the policymaking process has led one scholar to conclude that "for many areas of European and national policy, knowing the position of the ECJ is as important as knowing the position of the member states and national interest groups."[19] The Court performs an important role in the policymaking process, as we discuss later.

The Single Currency and the European Central Bank

Economic and Monetary Union (EMU) had been discussed since the late 1960s, and the Maastricht Treaty finally established a timetable and made a serious commitment to move ahead. The EU established a **single currency** and a **European Central Bank** in

1999, and citizens began using the common currency (the **euro**) in January 2002.

The political dynamics behind EMU were clear to political elites, but difficult to explain to the general public. Under the previous European Monetary System (EMS) established in 1979, currencies were allowed to fluctuate only within an agreed-upon range. The German Bundesbank was the dominant decisionmaker. The German currency, the Deutsche mark, became the "anchor currency." That is, when the Bundesbank raised interest rates, the other EMS members had to follow in order to keep their currencies within the range to which they had agreed. When such a need arose during a recession, this had a harmful impact on national economies. The high interest rates in a recession exacerbated high unemployment and therefore were very painful.

The high cost of German unification led the German Bundesbank to raise interest rates while many other EMS members were in a recession. The French and the Italians in particular realized that they needed to gain a voice in European monetary policy. To do so, they had to give up their own monetary sovereignty (largely illusory in any case because of the dynamics of the EMS) and convince the Germans to do likewise. This would occur within the framework of a European central bank in which each member state's central bank would have equal representation.

Although the Bundesbank was reluctant to embrace EMU, Chancellor Kohl was anxious to show that unification was not leading Germany away from the EU and agreed to economic and monetary union. The decision over EMU fell within the "Chancellor's prerogative."[20] That is, the ultimate decision about EMU was the chancellor's. The Maastricht Treaty embodied that agreement. The German government, however, insisted on certain conditions in order to ensure that the new currency, the euro, would be as "strong" a currency as the Deutsche mark, which the Germans were to give up. In particular, the European Central Bank was to have price stability (rather than, for example, low unemployment or high rates of economic growth) as its primary objective. Countries were not allowed to join EMU unless their deficits were at 3 percent of GDP or lower.

Years of brutal budget cutting were required for many countries (such as Italy) to qualify. In 1999 eleven countries joined what became known as the Eurozone; the UK, Sweden, and Denmark stayed out. Greece joined in 2001, Slovenia in 2007, Cyprus and Malta in 2008, and Slovakia in 2009.

The European Central Bank, established in Frankfurt, is composed of the governors of the national central banks. It is extremely independent of all the other EU institutions, as well as of the member state governments. It is arguably the most independent central bank in the world. In fact, that independence has been criticized by countries such as France that believe there should be greater emphasis on stimulating economic growth. However, the European Central Bank believes it is necessary to convince the financial markets that it will not pursue a monetary policy that would allow inflation. Price stability is its policy mantra.

NATIONAL GOVERNMENTS AS ACTORS

As already indicated in our discussion of the EU's institutions, national governments play a key role in the EU's policymaking process. Their influence is felt directly in the Council of Ministers and through the power of appointment in the European Commission and the European Court of Justice. Typically, the focus on understanding how and why national governments operate within the EU highlights the role of ruling parties and bureaucracies. National governments are able to defend their national interest in all the EU's institutions in one fashion or another. The opportunity to defend one's national interest has lubricated the path of integration for the member states.

The need to prepare the EU's institutions for enlargement highlighted the disproportionate power of the small member states. This issue had not been the subject of controversy since the Treaty of Rome. As the negotiations proceeded for the Treaty of Nice, the disproportionality of size became the object of intense political conflict among the current member states. Simply put, the negotiations for the Treaty of Nice forced the question of *which* governments could adequately defend their national interests in the future. In addition to wielding disproportionate power within the EU, as indicated by Table 12.1, small countries have a formal status largely equal to that of the large countries in the European Court of Justice, the European Council, and the governing council of the European Central Bank. Given that many new small countries would join the EU through enlargement, the large member states in 2000 sought to redress the balance in the negotiations leading to the Treaty of Nice.

Distribution of Power in the EU

TABLE 12.1

Small states wield disproportionate power in the EU

Member States	Number of Commissioners	Number of Votes in Council of Ministers	Number of Members of Parliament (MEPs)
Germany	1	29	99
France	1	29	78
United Kingdom	1	29	78
Italy	1	29	78
Spain	1	27	54
Poland	1	27	54
Romania	1	14	35
Netherlands	1	13	27
Greece	1	12	24
Portugal	1	12	24
Belgium	1	12	24
Czech Republic	1	12	24
Hungary	1	12	24
Sweden	1	10	19
Austria	1	10	18
Bulgaria	1	10	18
Denmark	1	7	14
Slovakia	1	7	14
Finland	1	7	14
Ireland	1	7	13
Lithuania	1	7	13
Latvia	1	4	9
Slovenia	1	4	7
Estonia	1	4	6
Cyprus	1	4	6
Luxembourg	1	4	6
Malta	1	3	5

The small states feared being "pushed around" by the large states and rejected many of the demands made by the four large states (France, Germany, Italy, and the UK). The last half of 2000 was filled with acrimony as the small states accused the large ones of trying to weaken the European Commission (which the small states view as an ally) in the name of efficient decisionmaking. They accused the large states of trying to make the EU more intergovernmental so that the large states would have more influence. The large states, for their part, adamantly demanded more power within the Council of Ministers (through a reallocation of voting weights) and wanted more representation in the European Parliament. Furthermore, they viewed their proposals for the Commission as strengthening it by making it more effective. In brief, the large member states wanted to ensure that the next enlargement did not privilege small countries even further. The small member states worried that if the large member states gained too much power, the EU would become more like an international organization (in which small countries fare very badly) and less like a federation (in which small subfederal units exercise disproportionate power, as in the United States). The small countries wanted the policymaking process to respect their wishes as it had since the Treaty of Rome. The final compromise gave the large states less power than they had desired, but nonetheless more than they had in the pre-Nice period. Poland and Spain (by exploiting their position as "medium-size" countries, as well as by engaging in very tough bargaining) gained an especially privileged position.

The issue of the appropriate balance between large and small states reemerged during the negotiations over the Constitution for Europe (which was actually a constitutional treaty). The final compromise, reached in June 2004, would have given the large member states more power than they had had under the Treaty of Nice, but less than they had desired. After the French and Dutch voters rejected the constitutional treaty, many of its provisions were adopted by the Lisbon Treaty (whose ratification is in doubt), but only after Poland engaged in a fierce fight for its voting rights in the Council of Ministers.

POLITICAL PARTIES

Political parties do not play the same role in EU politics as they do in the national politics of the European countries described in this book (see Chapter 3). On the one hand, political parties in national elections often do not offer alternative policies and analyses at the European level. In almost every member state, the focus of party competition in national elections continues to be domestic politics.[21] Thus, while national elections may determine which party controls the government that chooses representatives to the European Commission and the Council of Ministers, the electoral debate seldom focuses on the EU policies of those representatives. Even direct elections to the European Parliament primarily operate as referendums on the domestic achievements and promises of the competing parties.

On the other hand, this inattention is encouraged because election outcomes do not directly determine the control of the EU's governing institutions. Some observers argue that the control of at least some institutions should be politicized and made the object of European-wide political campaigns. For instance, based on the European Parliament's existing power to approve the president of the European Commission, the Parliament elections could become elections for the president of the Commission, with European parties campaigning in support of their candidate for the job.[22] This would follow the parliamentary model of many national governments within the EU.

This would also help create a truly European political sphere, with political divisions played out at the European level by European parties. As things are now, however, politics in the EU revolves more around broad territorial (national) divisions than the socioeconomic divisions of national party politics. The "left-right" division so pivotal in structuring political party positions at the national level manifests itself less often and in different ways in Brussels. Divisions on European integration crosscut the left-right cleavage at the European level, as both the left and the right blocs in the European Parliament are internally divided on how and how far European integration should proceed.[23] Thus, it is mainly through national governments that political parties influence European affairs.[24]

The histories of national political parties are not rooted in conflicts over European integration. Until voters in some member states became concerned with the impact of integration, parties did not address EU policy issues. Even after integration became more politicized, many major parties did not take clear positions on the issues they would face in the Council of Ministers. On the contrary, they cloaked their actions in the garb of national interest: "Instead of defending their participation in European regulatory decision-making on the grounds of fulfilling an electoral mandate, ruling parties have consistently defended such actions on the grounds that they have done their best to protect national interests, thus casting European politics as a zero-sum game between the member states."[25]

Nonetheless, parties are organizing a bit more extensively on the European level than they have in the past. In 1992 and 1993, all the major transnational party federations institutionalized themselves to a greater degree. Furthermore, the transnational federations meet right before the European Council meetings, so that prime ministers, members of the European Parliament, and commissioners from each of the leading political parties discuss EU issues.[26] Whether and how quickly transnational parties will evolve is still an open question.

The issues with which the EU deals typically have a strong economic component that often manifests itself in technical issues not usually the subject of political discourse. That economic component is shaped by the Treaty of Rome and the Single European Act, both of which embody a certain model of economics. Expanding cross-border trade and competition and opening economies and markets are the EU's key economic objectives. That model does not easily address political problems in the way that parties have traditionally done so in national contexts. Finally, much national party competition revolves around issues related to the welfare state. The EU does not directly legislate on welfare state issues, which means that a central element of national political party conflict is not even on the EU agenda.

Parliamentary Elections

Elections to the European Parliament differ from national parliamentary elections in a variety of ways. Most centrally, they do not influence government formation in the same way as do national elections in the member states. Turnout is higher in national (and sometimes even in subnational) elections. The large parties typically do better in national elections, while small parties do better in elections to the European Parliament. This indicates that citizens often just cast a protest vote in European Parliament elections. Worrisome for those concerned about the "democratic deficit" (discussed later in this chapter), in most countries the turnout for parliamentary elections has declined since the elections of 1979. The lowest turnout was in the 2004 elections, although with significant differences across the member states (see Figure 12.3).

European elections are described as "pale reflections of national elections."[27] The electoral campaign does not highlight choices to be made at the European level, but rather emphasizes the kinds of issues typically debated within the voters' normal national party context.

Analysts often view national elections as "first-order" elections. Elections to the European Parliament are "second-order" elections because no actual executive power is at stake. Rather than focusing on European issues, elections to the Parliament often provide a forum for voters to express their support of, or discontent with, national parties.

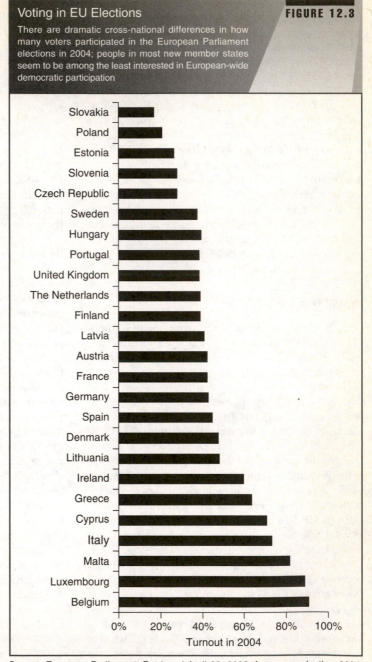

Voting in EU Elections

FIGURE 12.3

There are dramatic cross-national differences in how many voters participated in the European Parliament elections in 2004; people in most new member states seem to be among the least interested in European-wide democratic participation

Turnout in 2004

Source: European Parliament. Retrieved April 22, 2009, from www.elections2004.eu.int/ep-election/sites/en/results1306/turnout_ep/turnout_table.html.

National cues, rather than the specific policies of the European Union, are paramount in shaping how voters cast their ballots.

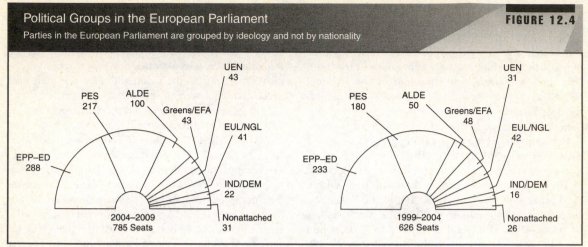

Political Groups in the European Parliament

FIGURE 12.4

Parties in the European Parliament are grouped by ideology and not by nationality

2004–2009
785 Seats

EPP–ED 288 · PES 217 · ALDE 100 · Greens/EFA 43 · UEN 43 · EUL/NGL 41 · IND/DEM 22 · Nonattached 31

1999–2004
626 Seats

EPP–ED 233 · PES 180 · ALDE 50 · Greens/EFA 48 · UEN 31 · EUL/NGL 42 · IND/DEM 16 · Nonattached 26

Key to acronyms: EPP-ED: European People's Party (Christian Democrats) and European Democrats; PES: Party of European Socialists; ALDE: Alliance for Liberals and Democrats for Europe; Greens/EFA: Greens/European Free Alliance; UEN: Union for a Europe of Nations; EUL/NGL: European United Left/Nordic Green Left; IND/DEM: Independence/Democracy.

Source: European Parliament. Retrieved April 22, 2009, from www.europarl.europa.eu/members/expert.do?language=EN (for 2004–2009); www.europarl.europa.eu/press/sdp/pointses/en/1999/p990720s.htm (for 1999–2004).

Parties in the European Parliament

Within the EU's institutions, political parties are most visible in the European Parliament. Europe's extraordinary cultural and political diversity appears in over 164 parties that are represented in the European Parliament. These parties combine into Political Groups that are the centers of power within the Parliament (see Figure 12.4). Seven Political Groups emerged after the 2004 parliamentary elections:

- *European People's Party and European Democrats (EPP–ED):* Christian Democratic and Conservative parties
- *Party of European Socialists (PES):* most major socialist parties
- *Alliance for Liberals and Democrats for Europe (ALDE):* centrist free-market parties
- *Greens/European Free Alliance (Greens/EFA):* most of the major green parties
- *Union for a Europe of Nations (UEN):* Conservative non-Christian-Democratic parties, against further European integration (Euroskeptic)
- *European United Left/Nordic Green Left (EUL/NGL):* extreme left
- *Independence/Democracy (IND/DEM):* extreme right, against further European integration (Euroskeptic)

Each Political Group includes MEPs that share a political affinity and come from at least two member states. The groups set the parliamentary agenda and de facto choose the parliament's president and fourteen vice presidents as well as the chairs, vice-chairs, and rapporteurs of the various committees.

Political Groups are organized not along national lines, but, just like in national parliaments, along ideological ones. They do not perform the same role as do parties in national parliaments. The appointment of the executive—that is, the Commission—is not formally determined by the Parliament. However, in 2004 Commission President Barroso came from the political group that had the largest number of seats in the European Parliament. The groups also do not influence the portfolios that the individual commissioners receive, nor do they influence the partisan coloring of the ministers in the Council of Ministers. National governments choose both the commissioners and the ministers in the Council of Ministers. To understand the difference between a party in a national parliament and a Political Group in the European Parliament, it is important to remember that European elections do not initiate a process of government formation, as they do in most parliamentary democracies.

The Political Groups provide an important channel of information for national parties. They are also important in organizing meetings, typically held before European Council meetings. At these sessions heads of government and commissioners from the party, party leaders, and the chair of the Political Group try to achieve a consensus on key issues affecting European integration.

The two largest Political Groups are the center-right European People's Party (EPP; previously named the Christian Democrats) and the center-left Party of European Socialists. Until the parliamentary elections of 1999, the Socialists were the dominant party within the Parliament. Much to the shock of the Socialists, the EPP won 233 seats in 1999, while the Socialists won only 180. The trend continued in 2004, when the EPP won 278 seats and the Socialists won 199. Whereas the Socialists and the EPP previously had engaged in a kind of "grand coalition" and shared the committee chairmanships and the presidency of the Parliament among themselves, in 1999 the EPP pursued a different strategy. It concluded an informal alliance with the third largest party, the Alliance of Liberals and Democrats for Europe (with 51 seats), and shared the presidency of the Parliament with the Liberals. Most importantly, the EPP stressed the left-right division within the Parliament and the Commission. The Parliament became more "politicized." Rather than subordinating partisan conflict to the desire to increase the Parliament's power vis-à-vis the Commission and the Council of Ministers, the EPP highlighted the policy differences between the Socialists and the center-right parties. The EPP views government intervention in the market less favorably than do the Socialists. In fact, under EPP leadership the Parliament voted more pro-business and less environmentally friendly than had past Parliaments. After the 2004 elections, the EPP and the Socialists again shared the committee chairmanships and the presidency of the Parliament among themselves, so that the "grand coalition" has reemerged.

It is important to note that the party families (especially the EPP and the Socialists) have traditionally cooperated with one another. The EPP, the Socialists, and the Liberals still need to cooperate because none alone has the majority needed under parliamentary procedures. Given the necessity to cooperate, the Parliament is not the forum for the kinds of partisan clashes found in the British House of Commons (see Chapter 5). Nonetheless, adversarialism is now present in the Parliament to a greater degree, especially since the 1999 elections. Partisan divides tend to dilute the Parliament's power when dealing with the other institutions. For example, when the partisan divisions between right and left are highlighted on an issue, the Parliament is in a weaker position when entering conciliation talks with the Council than when there is a unitary parliamentary position.

In general, politics within the Parliament is now less predictable and more fluid than had been the case in the past. The EPP itself is divided between members from the Christian Democrats, who have traditionally favored European integration, and Euroskeptics. This means that the political dynamics of the Parliament are very complex. Importantly, partisan divisions tend to be more important than nationality differences in determining the voting behavior of MEPs.[28] This is an indication that the European Parliament is functioning more and more like a "normal" national parliament.[29]

The 2004 elections were marked by a low turnout (in the ten new countries, overall participation was only at 26 percent, with notable exceptions in Malta and Cyprus (see Figure 12.3). The elections also showed a clear gain for smaller, Euroskeptic, or populist parties. In the UK, for instance, the UK Independence Party (UKIP), whose agenda calls for complete withdrawal of the UK from the EU, placed third after the Conservatives and the Labour Party, with 17 percent of the votes. In Sweden, Poland, and Denmark, Euroskeptic parties also gained ground. Voters punished their government either because of its support of the Iraq war (in the UK) or because of its poor economic performance (in France and Germany).

INTEREST GROUPS

As the EU has expanded the range of policies about which it can legislate, lobbying activities in Brussels have experienced a veritable boom.[30] Research is still trying to catch up with the growth and activity of groups, and scholars understand the role of interest groups in national systems better than in the EU. What is clear is that the system of policymaking within the EU is so open that interest groups can participate in the process of making public policy.

Interest groups interact with the EU's institutions in relatively unpredictable ways and at different points in the policy process. They lobby the Parliament for favorable amendments to Commission and Council of Ministers proposals, as well as the relevant Commission officials. They have become an integral part of the policy process in Brussels, much as they are in the UK, Germany, the Netherlands, Denmark, and Sweden. Although groups representing a variety of interests are becoming ever more numerous in Brussels, the structure of interest group interaction is not "corporatist," as it is in several European nations (see Chapter 4). That is, business and labor groups do not work with government officials in a structured way to make policy.

Interest groups have become so numerous (in 2008 there were 15,000 lobbyists working in Brussels) that both the Commission and the Parliament feel the need to regularize their activities in some fashion. The Parliament in 1996 established a register of interest groups. Once an interest group has registered and accepted a code of conduct, it receives a one-year pass giving access to the Parliament. However, this has proven insufficient to make the relationships between MEPs and lobbyists transparent enough. In 2008 Parliament proposed more stringent rules, although glaring loopholes remain (in particular, under the proposal lawyers are exempt from the new rules).[31]

The Commission developed guidelines to guide Commission officials in their dealings with representatives of interest groups and to improve transparency.[32] However, these rules have also not been enough. Between 2005 and 2008, the Commission further revised them, introducing a voluntary registry in 2008. The Commission, which is the object of most of the lobbying, has found it particularly difficult to maintain access to its relatively small staff without being overwhelmed by the demands on its time and attention. Although regulation exists, there are no uniform rules across EU institutions on the participation of interest groups in the EU decisionmaking process.

Political parties are not the key actors in Brussels as they are in national political systems and there is no "government" in the traditional sense; instead, the Commission has become the key target of interest groups because of its role in initiating legislation. The Commission subsidizes European-level groups—such as citizen groups, trade associations and unions—as it sees them as a way to support further integration.[33] These groups are transnational actors—that is, they bring together national associations so as to form a European group. Transnational groups are not as important as many assume, at least partially because national associations often find it difficult to agree on a common position. Many such groups are much weaker than their national counterparts. National organizations, rather than the European federations of

such organizations, often possess the information that is the interest group's chief asset and the resource most valuable to the Commission as it attempts to formulate policy.

Although it is difficult to gauge precisely the relative power and influence of diverse groups, many analysts argue that business interests have the most access and are the most influential.[34] Trade unions, although members of the European Trade Union Conference, have been unable to organize as effectively, and in general labor representatives are less visible in policy debates. Environmental and consumer groups, although nurtured and supported by the Commission, are still much weaker in general than are business groups.

In fact, business interests form the overwhelming majority of interests represented in Brussels (see Figure 12.5). According to the latest count, there are more that 1,300 corporations (including many from the United States, such as McDonald's and defense and aerospace giant Northrop Grumman), organizations representing business interests (from the Association of the European Self-Medication Industry to the Tattoo Ink Manufactures of Europe), and chambers of commerce working with the EU. Conversely, only twenty-three labor unions are represented in Brussels. However, interest representation is not limited to economic interests: 439 nongovernmental organizations (from Amnesty International to the World Wildlife Fund) operate in Brussels alongside the representatives of 88 regional governments (including some from the United States and Canada) and 117 international organizations.[35]

In spite of the number of interest groups operating in Brussels and their varied activities, it is important not to overestimate their influence. As indicated earlier, the Economic and Monetary Union represents a historic milestone for European integration. The new European Central Bank and the euro are key changes in the economic landscape of the EU. Yet interest groups were not involved at key points in these decisions. Business groups, labor representatives, and associations representing banks were all excluded. Heads of state and government and their finance ministers, along with their advisors and civil servants, were the key negotiators on EMU, not interest groups. The same general argument can be made about all the treaties, up to and including the Lisbon Treaty.

Although interest groups are not necessarily included in the "historic" decisions, they are typically woven into the EU's policy process. In particular,

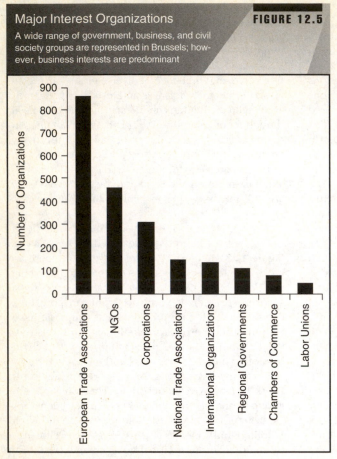

Major Interest Organizations

FIGURE 12.5

A wide range of government, business, and civil society groups are represented in Brussels; however, business interests are predominant

Source: Dods, *The European Public Affairs Directory* (London: Dods, 2007).

across European, national, and subnational levels, as EU laws need to be transposed into national laws.

PUBLIC OPINION—DOES IT MATTER?

The European Union is different from the national political systems in the role that mass politics plays. Citizens have an ambiguous role, and scholars are still determining how public opinion intersects with the EU's policymaking process. In the EU the voters transmit their wishes primarily through national governments. In national systems the voters directly choose those in power. Because the EU involves negotiations among governments, similar in that sense to international relations, governments can pursue policies somewhat independently from the wishes of voters.

Governments, once in power, have more discretion on issues related to integration than they do on national issues centrally identified with their political party. The question of "Europe" is not clearly positioned within national political systems. It divides political parties internally, rather than separating one party from another. Prime ministers therefore exercise considerable discretion when deciding broad issues of European integration. In countries where referendums are common (Denmark and Sweden, for example), voters can express their views more directly and have them be more binding than can voters in countries without referendums (such as Germany). In some cases, where referendums are possible, but infrequent (France), the results can be surprising. This was evident when President Mitterrand, assuming that the French would support the Maastricht Treaty, called for a referendum—only to see the treaty supported by the thinnest of margins. Even when referendums are used, the substantive results can be somewhat surprising. Norwegian voters twice rejected membership in the EC. Still, Norwegian governments have tried to pass legislation and pursue economic policies compatible with EU legislation. If one examined selected aspects of Norwegian public policy, it would not be immediately obvious that Norway is not a member of the EU.

sophisticated groups lobby at both the national and the European levels. They lobby the Commission for favorable provisions when it is drafting the legislation, they lobby the Parliament for favorable amendments when it is considering the legislation, and they lobby the national officials who will be involved when the issue reaches the Council of Ministers. The EU has many access points for groups or individual actors, and they are increasingly taking advantage of all of them. A large business firm's lobbying effort may use its national association—which has an office in the national capital as well as an office in Brussels, a Euro-association that brings together national associations, and the firm's own office in Brussels. It can thus lobby a variety of officials using a variety of venues and strategies. To be effective, lobby groups also need to coordinate

Public opinion does not constrain political leaders as directly as it does in national, strictly domestic, politics. Rather, the constraint of public opinion is more subtle and diffuse. Public opinion as expressed in the elections to the European Parliament is also diluted, since the Parliament does not form the government.

Although compromise is a normal part of the democratic process, especially in systems with coalition governments, national politicians do not feel comfortable explaining their EU policy positions to their electorate. While political elites understand the necessity for compromise, the EU's decisionmaking process is often presented to the public as one in which countries lose or win. Depending on the circumstances, ministers either claim to have "won" (when carrying out popular policies) or claim to have been "forced" by the EU to take an (unpopular) action.

Even when taking an unpopular action, it is quite likely that the national government voted in favor of that unpopular action, but conveniently does not mention that fact. "Scapegoating" Brussels is easy because the legislation approved by the Council of Ministers often does not take effect until several years later. Only the most sophisticated newspaper reporter is likely to track the legislative history of an EU law, which is criticized by national politicians when it goes into effect.

The lack of a direct transmission belt between public opinion and the EU executive has led many to argue that a "democratic deficit" exists. Some argue that a much stronger European Parliament is necessary to remedy the deficit. Others argue that national parliaments need a stronger role in the EU policy process.[36] Ironically, considering its rejection by Irish voters in 2008, the Lisbon Treaty considered both positions by increasing the power of the European Parliament and giving national parliaments a greater role in EU policymaking. Yet, neither of these two positions confronts the fact that the EU is not a state. As long as the policy process involves bargaining among legally constituted national governments, the influence of public opinion will face many of the same constraints that exist in the making of foreign policy. Multilateral decisionmaking that requires bargaining with foreigners is not the same as decisionmaking within national systems in which foreigners do not play a role. That difference raises difficult issues in fixing the democratic deficit. First, the institutional structure of the EU is mind-bogglingly complex and very distant from the clear lines of responsibility of parliamentary democracy (the standard form of democracy with which most Europeans are familiar). Second, the lack

of a truly European-wide public opinion reduces the significance of European elections. For this reason the innovations introduced by the Lisbon Treaty—even if it were to be finally ratified—might not be sufficient to address the democratic deficit. Some suggest further reforms—for instance, to raise the selection of the European Commission to a significant political issue for European voters, with real cross-European campaigns by the candidates for the position of Commission president.[37]

The Council of Ministers operates in a great deal of secrecy, and that secrecy helps political leaders operate in Brussels with less scrutiny than they receive in their national capitals. Minutes of Council meetings, even when accessible to the public, are often not very revealing of the political dynamics that led to the decision being reported in the minutes.[38] The deals made between ministers are often not revealed to the press. Each minister may well claim "victory" for his or her position, but what is typically not revealed is what concessions were made by that same minister. Even though the Council of Ministers could not reach a decision without each national government being willing to compromise, ministers do not publicize their role in reaching a compromise.

The secrecy accompanying Council of Ministers decisionmaking has led many critics to identify such secrecy as a contributor to the democratic deficit. Citizens do not know what kinds of concessions their national government made or even how their government voted on a particular piece of legislation. This leads to a lack of transparency in the EU's operations, which many see as intrinsically undemocratic. Again, secrecy in decisionmaking is more characteristic of international relations than of domestic politics. Many international "deals" are made away from public scrutiny. Foreign policymaking is one of the least transparent policy areas within national systems. International diplomacy has historically been rooted in secrecy, partially so that negotiators can protect their negotiating flexibility and thereby arrive at a compromise. Although the EU exhibits a great deal of integration and negotiations within the Council of Ministers differ in significant ways from those in other international forums, such negotiations are nonetheless different from their domestic counterparts. The EU is composed of states that still regard each other as foreign. That basic fact affects the dynamics of negotiation and raises difficult questions about whether such a system can be democratized without paralyzing its decisionmaking capacity.

As Brussels penetrates more and more deeply into domestic political systems and wields greater power in policy areas traditionally seen as domestic, the lack of open decisionmaking is increasingly problematic. Given the lack of strong European transnational parties that could claim some legitimacy in the tradition of "party government" and the lack of oversight by national parliaments over the EU's executive levels, the Council of Ministers is open to the charge that it is "undemocratic." But can multilateral decisionmaking involving foreign governments be democratic in the same way in which national systems are? Can public opinion be as influential?

The current policy process does not allow public opinion, defined either ideologically or nationally, to be directly transmitted into decisionmaking. The relative absence of transnational political parties and the discretion exercised by national ministers both dilute the impact of public opinion. It is therefore difficult to predict the position a national government will take by looking at the state of public opinion. Chancellor Helmut Kohl, for example, strongly supported the drive for a single currency even though at times a majority of Germans opposed it. While elections that bring in new political parties can certainly change a government's position on integration, such change is not automatic.

In spite of the relative insulation policymaking has enjoyed, public opinion became far more important during the ratification of the Maastricht Treaty. That ratification process politicized the issue of European integration, so much so that elites negotiating the Treaty of Amsterdam in 1997 had to keep public opinion in the forefront of their calculations. That is particularly true for political leaders in countries that use referendums for ratification, as a series of defeats in national referendums—over the Nice Treaty (2001) and the Lisbon Treaty (2008) in Ireland and the constitutional treaty in France and the Netherlands (2005)—has amply shown. The referendum, however, is a dull tool to use when deciding complex institutional questions. In the 2008 Irish referendum on the Lisbon Treaty, the main reason why voters voted "no" was because they felt they did not have enough information on the treaty.[39]

Although it can be argued that adverse public opinion has mainly slowed down the progress of integration, rather than changing its orientation in any fundamental way, there is no doubt that political leaders now take it into account tactically, if not strategically. However, outside of a referendum, public opinion becomes most influential when political parties mobilize it. European political parties are divided by religion, the proper role of government in the economy, and the limits of social welfare, rather than by issues linked to European integration. Thus, they have not capitalized on different opinions about integration within the mass electorate. In addition, they have not engaged in a sustained debate about the policy choices presented by integration. Consequently, public opinion has less impact on the European arena than it does on the national, except when referendums are involved.

Cross-National Differences

Support for European integration depends on socioeconomic status, with the more affluent being more supportive of integration (see Figure 12.6). Support is higher among upper-status professionals such as managers and salaried employees (and students) and lower among the unemployed and retired.

Typically, support for Europe also varies crossnationally, as does participation in European elections. It is important to remember that there is no "European" public opinion; there is instead only public opinion within twenty-seven different national political discourses. The lack of "European" media reinforces such segmentation. Nationally based newspapers and television reporting strengthen the notion of national opinion, national electorates, and national victories and losses within the EU. In a similar vein, the notion of a "European identity" gains more support in some member states than others, but is secondary to national identity.

A majority of European citizens support European integration. In general, the citizens of the founding six members are more supportive of European integration than are the citizens of the UK (Figure 12.7). The citizens of states that joined in 1981 and 1986 (Greece, Spain, and Portugal) have consistently been far more favorable than the British. For members such as the Irish, the Spanish, and the Portuguese, favorable attitudes may be rooted in the view that the modernization of the economic and political system is linked to membership in the EU. Analysts view modern Spain and Ireland as intrinsically "European," while the traditional Spain and Ireland were outside of the European mainstream. In general, attitudes in Greece, Spain, Portugal, and Ireland are now as favorable toward integration as are attitudes in the original six members. Among the

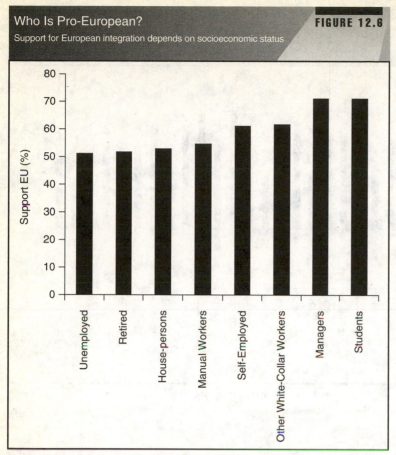

Who Is Pro-European?

Support for European integration depends on socioeconomic status

FIGURE 12.6

Note: The figure shows the percentage in the EU 27 that says membership in the EU is a good thing.

Source: European Commission. *Eurobarometer 68* (Brussels: European Union, December 2007).

91 percent (Slovenia, probably in connection with the country's recent entry in the Eurozone) and a low of 41 percent (Greece). By contrast, most Europeans favor a common foreign and security policy.

Public opinion was especially salient during the process of ratifying the Maastricht Treaty. Given the broad consensus among all the key political parties in the member states, the leaders meeting in Maastricht expected no trouble during ratification of the treaty. Much to the surprise of political elites, the Danish electorate voted "no" on Maastricht in June 1992. The Danes voted "yes" only in May 1993 after the Danish government had obtained key opt-outs from central provisions of Maastricht. Even more troubling was the French reaction to Maastricht. In October 1992 the French barely approved the ratification of Maastricht. The shock waves from the Danish and French results obscured the fact that the Irish electorate approved the treaty by a substantial margin. Denmark and France became the symbols of a troubled European integration, whereas the Irish results were largely discounted.

Most analysts interpreted the results of the Maastricht referendums as a warning light that mass electorates were either hostile to or deeply skeptical about further European integration. Within the European Commission itself, a new sense of caution and circumspection emerged. National politicians clearly interpreted the referendums as a vote on integration, and the importance of public opinion in setting the parameters for elite action increased. In 2001 the Irish rejected the Nice Treaty and accepted it only in a second referendum. In 2005 French and Dutch voters rejected the proposed constitutional treaty, and, as we have seen, in 2008 the Irish rejected the Lisbon Treaty.

In sum, the role of public opinion concerning integration is still ambiguous. How to mobilize public

countries that joined since 2004, Latvia, Hungary, and Cyprus are the least "Euro-enthusiastic," while Poland and Romania are much more satisfied with European integration.

Support for the euro has been volatile and is currently higher than support for EU membership. Average support was 64 percent in 2007. In September 2000, 53 percent of Danes voting in a referendum on the euro voted against Danish membership; in 2007, however, a majority of Danish voters supported the euro. Conversely, the Swedes rejected the euro in 2003 and remain opposed to it, as are the British (less than a third of UK voters favor the euro). Among the countries that have adopted the euro, in 2007 support for the common currency varied between a high of

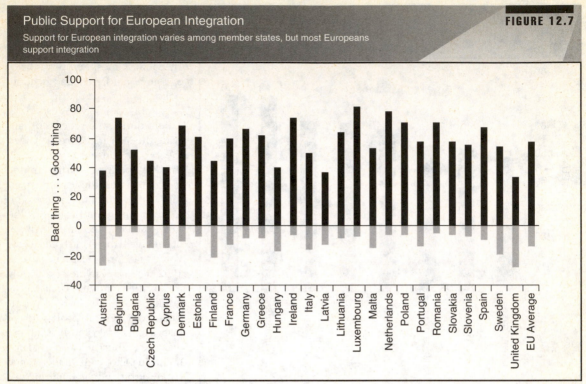

Public Support for European Integration

Support for European integration varies among member states, but most Europeans support integration

FIGURE 12.7

Note: The figure plots the percentages of the public in each member state that say membership in the EU is a "good thing" or a "bad thing."

Source: European Commission, *Eurobarometer 68* (Brussels: European Union, December 2007).

opinion in a system of multilateral decisionmaking involving foreigners is still an open question. The issues linked to European integration, although more than fifty years old, have not yet found their place on the national political agenda as shaped by national political parties.

THE POLICYMAKING PROCESS

Given the institutional complexity of the EU—its unusual institutions, its differing decisionmaking procedures across pillars—the policymaking process is more variegated, segmented, and less uniform than in European nation-states. The system itself is in flux, and the cast of political characters is often unpredictable. Nonetheless, certain key characteristics of the EU make that process more understandable.

First, small states wield a surprising amount of power within the EU. The large countries have more administrative resources to bring to bear in the EU's policymaking process, but the national governments of small member states typically focus on issues of particular concern to them. They often do extraordinarily well in defending their national interests in those specific policy areas. Especially in pillar one, where the small member states view the Commission as an ally to protect them from the pressure of overly aggressive large countries, government officials of small member states can be quite important in policymaking. The new Lisbon Treaty will introduce greater correspondence between demographic weight and representation of the member states in the EU institutions (and in particular, in the Council of Ministers), but the smaller states will still be overrepresented in those institutions (see Table 12.1).

Second, Germany disproportionately pays the highest net financial contributions to the EU, as Table 12.2 indicates. If Germany refuses to support a new initiative that requires new expenditure, its opposition is particularly important because of Germany's role as paymaster.

Member States' Budget Shares, 2007	TABLE 12.2

Germany remains the largest contributor to the EU budget

Country	Share of EU Budget (%)
Austria	2.0
Belgium	4.0
Bulgaria	0.3
Cyprus	0.2
Czech Republic	1.1
Denmark	2.0
Estonia	0.2
Finland	1.5
France	15.4
Germany	19.7
Greece	2.7
Hungary	0.8
Ireland	1.4
Italy	12.8
Latvia	0.2
Lithuania	0.2
Luxembourg	0.3
Malta	0.1
Netherlands	5.7
Poland	2.6
Portugal	1.3
Romania	1.0
Slovakia	0.5
Slovenia	0.3
Spain	8.9
Sweden	2.7
United Kingdom	12.2

Source: EU Commission, *EU Budget 2006 Financial Report* (Luxembourg: European Commission, 2007).

The EU's budget is actually very small, compared with that of the member states. It stands at about 1 percent of the member states' GDP. The lack of money encourages the EU to use regulations rather than expenditures as an instrument of policy. While expenditures are comparatively small, they are very important for the smaller, poorer countries, and especially for the more recently added member states. In 2006 EU funds accounted for 2.5 percent of Hungarian GDP, 2.4 percent of Polish GDP, 2.0 percent of Slovak GDP, and 1.4 percent of Czech GDP.[40]

Third, questions about expenditures and financial resources invariably raise the issue of compulsory expenditure for the Common Agricultural Policy (CAP). CAP has historically dominated the EU's budget. However, CAP spending has declined significantly—from roughly 70 percent of its budget in 1984 to 34 percent in 2009 (see Figure 12.8). It now represents the second largest expenditure item after cohesion policies, which reduce inequality among regions in the EU and stimulate economic development. External policies, which include foreign aid, account for only 5 percent of the 2009 budget.

Designed as a key element of the European postwar welfare state, the CAP maintains the incomes of farmers by keeping food prices high and cheaper agricultural products out of the EU's market. The international community (the United States especially), as well as some member states (the UK, in particular), has consistently criticized it. The General Agreement on Tariffs and Trade (GATT) Agreement on Agriculture and reforms that the Commission had been successful in promoting in 1992 reduced the budgetary burden of agriculture, but a great deal more change is necessary if the accession of the postcommunist countries with their large agricultural sectors is not to intolerably strain the EU's finances.

Although the Commission had hoped for more reform, the Berlin European Council meeting of 1999 agreed on only relatively modest changes. Germany, facing very strong French resistance to major changes in the financing of the CAP, agreed to continue its role as paymaster of the EU. Even though Germany is the largest contributor to the EU budget, it receives only 13.2 percent of CAP monies. France receives 20.3 percent of the CAP, but contributes only 16.3 percent of the EU's budget (2006 data).[41] Enlargement to include the poorer and more agricultural countries of Eastern Europe has produced some changes in the CAP, both in the redistribution of funds (from the old to the new member states) and in the nature of the policy. The CAP now emphasizes support to rural development, rather than support to production.

Fourth, the policy process is rooted in a culture in which consensus building is highly valued. Even when qualified majority voting is permissible, the Commission and member states try to develop legislation that is acceptable to all twenty-seven member states. The consensual decisionmaking style reflects the norm in many of the member states, but is clearly different from the more adversarial political cultures in the UK and France.

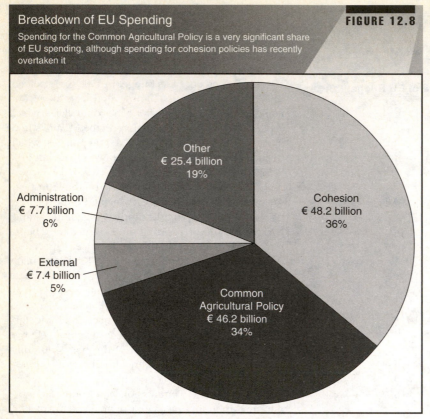

Breakdown of EU Spending   FIGURE 12.8

Spending for the Common Agricultural Policy is a very significant share of EU spending, although spending for cohesion policies has recently overtaken it

Other
€ 25.4 billion
19%

Administration
€ 7.7 billion
6%

External
€ 7.4 billion
5%

Cohesion
€ 48.2 billion
36%

Common
Agricultural Policy
€ 46.2 billion
34%

Note: Figure entries are budget forecasts for 2009 spending.

Source: European Commission, *General Budget of the European Union for the Financial Year 2008* (Luxembourg: Office for Official Publications of the European Communities, 2008).

both the Parliament and the Council. The Commission is the focal point of attention in the policymaking system because it shapes the agenda of the other institutions. The Commission's "work in progress" is an excellent predictor of the issues that the Council and the Parliament will debate in the future.

The Commission attends all meetings within the Council of Ministers and the Parliament. However, neither the Council nor the Parliament is represented at Commission meetings. The Commission is so visible in the Council that it is sometimes called the "twenty-eighth member state." The Commission plays such a powerful role in various stages of the policymaking process that it is a "co-player" with the Council of Ministers: "neither institution can act without the other."[43] In most policy areas, however, the European Parliament has become a "third co-player," and its role will be further strengthened if the Lisbon Treaty is eventually ratified.

Finally, the EU has such diversity of interests, administrative and political cultures, and regulatory arrangements that policy outcomes show the influence of several models. No national government can impose its own framework on others, and no national government is consistently forced to accept models alien to its own traditions. In the field of regulation, the outcome is a "patchwork" that incorporates aspects of varied traditions.[42] In a similar vein, no national government consistently loses in terms of policy outcomes.

Policy Initiation

The European Commission formally initiates all policy proposals. During the policy process, it interacts closely with both the Council of Ministers and the European Parliament. The Commission is the spoke in the wheel, with constant and routine contacts with

The Commission President The **president of the Commission** plays a critical role in the policy process (in pillar one) because of the visibility and the intensely political nature of the position. In practice, the power of the president depends on the context in which he or she operates, and in particular on whether the member states are willing to cede some control of the agenda to the Commission.[44] The president is appointed as a commissioner by his home country, but is chosen (in practice) as president by consensus by the twenty-seven heads of state and has to be approved by the European Parliament. Jacques Delors, the president from 1985 to 1995, was a commissioner from France and the longest-serving Commission president in the EU's history. He was followed by Jacques Santer, appointed in 1995, who had been the prime minister of Luxembourg. Santer was forced to resign, along with the entire Commission, in March 1999. Romano Prodi, the former prime minister of Italy, succeeded him. In 2004, Jose Manuel Barroso, the prime minister of Portugal, became the next president.

Choosing a president of the Commission is a delicate, intensely political task. The chief executives of the member governments, meeting in the European Council, choose the president. Delors was chosen because UK Prime Minister Margaret Thatcher and German Chancellor Helmut Kohl opposed another Frenchman, Claude Cheysson. Jacques Santer of Luxembourg was chosen because John Major (the UK prime minister) vetoed the choice of the French and Germans, Jean-Luc Dehaene (the prime minister of Belgium). Santer was a candidate who could receive unanimous support. Barroso was chosen because the UK considered the Franco-German choice, Guy Verhofstadt (the prime minister of Belgium), too federalist; Jean-Claude Juncker, the prime minister of Luxembourg, refused to be a candidate; and Chris Patten, the British choice, did not speak good French and did not come from a country that participates in the Eurozone (France's requirements for the new president).

Jacques Delors was especially important in increasing the prestige and political weight of the Commission, both within the EU and in the international arena. His admirers described him as strategic, brilliant, intellectual, and visionary, while his critics argued that he was arrogant and too much of a centralizer and did not sufficiently consider the wishes of national governments or the other Commissioners. Both his critics and his admirers would agree, however, that under his leadership the EU made some of its most important steps toward further integration. His advocacy and implementation of the *1992 Project,* the initiative to create a single market, will undoubtedly give him a firm place in the history of European integration. It is in fact possible that future histories of the EU will identify Monnet and Delors as the two most important individuals associated with the project of European integration in the twentieth century. Delors's immediate successors were not nearly as successful: Santer had to resign under a cloud, and Prodi was considered well intentioned, but ineffectual.

Civil Service The Commission's civil service is organized by a directorate-general (DG), rather than by ministry, as in national executives. The Commission's secretary-general plays an important, albeit discreet, role in coordinating the work of the various directorates-general. The secretary-general is responsible for the relations among the Commission, the Parliament, and the Council of Ministers and is the only noncommissioner who sits with the commissioners when the College meets.

National Governments The relationship between the Commission and the national governments is critical. A national government works especially closely with the Commission President when it holds the six-month rotating EU Presidency The politics of Brussels and the politics of key national capitals, including that of the country holding the Presidency, are entangled. Power in a national political system, especially within the French or German system, is a tremendous asset when operating within the EU's policymaking system.

The Commission is in constant contact with national executives during the routine of policy initiation. The commissioners have political contacts at the highest national level, while Commission officials have frequent contact with their national counterparts. In fact, the Commission often introduces proposals at the behest of a national government. The Commission president must deal with the national governments as soon as the appointments process begins in national capitals. Although Prodi was in a stronger position to bargain with the national governments because of the increased powers given to the president by the Treaty of Amsterdam and Barroso was in an even stronger position, there were definitely limits to their ability to persuade the national governments to appoint the people they would have preferred. Barroso was pleased that more women were appointed to his Commission than had been the case previously (there are eight out of twenty-seven), but he could not himself appoint any female commissioners.

After negotiations between the Commission president and national governments, each commissioner is given a portfolio—a specific policy area for which he or she is primarily responsible. For example, one commissioner is in charge of environmental policy, while another oversees the internal market and another is responsible for transportation programs. As in a national cabinet, some portfolios are more attractive and prestigious than others. Those dealing with external relations are always desirable, as are those dealing with economic matters. At the beginning of each new term, the president assigns portfolios with an eye to seniority, national government pressure, expertise, and political clout back home. In assigning a policy area to each commissioner, President Barroso has acted more independently from the member states than many had expected. He has not given the large member states the posts they were seeking for their commissioners. For instance, France was pushing for the powerful competition (antitrust) post, but was given the transport post. When the Italian commissioner gave up the Justice, Freedom and Security portfolio to join the Italian government in 2008, Barroso shifted the transport portfolio to Italy (and gave the Justice portfolio to France) over the protests of Italy.

The policy initiation process, broadly defined, is complex because commissioners must deal with their national governments, other national governments in the areas of their policy responsibilities, and the institutions of the EU. Since the Commission is involved in nearly all phases of the policy process in pillar one, officials are in contact with countless actors as a proposal is drafted, refined, accepted by the College of Commissioners, and then shepherded through the EU's institutional process.

Although commissioners are required formally to represent the European interest, they need to keep their prime ministers at home happy if they want to be reappointed. In general, commissioners try to represent both the European and the national interest within certain boundaries. While they do not accept instructions from their government, they typically do put forth some policy positions that are recognizable as "national" positions.

Keeping a political master minimally satisfied without sacrificing one's European credentials can be difficult. Typically, an effective commissioner will be able to inform his colleagues in Brussels when a proposed piece of legislation will run into severe political trouble with his national government. Conversely, he will be able to keep his capital well informed about developments within the Commission so that the national capital is not surprised. Finally, he will be able to mobilize his colleagues in the College of Commissioners to support the positions he advocates, positions that his national government is likely to support.

Once the College of Commissioners approves draft legislation by majority vote, it goes to the Council of Ministers and often the Parliament. In both cases the Commission's proposal will undergo amendments, although usually the main lines of the Commission's proposal are accepted. Depending on the subject matter, the Council can legislate by itself, or it approves a draft of the legislation, which then will be amended by the Parliament under the co-decision procedure. In the latter case, both the Council and the Parliament need to agree in order for a bill to become a law. If the Council agrees on a piece of legislation, but the Parliament and the Council cannot jointly come to an agreement, the legislation dies and is not enacted.

The Commission does not have the political clout in relation to the Council of Ministers that, say, the German chancellor or the U.S. president has in relation to the Bundesrat or the Senate, respectively. The Commission's leverage over the collectivity of national governments comes more from the power that accompanies the setting of the policy agenda and the definition of problems than from the formal powers typically associated with a cabinet or executive branch.

COREPER When ministers fly into Brussels for Council of Ministers meetings, they consider only the most difficult issues, those that need compromise at the high political level of a minister. The **Committee of Permanent Representatives** (known as *COREPER,* its French acronym) has already negotiated most of the other issues.

COREPER is critical to the successful functioning of the Council of Ministers as an institution. Some view it as "the contemporary battlefield on which the nations of Europe settle their differences."[45] This group, made up of the ambassadors to the EU from each of the member states, resolves all but the most politically sensitive issues in the legislation passed by the Council of Ministers.[46] The group meets weekly on Wednesday or Thursday, with the Commission and the Secretariat of the Council of Ministers both represented. At least once a month, they have a very private lunch at which time no interpreters and no note takers are present; English and French are the only languages spoken. That kind of privacy allows the real deals to be made, as both the Commission representatives and the ambassadors can select what they report back to their superiors. In the words of one participant, "It's very simple, there are no spies."[47]

COREPER represents the views of national capitals in Brussels and gives officials in those same capitals a sense of which arguments the other national governments within the Council of Ministers are likely to accept. COREPER officials play a key role in the entanglement of the "European" and the "national." Both national and EU officials take them seriously.[48] COREPER operates in pillar one, while the

Political and Security Committee (COPS, from its French acronym) plays a similar function in security-related issues of pillar two. According to the Nice Treaty, COPS monitors the international situation covered by the areas of the second pillar. It also contributes to the definition of the CFSP by giving opinions to the Council. The COPS is composed of senior ambassadors from the national permanent representations to the EU.

The Parliament is now a much more important legislative actor in many policy areas. The triangular relationship of the Commission, the Council, and the Parliament is one in which the Commission and the Parliament have typically been allies. Increasingly, the Council and the Parliament are participating in direct relations, as the co-decision procedure forces the Council to take the Parliament seriously. Given the Parliament's significant budgetary powers, the three institutions are inextricably linked when fashioning budgetary policy,[49] and this will be especially true if the Lisbon Treaty puts the Parliament's budgetary powers on a par with those of the Council of Ministers.

Policy Implementation

While the Commission is the "motor" of European integration, it is not the implementor of EU legislation. That function falls to the member states. The Commission's civil service is too small to carry out the monitoring and enforcement duties of a national bureaucracy.

The Commission is largely restricted to the use of legal instruments in its efforts to oversee implementation. In particular, it can bring a member state before the ECJ if a directive passed by the Council of Ministers has not been appropriately "transposed" into national law. It can also bring a member state before the ECJ if the implementation of an EU directive is not being properly pursued (in 2008 the Commission threatened to do just that in connection with a garbage disposal crisis in Naples, accusing the Italian government of having failed to implement the waste framework directive). Such an action is difficult, however, as the Commission does not have the power physically to enter a member state to gather the kind of evidence it would need to persuade the judges of the ECJ. Nongovernmental groups and private citizens do, however, write to the Commission with complaints of infringements of EU law, and the Commission often uses informal pressure on a national government to improve the execution of directives on the ground.

Sometimes the domestic implementation goes even beyond the letter and the spirit of the European legislation, thus generating unnecessary frictions with the citizens (see Box 12.3).

Judicial Review

The ECJ has evolved in a way that the member states did not expect. Established to ensure that the Commission did not overstep its authority, the ECJ

Goldplating

BOX 12.3

The United Kingdom has often been excessive in its implementation of EU directives, exhibiting a zeal that its "Euro-skeptic" population often refers to as "goldplating." The introduction of metric measurement is an example of goldplating: Metric measures were to serve as the common system of measurement within Europe and thus facilitate trade among EU members. But many in Britain viewed such as change in the traditional system of measurement as an assault on British sovereignty and the British way of life. In 1980 directive 80/181/EEC introduced the requirement of metric units. The directive was

implemented in Britain in 1994 with the "Units of Measurement Regulation 1995."

The regulation went well beyond the original directive, however, contributing to the image of the EU as an unreasonable behemoth. In 2003, for instance, a farmer selling potatoes at a local market was warned by the authorities that he was in breach of the law: He was selling his potatoes in bags labeled both in imperial and in metric units, as required by EU regulation. However, the bags weighed 25.4 kilograms, while the British regulation—not the EU directive—prescribed that bags should weigh either 25 or 20 kilograms.

expanded the scope of EU authority in several ways. Most importantly, it declared that EU law was supreme—that is, superior to member states' law[50]—and that it conferred judicially enforceable rights to individual citizens and firms, even vis-à-vis their own governments.[51]

The sweep and direction of the ECJ's decisions have been so important that some analysts view the ECJ as another "motor" of European integration at times when national governments were reluctant to move integration forward and to allow the Commission to pursue further integration. Although, like all courts, constraints limit its power, the ECJ has gradually attained the unique legitimacy enjoyed by courts. The process of integration would have proceeded much more slowly, and in some areas might not have proceeded at all, without the ECJ's activism. In sum, the ECJ has led to the constitutionalization of Europe. As Alec Stone Sweet has put it, through the activity of the ECJ, "[t]he Rome Treaty evolved from a set of legal arrangements binding upon sovereign states into a vertically integrated legal regime conferring judicially enforceable rights and obligations on legal persons and entities, public and private, within EC territory."[52]

Several factors have helped the ECJ in its integrationist project. First, the use of legal reasoning and argument seems apolitical. In that sense the very language and procedures of the judiciary and the legal profession help mask the political consequences of legal decisions. Second, it has been very difficult for the member states to agree to pass legislation overriding ECJ decisions. In fact, the supranational institutions in general benefit because each one typically has allies on any issue among at least several states. Dissenting states therefore find it difficult to reverse "integrationist" decisions or processes once they are established.[53]

Third, the ECJ benefits from the use of national courts (through what is known as the preliminary ruling system) in implementing EU law. Once national judges accepted the legitimacy of the rulings of the ECJ, the national governments' room to maneuver narrowed considerably. It is difficult for national governments to ignore the decisions of their own national courts, so the ECJ's use of national judges has given it powerful allies within the member states themselves.

The ECJ has been a powerful instrument of integration (see Box 12.4). Until very recently it typically promoted further integration through its decisions

and was a powerful ally of the Commission, as well as of the Parliament. In policy terms it set the stage for the single market with groundbreaking decisions, granted the Commission external power in those areas in which the EU was allowed to legislate internally, decided the boundaries within which environmental protection could act as a nontariff barrier, and promoted gender equality in the workplace.

Although environmental policy is now a major concern of the EU, the EC lacked competence until the SEA. However, the ECJ intervened in this policy area even before the signing of the SEA. Already in 1983, the ECJ declared that environmental protection was one of the core goals of the EC.[54] Later, as the EU began to include environmental policy among its competences, the ECJ ensured that the member states—as in all other areas in which the EU has competence—fully implemented the European legislation. In this way it has been an agent of Europeanization (see below), as it transmits the impetus for change originating from the European institutions to the policies actually carried out in the member states.[55]

As for gender discrimination, the ECJ began to act beginning in the early 1970s. A Belgian air attendant brought a case against the practices of the Belgian flag airline of compensating female attendants less than males, forcing them to retire earlier than men, and paying pensions to men but not women, even though male and female attendants did the same job. The principle of nondiscrimination between men and women over pay was already in the Treaty of Rome, but the member states had refused to consider it anything more than a vague declaration of principles. The ECJ, with this and successive cases, made the principle of pay equality directly applicable to individual women across the EC. Over time—and often in conflict with member states (such as the UK) that defended the discriminatory practices of their industries—the ECJ has clarified that a wide array of benefits beyond the monetary salary, including access to promotion, should be equal for men and women doing the same job.[56]

In sum, the ECJ has provided the EU with a legal order in which EC law is supreme to national law, a supremacy accepted by national judges. The ECJ, in the words of one of its distinguished judges, has sought "to fashion a constitutional framework for a quasi-federal structure in Europe."[57]

Many of the landmark cases through which the European Court of Justice has driven European integration have to do with food and alcoholic beverages. While the principle of the supremacy of European law over domestic law was first established with the Costa case (Costa, ECJ 6/64, 1964), it was with the Simmenthal case that supremacy was given its bite. This case (Simmenthal, ECJ 106/77, 1978) involved the importation of French beef into Italy by the Simmenthal company. The company had to pay substantial fees for border health inspections required by the Italian authorities. The company's attempt to see the fees declared in contravention of the rules of the common market eventually led to the referral of the case to the European Court of Justice, which found in favor of Simmenthal. Still, the Italian Constitutional Court balked by arguing that only it had the power to declare Italian legislation invalid. If this position had been allowed to stand, the supremacy principle would hardly have been applicable in practice. The European Court of Justice, however, rebutted the Italian court's position, declaring that its judgments were immediately enforceable throughout the European Community.

Although the signatories to the Treaty of Rome had committed to the creation of a common market and thus to the elimination of obstacles to trade among them, they continued to try to protect their own industries by supporting a minimalist interpretation of this commitment. In particular, they argued that only rules that could actually be proved to restrict trade should be eliminated, thus placing a heavy burden of proof on the traders. The European Court of Justice weighed in with the Dassonville case (ECJ 8/74, 1974).

Mr. Dassonville had imported into Belgium a dozen bottles of Johnny Walker Scotch Whisky, which he had purchased from a French supplier who, in turn, had imported them from Britain. He soon found himself in a Belgian court, accused by the government of violating regulations that allowed the importation of spirits only from countries that had customs rules similar to those of Belgium. The case reached the European Court of Justice, which found in favor of Mr. Dassonville, arguing that all measures that can even just potentially disrupt trade should in principle be considered in violation of common market rules.

Member states had also reserved for themselves the right to prevent the importation of goods that had been produced in other member states under national regulations that differed from their own. Under the guise of protecting consumers' health, this practice was clearly open to abuse as a protectionist measure. The European Court of Justice eventually reacted with what is known as the "mutual recognition" principle, whereby products that have been lawfully produced in a member state must be allowed to be marketed in other member states. This ruling came out of the Cassis de Dijon case (ECJ 120/78, 1979). Cassis de Dijon is a French black currant syrup usually mixed with white wine as an aperitif. Germany had prohibited its importation on the ground that its alcoholic content was too low to be classified as a liquor under German legislation and that this was somehow a threat to the health of German consumers. The European Court of Justice, however, found against Germany, in the process establishing the key principle of mutual recognition.

EXTERNAL RELATIONS

The powers of the EU in external relations have been growing. The Treaty of Rome specifically identified the Commission as representing the EU in organizations such as the Organization for Economic Cooperation and Development (OECD) and the United Nations Economic Commission for Europe (UNECE); the Commission thus had an external role very early. Furthermore, the fact that the Commission was the sole negotiator for the EU in the various rounds of the General Agreement on Tariffs and Trade (GATT) enhanced the EU's presence in the field of international economic relations. It, along with the member states, became a contracting party to the World Trade Organization (WTO).

The Lisbon Treaty would introduce important institutional changes in the area of external relations. In particular, it would merge two preexisting positions (the high representative for CFSP and the European commissioner for external relations) to create the position of high representative of the EU for foreign affairs and security policy, with a European diplomatic service (formally the European External Action Service) at the high representative's disposal.

The EU has struggled to gain recognition in the United Nations. It has an observer status, but has negotiated very hard to be treated as an equal negotiating partner in, for example, international environmental negotiations. In the case of global agreements (such as the Montreal Protocol limiting CFCs), the Commission bargained hard and long to be recognized as a signatory.[58] This should change with the Lisbon Treaty, which gives the EU legal personality and thus empowers it to be part of international conventions or organizations. Generally, outside of the trade area, the member states have regarded treaties as "mixed" agreements in which the Commission signs on behalf of the EU and the member states sign as well.

ENTANGLEMENT OF THE "NATIONAL" AND THE "EUROPEAN"

The coexistence of *intergovernmental* and *supranational* elements within the EU makes it clearly distinct from any of the nation-states that belong to the EU. The institutions are in a delicate balance. Some institutions (such as the Council of Ministers) are intended to ensure that national governments' views are respected and that integration does not proceed further than what is permitted by the "permissive consensus" that national governments accept. Other institutions (the Commission, the ECJ, and the Parliament) push the goal of integration by setting the agenda, raising issues, and keeping the pressure on to further integrate. These institutions test the boundaries of the permissive consensus. They project a broad strategic "European" perspective that does not match the views of any of the national governments per se, but that represents the interest of the European collectivity. They are the supranational component of the EU. Proponents of a more federal Europe see the ECJ, the Parliament, and the Commission as the institutions that should gain more power, while proponents of an intergovernmental Europe wish to increase the power of the Council of Ministers and the European Council.

The EU is, above all, its institutions, for there is not an EU political culture, media following, party system, electoral system, welfare state, or society. National diversity in all those areas is so great that the EU is identified more by its institutions than by those societal and cultural factors so important in shaping national polities.[59] In brief, there is no EU "public" or "culture" as such.

Because of the delicate balance between institutions and the still evolving nature of the EU, it is not surprising that much of the "politics" observed in Brussels involves the various institutions jockeying for institutional power. The Council of Ministers, the Commission, and the Parliament constantly try to maximize their institutional reach and influence as they collectively struggle to reach a consensus on proposed legislation. The Commission tries to protect itself from encroachments from both the Parliament and the Council of Ministers, and the Council and the Parliament eye each other warily. Rather than being based on some kind of balance of power between the executive and the legislative branches as in the United States, the EU's political system is based on a balance in the representation of both national interests and "European" interests. That is, the national interest and the supranational interest coexist, but are in constant tension. In that sense, the EU is more recognizable to students of federal systems than of unitary systems, for in federal systems the states and the federal government are typically struggling to maximize their own power.

In a parallel vein, those institutions representing national governments are "Europeanized," so that national governments, when operating within them, are enmeshed in a decisionmaking machinery that is significantly different from that of a traditional international organization and from that at the national level. For instance, in the Council of Ministers there is a strong norm favoring reaching a consensus when deciding policy, so that governments are not outvoted by other member states' governments.[60] This is a far cry from the unilateral decisionmaking role of governments at the national level, as it requires them to some extent to internalize the preferences of the other governments.

The member governments of the EU collectively work together so that each individual national government has submitted to the "European" collectivity in forgoing unilateral decisionmaking. A national government operates within the boundaries of the EU's institutional structure in a qualitatively different manner from the way it operates unilaterally in other international forums or at home. In brief, France in the European Union acts differently from France in the rest of the world, as does Paris acting as the sole decisionmaker in French national politics.

The *supranational* and the *intergovernmental* institutions are both integral to the project of European integration. The Council of Ministers, the main intergovernmental body, is there to bring the member states to a collective view, in contrast to the unilateral national decisionmaking that would take place if the European Union did not exist. National government action within the Council of Ministers is not unilateral action. The EU's institutions, whether representing national governments or the "European" interest, all implicitly reject the exercise of unilateral national power.

That rejection of unilateral national power across a broad range of issues makes the EU so distinctive when viewed from the outside. Even when the member states decide to cooperate within the Council of Ministers, downgrade the Commission's role, and exclude the ECJ, the degree of integration that they accept is far greater than that found in other parts of the world. Even when an arrangement is considered to be intergovernmental by Europeans, it would be considered far too integrationist for a country such as the United States to accept. The debate between the intergovernmental states (such as the UK and Denmark) and the federalist states (such as the Benelux states, Germany, and Italy) takes place within a context in which the rejection of the exercise of unilateral national decisionmaking is much more commonly accepted than it is anywhere else in the world. In brief, an intergovernmental posture within the EU would typically be considered as radically integrationist or federalist in Asia, North America, or Latin America.[61]

It is a testament to the high level of integration reached in the EU that many observers speak of multilevel governance with reference to many areas of EU policymaking.[62] This refers to the fact that decisionmaking in many policy areas not only involves actors from different levels of government (from the supranational—that is, the EU level—to the national and the regional levels), but also brings together both government and private (civil society) actors. An important area that operates through multilevel governance is cohesion policy—namely, the policy area concerned with economic development in the EU regions that are lagging behind.[63]

Moreover, the relationship between the member states and the EU is not static. The member states affect the policies and the institutional shape of the EU even as EU policies and institutions influence the policies and even institutions of the member states. The EU requires or suggests policy changes at the domestic level that lead to or facilitate changes in the way national institutions work. By now a vast literature exists that studies the so-called Europeanization of—for instance—national executives,[64] political parties,[65] and parliamentary institutions.[66]

POLICY PERFORMANCE

National governments provide social services; the EU makes laws, but it does not engage, with a few exceptions (in the fields of agriculture and regional policy), in activities that involve large public expenditure. The EU's comparatively small budget keeps it from engaging in the kinds of activities traditionally the province of national governments.

The EU engages in regulation, for the costs of regulation are borne by the objects of regulation rather than the regulators.[67] With the creation of the single market, the EU became an important regulator of economic activity. Its role consisted of removing national regulations that impeded cross-border trade and re-regulating at the EU level to ensure, for example, the setting of safety standards. The process of regulatory reform therefore empowered the EU, while eliminating many national nontariff barriers to trade.

The Single-Market Program

As already mentioned, the Single European Act allowed the member states to create a true single market. The single-market program involved the removal of nontariff barriers from the EU's economy. That is, it has largely dismantled the regulatory barriers that protected national markets from competition from goods and services produced in other EU countries. The 1992 Project as it was known (the goal was to approve nearly 300 pieces of single-market legislation in Brussels by 1992, a goal largely achieved) was the foundation stone of the more integrated European economy with which Europe entered the twenty-first century. Its effects in both the economic and the political spheres were huge. Once firms no longer benefited from protected national markets, they realized they had to become global, rather than being simply European players, to survive the competition from American firms. American firms were attracted to the single market, invested huge sums in building production facilities in Europe, and bought promising European firms. European firms therefore entered the American market in a sustained fashion, set up production facilities in the United States, and bought promising American firms. Interestingly, the relationship became quite symmetrical—the number of Americans working for European firms roughly equaled the number of Europeans working for American firms.[68]

Although there are still a few areas in which agreement has not been reached, the EU's legislative program for the single market is largely finished. In 1980 a citizen from one EU country was stopped when crossing the border into another EU state; by 2008 one could travel from Estonia to Portugal without any interruption. Capital now moves freely without capital controls by national governments. Firms based in one country can acquire firms in other member states, and banks can set up offices outside their home country. Airlines that were previously protected from each other now compete with one another, and low-cost carriers have emerged (symbolized by Ryanair). The telecommunications sector is now open to fierce competition, whereas previously it was a state monopoly. As a result of the competitive forces unleashed by the single market, the member states have privatized previously nationalized industries and so transformed the European economy. The single-market program was such a pivotal program for the process of European integration that the proponents of the single currency argued that a single market required a single currency—"one market, one currency."

A properly working market requires a level playing field. For this reason, antitrust is a key EU policy, and one of the few in which the European Commission can act directly without the intermediation of the member states. The DG in charge of antitrust (DG Competition) is one of the most powerful and best regarded directorates-General of the Commission. The Commission tussles frequently with both firms and states over alleged anticompetitive behavior. In 2008, for instance, Microsoft was fined € 899 million, and EU regulators have often sparred with Spain, Italy, and especially France over the way in which they try to protect national firms from foreign takeovers or give them illegal state aid.

External Relations

Since the implementation of the single-market program, the EU has become far more active in the area of external relations. The EU has been involved in external relations since the Rome treaties, through the role of the Commission in trade negotiations, as well as through the EU role in development policy. The EU's development policy dates from the special

relationship (primarily in the area of trade) that France insisted should exist between the EU and France's colonies and overseas territories. The special relationship was strengthened when the UK joined the EC, as its former colonies also benefited from that relationship. The first Lome Convention of 1975 established the cooperative framework between the EC and the developing world with links to Europe. The EU also strengthened its relations with countries of the Maghreb and the Masreq.

Today the EU is the world's leading development partner in terms of aid, trade, and direct investment. In 2006 the EU and its member states provided more than 55 percent of all official international development aid—and more than twice what the United States provided. Since the vast majority of aid is directly provided by the member states, the EU (and in particular the European Commission) has increasingly, and successfully, focused on coordinating the aid policies of the member states.[69] As part of this coordination effort, in 2005 the Council of Ministers, the European Parliament, and the European Commission agreed to a common strategy, the so-called European Consensus on Development, which emphasizes the centrality of human rights, the rule of law, and democracy to the development goals of the EU.

The promotion of human rights and democracy is part of the enlargement process and of the so-called European Neighborhood Policy. This policy offers "good neighborly relations," but not full-fledged membership, to countries mostly in central Asia and along the southern shore of the Mediterranean. In both cases the EU has connected the benefits of joining or having a preferential relationship with the EU to domestic changes promoting the rule of law, human rights, minority rights, and democracy. These four criteria— known as the Copenhagen Criteria, from the 2002 Copenhagen European Council that formulated them—are part of the express requirements for membership. In 2008 the prospect of eventual membership was even used in a not so subtle manner to sway elections in Serbia in favor of a pro-Western candidate.[70]

Turkey is a clear case of how this approach works. In spite of the many bumps on the road to eventual membership, Turkey has made significant changes in order to bring its policies and institutions in line with EU requirements. The Kurdish minority has been given cultural rights, and in 2008 Turkey's parliament passed laws returning confiscated property to religious minorities and eliminating the crime of "insulting Turkishness," which had been used in recent years to prosecute intellectuals criticizing the country.[71]

However, the European Neighborhood Policy has been only partially successful in promoting democracy and human rights,[72] and there are signs of backsliding even among the new member states. In 2008 Bulgaria's interior minister was forced to retire after he admitted to contacts with crime bosses; in 2007 the EU was disappointed when Romania's justice minister was removed from government for her excessive enthusiasm in fighting corruption.[73] In Poland a law requiring the media to respect Christian values has been used to prosecute journalists criticizing the Pope.[74] After all, once membership in the EU is achieved, the incentives to adapt to the EU principles might well weaken.

In foreign policy the EU has been slower in acquiring a role, first because foreign policy and international security touch the core of national sovereignty and second because the defense of Europe was left to NATO. The end of the Cold War and the uncertainty of a continued U.S. military involvement in Europe, along with the poor military performance of member states (particularly France) during the first Gulf War led to the creation of the Common Foreign and Security Policy during the Maastricht negotiations.[75] Although the Commission has a role in the CFSP decisionmaking process, since it can make proposals to the Council of Ministers, the CFSP maintains a mostly intergovernmental nature. The Council of Ministers (acting based on unanimity) is the sole CFSP decisionmaker. The Lisbon Treaty, however, would introduce some new elements that point to a certain degree of pooled sovereignty. Although some countries that are particularly jealous of national prerogatives have stressed that the position is not that of a minister of foreign affairs,[76] the establishment of a high representative of the EU for foreign affairs and security policy goes a long way toward answering Henry Kissinger's famous query about whose number one should call when one wants to speak with Europe. Moreover, the European Parliament would get a foot into the door of the CFSP because the new European diplomatic service is funded by the EU budget and the European Parliament is called to approve the budget.

To this day the EU maintains its nature as a "civilian" power—namely, one that tends to avoid the use of coercive means. However, since its first formulation in the Maastricht Treaty, the CFSP also entails the eventual creation of a genuine EU defense policy, although not in competition with NATO. The first test of the EU's new CFSP was the Yugoslav wars of the early 1990s, in which the EU did not fare well, except in the area of humanitarian aid. The wars ended only when the United States and NATO became involved.

The Treaty of Amsterdam strengthened the commitment of the member states to the CFSP, but it did not become a major area of EU policy until the UK and France, the two major actors in European defense, reached an agreement at a Franco-British summit at St. Malo, France, in December 1998.

Essentially, the UK, a traditional supporter of NATO and concerned that a European defense policy would weaken NATO, agreed to cooperate with European efforts to develop a European capability in security and defense policy. France, which traditionally supported a European defense posture independent of NATO, agreed that such efforts should not weaken NATO. The EU would develop a common defense policy within the framework of the CFSP through summit meetings of foreign affairs and defense ministers. For the first time, defense ministers, who previously had operated solely within NATO, would be brought under the EU's umbrella, although still meeting informally.

Once the Franco-British bargain had been struck—with the UK willing to become more European in its defense policy in return for France's accepting NATO's crucial role in Europe's collective defense—movement came quickly. The Helsinki European Council in December 1999 agreed to develop by 2003 a collective European capability to deploy a rapid-reaction force of 60,000 troops for crisis management operations. These troops would be capable of being deployed at sixty days' notice and remain operational for one year. They would intervene in humanitarian and rescue tasks, as well as in peacekeeping and crisis management (what is referred to in the EU jargon as the Petersberg tasks). Since March 2000 a Political and Security Committee (known as COPS from its French acronym) meets weekly at the ambassadorial level, and a military committee (Military Committee of the EU or EUMC) and a military staff (Military Staff of the EU or EUMS) have been established within the Council's structures to provide the Council of Ministers with military expertise.

The major challenge to the European Security and Defense Policy (ESDP) is in the area of military capabilities. The Europeans, with the exception of France and the United Kingdom, are extremely weak in what is called C3I (control, command, communication, and intelligence). In 2004 the Council of Ministers set up the European Defense Agency (EDA) to address this issue. The EDA's tasks include creating a competitive armament market in Europe, promoting cooperation within the European defense industry, and promoting research and development in defense technology.

Since the goal of the ESDP is not to create a European army, EU–NATO relations are critical. Yet these two organizations had no formal relationship throughout the entire postwar period. Although France initially wanted to keep NATO at arm's length from the ESDP, it reversed its position in 2000 and agreed to establish four ad hoc EU–NATO working groups. In September 2000, for the first time, the Interim Political and Security Committee and NATO's Permanent Council met—the first formal high-level contact between the EU and NATO. In December 2002 the EU and NATO reached an agreement whereby the EU may use NATO military assets in operations in which NATO as a whole is not involved. Assurances were given that the ESDP would not affect any vital interest of a non-EU NATO member.

The 2002 agreement allows the EU to launch its own operations under the ESDP. The first military operation began on April 2003, when the EU took over from NATO in Macedonia. A second military operation, without the use of NATO assets, was launched in June 2003 in the Republic of Congo. At the end of 2004, the EU took over the NATO peacekeeping operation in Bosnia. Between 2003 and 2008, the EU has engaged in approximately twenty ESDP operations (not all military, as many involve police forces or trainers in the implementation of the rule of law) and is currently present in places such as Guinea-Bissau, Congo, Afghanistan, and Iraq (although in the latter case most of the EU team is actually based in Brussels). These increased capabilities and willingness to intervene beyond the EU border should not make one forget that cooperation in the CFSP and EDSP remains rather fragile when the EU is subject to strong external pressure. A case in point was the second Iraq war, where U.S. intervention provoked deep fissures—exacerbated by the United States—between member states in favor of it and those opposing it.

DOES THE EUROPEAN UNION MAKE A DIFFERENCE?

The EU now affects a great many people, some of them more directly than others. It makes the most difference for the farmer whose prices and subsidies largely depend on the decisions made by the Council of Agricultural Ministers and the Commission. Fishermen's catches and allotments are significantly influenced by Brussels. Businesspeople are affected by the provisions of the single market (especially the mobility of capital and the liberalization of numerous once-protected markets), the move to the euro, the Commission's robust antitrust policy (coordinated with the antitrust policy of the United States in relevant cases), and the EU's environmental policy. Bankers and investors are affected by the policies of the European Central Bank and the move to a common currency. Environmentalists want to increase environmental protection. Consumers are worried about the safety of the food they eat; soccer players now enjoy "free agency" because of the EU. Women seek equal pay for equal work. Airline passengers benefit from airline deregulation. Retirees can decide to live in another member state. Regional government officials receive funds from Brussels to help their region develop roads and jobs. Patients benefit from more rapid approval of new medicinal drugs now that they fall under the jurisdiction of the EU. Telephone users benefit enormously in terms of both price and level of service from the deregulation of the telecommunications sector pushed through by the Commission. By 2008 everyone living in the fifteen member states using the euro was accustomed to paying their bills with a new currency and relinquishing their old familiar national currency.

By contrast, in areas such as the provision of health care, education, urban policies, social security, and unemployment compensation, national governments retain the right to unilaterally make policy. The EU only indirectly affects these policy areas. The welfare state is largely still under the unilateral control of national policymakers (although its financing is affected by the policies of the European Central Bank). In areas related to economic activity and social regulation (consumer and environmental protection, for example), rather than social services, the EU is particularly relevant. Thus, the EU does not legislate the health benefits that any citizen of any member state is entitled to enjoy. However, the fact that the doctor chosen by a patient may be of a different nationality from the patient occurs because EU regulations recognize medical degrees across borders. The drugs that the doctor prescribes are under EU regulations if they are new to the market, and the competition among firms selling that drug is shaped by EU rules.

Countries outside of the EU are also particularly aware of the EU. The United States must bargain with the EU in important global forums such as the World Trade Organization. Developing countries in Africa and Latin America, for example, compete to export bananas to EU member states. Countries such as Turkey and Israel have negotiated special trade agreements with the EU.[77] Although at this point in time the EU is not yet a true "military" power, its economic reach and power make it an important international actor.

From the beginning the external economic role that "Europe" would play if organized into a relatively integrated unit was an important consideration for European policymakers. In the field of agriculture, for example, the Common Agricultural Policy allowed the EC to ward off strong American pressure to open up the European agricultural market.[78] This external role was particularly important because the initial EC member states were not "self-confident" states. Their capacities were not in any way similar to that of the United States, a superpower with enormous resources and global power. European integration allowed these states to have much greater influence in the international environment than if they had exercised traditional sovereignty. Public opinion surveys of attitudes among mass electorates, in fact, show high degrees of support for EU activity in the global political arena in all policy areas, not simply those having to do with economics. European elites may emphasize the difficulties of coordinating foreign and defense policies among the European states, but European publics see this as a natural area of joint action.[79] In fact, as we have seen, the leaders of the EU member states are following the lead of public opinion in cooperating more extensively in the field of foreign and security policy.

The EU reflects and fosters the great developments that have changed Europe in the past sixty years: economic progress, democracy, and peace. The common market—created under the military umbrella of the United States that protected Western Europe from potential Soviet aggression—spurred fast economic growth by facilitating trade among its member states. In turn, economic development contributed to the rooting of democracy in those among the original member states that had been fascist dictatorships (Italy and Germany); eventually, the attraction of this area of prosperity facilitated democratic transition both in Southern Europe (Portugal, Spain, Greece) and in the countries under former Soviet domination. Trade, common democratic values, cultural exchanges, and travel, all promoted by European integration, have made armed conflict among the member states unthinkable.

This does not mean that the process of integration has been free of problems. Just like many democracies in Europe and beyond, the EU struggles with a widespread sense of dissatisfaction among its citizens with the way the democratic process works. This discontent is heightened by the often baroque and opaque institutional arrangements that have evolved over time and that reveal the persisting preoccupation of sovereign states with retaining power. Moreover, European integration is far from complete. Only twenty-seven of the forty-one countries of Europe are EU member states. Further enlargement is made difficult not only by economic factors (the uneven development prospects of some nonmembers) and institutional considerations (the absorption capacity of the EU), but also by cultural concerns (as in the case of Turkey) and geopolitical problems (the resurgent confrontation between Russia and the West).

However, if one considers the evolution of the EU over time, one can see that it has tended to deal with some of the key concerns of Europe's citizens. It addressed economic development in the 1950s (the common market), inflation in the 1970s (the beginning of monetary integration), the environment in the 1980s and 1990s, and issues such as immigration and security in more recent years. If the past is any guidance, the EU will find in itself the flexibility needed to face the problems that Europe's citizens will consider fundamental in the future.

REVIEW QUESTIONS

- What are the challenges brought about by enlargement?

- What are the issues raised by the prospect of Turkey's accession?

- Why was European integration connected to the "German Question?"

- Which EU institutions are considered the "motors" of European integration?

- Discuss the evolution of the powers and role of the European Parliament in EU policy making.

- Discuss the role of political parties in European Union governance.

- Discuss the evolution of the Common Agricultural Policy.

- What interests are best represented in Brussels?

- In what ways does the EU "protect" small member states from large member states?

- What are the main goals of the EU's Neighborhood Policy?

- Discuss examples of supranational and intergovernmental governance in the EU.

KEY TERMS

Committee of Permanent Representatives (COREPER)

Common Foreign and Security Policy (CFSP)

Council of Ministers (Council of the European Union)

Economic and Monetary Union (EMU)

European Central Bank

European Commission

European Council

European Court of Justice

European Economic Community (EEC)

European Parliament

European Union (EU)

intergovernmental

Intergovernmental Conference (IGC)

Justice, Freedom and Security

Maastricht Treaty (Treaty of European Union)

Marshall Plan

Members of the European Parliament (MEPs)

North Atlantic Treaty Organization (NATO)

Political and Security Committee (PSC)

presidency of the European Council and the Council of Ministers

President of the Commission

Schuman Plan

single currency (euro)

Single European Act (SEA)

supranational

Treaty of Amsterdam

Treaty of Lisbon

Treaty of Nice

Treaty of Rome

SUGGESTED READINGS

Bomberg, Elizabeth, and Alexander Stubb, eds. *The European Union: How Does It Work?* 2nd ed. New York: Oxford University Press, 2008.

Cini, Michelle, ed. *European Union Politics*. 2nd ed. Oxford, England: Oxford University Press, 2007.

Corbett, Richard, Francis Jacobs, and Michael Shackleton. *The European Parliament*. 7th ed. London: John Harper, 2007.

Cowles, Maria, Thomas Risse, and James Caporaso, eds. *Transforming Europe*. Ithaca, NY: Cornell University Press, 2001.

Dinan, Desmond. *Europe Recast: A History of European Union*. New York: Palgrave Macmillan, 2004.

Gilbert, Mark. *Surpassing Realism—The Politics of European Integration Since 1945*. Lanham, MD: Rowman and Littlefield, 2003.

Hayes-Renshaw, Fiona, and Helen Wallace. *The Council of Ministers*. 2nd ed. Houndsmills, England: Palgrave Macmillan, 2006.

Hix, Simon. *The Political System of the European Union*. 2nd ed. Houndsmills, England: Palgrave Macmillan, 2005.

Hix, Simon, Abdul G. Noury, and Gérard Roland. *Democratic Politics in the European Parliament*. Cambridge, England: Cambridge University Press, 2007.

McCormick, John. *The European Union—Politics and Policies*. Boulder, CO: Westview Press, 2004.

Moravcsik, Andrew. *The Choice for Europe: Social Purpose and State Power from Messina to Maastricht*. Ithaca, NY: Cornell University Press, 1998.

Parsons, Craig. *A Certain Idea of Europe*. Ithaca, NY: Cornell University Press, 2003.

Peterson, John, and Michael Shackleton, eds. *The Institutions of the European Union*. New York: Oxford University Press, 2006.

Rosamond, Ben. *Theories of European Integration*. New York: St Martin's, 2000.

Ross, George. *Jacques Delors and European Integration*. Oxford, England: Oxford University Press, 1995.

Smith, Michael E. *Europe's Foreign and Security Policy: The Institutionalization of Cooperation.* New York: Cambridge University Press, 2004.

Trachtenberg, Marc. *A Constructed Peace: The Making of the European Settlement 1945–63.* Princeton, NJ: Princeton University Press, 1999.

Wallace, Helen, William Wallace, and Mark A. Pollack, eds. *Policy-Making in the European Union.* 5th ed. Oxford, England: Oxford University Press, 2005.

Winand, Pascaline. *Eisenhower, Kennedy, and the United States of Europe.* New York: St. Martin's, 1993.

INTERNET RESOURCES

The European Commission: **ec.europa.eu**

The European Parliament: **www.europarl.europa.eu**

The Council of the EU: **www.consilium.europa.eu**

Commission Delegation in Washington, DC: **www.eurunion.org**

EU-Related News: **www.eupolitix.com; euobserver.com**

ENDNOTES

1. Based on forecast values from Eurostat (retrieved April 22, 2009), http://epp.eurostat.ec.europa.eu/portal/page?_pageid=1996,45323734&_dad=portal&_schema=PORTAL&screen=welcomeref&open=/t_na/t_nama/t_nama_gdp&language=en&product=REF_TB_national_accounts&root=REF_TB_national_accounts &scrollto=174.

2. European Commission, *Eurobarometer—Post-referendum Survey in Ireland* (Luxembourg: European Commission, 2008).

3. Many scholars have debated whether national governments are the only real decisionmakers in the EU, with the EU institutions, which do not represent state interests, being in fact agents of the national governments or whether national governments share their decisionmaking power with those other "non-state-centric" institutions. For example, see Andrew Moravcsik, *The Choice for Europe* (Ithaca, NY: Cornell University Press, 1998); Gary Marks, Liesbet Hooghe, and Kermit Blank, "European Integration from the 1980s: State-Centric v. Multi-Level Governance," *Journal of Common Market Studies* 34, no. 3 (September 1996): 341–378; James A. Caporaso and John T. S. Keeler, "The European Union and Regional Integration Theory," in *Building a European Polity?* ed. Carolyn Rhodes and Sonia Mazey (Boulder, CO: Lynne Rienner, 1995), 29–62.

4. F. Roy Willis, "Schuman Breaks the Deadlock," in *European Integration,* ed. F. Roy Willis (New York: New Viewpoints, 1975), 27.

5. Derek W. Urwin, *The Community of Europe: A History of European Integration Since 1945,* 2nd ed. (New York: Longman, 1995), 21.

6. David Armstrong, Lorna Lloyd, and John Redmond, *From Versailles to Maastricht: International Organization in the Twentieth Century* (New York: St. Martin's, 1996), 159.

7. Stephen Wilks, "Competition Policy: Challenge and Reform," in *Policy-Making in the European Union,* 5th ed., ed. Helen Wallace, William Wallace, and Mark A. Pollack (Oxford, England: Oxford University Press, 2005), 114–139.

8. Giandomenico Majone, "The Rise of the Regulatory State in Europe," *West European Politics* 17, no. 3 (July 1994): 77–101.

9. The Schengen area (from the locality where the first agreement was signed in 1985) refers to the EU countries that have eliminated border controls for travel to and from each other. In March 2008, with the inclusion of Estonia, the Czech Republic, Lithuania, Hungary, Latvia, Malta, Poland, Slovakia, and Slovenia, Schengen included twenty-four of the twenty-seven EU countries.

10. Damian Chalmers and Erika Szysczak, *European Union Law: Towards a European Polity?* Vol. 2 (Brookfield, VT: Ashgate, 1998), 146–147.

11. Alberta M. Sbragia "Conclusion to Special Issue on the Institutional Balance and the Future of EU Governance: The Treaty of Nice, Institutional Balance, and Uncertainty," *Governance* 15 (July 2002): 393–412.

12. "The Square Root or Death," *The Economist,* June 14, 2007.

13. "The Polish Farewell," *The Economist,* November 29, 2007.

14. Fiona Hayes-Renshaw and Helen Wallace, *The Council of Ministers* (London: Macmillan, 1997), 163.

15. Martin Westlake, "A Paradoxical Parliament?" *European Political Science* 6 (December 2007): 341–351.

16. Luca Verzichelli and Michael Edinger, "A Critical Juncture? The 2004 European Elections and the Making of a Supranational Elite," *Journal of Legislative Studies* 11 (March 2005): 254–274.

17. As of March 2005, according to the Interparliamentary Union. Retrieved April 22, 2009 from www.ipu.org/wmn-e/regions.htm.

18. Amy Kreppel, "Understanding the European Parliament from a Federalist Perspective: The Legislatures of the United States and the European Union Compared," in *Comparative Federalism: The European Union and the United States in Comparative Perspective,* ed. Anand Menon and Martin A. Schain (Oxford, England: Oxford University Press, 2006), 245–273.

19. Karen J. Alter, "The European Court's Political Power," *West European Politics* 19, no. 3 (July 1996): 458.

20. Beate Kohler-Koch, "Germany: Fragmented but Strong Lobbying," in *National Public and Private EC Lobbying,* ed. M. P. C. M. van Schendelen (Brookfield, England: Dartmouth, 1993), 32.

21. Denmark is an exception: The People's Movement against the European Community competes in European parliamentary elections—but not in domestic elections—on an anti-integration platform. Vernon Bogdanor, "The European Union, the Political Class, and the People," in *Elitism, Populism, and European Politics,* ed. Jack Hayward (Oxford, England: Clarendon, 1996), 110.

22. Simon Hix, *What's Wrong with the European Union and How to Fix It* (Cambridge, England: Polity, 2008).

23. Simon Hix, *The Political System of the European Union* (Houndsville, England: Palgrave Macmillan, 2005).

24. John Gaffney, "Introduction: Political Parties and the European Union," in *Political Parties and the European Union,* ed. John Gaffney (London: Routledge, 1996), 13.

25. Mark Franklin and Cees van der Eijk, "The Problem: Representation and Democracy in the European Union," in *Choosing Europe? The European Electorate and National Politics in the Face of Union,* ed. Cees van der Eijk and Mark N. Franklin (Ann Arbor: University of Michigan Press, 1996), 8.

26. Simon Hix, "Parties at the European Level and the Legitimacy of EU Socio-economic Policy," *Journal of Common Market Studies* 33, no. 4 (December 1995): 545; Robert Ladrech, "Partisanship and Party Formation in European Union Politics," *Comparative Politics* 30 (January 1997): 176.

27. Mark Franklin, "European Elections and the European Voter," in *European Union: Power and Policymaking,* ed. Jeremy J. Richardson (London: Routledge, 1996), 187.

28. Simon Hix, Abdul Noury, and Gérard Roland, *Democratic Politics in the European Parliament* (Cambridge, England: Cambridge University Press, 2007).

29. It should also be noted that in cases where strong national interests are at stake, MEPs sometimes revert to voting along national lines. This was the case, for instance, with the failed takeover directive. Helen Callaghan and Martin Höpner, "European Integration and the Clash of Capitalisms: Political Cleavages over Takeover Liberalization," *Comparative European Politics* 3 (September 2005): 165–189.

30. Andreas Broscheid and David Coen, "Insider and Outsider Lobbying of the European Commission," *European Union Politics* 4 (June 2003): 165–189

31. Honor Mahony, "MEPs Vote to Tighten Up Rules for Brussels Lobbyists," *EUobserver,* May 9, 2008.

32. European Commission, *Towards a Reinforced Culture of Consultation and Dialogue—COM (2002) 704 Final* (Brussels: European Commission, 2002).

33. Christine Mahoney, "The Power of Institutions: State and Interest Group Activity in the European Union," *European Union Politics* 5 (December 2004): 441–466.

34. Mahoney, "The Power of Institutions," 444.

35. Dods, *The European Public Affairs Directory* (London: Dods, 2007).

36. While the democratic deficit is a problem for many observers, both among academics and in the mass media, it should be noted that not all agree that it is indeed a problem. See, in particular, Giandomenico Majone, "The European Commission: The Limits of Centralization and the Perils of Parliamentarization," *Governance* 15 (July 2002): 375–392; and Andrew Moravcsik, "The EU Ain't Broke" *Prospect* 8 (March 2003): 38–45.

37. Hix, *What's Wrong with the European Union.*

38. See EC Regulation No. 1049/2001 of the European Parliament and of the Council of 30 May 2001 regarding public access to European Parliament, Council, and Commission documents; Council decision of 29 November 2001 amending the Council's Rules of Procedure (2001/840/EC); and Council decision of 22 March 2004 adopting the Council's Rules of Procedure (2004/338/EC).

39. European Commission, *Eurobarometer—Post-referendum Survey in Ireland* (Luxembourg: European Commission, 2008).

40. GDP data are from World Bank, *World Development Indicators* (Washington, DC: World Bank, 2006); data on EU funds are from European Commission, *EU Budget 2006—Financial Report* (Luxembourg: European Commission, 2006), based on the European Central Bank euro–U.S. dollar exchange rate for May 20, 2008.

41. European Commission, *EU Budget 2006—Financial Report* (Luxembourg: European Commission, 2006).

42. A. Heritier, "The Accommodation of Diversity in European Policy-Making and Its Outcomes: Regulatory Policy as a Patchwork," *Journal of European Public Policy* 3, no. 2 (1996): 149–167.

43. Dietrich Rometsch and Wolfgang Wessels, "The Commission and the Council of Ministers," in *The European Commission,* ed. Geoffrey Edwards and David Spence (Essex, England: Longman, 1994), 221.

44. John Peterson, "The College of Commissioners," in *The Institutions of the European Union,* ed. John

Peterson and Michael Shackleton (Oxford, England: Oxford University Press, 2006), 81–103.

45. Lionel Barber, "The Men Who Run Europe," *Financial Times,* March 11–12, 1995, sect. 2, I.

46. To be precise, COREPER meets in two different forms. The ambassadorial-level COREPER mentioned in the text is known as COREPER II.

47. Barber, "The Men Who Run Europe," II.

48. Jeffrey Lewis, "National Interests—COREPER," in *The Institutions of the European Union,* ed. John Peterson and Michael Shackleton (Oxford, England: Oxford University Press, 2006), 272–292.

49. Brigid Laffan and Johannes Lindner, "The Budget," in *Policy-Making in the European Union*, 5th ed., ed. Helen Wallace, William Wallace, and Mark A. Pollack (Oxford, England: Oxford University Press, 2005), 191–212.

50. Tom Kennedy, "The European Court of Justice," in *The Institutions of the European Union,* ed. John Peterson and Michael Shackleton (Oxford, England: Oxford University Press, 2006), 125–143.

51. Alec Stone Sweet, *The Judicial Construction of Europe* (Oxford, England: Oxford University Press, 2004).

52. Stone Sweet, *The Judicial Construction of Europe*, 65.

53. Karen Alter, "Who Are the 'Masters of the Treaty'? European Governments and the European Court of Justice," *International Organization* 52, no. 1 (Winter 1998): 121–148; Alec Stone Sweet and Thomas L. Brunell, "Constructing a Supranational Constitution: Dispute Resolution and Governance in the European Community," *American Political Science Review,* 92, no. 1 (March 1998): 63–81.

54. Stone Sweet, *The Judicial Construction of Europe*, 200.

55. Diana Panke, "The European Court of Justice as an Agent of Europeanization?" *Journal of European Public Policy* 14 (September 2007): 847–866.

56. Stone Sweet, *The Judicial Construction of Europe*, 152–159.

57. C. Federico Mancini, "The Making of a Constitution for Europe," in *The New European Community,* ed. Stanley Hoffman and Robert O. Keohane (Boulder, CO: Westview Press, 1991), 178.

58. Alberta Sbragia, "Institution-Building from Above and from Below: The European Community in Global Environmental Politics," in *European Integration and Supranational Governance,* ed. Wayne Sandholtz and Alec Stone (Oxford: Oxford University Press, 1998), 283–303.

59. Thomas Risse, "European Institutions and Identity Change: What Have We Learned?" in *Transnational Identities,* ed. Richard Herrmann, Thomas Risse, and Marilynn Brewer (Lanham, MD: Rowman & Littlefield, 2004), 247–271.

60. Elisabeth Bomberg and Alexander Stubb, "The EU's Institutions," in *The European Union—How Does It Work?* ed. Elisabeth Bomberg, John Peterson, and Alexander Stubb (Oxford, England: Oxford University Press, 2008), 45–70.

61. For example, see Miles Kahler, *Regional Futures and Transatlantic Economic Relations* (New York: Council on Foreign Relations Press, 1995).

62. Beate Kohler-Koch and Berthold Rittberger, "Review Article: The Governance Turn in EU Studies," *Journal of Common Market Studies* 44 (March 2006): 27–49.

63. Ian Bache and Matthew Flinders, eds., *Multi-level Governance* (Oxford, England: Oxford University Press, 2004).

64. Hussein Kassim, Anand Menon, Guy B. Peters, and Vincent Wright, *The National Co-ordination of EU Policy* (Oxford, England: Oxford University Press, 2001).

65. Robert Ladrech, "Europeanization and Political Parties," *Party Politics* 8 (July 2002): 389–403.

66. Katrin Auel and Arthur Benz, "The Politics of Adaptation: The Europeanization of National Parliamentary Systems," *Journal of Legislative Studies* 11 (October 2005): 372–393.

67. Martin Lodge, "Regulation, the Regulatory State and European Politics," *West European Politics* 31 (January 2008): 280–301.

68. Alberta Sbragia, "The Transatlantic Relationship: A Case of Deepening and Broadening," in *The European Union in the World Community,* ed. Carolyn Rhodes (Boulder, CO: Lynne Rienner, 1998), 147–164.

69. Maurizio Carbone, *The European Union and International Development* (London: Routledge, 2007).

70. Dan Bilefsky and Stephen Castle, "Europe Offers Serbia Deal to Sway Vote," *New York Times,* January 29, 2008.

71. Sabrina Tavernise, "Turkey: Parliament Backs Return of Minorities' Properties," *New York Times,* February 21, 2008; Associated Press, "Turkish Law Easing Curbs on Speech Wins Praise," *New York Times,* May 1, 2008.

72. Frank Schimmelfennig, "European Neighborhood Policy: Political Conditionality and Its Impact on Democracy in Non-candidate Neighboring Countries" (paper prepared for the EUSA Ninth Biennial International Conference Austin, TX, March 31–April 2, 2005.

73. "Europe's Marxist Dilemma," *The Economist*, April 24, 2008.

74. Umut Korkut, "Reversing the Wave," *Europe-Asia Studies* (forthcoming 2009).

75. William Wallace, "Foreign and Security policy," in *Policy-Making in the European Union*, 5th ed., ed. Helen Wallace, William Wallace, and Mark A. Pollack (Oxford, England: Oxford University Press, 2005), 429–456.

76. James Blitz, "London Confident 'Red Lines' Will Hold Out," *Financial Times*, June 22, 2007.

77. To get a sense of the policy areas in which the European Union is most important, see Wallace,

Wallace, and Pollack *Policy-Making in the European Union,* 5th ed; Desmond Dinan, *Ever Closer Union,* 3rd ed., (Houndsville, England: Palgrave Macmillan, 2005).

78. Elmar Rieger, "The Common Agricultural Policy," in Wallace, Wallace and Pollack, *Policy-Making in the European Union,* 5th ed., 161–190.

79. Russel J. Dalton and Richard C. Eichenberg, "Citizen Support for Policy Integration," in Sandholtz and Stone, *European Integration and Supranational Governance,* 260.